THE U.S. HEALTHCARE CERTIFICATE OF NEED SOURCEBOOK

THE U.S. HEALTHCARE CERTIFICATE OF NEED SOURCEBOOK

ROBERT JAMES CIMASI
ASA, CBA, AVA, FCBI, CM&A, CMP

Beard Books
Washington, D.C.

Printed in the United States of America

DISCLAIMER

This work offers a detailed treatment of basic characteristics related to the various states' Certificate Of Need ("CON") statutes, regulations, and program administration and is intended to provide only a general overview of CON. This information is provided with the understanding that the author and publisher are not rendering legal advice and services. The author has made every attempt to verify the completeness and accuracy of the information, however, neither the author nor publisher can guarantee, in any way whatsoever, the validity of the information found herein. This work does not intend to provide specific descriptions of each state's complex CON regulatory scheme. Further, this work is not intended as legal advice or a substitute for a state's CON statutes or regulations. It is important to acquire a specific state's statutes and regulations before filing a CON application.

To my wife
Laura M. Baumstark, CAE

PREFACE

Certificate of Need (CON) has had a broad impact on healthcare providers and markets for over three (3) decades. As the bibliographies and other resources in this book illustrate, there is a large amount of literature documenting CON regulation over the years. However, the literature is sporadic in it's coverage of certain key aspects of CON including: directories and data for individual states CON programs and their impact, private studies on CON, legal and case law analyses, and several other areas.

This work is the result of over two (2) years of dedicated, focused research resulting in a comprehensive reference manual and sourcebook encompassing the statutory, regulatory, administrative, and legal aspects CON regulation from its inception in the late 1960's to the present.

"The U.S. Healthcare Certificate of Need Sourcebook" provides detailed descriptions, on a state-by-state basis, of CON regulatory requirements, including application thresholds, contact information and utilization data. Comprehensive bibliographies are also included with thousands of published monographs, serials, professional and trade journal, as well as general press articles, research studies, published case law, law review, and bar journal coverage of CON. The work also includes compendiums of Internet-based and other data resources, a thorough glossary of CON terminology, and reviews of major research organizations and economists. The book is supplemented with numerous appendices. Based on a proprietary database, the work is designed to support periodic publication updates.

"The U.S. Healthcare Certificate of Need Sourcebook" is unique in its scope and comprehensive treatment of the topic of CON, which is a growing and increasingly contentious competitive, political, and legal healthcare policy issue.

ACKNOWLEDGEMENTS

I would like to acknowledge the assistance and support of a number of Health Capital Consultants (HCC) staff and colleagues who have helped facilitate the publication of this Sourcebook. Tim Alexander, MLS, HCC's Vice President of Library and Research Services, was central to the development of this project, both in conducting and directing the research for this book and coordinating the efforts of all those who have contributed to this project. Other researchers on this book include Jennifer A. Turner, MBA, Esq.; Anne C. Porter, St. Louis University School of Law (3L); and, HCC's other library and research staff members. In addition, I would like to thank Todd A. Zigrang, MHA, MBA, CHE, HCC Vice President, who has excelled in representing HCC throughout numerous healthcare regulatory client engagements and has greatly assisted in contributing to this work. Finally, thanks to HCC's consulting and administrative support team, who were of great assistance during my research and writing efforts.

ROBERT JAMES CIMASI, ASA, CBA, AVA, FCBI, CM&A, CMP

Robert James Cimasi, ASA, CBA, AVA, FCBI, CM&A, CMP is President of HEALTH CAPITAL CONSULTANTS (HCC) with over twenty years (20) of experience in serving clients, in over forty five (45) states, with a professional focus on the financial and economic aspects of healthcare service sector entities including: valuation consulting; litigation support; business intermediary and financing services; certificate-of-need consulting; and, healthcare transactions including sales, mergers, and acquisitions. Mr. Cimasi holds the Accredited Senior Appraiser (ASA) designation in Business Valuation, as well as, the Certified Business Appraiser (CBA), Accredited Valuation Analyst (AVA), Certified Business Intermediary (Fellow) (FCBI), the Alliance of Merger & Acquisition Advisors CM&A, and the Certified Medical Planner (CMP) designations.

Mr. Cimasi is a nationally known speaker on healthcare industry topics, who has served as conference faculty or presenter such organizations as the American Society of Appraisers (ASA), Institute of Business Appraisers (IBA), International Business Brokers Association (IBBA), American Institute of Certified Public Accountants (AICPA), Academy Health, Healthcare Financial Management Association (HFMA), American College of Healthcare Executives (ACHE), National Association of Healthcare Consultants (NAHC), National CPA Health Care Advisors Association, National Litigation Support Services Association (NLSSA), and many other national and state healthcare companies and organizations, as well as industry associations and professional societies.

He has been certified and has served as an expert witness on cases in several states, and has provided testimony before federal and state legislative committees. He is the author of *A Guide To Consulting Services for Emerging Healthcare Organizations* (John Wiley & Sons, 1999), *The Valuation of Healthcare Entities in a Changing Regulatory and Reimbursement Environment* (IBA Course 1011 text - 1999), and the author of *An Exciting Insight Into the Health Care Industry and Medical Practice Valuation* (AICPA Business Valuation course text 1997, rev. 2004.) He has written chapters on medical practice valuation in *The Handbook of Business Valuation* (John Wiley & Sons), *Valuing Professional Practices and Licenses: A Guide for the Matrimonial Practitioner, 3rd ed., 1999* (Aspen Law & Business), and *Valuing Specific Assets in Divorce* (Aspen Law & Business) and has been a contributor to *The Guide to Business Valuations* (Practitioners Publishing Company) and *Physician's Managed Care Success Manual: Strategic Options, Alliances, and Contracting Issues* (Mosby).

FOREWORD

As a young attorney in the general counsel's office of the U.S. Department of Health and Human Services during the late 1970s, I first learned of the federal government's quixotic efforts to rein in the rapid growth of our Nation's healthcare industry. With its whimsical acronyms and labyrinth of regulatory protocols, the Certificate of Need (CON) program became my ticket out of government service into the private practice of law. Indeed, for much of the next ten years I found myself in the middle of a fierce battle between regulators and competing healthcare organizations fighting over who should receive the government's franchise for the newest technology or facility to put it in.

Looking back from the vantage of today's healthcare system, it seems remarkable that at one point almost every state had some form of CON program and had accepted the premise that governments could do a better job of matching supply and demand than the healthcare marketplace. Although a large number of states have either abandoned or fundamentally revised their CON programs, where they exist, CON programs remain a major hurdle for providers seeking to expand, modernize or reshape their service capabilities. Success in scaling this hurdle requires a combination of resources including the expertise of professionals like Bob Cimasi who have dedicated their careers to understanding the inner workings of the regulatory process and its effect on the private sector.

When CON was a larger part of my legal practice than it is today, there was no single source containing a reliable summary of each state's law and how it has been interpreted and applied. Nor was there a directory of the contact people who ran the CON programs or were available for consultation or representation on a project. Those of us who did quite a lot of this work treated such information as highly proprietary and only shared it with our clients. Mr. Cimasi's book ***The U.S. Healthcare Certificate of Need Sourcebook*** fills that void in the literature and provides a useful research tool for both the neophyte and seasoned professional. Healthcare providers, both institutional and non-institutional, whether for-profit or not-for-profit, will find this work to be a vital part of their libraries.

Having had the pleasure to work with Bob Cimasi on many occasions, I know first-hand the depth of his knowledge and experience with complex subjects. I am delighted that he has taken the time to share some of his wisdom through this excellent book.

Peter A. Pavarini, Esq.
Schottenstein, Zox & Dunn
September 2004

CONTENTS

CON NARRATIVE HISTORY AND BACKGROUND

"We call it a Society; and go about professing openly the totalest separation, isolation. Our life is not a mutual helpfulness; but rather, cloaked under due laws-of-war, named "fair competition" and so forth, it is a mutual hostility."

— Thomas Carlyle (1795–1881. Past and Present, bk. 3, ch. 2 (1843)

I INTRODUCTION

In response to growing healthcare costs in an environment of budgetary restraints, there has been, in recent years, a resurgence of interest in government intervention to exert control over the supply and containment of health services, in the quest to control costs. Government mandated health planning has been based on the assumptions that health providers should not have sole control over the provision of healthcare services, and that decisions about healthcare access and choice should be made in a public, community forum because of their significant potential impact on the public welfare.[1]

One traditional method of government health policy intervention is the promulgation and enforcement of Certificate of Need statutes and regulations ("CON"), which specify those healthcare facilities, medical equipment, and services which require applications and approval to operate. This regulatory policy has been highly contentious in the state legislative arenas for many years, and has been the subject of significant administrative agency study and review. Beyond these activities, the grant or denial of a CON application has frequently resulted in complex and costly litigation. In the four (4) decades that CON has existed, approximately 800 reported legal cases have involved CON issues. (Refer to the CON Case Law Indexes). During this period CON has also been the subject of numerous academic and governmental scientific research studies, as well as the subject of thousands of news and journal articles.

While current CON laws were modeled after federal legislation, CON regulation is currently based on various state statutes and rules and regulations which designate an agency or board to administer the approval process of reviewing CON applications and give authority to the CON regulatory review board or commission to promulgate regulations specifying the criteria by which CON applications are evaluated. These criteria are commonly required to be created in conjunction with the state's long term health plan and goals. In the states where CON regulation is still in effect, CON regulation traditionally constitutes the most prevalent form of state health planning.

The intent of CON was to control costs by regulating major capital expenditures and changes in healthcare services capacity.[2] CON regulatory policy was designed to prevent *duplication* of healthcare services or *excessive competition* between healthcare providers. CON is based on the theory that in an unregulated market, healthcare providers will provide the latest costly technology and equipment, regardless of duplication or need. Although, since its inception in the early 1970's, CON was intended to reduce healthcare costs by preventing duplication of services, healthcare costs have continued to rise.

---

[1] *See* Herbert Harvey Hyman, Health Regulation: Certificate of Need & 1122 32 (Aspen Systems Corp., 1977).

[2] *See* Chayet & Sonnenreich, P.C., Medicine In the Public Interest, Inc., Certificate of Need: An Expanding Regulatory Concept 1 1978).

II THE THEORETICAL BASIS FOR CERTIFICATE OF NEED

II.A The Roemer Effect

Cited in the establishment of many CON laws restricting the construction and expansion of healthcare facilities was the "Roemer Effect." In their 1959 study, Roemer and Shain argued that hospital beds would be intentionally filled by providers who induce ill-informed patients into hospital stays.[3] While the basis of the argument for this set of circumstances, i.e. "*supply and demand,*" may have been valid during the "cost-plus reimbursement era" before the implementation of the prospective payment system ("PPS") for hospitals in 1983, it is widely asserted that it has not been demonstrated to be the case today, in an era characterized by the shifting of financial risk to providers.

II.B Prospective Pricing Systems

In response to rising healthcare costs, Medicare has gradually transitioned from reimbursing providers on a cost-plus or fee-for-service basis to the PPS, under which reimbursement is set before the service is provided.[4] Medicare and Medicaid originally paid for hospital services using a "cost plus" reimbursement basis, where hospitals were paid for all of their costs and more. Under this reimbursement system, hospital profits were directly linked with patient volumes. In 1983, "cost-plus" reimbursement was replaced by a prospective payment system measured by "diagnosis-related groups" ("DRGs") based on the patient's primary diagnosis.[5] Under this reimbursement system, hospitals have the financial risk of providing services efficiently under a set fee scale for a set diagnosis.

II.C Excess Capacity and Duplication of Services

The fundamental idea of CON was simple: lower costs by reducing duplication. The term duplication is often used in the assertion that societal costs increase when there are "*too many*" providers of the same health services, often labeled as "excess capacity."[6] However, *excess capacity* is on a basic level, a value-laden term, not an absolute standard. In a recent article published in *Health Services Research* (February 1999), Professor Carolyn Madden summarized a number of studies of excess capacity saying, "Without a clear statement of this standard [e.g., the *correct* number of hospital beds], we cannot determine what constitutes *too many*. The research literature provides no clear statement."[7]

II.D Competition

A central argument against CON regulatory policy is that in intervening in the market, it disrupts the natural market forces and is significantly anti-competitive. As a result, CON often serves as a barrier to new market entrants and has been viewed by many healthcare economists as a strong disincentive of the benefits of the introduction of new technologies. *"In industry after industry, the underlying dynamic is the same: competition compels companies to deliver increasing value to customers. The fundamental driver of this continuous quality improvement and cost reduction is innovation. Without incentives to sustain innovation in health care, short-term cost savings will soon be overwhelmed by the desire to widen access, the growing health needs of an aging population, and the unwillingness of Americans to settle for anything less than the best treatments available.*

---

[3] Carolyn W. Madden, *Excess Capacity: Markets, Regulation, and Values* 33: 6 HEALTH SERVS. RESEARCH 1651, 1653 (Feb. 1999).

[4] "Prospective Payment System" ON-LINE MEDICAL DICTIONARY, *available at* cancerweb.ncl.ac.uk/cga-bin/omd?query=prospective+payment+system, (last visited June 10, 2003).

[5] Michael Millenson, VISITING SCHOLAR INSTITUTE FOR HEALTH SERVICES RESEARCH AND POLICY STUDIES, AMERICA'S HEALTH CARE CHALLENGE: RISING COSTS 9 (Jan. 22, 2002).

[6] Carolyn W. Madden, *Excess Capacity: Markets, Regulation, and Values* 33: 6 HEALTH SERVS. RESEARCH 1651, 1652 (Feb. 1999).

[7] Carolyn W. Madden, *Excess Capacity: Markets, Regulation, and Values* 33: 6 HEALTH SERVS. RESEARCH 1651, 1652 (Feb. 1999).

Inevitably, the failure to promote innovation will lead to lower quality or more rationing of care – two equally undesirable results."[8]

In the same manner, there is continuing consensus among health economic analysts that competition between providers drives patient quality of care and beneficial outcomes, as well as cost efficiency. According to Professor Madden, "*there is ... agreement across all perspectives of [health economics theory] on one issue: the negative consequences of too much concentration of economic power.*"[9] Hospitals in more competitive markets have been demonstrated to have average costs below those of less competitive markets.[10] Healthy competition appears to work in giving economic power to patients and payers by creating choices for consumers and raising quality standards as providers compete for patient loyalty. When patient choice is diminished, decisions about access, quality, and beneficial outcomes become the sole purview of oligopoly market players who, as decision makers acting in the absence of healthy competition, are free to ignore patient demands and needs.

CON is an example of a governmental regulatory policy that is often in conflict with the goals of antitrust enforcement, and has been regularly denounced by the FTC, the agency for federal antitrust enforcement. Seeking to preserve competition in healthcare markets, the FTC has consistently denounced CON, most recently in a joint study and report with the Department of Justice ("DOJ"), as a failed public health regulatory policy which creates barriers to new market competitors.

II.E Quality Enhancement Through Concentration of Experience

II.E.1 The Dartmouth Atlas of Healthcare

Several studies have attempted to link higher procedural volume with better outcomes. CON proponents have asserted that CON, by limiting the supply of healthcare services and facilities through CON regulation, is actually improving the quality of outcomes for those procedures that may be affected by facility or provider volume. In a novel approach to promoting CON regulation, the "Dartmouth Atlas of Health Care,"[11] was cited by CON proponents soon after its publication in 1999, as determining that more hospital care is not linked with better outcomes.[12]

In fact, the Dartmouth Atlas's findings indicated that there was no evidence that more intensive care achieved better outcomes, that physicians' were unaware of low hospital resource supply, and that hospital care is itself a health risk. Physicians' awareness of health facilities is not a CON related issue.[13] While these issues are serious, no direct reference is made, or evidence provided, nor has any efficacious inference been drawn by the study that correlates the effect of CON to the value of access to hospital resources.

The issues of medical error and the associated risk of hospitalization is a completely separate, although serious, issue unrelated to CON or the value of access to hospital resources. In 2000, the "*Institute of Medicine reported that medical errors kill up to 98,000 Americans each year.*"[14] Medical errors may be the third leading cause of death in the U.S.[15] and may kill approximately 44,000 patients in U.S. hospitals each

[8] Michael Porter, et. al., *Making Competition in Health Care Work*, 72(4) HARV. BUS. REV. 131, 131 (1994).

[9] Carolyn W. Madden, *Excess Capacity: Markets, Regulation, and Values* 33: 6 HEALTH SERVS. RESEARCH 1651, 1663 (Feb. 1999).

[10] J. Zwanziger, G. Melnick G, & A. Bamezai, *California Providers Adjust to Increasing Price Controls, in* HEALTH POLICY REFORM: COMPETITION AND CONTROLS 254-55, 241-258 (R. Helms, ed., Washington, DC: AEI Press, 1993).

[11] THE QUALITY OF MEDICAL CARE IN THE UNITED STATES: A REPORT ON THE MEDICARE PROGRAM, THE DARTMOUTH ATLAS OF HEALTH CARE 93(AHA Press, 1999).

[12] Michael Smith-Mello, Kentucky Long Term Policy Research Center, *Health Care Costs Compel Fresh Look at Old Regulatory Lever*, 10(4) *FORESIGHT* 1, 3 (2004) *available at www.kltprc.net/foresight/Chpt_74.htm* (last visited Dec. 1, 2004).

[13] THE QUALITY OF MEDICAL CARE IN THE UNITED STATES: A REPORT ON THE MEDICARE PROGRAM, THE DARTMOUTH ATLAS OF HEALTH CARE 93(AHA Press, 1999).

[14] "The Hospital Industry: An Uncertain Future." The Sourcebook, 2001. p.1-3.

[15] "Is US Really the Best in the World?" JAMA, Vol. 284, no. 4 (7/26/00), p. 485-487.

year.[16] A recent study by the U.S. Agency for Healthcare Research on 18 types of hospital complications *"sometimes caused by medical errors"* found that *"postoperative infections, surgical wounds accidentally opening and other often-preventable complications lead to more than 32,000 U.S. hospital deaths and more than $9 billion in extra costs annually."*[17]

Another complication to utilizing the Dartmouth Studies to promote the utility of CON, is that surgical volume per capita for individual facilities and in a community is known to vary across markets for a variety of reasons. In this well known study of clinical geographic variation, The Dartmouth Atlas of Health Care, it states, *"Although regional variation in health care is ubiquitous, not all surgical procedures vary to the same degree. Procedures which are not very variable are generally applied to clinical conditions for which treatment is constrained to a single clinical approach."*[18] The report goes on to state, *"The amount of regional variation for most procedures, however, is too large to attribute to chance or variation in illness rates ... Variations in the rates of the use of these procedures reflect variations in practice style and in how physicians diagnose and treat common clinical conditions."* The causes of these variations include: variations in the intensity of the utilization of diagnostic testing; gaps in medical science and professional uncertainty; and, a lack of consideration for patient preferences.[19] *"Several studies have attempted to understand the relationship between inappropriate use of care, as defined by panels of experts, and geographic variations in surgical rates. While many researchers had assumed that areas with high rates of surgery would have a greater percentage of unnecessary care, the studies failed to confirm that hypothesis. Overuse as defined by experts accounts for very little of the variation."*[20]

Several recent articles have been published that contradict the assertions of CON proponents related to the examination of whether CON can improve outcomes by increasing facility volumes.[21] One of the most recent meta studies of the published literature related to this phenomenon concluded that the improvements in outcomes related to hospital volume were supported but that the causes of this correlation and any related policy implications were unclear. Thus, it remains uncertain as to what extent improved outcomes depends on physician volume or experience rather than hospital volume. *"Therefore, policies advocating selective referral to high-volume providers based solely on hospital (or physician) volume may not achieve their intended effect; a low-volume surgeon at a high-volume hospital may have significantly poorer results than a moderate-volume surgeon at a moderate-volume hospital."*[22] Furthermore, there was no consensus of what defines high volume or low volume levels amongst the survey reviewed. The relationship between volumes and outcomes in the 135 studies analyzed varied greatly among individual procedures and conditions and also noted was the wide variance between individual hospitals and physicians. However, this review of the literature concludes by cautioning that, *"The clinical and policy significance of this finding is complicated by the methodologic shortcomings of many studies."*[23]

---

[16] "Preventing Death and Injury from Medical Errors Requires Dramatic, System-Wide Changes" The National Academies, (11/29/99), www4.nationalacademies.org/news.nsf/isbn/0309068371?OpenDocument (Accessed 9/30/03).

[17] "Med complications may cost $9B per year." YAHOO! NEWS, Oct. 7, 2003 (news.yahoo.com/news?tmpl=story2&cid=534&u=/ap/2003100/ /ap_on_he_me/costly_complications&printer=1, accessed 10/8/03).

[18] THE QUALITY OF MEDICAL CARE IN THE UNITED STATES: A REPORT ON THE MEDICARE PROGRAM, THE DARTMOUTH ATLAS OF HEALTH CARE 142 (AHA Press, 1999).

[19] THE QUALITY OF MEDICAL CARE IN THE UNITED STATES: A REPORT ON THE MEDICARE PROGRAM, THE DARTMOUTH ATLAS OF HEALTH CARE 142-144 (AHA Press, 1999).

[20] THE QUALITY OF MEDICAL CARE IN THE UNITED STATES: A REPORT ON THE MEDICARE PROGRAM, THE DARTMOUTH ATLAS OF HEALTH CARE 223 (AHA Press, 1999).

[21] Ethan A. Halm, et. al., *Is Volume Related to Outcome in Health Care? A Systematic Review and Methodologic Critique of the Literature,* 137 ANNALS OF INTERNAL MED. 511 (2002).

[22] Ethan A. Halm, et. al., *Is Volume Related to Outcome in Health Care? A Systematic Review and Methodologic Critique of the Literature,* 137 ANNALS OF INTERNAL MED. 511, 516 (2002).

[23] Ethan A. Halm, et. al., *Is Volume Related to Outcome in Health Care? A Systematic Review and Methodologic Critique of the Literature,* 137 ANNALS OF INTERNAL MED. 511, 517 (2002).

III DEVELOPMENT OF FEDERAL REGULATIONS

State and federal involvement in enforced planning for health facilities has an extensive and well-documented history. Regulation of healthcare resources began after World War II with the passage of the Hospital Survey and Construction Act,[24] commonly known as the Hill-Burton Act in 1946. The enactment of federally mandated CON related laws were the genesis of government mandated health policy planning efforts. While federal regulations provided legislation and enforcement provisions, program development and implementation generally took place on the state or local level.[25]

III.A Hill-Burton Act

The passage of the Hill-Burton Act marked the beginning of forty (40) plus years of federally funded health policy planning.[26] It was intended to encourage the development of hospitals in rural areas because of a perceived shortage of healthcare facilities following the Depression and World War II.[27] The Act required states to institute health policy planning in order to receive federal funding for hospital construction.[28] In addition to producing a healthcare plan delineating its healthcare needs, states were required to inventory existing healthcare facilities and designate a single agency responsible for health policy planning.[29] Between 1946 and 1971, the Hill-Burton program provided financial assistance to sixty percent (60%) of American hospitals.[30]

III.B Section 1122

Mandatory federal health policy planning did not exist before 1970 and only five (5) states had health policy planning regulations. However, despite the rarity of health policy regulation before 1970, within four (4) years, twenty-four (24) states had enacted CON laws in response to the passage of Section 1122 of the 1972 Social Security Amendments.[31] Section 1122 allowed the Secretary of Health, Education, and Welfare to enter into agreements with states with a "designated planning agency" responsible for determining whether healthcare facilities could make capital expenditures.[32] Similar to CON, Section 1122 forced states to review capital expenditures exceeding $100,000, bed capacity changes, or "substantial" changes in services.[33] It covered all major healthcare institutions and was much more comprehensive than existing state CON laws.[34] States failing to institute health policy planning programs could lose Medicare and Medicaid cost reimbursement because the costs of facilities constructed without CON approval could be excluded when

---

[24] *See* ANDREW BRYSON DUNHAM, HEALTH AND POLITICS: THE IMPACT OF CERTIFICATE OF NEED REGULATION 141 (University of Chicago, 1981).

[25] *See generally* Patrick John McGinley, *Beyond Health Care Reform: Reconsidering Certificate of Need Laws in a "Managed Competition" System*, 23 FLA. ST. U. L. REV. 141, (1995). After World War II there was a shortage of hospital beds, physicians, and supporting healthcare workers resulting in high mortality rates and an inability to develop effective disease treatments. *See SEE* HERBERT HARVEY HYMAN, HEALTH REGULATION: CERTIFICATE OF NEED AND 1122 7, (Aspen Systems Corp., 1977).

[26] *See* FRANK A. SLOAN, ET. AL., COST, QUALITY, AND ACCESS IN HEALTH CARE: NEW ROLES FOR HEALTH PLANNING IN A COMPETITIVE ENVIRONMENT 21 (Josey-Bass Publishers 1988).

[27] *See* ANDREW BRYSON DUNHAM, HEALTH AND POLITICS: THE IMPACT OF CERTIFICATE OF NEED REGULATION 141 (University of Chicago, 1981).

[28] *See* FRANK A. SLOAN, ET. AL., COST, QUALITY, AND ACCESS IN HEALTH CARE: NEW ROLES FOR HEALTH PLANNING IN A COMPETITIVE ENVIRONMENT 30 (Josey-Bass Publishers 1988).

[29] *See* ANDREW BRYSON DUNHAM, HEALTH AND POLITICS: THE IMPACT OF CERTIFICATE OF NEED REGULATION 141 (University of Chicago, 1981).

[30] *See* ANDREW BRYSON DUNHAM, HEALTH AND POLITICS: THE IMPACT OF CERTIFICATE OF NEED REGULATION 141, 142 (University of Chicago, 1981).

[31] *See* HERBERT HARVEY HYMAN, HEALTH REGULATION: CERTIFICATE OF NEED AND 1122 27, (Aspen Systems Corp., 1977).

[32] *See* Chayet & Sonnenreich, P.C., MEDICINE IN THE PUBLIC INTEREST, INC., CERTIFICATE OF NEED: AN EXPANDING REGULATORY CONCEPT 1,2 (1978).

[33] Daniel M. Mendelson & Judith Arnold, *Certificate of Need Revisited* 66(1) SPECTRUM 36, 36. (1993).

[34] *See* HERBERT HARVEY HYMAN, HEALTH REGULATION: CERTIFICATE OF NEED AND 1122 31, (Aspen Systems Corp., 1977). Some state CON laws enacted after 1122 were more stringent in that they "regulated capacity and service changes whether or not a capital expenditure was involved." *SEE* HERBERT HARVEY HYMAN, HEALTH REGULATION: CERTIFICATE OF NEED AND 1122 32, (Aspen Systems Corp., 1977).

determining Medicare or Medicaid reimbursement.[35] Therefore, hospitals would comply with state CON laws and not provide new services without state approval because Medicare and Medicaid reimbursement is a significant source of revenue for almost all healthcare facilities. "*Two years after the passage of the '1122' amendments, 37 states had opted to establish a state-designated agency for the purpose of implementing the federal law.*"[36]

The 1972 Amendments also established Professional Standards Review Organizations ("PSROs") to control utilization of services and to review procedures according to professional standards.[37] PSROs preceded Professional Review Organizations ("PROs"), established in the mid-1980's to evaluate the reasonableness and necessity of inpatient services provided to Medicare patients.[38] Although advocates of PSROs argue that they improved healthcare quality, the majority of evidence indicates that PSROs were used primarily to control costs rather than promote quality.[39] A 1979 PRSO Program Evaluation study found that each dollar spent on CON review yielded approximately ninety cents in reimbursement savings, corresponding to a savings-to-cost ratio of about 0.9-to-1.[40] However, 1978 data indicated that only forty percent (40%) of the cost of PSRO review was recouped.[41] Thus, these savings were estimated by PSRO review costs.[42]

III.C National Health Planning and Resources Development Act

The National Health Planning and Resources Development Act, enacted in 1974, pushed CON regulations to the forefront of government healthcare cost containment efforts. The Act was designed to develop a "*national health planning policy*"[43] *in response to "the lack of uniformly effective methods of delivering health care,"*[44] *"the substitution of ambulatory and intermediate care for inpatient hospital care,"*[45] *and the lack of "basic knowledge regarding personal health care and methods for effective use of available health services."*[46] *The Act required that federal agencies pass health policy planning guidelines and establish "specific goals, priorities, and success criteria."*[47] It prompted states to enact CON programs by guaranteeing federal funding for state CON review programs and conditioning the receipt of certain healthcare funding on enacting CON programs.[48] It also specified that state CON programs must meet federal guidelines in order to receive federal funding.[49]

---

[35] *See* Chayet & Sonnenreich, P.C., MEDICINE IN THE PUBLIC INTEREST, INC., CERTIFICATE OF NEED: AN EXPANDING REGULATORY CONCEPT 2, 32 1978).

[36] HERBERT HARVEY HYMAN, HEALTH REGULATION: CERTIFICATE OF NEED AND 1122 7, (Aspen Systems Corp., 1977).

[37] J.L. Ashby, *The Impact of Hospital Regulatory Programs on Per Capita Costs, Utilization and Capital Investment* 21(1) INQUIRY 45, 46 (1984).

[38] *See* FRANK A. SLOAN, ET. AL., COST, QUALITY, AND ACCESS IN HEALTH CARE: NEW ROLES FOR HEALTH PLANNING IN A COMPETITIVE ENVIRONMENT 111 (Josey-Bass Publishers 1988).

[39] *See* FRANK A. SLOAN, ET. AL., COST, QUALITY, AND ACCESS IN HEALTH CARE: NEW ROLES FOR HEALTH PLANNING IN A COMPETITIVE ENVIRONMENT 112 (Josey-Bass Publishers 1988). *See generally*, P.E. Dans. et al., *Peer Review Organizations: Promises and Potential Pitfalls*, 313 NEW ENG. J. OF MED., 1131 (1985).

[40] *See* CONGRESS OF THE UNITED STATES CONGRESSIONAL BUDGET OFFICE, THE IMPACT OF PSROS ON HEALTH-CARE COSTS: UPDATE OF CBO'S 1979 EVALUATION xiv (1981). *See also* Sloan, Frank A. et al., Cost, Quality, and Access in Health Care: New Roles for Health Planning in a Competitive Environment 112, (Jossey-Bass Publishers, 1988).

[41] CONGRESS OF THE UNITED STATES CONGRESSIONAL BUDGET OFFICE, THE IMPACT OF PSROS ON HEALTH-CARE COSTS: UPDATE OF CBO'S 1979 EVALUATION xiii (1981).

[42] *See* U.S. CONGRESS, CONGRESSIONAL BUDGET OFFICE, THE IMPACT OF PSROS ON HEALTH-CARE COST: UPDATE OF CBO'S 1979 EVALUATION xiv (U.S. Gov't Printing Office 1981).

[43] National Health Planning and Resource Development Act of 1974, Pub. L. No. 93-641, 88 Stat. 2225 (1975).

[44] National Health Planning and Resource Development Act of 1974, Pub. L. No. 93-641, 88 Stat. 2225, Sec. (-2)(A)(3)(A) (1975).

[45] National Health Planning and Resource Development Act of 1974, Pub. L. No. 93-641, 88 Stat. 2225, Sec. (2)(A)(4) (1975).

[46] National Health Planning and Resource Development Act of 1974, Pub. L. No. 93-641, 88 Stat. 2225, Sec. (2)(A)(6) (1975).

[47] *See* FRANK A. SLOAN, ET. AL., COST, QUALITY, AND ACCESS IN HEALTH CARE: NEW ROLES FOR HEALTH PLANNING IN A COMPETITIVE ENVIRONMENT 31 (Josey-Bass Publishers 1988).

[48] Patrick John McGinley, *Beyond Health Care Reform: Reconsidering Certificate of Need Laws in a "Managed Competition" System*, 23 FLA. ST. U. L. REV. 141,148 (1995).

[49] Carolyn W. Madden, *Excess Capacity: Markets, Regulation, and Values* 33: 6 HEALTH SERVS. RESEARCH 1651, 1658 (Feb. 1999).

As enacted, this federal oversight plan created huge disincentives for noncompliance with the mandated establishment of CON review programs. Accordingly, most states replaced their Section 1122 review provisions with a CON regulatory scheme. By 1980 almost every state had developed some form of CON review program under these guidelines.[50]

The ostensible reason for the federal push of CON regulation during the 1970's was Congress' belief that the healthcare industry suffered from a version of the "Roemer effect," i.e. exhibited a phenomenon described as *"supply created demand,"* which malady Congress intended to correct through a mandate for state government intervention in the market.[51] State health policy planning agencies were required to "*take actions . . . to allocate the supply of [inpatient health services and other institutional health services].*"[52] Although the Act claimed to regulate only the segments of the healthcare industry believed to be unresponsive to competition, they suggest a lack of faith in market forces' ability to control costs. Additionally, despite the fact that some states developed CON programs prior to national legislation,[53] these federal laws were clearly the catalyst for most state CON programs. States that subsequently questioned the wisdom of CON had, as a practical matter, no choice but to comply with federal guidelines.

In the 1980s, however, the deregulation movement set the stage for the elimination of federal CON regulations. Federal support for CON ended in 1986 with the repeal of the National Health Planning and Resources Development Act of 1974.[54] Legislators were concerned that CON "*failed to reduce the nation's aggregate health care costs, and it was beginning to produce a detrimental effect in local communities.*"[55] After the Act's repeal, state CON programs would no longer be subsidized by federal funding.[56]

IV STATE REGULATIONS

Subsequent to federally mandated CON regulations, state CON regulations have slowly evolved and diverged with many states eliminating or minimizing their CON regulations.

IV.A Development of State CON Programs

In response to The National Health Planning and Resources Development Act of 1974, the states developed some form of CON review program replacing their Section 1122 guidelines.[57] In 1974, 23 states had CON programs, and by 1980, 49 states had enacted CON review. (Refer to the "States with CON Programs" table for further information).

IV.B Structure of State Programs

State CON programs are administered according to statutes and regulations controlling market entry for regulated facilities, services, and equipment. Hospitals, nursing homes, some freestanding clinics, home health agencies, and ambulatory care surgery centers are often among the healthcare facility providers covered by CON.[58] CON also often applies to healthcare services including the change of one service to another, the

---

[50] Frank A. Sloan, *Government and the Regulation of Hospital Care* 72(2) The Am. Econ. Rev. 196, 198 (1982).

[51] L.H. Wolfson., *State Regulation of Health Facility Planning: The Economic Theory and Political Realities of Certificates of Need*, 4 DePaul J. of Health Care Law 261, 267 (2001).

[52] *See generally*, National Health Planning and Resource Development Act of 1974, Pub. L. No. 93-641, 88 Stat. 2225 (1975).

[53] Frank A. Sloan, *Government and the Regulation of Hospital Care* 72(2) The Am. Econ. Rev. 196 (1982).

[54] Carolyn W. Madden, *Excess Capacity: Markets, Regulation, and Values* 33: 6 Health Servs. Research 1651, 1659 (Feb. 1999).

[55] Patrick John McGinley, *Beyond Health Care Reform: Reconsidering Certificate of Need Laws in a "Managed Competition" System*, 23 Fla. St. U. L. Rev. 141, 157 (1995).

[56] Patrick John McGinley, *Beyond Health Care Reform: Reconsidering Certificate of Need Laws in a "Managed Competition" System*, 23 Fla. St. U. L. Rev. 141, 148 (1995).

[57] Frank A. Sloan, *Government and the Regulation of Hospital Care* 72(2) The Am. Econ. Rev. 196, 197-198 (1982).

[58] Frank A. Sloan, Cost, Quality, and Access in Health Care, 44 (Jossey-Bass, 1988).

purchase of medical equipment, and new technology. State CON programs generally have two (2) functions: to develop a health plan promoting equitable access to healthcare services; and, to review CON applications submitted by healthcare providers. There has been a significant ongoing controversy as to whether the first function has been adequately addressed, or whether, through "agency capture," the CON regulatory process has been highjacked to promote the objectives of oligopoly market players.[59]

V SELECTED CON RESEARCH STUDIES

The following are brief descriptions of selected representative studies related to the effectiveness of CON regulations. Summaries of the most recent studies' findings will be discussed first followed by a description of findings from older studies. These summaries are provided only as an illustration of the types and depth of research which has been conducted regarding CON topics. Refer to the CON Books Bibliography and CON Articles Bibliography for a more complete list of the published CON literature.

V.A 2004 Detroit "Big Three Automakers" Study

CON proponents have recently cited assertions by the "big three automakers," that the employee healthcare costs for these automakers are less in CON States than in Non-CON States where they operate.[60] These purported results have been provided in several States' legislative hearings on CON including Indiana, Missouri, and Ohio.[61] Nonetheless, CON proponents have as yet not published or otherwise submitted the underlying empirical data set or methodology for peer review of this study. From the information that has been made publicly available on the Missouri CON website, these studies include the following characteristics, some of which have been challenged by CON opponents. Only eight (8) states are sampled: three (3) non-CON (Wisconsin, Ohio, and Indiana) and five (5) CON states (Delaware, Kentucky, Missouri, Michigan, and New York). A sample of only five (5) CON states may not be statistically valid or representative of indications of the cost of healthcare for all CON states, and the selection of a sub-set of "extremes" of these few states (e.g., only the "high" and "low" of two (2) CON states and two (2) Non-CON states) may further exacerbate these shortcomings. Also, the survey data was limited to healthcare expenses for employees of automakers which may not be representative of the total healthcare expenses in these States.

As a review of the automakers' claims, Health Capital Consultants (HCC) evaluated a data sample that includes hospital expenses per capita for CON States as compared to Non-CON States, and also selected CON and Non-CON States including all of the States included in the automakers' study. The results of the HCC analysis clearly indicated that hospital expenses per capita for Non-CON States are considerably less than hospital expenses per capita for CON States. Furthermore, hospital expenses per capita for all of the five (5) CON states selected for the automakers' study, were higher than in Non-CON States overall.[62]

V.B 2002 Health Capital Consultants (HCC) Hospital CON Study

In a 2002 study of CON regulatory policy, HCC analyzed hospital financial and utilization data for CON States and Non-CON States for the years 1989, 1994, and 1999. The study was designed within the context of stated CON theory, that asserts that the appropriate management of and implementation of CON controls on inpatient care supply should reduce the cost of care. The objective of the study was to: (a) describe characteristics of the U.S. healthcare system, stratified by CON policy; and, (b) compare inpatient costs,

---

[59] Michael M. Morrisey, *State Health Care Reform: Protecting the Provider, in* American Health Care, Government Market Processes, and the Public Interest 229, 238-239, 244-247 ((The Independent Institute 2000).

[60] Missouri Health Facilities Review Committee, Benefits Flier *available at www.dhss.mo.gov/CON/conbenefits.pdf* (last visited Dec. 28, 2004).

[61] Lee Hawkins, Jr., *Detroit Auto Makers Fight Local Hospitals' Building Plans*, Wall St. J. at B1, Jan. 20, 2004, *available at* online.wsj.com/article_print/0,,SB107454982298405576.

[62] HCC Findings, Internal references.

utilization, and capital indicators between States with and without CON laws over the period of the most recent decade of reported data, utilizing five year points-in-time, i.e., 1989,1994, and 1999.

Case definitions for the 2002 HCC CON Study terms included: the term "*CON State*", which was defined as any state that had an acute care CON law in effect during the analysis period years 1989-1999; the term "*NON Con State*", which was defined as any state that did not have an acute care CON law in effect during the analysis period years1989-1999; the term "*Included States*", which was defined as those 47 States and the District of Columbia, whose status related to whether CON regulations were in effect did not change during the analysis period years 1989-1999; and, the term "*Excluded States*", which referred to the states of Indiana, North Dakota, and Pennsylvania, which were exclude because of significant changes to their CON status between1989 and 1999.

The methodology for the 2002 HCC CON Study was based on a statistical analysis, employing a one-way analysis of variation (ANOVA), comparing each of the study variables, i.e.: *Beds per1000; Admissions per1000; average length of stay (ALOS); Expenses per Admission; Expenses per Capita; Cost per 1000; Total Profit Margins*; *Average Age of Plant*; and *Debt per Bed*, by State CON law status, across three time points – 1989, 1994, and 1999. Confidence *p-values* were calculated for each variable for each variable pair (CON and Non-CON) for each year. A standard statistical significance cut-off of .05 was utilized.

Data selected and analyzed for the 2002 HCC CON Study was derived from three (3) widely recognized sources, i.e.: (a) "*Hospital Statistics*", published by the American Hospital Association (AHA), which compiles hospital data derived from replies to the AHA Annual Survey, sent to all AHA-registered and non-registered hospitals in the U.S. and its associated areas; (b) "*The Almanac of Hospital Financial & Operating Indicators*", published by The Center for Healthcare Industry Performance Studies (CHIPS), which annually reports the financial position of the hospital industry; and, (c) "*The Comparative Performance of U.S. Hospitals: The Sourcebook*", published and produced jointly by Health Care Investment Analysts (HCIA) and Deloitte & Touche, which presents current and historical information on the financial performance of the U.S. hospital industry.

Several limitations of the 2002 HCC CON Study were disclosed, including: "*(a) the complexity of the healthcare economy, subject to the impact of multiple variables, complicates efforts to isolate CON as the driving variable in the analysis of health system costs, utilization, or access amid market forces such as the impact of government policy and managed care on reimbursement; evolving technology; and, shifting patient population demographics and expectations; (b) CON is not a "Yes/No" variable because States subject to CON are also subject to other significant variations including facilities and services regulated; CON geographic market definitions; CON review thresholds and criteria; demographic and epidemiological characteristics; and, CON administrative processes; and, (c) the accuracy, validity, and efficacy of the study's statistical analysis was dependent upon the accuracy, validity, and scope of the reported data utilized.*"

Among the several conclusions drawn from the 2002 HCC CON Study analysis, based on comparing data from CON States with Non-CON States during the analysis period years 1989, 1994, and 1999, were that: (a) the data examined indicated that CON regulation does not reduce *Beds per1000; Admissions per1000; ALOS, Expenses per Admission; or, Expenses per Capita;* (b) there is no evidence that CON States have achieved greater *Total Profit Margins* at less *Cost per 1000*; (c) there is no statistically significant evidence that CON States have achieved a lower *Average Age of Plant* as an indicator of acceleration in new construction activity or retirement of existing, aging facilities; and, (d) there is statistically significant evidence that CON States have higher *Debt per Bed* than Non-CON States in 1999 as an indicator of increased cost due to debt load.

V.C Feldman's 2000 Meta-study of CON and Government Market Processes

Roger Feldman's 2000 meta-study of CON and Government market processes concludes that the empirical literature on CON laws is extensive, and virtually unanimous in its consensus that CON regulation has neither controlled hospital costs nor restrained service diffusion. The specific studies reviewed by Feldman indicate that CON laws have resulted in higher profits by for-profit hospitals, and have prevented entry of new providers into the markets to the benefit of existing providers.[63] This restriction into the market is described as especially significant given the increased competitiveness due to the spread of managed care entities. Moreover, recent studies indicate that CON programs tend to increase costs, rather than achieve their designed purpose of controlling costs, with hospitals in states regulated by CON having costs 20.6 percent higher than those in states with no CON regulation.[64]

The empirical literature reviewed in the Feldman meta-study also suggests that CON has not been effective in restricting the diffusion of new technologies, including open-heart surgery, renal dialysis programs, and CT scanners.[65] Case studies from Policy Analysis-Urban Systems (1980), cited by Feldman, suggest this lack of effectiveness resulted from hospitals being able to avoid CON by leasing CT scanners, purchasing mobile units, or purchasing units right below CON regulatory threshold.[66]

V.D 1998 Washington State Study of Healthcare Costs and CON

In 1998, the Joint Legislative and Audit Review Committee and the Health Policy Analysis Program of the University of Washington's School of Public Health and Community Medicine conducted a study of the CON program in the state of Washington aimed at examining the effects of CON and its possible repeal on the cost, quality, and availability of healthcare services, as well as CON's effect on charity care and access to health services in rural areas.[67] Results based on a literature review, interviews and information from healthcare providers and healthcare economic experts in the state, as well as the analysis of states that completely or partially repealed their CON laws, indicated that there is strong evidence that CON is not an effective mechanism for controlling overall healthcare spending and is not always effective in controlling supply.[68] This study found that while CON laws can slow the expansion of some healthcare services, there are other factors affecting healthcare costs that CON does not control. Additionally, CON was found to not always be effective in controlling supply. While CON has restricted the supply of some specific services, there is no convincing evidence that CON limits the number of hospitals and other providers for managed care.[69]

Further, the evidence gathered in this study, regarding the effect of CON on quality, and the ability of CON to improve quality by concentrating volume of specialized services is weak and inconclusive, with only

---

[63] Roger D. Feldman, American Health Care, Government Market Processes, and the Public Interest 245-246 (The Independent Institute 2000).

[64] Roger D. Feldman, American Health Care, Government Market Processes, and the Public Interest 230, 245 (The Independent Institute 2000).

[65] Roger D. Feldman, American Health Care, Government Market Processes, and the Public Interest 246 (The Independent Institute 2000).

[66] Roger D. Feldman, American Health Care, Government Market Processes, and the Public Interest 246 (The Independent Institute 2000).

[67] State of Washington Joint Legislative and Audit Review Committee, Effects of Certificate of Need and Its Possible Repeal i (January 8, 1999).

[68] State of Washington Joint Legislative and Audit Review Committee, Effects of Certificate of Need and Its Possible Repeal i (January 8, 1999).

[69] State of Washington Joint Legislative and Audit Review Committee, Effects of Certificate of Need and Its Possible Repeal -910 (January 8, 1999).

some indirect evidence suggesting that CON may protect quality in home health and hospice by keeping out unprepared or unqualified providers, mainly due to the fact that CON does not provide an ongoing mechanism to monitor quality.[70]

Similarly, this study found conflicting evidence regarding the effect of CON or its repeal on access to health services, particularly in rural areas. Although CON has been used to protect existing facilities in inner city areas or to prompt providers to locate in those areas; CON appears to restrict access by preventing the development of new facilities. Additionally, the relationship between CON and access varies by service, as well as by state, with no ongoing mechanism to monitor access.[71]

Finally, while some states are more likely to grant a CON to facilities offering more charity care, the CON program in Washington and most other states does not include monitoring for compliance. No studies were identified that measured the effect of CON on levels of charity care, while the study reported that financial and market pressures make it increasingly difficult for all types of providers to offer charity care.[72]

The study determined that the available evidence did not support making a recommendation as to whether Washington should repeal or retain its CON program. However, the study did provide specific options for policy makers depending on their decision as to the CON program's future. Should Washington decide to reform the program, the study suggested: reassessing legislative and regulatory goals in relation to new conditions and needs in healthcare system; establishing policy oversight or an advisory board to make CON more responsive to changes in the healthcare system, e.g. create policy oversight or advisory board; and improving data collection to allow for ongoing monitoring and oversight of quality, access, and community benefits, including charity care.[73] Should the program be repealed, the study suggested: identifying policy goals for cost, quality, access, and accountability along with alternative methods of attaining these goals; strengthening data collection and reporting to monitor the effects of repeal on quality, access, and community benefits; and conducting economic analysis to estimate the effects of deregulation and to guide the policy changes.[74]

V.E 1998 Impact of CON Repeal on Health Care Spending

A 1998 empirical study by Christopher Conover and Frank A. Sloan Ph.D. entitled "*Does Removing Certificate-of-Need Regulations Lead to a Surge in Health Care Spending?*" examined health spending between the late 1970's and 1993, including spending prior to and directly after state CON laws were repealed, stated, "*The major findings about CON can be summarized as follows: first, we found no surge in expenditures after CON was lifted; second, despite a statistically significant reduction by mature programs on acute spending per capita, there was no corresponding reduction in total per capita spending (apparently due to offsetting expenditures on non-hospital services).*"[75] "*We found that mature CON reduced hospital bed supply per capita population, but*

[70] STATE OF WASHINGTON JOINT LEGISLATIVE AND AUDIT REVIEW COMMITTEE, EFFECTS OF CERTIFICATE OF NEED AND ITS POSSIBLE REPEAL 15 (January 8, 1999).

[71] STATE OF WASHINGTON JOINT LEGISLATIVE AND AUDIT REVIEW COMMITTEE, EFFECTS OF CERTIFICATE OF NEED AND ITS POSSIBLE REPEAL 19 (January 8, 1999).

[72] STATE OF WASHINGTON JOINT LEGISLATIVE AND AUDIT REVIEW COMMITTEE, EFFECTS OF CERTIFICATE OF NEED AND ITS POSSIBLE REPEAL 22 (January 8, 1999).

[73] STATE OF WASHINGTON JOINT LEGISLATIVE AND AUDIT REVIEW COMMITTEE, EFFECTS OF CERTIFICATE OF NEED AND ITS POSSIBLE REPEAL 29 (January 8, 1999).

[74] STATE OF WASHINGTON JOINT LEGISLATIVE AND AUDIT REVIEW COMMITTEE, EFFECTS OF CERTIFICATE OF NEED AND ITS POSSIBLE REPEAL 30 (January 8, 1999).

[75] Christopher Conover & Frank Sloan, *Does Removing Certificate-of-Need Regulations Lead to a Surge in Health Care Spending?*, 23 J. of HEALTH POL., POL'Y & LAW 455, 473-474 (1998).

could detect no increase in bed supply following the removal of CON."[76] Furthermore, the study authors found that established CON programs increased cost per adjusted patient day and also cost per admission. [77]

V.F 1993 CON Evidence of Poor Health Care Policy

A 1993 study conducted by Terree Wasley entitled *"Certificate of Need: Poor Health Care Policy"* published by the Mackinac Center for Health Care Policy, questioned the effectiveness of CON stating, "*Extensive research, however, strongly suggests that CON programs have not worked as originally intended. It appears, in fact, that they may have boosted the very costs they were supposed to control for these reasons: 1) they restrict competition among hospitals, and 2) by curtailing efficient capital investments they actually raise operating costs.*"[78] Thus, this study supports the other earlier studies reported and builds consensus that CON regulation has not only failed to control costs, but it has actually increased costs.

V.G 1992 Relationship Between Capital Investment and Hospital Operating Expenditures

A 1992 Gerard Anderson study examined the effect of CON on hospital capital investment and operating expenditures in his article entitled *"Examining the Relationship Between Capital Investment and Hospital Operating Expenditures."* Many previous studies have found that hospital capital investments significantly raise operating costs. However, a 1987 assessment of prior studies found that although current capital expenditures increased future operating expenditures, it estimated that the overall effect was much less than previously reported.[79] The study further advised, "*As Congress debates whether to incorporate capital into the Medicare Prospective Payment System, our results suggest that controlling the rate of increase in operating expenses may only negligibly deter capital expansion by hospital administrators.*"[80]

V.H 1986-1988 Federal Trade Commission (FTC) Studies

During the late 1980s, the FTC conducted the first of several studies on CON concluding that, "*Market forces generally allocate society's resources far better than decisions of government planners,*"[81] and recommended that states remove their CON regulations. Later studies were conducted in 1987 and 1998 as described below.

V.H.1 1986 CON Regulation of Home Health Care

A study conducted by Keith B. Anderson and David I. Kass entitled *"Certificate of Need Regulation of Entry Into Home Health Care"* examined the justification for requiring CON approval before new firms can begin providing home health care services.[82] Like studies of the impact of CON regulation on hospitals, this study found no evidence that CON regulation contributes to lowers costs for the provision of home health care services and, if anything CON regulation is associated with on average two percent higher costs for firms

[76] Christopher Conover & Frank Sloan, *Does Removing Certificate-of-Need Regulations Lead to a Surge in Health Care Spending?*, 23 J. of HEALTH POL., POL'Y & LAW 455, 469 (1998).

[77] Christopher Conover & Frank Sloan, *Does Removing Certificate-of-Need Regulations Lead to a Surge in Health Care Spending?*, 23 J. of HEALTH POL., POL'Y & LAW 455, 466 (1998).

[78] TERREE WASLEY, CERTIFICATE OF NEED: POOR HEALTH CARE POLICY, Mackinac Center for Health Care policy (1993).

[79] Gerard Anderson, et. al., Examining the Relationship Between Capital Investment and Hospital Operating Expenditures, 69(4) The Rev. of Econ. & STATS. 709, 712 (1992).

[80] Gerard Anderson, et. al., Examining the Relationship Between Capital Investment and Hospital Operating Expenditures, 69(4) THE REV. OF ECON. & STATS. 709, 712-713 (1992).

[81] Press Release, FTC (Aug. 10, 1987).

[82] KEITH B. ANDERSON & DAVID I. KASS, CERTIFICATE OF NEED REGULATION OF ENTRY INTO HOME HEALTH CARE 2-3 (Bureau of Economics, Federal Trade Commission, 1986).

operating in regulated states.[83] Moreover, a CON program for home health firms necessarily involved administrative costs in addition to the seeming lack of cost containment benefits.[84]

V.H.2 1987 Competition Among Hospitals

Next, a 1987 study conducted by Monica Noether entitled *"Competition Among Hospitals"* reported that CON regulation significantly impacts entry into the hospital market. While for-profit institutions were once subject to more stringent CON regulation than non-profit institutions, non-profits no longer have this advantage.[85] Studies show that where entry into the market is regulated by CON law, both prices and expenses are higher than in areas without such regulation. Despite CON law's function as a potential entry barrier, its primary effect is less efficient resource utilization which is then passed on in the form of higher prices.[86] States with CON laws on average have higher prices and expenses averaging 1.8 to 2.6 percent and 1.2 to 2.4 percent higher, respectively, than those without.[87] Additionally, this study found no evidence that CON laws have resulted in the resource savings they were designed to provide. Thus, it concludes recent plans and decisions to repeal CON laws in some states should, in theory, increase consumer welfare.[88]

V.H.3 1988 The Effect of State CON Laws on Hospital Costs: An Economic Policy Analysis

In 1988, an economic policy study conducted by Daniel Sherman entitled "*The Effect of State CON Laws on Hospital Costs: An Economic Policy Analysis*" analyzed data from 1983-84 provided by the "1984 Annual Survey of Hospitals" conducted by American Hospital Association (AHA). Data from approximately 6,300 short-term, general acute care hospitals, covering a 12-month period, were included in the survey.[89] Output costs were measured by five (5) variables: total number of inpatient days spent in acute care; total number of inpatient days spent in intensive care; patient days spent in sub-acute care or other departments; all visits to hospital emergency rooms; and, clinic and other outpatient visits made to hospitals.[90]

Results of the study indicated that as states review fewer hospital expenditures, hospital costs do not increase.[91] Rather, hospital costs are lower in those states which set higher review thresholds for all types of hospital expenditures. Moreover, if states were to significantly relax their regulatory constraints by doubling the thresholds at which hospital expenditures were subject to CON review, total hospital costs would decline by 1.4 percent.[92] The study posits that the reason for increased costs despite CON review is because CON regulation implicitly assumes that by reducing the amount of capital and equipment available to hospitals, the total cost of resources will decrease. This falsely assumes that other inputs, such as labor, cannot be

---

[83] KEITH B. ANDERSON & DAVID I. KASS, CERTIFICATE OF NEED REGULATION OF ENTRY INTO HOME HEALTH CARE 90 (Bureau of Economics, Federal Trade Commission, 1986).

[84] KEITH B. ANDERSON & DAVID I. KASS, CERTIFICATE OF NEED REGULATION OF ENTRY INTO HOME HEALTH CARE 87 (Bureau of Economics, Federal Trade Commission, 1986)

[85] MONICA NOETHER, COMPETITION AMONG HOSPITALS 24-25, Staff Report of the Bureau of Economics, Federal Trade Commission 1987).

[86] MONICA NOETHER, COMPETITION AMONG HOSPITALS 3, 77, 82, Staff Report of the Bureau of Economics, Federal Trade Commission 1987).

[87] MONICA NOETHER, COMPETITION AMONG HOSPITALS 25, Staff Report of the Bureau of Economics, Federal Trade Commission 1987). MONICA NOETHER, COMPETITION AMONG HOSPITALS 74, Staff Report of the Bureau of Economics, Federal Trade Commission 1987).

[88] MONICA NOETHER, COMPETITION AMONG HOSPITALS 3, Staff Report of the Bureau of Economics, Federal Trade Commission 1987).

[89] Daniel Sherman, THE EFFECT OF STATE CERTIFICATE-OF-NEED LAWS ON HOSPITAL COSTS: AN ECONOMIC POLICY ANALYSIS, 28 (Bureau of Economics, Federal Trade Commission 1988).

[90] Daniel Sherman, The Effect of State Certificate-of-Need Laws On Hospital Costs: An Economic Policy Analysis 48 (Bureau of Economics, Federal Trade Commission 1988).

[91] Daniel Sherman, The Effect of State Certificate-of-Need Laws On Hospital Costs: An Economic Policy Analysis vi (Bureau of Economics, Federal Trade Commission 1988).

[92] Daniel Sherman, THE EFFECT OF STATE CERTIFICATE-OF-NEED LAWS ON HOSPITAL COSTS: AN ECONOMIC POLICY ANALYSIS vi (Bureau of Economics, Federal Trade Commission 1988).

substituted for the restricted inputs. Rather, by restricting the use of capital and equipment, CON laws may actually encourage hospitals to switch to less capital-intensive but more expensive ways of treating patients.[93]

V.I 1988 CON Impact on Costs, Quality and Access in Healthcare

A 1988 study conducted by Frank A. Sloan Ph.D., et. al, published in the book *"Cost, Quality, and Access to Health Care: New Roles for Health Planning in a Competitive Environment"* evaluated several of the past arguments made by supporters of CON. One past argument in support of CON is that "*in the absence of regulation, firms will drop prices so low that most will fail, leaving the market to a monopolist or a few oligopolists.*"[94] Providers have been shown to accelerate investments in facilities and equipment in anticipation of the implementation of CON laws.[95] Such behavior is cited as demonstrating the willingness of providers to "play the system". Thus, existing providers support CON laws to prevent competition.

Another study, by Frank A. Sloan, PhD and Bruce Steinwald, found a 1.4 percent additional increase in bed supply in the year prior to CON implementation and attributed to the anticipatory effects of CON implementation.[96] After CON implementation, providers shifted investment to those areas not covered by CON, such as hospital equipment. Additionally, the labor input regressions indicated that CON tends to increase labor employment as an unintended, although, compensatory effect of CON regulation. This continued investment contributes to the increase of expenditures per bed. The study observed 1,228 U.S. hospitals between 1969-1975, including labor inputs and simultaneous assessment of several concurrent regulatory programs in an attempt to isolate the effects of CON laws from those of other regulatory programs in place.[97]

However, opponents point out that the remaining firms would be unable to raise prices to monopoly levels because competitors could easily enter the market. "Attempts by providers to reduce costs, gain efficiencies of scale, and position themselves aggressively in the marketplace have resulted in the formation of vertically integrated delivery systems of such providers."[98]

To arrive at an understanding of what CON might provide in terms of cost savings, (if any), valid data and a scientific methodology are required. A common methodology used by CON proponents appears to be based on comparison of dollar amounts of disapproved applications to total dollar amounts of applications as submitted for review.[99] For example, the State of Missouri's CON Program claims that the proposed capital investments of denied applications is in fact a CON savings.[100]

In this study, Frank A. Sloan Ph.D., identifies the following three (3) flaws in this type of calculation of CON cost savings:

1. There is a built in bias toward showing savings. Agencies can reasonably be expected to deny some applicants and some claimed savings will be shown as a result.

---

[93] Daniel Sherman, THE EFFECT OF STATE CERTIFICATE-OF-NEED LAWS ON HOSPITAL COSTS: AN ECONOMIC POLICY ANALYSIS 12 (Bureau of Economics, Federal Trade Commission 1988).

[94] *See* FRANK A. SLOAN, ET. AL., COST, QUALITY, AND ACCESS IN HEALTH CARE: NEW ROLES FOR HEALTH PLANNING IN A COMPETITIVE ENVIRONMENT 45 (Josey-Bass Publishers 1988).

[95] FRANK A. SLOAN, *Containing Health Expenditures: Lessons Learned from Certificate-of-Need Programs, in* COST, QUALITY, AND ACCESS IN HEALTH CARE, 48-49 (Jossey-Bass, 1988).

[96] "Insurance, Regulation, and Hospital Costs" By Frank A. Sloan and Bruce Steinwald. Lexington Books, 1980, p. 169.

[97] "Insurance, Regulation, and Hospital Costs" By Frank A. Sloan and Bruce Steinwald. Lexington Books, 1980, pp. 150, 169.

[98] Braulio Montesino, *Anatomy of a Roadblock*, 29 HEALTH SYSTEMS REVIEW 30, 30 (1996).

[99] *See generally*, MISSOURI HEALTH FACILITIES REVIEW COMMITTEE, CERTIFICATE OF NEED: EFFECTIVE, EFFICIENT, ACCOUNTABLE (2002) *available at* www.dhss.mo.gov/CON/coninfo.pdf (last visited Dec. 28, 2004).

[100] MISSOURI HEALTH FACILITIES REVIEW COMMITTEE, CERTIFICATE OF NEED: EFFECTIVE, EFFICIENT, ACCOUNTABLE (2002) *available at* www.dhss.mo.gov/CON/coninfo.pdf (last visited Dec. 28, 2004).

2. Litigation and administrative costs incurred by hospitals as a result of the CON application process and the agency costs of administering the program are not considered as offsets to savings.
3. Finally, there are "compensatory effects" inherent in the expectation of regulation. Existing hospitals may undergo construction in order to prevent competitors from establishing a need for facilities or equipment. Hospitals may also accelerate construction in anticipation of CON as described earlier or make false CON applications to bog down the review process.[101]

V.J 1979 CON Impact on Investment, Costs, and Use 1979

A 1979 study conducted by Salkever and Bice entitled *"Hospital Certificate-of-Need Controls, Impact on Investment, Costs, and Use"* demonstrated that CON regulation from 1968-1972 had no appreciable effect on total hospital investment but did result in a decrease in the rate of growth in bed supply and an increase in investment in quality enhancing projects.[102] Additionally, analyses based on all states combined, over the time period 1968-1972, found that CON controls applied to a typical state would have reduced the number of inpatient days, a small increase in inpatient cost per inpatient day, and at best, a very modest reduction in hospital costs per capita.[103] Moreover, no significant savings in hospital costs were achieved through CON programs as any savings from lower admission rates and hospital stays resulting from control over bed growth were approximately offset by higher than average per diem costs resulting from upgrading the level of care.[104] The scope of the study was limited to the impact of CON controls on hospital investment and costs. Additionally, researchers expressed some concern over validity of data relied upon as there were no means to identify inaccuracies in the cost data supplied. Finally, the authors expressed wariness over extrapolation of the findings due to the large amount of regulatory change during the late 1970's.[105]

VI SELECTED CON SURVEYS

VI.A National Directory of Health Planning, Policy and Regulatory Agencies

The *National Directory of Health Planning, Policy and Regulatory Agencies* is an ongoing survey of state CON and health policy planning agencies conducted by the American Health Planning Association (AHPA), an association of healthcare executives, researchers, consumers, providers, and others interested in health policy planning.[106] The directory lists names and addresses of state agency contacts, information on local planning agencies, and a summary of CON programs in the thirty-six (36) states and the District of Columbia that continue to operate such programs.[107] It also includes data on the relative scope and thresholds of CON regulated services; CON fees; and the duration of CON regulation, as self-reported by the various states surveyed.[108]

---

[101] Frank A. Sloan, *Containing Health Expenditures: Lessons Learned from Certificate-of-Need Programs, in* Cost, Quality, and Access in Health Care, 48-49 (Jossey-Bass, 1988).

[102] David S. Salkever & Thomas W. Bice, Hospital Certificate-of-Need Controls, Impact on Investment, Costs, and Use (Am. Enter. Inst. for Pub. Pol'y Research, 1979).

[103] David S. Salkever & Thomas W. Bice, Hospital Certificate-of-Need Controls, Impact on Investment, Costs, and Use 73 (Am. Enter. Inst. for Pub. Pol'y Research, 1979).

[104] David S. Salkever & Thomas W. Bice, Hospital Certificate-of-Need Controls, Impact on Investment, Costs, and Use 75 (Am. Enter. Inst. for Pub. Pol'y Research, 1979).

[105] David S. Salkever & Thomas W. Bice, Hospital Certificate-of-Need Controls, Impact on Investment, Costs, and Use 76-77 (Am. Enter. Inst. for Pub. Pol'y Research, 1979).

[106] American Health Planning Association, National Directory of Health Planning, Policy and Regulatory Agencies, (15th ed. 2004).

[107] American Health Planning Association, National Directory of Health Planning, Policy and Regulatory Agencies, (15th ed. 2004).

[108] American Health Planning Association, National Directory of Health Planning, Policy and Regulatory Agencies, (15th ed. 2004).

VI.B 1978 Chayet and Sonnreich Compilation "Certificate of Need: An Expanding Regulatory Concept"

The 1978 Chayet and Sonnreich compilation entitled *"Certificate of Need: An Expanding Regulatory Concept,"* (updated in 1979) is a collections of CON regulatory information including a history of the Federal laws, a state by state summary of CON, and the text of the CON laws for all states. The introduction to the book contains a review of CON legislation enacted up to 1978 and an evaluation of the evidence concerning CON as a cost containment measure. The study found it noteworthy that no hard data had demonstrated its effectiveness in controlling costs.[109] Moreover, estimates of any savings vary sharply even within the same state.[110] Additionally, the book states that there is mounting evidence that CON regulation is causing unanticipated problems, including regulatory expansion of coverage to including, in some cases, facilities that were not seeking CON review or approval.[111]

VII RECENT DEVELOPMENTS

VII.A Recent State Legislation and News

In response to recent budget crises, many states are considering CON as a familiar healthcare cost-containment tool. Alabama, Connecticut, Florida, Georgia, Illinois, Louisiana, Maine, Massachusetts, New Hampshire, and Ohio have all recently considered or passed legislation related to their CON programs.

VII.A.1 Alabama

The Alabama legislature exempted MRIs and PET scanners from CON review in late 2003,[112] however recent legislation proposes reinstating CON review for both MRI & PET.[113] Perhaps as a result of a recent scandal involving the approval of a HealthSouth digital hospital, the chairman of Alabama's CON Review Board and the governor have "*batted around the idea of abolishing the CON process.*"[114] Alabama state legislation allowed a one (1) time exemption from the customary CON review process for the HealthSouth hospital.[115]

VII.A.2 Connecticut

CON requirements for outpatient surgical facilities using levels of sedation or anesthesia were set to expire in July of 2004 but were made permanent by legislation signed by Governor John G. Rowland in June of 2004. This legislation was supported by Connecticut Hospital Association ("CHA") but opposed by the Connecticut State Medical Society ("CSMS").[116]

VII.A.3 Florida

Florida Governor Jeb Bush's administration has proposed major deregulation of the healthcare industry. In 2003, the Florida legislature attempted to bypass the state's CON program by granting open-heart surgery

---

[109] *See* Chayet & Sonnenreich, P.C., Medicine In the Public Interest, Inc., Certificate of Need: An Expanding Regulatory Concept vi (1978).

[110] *See* Chayet & Sonnenreich, P.C., Medicine In the Public Interest, Inc., Certificate of Need: An Expanding Regulatory Concept vi (1978).

[111] *See* Chayet & Sonnenreich, P.C., Medicine In the Public Interest, Inc., Certificate of Need: An Expanding Regulatory Concept vi-vii (1978).

[112] H.R. 322, Reg. Sess. (Ala. 2003).

[113] S 505 Reg. Sess. (Ala. 2004).

[114] Anna Velasco, *State Hospitals Likely to Keep Certificate of Need Programs*, Birmingham News, Aug. 4, 2004, *available at* www.al.com/printer/printer.ssf?/base/living/1091613250179920.xml (last visited August 12, 2004).

[115] Tom Bassing, *Rivals Get CON Review in 'Digital Hospital' Tift*, Birmingham Bus. J., April 9, 2004, *available at* birmingham.bizjournals.com/birmingham/stories/2004/04/12/story6.html (last visited Dec. 28, 2004).

[116] H.R. 5531, Reg. Sess. (Conn. 2004) (Report on Bills Favorably Reported by Committee March 16, 2004), *available at* www.cga.ct.gov/2004/jfr/h/2004HB-05531-R00PH-JFR.htm (last visited Dec. 28, 2004).

one to five (5) hospitals. The bill was later found to be unconstitutional.[117] In 2004, the Florida legislature passed legislation exempting some nursing homes from CON review and the expedited review process for proposed nursing home replacement beds was revised.[118] Hospitals without open heart surgery programs seeking to provide emergency percutaneous coronary interventions are now exempted from CON review.[119] However, proposals to exempt the transfer of acute care beds from CON review died in committee.[120]

VII.A.4 Georgia

In April 2004, Georgia's former state attorney general filed suit seeking a declaratory judgment that Georgia's CON laws are unconstitutional because they discourage competition. This came after several unprecedented actions against ambulatory surgery centers in Georgia by the state board. The state recently ordered two (2) imaging centers to cease operations because they allegedly exceeded spending limits without state approval.[121] However, the Georgia Supreme Court unanimously upheld the state's CON regulations in a late 2004 ruling. The court found that CON regulations were "neither unreasonable nor unconstitutional" and "can be adopted without procedural requirements necessary for the passage of legislation."[122]

VII.A.5 Illinois

In 2004, a federal whistleblower lawsuit alleged some Illinois Health Facilities Planning Board ("IHFPB") members tried to "shakedown" CON applicants by steering contracts to a construction company and bond brokerage house. In an unparalleled response to the allegations, Governor Rod Blagojevich suspended the nine (9) member board and the Illinois House and Senate approved a bill overhauling the state board.[123] The board was downsized from nine (9) to five (5) members and guards established against conflicts of interest. Board members are now prohibited from having financial ties to any healthcare facility.[124] The full repercussions of this scandal on Illinois and national CON regulations and healthcare competition remain to be seen.

VII.A.6 Louisiana

Louisiana abolished almost all of their CON requirements in 1987 after then Governor Edwin Edwards was accused of selling hospital construction permits. However, it appears there is a move towards reinstating CON in Louisiana.[125] Legislation requiring certain facilities, including ambulatory surgery centers, to have CON approval was proposed in 2003[126] and the Louisiana Hospital Association ("LHA") recently proposed that legislators impose a moratorium on all new hospital licenses. However, the moratorium is opposed by

---

[117] John Dorschner, *State May Deregulate Hospitals,* MIAMI HERALD, Nov. 21, 2003, *available at* www.miami.com/mld/miamiherald/business/7313178.htm?1c (last visited Nov. 3, 2004).

[118] H.R. 1062, Reg. Sess. (FLA. 2004).

[119] S. 182, Reg. Sess. (FLA. 2004).

[120] S. 1306, Reg. Sess. (FLA. 2004).

[121] Megan Woolhouse, *State's CON Law Being Challenged,* ATLANTA BUS. CHRON., May 1, 2004 *at* http://atlanta.bizjournals.com/atlanta/stories/2004/05/17/story6.html (last visited Aug. 12, 2004).

[122] Megan Woolhouse *Struggling Hospital Files for Bankruptcy Protection,* ATLANTA BUS. CHRON. Sept. 17, 2004. *at* www.bizjournals.com/atlanta/stories/2004/09/20/newscolumn2.html?t=printable (last visited Nov. 30, 2004).

[123] Jeff Kolkey, *Federal Investigation Mires Mercy,* NORTHWEST HERALD, July 26, 2004 *at* www.nwherald.com/MainSection/281062296558626.php (last visited Aug. 12, 2004).

[124] "State Makes Changes to Health Board" THE HERALD NEWS, August 10, 2004, www.suburbanchicagonews.com/heraldnews/top/j10health.htm (last visited 8/12/04).

[125] Philip Betbeze, *Too Many Beds,* HEALTHLEADERS, September 1, 2004 *at* www.healthleaders.com/magazine/print.php?contentid=57885 (last visited Nov. 3, 2004).

[126] H.R. 612, Reg. Sess. (LA. 2003).

associations of physician-owned facilities noting that the proposal would not limit the expansion of existing hospitals.[127]

VII.A.7 Maine

In the eight (8) weeks following the expiration of Maine's CON moratorium in May 2004, $214 million in new capital expenditures were proposed through Letters of Intent.[128] A dramatic increase for Maine, this year's proposed spending is 229 percent greater than the average $65 million annually approved for CONs between 2001 and 2003.[129] The Governor's Office of Health Policy and Finance (GOHPF), the governing regulatory body, created a "Capital Investment Fund" (CIF) and new CON cost criteria through its emergency rulemaking authority in response to the proposed rise in healthcare investment. [130]

The CIF acts as a budget for potential CON approvals. Interestingly, the CIF only analyzes the projected third-year operating costs, and their relationship to the initial capital investment, when reviewing CON applications. Third-year operating costs, rather than capital investment costs, are thought to be a better predictor of the long-term impact on the cost of care.[131] Notably, hospital CON projects are assigned the bulk of the CIF budget and only 12.5 percent is reserved for non-hospitals.[132]

The emergency rule is now proposed as a new rule under this agency's traditional rulemaking authority. Notice has been filed, requests for public comment are being accepted and the public hearing is scheduled for September 15, 2004.[133]

VII.A.8 Texas

The booming specialty hospital market has the American Hospital Association as well as many state hospitals groups, including the Texas Hospital Association (THA), seeking to regulate competition from specialty hospitals through expanded CON regulations.[134] While, the THA is considering recommending that Texas bring back its CON regulation for new hospital construction, the Executive Director believes the concerns over specialty hospitals can best be addressed by lawmakers.[135]

VII.B The Specialty Hospital Moratorium and CON

CON also serves as a barrier to market entry for specialty and niche providers, such as surgical and specialty hospitals, into healthcare markets. This has led to renewed interest in health planning regulations.

---

[127] Philip Betbeze, *Too Many Beds*, HEALTHLEADERS, Sept. 1, 2004, *available at* www.healthleaders.com/magazine/print.php?contentid=57885 (last visited Nov. 3, 2004).

[128] *Capital Investment Fund Amount for Health Care Spending Released,* 127 BOOTHBAY REGISTER, 33 Aug. 12, 2004 *at* boothbayregister.maine.com/2004-08-12/health care spending.html (last visited Dec. 22, 2004).

[129] *Capital Investment Fund Amount for Health Care Spending Released,* 127 BOOTHBAY REGISTER, 33 Aug. 12, 2004 *at* boothbayregister.maine.com/2004-08-12/health care spending.html (last visited Dec. 22, 2004).

[130] *Capital Investment Fund Amount for Health Care Spending Released,* 127 BOOTHBAY REGISTER, 33 Aug. 12, 2004 *at* boothbayregister.maine.com/2004-08-12/health care spending.html (last visited Dec. 22, 2004).

[131] *Capital Investment Fund Amount for Health Care Spending Released,* 127 BOOTHBAY REGISTER, 33 Aug. 12, 2004 *at* boothbayregister.maine.com/2004-08-12/health care spending.html (last visited Dec. 22, 2004).

[132] *Capital Investment Fund Amount for Health Care Spending Released,* 127 BOOTHBAY REGISTER, 33 Aug. 12, 2004 *at* boothbayregister.maine.com/2004-08-12/health care spending.html (last visited Dec. 22, 2004).

[133] *Capital Investment Fund Amount for Health Care Spending Released,* 127 BOOTHBAY REGISTER, 33 Aug. 12, 2004 *at* boothbayregister.maine.com/2004-08-12/health care spending.html (last visited Dec. 22, 2004).

[134] Colin Pope, *One Nibble at a Time: Boutique Hospitals, Scott & White Expansion Eat Away at Revenue for Seton, St. David's*, AUSTIN BUSS. J., Nov. 11, 2002, *available at* austin.bizjournals.com/austin/stories/2002/11/11/focus1.html?t=printable, (last visited June 20, 2003).

[135] Colin Pope, *One Nibble at a Time: Boutique Hospitals, Scott & White Expansion Eat Away at Revenue for Seton, St. David's*, AUSTIN BUSS. J., Nov. 11, 2002, *available at* austin.bizjournals.com/austin/stories/2002/11/11/focus1.html?t=printable, (last visited June 20, 2003).

All states currently license and regulate, under CON, surgical and specialty hospitals in the same manner as general acute care hospitals. However, in a recent presentation entitled, "*Specialty Hospitals: Competition or Cream-Skimming, Regulatory Perspective: Certificate of Need Affects*", Tom Piper, Director of the Missouri CON Program, summarized the potential for the development of specific CON criteria and standards for surgical and specialty hospitals. The presentation notes that several states are considering adding special criteria and standards for these facilities or otherwise dealing with the issue of specialty hospitals. These states include Hawaii, Michigan, New Jersey, New York, Oregon, Rhode Island, and Virginia.[136]

Given the renewed interest in health planning regulations and their barrier to market entry of specialty hospitals, the American Medical Association recently announced its official position in support of state efforts to repeal their CON legislation. "Consistent with Council on Ethical and Judicial Affairs Opinion E-8.032, the board continues to support health facility ownership by physicians if they directly provide care or services at the facility. The board also supports competition between and among health care facilities because it promotes the delivery of high-quality, cost-effective health care. On the other hand, many hospitals are aggressively attempting to thwart physician competition, not only through self-referral prohibitions, but also though states' CON programs. Although CON laws have failed to achieve their intended purpose, i.e., the reduction of health care costs, only 14 states have repealed their programs. Hospitals are increasingly attempting, and have achieved some recent successes, in extending CON requirements to physician ventures such as ambulatory surgery centers and diagnostic imaging facilities. Based on current AMA policy and the recent FTC/DOJ recommendation for states to reconsider their CON programs, the board opposes enactment of a federal certificate-of-need program, supports efforts to rescind state CON legislation, and opposes efforts to reinstate it or expand it to include physician-owned ambulatory care facilities."[137]

VII.C The Federal Trade Commission and CON

The FTC has evaluated the impact of CON on competition for many years. As early as 1988, an FTC press release stated, "*State certificate-of-need (CON) regulations may have raised hospital costs instead of producing intended resource savings, according to a study issued today by the Federal Trade Commission's Bureau of Economics.*"[138] This FTC study estimated that total hospital costs might decline by 1.4 percent, or $1.3 billion per year, if all states with CON laws doubled the dollar thresholds at which they require CON review of hospital expenditures.[139]

In a 1987 letter to Virginia officials they stated, "*Any potential benefits of CON regulation are likely to be outweighed by the adverse effects of such regulation on competition in health care markets. Consequently, CON regulation is likely to harm consumers on balance by increasing the price, and decreasing the quality, of health services in Virginia.*"[140]

Reiterating their public position regarding CON, the FTC stated that CON is "*contrary to the interests of health care consumers in Michigan" and advised its state legislatures that, "any potential benefits of CON regulation are likely to be outweighed by its adverse effects on competition in health care markets."*[141] *Likewise, the FTC expressed similar sentiments before the Georgia General Assembly. "The Federal Trade Commission staff said that a proposal before the Georgia General Assembly to relax temporarily part of the state's "Certificate-of-Need"*

[136] Thomas R. Piper, MoCONP and AHPA, *Specialty Hospitals: Competition or Cream-Skimming, Regulatory Perspective: Certificate of Need Affects*, (2004), *available at* www.ahpanet.org/Images/NASHPpiper.pdf (last visited Dec. 28, 2004).

[137] Mike Norbut, *Cutting Through the CONfusion: Movement to Relax the Limits*, AMNews (Feb. 7, 2005), *available at* www.ama-assn.org/amednews/2005/02/07/bisa0207.htm (last visited Feb. 9, 2005).

[138] Press Release, FTC, FTC Economics Study Finds State Certificate-Of-Need Regulations Increase Hospital Costs (Feb. 4, 1988).

[139] Press Release, FTC, FTC Economics Study Finds State Certificate-Of-Need Regulations Increase Hospital Costs (Feb. 4, 1988).

[140] Press Release, FTC, (Aug.10, 1987).

[141] Press Release, FTC (Mar. 9, 1988)

(CON) regulation "represents a worthwhile undertaking which may lead to greater diversity and better quality in health care services and increased price competition in the health care market." Additionally, the FTC has recommended that Virginia eliminate its CON regulation reasoning that such regulation is "contrary to the interests of health care consumer" in the state. "Any potential benefits of CON regulation are likely to be outweighed by the adverse effects of such regulation on competition in health care markets. Consequently, CON regulation is likely to harm consumers on balance by increasing the price, and decreasing the quality, of health services in Virginia...as market forces generally allocate society's resources far better than decisions of government planners."[142]

In November, 2002, FTC Chairman, Timothy J. Muris, announced that the FTC would hold joint hearings with the DOJ on competition in healthcare in 2003.[143] On July 23, 2004, following the conclusion of the hearings lasting over six (6) months, the FTC and DOJ ("agencies") issued a joint report, entitled "*Improving Health Care: A Dose of Competition*" in which the agencies recommended that states decrease barriers to entry into provider markets. The agencies encourage states to reconsider whether CON programs "*best serve their citizens' health care needs.*"[144]

Following testimony at numerous hearings from industry representatives and legal, economic, and academic experts on the healthcare industry and health policy, the agencies concluded that the burdens placed on competition by CON programs "generally outweigh" its "purported economic benefits." The agencies suggested that instead of reducing costs, there is evidence that CON programs actually drive up costs by "*fostering anticompetitive barriers to entry.*"[145] *"More importantly, CON regulation tends to foster higher prices, lower quality and reduced innovation in health care markets."*[146]

The agencies expressed concern that CON programs drive up healthcare costs because they depress supply and protect healthcare providers from competition. The agencies expressed further concern that CON programs prevent entry into the market by entities that can provide higher quality care, and contended that CON programs may delay the introduction of new technology. In support of their conclusions, the agencies relied upon empirical studies that showed CON programs generally failed to control costs and actually result in higher healthcare costs.[147]

Regarding Ambulatory Surgery Centers (ASCs) (relatively new market entrants and hospital competitors) the agencies stated their belief that ASCs are beneficial for consumers and that state CON laws pose an anticompetitive barrier to entry. In response to ASC provider allegations that general hospitals have attempted to use CON laws to prevent ASCs from entering the market, the agencies committed to "aggressively pursue" activities of anticompetitive conduct. However they acknowledged that antitrust laws do not prevent individual hospitals from unilaterally approaching state governments in connection with CON proceedings.[148]

The FTC has also recognized the potential for competitive abuse in CON by stating, "*...state law frequently requires a hospital to obtain a "certificate of need" (CON) before it can build a new facility. The Commission has discovered that existing hospitals have sometimes opposed these CON applications, not in good*

[142] Press Release, FTC (Aug. 10, 1987)

[143] Press Release, FTC, FTC Chairman Announces Public Hearings on Health Care and Competition Law and Policy to Begin in February 2003 (Nov. 7, 2002) *at* www.ftc.gov/opa/2002/11/murishealthcare.htm (last visited Aug. 5, 2004).

[144] Fed. Trade. Comm.& Dept. of Just., Improving Health Care: A Dose of Competition" A Report by the Federal Trade Commission and the Department of Justice 22 (2004).

[145] Fed. Trade. Comm.& Dept. of Just., Improving Health Care: A Dose of Competition" A Report by the Federal Trade Commission and the Department of Justice 1-2 (2004).

[146] Press Release, FTC (Mar. 9, 1988)

[147] Fed. Trade. Comm.& Dept. of Just., Improving Health Care: A Dose of Competition" A Report by the Federal Trade Commission and the Department of Justice 4 (2004).

[148] Fed. Trade. Comm.& Dept. of Just., Improving Health Care: A Dose of Competition" A Report by the Federal Trade Commission and the Department of Justice 27 (2004).

faith, but merely to delay the entry of a new competitor and to burden it with heavy costs."[149] Additionally, *"'there is near universal agreement' among health care economists that Certificate of Need Regulation 'has been unsuccessful in containing health care costs.'"*[150] This consensus is based on several reasons, including the fact that CON restricts new firms from entering a healthcare market in competition against incumbent providers. *"One reason that CON may have been unsuccessful in constraining health care costs is that it restricts the ability of new firms to enter a health care market and compete against incumbent providers.' Because it tends to protect existing providers from competition, the CON process may increase prices to consumers and interfere with improvements in the quality of care. In addition, 'while health care providers and insurers may have lacked adequate incentives to control costs 15 to 20 years ago, substantial progress has been made in providing the incentives that will lead unregulated health care markets to control costs.' Kindt concluded, 'the available economic evidence suggests that CON regulation has not been successful in controlling health care costs. CON may have anticompetitive effects. Recent changes in health care markets should be increasing the ability of health care markets to function effectively and efficiently.'"*[151]

Therefore, in light of these previous FTC pronouncements, it remains to be seen what impact this report will actually manifest on the continuing existence or enforcement of state CON legislation. Nonetheless, this Federal report is perhaps, the most significant development in the last several years in the ongoing battle to eliminate CON and support a level playing field for market competition in healthcare.

VIII SUMMARY

CON has been in effect, in some form, for as long as four (4) decades in a large percent of U.S. states. The effectiveness and burdens of CON regulatory policy during this time have been studied extensively by federal and state governments, academic institutions, and other researchers and organizations. From a market economy perspective, CON laws appear to have failed to control costs. In an article reviewing CON and its application to modern markets, Patrick J. McGinley wrote, "*In searching the scholarly journals, one cannot find a single article that asserts that CON laws succeed in lowering healthcare costs.*"[152]

Nonetheless, CON continues to be the subject of lively and often contentious debate in legislatures, the healthcare literature, and general media. As this book goes to print, several other states, including Missouri and Indiana, are considering the reinstatement of all or part of their CON laws. Despite repeated FTC criticism of CON regulations as anti-competitive, it seems unlikely that Federal action will mandate the repeal of CON regulatory policy and, lacking that action on a Federal level, there is little likelihood that CON laws will be repealed at the state level any time in the foreseeable future.

[149] Press, Release, FTC, Calvani Outlines FTC's Concerns in Health-Care Competition (Feb. 21, 1986).

[150] Press Release, FTC (June 22, 1989).

[151] Press Release, FTC (June 22, 1989).

[152] Patrick John McGinley, *Beyond Health Care Reform: Reconsidering Certificate of Need Laws in a "Managed Competition" System*, 23 FLA. ST. U. L. REV. 141, 157 (1995).

STATES WITH CON PROGRAMS

YEAR:	1962	1963	1964	1965	1966	1967	1968	1969	1970	1971	1972	1973	1974	1975	1976	1977	1978	1979	1980	1981	1982	1983
Total States with CON:	1	1	1	1	2	2	4	5	5	14	18	23	23	29	30	33	38	47	49	49	49	48
Alabama																	CON	CON	CON	CON	CON	CON
Alaska															CON	CON	CON	CON	CON	CON	CON	CON
Arizona (1)										CON	CON	CON	CON	CON	CON	CON	CON	CON	CON	CON	CON	CON
Arkansas														CON	CON	CON	CON	CON	CON	CON	CON	CON
California (1)								CON	CON	CON	CON	CON	CON	CON	CON	CON	CON	CON	CON	CON	CON	CON
Colorado (1)												CON	CON	CON	CON	CON	CON	CON	CON	CON	CON	CON
Connecticut (1)												CON	CON	CON	CON	CON	CON	CON	CON	CON	CON	CON
Delaware																	CON	CON	CON	CON	CON	CON
District of Columbia (1)							CON	CON	CON	CON	CON	CON	CON	CON	CON	CON	CON	CON	CON	CON	CON	CON
Florida												CON	CON	CON	CON	CON	CON	CON	CON	CON	CON	CON
Georgia																		CON	CON	CON	CON	CON
Hawaii														CON	CON	CON	CON	CON	CON	CON	CON	CON
Idaho (1)																			CON	CON	CON	
Illinois														CON	CON	CON	CON	CON	CON	CON	CON	CON
Indiana (1)																			CON	CON	CON	CON
Iowa																	CON	CON	CON	CON	CON	CON
Kansas (1)											CON	CON	CON	CON	CON	CON	CON	CON	CON	CON	CON	CON
Kentucky											CON	CON	CON	CON	CON	CON	CON	CON	CON	CON	CON	CON
Louisiana (1)(2)																		SEC 1122	SEC 1122	SEC 1122	SEC 1122	SEC 1122
Maine																	CON	CON	CON	CON	CON	CON
Maryland	CON	CON	CON	CON	CON	CON	CON	CON	CON	CON	CON	CON	CON	CON	CON	CON	CON	CON	CON	CON	CON	CON
Massachusetts											CON	CON	CON	CON	CON	CON	CON	CON	CON	CON	CON	CON
Michigan																	CON	CON	CON	CON	CON	CON
Minnesota (1)										CON	CON	CON	CON	CON	CON	CON	CON	CON	CON	CON	CON	CON
Mississippi																		CON	CON	CON	CON	CON
Missouri (1)																		CON	CON	CON	CON	CON
Montana														CON	CON	CON	CON	CON	CON	CON	CON	CON
Nebraska																		CON	CON	CON	CON	CON
Nevada (1)										CON	CON	CON	CON	CON	CON	CON	CON	CON	CON	CON	CON	CON
New Hampshire																						CON

New Jersey (1)										CON	CON	CON	CON	CON	CON	CON	CON	CON	CON	CON	CON	CON
New Mexico (1)																	CON	CON	CON	CON	CON	
New York					CON	CON	CON	CON	CON	CON	CON	CON	CON	CON	CON	CON	CON	CON	CON	CON	CON	CON
North Carolina																		CON	CON	CON	CON	CON
North Dakota (1)										CON	CON	CON	CON	CON	CON	CON	CON	CON	CON	CON	CON	CON
Ohio														CON	CON	CON	CON	CON	CON	CON	CON	CON
Oklahoma (1)										CON	CON	CON	CON	CON	CON	CON	CON	CON	CON	CON	CON	CON
Oregon										CON	CON	CON	CON	CON	CON	CON	CON	CON	CON	CON	CON	CON
Pennsylvania (1)																		CON	CON	CON	CON	CON
Rhode Island							CON	CON	CON	CON	CON	CON	CON	CON	CON	CON	CON	CON	CON	CON	CON	CON
South Carolina (1)										CON	CON	CON	CON	CON	CON	CON	CON	CON	CON	CON	CON	CON
South Dakota (1)											CON	CON	CON	CON	CON	CON	CON	CON	CON	CON	CON	CON
Tennessee												CON	CON	CON	CON	CON	CON	CON	CON	CON	CON	CON
Texas (1)														CON	CON	CON	CON	CON	CON	CON	CON	CON
Utah (1)																		CON	CON	CON	CON	CON
Vermont																		CON	CON	CON	CON	CON
Virginia (1)												CON	CON	CON	CON	CON	CON	CON	CON	CON	CON	CON
Washington										CON	CON	CON	CON	CON	CON	CON	CON	CON	CON	CON	CON	CON
West Virginia																CON	CON	CON	CON	CON	CON	CON
Wisconsin																CON	CON	CON	CON	CON	CON	CON
Wyoming (1)																CON	CON	CON	CON	CON	CON	CON

SOURCES:
Unless noted, data for the 50 states (except Washington D.C.) through 2001 is from "Major health care policies, 50 state profiles," National Conference of State Legislators, Health Policy Tracking Service, 2001.
Data from 2002-2004 is was gathered directly from the state laws and regulations.
(1) Data on the beginning dates for CON for these states were obtained from "National directory of health planning, policy and regulatory agencies," 15th ed., American Health Planning Association, 2004, p. 80.
(2) Section 1122 is a psuedo CON law based on the Federal mandate.

STATES WITH CON PROGRAMS (CONTINUED)

YEAR:	1984	1985	1986	1987	1988	1989	1990	1991	1992	1993	1994	1995	1996	1997	1998	1999	2000	2001	2002	2003	2004
Total States with CON:	46	42	42	40	39	39	39	39	39	39	39	38	36	37	37	36	36	36	36	36	36
1 Alabama	CON	CON	CON	CON	CON	CON	CON	CON	CON	CON	CON	CON	CON	CON	CON	CON	CON	CON	CON	CON	CON
2 Alaska	CON	CON	CON	CON	CON	CON	CON	CON	CON	CON	CON	CON	CON	CON	CON	CON	CON	CON	CON	CON	CON
3 Arizona (1)	CON																				
4 Arkansas	CON	CON	CON	CON	CON	CON	CON	CON	CON	CON	CON	CON	CON	CON	CON	CON	CON	CON	CON	CON	CON
5 California (1)	CON	CON	CON																		
6 Colorado (1)	CON	CON	CON																		
7 Connecticut (1)	CON	CON	CON	CON	CON	CON	CON	CON	CON	CON	CON	CON	CON	CON	CON	CON	CON	CON	CON	CON	CON
8 Delaware	CON	CON	CON	CON	CON	CON	CON	CON	CON	CON	CON	CON	CON	CON	CON	CON	CON	CON	CON	CON	CON
9 District of Columbia (1)	CON	CON	CON	CON	CON	CON	CON	CON	CON	CON	CON	CON	CON	CON	CON	CON	CON	CON	CON	CON	CON
10 Florida	CON	CON	CON	CON	CON	CON	CON	CON	CON	CON	CON	CON	CON	CON	CON	CON	CON	CON	CON	CON	CON
11 Georgia	CON	CON	CON	CON	CON	CON	CON	CON	CON	CON	CON	CON	CON	CON	CON	CON	CON	CON	CON	CON	CON
12 Hawaii	CON	CON	CON	CON	CON	CON	CON	CON	CON	CON	CON	CON	CON	CON	CON	CON	CON	CON	CON	CON	CON
13 Idaho (1)																					
14 Illinois	CON	CON	CON	CON	CON	CON	CON	CON	CON	CON	CON	CON	CON	CON	CON	CON	CON	CON	CON	CON	CON
15 Indiana (1)	CON	CON	CON	CON	CON	CON	CON	CON	CON	CON	CON	CON		CON	CON						
16 Iowa	CON	CON	CON	CON	CON	CON	CON	CON	CON	CON	CON	CON	CON	CON	CON	CON	CON	CON	CON	CON	CON
17 Kansas (1)	CON																				
18 Kentucky	CON	CON	CON	CON	CON	CON	CON	CON	CON	CON	CON	CON	CON	CON	CON	CON	CON	CON	CON	CON	CON
19 Louisiana (1)(2)	SEC 1122	SEC 1122	SEC 1122	SEC 1122	SEC 1122	SEC 1122	SEC 1122	CON	CON	CON	CON	CON	CON	CON	CON	CON	CON	CON	CON	CON	CON
20 Maine	CON	CON	CON	CON	CON	CON	CON	CON	CON	CON	CON	CON	CON	CON	CON	CON	CON	CON	CON	CON	CON
21 Maryland	CON	CON	CON	CON	CON	CON	CON	CON	CON	CON	CON	CON	CON	CON	CON	CON	CON	CON	CON	CON	CON
22 Massachusetts	CON	CON	CON	CON	CON	CON	CON	CON	CON	CON	CON	CON	CON	CON	CON	CON	CON	CON	CON	CON	CON
23 Michigan	CON	CON	CON	CON	CON	CON	CON	CON	CON	CON	CON	CON	CON	CON	CON	CON	CON	CON	CON	CON	CON
24 Minnesota (1)																					
25 Mississippi	CON	CON	CON	CON	CON	CON	CON	CON	CON	CON	CON	CON	CON	CON	CON	CON	CON	CON	CON	CON	CON
26 Missouri (1)	CON	CON	CON	CON	CON	CON	CON	CON	CON	CON	CON	CON	CON	CON	CON	CON	CON	CON	CON	CON	CON
27 Montana	CON	CON	CON	CON	CON	CON	CON	CON	CON	CON	CON	CON	CON	CON	CON	CON	CON	CON	CON	CON	CON
28 Nebraska	CON	CON	CON	CON	CON	CON	CON	CON	CON	CON	CON	CON	CON	CON	CON	CON	CON	CON	CON	CON	CON
29 Nevada (1)	CON	CON	CON	CON	CON	CON	CON	CON	CON	CON	CON	CON	CON	CON	CON	CON	CON	CON	CON	CON	CON

30 New Hampshire	CON	CON	CON	CON	CON	CON	CON	CON	CON	CON	CON	CON	CON	CON	CON	CON	CON	CON	CON	CON	CON
31 New Jersey (1)	CON	CON	CON	CON	CON	CON	CON	CON	CON	CON	CON	CON	CON	CON	CON	CON	CON	CON	CON	CON	CON
32 New Mexico (1)																					
33 New York	CON	CON	CON	CON	CON	CON	CON	CON	CON	CON	CON	CON	CON	CON	CON	CON	CON	CON	CON	CON	CON
34 North Carolina	CON	CON	CON	CON	CON	CON	CON	CON	CON	CON	CON	CON	CON	CON	CON	CON	CON	CON	CON	CON	CON
35 North Dakota (1)	CON	CON	CON	CON	CON	CON	CON	CON	CON	CON	CON										
36 Ohio	CON	CON	CON	CON	CON	CON	CON	CON	CON	CON	CON	CON	CON	CON	CON	CON	CON	CON	CON	CON	CON
37 Oklahoma (1)	CON	CON	CON	CON	CON	CON	CON	CON	CON	CON	CON	CON	CON	CON	CON	CON	CON	CON	CON	CON	CON
38 Oregon	CON	CON	CON	CON	CON	CON	CON	CON	CON	CON	CON	CON	CON	CON	CON	CON	CON	CON	CON	CON	CON
39 Pennsylvania (1)	CON	CON	CON	CON	CON	CON	CON	CON	CON	CON	CON	CON									
40 Rhode Island	CON	CON	CON	CON	CON	CON	CON	CON	CON	CON	CON	CON	CON	CON	CON	CON	CON	CON	CON	CON	CON
41 South Carolina (1)	CON	CON	CON	CON	CON	CON	CON	CON	CON	CON	CON	CON	CON	CON	CON	CON	CON	CON	CON	CON	CON
42 South Dakota (1)	CON	CON	CON	CON																	
43 Tennessee	CON	CON	CON	CON	CON	CON	CON	CON	CON	CON	CON	CON	CON	CON	CON	CON	CON	CON	CON	CON	CON
44 Texas (1)	CON																				
45 Utah (1)																					
46 Vermont	CON	CON	CON	CON	CON	CON	CON	CON	CON	CON	CON	CON	CON	CON	CON	CON	CON	CON	CON	CON	CON
47 Virginia (1)	CON	CON	CON	CON	CON	CON	CON	CON	CON	CON	CON	CON	CON	CON	CON	CON	CON	CON	CON	CON	CON
48 Washington	CON	CON	CON	CON	CON	CON	CON	CON	CON	CON	CON	CON	CON	CON	CON	CON	CON	CON	CON	CON	CON
49 West Virginia	CON	CON	CON	CON	CON	CON	CON	CON	CON	CON	CON	CON	CON	CON	CON	CON	CON	CON	CON	CON	CON
50 Wisconsin	CON	CON	CON	CON	CON	CON	CON	CON	CON	CON	CON	CON	CON	CON	CON	CON	CON	CON	CON	CON	CON
51 Wyoming (1)	CON																				

SOURCES:
Unless noted, data for the 50 states (except Washington D.C.) through 2001 is from "Major health care policies, 50 state profiles," National Conference of State Legislators, Health Policy Tracking Service, 2001.
Data from 2002-2004 is was gathered directly from the state laws and regulations.
(1) Data on the beginning dates for CON for these states were obtained from "National directory of health planning, policy and regulatory agencies," 15th ed., American Health Planning Association, 2004, p. 80.
(2) Section 1122 is a psuedo CON law based on the Federal mandate.

STATE CON STATUS MAPS

States With Ambulatory Surgery Center (ASC) CON Regulations

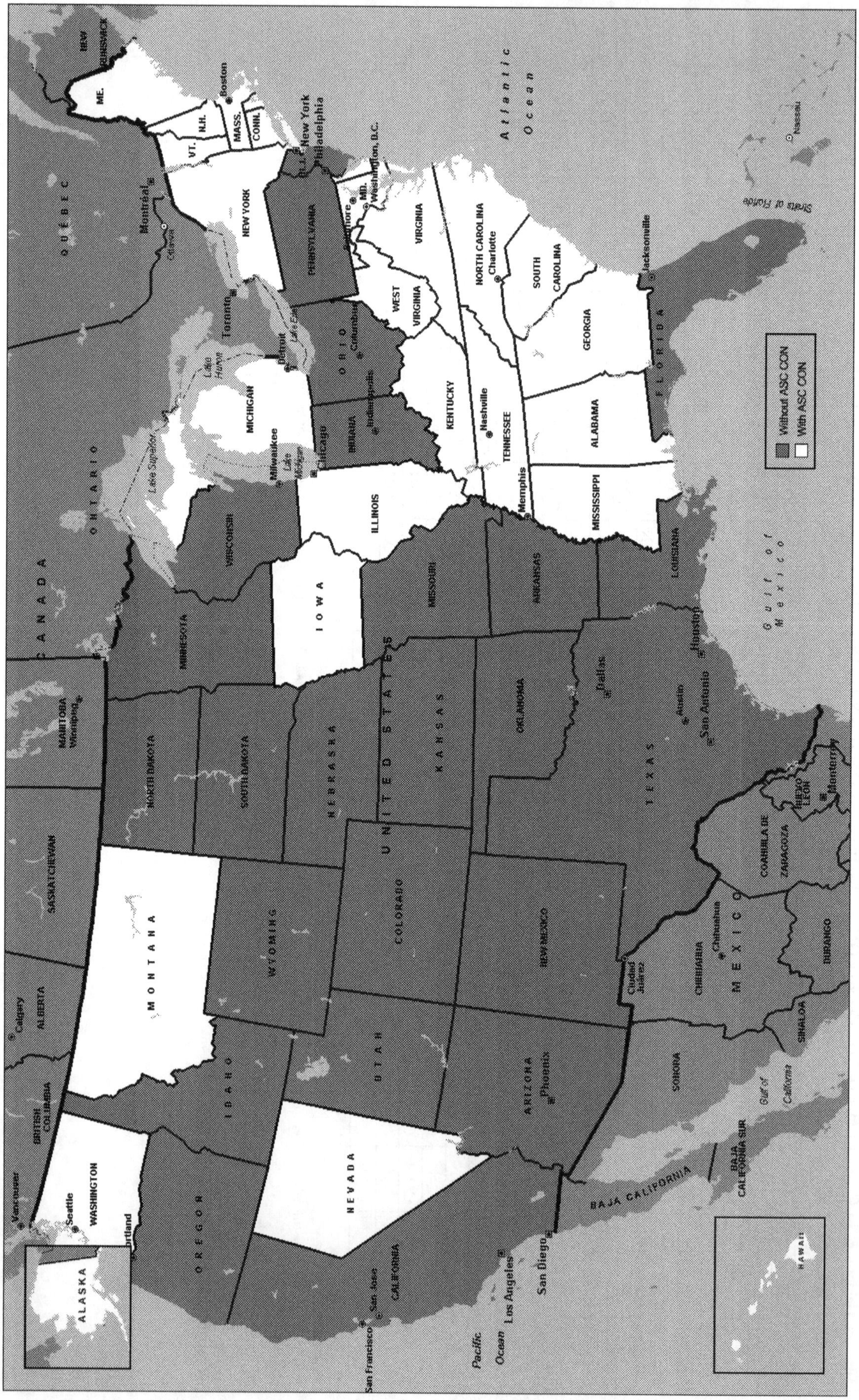

STATE CON STATUS MAPS

States With Medical Equipment CON Regulations

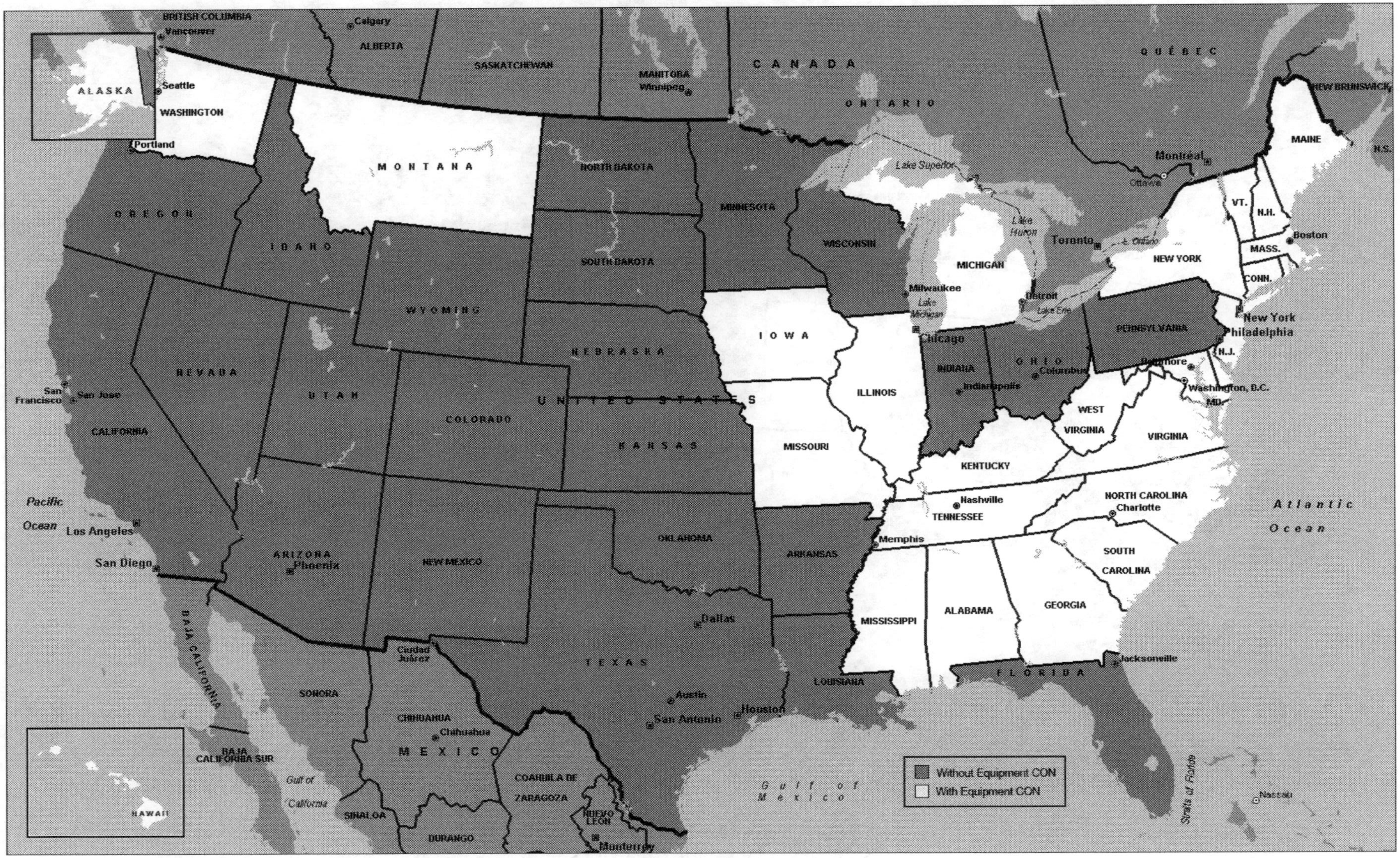

STATE CON STATUS MAPS
States With Hospital CON Regulations

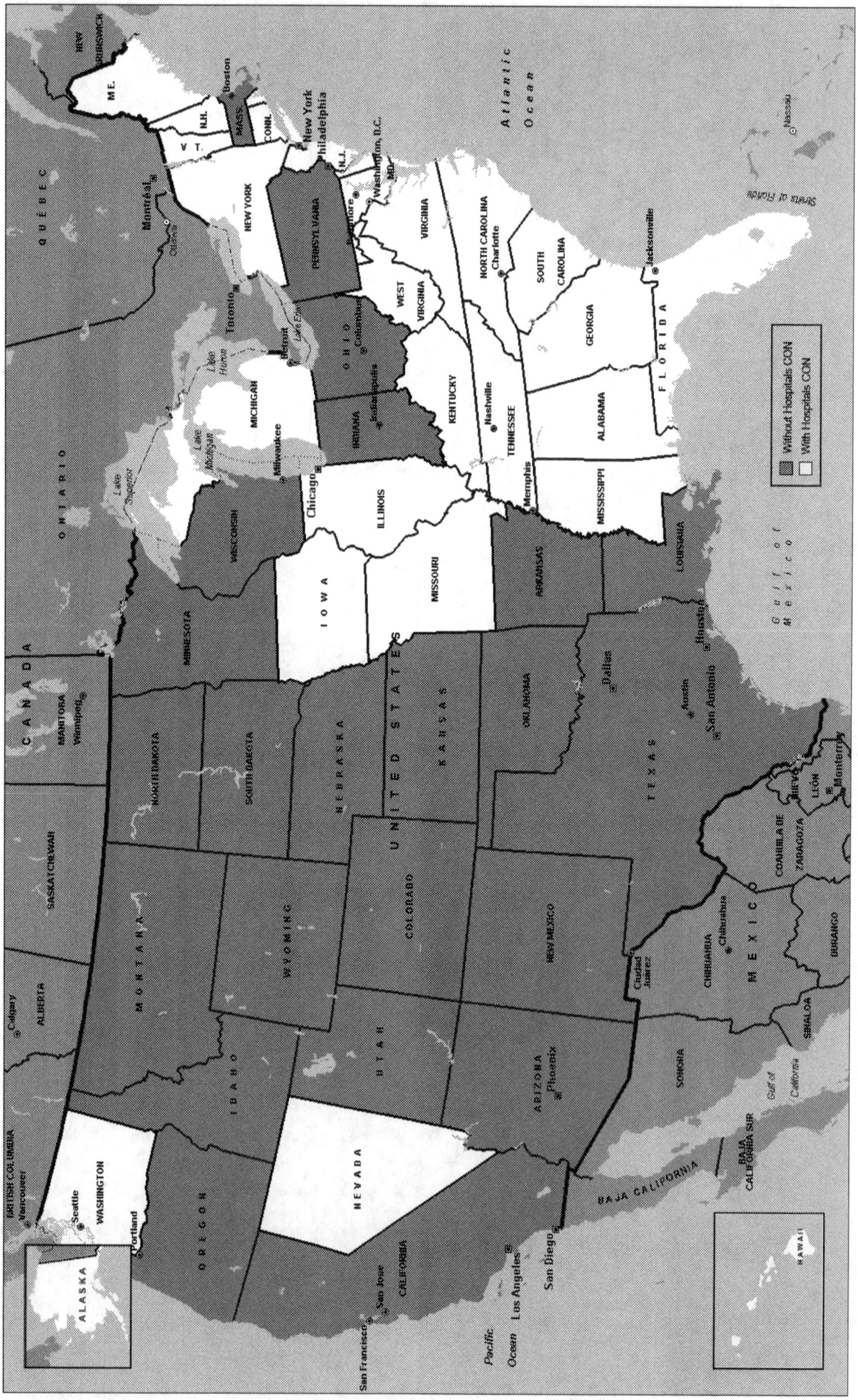

STATE CON STATUS MAPS

States With Long Term Care CON Regulations

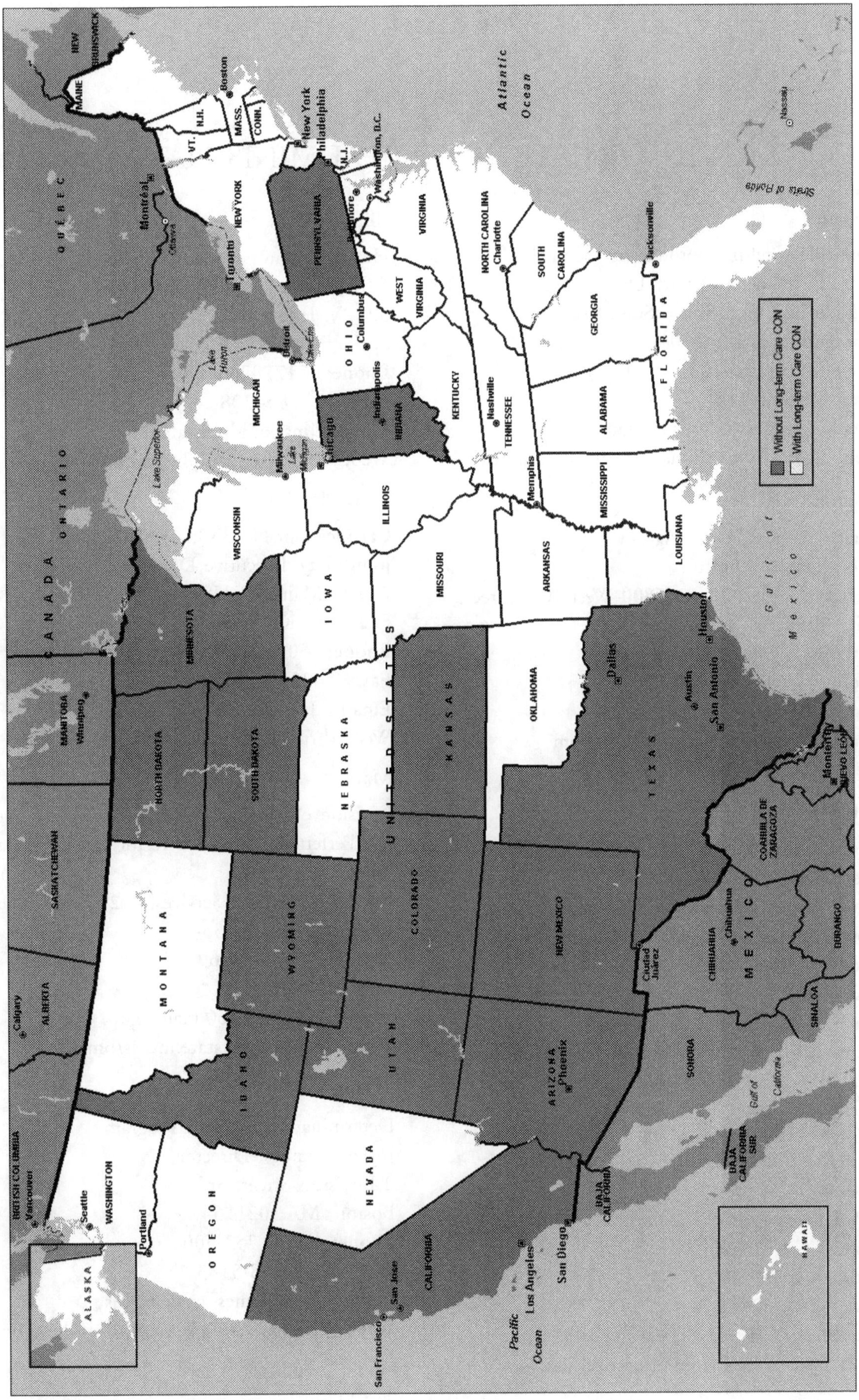

CONTACT INFORMATION – CON ADMINISTRATIVE AGENCIES

Alabama

Statewide Health Coordinating Council
James E. Sanders, Deputy Director
100 North Union Street, Suite 870
Montgomery, AL 36104-
Phone: 3342424103
Fax: 3342424113
Email: jsanders@shpda.state.al.us
Web: http://www.shpda.state.al.us/main.htm

Arkansas

Health Services Permit Agency
Debra Frazier, Director
Freeway Medical Tower, 5800 West 10th Street, Suite 805
Little Rock, AR 72205-
Phone: (501) 661-2509
Fax: (501) 661-2399
Email: dfrazier@healthyarkansas.com
Web: http://www.arhspa.org/

Delaware

Bureau of Health Planning & Resource Management
Kae Johnson, Director
655 S. Bay Road, Blue Hen Corporate Center
Dover, DE 19910-
Phone: (302) 741-2960
Fax: (302) 741-2970
Email: kae.johnson@state.de.us
Web: http://www.state.de.us/dhss/dph/index.html

Georgia

Division of Health Planning
Rathelia Stroud, Director Certificate of Need Program
2 Peachtree Street NW, 40th Floor
Atlanta, GA 30303
Phone: 4046560436
Fax: 4046560442
Email: rstroud@dch.state.ga.us
Web: http://www.communityhealth. state.ga.us

Illinois

Health Facilites Planning Board
Jeffrey Mark, Executive Secretary
525 W. Jefferson St.,
Springfield, IL 62761-
Phone: 2177823516
Fax: 2177854308
Email: jmark@idph.state.il.us
Web: http://www.idph.state.il.us/about/hfpb.htm

Kentucky

Certificate of Need Office
John Gray, Executive Director
275 E. Main St., HS1E-D
Frankfort, KY 40621-
Phone: 5025649589
Fax: 5025640302
Email: John.Gray@mail.state.ky.us
Web: http://chs.state.ky.us/cofn/

Maine

Division of Finance & Reimbursement Services
Bill Perfetto, Assistant Director and Certificate of Need
Bureau of Medical Services, 422 Civic Center Drive
Augusta, ME 04333-
Phone: 2072872769
Fax: 2072871788
Email: bill.perfetto@maine.gov
Web: http://www.state.me.us/bms/

Massachusetts

Determination of Need Program
Joyce E. James, Director
2 Boylston Street, 3rd
Boston, MA 02116-
Phone: (617) 753-5002
Fax: (617) 338-5183
Email: Joyce.James@state.ma.us
Web: http://www.state.ma.us/dph/dhcq/don.htm

Mississippi

State Department of Health
Rachel Pittman, Chief
570 E. Woodrow Wilson, PO Box 1700
Jackson, MS 39215-
Phone: 6015767874
Fax: 6015767530
Email: rachel.pittman@msdh.state.ms.us
Web: http://www.msdh.state.ms.us/msdhsite/index.cfm/30,0,84,html

Montana

Certificate of Need Program
Pamela Sourbeer, Admin. Officer
Dept of Public Health and Human Services, P.O. Box 202953
Helena, MT 59620-
Phone: 4064449519
Fax: 4064441742
Email: psourbeer@state.mt.us
Web: http://www.dphhs.state.mt.us/about_us/divisionsquality_assurance/certificate_of_need/certificate_of_need.htm

Nevada

Bureau of Health Planning & Statistics
Mary Griffith, RN, Health Resource Analyst
505 E. King St., Room 102
Carson City, NV 89701-
Phone: 7756844180
Fax: 7756844156
Email: mgriffith@nvhd.state.nv.us
Web: http://health2k.state.nv.us/vs/letter.htm

New Jersey

State Health Planning Board
John Calabria, Director
P.O. Box 360, John Fitch Plaza,
Trenton, NJ 8625
Phone: 6092928773
Fax: 6092923780
Email: john.calabria@doh.state.nj.us
Web: http://www.state.nj.us/health/hcsa/hcsadmin.htm#CN

North Carolina

Certificate of Need Section
Lee Hoffman, Chief
Certificate of Need Section, 2704 Mail Service Center
Raleigh, NC 27699
Phone: 9198553763
Fax: 9197338139
Email: Lee.Hoffman@ncmail.net
Web: http://facility-services.state.nc.us/conpage.htm

Oklahoma

Health Facility Systems
Henry F. Hartsell, Jr PhD, Chief
Oklahoma State Department of Health, 1000 NE 10th St
Oklahoma City, OK 73117-
Phone: 4052716868
Fax: 4052717360
Email: hank@health.state.ok.us
Web: http://www.health.state.ok.us/program/condiv

Rhode Island

Office of Health Systems Development
John X. Donahue, Chief
Three Capitol Hill, Room 407,
Providence, RI 2908
Phone: 4012222788
Fax: 4012734350
Email: JohnD@doh.state.ri.us
Web: http://www.health.ri.gov/hsr/healthsystems/Home.htm

Tennessee

Certificate of Need Program
Melanie Hill, Acting Executive Director
500 Deaderick Street, Suite 850
Nashville, TN 37243-
Phone: 6157412364
Fax: (615) 532-9884
Email: Melanie.Hill@state.tn.us
Web: http://www.tn.gov/hsda/cert_need_sum.html

Virginia

Certificate of Public Need Program
Erik Bodin, Director
3600 W. Broad St., Suite 216
Richmond, VA 23230
Phone: 8043672126
Fax: 8043672206
Email: erik.bodin@vdh.virginia.gov
Web: http://www.vdh.state.va.us/quality/copn

Washington D.C.

State Health Planning and Development Agency
Amha Selassie, Chief of Project Review
825 North Capitol Street NE,
Washington, DC 20002-
Phone: (202) 442-5875
Fax: (202) 442-9035
Email: aselassie@dchealth.com
Web: http://dchealth.dc.gov/services/administration_offices/shpda/services.shtm

Wisconsin

Bureau of Health Care Benefits
C. David Lund, Chief, Nursing Home Section
1 West Wilson St.,
Madison, WI 53702-
Phone: (608) 266-2021
Fax: (608) 267-2832
Email: lundcd@dhfs.state.wi.us
Web: http://dhfs.wisconsin.gov/aboutDHFS/DHCF/dhcf.htm

CON INFORMATION – RESEARCH GROUPS

Academy Health

1801 K Street NW #701-L
Washington, DC 20006
Phone: (202) 292-6700
Fax: (202) 292-6800
Email: info@academyhealth.org
URL: www.academyhealth.org

Academy Health, drawing upon the strengths of its two predecessor organizations, is advancing the fields of health services research and health policy through the transfer of relevant information across the research and policy arenas.

Agency for Healthcare Research and Quality

540 Gaither Road
Rockville, MD 20850
Phone: (301) 427-1364
Email: info@ahrq.gov
URL: www.ahrq.gov

The Agency for Healthcare Research and Quality (AHRQ) research provides evidence-based information on health care outcomes; quality; and cost, use, and access. Information from AHRQ's research helps people make more informed decisions and improve the quality of health care services.

American Enterprise Institute for Public Policy Research

1150 Seventeenth Street, N.W.
Washington, D.C. 20036
Phone: (202) 862- 5800
Fax: (202) 862- 7177
URL: www.aei.org

The American Enterprise Institute for Public Policy Research is an independent, non-profit organization interested in preserving America's cultural and political institutions. The Institute publishes many reports and articles each year and consults with all three branches of government.

American Health Care Association

1201 L Street NW
Washington, DC 20005
Phone: (202) 842-4444
Fax: (202) 842-3860
URL: www.ahca.org

AHCA represents the long term care community to the nation at large – to government, business leaders, and the general public. It also serves as a force for change within the long term care field, providing information, education, and administrative tools that enhance quality at every level.

The American Health Planning Association
7245 Arlington Boulevard, Suite 300
Falls Church, VA 22402
Phone: (703) 573- 3103
Email: ahpanet@aol.com
URL: www.ahpanet.org

The American Health Planning Association is a non-profit organization committed to health policy education. The Association provides healthcare data and analysis on a variety of issues including healthcare access, planning, quality and regulations.

The American Hospital Association

One North Franklin
Chicago, IL 60606
Phone: (312) 422-3000
URL: www.aha.org

AHA leads, represents, and serves healthcare provider organizations that are accountable to the community and committed to health improvement.

The American Public Health Association

800 I Street, N.W.
Washington, D.C. 20001-3710
Phone: (202) 777-2742
Fax: (202) 777-2534
Email: comments@apha.org
URL: www.apha.org

APHA is an Association of individuals and organizations working to improve the public's health and to achieve equity in health status for all.

Association for Community Health Improvement

180 Montgomery Street, Suite 1520
San Francisco, CA 94104
Phone: (415) 248- 8408
Fax: (415) 296- 0519
Email: communityhlth@aha.org
URL: www.communityhlth.org

The Association for Community Health works to strengthen healthcare through education. The Association is focused on effective planning, measurement, and delivery of healthcare services.

The Association of State and Territorial Health Officials (ASTHO)

1275 K. St., N.W. Suite 800
Washington, D.C. 20005-4006
Phone: (202) 371-9090
Fax: (202) 371-9797
URL: www.astho.org

The Association of State and Territorial Health Officials (ASTHO) is the national nonprofit organization representing the state and territorial public health agencies of the United States, the U.S. Territories, and the District of Columbia. ASTHO's members, the chief health officials of these jurisdictions, are dedicated to formulating and influencing sound public health policy, and to assuring excellence in state-based public health practice.

California HealthCare Foundation

476 Ninth Street
Oakland, CA 94607
Phone: (510) 238-1040
Fax: (510) 238-1388
URL: www.chcf.org

The California HealthCare Foundation is an independent philanthropy committed to improving the way health care is delivered and financed in California, and helping consumers make informed health care and coverage decisions.

The Cato Institute

1000 Massachusetts Avenue, N.W.
Washington, D.C. 20001-5403
Phone: (202) 842-0200
Fax: (202) 842-3490
Email: service@cato.org
URL: www.cato.org

The Cato Institute seeks to broaden the parameters of public policy debate to allow consideration of the traditional American principles of limited government, individual liberty, free markets and peace. Toward that goal, the Institute strives to achieve greater involvement of the intelligent, concerned lay public in questions of policy and the proper role of government.

The Center for Studying Health System Change

600 Maryland Avenue SW #550
Washington, DC 20024
Phone: (202) 484-5261
Fax: (202) 484-9258
Email: hscinfo@hschange.org
URL: www.hschange.com

The mission of the Center for Studying Health System Change (HSC) is to inform health care decision makers about changes in the health care system at both the local and national levels and the effects of such changes on people.

The Century Foundation

41 East 70th Street
New York, NY 10021
Phone: (212) 535-4441
Fax: (212) 535-7534
URL: www.tcf.org

Our mission is to persuade those who care about issues such as economic inequality, population aging, homeland security, discontent with government and politics, and national security that significant improvements are possible even when the conventional wisdom says they are not.

The Commonwealth Fund

One East 75th Street
New York, NY 10021
Phone: (212) 606-3800
Fax: (212) 606-3500
Email: cmwf@cmwf.org
URL: www.cmwf.org

The Commonwealth Fund is a private foundation that supports independent research on health and social issues and makes grants to improve health care practice and policy.

Community Service Society

105 East 22nd Street
New York, NY 10010
Phone: (212) 254-8900
Email: info@cssny.org
URL: www.cssny.org

The Community Service Society of New York is an independent, nonprofit organization that for more than 150 years has helped New Yorkers in need to defeat the problems of poverty and strengthen community life for all.

The Fraser Institute

1770 Burrard Street, 4th Floor
Vancouver, B.C. V6J 3G7 Canada
Phone: (604) 688-0221
Fax: (604) 688-8539
Email: info@fraserinstitute.ca
URL:www.fraserinstitute.ca

As an independent public policy organization, The Fraser Institute focuses on the role competitive markets play in providing for the economic and social well-being of all Canadians.

The Heartland Institute

19 South LaSalle, Suite 903
Chicago, IL 60603
Phone: (312) 377-4000
Fax: (312) 377-4800
Email: think@heartland.org
URL: www.heartland.org

*Heartland's **mission** is to help build social movements in support of ideas that empower people. Such ideas include parental choice in education, choice and personal responsibility in health care, market-based approaches to environmental protection, privatization of public services, and deregulation in areas where property rights and markets do a better job than government bureaucracies.*

The Heritage Foundation

214 Massachusetts Avenue, N.E.
Washington, D.C. 20002-4999
Phone: (202) 546-4400
Fax: (202) 546-8328
Email: info@heritage.org
URL: www.heritage.org

Founded in 1973, The Heritage Foundation is a research and educational institute, "a think tank" whose mission is to formulate and promote conservative public policies based on the principles of free enterprise, limited government, individual freedom, traditional American values, and a strong national defense.

The James Madison Institute

PO Box 37460
Tallahassee, FL 32315
Phone: (850) 386-3131
Fax: (850) 386-1807
Email: jmi@jamesmadison.org
URL: www.jamesmadison.org

The James Madison Institute is a Florida-based research and educational organization engaged in the battle of ideas. The Institute's ideas are rooted in a belief in the U.S. Constitution and such timeless ideals as limited government, economic freedom, federalism, traditional values, and individual liberty coupled with individual responsibility.

The Lewin Group

3130 Fairview Parke Drive, Suite 800
Falls Church, VA 22042
Phone: (703) 269-5500
Fax: (703) 269-5501
URL: www.lewin.com

The Lewin Group is a healthcare consulting firm concerned with health technology, regulation and healthcare practice. The Group evaluates programs to improve the financing and delivery of healthcare.

Kaiser Family Foundation

2400 Sand Hill Road
Menlo Park, CA 94025
Phone: (650) 854-9400
Fax: (650) 854-4800
URL: www.kff.org

The Henry J. Kaiser Family Foundation is an independent philanthropy focusing on the major health care issues facing the nation. The Foundation is an independent voice and source of facts and analysis for policymakers, the media, the health care community, and the general public.

The Mackinac Center for Public Policy

140 West Main Street, PO Box 568
Midland, MI 48640
Phone: (989) 631-0900, (800) 224-3327
Fax: (989) 631-0964
Email: mcpp@mackinac.org
URL: www.mackinac.org

*The **Mackinac Center for Public Policy** is a nonpartisan research and educational organization devoted to improving the quality of life for all Michigan citizens by promoting sound solutions to state and local policy questions.*

Mathematica Policy Research, Inc.

P.O. Box 2393
Princeton, NJ 08543-2393
Phone: (609) 799-3535
Fax: (609) 799-0005
E-mail: info@mathematica-mpr.com
URL: www.mathematica-mpr.com

Along with its research affiliate, the Center for Studying Health System Change, is a researcher of issues related to social policy problems. The company has been in operation for 35 years and conducts studies of healthcare, welfare, education, employment, nutrition, and early childhood policies and programs. Healthcare policy analysis is done for federal and state agencies and involves the collection and analysis of data, evaluation of programs, summarization of policy implications, and offering practical solutions.

National Association of City and County Health Officials

1100 17th Street, Second Floor
Washington, D.C. 20036
Phone: (202) 783-5550
Fax: (202) 783-1583
URL: www.naccho.org

The National Association of County and City Health Officials (NACCHO) is the national nonprofit organization representing local public health agencies (including city, county, metro, district, and Tribal agencies).

The National Center for Policy Analysis

12770 Colt Road, Suite 800
Dallas, TX 75251
Phone: (972) 386-6272
Fax: (972) 386-0924
Email: ncpa@ncpa.org
URL: www.ncpa.org

The National Center of Policy Analysis (NCPA) is a nonprofit, nonpartisan public policy research organization, established in 1983. The NCPA's goal is to develop and promote private alternatives to government regulation and control, solving problems by relying on the strength of the competitive, entrepreneurial private sector. Topics include reforms in health care, taxes, Social Security, welfare, criminal justice, education and environmental regulation.

National Conference of State Legislatures

7700 East First Place
Denver, CO 80230
Phone: (303) 364-7700
Fax: (303) 364-7800
Email: info@ncsl.org
URL: www.ncsl.org

NCSL is your forum for advancing ideas in your home state, across other states, and on Capitol Hill; for promoting information-sharing, one-on-one and collectively; and for providing you with the knowledge and resources you need to get America's ideas working.

The National Institutes of Health

9000 Rockville Pike
Bethesda, MD 20892
Phone: (301) 496-4000
Email: NIHInfo@OD.NIH.GOV
URL: www.nih.gov

The National Institutes of Health is the steward of medical and behavioral research for the Nation. It is an Agency under the U.S. Department of Health and Human Services.

The Performance Institute

1515 North Courthouse Road, Suite 600
Arlington, VA 22201
Phone: (703) 894- 0481
Fax: (703) 894- 0482
Email: info@performanceweb.org
URL: www.performanceweb.org

The Performance Institute is a private research organization focused on identifying solutions to the nation's healthcare problems. The Institute studies program management and funding for many public health services.

RAND

1700 Main Street PO Box 2138
Santa Monica, CA 90407-2138
Phone: (310) 393-0411
Fax: (310) 393- 4818
Email: correspondence@RAND.org
URL: www.rand.org

RAND is a nonprofit institution that helps improve policy and decision-making through research and analysis. Areas of expertise include children and adolescents, civil justice, education, energy and the environment, healthcare, international affairs, U.S. national security, population and aging, public safety, science and technology, substance abuse, terrorism, and transportation and infrastructure.

Robert Woods Johnson Foundation

College Road East and Route 1
PO Box 2316
Princeton, NJ 08543
Phone: (888) 631-9989
URL: www.rwjf.org

The Robert Wood Johnson Foundation seeks to improve the health and health care of all Americans. Rather than paying for individual care, we concentrate on health care systems and the conditions that promote better health.

The Urban Institute

2100 M Street, N.W.
Washington, D.C. 20037
Phone: (202) 833-7200
Email: paffairs@ui.urban.org
URL: www.urban.org

The Urban Institute is a nonprofit nonpartisan policy research and educational organization established to examine the social, economic, and governance problems facing the nation. It provides information and analysis to public and private decision makers to help them address these challenges and strives to raise citizen understanding of the issues and tradeoffs in policy making.

W.K. Kellogg Foundation

One Michigan Avenue East
Battle Creek, MI 49017
Phone: (269) 968-1611
Fax: (269) 968-0413
URL: www.wkkf.org

The W.K. Kellogg Foundation is a nonprofit organization whose mission is to apply knowledge to solve the problems of people. Since its beginning the Foundation has continuously focused on building the capacity of individuals, communities, and institutions to solve their own problems.

LEADING CON HEALTHCARE ECONOMISTS

Anil Bamezai Ph.D
Assistant Professor
Villanova University
Phone: 610-519-4847
Fax: 610-519-7863
Email: anil.bamezai@villanova.edu

Dr. Bamezai received his Ph.D. from All India Institute of Medical Sciences, New Delhi. He is currently an assistant professor at Villanova University teaching Immunobiology. Dr. Bamezai has several published articles regarding his research within this area.

Zwanziger J, Melnick G, Bamezai A. "California providers adjust to increasing price controls." In *Health Policy Reform: Competition and Controls.* Edited by R. Helms, pp. 241-58. Washington, DC: AEI Press, 1993.

Thomas W. Bice, Ph.D
The Yankee Institute for Public Policy, Inc.
bice@yankeeinstitute.org

Bice, Thomas W., PhD, and David S. Salkever, PhD. *Certificate-of-Need programs: Cure or cause of inflated costs?* St. Louis, MO: Hospital Progress, July 1977.

Salkever, David S. and Thomas W. Bice. *Impact of state certificate-of-need laws on health care costs and utilization.* Rockville, MD: U.S. Department of Health, Education, and Welfare, 1/31/1976.

Salkever, David S. and Thomas W. Bice. *Certificate-of-need legislation and hospital costs.*

Salkever, David S. and Thomas W. Bice. *The Impact of Certificate-of-Need controls on hospital investment.* MMFQ, Spring 1976.

Salkever, David S. and Thomas W. Bice. *Hospital certificate-of-need controls:_Impact on investment, costs, and use.* Washington, D.C.: American Enterprise Institute for Public Policy Research, 1979.

Randall R. Bovbjerg
Urban Institute
2100 M. Street, NW
Washington, DC 20037

Bovbjerg, Randal R. and Jill A. Marsteller, *Health care market competition in six states: Implications for the poor.* Occasional Paper Number 17 Washington, D.C.: The Urban Institute, 1998.

Sloan, Frank A., James F. Blumstein, James M. Perrin, Clark C. Havighurst, Laurence R. Tancredi, C. Arden Miller, Joseph N. Onek, Terry Calvani, M. Elizabeth Gee, Randall R. Bovbjerg, and May W. Shayne. *Cost, quality, and access in health care: New roles for health planning in a competitive environment.* The Jossey-Bass Health Series The Jossey-Bass Public Administration Series. San Francisco CA: Jossey-Bass Publishers, c1988.

Albert F. Cacozza
Ropes & Gray
One Metro Center
700 12th Street, NW, Suite 900
Washington, DC 20005
Phone: 202-508-4611
Fax: 202-508-4650
Email: acacozza@ropesgray.com

Al Cocozza is a partner at Ropes & Gray. His practice focuses on providing advice to healthcare clients on legislative, regulatory and corporate matters. One of his many projects include managing an internal Food and Drug administration safety audit for a national non-profit health organization; employment agreements and university conflict of interest policies; and coordinating efforts of a major health care corporation regarding competitive issues before the FTC; and counseling multinational pharmaceutical corporations regarding compliance with information privacy requirements.

Cacozza, Albert F. *Certificate of need litigation: 1966-1979 case briefs.* Washington, D.C.: The Urban Institute, 1979.

William S. Custer, Ph.D.
Associate Professor, J. Mack Robinson College of Business, Georgia State University
Risk Management and Insurance Department
Institute of Health Administration
Email: wcuster@gsu.edu

Dr. Custer is an Associate Professor at the J. Mack Robinson College of Business at Georgia State University. He is an expert in employee benefits, health care financing and health insurance. Dr. Custer has written numerous articles and studies on the healthcare delivery system, insurance, retirement income security and employee benefits. Dr. Custer has also worked as an economist in the research program for Health Policy Research at the American Medical Association.

Custer, William S. *Certificate of need regulation and the health care delivery system.* Atlanta, GA: Center for Risk Management and Insurance Research, Feb. 1997.

Elizabeth Devore
National Council on State Legislatures
444 North Capitol Street. N.W., Suite 515
Washington D.C. 20001
Phone: 202-624-5400

Elizabeth Devore currently works for the National Council on State Legislatures on Long Term Care issues.

Devore, Elizabeth. *Certificate of Need.* Washington DC: Health Policy Tracking Service, National Conference of State Legislatures, Dec. 31, 2001.

Michael F. Drummond
Professor of Economics and Director of the Centre for Health
University of York, UK
Email: chedir@york.ac.uk

Michael Drummond has been the Director of the Center of Health Economics at the University of York since 1995. His area of interest includes the economic evaluation of health care treatments and programs. Dr.

Drummond is the author of two major textbooks and more than 450 scientific publications. His current projects focus on economic evaluations and their use in health care decision making.

Drummond, Michael, F. and Bernie J. O'Brien; Stoddart, Greg L.; Torrance, George W. *Methods for the economic evaluation of health care programmes.* Second Edition New York: Oxford University Press, 1997.

Donna O. Farley Ph.D
201 North Craig Street
Pittsburgh, PA 15213-1516
Phone: 412-683-2300, ext. 4633

Dr. Farley is a Senior Health Policy Analyst at RAND and has over 27 years of professional experience. She focuses on policy research interests in managed care, insurance coverage for vulnerable populations, Medicare policy, military health, evaluation of payment designs, and international health policy issues. Dr. Farley has over sixty publications in relation to healthcare.

Farley, Donna O., Lisa R. Shugarman, Feng Zeng, Pat Taylor, and J. Scott Ashwood. *Trends in supply and utilization of rural hospitals with special medicare payments.* RAND, c2000.

John C. Goodman Ph.D
President and Founder of the NCPA
Phone: 800-859-1154
Email: jcgoodman@ncpa.org
Gerald L. Musgrave

President of Economics America, Inc. in Ann Arbor, Michigan. Mr. Musgrave is a teacher and researcher at the California State University, Michigan State University, the U.S. Naval Postgraduate School, Stanford University and the University of Michigan. Musgrave is the author/co-author of over sixty publications including Patient Power, a book he wrote with National Center for Policy Analysis President John Goodman.

Goodman, John C. and Gerald L. Musgrave. *Patient Power: Solving America's health care crisis.* Washington DC: Cato Institute, c1992.

Paul Gross
Chairman
Health Group Strategies Pty. Ltd.
P.O. Box 1095
Dee Why N.S.W 2099
Phone: 612-9977 1054
Fax: 612-8966 9018
Email: iheta@ozemail.com.au

Gross, Paul F., Peter Duffy, and Ronald Kotzmann. *Certificate of need as a method of cost control in hospitals: In theory good, in practice unproven.* Sydney, Australia: Institute of Health Economics and Technology Assessment, c1985.

Paul L. Joskow
Massachusetts Institute of Technology (MIT)- Department of Economics
50 Memorial Drive
E52-373A
Cambridge, MA 02142
United States
Phone: 617-253-6664
Fax: 617-258-7070

Joskow, Paul L. *Controlling hospital costs: The role of government regulation.* Cambridge, MA: MIT Press, 1984.

Jill A. Marsteller
Urban Institute
2100 M. Street, NW
Washington, DC 20037

Jill Marsteller is currently a researcher at the Urban Institute. She has written several papers on Healthcare and related issues.

Bovbjerg, Randal R. and Jill A. Marsteller, *Health care market competition in six states: Implications for the poor.* Occasional Paper Number 17 Washington, D.C.: The Urban Institute, 1998.

Mara Melum
Minerva Leadership Institute, Inc.
St. Paul, MN.
Email: Minerva@visi.com

Locke, Sheryl, Thomas Erickson, and Mara Melum. *Position Paper: Certificate of Need.* Minneapolis, MN: Minnesota Hospital Association, 1979.

Glenn Melnick Ph.D
Ralph and Goldy Lewis Hall 307
Los Angeles, CA 90089-0626
Phone: 213-821-1408
Fax: 213-821-1331
Email: gmelnick@usc.edu

Dr. Melnick is a Blue Cross of California Professor of Healthcare Finance and Master of International Public Policy and Management program. He is a renowned expert in healthcare and finance. He was on the board at the UCLA School of Public Health as a consultant and served as an expert witness to the Federal Trade Commission.. Dr. Melnick is a widely published author on Healthcare and financial topics.

Zwanziger J, Melnick G, Bamezai A. "California providers adjust to increasing price controls." In *Health Policy Reform: Competition and Controls.* Edited by R. Helms, pp. 241-58. Washington, DC: AEI Press, 1993.

Michael A. Morrisey, M.A., Ph.D
Professor of Health Care Organization and Policy
Ryals 330
Phone: 205-975-8966
Email: morrisey@uab.edu

Backround: Michael Morrisey is currently a professor in the Dept. of Health Care Organization and Policy in the UAB school of Public Health, with secondary faculty appointments in the Department of Economics, the Department of Health Services Administration, and the Department of Sociology. Dr. Morrisey is the director of the UAB Lister Hill Center for Health Policy and is the senior scientist in the Center for Aging, the Injury Control and Research Center, the Multipurpose Arthritis and Musculoskeletal Disease Center and the Center for Telecommunications Education and Research. Dr. Morissey is the first recipient of the John Thompson Prize in Health Services Research awarded by the Association of University Programs in Health Administration. He teaches courses in health economics, and health insurance and managed care.

Morrisey, Michael A. "Competition in Hospital and Health Insurance Markets." *Health Services Research.* April 2001.

Bernie O'Brien , DOD: 2/13/04
Please contact: Veronica McGuire, Media Relations
Phone: 905-525-9140, ext. 22169

Bernie O'Brien was a professor in the department of clinical epidemiology and biostatistics at McMaster University. He was also the director of clinical effectiveness research for the Father Sean O'Sullivan Research Centre and associate director of the Centre for Evaluation of Medicines at St. Joseph's Healthcare Hamilton, and an associate of the Centre for Health Economics and Policy Analysis at McMaster. Dr. O'Brien received many awards and recognition for his research work.

Drummond, Michael, F. and Bernie J. O'Brien; Stoddart, Greg L.; Torrance, George W. *Methods for the economic evaluation of health care programmes.* Second Edition New York: Oxford University Press, 1997.

Eleanore Rothenberg Ph.D
New York Institute for Psychological Change
180East 79th Street, Suite 1C
NY, NY 10021
Phone: 212-744-3700

Dr. Rothenberg is a New York state licensed Clinical Psychologist Clinical Social Worker and a Certified Group Psychotherapist. She is the Clinical Director of the Sibling Center for Sisters and Brothers of People with Disabilities. Dr. Rothenberg's specializes in clinical work with siblings of disabled people and their families.

Rothenberg, Eleanore. *Regulation and expansion of health facilities: The certificate of need experience in New York State.* New York, NY: Praeger Publishers, 1976.

David S. Salkever, PhD
Johns Hopkins University - Bloomberg School of Public Health
624 N. Broadway
Department of Health Policy and Management
Baltimore, MD 21205

Bice, Thomas W., PhD, and David S. Salkever, PhD. *Certificate-of-Need programs: Cure or cause of inflated costs?* St. Louis, MO: Hospital Progress, July 1977.

Salkever, David S. and Thomas W. Bice. *Impact of state certificate-of-need_laws on health care costs and utilization.* Rockville, MD: U.S. Department of Health, Education, and Welfare, 1/31/1976.

Salkever, David S. and Thomas W. Bice. *Certificate-of-need legislation and hospital costs.*

Salkever, David S. and Thomas W. Bice. *The Impact of Certificate-of-Need controls on hospital investment.* MMFQ, Spring 1976.

Salkever, David S. and Thomas W. Bice. *Hospital certificate-of-need controls: Impact on investment, costs, and use.* Washington, D.C.: American Enterprise Institute for Public Policy Research, 1979.

John R. Selser, Esq.
J.R. Selser Dispute Resolution Services
P.O. Box 189, Readfield, ME 04355
Phone: 685-4054
Fax: 685-4054
Email: jrselser@ezsg.com

Backround: John Selser has been a licensed attorney since 1977. His areas of practice are Divorce/Family, Employment, Labor, EEOC/ADA, Consumer, Community/Neighborhood, Public Policy, Regulatory/Admin, Civil/Human Rights, Schools/Education, Workers Comp.

Selser, John R. *Certificate of need study of the human resources committee of the 112th legislature.* Augusta, ME: Office of Policy and Legal Analysis, 1986.

Frank Sloan
Professor
Duke University
Office: 233 Social Sciences
Phone: 919-660-1820
Email: fsloan@econ.duke.edu

Dr. Sloan is the J. Alexander McMahon professor of Health Policy and Management and Professor of Economics at Duke University since 1993. Prior to his current positions he was a Research Economist at the Rand Corporation and served on the faculty at the University of Florida and Vanderbilt University. His current research includes alcohol use prevention, long-term care, medical malpractice, and cost-effectiveness analyses of medical technologies. Dr. Sloan has several published articles relating to his research.

Sloan, Frank and Judith D. Bentkover. *Access to ambulatory care and the U.S. economy.* Lexington MA: Lexington Books, c1979.

Sloan, Frank A., James F. Blumstein, James M. Perrin, Clark C. Havighurst, Laurence R. Tancredi, C. Arden Miller, Joseph N. Onek, Terry Calvani, M. Elizabeth Gee, Randall R. Bovbjerg, and May W. Shayne. *Cost, quality, and access in health care: New roles for health planning in a competitive environment.* The Jossey-Bass Health Series The Jossey-Bass Public Administration Series. San Francisco CA: Jossey-Bass Publishers, c1988.

Sloan, Frank A. and Bruce Steinwald. *Insurance, regulation, and hospital costs.* Lexington MA: D C Heath and Company, c1980.

David G. Stevenson
Harvard Medical School
Assistant Professor of Health Economics
180 Longwood Avenue
Health Care Policy
Boston, MA 02115
Phone: 617-432-3905
Email: Stevenson@hcp.med.harvard.edu

Wiener, Joshua M. and David G. Stevenson. *Long-term care for the elderly: Profiles of thirteen states.* Occasional Paper Number 12 Washington, D.C.: The Urban Institute, 1998.

Wiener, Joshua M. and David G. Stevenson. *Long-term care for the elderly in the District of Columbia: Issues and prospects.* Washington, D.C.: The Urban Institute, 1999.

Wiener, Joshua M., David G. Stevenson, and Susan M. Goldenson. *Controlling the supply of long-term care providers at the state level.* Occasional Paper Number 22 Washington, D.C.: The Urban Institute, 1998.

Greg Stoddart, Ph.D
Health Sciences Center/Room 2D1
McMaster University
1200 Main Street West
Hamilton, ON L8N 3Z5
Phone: 905-525-9140
Fax: 905-529-5742
Email: Stoddart@mcmaster.ca

Drummond, Michael, F. and Bernie J. O'Brien; Stoddart, Greg L.; Torrance, George W. *Methods for the economic evaluation of health care programmes.* Second Edition New York: Oxford University Press, 1997.

Constance Thomas
Faculty of Nursing
University of Alberta
3rd Floor Clinical Sciences Building
Edmonton, Alberta
T6G 2G3 Canada

Thomas, Constance. *Certificate of need: an overview of 1992 legislative activity.* c1993.

Thomas, Constance. *A Summary of CON laws from the 1987-1988 legislative sessions.* Washington, D.C.: Intergovernmental Health Policy Project, c1993.

George Torrance, Ph.D
Vice President, Scientific Affairs
Innovus Research (U.S) Inc.
10 Cabot Road, Suite 102
Medford, MA 02155
Phone: 781-338-9700
Fax: 781-338-9522

Dr. Torrance is Professor Emeritus of Clinical Epidemiology and Biostatistics and Management Science at McMaster University. As Vice President of Innovus Research Inc. his responsibilities include strategic direction of the health economic and outcomes activities as well as consulting and overseeing the technical parts of those projects.

Drummond, Michael, F. and Bernie J. O'Brien; Stoddart, Greg L.; Torrance, George W. *Methods for the economic evaluation of health care programmes.* Second Edition New York: Oxford University Press, 1997.

Carolyn A. Watts, Ph.D [new Madden]

Professor/ University of Washington
University of Washington
1959 NE Pacific Street
Box: 357660
Seattle, WA 98195
Phone: 206-616-29896
Fax: 206-543-3964
Email: Watts@u.washington.edu

Madden CW. "Excess capacity: markets, regulation, and values." *Health Services Research.* February, 1999.

Joshua M. Wiener

RTI International
1615 M Street, NW, Suite 740
Washington D.C. 20036-3209
Phone: 202-728-2094
Email: jwiener@rti.org

Dr. Wiener received his Ph.D. from Harvard University and has over 25 years of experience as a health care researcher and government official. Since the 1970's he has been involved in federal, state, and local government policy issues. His specialties are long term care, Medicaid, and health care for the elderly. Dr. Wiener is the author or editor of eight books and more than 100 publications.

Wiener, Joshua M. and David G. Stevenson. *Long-term care for the elderly: Profiles of thirteen states.* Occasional Paper Number 12 Washington, D.C.: The Urban Institute, 1998.

Wiener, Joshua M. and David G. Stevenson. *Long-term care for the elderly in the District of Columbia: Issues and prospects.* Washington, D.C.: The Urban Institute, 1999.

Wiener, Joshua M., David G. Stevenson, and Susan M. Goldenson. *Controlling the supply of long-term care providers at the state level.* Occasional Paper Number 22 Washington, D.C.: The Urban Institute, 1998.

Jack Zwanziger

University of Rochester
Adjunct Associate Professor Community & Preventitive Medicine
255 Crittenden Blvd.
RM 4W-204
Phone: 585-275-2192

Zwanziger J, Melnick G, Bamezai A. "California providers adjust to increasing price controls." In *Health Policy Reform: Competition and Controls.* Edited by R. Helms, pp. 241-58. Washington, DC: AEI Press, 1993.

Glenn, Melnick, Emmett Keeler, Jack Zwanziger, Market Power and Hospital Pricing: Are Nonprofits Different?, Health Affairs, Vol. 18 Num. 3 at 167, 170 (1999).

CON RELATED INTERNET WEBSITES

State CON Programs:

Alabama State Health Planning and Development Agency
http://shpda.state.al.us/

Alaska Department of Health and Social Services
http://health.hss.state.ak.us/dph/chems/cert_of_need

Arkansas Health Services Permit Agency
http://www.arhspa.org

Connecticut Office of Health Care Access
http://www.ohca.state.ct.us/certificateofneed.htm

Delaware Health and Social Services
http://www.state.de.us/dhss

Florida Health and Human Services
http://www.fdhc.state.fl.us/MCHQ/CON_FA/who/review.shtml

Georgia Department of Community Health
http://www.communityhealth.state.ga.us

Hawaii State Health Planning and Development Agency
http://www.state.hi.us/health/shpda/index.htm

Illinois Department of Public Health
http://www.idph.state.il.us/about/hfpb.htm

Iowa Department of Public Health
http://www.idph.state.ia.us/do/cert_of_need.asp

Kentucky Cabinet of Health Services
http://www.chs.ky.gov/cofn

Louisiana Department of Health and Hospitals
http://www.dhh.state.la.us

Maine Department of Human Services
http://www.maine.gov/bms/

Maryland Health Care Commission
http://www.mhcc.state.md.us/mhccinfo/certificate_of_need/certificateofneed.htm

Massachusetts Department of Public Health
http://www.mass.gov/dph/dhcq/don.htm

Michigan Department of Community Health
http://www.michigan.gov/mdch/0,1607,7-132-2945_5106—,00. html

Mississippi Department of Health
http://www.msdh.state.ms.us/msdhsite/index.cfm/15,html

Missouri Department of Health and Senior Services
http://www.dhss.state.mo.us/con

Montana Department of Health & Human Services
http://www.dphhs.state.mt.us/about_us/divisions/quality_assurance/certificate_of_need/certificate_of_need.htm

Nebraska Department Of Health and Human Services (Regulation and Licensure)
http://www.hhs.state.ne.us/crl/need.htm

Nevada Bureau of Health Planning
http://health2k.state.nv.us/vs/letter.htm

New Hampshire Health Services Planning and Review Board
http://www.dhhs.state.nh.us/DHHS/HSPR/default.htm

New Jersey Certificate of Need Acute Care Licensure
http://www.state.nj.us/health/hcsa/hcsadmin.htm

New York Division of Health Facility Planning
http://www.health.state.ny.us/nysdoh/cons/main.htm

North Carolina Division of Facility Services
http://facility-services.state.nc.us/conpage.htm

Ohio Department of Health
http://www.odh.state.oh.us/ODHPrograms/CERTN/certneed1.htm

Oklahoma Department of Health/Health Resources Development Services
http://www.health.state.ok.us/program/condiv/

Oregon Health Service's Certificate of Need
http://www.dhs.state.or.us/publichealth/hsp/certneed/index.cfm

Rhode Island Office of Health Systems Development
http://www.health.state.ri.us/hsr/healthsystems/Home.htm

South Carolina Department of Health & Environmental Control/Health Facilities & Services
http://www.scdhec.net/hr/cofn

Tennessee Health Facilities Commission
http://www2.state.tn.us/health/HCF

Vermont Health Care Administration
http://www.bishca.state.vt.us/HcaDiv/CON_/CON_Main_Index.htm

Virginia Certificate of Public Need Program
http://www.vdh.state.va.us/quality/COPN

Washington Department of Health/Facilities & Services Licensing
http://www.doh.wa.gov/hsqa/fsl/crs/certificate_need.htm

Washington D.C. State Health Planning and Development Administration
http://dchealth.dc.gov/services/administration_offices/shpda/services.shtm

West Virginia Health Care Authority
http://www.hcawv.org/con1.htm

Wisconsin Department of Health and Family Services
http://www.dhfs.state.wi.us/index.htm

Other Websites:

American Academy of Orthopedic Surgeons
http://www.aaos.org

American Association of Ambulatory Surgery Centers
http://www.aaasc.org

American College of Cardiology
http://www.acc.org

American Enterprise Institute for Public Policy Research
http://www.aei.org

American Health Planning Association
http://www.ahpanet.org

American Surgical Hospital Association
http://www.surgicalhospital.org

A Perfect Cause
http://www.aperfectcause.org

Assisted Living Federation of America
http://www.alfa.org

Center for Studying Health Change
http://www.hschange.com

Centers for Medicare and Medicaid Services
http://www.cms.hhs.gov

Community Catalyst
http://www.communitycatalyst.org

Department of Health and Human Services
http://www.dhhs.gov

Federation of American Hospitals
http://www.fahs.com

The Heartland Institute
http://www.heartland.org

Kaiser Family Foundation
http://www.kff.org

Mackinac Center for Public Policy
http://www.mackinac.org

Medicare Payment Advisory Commission
http://www.medpac.gov

National Congress of State Legislatures
http://www.ncsl.org

Robert Wood Johnson Foundation
http://www.rwjf.org

Society for Healthcare Strategy and Market Development
http://www.shsmd.org

The Urban Institute
http://www.urban.org

BOOK BIBLIOGRAPHY

ACADEMY OF HEALTH CARE CONSULTANTS, CERTIFICATE OF NEED, (Teach'em, 1977).

AGENCY FOR HEALTH CARE ADMINISTRATION, FLORIDA NEED PROJECTIONS FOR HOSPICE PROGRAMS: BACKGROUND INFORMATION FOR USE IN CONJUNCTION WITH THE APRIL 2002 BATCHING CYCLE FOR THE JULY 2003 HOSPICE PLANNING HORIZON, (Agency for Health Care Administration, 2002).

AGENCY FOR HEALTH CARE ADMINISTRATION, FLORIDA NURSING HOME BED NEED PROJECTIONS BY DISTRICT AND SUBDISTRICT: BACKGROUND INFORMATION FOR USE IN CONJUNCTION WITH THE JANUARY 2004 PLANNING HORIZON, (Agency for Health Care Administration, 2001).

AGENCY FOR HEALTH CARE ADMINISTRATION, FLORIDA NURSING HOME UTILIZATION PROJECTIONS BY DISTRICT AND SUBDISTRICT: JANUARY 2001-DECEMBER 2001, (Agency for Health Care Administration, 2002).

AGENCY FOR HEALTH CARE ADMINISTRATION, INTERIM REPORT OF THE FLORIDA CON WORKGROUP, (2001).

AGENCY FOR HEALTH CARE ADMINISTRATION, NURSING HOME REPORTING SYSTEM: FINANCIAL DATA, (Agency for Health Care Administration, 2000).

AMERICAN COLLEGE OF HEALTHCARE ADMINISTRATORS, CERTIFICATE OF NEED AND APPROPRIATENESS REVIEW.

AMERICAN HEALTH PLANNING ASSOCIATION, CERTIFICATE OF NEED REGULATION OF HOME HEALTH AND HOSPICE SERVICES IN THE UNITED STATES, 1966-2000: SURVEY AND STUDY CONDUCTED BY THE AMERICAN HEALTH PLANNING ASSOCIATION FOR THE DIVISION OF HEALTH RESOURCES MARYLAND HEALTH CARE COMMISSION, (American Health Planning Association, 2000).

AMERICAN HEALTH PLANNING ASSOCIATION, CERTIFICATE OF NEED REGULATION OF NURSING HOME SERVICES IN THE UNITED STATES, 1966-2000, (American Health Planning Association, 2000).

AMERICAN HEALTH PLANNING ASSOCIATION, NATIONAL DIRECTORY OF HEALTH PLANNING, POLICY AND REGULATORY AGENCIES, (American Health Planning Association, (1989-2004).

AMERICAN HOSPITAL ASSOCIATION, AHA SURVEY REPORT: REVIEW OF 1971 STATE CERTIFICATE-OF-NEED LEGISLATION, (Catholic University of American Libraries, 1971).

AMERICAN HOSPITAL ASSOCIATION, GUIDELINES FOR IMPLEMENTATION OF CERTIFICATION OF NEED FOR HEALTH CARE FACILITIES AND SERVICES, (American Hospital Association, 1972).

AMERICAN HOSPITAL ASSOCIATION, SURVEY REPORT: REVIEW OF 1971 STATE CERTIFICATE-OF-NEED LEGISLATION, (American Hospital Association, 1972).

ANDERSON, KEITH B. & KASS, DAVID I., CERTIFICATE OF NEED REGULATION OF ENTRY INTO HOME HEALTH CARE, (Bureau of Economics, Federal Trade Commission, 1986).

AN EVALUATION OF THE CERTIFICATE OF NEED PROCESS AND RELATED PROCEDURAL AND POLICY ISSUES: HEARING BEFORE THE ASSEMBLY HEALTH AND HUMAN SERVICES COMMITTEE, (1993) (statement of Bruce Siegel, M.D., M.P.H., Commissioner of Health).

ASSOCIATION OF COMMUNITY HOSPITALS AND HEALTH SYSTEMS OF FLORIDA, CHHS CERTIFICATE OF NEED (CON) WHITE PAPER, (Association of Community Hospitals and Health Systems of Florida, 1998).

BICE, THOMAS W., PHD & SALKEVER, DAVID S. PHD., CERTIFICATE-OF-NEED PROGRAMS: CURE OR CAUSE OF INFLATED COSTS?, (Hospital Progress, 1977).

BLUE RIBBON COMMISSION ON HEALTH CARE, THE COST OF HEALTH CARE IN MAINE: AN ANALYSIS OF HEALTH CARE COSTS, FACTORS THAT CONTRIBUTE TO RISING COSTS, AND SOME POTENTIAL APPROACHES TO STABILIZE COSTS, (Maine Development Foundation, 2000).

BOGUE, TED, MODEL STATE HEALTH PLANNING AND CERTIFICATE OF NEED STATUTE, (Public Citizen's Health Research Group, 1977).

BOVBJERG, RANDAL R. & MARSTELLER, JILL AL, HEALTH CARE MARKET COMPETITION IN SIX STATES: IMPLICATIONS FOR THE POOR, (The Urban Institute, 1998).

BROWN, JONATHON B. ET AL., EXCHANGE OF INFORMATION BETWEEN HOSPITAL RATE SETTING AND CERTIFICATE OF NEED AGENCIES: SELECTED STATE EXPERIENCES, (Harvard University Center for Community Health and Medical Care, 1976).

BURWELL, BRIAN O. & CROWN, WILLIAM H., PUBLIC FINANCING OF LONG-TERM CARE: FEDERAL AND STATE ROLES, (SysteMetrics, 1994).

CACOZZA, ALBERT F., CERTIFICATE OF LITIGATION: 1966-1979 CASE BRIEFS, (The Urban Institute, 1979).

CAIN, H.P. & THORNBERRY, H.N., HEALTH PLANNING IN THE UNITED STATES: WHERE WE STAND TODAY, (Westview Press for the American Association for the Advancement of Science, 1977).

CENTER FOR LOCAL PUBLIC HEALTH SERVICES, MISSOURI DEPARTMENT OF HEALTH, DEFINING PUBLIC HEALTH FOR MISSOURI, (Missouri Department of Health, 1999).

CERTIFICATE OF NEED TASK FORCE, REPORT OF ACTIONS OF CERTIFICATE OF NEED TASK FORCE, (2001).

CERTIFICATE OF NEED TASK FORCE, CERTIFICATE OF NEED TASK FORCE REPORT FOR 2001, (2001).

CHAYET & SONNENREICH, P.C., CERTIFICATE OF NEED: AN EXPANDING REGULATORY CONCEPT: SUPPLEMENT, Fall 1978, (Medicine in the Public Interest MIPI, 1978).

COMMUNITY SERVICE SOCIETY, AN APPLICANT'S GUIDE TO THE NEW YORK STATE CERTIFICATE OF NEED REVIEW PROCESS FOR AMBULATORY CARE FACILITIES, (Community Service Society, 1981).

CURRAN, WILLIAM J., NATIONAL SURVEY AND ANALYSIS OF CERTIFICATION-OF-NEED LAWS: HEALTH PLANNING AND REGULATION IN STATE LEGISLATURES, (American Hospital Association, 1972).

CUSTER, WILLIAM S., CERTIFICATE OF NEED REGULATION AND THE HEALTH CARE DELIVERY SYSTEM, (Center for Risk Management and Insurance Research, 1997).

DEVORE, ELIZABETH, PROVIDERS, (Health Policy Tracking Service, 2001).

DRUMMOND, MICHAEL F. ET AL., METHODS FOR THE ECONOMIC EVALUATION OF HEALTH CARE PROGRAMS, (2d ed., 1997).

DUNHAM, ANDREW BRYSON, HEALTH AND POLITICS: THE IMPACT OF CERTIFICATE OF NEED REGULATION, (National Center for Health Service Research, 1981).

FARLEY, DONNA O. ET AL., TRENDS IN SUPPLY AND UTILIZATION OF RURAL HOSPITALS WITH SPECIAL MEDICARE PAYMENTS, (RAND, 2000).

FISHER, ELLIOT S., HEALTH CARE IN AMERICA: IS MORE BETTER, (1998).

FLETCHER ALLEN HEALTHCARE, INTERNAL REVIEW BLASTS VT. HOSPITAL'S MANAGEMENT, (Fletcher Allen Health Care, Inc., 2002).

GIEL, DAVE & SCANDRETT, MICHAEL, HOSPITAL AND NURSING HOME SYSTEM GROWTH: MORATORIA, CERTIFICATE OF NEED, and Other Alternatives, (Senate Counsel and Research, 1986).

GOODMAN, JOHN C. & MUSGRAVE, GERALD L., PATIENT POWER: SOLVING AMERICA'S HEALTH CARE CRISIS, (Cato Institute, 1992).

GROSS ET AL., CERTIFICATE OF NEED AS A METHOD OF COST CONTROL IN HOSPITALS: IN THEORY GOOD, IN PRACTICE UNPROVEN, (Institute of Health Economics and Technology Assessment, 1985).

HACKEY, ROBERT B., & ROCHEFORT, DAVID A., THE NEW POLITICS OF STATE HEALTH POLICY, (University Press of Kansas, 2001)

HACKEY, ROBERT B., RETHINKING HEALTH CARE POLICY: THE NEW POLITICS OF STATE REGULATION, (Georgetown University Press, 1998).

HEALTH PLANNING COMMISSION, CRITERIA AND STANDARDS FOR CERTIFICATE OF NEED, (Tennessee Health Planning Commission, 2000).

HEALTH POLICY ANALYSIS PROGRAM, CERTIFICATE OF NEED: AN ASSESSMENT OF CURRENT PROGRAMS AND POLICY ISSUES, (Health Policy Analysis Program, 1978).

HEALTH POLICY ANALYSIS PROGRAM OF THE UNIVERSITY OF WASHINGTON'S SCHOOL OF PUBLIC HEALTH AND COMMUNITY MEDICINE, EFFECTS OF CERTIFICATE OF NEED AND ITS POSSIBLE REPEAL : REPORT 99-1, (University of Washington's School of Public Health and Community Medicine, 1999).

HEALTH POLICY TRACKING SERVICES, MAJOR HEALTH CARE POLICIES: 50 STATES PROFILES, 2001, (National Conference of State Legislatures, 2002).

HEALTH POLICY TRACKING SERVICES, MAJOR HEALTH CARE POLICIES 50 STATES PROFILES, 2000, (National Conference of State Legislatures, 2001).

HEALTH POLICY TRACKING SERVICE, STATE HEALTH PRIORITIES SURVEY, (National Conference of State Legislatures, 2002).

HEARINGS ON GLOBAL AND INNOVATION-BASED COMPETITION, (1995).

HYMAN, HERBERT H., HEALTH REGULATION: CERTIFICATE OF NEED AND 1122, (Aspen Systems Cooperation, 1977).

ILLINOIS DEPARTMENT OF PUBLIC HEALTH, HOSPITAL BEDS IN ILLINOIS: ALTERNATIVE SYSTEMS AND BED COUNTS, (Illinois Department of Public Health, 1987).

ILLINOIS HEALTH CARE COST CONTAINMENT COUNCIL, REPORT OF THE ILLINOIS HEALTH CARE COST CONTAINMENT COUNCIL TO THE GOVERNOR AND THE ILLINOIS GENERAL ASSEMBLY ON THE EFFECTIVENESS OF CERTIFICATE OF NEED REVIEW, (Illinois Health Care Cost Containment Council, 1987).

ILLINOIS HEALTH CARE COST CONTAINMENT COUNCIL, REPORT TO ILLINOIS GENERAL ASSEMBLY REGARDING THE STATUS OF HEALTH CARE IN ILLINOIS, (1988).

JOINT LEGISLATIVE AUDIT AND REVIEW COMMISSION, THE CERTIFICATE-OF-NEED IN VIRGINIA: A REPORT IN A SERIES FOCUSING ON MEDICAL ASSISTANCE PROGRAMS IN THE COMMONWEALTH OF VIRGINIA, (Joint Legislative Audit and Review Commission, 1979).

JOSKOW, PAUL L., CONTROLLING HOSPITAL COSTS: THE ROLE OF GOVERNMENT REGULATION, (MIT Press, 1984).

LEG. BUDGET AND FINANCE COMM., INTERIM REPORT OF THE FLORIDA CON WORKGROUP, (1986).

LEG. BUDGET AND FINANCE COMM., REPORT ON A STUDY OF PENNSYLVANIA'S CERTIFICATE OF NEED PROGRAM, (1987).

LEG. COUNS. COMM., STUDY ON HEALTH PLANNING AGENCIES AND CERTIFICATE OF NEED LEGISLATION CONCERNING HEALTH FACILITIES: FINAL REPORT OF THE LEGISLATIVE COUNCIL COMMITTEE, (1973).

LEWIN AND ASSOCIATES, INC., EXPERIENCE WITH THE SECTION 1122 CAPITAL EXPENDITURE REVIEW PROGRAM.

LEWIN-VHI, INC., NURSING HOME BED SUPPLY: A SYNTHESIS OF THE LITERATURE AND STATE INITIATIVES, (1996).

LITTLE, ARTHUR D., DEVELOPMENT OF AN EVALUATION METHODOLOGY FOR USE IN ASSESSING DATA AVAILABLE TO THE CERTIFICATE-OF-NEED (CON) AND HEALTH PLANNING PROGRAMS, (Arthur D. Little, Inc.).

LOCKE, SHERYL ET AL., POSITION PAPER: CERTIFICATE OF NEED, (Minnesota Hospital Association, 1979).

MACRO SYSTEMS, INC., THE CERTIFICATE-OF-NEED EXPERIENCE: AN EARLY ASSESSMENT, (Macro Systems, 1974).

MAINE DEPARTMENT OF LABOR, LICENSING AND REGULATION, CERTIFICATE OF NEED REPORT: APPROVED BEDS IN HOSPITALS AND NURSING HOMES, (Maine Department of Labor, Licensing and Regulation, 1998).

MANARD, BARBARA B. & CAMERON, ROSEMARY, A NATIONAL STUDY OF ASSISTED LIVING FOR THE FRAIL ELDERLY: REPORT ON IN-DEPTH INTERVIEWS WITH DEVELOPERS, (The Lewin Group, Inc., 1997).

MARYLAND DEPARTMENT OF LABOR, LICENSING AND REGULATION, HEALTH SERVICES INDUSTRY IN MARYLAND 1998 UPDATE, (Maryland Department of Labor, Licensing and Regulation, 1998).

MARYLAND HEALTH CARE COMMISSION, AN ANALYSIS AND EVALUATION OF CERTIFICATE OF NEED REGULATION IN MARYLAND: FINAL REPORT TO THE MARYLAND GENERAL ASSEMBLY, (1st Sess., 2001).

MARYLAND HEALTH CARE COMMISSION, CERTIFICATE OF NEED REGULATION OF HOME HEALTH AND HOSPICE SERVICES IN THE UNITED STATES, (Maryland Health Care Commission, 2000).

MARYLAND HEALTH CARE COMMISSION, CERTIFICATE OF NEED REGULATION OF NURSING HOME SERVICES IN THE UNITED STATES, (Maryland Health Care Commission, 2000).

MARYLAND HEALTH CARE COMMISSION, MARYLAND HEALTH PLANNING NEWS, (Maryland Health Care Commission, 1990).

MARYLAND HEALTH PLANNING COMMISSION, WORKING PAPER: ACUTE INPATIENT OBSTETRIC SERVICES, (Maryland Health Care Commission, 2001).

MARYLAND HEALTH CARE COMMISSION, WORKING PAPER: CARDIAC SURGERY AND THERAPEUTIC CATHETERIZATION SERVICES, (Maryland Health Care Commission, 2001).

MARYLAND HEALTH CARE COMMISSION, WORKING PAPER: CHILD AND ADOLESCENT INPATIENT PSYCHIATRIC AND RTC SERVICES, (Maryland Health Care Commission, 2001).

MARYLAND HEALTH CARE COMMISSION, WORKING PAPER: HOSPICE SERVICES, (Maryland Health Care Commission, 2000).

MARYLAND HEALTH CARE COMMISSION, WORKING PAPER: INPATIENT ACUTE CARE HOSPITAL SERVICES, (Maryland Health Care Commission, 2001).

MARYLAND HEALTH CARE COMMISSION, WORKING PAPER: INPATIENT PSYCHIATRIC SERVICES, (Maryland Health Care Commission, 2001).

MARYLAND HEALTH CARE COMMISSION, WORKING PAPER: INTERMEDIATE CARE FACILITIES FOR ALCOHOLISM AND DRUG ABUSE, (Maryland Health Care Commission, 2001).

MARYLAND HEALTH CARE COMMISSION, WORKING PAPER: INTERMEDIATE CARE FACILITIES- MENTAL RETARDATION (ICF/MR) SERVICES, (Maryland Health Care Commission, 2001).

MARYLAND HEALTH CARE COMMISSION, WORKING PAPER: NURSING HOME SERVICES, (Maryland Health Care Services, 2000).

MARYLAND HEALTH CARE COMMISSION, WORKING PAPER: ORGAN TRANSPLANT SURGERY, NEONATAL INTENSIVE CARE SERVICES, AND BURN SERVICES, (Maryland Health Care Commission, 2001).

MARYLAND HEALTH CARE COMMISSION, WORKING PAPER: REHABILITATION HOSPITAL AND CHRONIC HOSPITAL SERVICES, (Maryland Health Care Commission, 2001).

MICHIGAN DEPARTMENT OF COMMUNITY HEALTH, CERTIFICATE OF NEED: ADMINISTRATIVE RULES, (Michigan Department of Community Health, 2001).

MICHIGAN DEPARTMENT OF PUBLIC HEALTH, MICHIGAN STATE MEDICAL FACILITIES PLAN, (Division of Health Facility Planning & Construction, 1979).

MINNESOTA DEPARTMENT OF HEALTH, CERTIFICATE OF NEED REVIEW IN MINNESOTA: PAST EFFECTIVENESS AND ISSUES FOR THE FUTURE, (Minnesota Department of Health, 1984).

MINNESOTA DEPARTMENT OF HEALTH, A REVIEW AND ANALYSIS OF THE CERTIFICATE OF NEED EXPERIENCE IN MINNESOTA, 1972-1978, (Minnesota Department of Health, 1979).

MISSOURI HEALTH FACILITIES RESOURCE COMMITTEE, CERTIFICATE OF NEED: EFFECTIVE, EFFICIENT, ACCOUNTABLE, (Missouri Health Facilities Resource Committee, 2002).

NATIONAL CLEARINGHOUSE FOR LEGAL SERVICES, CERTIFICATE OF NEED: BACKGROUND AND REVIEW OF RECENT CHANGES IN FLORIDA'S LAW, (National Clearinghouse for Legal Services, 1987).

NOETHER, MONICA, COMPETITION AMONG HOSPITALS, (Bureau of Economics, Federal Trade Commission, 1987).

OFF. OF THE ASSISTANT SECRETARY FOR PLANNING & EVALUATION, STATE ASSISTED LIVING POLICY: 1998 SECTION I, (1998).

OFF. OF THE ASSISTANT SECRETARY FOR PLANNING & EVALUATION, STATE ASSISTED LIVING POLICY: 1998 SECTION III, (1998).

OFF. OF HEALTH PLANNING, BUREAU OF HEALTH MAINTENANCE ORG. AND RESOURCES DEV., (1085).

OHIO DEP'T OF HEALTH, STATE HEALTH RESOURCES PLAN: 1999, (1998).

OKLAHOMA HEALTH PLANNING COMMISSION, CAPITAL INVESTMENT REVIEWS OF PROPOSED INSTITUTIONAL HEALTH SERVICES AND CAPITAL EXPENDITURE PROJECTS IN OKLAHOMA DURING FISCAL YEAR 1978, (Oklahoma Health Planning Commission, 1978).

OKLAHOMA HEALTH PLANNING COMMISSION, PROCEDURES FOR PROJECT REVIEW UNDER THE STATE CERTIFICATE OF NEED LAWS, (Oklahoma Health Planning Commission, 1982).

OKLAHOMA HEALTH PLANNING COMMISSION, PROCEDURES FOR PROJECT REVIEW UNDER THE STATE CERTIFICATE OF NEED LAWS, OHPC REVIEW NOTICE #32, (Oklahoma Health Planning Commission, 1984).

OKLAHOMA HEALTH PLANNING COMMISSION, PROCEDURES FOR PROJECT REVIEW UNDER THE STATE CERTIFICATE OF NEED LAWS: OHPC REVIEW NOTICE #23, (Oklahoma Health Planning Commission, 1981).

PEER COMM., A REVIEW OF MISSISSIPPI'S LONG-TERM CARE FACILITY LICENSING AND CERTIFICATION, THE EFFECT OF FEDERAL DEREGULATION ON THE CERTIFICATE OF NEED PROGRAM, AND AN INVESTIGATION OF RELATED BUSINESS ACTIVITIES OF A FORMER BOARD OF HEALTH EMPLOYEE, (1990).

POLICY ANALYSIS, INC. EVALUATION OF THE EFFECTS OF CERTIFICATE OF NEED PROGRAMS, (Policy Analysis, Inc.).

PUBLIC HEALTH RESOURCE GROUP, INC., CERTIFICATE OF NEED PROJECT REPORT, (Public Health Resource Group, Inc., 2001).

ROTHENBERG, ELEANORE, REGULATION AND EXPANSION OF HEALTH FACILITIES: THE CERTIFICATE OF NEED EXPERIENCE IN NEW YORK STATE, (Praeger Publishers, 1976).

SALKEVER, DAVID S. & BICE, THOMAS W., CERTIFICATE-OF-NEED LEGISLATION AND HOSPITAL COSTS.

SALKEVER, DAVID S. & BICE, THOMAS W., HOSPITAL CERTIFICATE-OF-NEED CONTROLS: IMPACT ON INVESTMENT, COSTS, AND USE, (American Enterprise Institute for Public Policy Research, 1979).

SALKEVER, DAVID S. & BICE, THOMAS W., THE IMPACT OF CERTIFICATE-OF-NEED CONTROLS ON HOSPITAL INVESTMENT, (MMFQ, 1976).

SALKEVER, DAVID S. & BICE, THOMAS W., IMPACT OF STATE CERTIFICATE-OF-NEED LAWS ON HEALTH CARE COSTS AND UTILIZATION, (U.S. Department of Health, Education, and Welfare, 1976).

SCHNEITER, ELLEN JANE ET AL., RISING HEALTH CARE COSTS: STATE HEALTH COST CONTAINMENT APPROACHES, (National Academy for State Health Policy, 2002).

SELSER, JOHN R. & OFFICE OF POLICY AND LEGAL ANALYSIS, CERTIFICATE OF NEED STUDY OF THE HUMAN RESOURCES COMMITTEE OF THE 112TH LEGISLATURE, (Maine Office of Policy and Legal Analysis, 1986).

SENATE COMMITTEE ON HEALTH CARE, CERTIFICATE OF NEED REGULATION: A REVIEW OF HOME HEALTH AGENCY, (Senate Committee on Health Care, 1995).

SHERMAN, DANIEL, THE EFFECT OF STATE CERTIFICATE-OF-NEED LAWS ON HOSPITAL COSTS: AN ECONOMIC POLICY ANALYSIS, (Bureau of Economics, Federal Trade Commission, 1988).

SIMPSON, JAMES B. & BOGUE, TED, GUIDE TO HEALTH PLANNING LAW: A TOPICAL DIGEST OF HEALTH PLANNING AND CERTIFICATE OF NEED CASE LAW, (3rd ed., 1985).

SIMPSON, JAMES B. & BOGUE, TED, GUIDE TO HEALTH PLANNING LAW: A TOPICAL DIGEST OF HEALTH PLANNING AND CERTIFICATE OF NEED CASE LAW, (U.S. Department of Health and Human Services, 1984).

SLOAN, FRANK & BENTKOVER, JUDITH D., ACCESS TO AMBULATORY CARE AND THE U.S. ECONOMY, (Lexington Books, 1979).

SLOAN, FRANK A. ET AL., COST, QUALITY, AND ACCESS IN HEALTH CARE: NEW ROLES FOR HEALTH PLANNING IN A COMPETITIVE ENVIRONMENT, (Jossey-Bass Publishers, 1988).

SLOAN, FRANK A. & STEINWALD, BRUCE, INSURANCE, REGULATION, & HOSPITAL COSTS, (Health and Company, 1980).

TASK FORCE, CERTIFICATE OF NEED, STATE HEALTH PLANNING, AND THE STATE BONDING AUTHORITY FOR HEALTH FACILITIES CONSTRUCTION AND DEVELOPMENT, (Task Force, 1986).

THOMAS, CONSTANCE, A SUMMARY OF CON LAWS FROM THE 1987-1988 LEGISLATIVE SESSIONS, (Intergovernmental Health Policy Project, 1988).

THOMAS, CONSTANCE, CERTIFICATE OF NEED: AN OVERVIEW OF 1992 LEGISLATIVE ACTIVITY, (1993).

UNITED STATES GENERAL ACCOUNTING OFFICE, ANTITRUST ENFORCEMENT UNDER MARYLAND'S HOSPITAL ALL-PAYER SYSTEM, (United States General Accounting Office, 1994).

UNITED STATES GENERAL ACCOUNTING OFFICE, HEALTHCARE FACILITIES: CAPITAL CONSTRUCTION EXPENDITURES BY STATE, (United States General Accounting Office, 1986).

HEALTH COMMUNICATIONS NETWORK, UPDATE ON HEALTH PLANNING IN SOUTH CAROLINA, (Health Communications Network).

URBAN SYSTEMS RESEARCH AND ENGINEERING, CERTIFICATE OF NEED PROGRAMS: A REVIEW, ANALYSIS, AND ANNOTATED BIBLIOGRAPHY OF THE RESEARCH LITERATURE, (U.S. Department of Health, Education, and Welfare, 1978).

UZKURATITIS, VINCENT, EVALUATION OF NEW MEXICO CERTIFICATE OF NEED LEGISLATION, (Amherst Associates, Inc., 1984).

VALUING HEALTH CARE: COSTS, BENEFITS, AND EFFECTIVENESS OF PHARMACEUTICALS AND OTHER MEDICAL TECHNOLOGIES, (Cambridge University Press, 1995).

WASHINGTON STATE DEPARTMENT OF HEALTH, CERTIFICATE OF NEED OPEN HEART SURGERY METHODOLOGY REVIEW, (Washington State Department of Health, 2000).

WASHINGTON STATE SENATE, THE IMPACT OF CERTIFICATE OF NEED: SUBSTANTIAL ACQUISITION ON NURSING HOMES IN WASHINGTON STATE, (Wash. State Sen. Comm. on Social and Health Services, 1975).

WEINER, JOSHUA M. ET AL., CONTROLLING THE SUPPLY OF LONG-TERM CARE PROVIDERS AT THE STATE LEVEL, (The Urban Institute, 1998).

WIENER, JOSHUA M. & STEVENSON, DAVID G., LONG-TERM CARE FOR THE ELDERLY IN THE DISTRICT OF COLUMBIA: ISSUES AND PROSPECTS, (The Urban Institute, 1998).

ARTICLE BIBLIOGRAPHY

Abrams HL; McNeil BJ, *Computed tomography: cost and efficacy implications,* 131. AM. J. OF ROENTGENOLOGYp. 81-7 (1978 Jul).

Aday, L.A.; Anderson, R, *A Framework for the Study of Access to Medical Care,* 9 (1974).

Adem, Antoine M.; [et al.], *Stop being conned,* ST. LOUIS BUS. J, May 9, 2003.

Adler, Neil, *Health commish questions need for Germantown ER,* WASHINGTON BUS. J.

AGENCY FOR HEALTH CARE ADMINISTRATION, INTERIM REPORT OF THE FLORIDA CON WORKGROUP, (2001).

Ahern M, *Changes in Wisconsin's Certificate-Of-Need Law; challenged moratorium extended,* 6. HEALTH L. VIGILp. 10-Sep (1983 Sep 2).

Aizer, Anna; Lyons, Barbara; Schoen, Cathy, *Health insurance expansion through states in a pluralistic system,* 26. J. OF HEALTH POLITICS p. 581-615 (June 2001).

Alexander, Donna A, *UPMC Mergers under antitrust law: An Analysis of the application of the federal antitrust laws to non-profit hospital mergers* DUQ. L. +REV. Vol. 38, no. 77 (1999) *available at*- http://80-web.lexis-nexis.com.

Allen HH Jr., *Virginia's outdated COPN law,* 122. VA. MED. Q.p.138-9 (1995 Summer).

American Bar Association, *Antitrust Health Care Chronicle: Fall 2000* ANTITRUST HEALTH CARE CHRON.

American Bar Association, *Antitrust Health Care Chronicle: Summer 2003* ANTITRUST HEALTH CARE CHRON.

American Business Journals, *Headliners: People on the news the past year: Bob Ramsey, owner, American LifeStar Ambulance Co,* BUS. J. OF PHOENIX, October 14, 2002, at 5.

Anderson TJ; Franco B, *Certificate of need—how it is affecting the practice of medicine in Georgia,* 68. J. OF THE MED. ASS'N OF GA.p.1057-9 (1979 Dec).

Anderson, Charles E, *Hospital Production—Can costs be contained?,* THE AMERICAN ECONOMIC REV, May 1979, at p.293-297.

Anderson, Gerald,; Jane Erickson,; Susan Feigenbaum, *Examining the Relationship between Capital Investment and Hospital Operating Expenditures,* 69. REV. OF ECONOMIC & STAT. (November 1987).

Anderson, R.A,; McCuthcheon, R,; Aday, L.A,; Chin, G,; Bell, R, *Exploring Dimensions of Access to Medical Care,* 18 (1983).

Andrus. D,; Kohout, F.J, *The Effect of Rural Consumer Satisfaction on Outshopping for Medical Services,* 2. MARKETING AMBULATORY CARE SERV. (February 1985).

Antel, J.J,; Ohsfeldt, R.L,; Becker, E.R, *State Regulation and Hospital Costs,* 77. REV. OF ECONOMIC & STAT. (August 1995).

Antlitz AM; Boyer E, *Certificate of need: a physician concern,* 28. MD. ST. MED. J.p.45-7 (1979 Jun).

Ashby Jr, John L, *The Impact of hospital regulatory programs on per capita costs, utilization, and capital investment,* 21. IMPACT OF HOSP. REG. PROGRAMS p 45-59.

Ashby, John L, *The impact of hospital regulatory programs on per capita costs, utilization, and capital investment,* 21. INQUIRYp.45-59 (1984 Spring).

Associated Press, *Georgia to appeal mobile cardiac cath unit ruling*, MOD. HEALTHCARE, March 25, 1996, at p.66.

Atkinson SC, *Mobile medical facilities and CONs: maneuvering mobile medicine through a stationary statutory scheme,* 79. J. OF THE MED. ASS'N OF GA.p.249-52 (1990 Apr).

Babbitt, Bruce, *Building a better mousetrap: Health care reform and the Arizona program,* YALE J. ON REG. 243 Vol. 3, no. 243 (1986) *available at* http://80-web.lexis-nexis.com

Backhus, Stephen P. United States General Accounting Office, *VA Health Care: Supply of Nursing Home Beds is Sufficient to 2005 in the Detroit, Michigan, Area*, Aug. 16, 2000.

Bader N, *Michigan groups battle for better heart care,* BUS. & HEALTH, 1993 Sep, at 66, 68.

Bailey, Amy F, *House approves changes to certificate of need law*, THE MIAMI HERALD, Dec. 12, 2002.

Bailey, Scott W. *Moratorium may delay hospital's growth plan Planned facility expansion to create 250 jobs (November 5, 2004) available at* http://sanantonio.bizjournals.com.

Balaban, Dan, *Hospitals compete in affluent Northland,*, BUS. J, October 17, 1997.

Bank, F. Philip, *The 1997 amendments to Florida's certificate of need law* THE FLA. BAR p. 75 (12/17/03).

Bankhead CD, *Arizona data undercut claim deregulation ups mortality,* 29. MED. WORLD NEWSp.58-9 (1988 Aug 22).

Bankofier, Todd. *In depth: valley influential young guns,* THE BUS. J. OF PHOENIX *(November 5, 2004) available at* http://phoenix.bizjournals.com/phoenix/stories/2004/11/08/focus5.html?t=printable.

Barcousky, Len, *Butler Memorial officials plead case for new hospital*, POST-GAZZETTE.COM, Dec. 5, 2003.

Barnes Marc, *King to get $18 million hospital*, THE BUS. J, at p.1-3.

Barnes, Marc *High Point Endoscopy addition snagged by new CON law,* THE BUS. J. OF THE GREATER TRIAD AREA *(2002) available at* http://triad.bizjournals.com/triad/stories/2002/01/28/story8.html.

Barnes, Marc, *2002 medical facilities plan turns attention away from beds*, THE BUS. J.

Barnes, Marc, *Five medical facilities vie for right to buy new MRIs*, THE BUS. J, 3/18/2002.

Barnes, Marc, *King to Get $18 Million Hospital* (March 29, 2002), *available at* triad.bizjournals.com.

Barnes, Marc, *Lexington hospital to get fixed MRI*, THE BUS. J, 7/28/2004, at 1 p.

Barnes, Marc, *Novant Eyes Ambitious Growth* (August 9, 2002), *available at* triad.bizjournals.com.

Barnett GH, *Evolution and organization of a regional Gamma Knife Center,* 66. STEREOTACTIC & FUNCTIONAL NEUROSURGERYp.365-9 (1996).

Bartlett SW, *Influence of federal and state regulations on the acquisition and operation by hospitals of magnetic resonance imaging scanners,* 8. CARDIOVASCULAR & INTERVENTIONAL RADIOLOGYp.394-402 (1986).

Basanta, Eugene; Conley, Thomas P.; Emmons, Keith E.; Kane, Robert John; LeBlang, Theodore R.; Sherwood, William F, *Survey of Illinois law: health care*, 25. U. ILL. L. J. p.873-902 (Summer 2001).

Bassing, Todd, *Change to CON law eases capital investment bids*, BIRMINGHAM BUS. J, 8/11/03, at 3 p.

Bassing, Tom, *Agency chiefs await their fate*, BIRMINGHAM BUS. J, November 25, 2002, at pp. 3.

Bassing, Tom, *Baptist drops CON bid for scanner*, BIRMINGHAM BUS. J, December 6, 2002, at pp. 1-2.

Bassing, Tom, *Baptist plans $44M hospital for Sylacauga, available at* www.birmingham.bizjournals.com.

Bassing, Tom, *Baptist plans $44M hospital for Sylacauga*, BIRMINGHAM BUS. J, 12/23/2002, at 2 p.

Bassing, Tom, *Baptist spends big to go digital*, BIRMINGHAM BUS. J, September 16, 2002.

Bassing, Tom, *Baptist spends big to go digital: 10- hospital system will receive $25-$50M 'massive upgrade'*, BIRMINGHAM BUS. J, September 16, 2002, at 2.

Bassing, Tom, *Brookwood medical center plans $50M operating room expansion*, BIRMINGHAM BUS. J, 6/14/2004.

Bassing, Tom, *Carraway nears $7.2M psych expansion*, BIRMINGHAM BUS. J, 3/12/04.

Bassing, Tom, *Carraway rebounds strongly after hefty July loss*, BIRMINGHAM BUS. J, 10/27/03.

Bassing, Tom, *Carraway: Well enough to spend: Medical center launches $9M upgrade plan as it recovers*, BIRMINGHAM BUS. J, May 14, 2004.

Bassing, Tom, *Carraway-Norwood lease close to a 'done deal'*, BIRMINGHAM BUS. J, January 17, 2003, at 3 p.

Bassing, Tom, *Change to CON laws eases capital investment bids*, BIRMINGHAM BUS. J, Aug. 8, 2003.

Bassing, Tom, *'Digital' shell gets buttoned up: Health South puts two acute-care hospitals on the block*, BIRMINGHAM BUS. J, Apr. 11, 2003.

Bassing, Tom, *HealthMark unit has 'Bama plans'*, NASHVILLE BUS. J, Jun 28, 2004.

Bassing, Tom, *HealthSouth lawsuit is now in judge's hands*, BIRMINGHAM BUS. J, November 1, 2002, at 3 p.

Bassing, Tom, *Norwood regroups after clinic plan fails*, BIRMINGHAM BUS. J, September 30, 2002, at 3.

Bassing, Tom, *Nursing homes are in limbo: Four projects-worth $32.5 Million-are facing big hurdles*, BIRMINGHAM BUS. J, 3/12/04.

Bassing, Tom, *Nursing homes pushing for 310 additional beds in Shelby County*, BIRMINGHAM BUS. J, at 2 p.

Bassing, Tom, *Outpatient surgery firm targets city*, BIRMINGHAM BUS. J, Jun 21, 2004.

Bassing, Tom, *Paragon gets ok to build third assisted-living center*, BIRMINGHAM BUS. J, July 14, 2003.

Bassing, Tom, *Paragon plans $5.4M assisted-living facility*, BIRMINGHAM BUS. J, Mar. 10, 2003.

Bassing, Tom, *Paying state's CON game: Does process benefit the public- or stifle competition?*, BUS. J, 7/28/2004.

Bassing, Tom, *Playing state's CON game: Does process benefit the public - or stifle competition*, BIRMINGHAM BUS. J, Dec. 23, 2002.

Bassing, Tom, *Playing state's CON game: Does process benefit the public—or stifle competition?*, BIRMINGHAM BUS. J, at 5p.

Bassing, Tom, *Reimbursement drives strategy of pain specialist*, BIRMINGHAM BUS. J, 1/19/04.

Bassing, Tom, *St. Vincent's has tomorrow's hospital today*, BIRMINGHAM BUS. J, 1/31/2003, at 5 p.

Bassing, Tom, *Top court to hear HealthSouth rivals*, BIRMINGHAM BUS. J, 9/15/03, at 2 p.

Bassing, Tom, *UAB Medical West plans $5M surgery center*, BIRMINGHAM BUS. J, Dec. 15, 2003.

Bassing, Tom, *UAB, Children's pursuing $120M project*, BIRMINGHAM BUS. J, 8/18/2003, at 2 p.

Baydin, Lynda Diane, *The End-stage renal disease networks: An Attempt through Federal regulation to regionalize health care delivery*, 15. MED. CARE p. 586-98 (July 1977).

Bays, Carson W, *Patterns of hospital growth.: The case of profit hospitals*, 21. MED. CAREp.850-7 (1983 Sep).

Becker, Cinda, *Steamrolling Ahead: Two N.Y. Hospitals Don't Let a Little Paperwork Get in the Way*, MOD. HEALTHCARE, February 18, 2002, at p. 1.

Becker, Cinda, *Therapy on Target: Change in HCFA reimbursement helps advance a new radiation technology*, MOD. HEALTHCARE, 10/1/2004, at Pg.34.

Becker, Cinda, *Yale-New Haven seeks CON approval for cancer center*, MOD. HEALTHCARE, Jun. 2, 2004.

Becker, Scott, *New York and Kentucky ease certificate of need restrictions* BENDER'S HEALTH CARE L. MONTHLY p. 7-9 (Mar. 1998).

Begley, Charles; Schoeman, Milton; Traxler, Herbert, *Factors That May Explain Interstate Differences in Certificate-of-Need Decisions*, 3. HEALTH CARE FINANCING REV.p.87-94 (1982 Jun).

Belisle, Daniel J, *Closure one result of Arizona deregulation* PROVIDER p. 13-14 (Dec. 1987).

Bell, Jeff, *In face of criticism, hospitals say need fuels their cardiac expansions,* COLUMBUS BUS. FIRST, February 8, 2002.

Bell, Jeff, *Med centers trigger fear among hospitals, available at* Bizjournals.com.

Bell, Jeff, *Med centers trigger fear among hospitals, available at* Bizjournals.com.

Bell, Jeff, *Suite success: New Albany hospital survives obstacles, prepares to start,* BUS. FIRST OF COLUMBUS, Nov. 28, 2003.

Bellandi D, *Allina changes tune in new-hospital bid,* MOD. HEALTHCARE, 1999 Jul 12, at 16.

Bellandi D, *Columbia stirs storm over Fla. CON,* MOD. HEALTHCARE, 2000 Feb 21, at 22-3.

Benko, Laura B, *Shedding Few Tiers: Controversial plans are here to stay, insurers say,* MOD. HEALTHCARE, June 3, 2002, at p. 17.

Berg GH; Bicknell WJ, *Project planning without tears,* 30. TRUSTEEp.14-6 (1977 Feb).

Berg, Melissa, *Children's Mercy wins out $52 million project to nearly double hospital's size, get state panel's vote. Work is expected to take four years* (September 24, 1992).

Berg, Melissa, *Hospital regulation in spotlight Missouri governor wants to shift oversight to PSC.*

Berg, Melissa, *Hospital seeks to combine services, shopping in mall Saint Joseph facility would adjoin building.*

Berg, Melissa, *Review panel staff recommends three medical projects Medical Mall and MRI proposals will be considered in January.*

Berg, Melissa, *State board delays Children's Mercy plan; Officials expected no approval problems* (July 23, 1992).

Berg, Melissa, *State board rejects hospital project Saint Joseph had asked to build a health service mall.*

Berger S, *Bid to build hospital is greeted by stiff competition in Silicon Valley,* MOD. HEALTHCARE, 1984 Jul, at 248, 250.

Bergner, Marilyn, *Quality of life, health status, and clinical research,* 27. MED. CARE p. S148-S155.

Berlin L, *I'm betting my bundle on NMR: Undaunted by bureaucratic red tape, complex construction, and an unexpected financial restructuring, the author took less than a year to set up a pioneer nuclear magnetic resonance facility,* 61. MED. ECONOMICSp.108-12, 115 (1984 Jun 25).

Berlin L, *Our health planners are fiddling while I'm burning,* 57. MED. ECONOMICS p. 85-87 (1980 Apr 14).

Berliner H, *US health planning. Bye state planning—hello what?,* 97. THE HEALTH SERVICE J.p.38 (1987 Jan 8).

Berliner HS; Burlage RK, *The walk-in chains: the proprietarization of ambulatory care,* 17. INTERNATIONAL J. OF HEALTH SERVICESp.585-94 (1987).

Bernstein AH, *Antitrust litigation in the health care field,* 54. HOSP.p.10, 14, 89 (1980 Jun 1).

Bernstein AR, *HMOs, hospitals, and the law,* 53. HOSP.p.35, 38, 42 (1979 Dec 1).

Berretta, Giuliano, *Eetelsat shareholders approve streamlined corporate governance structure with nomination of board of directors* (10/13/2004), *available at* http://80-web.lexis-nexis.com.ezproxy.umuc.edu/universe/document?_m=129ab48270ebefa219823f....

Berriman WT, *No compromise reached on CON extension,* 8. HOSP. MED. STAFFp.26-9 (1979 Mar).

Berriman WT, *Regs control the planning process as well as the plan,* 54. HOSP.p.51-4 (1980 Apr 16).

Betbeze, Philip *Too many beds* HEALTHLEADERS (2004) *available at* http://www.healthleaders com/news

Betz RB; Hardy MJ; Gibson J, *Congress passes Health Science Promotion Act; clarifies and amends health planning law,* 3. HEALTH L. VIGIL p. 7-May (1980 Dec 26).

Bice TW; Salkever DS, *Certificate-of-need programs: cure or cause of inflated costs?*, 58. HOSP. PROGRESSp.65-7, 100 (1977 Jul).

Bice TW; Salkever DS, *Certificate-of-needs controls on hospital investment and costs,* 5. J. OF L. MED.p.41-5 (1977 Jun).

Bice, Thomas W, and Salkever, David S, *The Impact of certificate-of need controls on hospital investments*, 54. MILBANK MEMORIAL FUND Q. p 185-214.

Bice, Thomas W, Ph. D.; Salkever, David S, Ph. D, *Certificate-of-Need controls on hospital investment and cost,* 5. J. OF L. MED.p.4 p (06/1/1977).

Biles, Brian; Shramm, Carl; Atkinson, Graham, *Hospital Cost Inflation under State Rate-Setting Programs,* 303. NEW ENGLAND J. OF MED. (1980).

Birmingham Business Journal, *Group backs lawsuit against new HealthSouth hospital,* BIRMINGHAM BUS. J, June 27, 2002, at 1 p.

Birmingham Business Journals, *Two hospitals sue state over HealthSouth project*, BIRMINGHAM BUS. J, May 15, 2002, at 2 p.

Blackert, Robert, *Sizing Up New Technologies in Central Arizona*, MED. ECONOMICS ADMINISTRATIVE SERVICES, 1984 Jul-Aug, at p. 26-27.

Blackstone, Erwin, A. *Competitions within the physicians' services industry: Osteopaths and allopaths* AM. J. L. AND MED. Vol. 8, no.137 (1982) *available at* http://80-web.lexis-nexis.com

Bluestein, James F, *National health care reform on trial: Health care reform and competing visions of medical care* (12/17/2003), *available at* http://80-web.lexis-nexis.com.ezproxy.umuc.edu/universe/document?_m=9437330c7ff1.

Blumstein, James F, *Court action, agency reaction: The Hill-Burton Act as a case study*, 69. IOWA L. REV.p.1227-1261 (July 1984).

Blumstein, James F.; Sloan, Frank A, *Health planning and regulation through certificate of need: an overview*, 1978. UTAH L. REV. p. 1-37.

BNA, *Michigan: Alliance of competing hospitals fights proposed heart hospital's CON*, 8. BNA S HEALTH L. REPORTER.

BNA, *Mississippi: In pair of decisions, state high court approves one CON, strikes down another*, 8. BNA S HEALTH L. REPORTER.

Bogumil WA; Jones TH; Martin J, *Justify CON applications thoroughly*, 26. OSTEOPATHIC HOSP.p.14-7 (1982 Oct).

Bolze RS, *Health care planning is granted antitrust immunity*, 66. HEALTH PROGRESSp.34-5, 62 (1985 Nov).

Bolze RS, *Rex Hospital wins jury trial in antitrust action,* 8. HEALTH L. VIGILp.4-Feb (1985 Jan 11).

Bond, Martha, *Capacity management* HEALTH PLAN. TODAY p. 5 (2nd Quarter 2000).

Bondurant, Stuart; Ezra Susser. THE NEW YORK ACADEMY OF MEDICINE, *RWJF Goal: Cross-Cutting: Access/ Chronic/ Substance Abuse/Other.* (Jan 1999).

Boothbay Register, *Capital investment fund amount for health care spending released*, BOOTHBAY REG.

Borfitz D, *Florida CON criteria proposal examined,* 6. HOME HEALTH J.p.13, 16 (1985 May).

Borsody RP, *State certificate of need laws: practical problems of compliance,* 3. J. OF L. MED.p.24-7 (1975 Oct).

Bosack, Sean O'D *Antitrust immunity for health care providers in Wisconsin: The State action immunity doctrine and Wisconsin's health care cooperative agreement legislation* MARQ. L. REV. Vol. 80, no. 245 (1996) *available at* http://80-web.lexis-nexis.com

Boult Cumming Health Care Team, *HCFA finally releases stark II regulation, available at* http://www.bccb.com/publications/Files/HCFA%20FinallyReleasesStarkIIRegulations.aspx.

Bovbjerg, Randall, *Problems and prospects for health planning: the importance of incentives, standards, and procedures in certificate of need,* 1978. UTAH L. REV. p. 1-2, 83-121.

Bowen, Alma, *Precautionary tale of two hospitals highlights rural fiscal woes,* 4. GA. HEALTHCARE NEWS.

Bowen, Alma, *Statewide network quietly siphoning rural hospital patients,* 4. GA. HEALTHCARE NEWS.

Branas, Charles C, *A trauma resource allocation model for ambulance hospitals* (June 2000).

Branum, Richard D, *Hospital Planning: A Community Effort,* 36. TEX. HOSP. p. 38-41 (1980 Jun).

Brasfield JM, *Health planning reform: a proposal for the eighties,* 6. J. OF HEALTH POLITICS, POL'Y & L.p.718-38 (1982 Winter).

Braude, Michael, *Opinion: Plans for KU heart center promise to be high-touch as well as high-tech,* THE BUS. J, Sept. 27, 2004.

Braulio Montessino, *Anatomy of a Roadblock,* 29. HEALTH SYS. REV.p.30, 32 (1996 Jan-Feb).

Brazda JF, *CON compromise saves planning law,* 60. HOSP. PROGRESSp.19 (1979 Sep).

Breisch, Sandra Lee, *Hospital, orthopaedists end ASC battle,* AM. ACADEMY OF ORTHOPEDIC SURGEONS BULL.

Breo DL, *Nation's radiologists at the front in battle between technology and cost controls,* AM. MED. NEWS, 1980 Oct 10, at 6.

Broberg, Brad, *Eastside hospitals forego competition to stem the flow of patients to Seattle,* PUGET SOUND BUS. J, May 12, 2003.

Broccolo BM; Roach WH Jr, *Joint venture structures and legal issues,* 12. TOPICS IN HEALTH CARE FINANCINGp.55-76 (1986 Spring).

Bromberg MD, *Competition and CON: an incompatible combination?,* REV. - FEDERATION OF AM. HOSP, 1980 Aug, at 5.

Bromberg RS, *The legal perspective: leasing office space to physicians,* 33. TRUSTEEp.4-Dec (1980 Feb).

Brown JB; Saltman RB, *Health capital policy in the United States: a strategic perspective,* 22. INQUIRYp.122-31 (1985 Summer).

Brown, Eric, J.; Douglas Smith,; Jody Sindelar,, *Can we regulate the quality of care?: the case of dialysis in Connecticut,* 19. AM. J. OF KIDNEY DISEASESp.609-13 (1992 Jun).

Brown, Julie, *Healthy growth: SSM, BJC, St. Luke's plan expansion in St. Charles County to keep up with population explosion,* ST. LOUIS BUS. J, 1/5/04.

Brown, Lawrence D,, *Common Sense Meets Implementation: Certificate-of-Need Regulation in the States,* 8. J. OF HEALTH POLITICS, POL'Y & L.p.480-94 (Fall 1983).

Brown, M. Steele, *HCA entry could turn tide against Missouri CON law,* BUS. J. SERVING METROPOLITAN KAN. CITY, Mar. 10, 2003.

Brown, M. Steele, *HCA picks Independence hospital site,* BUS. J. SERVING METROPOLITAN KAN. CITY, 9/15/03, at 2 p.

Bryan, Julie, *New Heart Stent Could Cost Hospitals Millions* (6/19/03), *available at* atlanta.bizjournals.com/atlanta/stories/2002/12/09/newscolumn4.html ?t=printable.

Bryant LE Jr, *Avoiding antitrust compliance difficulties in mergers and acquisitions,* 47. HEALTHCARE FIN. MGMT. p.48-50, 52, 54-8 (1993 Aug).

Bryant, Jule, *Senate committee beings health-care debate,* ATLANTA BUS. CHRON, June 24, 2002.

Bryant, Julie *Piedmont hospital seeks authorization for expansion,* ATLANTA BUS. CHRON. *(2002) available at http://atlanta.bizjournals.com.*

Bryant, Julie, -DeKalb medical center to build hospital, ATLANTA BUS. CHRON. *(2002) available at*http://atlanta.bizjournals.com.

Bryant, Julie, *Atlanta Medical Center files CON application,* ATLANTA BUS. CHRON, Aug. 1, 2003.

Bryant, Julie, *Brawl over new hospital may lead to high court,* ATLANTA BUS. CHRON, 12/1/03.

Bryant, Julie, *Campus overhaul* ATLANTA BUS. CHRON.p.2 p. (10/13/03).

Bryant, Julie, *CON news,* ATLANTA BUS. CHRON, 11/10/03.

Bryant, Julie, *Cutting into profits: Outpatient surgery centers compete with hospitals,* ATLANTA BUS. CHRON, Feb. 17, 2003.

Bryant, Julie, *Fayette expansion planned* ATLANTA BUS. CHRON. (10/27/03).

Bryant, Julie, *Fayette Heart CON,* ATLANTA BUS. CHRON, 12/1/03.

Bryant, Julie, *Geography helped draw millions to Inhibitex,* ATLANTA BUS. CHRON. *(2002) available at* ATLANTA BUS. CHRON.

Bryant, Julie, *Georgia gets mixed checkup in ranking of states' health,* ATLANTA BUS. CHRON, 11/24/03.

Bryant, Julie, *Hospitals, doctors clash over centers,* ATLANTA BUS. CHRON, 9/29/03, at 3 p.

Bryant, Julie, *Not seeing eye to eye on PET scans,* ATLANTA BUS. CHRON, June 25, 2001.

Bryant, Julie, *Nursing homes: Keep 'need laws* (June 14, 2002), *available at* Bizjournals.com.

Bryant, Julie, *Piedmont, DeKalb to boost imaging services,* ATLANTA BUS. CHRON, 9/29/03, at 2 p.

Bryant, Julie, *Saint Joseph's asks state for $26M expansion,* ATLANTA BUS. CHRON, 1/12/04.

Bryant, Julie, *Southern Regional fighting rival's expansion* ATLANTA BUS. CHRON. (May 5, 2003).

Bryant, Julie, *State denies appeals against Emory Johns Creek Hospital,* ATLANTA BUS. CHRON, 7/28/2004, at 1 p.

Bryant, Julie. *Tenet will fight new Lithonia hospital* ATLANTA BUS. CHRON. *(March 12, 2002) available at* http://atlanta.bizjournals.com.

Brycs, Cindy L.; Cline, Kathryn Ellen, *The Supply and use of selected medical technologies: As hospitals add popular high-tech services to compete, what are the cost and quality implications? data from one large state-Pennsylvania-provide some answers,* 17. HEALTH AFF. p. 213-224 (Jan/Feb 1998).

Budetti, Peter P, *Public policy issues surrounding certificate of need,* 1978. UTAH L. REV. p. 1, 2, 40-57.

Burda D, *Baptists, Methodists spar in Tenn. arena,* MOD. HEALTHCARE, 1996 Mar 25, at 62.

Burda D, *CONspiracies to crush competition. Hospitals using CON laws to thwart rival's projects,* MOD. HEALTHCARE, 1991 Jul 8, at 28-30, 32-4, 36.

Burda D, *Counting the cost of complying with regulations,* MOD. HEALTHCARE, 1990 Aug 20, at 40, 43, 45-52.

Burda D, *Deal may include sub acute CON,* MOD. HEALTHCARE, 1994 Jan 24, at 14.

Burda D, *Fear of expansion keeps CON alive,* 61. HOSP.p.76 (1987 Jun 20).

Burda D, *Former Charleston, S.C, rivals open dialogue on affiliation,* MOD. HEALTHCARE, 1994 Aug 8, at 62, 64.

Burda D, *FTC investigating N.J. hospital purchase,* MOD. HEALTHCARE, 1994 Jan 3, at 4.

Burda D, *FTC testimony will hit CON laws in Mich, Pa,* MOD. HEALTHCARE, 1988 Mar 4, at 6.

Burda D, *Hospital construction boom not expected despite end of some state CON programs,* MOD. HEALTHCARE, 1987 Nov 6, at 134.

Burda D, *Mich. system awaits decision on $145 million building plans,* MOD. HEALTHCARE, 1992 Jul 27, at 30.

Burda D, *N.C. lawmakers may offer rescue for hospital deal,* MOD. HEALTHCARE, 1995 Jun 12, at 20.

Burda D, *Neb. judge reverses CON denial,* MOD. HEALTHCARE, 1994 May 30, at 16.

Burda D, *Quorum to proceed with Neb. deal,* MOD. HEALTHCARE, 1994 Jun 27, at 24.

Burda D, *S.C. hospitals offer price freeze,* MOD. HEALTHCARE, 1996 Jul 15, at 16, 21.

Burda D, *State agency's ruling sets back plans of for-profit chain Quorum to acquire not-for-profit hospital,* MOD. HEALTHCARE, 1993 Aug 9, at 26.

Burda D, *State's conditions guide merged hospital's actions,* MOD. HEALTHCARE, 1990 Mar 19, at 34.

Burda, David, *3 GA hospitals jockey for victory,* MOD. HEALTHCARE, July 8, 1991, at p. 32-33.

Burda, David, *Competitive Fires Still Burning: Healthcare's Building Boom Helps Counter Efforts to Carve Out Monopolies,* MOD. HEALTHCARE, April 15, 2002, at p. 24.

Burda, David, *Conspiracies to crush competition: hospitals using CON laws to thwart rivals' projects,* MOD. HEALTHCARE, July 8,1991, at p. 28-30, 32-34, 36.

Burda, David, *Flood shapes Tenn. CON law,* MOD. HEALTHCARE, July 8, 1991, at p. 29-30.

Burda, David, *Hospitals battle plan to replace beds,* MOD. HEALTHCARE, July 8, 1991, at p. 30, 32.

Burda, David, *Neb. CON filing sparks another,* MOD. HEALTHCARE, July 8, 1991, at p. 33-34.

Burda, David, *No pros in CONs: Certificate-of-need laws fail to protect communities, payers or patients,* MOD. HEALTHCARE, June 3, 2002, at p. 24.

Burda, David, *Wash. hospital line up for rehab,* MOD. HEALTHCARE, July 8, 1991, at p. 34, 36.

Burnes, Brian, *Hospital proposal worries residents: Two would close in Independence,* KANSAS CITY STAR, May 3, 2004.

Burns J, *Neb. CON review panel nixes sale of not-for-profit to Quorum,* MOD. HEALTHCARE, 1993 Sep 13, at 12.

Bushman FA; Cooper PD, *A process for developing new health services,* 5. HEALTH CARE MGMT. REV.p.41-8 (1980 Winter).

Business Wire, *ABIOMED, Inc. announces 500th customer for BVS Cardiac Assist System; New model supports patient transport; Improved reimbursement helps hospitals,* BUS. WIRE, Jan. 17, 2001.

Business Wire, *Agency for health care administration agrees to issue Cleveland Clinic Florida open heart surgery certificate of need,* BUS. WIRE, March 27, 1999.

Business Wire, *Community health systems executes definitive agreement to acquire Salem, New Jersey Hospital,* BUS. WIRE, Nov. 2, 2001.

Business Wire, *Info-X 'medical necessity' coding chosen for HMA hospitals; medical necessity dictionaries to be used system-wide,* BUS. WIRE, Dec. 13, 2001.

Business Wire, *Signet operates 16 multi-modality diagnostic imaging centers throughout Florida and Puerto Rico* (10/5/2004), *available at* http://www.80-web.lexis-nexis.com.ezproxy.umuc.edu.universe/document?_m=66c6a0123d2fcc....

Butcher, Laura, *Which way for health care?: Doctors and hospitals take contrary tacks to common problem of business pressures,* BUS. J. SERVING METROPOLITAN KAN. CITY, 3/19/04.

Butcher, Lola, *Fed diagnosis finds few pros with CON laws,* BUS. J. SERVING METROPOLITAN KAN. CITY, Aug. 27, 2004.

Butcher, Lola, *Feds pull plug on specialty hospitals,* BUS. J. SERVING METROPOLITAN KAN. CITY, 12/1/03.

Butcher, Lola, *HCA lines up political specialists for Independence hospital bid,* BUS. J. SERVING METROPOLITAN KAN. CITY, Jun. 4, 2004.

Butcher, Lola, *HCA lines up political specialists for independence hospital bid*, Bus. J. of Kan. City, Jun 19, 2004.

Butcher, Lola, *HCA selects Lee's Summit hospital site*, Bus. J. of Kan. City, Nov. 28, 2003.

Butcher, Lola, *HCA wastes little time in planning to rearrange hospital beds*, Bus. J. of Kan. City, 12/26/03.

Butcher, Lola, *Outpatient centers make strange foes of usual bedfellows*, Bus. J. of Kan. City, Jan. 9, 2004.

By Conrad F. Meier, *Missouri Debates Future of Certificate-of-Need.* Health Care News. (Jul 2001).

Cain HP; Darling HN, *Health planning in the United States: where we stand today*, 1. Health Pol'y Q.p.25-May (1979 Spring).

Callahan, John, *Development of laser operations; avoiding certificate of need requirements* Bender's Health Care L. Monthly p. 8-10 (Jul. 1996).

Cambell, Doug, *Consultant of need: Strategic Healthcare Consultants leave no stone unturned in pursuit of approval*, Bus. J. Serving the Greater Triad Area, Aug, 4, 2003.

Cambell, Doug, *Forsyth's women's center to cost $66M*, Bus. J. Serving the Greater Triad Area, http://triad.bizjournals.com/triad/stories/2003/09/22/story1.htm, at 2 p.

Cameron, Karen, *Health care costs: prophesizing the future, available at* www.ahpanet.org/articles.html.

Cameron, Karen, *What's the future of COPN in Virginia?* Health Plan. Today p. 7-8 (3rd Quarter 2000).

Campbell, Doug, *$2.4M upgrade on tap for Baptist's CompRehab*, Bus. J. of the Greater Triad Area, January 24, 2003, at 1 p.

Campbell, Doug, *ARMC appeals as state blocks Mebane project*, Bus. J. Serving the Greater Triad Area, Jan 19, 2004.

Campbell, Doug, *Begging for beds*, The Bus. J, at 1-3.

Campbell, Doug, *Cone, Forsyth seek high-tech scanners* (July 28, 2003), *available at* triad.bizjournals.com/triad/stories/2003/07/28/story7.html?t+printable.

Campbell, Doug, *Forsyth medical gets ok for $67M addition*, Bus. J. Serving the Greater Triad Area, Aug. 27, 2004.

Campbell, Doug, *State plan would give hospitals new beds*, Bus. J. Serving the Greater Triad Area, July 21, 2003.

Campbell, Ellen S,; Gary M. Fournier,, *Certificate-of-Need Deregulation and Indigent Hospital Care,*, 18. J. of Health Politics, Pol'y & L.p.905-25 (Winter 1993).

Campbell, Helen S,; Ahern, Melissa W, *Have Procompetitive Change Altered Hospital Provision of Indigent Care,*, 2. Health Economics p. 281-9 (1993 Oct).

Campbell, Matt, *Independence hospital drops application it had proposed a branch near I-170* (November 22, 1991).

Campbell, Matt, *Neighbors upset by surplus of group homes* (April 14, 1994).

Campbell, Matt, *State staff recommends against new hospital branch.*

Campbell-Eaton, Maja, *Antitrust and certificate of need: A doubtful prognosis*, 69. Iowa L. Rev. p. 1451-1481 (1984).

Canarie JD Jr, *MaldisTRIBUNEuted health care services: restructuring the current regulatory system,* 6. Am. J. of L. & Med.p.407-23 (1980 Fall).

Cancer consultants, *Lung cancer news: Integrated PET-CT improves staging of non-small cell lung cancer, available at* http://www.patient.cancerconsultants.com/lung_cancer_news.aspx?id=17976.

Caress B; Kotelchuck R, *Politics makes strange beds.* Health PAC Bull.p.1-10, 19-21 (1977 Jul-Aug).

Carey-York, Annamarie, *7 Practical tips for winning your CON* Outpatient Surgery (January 2004).

Carlyn M, *The MDPH challenge,* 22. MICH. HOSP.p.17-21 (1986 May).

Carnazzo JS, *Demand forecasting for magnetic resonance imaging services,* 30. HOSP. & HEALTH SERVICES ADMIN. p.84-91 (1985 Mar-Apr).

Carpenter ES; Paul-Shaheen P, *Implementing regulatory reform: the saga of Michigan's debedding experiment,* 9. J. OF HEALTH POLITICS, POL'Y & L.p.453-73 (1984 Fall).

Cartaya OA; Curran WJ, *A model certificate of need statue,* 2. HEALTH CARE MGMT. REV.p.31-41 (1977 Fall).

Carter, Diana Louise, *RGH gets expansion funds,* ROCHESTER DEMOCRAT & CHRON, 9/10/03, at 2 p.

Carter, Douglas L, *Judicial review of state health plans after the health planning and resources development amendments of 1979,* 1981. DUKE L. J. p. 404-415.

Castle, Nicholas G, *Replaced by fish: When a nursing home closes, what happens to the residents?,* 1. BALANCE p. 12-13, 28-29.

Catanoso, Justin, *What's the best way to market the Triad?, available at* Bizjournals.com.

Caudill, S.B,; Ford, J.M,; Kaserman, D. L, *Certificate-of-Need Regulation and the Diffusion of Innovations: A Random Coefficient Model,* 10. J. OF APPLIED ECONOMETRICS (Jan.-Mar, 1995).

Caudill, Steven B, Ford, Jon M, and Kaserman, David L, *Certificate-of-need regulation and the diffusion of innovations: a random coefficient model,* 10. J. OF APPLIED ECONOMETRICS p 73-78.

Center for Studying Health System Change, *An Update on the Community Tracking Study: a focus on the changing health system.* (February 1999).

Cerfolio, Robert Jemes. M.D,; Bryant, Ayesha s. MSPH, *The Role of PET and PET/CT in evaluating and staging patients with non-small cell lung cancer,* GEO INFO. SYS.

Cerne, F.; Montague, J, *Capacity Crisis,* 68. (October 5, 1998).

Chandler JA, *Court dismisses antitrust violation claim,* 8. HEALTH L. VIGILp.6 (1985 Aug 23).

Chandler, Kim, *Grand jury eyes denial of MRI request,* BIRMINGHAM NEWS, Jun 27, 2004.

Chandler, Kim, *New nursing home beds on hold in Medicaid crisis,* BIRMINGHAM NEWS, 11/25/03.

Charlene Harrington, Ph.D,; James H. Swan, Ph.D,; John A. Nyman, Ph.D,; Helen Carrillo, M.S,, *The effect of certificate of need and moratoria policy on change in nursing home beds in the United States,* 35. MED. CAREp.574-588 (1997 Jun).

Chassin MR, *The containment of hospital costs: a strategic assessment,* 16. MED. CAREp.Jan-55 (1978 Oct).

Chassin, Mark R, *Achieving and Sustaining Improved Quality: Lessons From New York State and Cardiac Surgery: Deaths from cardiac surgery fell 41 percent over the first four years of New York's reporting program and have continued to fall ever since,* 21. HEALTH AFF. p. 40-51 (July/August 2002).

Chazan JA, *Certificate of need: a concept whose time has passed,* 69. R.I. MED. J.p.273-5 (1986 Jun).

Cherskov M, *Hospitals hurdle CON barriers differently,* 60. HOSP.p.89 (1986 May 20).

Cherskov M, *Planning agencies' futures, funds uncertain,* 60. HOSP.p.79-80 (1986 Jun 20).

Ching-Yen Hsiung; Jia-Ming Wu; Chong-Jong Wang; Shih-Chang Kuo; Shyh-An Yeh; Hsuan-Chih Hsu; Eng-Yen Huang, *Attenuation of radiation dose by the skull base bone in patients with nasopharyngeal carcinoma:: Clinical importance* RADIOLOGY (2001).

Chitwood, Roy, *Salespeople with service ethic rise to the top,* PUGET SOUND BUS. J, Jul. 16, 2004.

Christakis, Nicholas A, M.D, M.P.H,; Jose Escarce, M.D,, *Survival of Medicare Patients After Enrollment in Hospice Programs,* NEW ENGLAND J. OF MED. (Jul 18, 1996).

Christensen, Clayton M.; Bohmer, Richard; Kenagy, John, *Will disruptive innovations cure health care: Heath care may be entrenched, change-averse industry in the United States. The innovations that will eventually turn it around are ready, in some cases - but they can't find backers.* HARVARD BUS. REV.p.102-112 p. (September-October 2000).

Chudler KM, *CON reform: its impact on construction,* 24. MICH. HOSP.p.56-7 (1988 May).

Cimasi, Robert James, *Improving health care: A Dose of competition* HEATLHCARE CONSULTANT.

Cimasi, Robert James, *No duplication with Women's Hospital,* ST. LOUIS BUS. J, June 19-25, 2000.

Cimasi, Robert James, *The Realities of Rising Healthcare Costs,* GREEN BAY PRESS-GAZETTE, Jan. 19, 1999.

Citizens Council of Michigan, *Certificate of need on research agenda* CRC E-CHRONICLE (7/28/04).

Claiborn SA, *Alternative financing approaches for health care institutions,* 11. TOPICS IN HEALTH CARE FINANCINGp. 33-41 (1985 Summer).

Cleary, Paul D,; Mark Schlesinger,; David Blumenthal,, *Factors Affecting the Availability and Use of Hemodialysis Facilities,*, 13. HEALTH CARE FINANCING REV. (Winter 1991).

Clemonds, Denise, *Response to certificate of need editorial* (2003).

Codner S, *Special report on licensure, accreditation and CON. Certificate of need laws: still alive and costing,* HEALTH CARE L. NEWS, 1994 Mar, at 5-Oct.

Coffey RJ, *Success in CON process depends on constructive attitudes and actions,* 56. HOSP.p.71-4 (1982 May 16).

Cohen AB; Cohodes DR, *Certificate of need and low capital-cost medical technology,* 60. THE MILBANK MEMORIAL FUND Q. HEALTH & SOC'Yp.307-28 (1982 Spring).

Cohen AB; Cohodes DR, *Certificate-of-need programs, mechanisms,* 70. AM. J. OF PUB. HEALTHp.290 (1980 Mar).

Cohen AB; Rock RC, *Changing health policies and clinical laboratory services,* 1. J. OF HEALTH CARE TECHNOLOGYp. 237-55 (1985 Spring).

Cohen HA; Atkinson JG, *Case mix and regulation,* 8. TOPICS IN HEALTH CARE FINANCINGp.21-8 (1982 Summer).

Cohen, Harris S, *Regulating health care facilities: the certificate-of-need process re-examined,* 10. INQUIRYp.9-Mar (1973 Sep).

Cohen, Irwin; Gold, Steven, *Merger, replacement & expansion of outdated nursing homes: A novel program by a Virginia provider results in more modern facilities and expanded services to the community,* COTEMPORARY LONGTERM CARE, 1988 Sep, at p. 90, 92.

Cohen, Joel W,; William D. Spector,, *The Effect of Medicaid Reimbursement on Quality of Care in Nursing Homes,*, 15. J. OF HEALTH ECONOMICS (1996).

Cohodes DR, *What to do about capital?,* 27. HOSP. & HEALTH SERVICES ADMIN.p.67-89 (1982 Sep-Oct).

Colby DC; Begley CE, *The effects of implementation problems on certificate of need decisions in Illinois,* 3. HEALTH POL'Y & EDUC.p.303-16 (1983 Apr).

Collier G, *Certificate of need requirements for home health services,* 3. CARINGp.19-27 (1984 May).

Collins, Barryzlabama Hospital Association, *CON our only Cost-Containment Process* (Spring 1998).

Community Catalyst, *Certificate of need: a chart comparing state laws,* COMMUNITY CATALYST, at 2 p.

Condon, Garret, *A Tug of war for hearts* (11/24/03), *available at* www.ctnow.com/news/custom/newsat3/hc-angio1124.artnov24,1,3571327.story?coll=hc-headlines-newsat3.

Condon, Garret, *Two hospitals seek ok to offer cardiac services* (Dec. 24, 2003), *available at* www.ctnow.com/news/local/hc-cardiac1224.artdec24,1,4986770.print.story?coll=h.

Cone, Kenneth, and Dranove, David, *Do state rate setting regulations really lower hospital expenses?* J. OF HEALTH ECONOMICS p 159-165.

Conn, Joseph, *Conflict in paradise: Virgin Islands hospital opposes certificate of need for competing surgery center,* MOD. HEALTHCARE, 4/1/2004, at 2 p.

Conn, Joseph, *Scan center's move violates Georgia CON laws,* MOD. PHYSICIAN, 1/22/04.

Conover, Christopher J, and Sloan, Frank A, *Does removing certificate-of-need regulations lead to a surge in health care spending?,* 23. J. OF HEALTH POLITICS, POL'Y & L. p 455-481.

Conover, Christopher J.; Frank A. Sloan, *Does removing certificate-of-need regulations lead to a surge in health care spending?,* 23. J. OF HEALTH POLITICS, POL'Y & L. p. 455-81 (June 1998).

Conrad SL, *The politics of getting a certificate of need,* 30. TRUSTEEp.35-8 (1977 May).

Conrad, Meier F, *More to dirigo than insurance, available at* http://www.heartland.org/PrinterFriendly.cfm?theType=artId&theID=15689.

Consedine JF; Jekel JF; Dunaye TM, *Certificate of need and the pitfalls of due process,* 17. INQUIRYp.348-56 (1980 Winter).

Cook K; Shortell SM; Conrad DA; Morrisey MA, *A theory of organizational response to regulation: the case of hospitals,* 8. ACAD. OF MGMT. REV.p.193-205 (1983 Apr).

Cook KS; Shortell SM; Conrad DA; Morrisey MA, *A theory of organizational response to hospital regulation: a reply to Smith and Mick,* 10. ACAD. OF MGMT. REV.p.337-43 (1985 Apr).

Cook, Robert, *Hospitals' motives questioned in quest for new cancer care center,* FOSTER'S SUNDAY CITIZEN, December 8, 2002, at p. 3.

Cooksey, Catherine L. *Surgical care center v. hospital service district no. 1: The Fifth circuit reins in parker immunity for hospital service districts in Louisiana* TUL. L. REV. Vol. 74, no. 717 (1999) *available at* http://80-web.lexis-nexis.com

Corey, Andrea, *Women's Hospital costs triple,* ST. LOUIS BUS. J, June 2, 2000.

Costich, Julia Field and Helton, Mike *The Kentucky health reform act* N. KY. L. REV. Vol. 22, no. 381 (1995) *available at* http://80-web.lexis-nexis.com

Court of Appeals of Missouri Western District, *EBG Healthcare III Inc. v. Missouri Health Facilities Review Comm.*

Crain DC, *Certificate of need,* 41. MED. ANNALS OF THE DISTRICT OF COLUMBIAp.2-Jan (1972 Sep).

Crane AB; Schoeman M, *Local hospitals: some experiences with the health planning program,* 6. J. OF HEALTH & HUM. RESOURCES ADMIN.p.373-99 (1984 Winter).

Crane SC, *Issues and trends in the regulation of office-based clinical laboratories,* 6. CLINICS IN LABORATORY MED.p.369-86 (1986 Jun).

Crane, Robert M, *Out of the Frying Pan and Into the Fire?: If current market trends continue, consumers could find themselves out of the managed care frying pan and into the cost-sharing fire.* HEALTH AFF.p.155-159.

Crum GE, *Getting your certificate of need approved* J. OF LONG TERM CARE ADMIN.p.23-6 (1985 Spring).

Cryan TV, *The MRI experience,* 7. RADIOLOGY MGMT.p.12-Aug (1985 Jun-Jul).

Curet, Monique, *Board denies SemperCare application,* MOBILE REG, Apr. 22, 2004.

Curran WJ, *A severe blow to hospital planning: certificate of need declared unconstitutional,* 288. NEW ENGLAND J. OF MED.p.723-4 (1973 Apr 5).

Curran WJ, *Health planning with clout: certificate of need legislation,* 62. AM. J. OF PUB. HEALTHp.1549 (1972 Nov).

Curran WJ, *Law-medicine notes. The health planners and computerized tomography: high technology, cost control, and judicial review,* 303. NEW ENGLAND J. OF MED.p.626-7 (1980 Sep 11).

Curran WJ, *Law-medicine notes: Health planning, Blue Cross, and the federal antitrust laws,* 305. NEW ENGLAND J. OF MED.p.1194-5 (1981 Nov 12).

D'Alessio, Alice, *Flint, MI, institutions join forces to build, operate MRI center,* HEALTH FACILITIES MGMT, at p. 12-13.

Dancer, Dingeman; Christopherson. PLC, *Stark realities: How the physician self-referral act affects group practice* (10/4/2004), *available at* http://www.library.lp.findlaw.com/articles/file/00635/000399/title/Subject/topic/Insurance_Life%20Insurance/....

Dandoy S, *Certificate of need program for health care institutions,* 32. ARIZ. MED.p.960 (1975 Dec).

Dasbach, Angie, *Retirement Centers Strain Under Law,* BUS. J, June 26, 1998.

D'Aunno, Thomas, *The role of institutional and market forces in divergent organizational change* ADMIN. SCI. Q. (Dec. 2000).

David C Grabowski, *Does an increase in the Medicaid reimbursement rate improve nursing home quality?,* 56B. J. OF GERONTOLOGY. SERIES B, PSYCHOLOGICAL SCI. & SOC. SCI.p.S84-93 (Mar 2001).

Davis CD, *Creating new facilities, services no longer requires THFC approval,* 41. TEX. HOSP.p.18-9 (1986 Mar).

Davis CD, *The Supreme Court upholds THFC procedure,* 39. TEX. HOSP.p.46-8 (1984 Apr).

Davis JE, *The major ambulatory surgical center and how it is developed,* 67. SURGICAL CLINICS OF NORTH AMERICAp. 671-92 (1987 Aug).

Davis, C. Dean, *The Health Systems Agency and Certificate of Need,* 36. TEX. HOSP. p. 45 (1980 Jun).

Davis, Mark S, *Certificate of need: Diagnosis and prescription,* COTEMPORARY LONGTERM CARE, 1988 Sep, at p. 40, 42, 44.

Davis, Mark S, *CON myths in nursing home development,* COTEMPORARY LONGTERM CARE, 1988 Jan, at P. 57, 75.

DBJ, *Anthem/Premier battle has ripples,* DAYTON BUS. J, Sept. 27, 2004.

DBJ, *Anthem/Premier battle has triples,* DAYTON BUS. J, Sept. 27, 2004.

Decker R, *Lack of CON laws may create cash squeeze,* 4. HOSP. PURCHASING MGMT.p.16-9 (1979 Nov).

Deemez, James A,; David W. Windus,; the St. Louis Nephrology group, Hemodialysis, *Prescription and Delivery in a Metropolitan Community,*, 41. KIDNEY INTERNATIONAL (1992).

Deering, Joseph, *[Summary of Committee on Health Care Policy meeting about HB 432]* (3/12/03).

DeGregory R, *Reproductive health: Eighth Circuit waives certificate of need for planned parenthood,* 25. J. OF L, MED. & ETHICSp.326-7 (1997 Winter).

Delmez, James A.; Windus, David W, *Hemodialysis prescription and delivery in a metropolitan community,* KIDNEY INTERNATIONAL, 1992, at p. 1023-1028.

Demers L, *The role of district health councils in the Independent Health Facilities Act,* 12. HEALTH L. CAN.p.42-5, 41 (1991).

Dem'ianova Epifantsev VI; Nikolaeva ES, *[Use of certification data for resolving the goals of ongoing and long-term planning for the development of the material and technological basis of a hospital network]* SOVETSKOE ZDRAVOOKHRANENIEp.11-Jul (1981).

Demkovich LE, *Health planning agencies face threat from deregulators,* 11. NAT'L J.p.687-90 (1979 Apr 28).

DeNyse RA, *Hospitals meet space and HSA criteria through merger,* 53. HOSP.p.137-8, 142, 145 (1979 Feb 16).

Deprez, Ronald and William B. Stanson, *Editorial piece by Ronald D. Deprez, PhD. MPH and William B. Stanson, MD, MS* PHRG.

Desloge, Rick, *BJC to invest $4.6 million in brain scanning devices,* ST. LOUIS BUS. J, Apr. 30, 2004.

Desloge, Rick, *CDI Sets Sights Here; To Open Two Imaging Centers* (July 5, 2002), *available at* stlouis.bizjournals.com.

Desloge, Rick, *Children's Hospital investing in MRI equipment upgrade,* ST. LOUIS BUS. J, Oct. 24, 2003.

Desloge, Rick, *Competitor SSM questions need for proposed BJC hospital,* ST. LOUIS BUS. J, Jan. 26, 2004.

Desloge, Rick, *Delmar Gardens Enterprises plans first Metro East site in O'Fallon,* ST. LOUIS BUS. J, 10/6/03, at 1 p.

Desloge, Rick, *Hirsch's group to build $5 million surgery center,* ST. LOUIS BUS. J, 2/20/04.

Desloge, Rick, *HMOs see healthy profits on hefty premium hikes,* ST. LOUIS BUS. J, December 6, 2002, at 3 p.

Desloge, Rick, *LSS seeks legislative help to expand Meramec Bluffs,* ST. LOUIS BUS. J, 2/13/04.

Desloge, Rick, *Physicians Group Taking on St. John's Mercy in Washington* (July 12, 2002), *available at* http:// stlouis.bizjournals.com.

Desloge, Rick, *Sunrise, Legacy join on Des Peres assisted living center,* ST. LOUIS BUS. J, July 28, 2003.

Desloge, Rick, *SurgCenter taps local investors: Drs. Barth, Brooks, Schmidt, buy into outpatient centers,* ST. LOUIS BUS. J, May 5, 2003.

Di Giovanni L; Gibofsky A, *Medicare fraud regulations and the implications for joint ventures: are we working at cross purposes?* L. MED.p.279-303 (1995).

Diller W, *States show new interest in regulated health planning,* BUS. & HEALTH, 1993 Feb, at 20-4.

DiPaolo V, *Public works funding will boost '79 building,* MOD. HEALTHCARE, 1979 Jun, at 13-4.

DiPaolo V, *Religious opposition raises cost of setting up 'test tube baby' lab,* MOD. HEALTHCARE, 1980 Feb, at 24, 28.

DiPaolo V, *See 14% design dollar volume rise; renovation's share grows rapidly,* MOD. HEALTHCARE, 1980 Feb, at 56-8.

Doherty, Peter, *Certificates of need: A Bad idea whose time has passed* J. OF THE JAMES MADISON INSTITUTE p. 10-15 (Winter 2001).

Dolan AK, *The antitrust status of health planning,* 1. HEALTH CARE PLAN. & MARKETINGp.23-Nov (1982 Jan).

Dolan, Andrew K, *Who has to standing appeal certificate-of-need decisions?,* 1978. UTAH L. REV. p. 1-2, 155-177.

Domanico L, *Long-range hospital development necessitates strategic planning,* 35. HOSP. FIN. MGMT.p.38-40, 42-4, 46 passim (1981 Jan).

Donahue, John X,; Donald C. Williams,; William J. Waters,; Barbara A. DeBuono,, *Affordability Considerations in Certificate-of-Need Hospital Capital Expenditures Review Determinations,,* 75. R.I. MED.p.403-6 (August 1992).

Dooley J, *The corruption of hospice. What price is hospice paying for survival?,* 40. PUB. WELFAREp.35-41 (1982 Spring).

Dore, Patricia A, *Access to Florida administrative proceedings* (12/29/2003), *available at* http://80-web-lexis-nexis.comezproxy.umuc.edu/universe/document?_m=6099f7c40a081.

Dorschner, John, *Cutthroat clinics: Hospitals turn hostile as healthcare margins tighten,* THE MIAMI HERALD, 8/31/03, at 4 p.

Dorschner, John, *State may deregulate hospitals,* THE MIAMI HERALD, 11/21/03.

Doughty A; Nash SI; Gift DA, *Deployment and utilization of MR imaging in Michigan: observations of a statewide data base,* 185. RADIOLOGYp.53-61 (1992 Oct).

Dranove, D,; Cone, K,, *Do State Rate Setting Laws Really Lower Hospital Expenses?,* 4. J. OF HEALTH ECONOMICS (June 1985).

Dreier, David, *Health care services - Certificate of need program,* CONGRESSIONAL REC.

Dritschilo A; Sherman D; Emami B; Piro AJ; Hellman S, *The cost effectiveness of a radiation therapy simulator: a model for the determination of need,* 5. INTERNATIONAL J. OF RADIATION ONCOLOGY, BIOLOGY, PHYSICSp.243-7 (1979 Feb).

Duke, K. S, *Hospitals in a Changing Health Care System,* 15. HEALTH AFF. (Summer 1996).

DuNah, Richard Jr,; Charlene Harrington, Ph.D,; Barbara Bedney, M.S.W,; Helen Carillo, M.S,, *Variations and Trends in State Nursing Facility Capacity,,* 17. HEALTH CARE FINANCING REV. (Fall 1995).

Dunkelberg JS; Furst RW; Roenfeldt RL, *State rate review and the relationship between capital expenditures and operating costs,* 20. INQUIRYp.240-7 (1983 Fall).

Durenberger D, *The principles of a competition advocate,* 1. HEALTH AFF.p.19-29 (1981 Winter).

Durr, Eric, *Saratoga hospital gets state approval to build radiation therapy center,* BUS. REV. SERVING N.Y.'S CAPITAL REGION, Dec. 29, 2003.

Durr, Eric, *Saratoga Hospital launches PR blitz for radiation center,* BUS. REV. SERVING N.Y.'S CAPITAL REGION, 8/18/2003, at 3 p.

Durr, Eric, *Will N.Y.'s politicians take on health care this year,* BUS. REV. SERVING NY'S CAPITAL REGION, Jan 3, 2003.

Eakin, B.K,, *Allocative Inefficiency in the Production of Hospital Services,* 58. SOUTHERN ECONOMIC J. (July 1991).

Eby, C.L,; Cohodes, D,, *What Do We Know about Rate-Setting?,* 10. J. OF HEALTH POLITICS, POL'Y & L. (1985).

Eckery KC, *Outlook cautious after California CON sunset,* 13. PROVIDERp.16, 20 (1987 Dec).

Eckery, Kevin C, *Outlook cautious after California CON sunset* PROVIDER p. 16, 20 (Dec. 1987).

Edgar, Julie, *Plan to change law may add hospitals in county,* DETROIT FREE PRESS (MI), December 10, 2002.

Elder, Shirley, *Case history: surgeons, hospital at odds: certificate of need is the key to case of surgeons vs. hospital,* BOSTON GLOBE, May 16, 1999.

Elhauge, Einer, *Symposium on regulating medical innovation: The Limited regulatory potential of medical technology assessment* (12/29/2003), *available at* http://80-web.lexis-nexis.comezproxy.umuc.edu/universe/document?_m=5e89dd21ac21.

Elizabeth Thompson Beckley,, *Looking back; Retrospective Reviews Replacing Pre-authorizations,* MOD. PHYSICIAN, Mar 2001.

Elkins, Ken, *Health-care battle looms in Lancaster,* CHARLOTTE BUS. J, 9/22/03, at 2 p.

Elkins, Ken, *Industry wrap-ups: Lowe's plans hickory store, but residents voice concerns,* BUS. J, 08/16/2004.

Elkins, Ken, *Salisbury hospital plans $17 million addition, renovation,* CHARLOTTE BUS. J, 10/21/2002, at 3.

Ellet, Van, *Planning: What Now?: A Look at how state planning is going* PROVIDER p. 12-13 (Dec. 1987).

Emmerich, Lisa, *Crowded hospitals to get relief: A New state law will allow more beds without the need to ask for permission,* ORLANDO SENTINEL, May 5, 2004.

Ennis, S,; Schoenbaum, M,; Keeler, T, *Optimal Prices and Costs for Hospitals with Excess Bed Capacity,* 32. APPLIED ECONOMICS (July 15, 2000).

Everton, Angus R,, *Health Resources Planning Commission regulation of ambulatory surgical care,* 44. MD. MED. J.p.125-8 (1995 Feb).

Ewing, Margaret F, *Health planning and deinstitutionalization:: Advocacy within the administrative process*, 31. STAN. L. REV. p. 679-715 (1979 Apr).

Ewing, Margaret F, *Health planning and reinstitution: Advocacy within the administrative process*, 31. STAN. L. REV. p. 679-715 (April 1979).

Fabro F, *Editorial: Certificate of need—Connecticut,* 37. CONN. MED.p.459-60 (1973 Sep).

Factiva, *Missouri - orders of rulemaking - Department of Health and Senior Services: 19 CSR 60-50* (Mar. 17, 2004), *available at* http://80-global.factiva.com/ezproxy.umuc.edu/en/arch/print_results.asp.

Falk, Brian, *Practices, hospital vie for state's approval for MRI,* CHARLOTTE BUS. J, December 2, 2002, at p. 1-2.

Fearnow, R. R, *Nursing Home Certificate of Need,* IND. LAWYER, May 28, 1997.

Fecht L, *Designing a laparoscopic operating room,* 8. SEMINARS IN PERIOPERATIVE NURSINGp.162-71 (1999 Oct).

Feder J; Scanlon W, *Regulating the bed supply in nursing homes,* 58. THE MILBANK MEMORIAL FUND Q. HEALTH & SOC'Yp.54-88 (1980 Winter).

Federation of American Hospitals, *The Planning maze: a CON game*, 13. FEDERATION OF AM. HOSP. REV. p. 3, 7-8, 23-31, 34-40, 49-50. (August 1980).

Feldman, Steven E, *Change is the only constant* HEALTH PLAN. TODAY p 4, 7 (4th Quarter 2000).

Feldstein, Paul J. Ph.D, *The Changing Structure of the Health Care Delivery System in the United States,* 1. J. OF MED. PRAC. MGMT. p. 13- 19 (1985 Jul).

Filaroski, P. Douglas; Manning, Margie, *Hospital law eased: Certificate-of-need process will be cut for expansion of beds, some medical programs,* BUS. J. OF JACKSONVILLE, May 14, 2004.

Fine J; Super KE, *Repeal of some states' CON laws spurs psych hospital construction,* MOD. HEALTHCARE, 1986 Oct 10, at 74, 76.

Firey, Thomas A, *Certificate of Need is indeed a CON* (May 09, 2004), *available at* http://www.mdpolicy.org/research/health/opinion/oped050904.shtml.

Fisher, E. S. et. al, *Associations Among Hospital Capacity, Utilization, and Mortality of U.S. Medicare Beneficiaries, Controlling for sociodemographic Factors*, 34 (February 2000).

Fisher, Jean P, *Raleigh hospitals call dibs on beds, available at* http://www.newsobserver.com/news/v-printer/story/1380707p-7503932c.html.

Fishman L, *Certificate of need,* 93. N.J. MED.p.8 (1996 Nov).

Fishman L, *Person of the year: Commissioner Len Fishman. Interview by Bill Berlin,* 93. N.J. MED.p.23-8 (1996 Dec).

Fletcher, Amy, *Fight for hospital patients shapes up in Boulder, available at* Bizjournals.com.

Flexer M, *The helicopter ambulance: essential medical service,* 61. HOSP. PROGRESSp.66-71 (1980 May).

Fligel, Sarah, *Independence short-lived for Christenbury's center,* CHARLOTTE BUS. J, November 29, 2002, at pp. 3.

Foley HA, *Assuring the nation's health resources,* 93. PUB. HEALTH REP.sp.627-36 (1978 Nov-Dec).

Fong, Tony, *HCA ends CON challenge of new Va. hospital.*

Fong, Tony, *HCA loses bid to build new Va. hospital.*

Fong, Tony, *Vt. system can survive, despite CON fiasco: report,* MOD. HEALTHCARE, May 1, 2003.

Foran, Janet W, *An interview with Dr. Hermann A. Ziel,* 14. MICH. HOSP. p. 2-4.

Forcina, Carolyn, *Medical Technology: Hospitals Juggle Quality, Cost and Legal Issues,* 2. N.J. HEALTHCARE p. 3-6 (1989 Sep-Oct).

Foreman, David, *Mayo moves on it new hospital,* BUS. J. OF JACKSONVILLE, August 30, 2002, at 2.

Foreman, David. *Mayo moves on its new hospital,* THE BUS. J. OF JACKSONVILLE *(Sept. 2, 2002) available at* http://jacksonville.bizjournals.com/jacksonville/stories/2002/09/02/story3.html?t=printable.

Fournier, G.; Campell, E, *Indigent Care as Quid Pro Quo in Hospital Regulation,* 79. REV. OF ECONOMIC & STAT. (1997).

Fox KS; Helms WD; Ginsburg S. United Hospital Fund of New York, *Policy and practice: certified home health care in New York City.* (1990 Aug).

Franczyk, Annemarie, *New health care panel turns down projects* (5/29/2004), *available at* http://www.bizjournals.com/industries/heath_care/physician_practice/2004/05/24/buffalo_story8....

Franczyk, Annemarie, *Nonprofit health care is big business in Buffalo,* BUFFALO BUS. FIRST, 11/17/03.

Franczyk, Annemarie, *Settlement clears way for hospital upgrade,* BUS. FIRST OF BUFFALO, Dec. 5, 2003.

Franczyk, Annemarie, *Zacher sells nursing home, consolidates two others,* BUFFALO BUS. FIRST, 11/3/03.

Franklin, Harriet, *Is certificate of need regulation extinct?,* PHYSICIAN'S NEWS DIG, Jan 1997.

Franko, Frederick P, *State laws and regulations for office-based surgery* AORN J. (April 2001).

Fraser I; Koontz T; Moran WC, *Medicare reimbursement for hospice care: an approach for analyzing cost consequences,* 23. INQUIRYp.141-53 (1986 Summer).

Frechette AL, *Massachusetts Determination of Need Program,* 301. NEW ENGLAND J. OF MED.p.218-9 (1979 Jul 26).

Freeman RA, *Implications of certificate of need legislation for institutional pharmacy practice,* 32. AM. J. OF HOSP. PHARMACYp.212-3 (1975 Feb).

Friedman BS; Hattis PA; Bogue RJ, *Tax exemption and community benefits of not-for-profit hospitals,* 11. ADVANCES IN HEALTH ECONOMICS & HEALTH SERVICES RES. (1990).

Friedman LD; Candidate JD, *Federal preclusion of state certificate-of-need exemptions for research and education expenditures,* 4. AM. J. OF L. & MED.p.91-110 (1978 Spring).

Friedman, Ben; Coffey, R.M, *The Effectiveness of State Regulation of Hospital Revenue in the 1980's.* (1993).

Friedman, Eli A, M.D,, *End-Stage Renal Disease Therapy: An American Success Story,,* 275. JAMA (April 10, 1996).

Gaffney, Mark; Zimmerman, Martin, *An old-fashioned way to control costs: Well-run certificate-of-need programs can help rein in rising healthcare spending,* MOD. HEALTHCARE, November 11, 2002, at 2 p.

Gale, Kevin, *Jm Family Enterprises Southern Wine & Spirits lead the list,* SOUTH FLA. BUS. J, July. 30, 2004.

Galewitz, Gale, *Heart centers set to double,* PALM BEACH POST, Jun 28, 2004.

Galewitz, Phil; Swartz, Kristi, *Heart surgery bill gets boost in legislature,* PALM BEACH POST, 3/24/04.

Gallagher P, *Back to the drawing board. Redefining some grand design,* 16. HEALTH PAC BULL.p.8-Jul (1986 Jun).

Gallagher P, *The Presbyterian story. The people pull the strings for a change,* 16. HEALTH PAC BULL.p.12-Sep (1986 Jun).

Galloro, Vince, *CON conflict: HMA wins Fla. ok but still may face hurdle,* MOD. HEALTHCARE, Oct. 13, 2003.

Galloro, Vince, *Finally.yes: Bon Secours wins long fight for new site,* MOD. HEALTHCARE, Feb, 3, 2003, at p. 25.

Galloro, Vince, *Finally.yes: Bon Secours wins long fight for new site,* MOD. HEALTHCARE, Feb. 3, 2003, at p. 25.

Galloro, Vince, *HCA, Cleveland Clinic resolve antitrust case,* MOD. HEALTHCARE, Apr. 30, 2003.

Galloro, Vince, *HCA's new uninsured policy pays off in Va. CON,* MOD. HEALTHCARE, March 12, 2004.

Galloro, Vince, *HealthSouth wants faster future,* MOD. HEALTHCARE, August 2001.

Galloro, Vince, *Keep competing: Fla. settles case involving noncompete CON clauses,* MOD. HEALTHCARE, May 5, 2003.

Galloro, Vince, *Pros and CONs: Tennessee Execs Looking for Down-home Recipe to Fix Certificate-of-Need Law,* MOD. HEALTHCARE, March 25, 2002, at p.22-23.

Galloro, Vince, *Quite quarrelsome: CON fight intensifies as Tennessee maps overhaul,* MOD. HEALTHCARE, at p. 36.

Galloro, Vince, *Tenn. partnership receives ok for surgery center,* MOD. HEALTHCARE, Nov. 20, 2003.

Galloro, Vince; Reily, Patrick, *Bon Secours beats HCA in fight over new hospital,* MOD. HEALTHCARE, Jan. 29, 2003.

Galtney L, *CONs and the Louisiana purchase,* 26. MED. WORLD NEWSp.32, 35 (1985 Jul 8).

Ganey, Terry, *Health agency under attack,* ST. LOUIS POST-DISPATCH, at 1-3.

Gardner E, *Certificate-of-need war erupts in Kentucky,* MOD. HEALTHCARE, 1989 Oct 6, at 4.

Gardner E, *Ga. planning agency to decide which of 4 rivals will build facility,* MOD. HEALTHCARE, 1992 Jun 22, at 7.

Gardner E, *Humana's one-county exemption to Ky.'s CON law struck down,* MOD. HEALTHCARE, 1991 Sep 16, at 3-Dec.

Gardner J, *CON law sparks battle between institutions,* MOD. HEALTHCARE, 1996 Feb 19, at 18.

Garella, S,, *The Costs of Dialysis in the USA* NEPHROLOGY DIALYSIS TRANSPLANTATION (1997).

Garloch, Karen, *State approves neonatal unit,* CHARLOTTE OBSERVER, Apr. 29, 2004.

Garnick, D.W.; Luft, H.S,; Robinson, J.C,; Tetreault, J, *Appropriate Measures of Hospital Market Areas,* 22 (1987).

Garrison LP Jr, *Assessment of the effectiveness of supply-side cost-containment measures* HEALTH CARE FINANCING REV. p.13-20 (1991).

Gaskill, M, *Effects of CON Repeal Still Unclear,* 44. HEALTHTEX. p. 9 (1989 Feb).

Gaumer G; Sumner M; Boland J, *Prospective reimbursement in Connecticut,* 6. TOPICS IN HEALTH CARE FINANCINGp. 51-7 (1979 Fall).

Gay PC; Dellinger RP; Shelhamer JH; Offord K, *The practice of critical care medicine. A national survey report. ACCP Council on Critical Care,* 104. CHESTp.271-8 (1993 Jul).

Gaynor D, *Lahey Clinic.* HEALTH PAC BULL.p.22-7 (1977 Jul-Aug).

Gaynor, M,; G.E. Anderson, *Uncertain Demand, The Structure of Hospital Costs, and The Cost of Empty Beds,* 14. J. OF HEALTH ECONOMICS (1995).

Gee, Preston, *Healthcare Extra: Are You Ready For 'Big Box' Healthcare?* (Sep 27, 2004), *available at* http://www.healthleaders.com/news/print.php?contentid=58603.

Gelber BR, *Certificate of Need and aviation,* 74. NEB. MED. J.p.171 (1989 Jul).

George, Eddie, *The need in this CON is real,* MOD. HEALTHCARE, June 24, 2002, at p. 21.

George, John, *Lawmakers start push to renew hospital restrictions,* BUS. J.

George, John, *N. J. hospitals fail in bid for cardiac programs,* PHILA. BUS. J, 2/27/04.

George, John, *State rejects 2 heart program proposals,* PHILA. BUS. J, Aug, 4, 2003.

George, John, *Yet another med center to offer open-heart, available at* Bizjournals.com.

George, John. *Lawmakers start push to renew hospital restrictions,* PHILADELPHIA BUS. J. *(Sept. 26, 2004) available at* http://msnbc.msn.com/id/6092598/.

Gerena, Charles, *Putting on the brakes: Certificate of need regulations try to steer health-care supplies, but it's hard to keep them from fishtailing* (10/23/2004), *available at* http://www.rich.frb.org/pubs/regionfocus/spring04/breaks.html.

Gershenfeld S, *Most-often-asked questions about swing beds under the new laws,* 25. MICH. HOSP.p.27-8 (1989 Feb).

Geuder L, *Health planning: states prepare for expected CON changes,* 56. HOSP.p.81-2, 84 (1982 Dec 16).

Gibson RW, *Is the psychiatrist expendable?: reflections thirteen years later,* 14. PSYCHIATRIC HOSP.p.2-Oct (1983 Winter).

Gibson, Ashley M, *Capital Health will invest $5M in Southeast growth,* CHARLOTTE BUS. J, September 20, 2002, at 2.

Gibson, Ashley M, *CHS buying Christenbury surgery centers,* CHARLOTTE BUS. J, 10/14/2004.

Gibson, Ashley M, *CHS expands and Presby breaks ground for new women's center: good news,* CHARLOTTE BUS. J, December 27, 2002, at 3 p.

Gibson, Ashley M, *CMC spreads its wings,* CHARLOTTE BUS. J, Apr. 4, 2003.

Gibson, Ashley M, *Ed Case leaves Presby as hospital pushes expansion,* CHARLOTTE BUS. J, 1/5/04.

Gibson, Ashley M, *Focusing on child care: Levine project at CHS steps up growing regional trend,* CHARLOTTE BUS. J.

Gibson, Ashley M, *Hospitals to boost care by nurse,* CHARLOTTE BUS. J, Sept. 24,2004.

Gibson, Ashley M, *Huntersville is siding with Presby in battle over hospital project,* CHARLOTTE BUS. J, August 23, 2002, at 2.

Gibson, Ashley M, *Huntersville still key for Presbyterian,* THE BUS. J, Mar. 11, 200.

Gibson, Ashley M, *Judge: State should withdraw Presby permit,* CHARLOTTE BUS. J, November 27, 2002.

Gibson, Ashley M, *NorthEast Medical wins MRI approval,* BUS. J.

Gibson, Ashley M, *Novant makes waves in Lake Norman market,* BUS. J. OF THE GREATER TRIAD AREA, September 16, 2002, at 3.

Gibson, Ashley M, *Presby Makes Waves in Lake Norman Market* (Aug. 2, 2002), *available at* charlotte.bizjournals.com.

Gibson, Ashley M, *State OKs new Presby hospital, available at* Bizjournals.com.

Gibson, Ashley M. *State oks Presby hospital in Huntersville,* CHARLOTTE BUS. J. *(2002) available at*http://charlotte.bizjournals.com.

Gibson, Ashley, *Gaston Hospice gets OK for new $2 million home,* CHARLOTTE BUS. J, 11/17/03.

Gil, Gideon, *MRI Centers open without state OK: Companies say law does not apply to them,* COURIER-J, 12/1/03.

Ginsburg DH, *Antitrust and the new competition in health care: excerpts,* 17. MEDICAL PRODUCT SALESp.39-42 (1986 Apr).

Gish, Ryan, *Measuring strategic success* HEALTHCARE FIN. MGMT. (August 2002).

Gitomer, Jeffery, *Time to ask yourself some life questions,* CINCINNATI BUS. J, Jul. 16, 2004.

Gittler, Josephine, *Hospital cost containment in Iowa: A Guide for state public policymakers,* 69. IOWA L. REV.p.1263-1349 (July 1984).

Glassman, M.L, *Can HMOs Wield Market Power? Assessing Antitrust Liability in the Imperfect Market for Health Care Financing,* 46. AM. U. L. REV. (1996).

Glover, Lynne, *As disease rises, so do centers: More heart centers could mean higher health care costs,* PITTSBURGH BUS. TIMES, Jun. 4, 2004.

Goins, Tony, *Legislators may tackle specialty hospitals*, DAYTON BUS. J, 02/26/2002, at 2 p.

Goins, Tony, *State legislators may take crack at a specialty hospitals* COLUMBUS BUS. FIRST *(2002) available at* http:/ /columbus.bizjournals.com

Goldberg LG; Greenberg W, *The determinants of HMO enrollment and growth,* 16 (1981 Winter).

Goldberg, L.G.; Greenberg, W, *The Response of the Dominant Firm to Competition,* 20. HEALTH CARE MGMT. REV. (1995).

Goldowsky SJ, *A full plate,* 71. R.I. MED. J.p.51-2 (1988 Feb).

Golub, Steven, *The Role of medicare reimbursement in contemporary hospital finance,* AM. J. L. AND MED. Vol. 11, no. 501 (1986) *available at* http://80-web.lexis.nexis.com

Gonzales, Angela, *Ambulance exec starting rival company, available at* Bizjournals.com.

Gonzalez, Gina, *Cardiac Care Services Expanding for Jerseyans,* 3. N.J. HEALTHCARE p. 8-10 (1990 Fall).

Gordan, Jennifer, *Kindred to open hospital within Frazier Rehab Institute: Officials plan to hire about 45 staff members, spend more than $1 million on facility renovations,* BUS. FIRST, Dec. 15, 2003.

Gordan, Jennifer, *Two health-care projects approved; moratorium is limiting CON filings,* BUS. FIRST THE WK. BUS. NEWSPAPER OF GREATER LOUISVILLE, Mar. 3, 2003.

Gordon, Jennifer, *$10 million personal-care facility planned for Middletown,* BUS. FIRST, Apr. 2, 2004.

Gordon, Jennifer, *Area sleep centers expand to meet increasing demand, available at* Bizjournals.com.

Gordon, Jennifer, *Baptist Hospital East updating its master plan: Plan calls for emergency room expansion, traffic pattern changes, additional MRI unit,* BUS. FIRST, 9/8/03, at 3 p.

Gordon, Jennifer, *Brown Center adding wing for new equipment,* BUS. FIRST, 9/22/03, at 2 p.

Gordon, Jennifer, *Caritas Opens Geriatric Psychiatry Unit at Peace Center: Texas Company Hired to Manage 20-Bed Unit After $900,000 Renovation* (June 28, 2002), *available at* louisville.bizjournals.com.

Gordon, Jennifer, *Crisis or competition?: Hospital officials voice concern that specialty centers erode profits,* BUS. FIRST, 9/8/03, at 4 p.

Gordon, Jennifer, *EPI Corp. to buy bed licenses, move them to East End: Relocation of personal-care beds one of $17.2 million in health care projects OK'd by state officials June 2,* BUS. FIRST OF LOUISVILLE, June 14, 2004.

Gordon, Jennifer, *EPI gets green light to move beds from Briarwood: Other CON applications would transfer personal care beds and,* BUS. FIRST THE WK. BUS. NEWSPAPER OF GREATER LOUISVILLE, June 30, 2003.

Gordon, Jennifer, *Hospital officials unsure of CON moratorium's effect,* BUS. FIRST OF LOUISVILLE, 1/24/2003, at 3 p.

Gordon, Jennifer, *Hospitals file CON applications to add MRI services,* BUS. FIRST, May 3, 2004.

Gordon, Jennifer, *Hospitals may be allowed to add MRIs,* BUS. FIRST OF LOUISVILLE, 2/27/04.

Gordon, Jennifer, *JHHS files plans for Bullitt County medical center,* BUS. FIRST, 7/28/20041, at 3 p.

Gordon, Jennifer, *JHHS plans $35.5 million Bullitt County med center,* BUS. FIRST OF LOUISVILLE, December 6, 2002, at 2.

Gordon, Jennifer, *Medicaid, CON are top health legislation priorities,* BUS. FIRST, Jan. 11, 2002.

Gordon, Jennifer, *Nearly $5 Million Being Invested at Norton Southwest: Projects Include Expansion of Emergency Room, New Women's Pavilion* (July 26, 2002), *available at* louisville.bizjournals.com.

Gordon, Jennifer, *Norton Suburban begins construction on cancer unit,* BUS. FIRST, Dec. 8, 2003.

Gordon, Jennifer, *Norton Suburban, Baptist East to add acute-care beads*, BUS. FIRST OF LOUISVILLE, September 30, 2002, at 3.

Gordon, Jennifer, *Norton suburban, Baptist east to add acute-care beds: Hospital officials cite need to convert existing units to accommodate increasing patient volume in east end*, BUS. FIRST OF LOUISVILLE *(September 27, 2002) available at*http://louisville.bizjournals.com/louisville/stories/2002/09/30/story4.html

Gordon, Jennifer, *Norton to expand Mount Washington practice* (November 1, 2002), *available at* louisville.bizjournals.com.

Gordon, Jennifer, *Norton to move beds at cost of $3.5 million*, BUS. FIRST, 12/1/03.

Gordon, Jennifer, *Pine Tree Villa receives state approval to relocate 186 beds*, BUS. FIRST, 9/8/03, at 2 p.

Gordon, Jennifer, *Proposals for rehab facilities challenged: concerns raised by state health plan; competitors could derail applications*, BUS. FIRST, at 1-3.

Gordon, Jennifer, *Providers file to relocate facilities: Norton, RMS Outpatient Therapy apply for state approval*, BUS. FIRST, 12/1/03.

Gordon, Jennifer, *Rehab agency move to enhance visibility*, BUS. FIRST, 12/1/03.

Gordon, Jennifer, *State officials approve three health care applications: projects include license and location changes, adding nursing beds*, BUS. FIRST OF LOUISVILLE, December 2, 2002, at pp. 2.

Gordon, Jennifer, *State requires formal review for rehab agency applications*, BUS. FIRST, Apr. 12, 2002.

Gordon, Jennifer, *Three hospitals file plans for new diagnostic services*, BUS. FIRST OF LOUISVILLE, December 27, 2002, at 2 p.

Gordon, Jennifer, *University hospital opens geriatric psychiatry unit*, BUS. FIRST OF LOUISVILLE, Jun 14, 2004.

Gordon, Jennifer. *Norton, U of L aim high with plans for cancer hospital,* BUS. FIRST OF LOUISVILLE *(2002) available at* http://louisville.bizjournals.com.

Gould, Perry. M.D, *Why I want imaging On-site: A Radiation oncologist explains why he elected to install imaging equipment in his freestanding cancer treatment facility, available at* http://www.imagingeconomics.com/library/tools/printengine.asp?printArticleID=200409-02.

Gousse GC; Nightingale CH; Dionne GP; Meehan J, *Applying for a certificate of need for unit dose and i.v. admixture services in a Connecticut hospital,* 41. AM. J. OF HOSP. PHARMACYp.2029-32 (1984 Oct).

Grabowski DC, *Medicaid reimbursement and the quality of nursing home care,* 20. J. OF HEALTH ECONOMICSp.549-69 (2001 Jul).

Grabowski, David; Morrisey, Michael, *Does the repeal of certificate-of-need laws pose a significant threat to state medicaid budgets?*, 13. INQUIRY p. 146-155 (Summer 2003).

Grabowski, David; Ohsfeldt, Robert L.; Morrisey, Michael A, *The Effects of CON repeal on Medicaid nursing home and long-term care expenditures* INQUIRY p. 146-155 (Summer 2003).

Graham J, *Cleveland Clinic's plans to build hospital in Florida worrying other facilities in state,* MOD. HEALTHCARE, 1987 Nov 6, at 110-1.

Graham, Scott, *Certificate of greed: State's regulatory approval program at forefront of debate over who can offer health care services*, BALT. BUS. J, 2/20/04.

Graham, Scott, *St. Agnes fighting to start open-heart surgery*, BALT. BUS. J, January 21, 2002.

Gramm P, *Congressman Gramm favors eventual abolishment of CON to pave way for competition model,* REV. - FEDERATION OF AM. HOSP, 1980 Aug, at 20-1.

Grayson, Mary, *The Second Time* H&HN p. 8 (August 2002).

Grazier, K.L, *Managed Care and Hospitals,* 44. J. OF HEALTHCARE MGMT. (1999).

Greaney, Thomas L, *Competitive reform in health care: The vulnerable revolution,* 5 (Winter 1988).

Green MJ, *Court to consider Medicare reimbursement for cost of compliance with CON condition,* 3. HEALTH L. VIGILp.6-May (1980 May 16).

Green MJ, *Federal district court upholds Medicare reimbursement of state-imposed certificate of need costs,* 5. HEALTH L. VIGILp.8-Jul (1982 Jun 11).

Green, L. V.; Nguyen, V, *Strategies for Cutting Hospital Beds: The Impact on Patient Service,* 36 (Jun 2001).

Greenberg, James; Kropf, Roger, *A Case-mix method for developing health planning criteria for hospital services,* 19. MED. CARE p. 1083-94 (Nov. 1981).

Greenberg, W, *Marshfield Clinic, Physician Networks, and the Exercise of Monopoly Power,* 33 (1998 Dec).

Greenberg, W, *Private Antitrust as a Public Good,* 8. LOY. CONSUMER L. REV. (1995-1996).

Greenblatt, Sarah, *St. Peter's wins round, but dispute over care continues* ROMAN CATHOLIC DIOCESE OF METUCHEN.

Greene J, *3 companies file CON requests for Fla. long-term-care ventures,* MOD. HEALTHCARE, 1995 Oct 2, at 6.

Greene J, *Capital expenditure law creates rift in Wisconsin,* MOD. HEALTHCARE, 1994 Jul 25, at 28, 30, 32.

Greene J, *Columbia/HCA plans new Florida hospital,* MOD. HEALTHCARE, 1994 Jul 11, at 30.

Greene J, *Fla. rejects Columbia's CON request,* MOD. HEALTHCARE, 1996 Jan 15, at 6.

Greene J, *Ga. hospitals duel over CON reform,* MOD. HEALTHCARE, 1995 Oct 2, at 29.

Greene J, *Ga. not-for-profits win CON battle,* MOD. HEALTHCARE, 1996 Mar 25, at 66.

Greene J, *Humana wins Ky. vote,* MOD. HEALTHCARE, 1990 Apr 9, at 3.

Greene J, *Judge overrules Miss. CON approval,* MOD. HEALTHCARE, 1994 Jun 13, at 24.

Greene J, *Miss. links CON, community benefit,* MOD. HEALTHCARE, 1994 Mar 28, at 22.

Greene J, *Mississippi lets smaller hospitals apply for CONs,* MOD. HEALTHCARE, 1994 May 9, at 32.

Greene J, *Ohio physicians face inquiries over MRIs,* MOD. HEALTHCARE, 1994 May 2, at 30.

Greene J, *Small obstetrical unit provokes big battle,* MOD. HEALTHCARE, 1993 Jan 25, at 6.

Greene, Jay, 'Ga, *Report Stirs the Pot on Charity Care Debate,* MOD. HEALTHCARE, June 24, 1996.

Greene, Jay, *Ga. report stirs the pot on charity-care debate,* MOD. HEALTHCARE, 1996, at p.64-65.

Greer, Jennifer, *Radiation therapy application from 2 hospitals are put on hold St. Mary's, North Kansas City involved in state ruling on costs.*

Greeson, Thomas W. J.D, *New stark rules address self-referral exceptions* (10/1/2004), *available at* http://www.80-web.lexis-nexis.com.ezproxy.umuc.edu/universe/document?_m=f88cc5f267d41865ee53925cd.

Griffin S; Peterson D; Brower HT, *The problems and payoffs of setting up a rural health clinic,* NURSING & HEALTH CARE PERSPECTIVES, 1986 Feb, at 78-82.

Griffiths, Robert I,; Neil R. Powe,; Darrell J. Gaskin,; Gerard F. Anderson,; Gregory V. de Lissovoy,; Paul K. Whelton,, *The Production of Dialysis by For-Profit versus Not-For-Profit Freestanding Renal Dialysis Facilities,,* 29 (October 1994).

Grimaldi PL, *Cluster approach allows budgeting, planning with DRGs,* 65. HOSP. PROGRESSp.73-9 (1984 Jul-Aug).

Grimaldi PL, *Misconceptions about case-mix payments for nursing homes,* 68. HEALTH PROGRESSp.42-7 (1987 Apr).

Groeller, Greg, *State may deregulate hospital industry,* ORLANDO SENTINEL, Dec. 4, 2003.

Gross, Benjamin, *Certificate of Need: Background and Review of Recent Changes in Florida's Law* U. FLA. J. L. & PUB. POL'Y p. 183- 210 (1988).

Grosser, R. C.; Armstrong, M. I.; Hornik, J. A, *Developing new certificate-of-need regulations for inpatient care of children in New York state* (Aug 1991), *available at* www.ncbi.nlm.nih.gov/entrez/query.fcgi?cmd=Retrieve&db=PubMed&list_uids=18.

Grube M, *Positioning against niche competitors to reduce revenue erosion,* 16. HEALTH CARE STRATEGIC MGMT. p.5-Dec (1998 Dec).

Gruca, Thomas S.; Nath, Deepika, *Regulatory change, constraints on adaptation and organizational failure: An empirical analysis of acute care hospitals,* 15. STRATEGIC MGMT. J. p. 345-363 (June 1994).

Guadagnino, Christopher. Ph.D, *Cancer center Competition intensifies, available at* http://www.physiciansnews.com/cover/302wp.html.

Gulley, O. David; Santerre, Rexford E, *The Effect of public policies on nursing home care in the united states,* 29. EASTERN ECONOMIC J. p. 93-104 (Winter 2003).

Haas Erwin J, MD, FACP,, *Certificate of Need Laws Increase Medical Care Costs, letter to the editor,,* 92. MICH. MED.p.6-May (1993 Mar).

Hackey, Robert B, *New Wine in Old Bottles Certificate of Need Enters the 1990s,,* 18. J. OF HEALTH POLITICS, POL'Y & L.p.927-35 (Winter 1993).

Hallam K, *A rivalry gets ugly. Florida hospital's antitrust suit bypasses state, federal regulators,* MOD. HEALTHCARE, 1998 May 11, at 41-2.

Hallam K, *Bon Secours plan to move Va. hospital,* MOD. HEALTHCARE, 1999 Jul 12, at 18.

Hallam K, *Charity care at issue in Bon Secours' CON,* MOD. HEALTHCARE, 1999 Nov 8, at 36.

Hallam K, *Growing strong. New government programs, building boom among positive vital signs for children's hospitals,* MOD. HEALTHCARE, 1999 Feb 1, at 26-8.

Hallam K, *Providers try to take Dare. Two teams vie for CON approval to build hospital in N.C,* MOD. HEALTHCARE, 1998 Sep 21, at 32.

Hallam K, *Some see contradictions in hospital's doings,* MOD. HEALTHCARE, 1999 Oct 25, at 9.

Hallam, Kristin, *Ga. hospital pays up over CON charges,* MOD. HEALTHCARE, June 29, 1998, at 1.

Halthon ML, *Hospice: the promises and the problems,* 17. NURSING MGMT.p.72-6 (1986 Apr).

Hamilton, Reed, *Barriers to hospital diversification: The regulatory environment,* 24. DUQUESNE L. REV. p. 425-453.

Hammer L, *Hospital diversification: evaluating alternatives,* 44. AM. J. OF HOSP. PHARMACYp.1051-5 (1987 May).

Hammer, Douglas J, *The review of institutional health services: the role and liability of the health systems agency governing body,* 1978. UTAH L. REV. p.1-2, 59-82.

Hannan EL; Racz M; Kavey RE; Quaegebeur JM; Williams R, *Pediatric cardiac surgery: the effect of hospital and surgeon volume on in-hospital mortality,* 101. PEDIATRICSp.963-9 (1998 Jun).

Hannan EL; Rouse RL; Barnett R; Uppal P, *Methods for developing relative need criteria to accompany a health care capital expenditure limit,* 12. J. OF HEALTH POLITICS, POL'Y & L.p.113-36 (1987 Spring).

Hansbarger, L. Clark, *West Virginia's department of health: Philosophy and direction,* 78. THE W.V. MEDICAL J. p. 41-5.

Hard R, *Voluntary tech assessment: a CON alternative?,* 65. HOSP.p.72 (1991 Jul 5).

Harner, Ivan C, *Corporate reorganization: Today's challenge,* at p. 60-68.

Harper, Jim, *CON commentary a laughter,* MOD. HEALTHCARE, December 2, 2002, at p. 24.

Harrington C; Carrillo H; Wellin V; Miller N; LeBlanc A, *Predicting state Medicaid home and community based waiver participants and expenditures, 1992-1997,* 40. GERONTOLOGISTp.673-86 (2000 Dec).

Harris S, *Certificate of need,* 7. J. AM. HEALTH CARE ASS'N.p.55-8 (1981 Jan).

Hash MM, *Health planning and the CON: changing directions,* 22. MICH. HOSP.p.27-32 (1986 Jul).

Hatch SW; Tuthill JP, *Hospitals should finance medical office buildings,* 53. HOSP.p.104-6, 108 (1979 Apr 16).

Haukebo, Kristen, *Jewish hospital can transfer certificate: Rival Norton Healthcare may appeal decision,* COURIER-J, at 1-2.

Havighurst, Clark C, *Doctors and hospitals in an antitrust perspective on traditional relationships* DUKE L. J. p. 1071-1163 (December 1984).

Havighurst, Clark C, *Health Maintenance Organizations and the Health Planners,* 1978. UTAH L. REV. p. 1-2, 123-154.

Hawkins, Lee, *Detroit auto makers fight local hospitals' building plans,* WALL STREET J, Jan. 20, 2004.

Hawryluk M, *Federal funds supplement assisted living,* 23. PROVIDERp.29-30 (1997 Oct).

Hawryluk M, *States reassess certificate of need statutes,* 23. PROVIDERp.21-2 (1997 Feb).

Health and Human services Department, *Healthy People 2010: Understanding and Improving Health.* (2000).

Health Care Advisory Board, *States without CON laws have higher CABG mortality rates,* THE DAILY BRIEFING, 2/12/02.

Health Resources Administration, Public Health Service, HHS, *Health Systems Agencies and State Health Planning and Development Agencies; Certificate of Need Reviews: Notice Regarding Adjustment of the Expenditure Minimum for Capital Expenditures and the Expenditure Minimum for Annual Operating Costs,* 47. FED. REG. p. 13414-5 (1982 Mar 30).

Health Resources and Services Administration, PHS, HHS, *Health System Agencies and State Health Planning Development Agencies; Certificate of Need Reviews: Notice Regarding Adjustment of the Expenditure Minimum for Capital Expenditures and the Expenditure Minimum for Annual Operating Costs,* 50. FED. REG. p. 14027 (1985 Apr 9).

Health Resources and Services Administration, Public Health Service, HHS, *Health Systems Agencies and State Health Planning and Development Agencies: Certificate of Need Reviews - Notice regarding adjustment of the expenditure minimum for capital expenditures and the expenditure minimum for annual operating costs,* 48. FED. REGISTER p. 15539 (1983 Apr 11).

Health Resources and Services Administration, Public Health Service, HHS, *Health Systems Agencies and State Health Planning Development Agencies: Certificate of Need Reviews - Notice regarding adjustment of the expenditure minimum for capital expenditures and the expenditure minimum for annual operating costs,* 49. FED. REGISTER p. 18899 (1984 May 3).

Healthcare Alabama, *Pros and CONS: Is there still a need for certificate of need?,* HEALTHCARE AL, Spring 1998, at p. 4-5, 7-8.

Healthcare Review, *PHRG evaluates CON in Maine* (Oct. 22, 2001).

HealthLeaders News, *Hospitals: A battle for Hearts and Market Share.*

Heaster, Randolph, *Missouri health panel approves projects for KC area hospitals* (March 27, 1992).

Heaster, Randolph, *State health agency OK's expansion at St. Joseph; Outpatient area was part of larger plan rejected in January* (March 24, 1992).

Heitler, George *Antitrust and third party insurers* AM. J. L. AND MED. Vol. 8, no. 251 (1982) *available at* http://80-web.lexis-nexis.com

Held, Philip J.; Port, Friedrich K.; Wolfe, Robert A.; Stannard, David C.; Carroll, Caitlin E.; Daugridas, John T.; Bloembergen, Wendy E.; Greer, Joel W.; Hakin, Raymond M, *The Dose of hemodialysis and patient mortality*, KIDNEY INTERNATIONAL, 1996, at p. 550-556.

Heller DL, *Structuring ambulatory care projects to minimize problems with regulatory constraints,* 11. J. OF AMBULATORY CARE MGMT.p.23-7 (1988 Nov).

Hellinger FJ, *The effect of certificate-of-need legislation on hospital investment,* 13. INQUIRYp.187-93 (1976 Jun).

Hempling, Randall, *CON a waste of effort*, MOD. HEALTHCARE, June 24, 2002, at p. 21.

Hensley S, *The patient or the wallet. N.H. hospitals battle over open-heart surgery CONs,* MOD. HEALTHCARE, 1997 Aug 25, at 24.

Hensley, Scott, *The Ghost of CON*, MOD. HEALTHCARE, Feb 17, 1997.

Hernandez, Ruben, *Mexican TV network now in Phoenix* (Jul. 26, 2004), *available at* http://phoenix.bizjournals.com/phoeniz/stories/2004/07/26/story4.html?t=printable.

Herr WW, *Taking a deep breath over capital payments,* 45. HEALTHCARE FIN. MGMT.p.18-9, 22-4, 26 passim (1991 Apr).

Herron, Sandra K. *Essential rural healthcare provider access act: Prohibit exclusion of essential rural health care providers from health benefits plans* GA. ST. U. L. REV. Vol. 15, no. 143 (1998) *available at* http://80-web.lexis-nexis.com

Hershey N; Robinson D, *Health planning and certificate of need: the quality dimension,* 1. HEALTH POL'Y Q.p.243-68 (1981 Winter).

Herzlinger R, *Can we control health care costs?*, 56. HARVARD BUS. REV.p.102-10 (1978 Mar-Apr).

Hesse, Gregory G. *More from the labor law front* ABI JNL. LEXIS Vol. 2000, no. 170 (2000) *available at* http://80-web.lexis-nexis.com

Heym RH, *Expansion planning and design: the vital process,* 13. J. OF LONG TERM CARE ADMIN.p.100-4 (1985 Fall).

Heym, Richard H, *Cost strategies for filing CONs: Balancing quality with cost efficiency,* COTEMPORARY LONGTERM CARE, 1990 Jan, at p. 40-2, 46, 82.

Hicok C, *Pushing ahead for CON reform,* 28. MICH. HOSP.p.19 (1992 Jan-Feb).

Hiland, Harriett, *Emory Clinic can't open heart lab, state rules, available at* Bizjournals.com.

Hill-Chinn L, *Health planning status reported by AHA's Office of Public Policy Analysis,* 7. HEALTH L. VIGIL p. suppl 1-6 (1984 Apr 13).

Hill-Chinn L, *State legal initiatives. Health planning status reported by AHA's Office of Public Policy Analysis,* 6. HEALTH L. VIGIL p. suppl 1-7 (1983 Sep 2).

Hill-Chinn L, *State legislators act on health planning despite Congressional delays,* 6. HEALTH L. VIGILp.2-Oct (1983 Apr 1).

Hill-Chinn L, *Status report: health planning and capital expenditure regulation,* 7. HEALTH L. VIGIL p. suppl 1-12 (1984 Dec 7).

Hillman AL; Schwartz JS, *The adoption and diffusion of CT and MRI in the United States. A comparative analysis,* 23. MED. CAREp.1283-94 (1985 Nov).

Himmelblau, Betty, *Texas Health Facilities Commission,* 38. TEX. HOSP. p. 17- 19 (1982 Dec).

Hirshfeld EB, *CONs shield hospitals from antitrust challenges,* MOD. HEALTHCARE, 1984 Jun, at 192-4.

Hirth RA; Chernew ME; Orzol SM, *Ownership, competition, and the adoption of new technologies and cost-saving practices in a fixed-price environment,* 37. INQUIRYp.282-94 (2000 Fall).

Hirth, Richard A, *Practice patterns, case mix, Medicare payment policy, and dialysis facility costs* (February 1999).

Hirth, Richard A,, *Competition Between For-Profit and Non-Profit Health Care Providers: Can it Help Achieve Social Goals?,* 54. MED. CARE RES. & REV. (December 1997).

Hitt DH, *What kind of payment? A community hospital perspective.* (1992).

Hoch LJ, *Recruiting physicians without inviting trouble,* 70. HEALTH PROGRESSp.50-4 (1989 May).

Hoerger, T.J, *'Profit' Variability in For-profit and Not-for-profit Hospitals,* 10. J. OF HEALTH ECONOMICS (October 1991).

Hogan AJ, *Long-range hospital capital requirements planning: the state of the art, a proposal for change,* 18. SOCIO-ECONOMIC PLAN. SCI.p.263-71 (1984).

Holcomb B, *Planners eye Michigan effort to trim 5,000 hospital beds,* 2. HEALTH CARE WK.p.1, 15 (1979 Jan 22).

Holoweiko, Mark, *How states plan to regulate physician supply: With health planners moving to control the number and kind of doctors in any area, you might one day have to certify that patients need you,* 57. MED. ECONOMICS p. 79-84.

Holyoke, Larry, *BJC, HealthSouth partner on rehab center,*, ST. LOUIS BUS. J, September 11, 1998.

Holyoke, Larry, *Gatesworth spends $3 million on expansion; considers Alzheimer's unit,* ST. LOUIS BUS. J.

Holyoke, Larry, *SSM backs off plan to build $8 million outpatient center* MONEY & MED. (September 6-12, 1999).

Holyoke, Larry, *Unity, state question need for new women's hospital* MONEY & MED. (September 6-12, 1999).

Holzberg, Harvey Fache A, *Opinion: Keeping the politics in health care* N.J. MED.

Honey RB, *A riled community attacks HSA plans,* 14. PATIENT CAREp.184, 186-7, 190 passim (1980 Aug 15).

Hong, Gary C.; Robinson, Cheryl L, *Independent ownership: Managing the price of quality* PROVIDER p. 14-16, 19 (July. 1990).

Hood, John, *Grassroots graft: Corruption in state governments* REASON (Aug./Sept. 1998).

Horty J, *Controversial decisions on CONs can generate lawsuits in protest,* MOD. HEALTHCARE, 1986 Mar 14, at 74.

Horty J, *Hospital exempt from antitrust liability because of exception to federal law,* MOD. HEALTHCARE, 1985 Aug 2, at 90.

Horty JF, *CON can't overrule M.D. staff procedure,* MOD. HEALTHCARE, 1978 Dec, at 57-8.

Horty JF, *CON process causes huge waste, duplication by providers, planners,* MOD. HEALTHCARE, 1980 Nov, at 104, 107.

Horty JF, *Court won't rule on CON inequity,* MOD. HEALTHCARE, 1979 Oct, at 90, 94.

Horty JF, *HSA must abide by its own rules, court says,* MOD. HEALTHCARE, 1979 Apr, at 70-1.

Horty JF, *Read laws as are, not as might be,* MOD. HEALTHCARE, 1980 Jun, at 88.

Horty, John F, *Court Quashes Humana Building Bid,* MOD. HEALTHCARE, 1984 Mar, at p. 178.

Hosp Community Psychiatry, *Developing new certificate-of-need regulations for inpatient care of children in New York State,* 42.p.829-33 (1991 Aug).

Hospital Purchasing News, *States Vary on CON Legislation,* 8. HPN HOSP. PURCHASING NEWS p. 42, 50-1 (1984 Sep).

Housewright, Ed, *Hospital boom intensifies need for additional nurses,* DALLAS MORNING NEWS, 11/30/03.

Howell JR, *Evaluating the impact of certificate-of-need regulation using measures of ultimate outcome: some cautions from experience in Massachusetts,* 19 (1984 Dec).

Howington, Patrick, *Medical center unveiled: Jewish Hospital's Bullitt County unit designed for expansion*, COURIER-J, May 12, 2004.

Hubbard, R. L, *The Allocation of Health Care Resources and its Effect on the Poor: Towards a Competitive Health Care System,* 683. FORDHAM URB. L. J. (Summer 1997).

Hudson T, *CON 'tailoring' comes to a head in Kentucky,* 64. HOSP.p.106 (1990 Apr 20).

Hudson, Terese, *Make no little plans. Community health planning is an antidote to a world in which the strong survive and the weak usually don't. But in an era of scaling back, does it have a future?,* 70. HOSP. & HEALTH NETWORKSp.47-8, 50, 52 (1996 May 5).

Hudson, Terese,, *State Laws: A Stumbling Block for Systems Integration*, 68.p.40-5 (1994 Apr 20).

Huff JW, *Certificate of Need and Public Law 93-641*, 65. J. OF THE MED. ASS'N OF GA.p.430-1 (1976 Nov).

Huff JW, *Certificate of need,* 64. J. OF THE MED. ASS'N OF GA.p.55-6 (1975 Feb).

Huff JW, *More on certificate of need,* 65. J. OF THE MED. ASS'N OF GA.p.468-9 (1976 Dec).

Hurst, O. Rey, *Texas Health Facilities Commission: Annual Reporting Requirements*, 36. TEX. HOSP. p. 9 (1981 Jan).

Hyland, Tim, *Surgery centers maybe next battleground*, BALT. BUS. J, Aug. 4, 2003.

Ikemoto, Lisa C, *When a hospital becomes Catholic* (12/29/2003), *available at* http://80-web.lexis-nexis.com/ezproxy.umuc.edu/universe/document?_m=01dfd3760e90d.

Imershein, Allen W.; Philip C. Rond III,; Mary P. Mathis, *Restructuring Patterns of Elite Dominance and the Formation of State Policy in Health Care,* 97. AM. J. OF SOCIOLOGY (Jan. 1992).

Intelligencer Journal, *Legislature kills law controlling PA health costs*, INTELLIGENCER J, December 4, 1996.

interview by AHPA Today in Health Planning (TIHP) with Thomas R. Piper, *CON Trends in America: A Panorama of change, available at* www.ahpanet.org.

Jackson, Cheryl, *Hospital Expansion Proposals to Face Fewer State Challenges*, AM. MED. NEWS CHICAGO, December 11, 2000.

Jackson, Cheryl, *Physicians build a hospital of their own*, AM. MED. NEWS, Oct. 16, 2000.

Jackson, Cheryl, *States rethinking need for certificate-of-need laws as fiscal health of hospitals wanes: A Boom in construction of new health care facilities has a few states fearing over saturation, leading them to reconsider tightening certificate-of-need rules* (Jul. 29, 2002), *available at* www.ama-assn.org/sci-pubs/amnews/pick_02/bisb0729.htm.

Jackson, Margaret, *Top docs, SSM to build hospital*, ST. LOUIS BUS. J, 7/9/99.

Jacobi, John V. *Competition law's role in health care quality* ANN. HEALTH L. Vol. 11, no. 45 (2002) *available at* http://80-web.lexis-nexis.com

Jacobson, Carol K, *Investor response to health care cost containment legislation: Is American health policy designed to fail?,* 37. ACAD. OF MGMT. J. p. 440-452 (April 1994).

Jaffe, Anna, *Care Providers Debate Need for CON Law*, BUS. J, April 20, 2001.

Jaffe, Anna, *Saint Luke's plans hospital in Lee's Summit*, BUS. J. OF KAN. CITY, Feb. 22, 2002, at p. 1-2.

Jaklevic, Mary C, *Cardiac-care Hotbed: Louisiana Gets Four New Facilities*, MOD. HEALTHCARE, at p.30-31.

James AE Jr, *Antitrust law and the practice of radiology,* 132. RADIOLOGYp.233-7 (1979 Jul).

James AE Jr; Sloan F; Blumstein J; Winfield AC; Pendergrass HP, *Certificate-of-need in an antitrust context,* 8. J. OF HEALTH POLITICS, POL'Y & L.p.314-9 (1983 Summer).

James AE Jr; Winfield AC; Rollo FD; Calvani T; Pendergrass HP, *Analysis of the combined effects of certificate-of-need legislation and changes in the granting of hospital privileges,* 145. RADIOLOGYp.229-31 (1982 Oct).

James, A. Everette,; Seymour Perry,; Susan E. Warner,; John E. Chapman,; Richard Zaner, *The Diffusion of Medical Technology: Free Enterprise and Regulatory Models in the U.S.A,* 17. J. OF MED. ETHICSp.150-5 (1991 Sep).

Japsen B, *Judge says Mich. hospital can't sue state to protest its rival's open-heart CON,* MOD. HEALTHCARE, 1993 Nov 22, at 32.

Japsen B, *Michigan hospital sues state over rival's open-heart CON; detractors question numbers,* MOD. HEALTHCARE, 1993 Nov 1, at 20.

Japsen B, *Plans for new Chicago hospital criticized,* MOD. HEALTHCARE, 1994 Jul 4, at 12.

Japsen B; Snow C, *Changing course. Columbia the buyer becomes Columbia the builder as the company seeks to overcome market impediments,* MOD. HEALTHCARE, 1997 Apr 14, at 50-2, 54-8, 60-2.

Japsen, Bruce, *Group challenges hospital agency seeks judicial review of board's decisions* (Dec. 1, 1998).

Japsen, Bruce, *How much did it cost?: Sales prices of some Columbia facilities may not be disclosed,* MOD. HEALTHCARE, Nov. 24, 1997, at p.16.

Japsen, Bruce,, *Ownership Counts, VHA Study Says,,* MOD. HEALTHCARE, November 24, 1997.

Jaspen, Bruce, *Board openings could affect decisions on hospital projects,* CHICAGO TRIBUNE, 3/11/04.

Jaspen, Bruce, *Columbia on media defense,* MOD. HEALTHCARE, at p. 56, 58.

Jaspen, Bruce, *Hospitals sick of planning board: Illinois regulatory panel exceeds its authority,* CHICAGO TRIBUNE, July 4, 1999.

Jaspen, Bruce, *Proposal would limit terms of health board,* CHICAGO TRIBUNE, February 22, 2000.

Jee M, *Perspectives. States rediscover certificate-of-need laws,* 47. MED. & HEALTH p. suppl 4 p. (1993 Feb 22).

Jee, Melissa, *Certificate-of-Need Laws Back in Style Again,,* 3. J. OF AM. HEALTH POL'Yp.59-61 (1993 Mar-Apr).

Jenkins, Colleen, *Hearts fixed here: Citrus Memorial Hospital is set to open the first open heart surgery center in the fast-growing county,* ST. PETERSBURG TIMES, 1/5/04.

Jergesen AD; Schulman EF, *What are the main junctures at which a hospital undertaking a construction project will need legal advice?,* 22. HOSP. F.p.34-5 (1979 Jul-Aug).

Johnson GC, *Assessment and approval of medical devices used in diagnostic imaging in the United States,* 22. ISR'L J. OF MED. SCI.p.505-18 (1986 Jul-Aug).

Johnson, Richard L, *Should hospital planning continue to be regulated?,* 2. HEALTH AFF.p.84-91 (Spring 1983).

Johnson, Spencer C, *Turning expectations into reality* MICH. HOSP. p. 5 (Feb. 1989).

Jones HM, *Certificate of need legislation for home health agencies in New York State.* NLN PUBLICATIONSp.9-Jan (1976).

Jordan, W. J.; Keenan, R. D, *An Early View of the Impact of Deregulation and Managed Care on Hospital Profitability and Net worth/Practitioner Application,* 46. J. OF HEALTHCARE MGMT. (May/June 2001).

Joskow, Paul L, *The Effects of competition and regulation on hospital bed supply and the reservation quality of the hospital,* 11. BELL J. OF ECONOMICS p. 421-447 (Autumn, 1980).

Journal of American Hospital Association, *Hospital agencies powers lie within law, court rules,* 53 (1979 Jun 1).

Kanaley, Reid, *Judge hints he'll OK Chesco hospital sale: The $100 million Phoenixville Hospital deal may be finalized by the end of the month* (Jun. 23, 2004), *available at* http://www.philly.com/mld/inquirer/news/local/8987687.htm?template=contentModules/printstor.

Kaplan, Mark E, *An economic analysis of Florida's hospital certificate of need program and recommendations for change*, 19. FLA. ST. U. L. REV. p.475-498 (Fall 1991).

Karash, Julius A, *Going up: Hospital expansions raise questions of need value*, THE KAN. CITY STAR, Nov. 30, 2003.

Karash, Julius A, *Hospital expansions raise questions of need, value* (11/30/03), *available at* www.kansascity.com/mld/kansascity/business/7377323.htm?template-contentModul.

Karash, Julius A, *Independence hospital proposal sent to state*, THE KAN. CITY STAR, Apr. 9, 2004.

Karash, Julius A, *Kansas City, Mo, Hospital sues over denial of application for new facility.* (July 3, 2002).

Karash, Julius A, *Medical center plan debated*, KANSAS CITY STAR, Jun 19, 2004.

Karash, Julius A, *St. Luke's proposal tests Missouri's certificate-of-need law* (May 20, 2003), *available at* www.kansascity.com/mld/business/5898269.htm?template=contentModul.

Karman III, John R, *Tumbleweed subsidiary buys former Kroger meat plant*, BUS. FIRST OF LOUISVILLE, Jul. 19, 2004.

Kass DI, *Economies of scale and scope in the provision of home health services*, 6. J. OF HEALTH ECONOMICSp.129-46 (1987 Jun).

Kasten: Braves, Hawks and Thrashers sale 'looms in future', ATLANTA BUS. CHRON, October 1, 2002, at 2.

Kates JA; Krella JM; Schoen EJ, *Developing mobile lithotripsy services*, 7. HEALTHSPANp.7-Nov (1990 Mar).

Katz, Aaron et al, *Insurers consolidate, hospitals struggle financially.*

Katzman, Mitchell, *Freestanding Emergency Centers: Regulation and Reimbursement*, 11. AM. J. OF L. & MED. p.105-29 (1985).

Kazon PM, *New Hampshire court permits outpatient services without CON*, BUS. & HEALTH, 1988 Sep, at 48.

Keefe J, *MR regulation: opportunity, risk and the freedom to fail*, 6. RADIOLOGY MGMT.p.30-2 (1984 Jun).

Keeler, T,; J. Ying, *Hospital Costs and Excess Bed Capacity: A Statistical Analysis*, 78. REV. OF ECONOMICS AND STATISTICS (1996).

Kelly, Margo P, *Is your organization operationally ready to be a Medicare PSO (provider-sponsored organization)* HEALTHCARE FIN. MGMT. (June 1998).

Kendix, Michael, Ph.D,, *Dialysis Modality Selection among Patients Attending Freestanding Dialysis Facilities*, 18. HEALTH CARE FINANCING REV. (Summer 1997).

Kendix, Michael, Ph.D,, *Provision of Home Dialysis by Freestanding Renal Dialysis Facilities,*, 17. HEALTH CARE FINANCING REV. (Winter 1995).

Kenney, Genevieve M.; Dubay, Lisa C, *Explaining area variation in the use of Medicare home health services*, 30. MED. CARE p. 43-57 (Jan. 1992).

Kessler, Howard B, M.D.; Andrew H. Shaer, M.D.; Michael R. Clair, M.D.; Steven Edell, D.O, *Business of imaging: Opportunities abound, even in tough market* (October 1, 2000).

Kiel, Joan M, *How State Policy Affects Rural Hospital Consortia: The Rural Health Care Delivery System*, 71. THE MILBANK Qp.625-43 (1993).

Kim, John J. and Turner, Kathryn A. *Survey: Development in Maryland Law 1985-86: VIII. Health care* MD. L. REV. Vol. 46, no. 782 (1987) *available at* http://80-web.lexis-nexis.com

Kimberly, James, *Edward cancer center to grow: $13.9 million expansion planned for Naperville hospital*, CHICAGO TRIBUNE, May 5, 2004.

Kimmey, James R, *Health Planning Agencies: Their Expanding Role in Containing Health Care Costs*, 32. PATHOLOGIST p. 553-557 (1978 Sep).

Kimmey, James R, *Who cares for the poor in St. Louis?* HEALTH PLAN. TODAY p. 3, 4 (2nd Quarter 2000).

Kimmith DV, *A national look at CON laws*, 25. MICH. HOSP.p.29-32 (1989 Feb).

Kinder, Peter, *To-Do lists for 2002: Security, health care, education top state needs*, ST. LOUIS POST-DISPATCH, Jan. 3, 2002, at p.B7.

Kinney ED, *Arizona business coalition seek initiative to impose rate-setting and CON on Arizona hospitals*, 6. HEALTH L. VIGILp.7-May (1983 Nov 25).

Kinney ED, *Coordinating rate setting and planning in states with mandatory hospital rate regulation. What makes a difference?*, 8. J. OF L. MED.p.397-435 (1987 Sep).

Kinney ED, *Court enjoins completion of a hospital parking lot because affiliated holding company failed to obtain a CON*, 6. HEALTH L. VIGILp.18-9 (1983 Oct 28).

Kinney ED, *Fourth Circuit requires limited rule of reason to be applied in hospital antitrust planning case*, 5. HEALTH L. VIGILp.7-Jun (1982 Nov 12).

Kinney ED, *Virginia Supreme Court requires CON for a hospital open heart surgery unit reactivated after one year*, 7. HEALTH L. VIGILp.1-Oct (1984 May 11).

Kirchheimer B, *A tale of two COPAs (Certificate of Public Advantage)*, MOD. HEALTHCARE, 2000 Jan 31, at 3-Dec.

Kirchheimer B, *Back in the feud. CON battle between Novant, Carolinas HealthCare continues to escalate*, MOD. HEALTHCARE, 2001 Feb 26, at 21.

Kirchheimer B, *CON dispute may lead to closure of Miss. hospital*, MOD. HEALTHCARE, 1999 Nov 8, at 2, 16.

Kirchheimer B, *CON ruling threatens hospital. Unless decision is reversed on appeal, 3-year-old Miss. hospital must close by year-end*, MOD. HEALTHCARE, 1999 Nov 22, at 12.

Kirchheimer B, *S.C. system can't COPA with limits*, MOD. HEALTHCARE, 2000 Nov 27, at 18.

Kirchheimer, Barbara, *Getting in on the inside: 'Hospital-within-a-hospital' idea catching on in N.C. for long-term acute care*, MOD. HEALTHCARE, 2001 Jun 4, at p. 28-9.

Kirchheimer, Barbara, *N.C. denies CON for two systems*, MOD. HEALTHCARE, 1999 Nov 8, at p. 35.

Kittredge FI, *Utility regulation of the health-care industry: certificate-of-need laws as access controls*. L. MED. ANN.p.423-38 (1978).

Klaus, Krista, *Cancer treatments are more image-makers than moneymakers for hospitals*, BUS. J. SERVING METROPOLITAN KAN. CITY, 11/17/03.

Kleiman M, *What's in it for us? A consumer analysis of the 1979 Health Planning Act amendments*, 4. HEALTH L. PROJECT LIBR. BULL.p.328-36 (1979 Oct).

Klein, Sarah A, *Health planning board conflicts grow*, CHICAGO BUS, 07/01/2004.

Knestrick, Adrienne P, *CON process ensures quality of health care*, MEMPHIS BUS. J, October 7, 2002, at 2.

Knowles EW Jr, *Certificate of need: an approach to the process*, 1. HEALTH CARE PLAN. & MARKETINGp.27-34 (1981 Oct).

Kolb DS; Krueger DJ, *Controlling expansion of the nursing home industry: effects of prospective payment systems on capital formation*, 10. TOPICS IN HEALTH CARE FINANCINGp.77-87 (1984 Spring).

Kolkey, Jeff, *Federal investigation mires Mercy* (8/12/2004), *available at* http://www.nwherald.com/MainSection/281062296558626.php.

Kopit WG; McCann RW, *Toward a definitive antitrust standard for nonprofit hospital mergers,* 13. J. OF HEALTH POLITICS, POL'Y & L.p.635-62 (1988 Winter).

Kopit, William G.; Krill, Edward J.; Bonnie, Karen F, *Hospital decertification: legitimate regulation or a taking of private property?,* 1978. UTAH L. REV. p. 1-2, 179-210.

Kornblatt ES, *Mental health in health planning agencies,* 21. SOC. SCI. & MED.p.377-81 (1985).

Kosterlitz J, *So long, planning,* 18. NAT'L J.p.2476 (1986 Oct 11).

Kotelchuck R, *HSAs and cost control* HEALTH PAC BULL. (1979).

Kravitz, Katherine Betz, *Nonprofit hospital mergers and federal antitrust law: the quest for compatibility* (12/17/20), *available at* http://80-web.lexis-nexis.comezproxy.umuc.edu.universe/ document?_m=5d7a8b1b87db.

Kretikos, Eleni, *Regal lineage: The Toyal Restaurant has been reborn a few times over its century-long history, brining in new generations of locals each time,* WASHINGTON BUS. J.

Kropf R; Greenberg J, *A case-mix approach to the control of hospital capital expenditures,* 7. HEALTH CARE MGMT. REV.p.17-24 (1982 Spring).

Krueger, Jill, *Florida hospital refiles to build new facility,* ORLANDO BUS. J, January 15, 2002.

Kuntz E, *P.L. 96-79 changes CON processes,* MOD. HEALTHCARE, 1979 Nov, at 50-1.

Kuntz EF, *Planning laws survive cuts, face changes,* MOD. HEALTHCARE, 1982 Mar, at 86.

Kuperberg JR; Vogt EM, *Health planning scenario: 2000 A.D,* 3. AM. J. OF HEALTH PLAN.p.28-33 (1978 Jul).

Kuttner, Robert,, *Columbia/HCA and the Resurgence of the For-Profit Hospital Business, Special Report [part one]* NEW ENGLAND J. OF MED. (Aug 1, 1996).

Kuttner, Robert,, *Columbia/HCA and the Resurgence of the For-Profit Hospital Business, Special Report [part two]* NEW ENGLAND J. OF MED. (Aug 1, 1996).

LaBar C, *Long term care. Home health care,* 1. LONG TERM CARE Q.p.i-iv, 1-15 (1986 Fall).

Ladika, Susan, *Hospitals and government: Deregulation could ease expansion process,* TAMPA BAY BUS. J, 2/20/04.

Ladika, Susan, *In Depth: Health care,* BUS. J.

Lagoe, Ronald J,; Cheryl M. Noetscher,; Mark E. Murphy, *Combined Benchmarking of Hospital Outcomes and Utilization,* 18. NURSING ECONOMICS (March 2000).

Lamb, Howard, *Opinion: Drop. 12 promises are coming true,* DALLAS BUS. J, Sept. 27, 2004.

Landau TP, *A methodology for the analysis of rural primary health care delivery systems,* 11. COMPUTERS IN BIOLOGY & MED.p.51-72 (1981).

Landon TE; Schwarz JL, *State regulation of hospitals: how does it affect nursing employment?,* 17. J. OF HEALTH & HUM. SERVICES ADMIN.p.284-302 (1995 Winter).

Landrum, Laura B, *CON modified in Illinois* HEALTH PLAN. TODAY p. 7 (2nd Quarter 2000).

Lanning, Joyce A,; Michael E. Morrisey,; Robert L. Ohsfeldt, *Endogenous Hospital Regulation and Its Effects on Hospital and Non-Hospital Expenditures,* 3. J. OF REGULATORY ECONOMICSp.137-154 (1991).

Larkin H, *Deregulation spurs market information demand,* 61. HOSP.p.58 (1987 Dec 20).

Larkin H, *Regulation, fiscal pressure expand CEO planning role,* 64. HOSP.p.24-30 (1990 Mar 5).

Lave JR, *Cost containment policies in long-term care,* 22. INQUIRYp.23-Jul (1985 Spring).

Law, Dennis, *Catheterization lab at Saratoga Hospital is poised for growth* (June 21, 2002), *available at* Bizjournals.com.

Law, Dennis, *Saratoga hospital eyes $10 million ambulatory outpatient surgery center,* BIZJOURNALS.COM.

Lawson, Robert A, *Taking the CON out of health care costs,* PERSPECTIVE, at p.1-3.

Lawthers-Higgins A; Taft C; Hodgman J, *The impact of certificate of need on CT scanning in Massachusetts,* 9. HEALTH CARE MGMT. REV.p.71-9 (1984 Summer).

Lee KE; Liu K, *Knowing a review agency's acceptability range' may help in obtaining CON approval,* 56. HOSP.p.42 (1982 Nov 1).

Lee, Judith, *Hospitals expansion plans caught in own tangled web: The Very argument a health system made to keep three competing surgery centers on the drawing board has come back to haunt it,* OUTPATIENT SURGERY MAG, May 2003.

Leeds, Helen S, *Certificate of need: up for revision* HEALTH SYS. REV. p. 26-29 (Jan/Feb. 1996).

Lefko LA, *New certificate of need rules increase regulatory pressures,* 59. HOSP. TOPICSp.4-Dec (1981 May-Jun).

Lesage AD; Cope SJ; Pezeshgi S, *Assessing the needs for care of non-psychotic patients. A trial with a new standardized procedure,* 26. SOC. PSYCHIATRY & PSYCHIATRIC EPIDEMIOLOGYp.281-6 (1991 Dec).

Lesparre M, *An interview with Sen. Richard Schweiker (R-PA),* 51. HOSP.p.16a-16b, 16d, 16f (1977 Sep 16).

Levit, K. et. al, *National health expenditures in 1997: More slow growth,* 17. HEALTH AFF. (Nov/Dec 1998).

Levy MG; Covaleski MA; Johnson AC, *Intra-organizational strategic decision model in the certificate-of-need application process,* 7. HEALTH CARE MGMT. REV.p.25-36 (1982 Spring).

Lewis HL, *Deregulated planning may increase competition,* 55. HOSP.p.39-40 (1981 Dec 1).

Lewis TJ, *Community participation in the certificate-of-need process: a look at ten-taxpayer groups in Massachusetts,* 5. AM. J. OF L. & MED.p.215-30 (1979 Fall).

Lewis, Bill, *HCA will fight Saint Thomas surgery center,* TENNESSEAN, 10/14/03, at 2 p.

Lewis, Bill, *HMD fighting agency's refusal to allow hospital,* TENNESSEAN, May 14, 2004.

Lewis, Bill, *Ruling sets up hospital battle* (11/20/03), *available at* xgi.tennessean.com/cgi-bin/print/pr.pl.

Lewis, Bill, *State agency quashes bid for hospital in Brentwood* (Apr. 29, 2004), *available at* http://cgi.tennesean.com/cgi-bin/print/pr.pl.

Lichiello, P.; Madden, C. W, *Context and Catalysts for Change in Health Care Markets,* 15. HEALTH AFF. (Summer 1996).

Lieb, David A, *certificate of need requirements under review by legislature,* SOUTHEAST. MISSOURIAN, March 18, 2002, at 1.

Lieb, David A, *Lawmakers eye revisions to certificate of need,* JEFFERSON CITY NEWS TRIBUNE, Mar. 19, 2002.

Liebers, Emily, *New Jersey appellate court applies CON regulations retroactively* BENDER'S HEALTH CARE L. MONTHLY p 9-11.

Liggett SP, *An attempt to prevent private practitioners and Bryan Memorial Hospital in performing renal transplantation,* 73. NEB. MED. J.p.81 (1988 Apr).

Limbacher PB, *Celebrating CON approval. After two denials, Florida hospital's bed transfer OK'd,* MOD. HEALTHCARE, 1998 Jan 12, at 26.

Limbacher PB, *Disney gets 2nd CON denial for Fla. hospital,* MOD. HEALTHCARE, 1997 Jul 21, at 21.

Limbacher PB, *Disney's dream,* MOD. HEALTHCARE, 1997 Oct 20, at 30-3.

Lippman, H, *The Bottom Line on Length of Stay,* 19. BUS. & HEALTH (April 2001).

Lipson MJ, *Medical legislation: its effect on rehabilitation programs,* 58. ARCHIVES OF PHYSICAL MED. & REHABILITATIONp.386-92 (1977 Sep).

Long, Ray and Yednak, Crystal, *Hospitals hire lobby clout: Law bans contact with state panel,* CHICAGO TRIBUNE, Jun. 30, 2004.

Long, Ray; Yednak, Crystal, *Governor halts work of hospital regulators,* CHICAGO TRIBUNE, 7/22/2004.

Lovern E, *Scrapped project may set trend,* MOD. HEALTHCARE, 2000 Oct 23, at 3-Dec.

Lovern, Ed, *CON gamble: Bon Secours ups ante in V. battle with HCA,* MOD. HEALTHCARE, October 22, 2001, at p.28.

Luft HS; Frisvold GA, *Decision making in regional health planning agencies,* 4. J. OF HEALTH POLITICS, POL'Y & L.p.250-72 (1979 Summer).

Lundine, Susan, *Hospital pinched for space: Nearly new Osceola facility will embark on $43 million expansion,* ORLANDO BUS. J, at p.1-4.

Lundine, Susan. *Heart surgery rule gets new life in Senate,* ORLANDO BUS. J. *(2002) available at* http://orlando.bizjournals.com/orlando/stories/2002/03/04/story2.html.

Lutz S, *Cleveland Clinic, Tenet team up in South Florida,* MOD. HEALTHCARE, 1995 Jul 31, at 2.

Lutz S, *Columbia seeks OK to build in Florida,* MOD. HEALTHCARE, 1995 Aug 28, at 16.

Lutz S, *CON adds to Omaha confusion,* MOD. HEALTHCARE, 1995 May 22, at 8.

Lutz S, *La. ponders novel way to plug its 'dispro hole',* MOD. HEALTHCARE, 1994 Jun 27, at 62.

Lynk, William J,, *Antitrust Analysis and Hospital Certificate-of-Need Policy,* ANTITRUST BULL. (Spring 1987).

Lyons, Marie, *Analysis of cost containment strategies involving medical technology,* Jan. 2002, at p. 1-6.

MacEachern, Lillian, *Certificate of need: Year end report-2003.*

MacLeod GK, *Hospital cost containment: a voluntary program for Pennsylvania,* 4. HEALTH L. PROJECT LIBR. BULL.p.251-6 (1979 Aug).

MacStravic RE, *Inpatient bed needs for psychiatric care,* 5. ADMIN. IN MENTAL HEALTHp.14-20 (1977 Fall-Winter).

Madden, C. W, *Excess Capacity: Markets, Regulation, and Values,* 33. HSR: HEALTH SERVICES RES. (February 1999).

Magid, Dennis J, *Opening your new health facility—a discussion of process,* CONCERN CARE AGING, at p. 24-31.

Magnussen, J.; Mobley, L. R, *The Impact of Market Environment on Excess Capacity and the Cost of an Empty Hospital Bed,* 6. INTERNATIONAL J. OF THE ECONOMICS OF BUS. (November 1999).

Mahler J, *Barriers to coordinating health services regulatory programs,* 6. J. OF HEALTH POLITICS, POL'Y & L.p.528-41 (1981 Fall).

Majewski, Sue, *A need to compete,* MOD. HEALTHCARE, April 29, 2002, at p. 26.

Makar, Scott D, *Antitrust immunity under Florida's certificate of need program,* 19. FLA. ST. U. L. REV. p.149-190 (Summer 1991).

Mala T, *Explaining Alaska's Certificate of Need program,* 34. ALA. MED.p.144 (1992 Jul-Sep).

Manasse HR Jr; Stewart JE; Johnson KW, *Certificate of need and statement of social impact as requirements for new drug approvals,* 17. J. OF THE AM. PHARMACEUTICAL ASS'Np.567-71 (1977 Sep).

Mandel MD; Getson J, *Mandated long-range planning for hospitals—where is it going and why?,* 4. HEALTH CARE MGMT. REV.p.21-Sep (1979 Winter).

Mannies, Jo, *Bill would end review of hospital projects: Measure leaves state out of expansion plans.*

Manninen, Charles O, *MDPH reforms: Is 'appropriate' care lost in the cracks?,* 20. MICH. HOSP. p. 17, 19-20.

Manning, Joe, *Cardiac care hospital coming to Glendale: area medical community says 32-bed MedCath facility is not needed*, MILWAUKEE J. SENTINEL, at 1-3.

Manning, Margie and Margaret Jackson, *Cancer centers investing $83 million along Hwy 40*, ST. LOUIS BUS. J, September 20, 2002, at 3.

Manning, Margie, *$15 million assisted living facility planned for Clayton Road: Harris to replant Little Flower on property owned by Sunrise*, ST. LOUIS BUS. J, January 3, 2003.

Manning, Margie, *$500 million worth of medical projects under way*, ST. LOUIS BUS. J, April 24, 1998.

Manning, Margie, *$7million hospital project,*, ST. LOUIS BUS. J, June 23, 2000.

Manning, Margie, *Arch Medical enters cancer treatment center battle*, ST. LOUIS BUS. J, at p.1-3.

Manning, Margie, *Arch Medical Enters Cancer Treatment Center Battle* (April 1, 2002), *available at* stlouis.bizjournals.com.

Manning, Margie, *BJC cuts deals with insurers, boots income*, ST. LOUIS BUS. J, September 30, 2002, at 2.

Manning, Margie, *BJC cuts scope of project*, ST. LOUIS BUS. J.

Manning, Margie, *BJC speaks out on hospital*, ST. LOUIS BUS. J, December 10, 1999.

Manning, Margie, *BJC, HealthSouth plan Gamma Knife,*, ST. LOUIS BUS. J, October 17, 1997.

Manning, Margie, *BJC, SLU cut deal to share Gamma Knife site,*, ST. LOUIS BUS. J, December 19, 1997.

Manning, Margie, *Brown got $1.9 million from BJC after he stepped aside: Pay included*, ST. LOUIS BUS. J, Jan. 29, 2001, at p. 1-2.

Manning, Margie, *Committee approves Ranken Jordan's Certificate of Need*, ST. LOUIS BUS. J, April 8, 2002.

Manning, Margie, *Committee reviews changes for oversight of hospitals: Group wants to make Certificate of Need process less cumbersome*, ST. LOUIS BUS. J, Sept. 28, 200.

Manning, Margie, *Committee Reviews Changes for Oversight of Hospitals*, ST. LOUIS BUS. J, Sept 28, 2001.

Manning, Margie, *Divided we prosper: Since dissolution of Unity Health, former member hospital see revenue jump, building projects increase*, ST. LOUIS BUS. J, June 7, 2002.

Manning, Margie, *Doctor-owned Cardiac Lab to Open at SSM St. Joseph*, ST. LOUIS BUS. J, August 24-30, 2001, at p. 1.

Manning, Margie, *Health-care benefits: Case, Brown cash in on way out*, ST. LOUIS BUS. J, Dec. 28, 2001, at p. 1-3.

Manning, Margie, *Hospital systems unite on effort to reform regulation,*, ST. LOUIS BUS. J, April 6, 2001.

Manning, Margie, *Hospitals face $21 billion cut in Medicare payments: Rocklage says AHA will continue intense lobbying efforts to keep government funding* MONEY & MED.p.1 (April 26-May 2, 2002).

Manning, Margie, *Hospitals seek approval for $17 million in projects,*, ST. LOUIS BUS. J, June 29, 2001.

Manning, Margie, *Law pumps life into cardiac care unit*, ORLANDO BUS. J, May 14, 2004.

Manning, Margie, *Legislature opens door for heart program at hospitals*, TAMPA BAY BUS. J, May 14, 2004.

Manning, Margie, *Ranken Jordan seeks pediatric specialty license*, ST. LOUIS BUS. J, Feb. 1-7, 2002, at p. 5.

Manning, Margie, *St. Anthony's to purchase $2.5 million scanning system*, TAMPA BAY BUS. J, Apr. 1, 2004.

Manning, Margie, *Stein, SSM to expand St. Charles County Surgery* MONEY & MED. (August 2-8, 1999).

Manning, Margie, *Tenet cuts out a new market, plans surgery center in Festus,*, ST. LOUIS BUS. J, June 5, 1998.

Manning, Margie, *Tenet sues state regulators over Festus surgery center,*, ST. LOUIS BUS. J, October 9,1998.

Maressa VA, *Should certificate of need legislation be repealed?*, 81. J. OF THE MED. SOC'Y OF N.J.p.185 (1984 Mar).

Margolies, Dan, *Defense attorneys facing complex legal challenges,*, BUS. J, November 8, 1996.

Margolies, Dan; Bonar Menninger, *Indictment in Corruption Probe Expected,*, BUS. J, October 4, 1996.

Margolis RE, *Competitors can take advantage of certificate of need proceedings, rules 9th Circuit,* 9. HEALTHSPANp. 22-3 (1992 Apr).

Mari Edlin, *Will the Market Build to Suit?* (Nov 5, 1997).

Marmor TR, *New York's Blue Cross and Blue Shield, 1934-1990: the complicated politics of nonprofit regulation,* 16. J. OF HEALTH POLITICS, POL'Y & L.p.761-92 (1991 Winter).

Marschall B, *[The value of daily allowance certificates for sociomedical treatment]*, 153. UGESKRIFT FOR L'GERp.3623-6 (1991 Dec 16).

Marsh, Peter, *A certificate to fleece health consumers*, SEATTLE TIMES, Feb. 25, 1998.

Marsh, Peter, *A Certificate to fleece health consumers*, SEATTLE TIMES, February 25, 1998.

Marshall WW Jr, *On a model certificate of need statute,* 3. HEALTH CARE MGMT. REV.p.9-Jul (1978 Spring).

Marshall, Roger J, *A Review of Methods for the Statistical Analysis of Spatial patterns of Disease,* 154. J. OF THE ROYAL STATISTICAL SOC'Y.p.421-441 (1991).

Martin, Shannon,; Mary Lee Seifert,; Mark Zezza, *Hospital, Employment, and Price Indicators for the Health Care Industry: Third Quarter 1999.* HEALTH CARE FINANCING REV. (Spring 2000).

Maryland Health Care Commission, *An Analysis and evaluation of Certificate of Need regulation in Maryland: Inpatient rehabilitation hospital and chronic hospital services* (Jul. 6, 2004), *available at* http://www.mhcc.state.md.us/certificateofneed/study_report/_studyreport.htm.

Matheussen JJ, *Heart transplantation services overdue for southern New Jersey,* 97. N.J. MED.p.23-4 (2000 Oct).

Mathews CL, *Cost-effectiveness of certificate of need,* 21. J. OF THE MISS. ST. MED. ASS'Np.268-72 (1980 Dec).

Matthew, Danya Bowen, *An economic model to analyze the impact of false claims act cases on access to healthcare for the elderly, disabled, rural and inner-city poor* AM. J. OF L. & MED. (Winter 2001).

Matthews, Peggy, *Madison hospital receives approval*, CLARION-LEDGER, 1/30/04.

May, Troy,, *Hospital Group Wants Building Moratorium,*, BUS. NEWS, Dec 15, 1997.

Mays, Glen P. et al, *Hospitals compete for specialty care* (Spring 2001).

McAuliffe WE; Breer P; Ahmadifar NW; Spino C, *Assessment of drug abuser treatment needs in Rhode Island,* 81. AM. J. OF PUB. HEALTHp.365-71 (1991 Mar).

McBeath, Gretchen, *Status report on Ohio after deregulation from certificate of need* (1/15/2003), *available at* www.bricker.com.

McCareins, R. Mark, *Evaluating secular/non-secular hospital affiliations: Lessons from Poughkeepsie*, 14. ANTITRUST HEALTH CARE CHRON. p. 3, 8-10 (Fall 2000).

McCarthy D, *Capital offense. New York's health care in the crunch,* 14. HEALTH PAC BULL.p.15-May (1983 Jul-Aug).

Mcclurg, Kelly, *Fiscal health of hospital is CEO's task: Baptist Montclair top exec seeks to grow market share*, BIRMINGHAM BUS. J, August 24, 2001, at 2 p.

McClurg, Kelly, *Local health care community has a new PET project, available at* Bizjournals.com.

McClurg, Kelly, *Medical Center East wants $68M expansion* (July 5, 2002), *available at* Birmingham.bizjournals.com.

McFall, Dennis N, *Utah provider hurting from unchecked growth,* 13. PROVIDER p. 20-21 (1987 Dec).

McGinley, Patrick John, *Beyond health care reform: reconsidering certificate of need laws in a managed competition system*, 23. FLA. ST. U. L. REV. p.143-188.

McGinley, Patrick John,, *Beyond Health Care Reform: Reconsidering Certificate of Need Laws in a Managed Competition System,* FLA. ST. U. L. REV. (1995).

McGuire Donna, *Plan to acquire nursing home could help Resthaven expand* (April 29, 1993).

McKay, Jim, *Health-care cost containment reviews shelved legislature adjourns before extending law on wasteful spending*, PITTSBURGH POST-GAZETTE, Nov. 28, 1996, at p. C-19.

McLaughlin CG; Merrill JC; Freed AJ, *The impact of HMO growth on hospital costs and utilization,* 5. ADVANCES IN HEALTH ECONOMICS & HEALTH SERVICES RES.p.57-93 (1984).

McLean RA, *Regulation of the health care marketplace: a review of the issues.* SOCIOECONOMIC ISSUES OF HEALTHp. 19-Mar (1980).

McPherson, Doug, *Conduct recording fast growth with faster recording*, DENVER BUS. J, Jul. 19, 2004.

Meadows G, *Geographical resource allocation for public mental health services in Victoria,* 31. AUSTRALIAN & NEW ZEAL. J. OF PSYCHIATRY p. 95-104 (1997 Feb).

Meeker RA, *CON: an added burden for smaller hospitals,* 23. MICH. HOSP.p.27-8, 30 (1987 Sep).

Melin CN; Rabkin MT, *Understanding the context for long-range planning in hospitals,* 2. HEALTH CARE MGMT. REV.p.13-20 (1977 Spring).

Mellen, Karen, *Hospitals defend proposals: 2 companies seek to build,* CHICAGO TRIBUNE, 3/19/04.

Mellen, Karen, *Orland Park hospital proposal debated: Affluent patients targeted, foes say,* CHICAGO TRIBUNE, 3/5/04.

Mellette, Peter M.; Towey, Emily W.G.; Hunt, Vaden J, *Healthcare law* (12/29/200), *available at* http://80-web.lexis-nexis.comezpropxy.umuc.edu/document?_m=32a91f868ff18f.

Mendelson, D. N.; Arnold, J. Spectrum:, *Certificate of Need Revisited,* 66. SPECTRUM: THE J. OF ST. GOV'Tp.36-44 (Winter 1993).

Menninger, Bonar, *3 appointees are named to CON group,,* BUS. J, November 22, 1996.

Menninger, Bonar, *CON program to be phased out,,* BUS. J, July 19, 1996.

Menninger, Bonar, *CON shutdown stalls health projects,,* BUS. J, September 20, 1996.

Menninger, Bonar, *Relief, anxiety greet Griffin charges,* BUS. J, November 8, 1996.

Merritt D, *States exert control over health costs through tighter capital spending regulation,* BUS. & HEALTH, 1984 May, at 42-3.

Merritt, Dick, *States exert control over health costs through tighter capital spending regulation* BUS. & HEALTH INSTITUTE p. 42- 43 (May 1984).

Merzel C, *Challenging the CON game,* 16. HEALTH PAC BULL.p.13-4 (1986 Jun).

Metzger PD, *Why should the physician bother with CMNs or orders?,* 97. PA. MED.p.20 (1994 Jun).

Meyberg L, *The impact of technology on hospital marketing,* 4. ISSUES HEALTH CAREp.46-9 (1983).

Michael Casey,, *The Battle For Dekalb County* MCI REP. (Oct 2001).

Michigan Health Association, *Current happenings—Michigan Department of Public Health,* 21. MICH. HOSP. p. 44-5.

Mihelic FJ, *Hospital design, construction, and renovation,* 80. J. OF THE MED. SOC'Y OF N.J.p.531-4 (1983 Jul).

Miller RW, *Hospitals and the antitrust laws.* 27. MEDICO-LEGAL BULL.p.6-Jan (1978 Mar-Apr).

Miller, Andy, *Children's hospital expansion approved: Opposition by Grady still a possible snag*, THE ATLANTA J.-CONST, Jun 19, 2004.

Miller, Andy, *Health care key topic for legislature*, THE ATLANTA J.-CONST, Jan 10, 1997, at p. F3.

Miller, R. H, *Competition in the Health System: Good News and Bad News*, 15. HEALTH AFF. (Summer 1996).

Miller-Jones M, *The construction manager can be the hospital trustee's ally*, 36. TRUSTEEp.33-4, 36 (1983 Feb).

Mintz E, *Providers issue brief: certificate of need.* ISSUE BRIEF HEALTH POL'Y TRACK SERV.p.9-Jan (2000 May 22).

Misek GI Reynolds RA, *Effects of regulation on the hospital industry*, 22. Q. REV. OF ECONOMICS & BUS.p.66-80 (1982 Autumn).

Missouri Association of Homes for the Aging, *Issue brief: Certificate of need (CON)* (2003).

Missouri Association of Homes for the Aging, *Mission Statement* (2003).

Missouri Certificate of Need Program, *CON is good: MHFRC statement* (Feb. 4, 2002).

Missouri Chamber of Commerce, *Chamber supports bill to extend, reform CON*, MISSOURI CHAMBER OF COMMERCE, 2/21/02, at 1.

Missouri State Medical Association, *Certificate of need repeal attempted* LEGISLATIVE REP. (Apr. 17, 2003).

Modern Healthcare, *Hospital Foes Rage On*, MOD. HEALTHCARE, March 25, 2002, at p. 23.

Moffit, Robert E.; Teske, Richard; Moses, Stephen, *How to cope with the coming crisis in long-term care* (April 27, 2000).

Mollmer, Mark, *MRI referrals targeted by Senate for possible cuts: Opponents say budget amendment would 'shackle free trade'*, BOSTON BUS. J, May 21, 2004.

Monroe, Stephen M, *Well-balanced growth adds luster to Florida: Outstanding demographics are offset, however, by state budget*, COTEMPORARY LONGTERM CARE, 1989 Oct, at p. 52-3.

Monroe, Stephen, *Low occupancy casts a pall over the market: Reimbursement rates compound problems*, COTEMPORARY LONGTERM CARE, 1993 Jul, at p. 26, 79.

Monroe, Stephen, *Low occupancy hurts Indiana market: Overbuilding diminishes acquisition interest*, COTEMPORARY LONGTERM CARE, 1991 Jan, at p. 26, 72.

Montgomery, Dean, *CON regulation of nursing home services* HEALTH PLAN. TODAY p. 7-8 (1st Quarter 2001).

Montrose GD, *Is the force on your side? Ambulatory surgical facilities in the competitive environment*, 31. MED. GROUP MGMT.p.48-50, 58 (1984 Nov-Dec).

Monypenny P; Colby DC; Baker DG, *The politics of legislative interference in certificate of need decisions*, 5. J. OF HEALTH & HUM. RESOURCES ADMIN.p.409-26 (1983 Spring).

Moody, Robin J, *Hospital expansions threaten over saturation*, BUS. J. PORTLAND, 11/10/03.

Moody, Robin J, *Renal Care Group expanding in Vancouver*, PORTLAND BUS. J, 7/28/2004, at 1 p.

Moomjian GT, *The legal aspects of homecare company acquisitions*, 6. HOME HEALTH J.p.16 (1985 Mar).

Moore JD Jr, *Device truce in St. Louis. Hospitals must cooperate to get single gamma knife*, MOD. HEALTHCARE, 1997 Dec 22-29, at 28-9.

Moore JD Jr, *Focus report. CON survival struggle. Certificate of need: gone in many states but not dead yet*, MOD. HEALTHCARE, 1997 Aug 11, at 32-3, 36.

Moore RB Jr; Worthem JC, *Market and financial planning in senior care*, 18. TOPICS IN HEALTH CARE FINANCINGp.72-9 (1992 Spring).

Moore, J. D, *Market Profile: Market Pressures? Say What?: St. Louis Providers Profit Amid Excess Capacity*, MOD. HEALTHCARE, Jun 29, 1998.

Moore, J. D, *MO. to cut back most of its CON law,* MOD. HEALTHCARE, June 3, 1996, at 28.

Moore, J. Duncan,, *Is JAMA Playing Politics? Plan to Publish Attack on Profits Anger Managed Care Execs,*, MOD. HEALTHCARE, December 1, 1997.

Moore, J.D, *$5.6 million hospital center OK'd; Outpatient facility on Holmes to help with increase in patients* (November 10, 1994).

Moore, J.D, *Canceled application by hospital raises eyebrows; Another proposal is developed for site* (June 6, 1993).

Moore, J.D, *Hospital to get high-cost tool to fight cancer* (December 9, 1993).

Moore, J.D, *Outpatient care plan is dropped; Independence Regional Health Center withdraws proposal prior to state hearing* (June 2, 1993).

Moore, J.D, *Showdown in a crowded health-care field; Independence Regional tries anew for a site further east* (June 1, 1993).

Moore, J.D, *State panel to decide on costly equipment; Hospital hopes to get expensive cancer tool to improve treatment* (December 8, 1993).

Moore, J.D, *Transforming mental treatment; Overbuilding in the 1980's was spurred by Kansas laws* (November 20, 1994).

Moore, Ray, *State approves surgery center at Southern Hills*, NASHVILLE BUS. J, Jun 28, 2004.

Moore, Roy, *Agency prepares to tweak CON process*, NASHVILLE BUS. J, Dec. 29, 2003.

Moore, Roy, *Doc groups come out against center's plans for $2.6M MRI*, NASHVILLE BUS. J, Dec. 12, 2003.

Moore, Roy, *Pain management practice braces for healthy expansion*, NASHVILLE BUS. J, 10/27/03.

Moore, Roy, *Surgery center conflicts heating up: Group proposing Smyrna facility faces loss from nearby center*, NASHVILLE BUS. J, 10/20/03.

Morone, James A.; Dunham, Andrew B, *Slouching towards national health insurance: The new health care politics*, 2. YALE J. ON REG. p.263-291 (Spring 1985).

Morrisey, Michael A, *Competition in hospital and health insurance markets: a review and research agenda: analysis information of both industries* (April 2001).

Morrissey, John,, *Conditional Approval; Mass. Activists Win Changes in Hospitals Consolidation*, MOD. HEALTHCARE, 1998 May 11, at 38.

Morse HN, *Hospital topical law: A certificate of need*, 60. HOSP. TOPICSp.2, 18, 28 passim (1982 Jan-Feb).

Mosberg WH Jr, *Neurosurgeons, computed tomographic scanners, and the health planning bureaucracy,* 8. NEUROSURGERYp.287-94 (1981 Feb).

Moskowitz, Daniel B, *The slow-me state* (Nov.-Dec. 2001).

Moyer NC; Calabria JA, *Planning long-term care services for the 1990's: the virtues and limitations of state regulation,* 10. FAM. & COMMUNITY HEALTHp.58-66 (1988 Feb).

Mullins LC; Mushel MF; Hermanns O, *Nursing homes in the United States: an historical view and contemporary description of facilities and residents,* 17. J. OF HEALTH & HUM. SERVICES ADMIN.p.136-47 (1994 Fall).

Murphy, Kevin Q, *Health-care project oversight criticized; Too much politics involved in certificate process, legislators say* (October 18, 1995).

Mycek S, *CON laws. Wishing upon Disney's star*, 72.p.42-3 (1998 Jan 5).

Nannie, Phillip, *NHC gets nod for 200-bed facility*, NASHVILLE BUS. J, 10/14/2002, at 2.

National Cancer Institute, *Quality patient care includes radiation oncology that is cross-cutting and multi disciplinary* THE CANCER ORG.

NCSL, *Certificate of Need Laws: A state legislative survey, available at* www.firedenver.org.

Nemes J, *Humana asks Ky. for HMO exemption,* MOD. HEALTHCARE, 1990 May 14, at 2.

Nemes J, *Humana won't need CON for Michael Reese,* MOD. HEALTHCARE, 1990 Nov 12, at 4.

Nemes J, *Humana's exemption from Ky. CON process approved,* MOD. HEALTHCARE, 1990 Jun 18, at 4-Mar.

Nemes J, *Ousted Humana lobbyist OK'd payment to ex-lawmaker,* MOD. HEALTHCARE, 1992 Nov 16, at 2.

Nestrud CR, *Arkansas court halts construction, upholds state health plan in CON proceeding,* 7. HEALTH L. VIGILp.4-Dec (1984 Jan 20).

Neumann BR; Kim J, *Use of cost prediction simulation models for CON affordability review,* 10. HEALTH CARE MGMT. REV.p.75-82 (1985 Winter).

Neurath, Peter, *Entry into cardiac surgery market may be eased,* PUGET SOUND BUS. J, Mar. 3, 2003.

Neurath, Peter, *Home care biz reels from cuts* (September 21, 1998), *available at* Bizjournals.com.

Neurath, Peter, *Kidney centers rekindle certification debate: Total Renal Care, Fresenius want to expand in Washington, but competitors could slow approval* (Nov. 28, 1997), *available at* Bizjournals.com.

Newberg, Joshua A. *In Defense of Aston park: The Case for state substantive due process review of health care regulation* N.C.L. REV. Vol. 68, no. 253 (1990) *available at* http://80-web.lexis-nexis.com

Newhouse, Joseph, *Towards a Theory of Non-profit Institutions: An Economic Model of a Hospital,* 6. AM. ECONOMIC REV. (1970).

Newman S, *Equal access to health care: health planning agencies' obligations,* 5. HEALTH L. PROJECT LIBR. BULL. p.201-14 (1980 Jul).

News Wire Association, *Siemens medical solutions today announced shipment of its new fourSight(TM)* (10/5/2004), *available at* http://www.80-web.lexis-nexis.com.ezproxy.umuc.edu/universe/document?_m=3100d9506cc69.

Niehaus, John,, *Hospitals Feeling CON's Demise,,* BUS. NEWS, June 2, 1997.

Nilsen, Kim, *Huffstetler and nine other lawyers leave Kilpatrick Stockton,* TRIANGLE BUS. J, Feb. 17, 2003.

Nilsen, Kim, *Rex sues to protect cancer niche, available at* Bizjournals.com.

Nodzenski, Thaddeus J, *Regulating managed care coverage: A New direction for health-planning agencies* ANN. OF HEALTH L.

Norbut, Mike, *States scrutinize big-ticket purchases by group practices: States are using certificate-of-need laws and other methods to keep a closer watch on health care spending, saying it's for quality and cost control.* (Dec. 23, 2002), *available at* www.ama-assn.org/sci-pubs/amnews/pick_02/bil21223.htm.

North Carolina Division of Facility Services, *Overview of CON process* (5/9/04), *available at* http://facility-services.state.nc.us/conpage.htm.

Norton JW, *A position paper from the state office of comprehensive health planning. The need for certificate of need authority towards building a model health system for Maine,* 64. J. OF THE ME. MED. ASS'Np.8 passim (1973 Jan).

O'Connor, Dan, *State should abolish cons, say government report,* OUTPATIENT SURGERY MAG, 8/1/2004, at 1 P.

O'Donnell JW, *The evolution of health planning in a competitive health care era,* 13. J. FOR HOSP. ADMITTING MGMT.p.1-Oct (1987 Autumn).

Ohsfeldt, Robert L, *The spread of state any willing provider laws: examining the role of regulation in an evolving healthcare marketplace* (December 1998).

Oliver D, *The heavy hand of regulation,* 6. ADMIN. RADIOLOGYp.14-7 (1987 Apr).

Onusko, Thomas J, *Keeping up with CON laws*, COTEMPORARY LONGTERM CARE, 1985 Jan, at p. 49-51.

O'Reilly B, *OR X-ray plan: new UCLA suites benefit surgeons, patients*, 14. CONTEMPORARY SURGERYp.71-3, 75-6 (1979 Mar).

Orlando Business Journal, *Other features: The Week in business*, ORLANDO BUS. J, 7/28/04.

Otrompke, John, *Hospitals without cardiac cath labs face hurdles to deliver needed care fast enough.*

Padiatr Padol, *[Guidelines for completing a medical certificate for obtaining a higher rate of family assistance in atopic dermatitis]*, 28. PADIATRIE AND PADOLOGIEp.A3-6 (1993).

Page, Leigh, *N.C. specialty hospital to get certificate of need*, MOD. PHYSICIAN, May 12, 2003.

Page, Leigh, *Ohio lawmakers soften proposed ban on specialty hospital investments*, MOD. PHYSICIAN, 8/27/03, at 2 p.

Paige, Jane, *Triangle heart centers grow to meet anticipated demand*, TRIANGLE BUS. J, 2/13/04.

Pallarito K, *Acquisitions tip scales*, MOD. HEALTHCARE, 1994 Aug 15, at 38-40, 42.

Pallarito K, *Change of heart. N.J. expansion of cardiac CONs proving controversial*, MOD. HEALTHCARE, 1998 Jul 20, at 44.

Pallarito K, *Conn. facilities in joint venture to build rehabilitation hospital*, MOD. HEALTHCARE, 1991 Jun 17, at 24.

Pallarito K, *Conn. hospital receives nod for scaled-back replacement*, MOD. HEALTHCARE, 1995 Mar 13, at 24.

Pallarito K, *Conn. hospitals scale down proposal for new facility*, MOD. HEALTHCARE, 1991 Jun 24, at 12.

Pallarito K, *Mass. seeks capital, free care link*, MOD. HEALTHCARE, 1992 Mar 9, at 6.

Pallarito K, *N.J. hospitals battle appeal of CON denial*, MOD. HEALTHCARE, 1991 Jan 14, at 12.

Pallarito K, *Sloan-Kettering the latest to try branching out*, MOD. HEALTHCARE, 1992 Mar 2, at 22.

Pallarito, Karen,, *N.J. Drops Most CON Reviews*, MOD. HEALTHCARE, July 6, 1998.

Pallarito, Karen,, *States Targeting CON Laws, But Few Changes Expected*, MOD. HEALTHCARE, 1995 May 1, at 31.

Paprocki SB, *Updated CON version will not impact all agencies*, 8. HOME HEALTH J.p.19 (1987 Aug).

Park, Carolyne, *Governor to ask for restructuring of health agency.*

Park, Jennifer, *Hospitals tangle over cancer units*, BIRMINGHAM BUS. J, September 3, 1999, at 3 p.

Park, Jennifer, *Northport Health plans $3M home in Shelby*, BIRMINGHAM BUS. J, February 2, 2001, at 2 p.

Park, Jennifer, *Shelby, Brookwood tangle over heart surgery*, BIRMINGHAM BUS. J, November 24, 2000, at 2 p.

Park, Young M, *Antitrust: monopoly of kidney dialysis services-Kottie v. Northwest Kidney Centers* AM. J. OF L. & MED. (Winter 1998).

Park, Young M, *Recent Court Decisions; Selected Recent Court Decisions*, 24. AM. J. OF L. & MED. (1998).

Patrick, Stephanie, *Study: Volume—not revenue—rises for docs, available at* Bizjournals.com.

Patten, Brad, *Things you can do to stop spam before it gets to you*, BUS. J. OF PHOENIX, Jul. 16, 2004.

Patterson, John, *Legislators want to fire hospital board* (8/12/2004), *available at* http://www.dailyherald.com/community/zone_story.sap?inID=3816842&zone=rmt.

Patton, Paul E, *The Establishment of a limited moratorium on the development and expansion of health care services, facilities and equipment* (8/4/03), *available at* chs.state.ky.us/cofn/publicnotice/moritorium.doc.

Paul-Shaheen P; Carpenter ES, *Legislating hospital bed reduction: the Michigan experience*, 6. J. OF HEALTH POLITICS, POL'Y & L.p.653-75 (1982 Winter).

Pautler, Paul A.; Vita, Michael G, *Hospital market structure, hospital competition, and consumer welfare: What can the evidence tell us?* J. OF CONTEMPORARY HEALTH L. & POL'Y (Spring 1994).

Payton S; Powsner RM, *Regulation through the looking glass: hospitals, Blue Cross, and certificate-of-need,* 79. MICH. L. REV.p.203-77 (1980 Dec).

Payton S; Powsner RM, *The CON game: high costs just what intended,* 80. MICH. MED.p.386, 382 (1981 Jul).

Pear, Robert, *States are moving to re-regulation on health costs,* N.Y. TIMES, May 11, 1992, at Section A, Page 1.

Penn W; Buntz CG, *State responses to federal health regulatory requirements,* 2. J. OF HEALTH & HUM. RESOURCES ADMIN.p.282-98 (1980 Feb).

Penner I, *Special report on licensure, accreditation and CON. JCAHO keeps pace with changing face of health care,* HEALTH CARE L. NEWS, 1994 Jan, at 17-22.

Perry L, *Hospital groups turning to adversarial campaigns to improve public image,* MOD. HEALTHCARE, 1991 Feb 25, at 24-6, 28.

Perry S, *Diffusion of new technologies: rational and irrational,* 1. J. OF HEALTH CARE TECHNOLOGYp.73-88 (1984 Fall).

Perry, Seymour and Chu, Flora *The Legal implications of health care cost containment: A Symposium: Commentary: Health care cost containment and technology assessment* CASE W. RES. Vol. 36, no. 884 (1986) *available at* http://80-web.lexis-nexis.com

Peruchietti CE; Bennane MJ, *Public health committee chairs share their views on the reform process,* 25. MICH. HOSP.p.23, 26 (1989 Feb).

Peters GR, *A guide to organizing joint ventures with physicians,* 67. HEALTH PROGRESS (1986 Dec).

Peters, Brian, *Anticipating wildcards,* 35. MICH. HEALTH & HOSPITALS p. 22.

Pfister, Shirley M, *Home oxygen therapy: Indications, administration, recertification, and patient education,* 20. NURSE PRACTITIONER p. 44-56 (July 1995).

Phillips DF, *Technology: the honeymoon is over,* 52. HOSP.p.159-63 (1978 Apr 1).

Pierce CF Jr, *HSA, hospital planning: arena of conflict offers room for cooperation,* 54. HOSP.p.63-6 (1980 Mar 16).

Pierce, David, *Certificate of Need and behavioral health planning* (Jul. 30, 2004), *available at* http://health.hss.state.ak.us/dph/chems/cert_of_need/.

Pies, Harvey E. and Speil, Steven G. *Highlights of federal legislative and executive action* AM. J. L. AND MED. Vol. 7, no. 219 (1981) *available at* http://80-web.lexis-nexis.com

Piotrowski, Julie, *Holdup for 'digital' hospital: Suit takes aim at law allowing HealthSouth plan,* MOD. HEALTHCARE, at p. 6.

Piotrowski, Julie, *Holdup for Digital Hospital: Suit Takes Aim at Law Allowing HealthSouth Plan,* MOD. HEALTHCARE, May 20, 2002, at p. 6.

Piotrowski, Julie, *Midwest system planning new 72-bed hospital,* MOD. HEALTHCARE.

Piotrowski, Julie, *Show me: System will challenge Missouri's CON law,* MOD. HEALTHCARE, Apr. 28, 2003.

Piper, Thomas R, *Certificate of need: A call for action,* xxiii. HEALTH PLAN. TODAY p. 8 (4th Quarter, 2001).

Piper, Thomas R, *Missouri CON futures* HEALTH PLAN. TODAY p. 9-10 (2nd Quarter 2001).

Piper, Thomas R, *Streamlining CON in Missouri* HEALTH PLAN. TODAY p. 7 (3rd Quarter 2001).

Piper, Thomas R. Missouri Certificate of Need program, *Memorandum to Missouri Health Facilities Review Committee* (July 25, 2002).

Piper, Thomas,.. *as such do laws elsewhere,* MOD. HEALTHCARE, June 17, 2002, at p. 58, 61.

Pope, G.C,; Burge, R.T, *Illegal Price-Fixing Charged in Danbury Hospital Suit,* N.Y. TIMES, September 14, 1995.

Port, Susan, *Martin memorial for St. Lucie hospital nixed,* PALM BEACH POST, Jun 19, 2004.

Potenza R, *Community cancer management*, 57. HOSP.p.80-2, 85 (1983 Jan 1).

PR Newswire, *Alliance for governmental action opposes Edward's for-profit cardiac center as unwarranted duplication of existing services*, PR NEWSWIRE, Aug. 23, 1999.

PR Newswire, *Despite state decision, novant isn't giving up fight for new hospital*, PR NEWSWIRE, Oct. 28, 1999.

PR Newswire, *Dover General Hospital - What happened to the $67 Million*, PR NEWSWIRE, Dec. 13, 1999.

PR Newswire, *Medical society's public opinion poll supports state government findings: we need to take better care of our commonwealth's health care system*, PR NEWSWIRE, June 18, 1999.

PR Newswire, *State hospital association files suit against health planning board*, PR NEWSWIRE, April 28, 1999.

Preston, Jennifer, *States ease restrictions on hospitals*, N.Y. TIMES.

Procknow ME, *Effective strategies for obtaining certificate of need approval*, 89. MICH. MED.p.45-6 (1990 Jan).

Pruchansky, Neal R, *Cost control and physicians: an examination of attitudes and behavioral expectations*, 21. MED. CARE p. 508-18 (May 1983).

Pryor, Rosie, *Competition and costs*, MOD. HEALTHCARE, June 24, 2002, at p. 21.

Public Health Service, *Health Systems Agencies and State Health Planning and Development Agencies: Certificate of Need Reviews*, 45. FED. REG. p. 12174- 12185 (1980 Feb 22).

Public Health Service, *Health Systems Agency and State Health Planning and Development Agency Reviews: Certificate of Need Program*, 45. FED. REG. p. 69740- 69473 (1980 Oct 21).

Public Health Service, HEW, *Health Systems Agency and State Health Planning and Development Agency Review of New Institutional Health Services: Final Regulations*, 44. FED. REG. p. 19305-19326 (1979 Apr 2).

Public Health Service, HEW, *Inclusion of Computed Tomographic Scanning Services: Interim Regulations*, 44. FED. REG. p. 24429-22430 (1979 Apr 25).

Public Health Service, HHS, *Health Systems Agency and State Health Planning and Development Agency Reviews: Certificate of Need Programs - Final Regulations*, 50. FED. REGISTER p. 2008- 2020 (1985 Jan 14).

Public Health Service, HHS, *Health Systems Agency and State Health Planning and Development Agency Reviews: Certificate of Need Programs - Notice of proposed rulemaking*, 48. FED. REGISTER p. 36402-36415 (1983 Aug 10).

Punch L, *States may ax emergicenters' growth*, MOD. HEALTHCARE, 1983 Oct, at 27-8.

Pyles JC, *The legal checklist for home care ventures*, 4. CARINGp.38-40 (1985 Jul).

Quinn CC, *Health care regulation and market forces*, 2. NURSING ECONOMIC$p.204-9 (1984 May-Jun).

Rabin, Michael W, *Local need overrides budget constraints, CON delays for SNF*, HEALTH FACILITIES MGMT, at p. 22-3.

Raiford, Dave, *Baby blues: Baptist Women's venture dropping obstetrics: Partnership with HealthMark lost $5M in past two years*, NASHVILLE BUS. J, September 20, 2002, at 2.

Raiford, Dave, *Baptist renovations to precede new surgical center, available at* www.nashville.bizjournals.com.

Raiford, Dave, *Cardiology group targets Brentwood, available at* Bizjournals.com.

Raiford, Dave, *Dueling doctors: Two surgical centers slated for Tullahoma*, NASHVILLE BUS. J, Feb. 1, 2002.

Raiford, Dave, *East Nashville hospital hearing delayed*, NASHVILLE BUS. J, May 5, 2003.

Raiford, Dave, *Fertility center unveils $2M expansion at Centennial site*, NASHVILLE BUS. J, July 21, 2003.

Raiford, Dave, *Gateway medical slates $55 million expansion in fast-growing Clarksville*, NASHVILLE BUS. J.

Raiford, Dave, *Gateway's $55 million expansion approved*, NASHVILLE BUS. J, September 6, 2002, at 3.

Raiford, Dave, *Green Hills Senior care center files for 30-bed, $1.5M project*, NASHVILLE BUS. J, June 9, 2003.

Raiford, Dave, *Health System Buys 34 Acres for Clinic: Sumner Regional Plans Diagnostic Center for Greensboro Village* (July 26, 2002), *available at* nashville.bizjournals.com.

Raiford, Dave, *Hospital drops deliveries: Tennessee Christian obstetrics a victim of demographic shifts*, NASHVILLE BUS. J, January 17, 2003, at 2 p.

Raiford, Dave, *Maury makes open-heart surgery bid* (October 25, 2002), *available at* nashville.bizjournals.com.

Raiford, Dave, *Maury Regional looks to regain patients with surgery center*, NASHVILLE BUS. J, Feb. 17, 2003.

Raiford, Dave, *Meth clinic proposal riles Donelson*, NASHVILLE BUS. J, December 2, 2002, at pp. 3.

Raiford, Dave, *No meeting for Health Services and Development Agency* (7/28/2004), *available at* http://nashville.biz.com/nashville/stories/2002/07/22/daily18.html?t=printable.

Raiford, Dave, *Nonprofit seeks to rehab Riverside Hospital*, NASHVILLE BUS. J, December 13, 2002, at 2 p.

Raiford, Dave, *Oncology groups seeks to plug PET scan void*, NASHVILLE BUS. J, January 3, 2003.

Raiford, Dave, *Outpatient endoscopy group seeks nod for Smyrna center*, NASHVILLE BUS. J, November 8, 2002, at 2.

Raiford, Dave, *Pain Management Group plans its own Antioch surgery center*, THE BUS. J.

Raiford, Dave, *Prognosis unclear: New health care agency begins with surgery center rejection*, NASHVILLE BUS. J, August 30, 2002, at 3.

Raiford, Dave, *Southern hills, skyline move to add cardiac surgery services, available at* Bizjournals.com.

Raiford, Dave, *Surgical Alliance, orthopedists teaming on surgery center*, NASHVILLE BUS. J, at 2.

Raiford, Dave, *Surgical alliance: Vanguard health care teaming on hospital project*, NASHVILLE BUS. J, 9/12/2002.

Raiford, Dave, *Tristar launches cath lab project: Health system to spend $2.8M on Centennial venture*, NASHVILLE BUS. J, June 23, 2003.

Raiford, Dave, *Williamson medical broadens expansion plans, available at* www.nashville.bizjournals.com.

RAND Center for the Study of Aging, *Government Policy and the Cost and Quality of Nursing Homes.* (May 1996).

Rauber, Chris, *Stuck in the waiting room: Hospitals slam state delays*, BOSTON BUS. J, May 21, 2004.

Regan WA, *Board refuses CON for cardiac surgery facility,* 59. HOSP. PROGRESSp.82, 84, 87 (1978 Apr).

Regan WA, *CON unnecessary when hospital resumes service*, 62. HOSP. PROGRESSp.68 (1981 Jan).

Regan WA, *Hospital awarded CON for shelled space,* 60. HOSP. PROGRESSp.84 (1979 Apr).

Regan WA, *Hospital purchased cat scanner without CON,* 60. HOSP. PROGRESSp.72 (1979 Oct).

Regan WA, *Public opinion influences decision on CON process,* 63. HOSP. PROGRESSp.95, 97 (1982 Jul).

Reider AE; Mason JR; Glantz LH, *Certificate of need: the Massachusetts experience,* 1. AM. J. OF L. & MED.p.13-40 (1975 Mar).

Reilly, Patrick, *Another Fla. hospital plans cardiac expansion*, MOD. HEALTHCARE, July 21, 2003.

Reilly, Patrick, *Fla. hospitals agree to hold off on heart units*, MOD. HEALTHCARE, July 25, 2003.

Reilly, Patrick, *Florida court finds CON exemptions unconstitutional*, MOD. HEALTHCARE.

Reilly, Patrick, *Tenet sues Fla. oven CON exemptions for rivals*, MOD. HEALTHCARE, July 17, 2003.

Reilly, Patrick, *Tenn. court blocks CON*, MOD. HEALTHCARE, February 2, 2004, at p. 5.

Reily, Patrick, *Opening the door: Fla. proposes softening its certificate-of-need process*, MOD. HEALTHCARE, November 24, 2003, at p. 4.

Reily, Patrick, *Tenn. surgery center OK'd*, MOD. HEALTHCARE, November 24, 2003, at p. 4.

Reily, Patrick, *Vt. hospital CON approved*, MOD. HEALTHCARE, November 24, 2003, at p. 4.

Reinfurt, Ed; Klein, David, *Seeking local control for local delivery of health care*, BUS. REV. SERVING N.Y.'S CAPITAL REGION, 8/18/03, at 2 p.

Reinhardt, U. E, *Perspective: Spending More Through 'Cost Control': Our Obsessive Quest to Gut the Hospital*, 15. HEALTH AFF. (Summer 1996).

Reiss JB, *Economic impact analysis for certificate of need applications*, 3. AM. J. OF HEALTH PLAN.p.18-23 (1978 Jan).

Restuccia JD; Payne SM; Lenhart G; Constantine HP; Fulton JP, *Assessing the appropriateness of hospital utilization to improve efficiency and competitive position,* 12. HEALTH CARE MGMT. REV.p.17-27 (1987 Summer).

Restuccia, Robert; Singleton, Sen. Marvin M.D.; Thorpe, Kenneth, *Are CON Laws Relevant Again as Niche Facilities Multiply?* H&HN p. 26 (August 2002).

Rettig, Richard A, Ph.D, *The Social Contract and the Treatment of Permanent Kidney Failure,*, 275. JAMA (April 10, 1996).

Rettig, Richard A, Ph.D,, *Dialysis in Connecticut*, XIX. AM. J. OF KIDNEY DISEASESp.614-6 (June 1992).

Richard MH; MacCallum JM, *Strong osteopathic identity yields some legal clout,* 28. OSTEOPATHIC HOSP.p.8-10, 20 (1984 Jan).

Richards CF, *'Report upon Inquiry into Certificate of Need Legislation'. Parliament of Victoria Social Development Committee, October 1984,* 8. AUSTRALIAN HEALTH REV.p.134-7 (1985).

Richards G, *Is this overbuilding, and why might it occur?*, 59. HOSP.p.70-2 (1985 Feb 1).

Richards NM, *New secretary of health stresses prevention,* 90. PA. MED.p.10, 12, 15-6 (1987 Jun).

Richman D, *Hospital Building Co. plans appeal in antitrust suit against Rex Hospital,* MOD. HEALTHCARE, 1 9 8 5 Feb 15, at 142.

Riley, Bob Governor, *Executive order number 14*, *available at* http://www.governorpress.state.al.us/pr/ex-14-2003-11-21.asp.

Rinek MA, *A record number of bills passed in 1987-88,* 88. MICH. MED.p.20-1 (1989 Feb).

Roark, Charles E, *Certificate Of Need.: Second in a Series on Planning*, 34. TEX. HOSP. p. 12- 13 (1978 Sep).

Roark, Charles E, *Certificate of Need: Fourth in a Series on Planning*, 34. TEX. HOSP. p. 24- 25 (1978 Nov).

Roark, Charles E, *Certificate Of Need: Third in a Series on Planning*, 34. TEX. HOSP. p. 15- 17 (1978 Oct).

Roark, Charles E, *Institutional Planning: The Future is Now*, 34. TEX. HOSP. p. 19- 21 (1978 Dec).

Roark, Charles E, *Texas Health Facilities Commission Application Costs*, 34. TEX. HOSP. p. 36- 38 (1979 May).

Roark, Charles E, *Thoughts on the Certificate of Need Process*, 34. TEX. HOSP. p. 25- 27 (1979 Jan).

Robertson, Kathy, *rival yolo hospitals add features to compete,* SACRAMENTO BUS. J. *(October 15, 2004) available at* http://sacramento.bizjournals.com/sacramento/stories/2004/10/18/focus2.html

Robertson, Kathy, *Rival Yolo hospitals add features to compete*, SACRAMENTO BUS. J, 111/19/2004, at 4 p.

Robinson JL; Nash DB; Moxey E; O'Connor JP, *Certificate of need and the quality of cardiac surgery,* 16. AM. J. OF MED. QUALITYp.155-60 (2001 Sep-Oct).

Robischon, Thomas, *CON as More Than a CT Pinch: Filing for Other Equipment*, 10. APPLIED RADIOLOGY p. 101-2, 104-5 (1981 Nov-Dec).

Robischon, Thomas, *Doing More Than Filing and Suing to Get CON Approval*, 10. APPLIED RADIOLOGY p. 25-28 (1981 May-Jun).

Robischon, Thomas, *Regulators' View of the CON*, 10. APPLIED RADIOLOGY p. 50, 53, 55-6 (1981 Jul-Aug).

Robischon, Thomas, *Taking Your CON Application Through the Administrative and Judicial Processes*, 10. APPLIED RADIOLOGY p. 49, 51-2 (1981 Jan-Feb).

Rogatz P, *Creative responses needed in controlled environment,* 52. HOSP.p.73-7 (1978 Aug 1).

Rogers, Steve, *Harvesting growth in Autumn: North Carolina company expands through careful acquisition and construction program*, COTEMPORARY LONGTERM CARE, 1986 Dec, at p. 32-4.

Rohrer JE, *Regulation of accountable health plans in rural areas,* 16. J. OF PUB. HEALTH POL'Yp.198-212 (1995).

Romano Michael, *Exception to the rule: Fla. gives CON break to facility of GOP conTRIBUNEutor*, MOD. HEALTHCARE, May 5, 2003.

Romano, Michael, *Exception to the CON rule: HealthSouth's exemption from certificate-of-need law draws Alabama Hospital Association into legal fray*, MOD. HEALTHCARE, October 14, 2002, at p. 4-5, 16.

Romano, Michael, *Pros and cons of certificates: American Health Planning Association directory suggests that certificate-of-need process is regulatory in theory, not in practice*, MOD. HEALTHCARE, Apr. 21, 2003, at p. 4-5.

Romansky MA; Millman DS, *Regulatory and legal aspects of outpatient surgery,* 14. UROLOGIC CLINICS OF NORTH AMERICAp.15-20 (1987 Feb).

Rosenberg CL, *What does society really want from doctors? Broader availability,* 55. MED. ECONOMICSp.136-42, 145, 148-9 (1978 May 29).

Rosenthal, Jill E, *State purchasing and regulatory strategies to reduce racial and ethnic health disparities* (November 12, 2002), *available at* apha.confex.com.

Rosoff AJ, *Health planning and certification of need under the new federal health planning act,* 20. HOSP. ADMIN. p.60-72 (1975 Summer).

Rossi RP, *The impact of government regulation on radiology,* 2. RADIOLOGY MGMT.p.22-30 (1980 Winter).

Rountree, George D, *The Certificate of Need: A Planning Process In Transition*, 36. TEX. HOSP. p. 25- 28 (1980 Jun).

Rovinsy, Michael, *Joint venture proposals strengthen hospital-physician relationship* HEALTHCARE FIN. MGMT. (December 2000).

Rowland, *Certificate-of-need programs harmful impact on health care industry*, CONGRESSIONAL REC.

Royer, David, *Mental health care providers form alliance to avert crisis*, MEMPHIS BUS. J, July 28, 2003.

Rubenstein AD, *Editorial: Another view of the certificate-of-need laws,* 292. NEW ENGLAND J. OF MED.p.1074-5 (1975 May 15).

Rubin JE, *Hospice of the Monterey Peninsula and its free-standing inpatient facility,* 5. FAM. & COMMUNITY HEALTHp. 30-8 (1982 Nov).

Rublee, Dale, *Data watch: Medical Technology in Canada, Germany, and the United States* HEALTH AFF.

Ruef, Martin, *An organizational field approach to resource environments in health care: comparing entries of hospitals and home health agencies in the San Francisco Bay region* (February 1998).

Ruggie, Mary, *The paradox of liberal intervention: Health policy and the American welfare state*, 97. AM. J. OF SOCIOLOGY p. 919-944 (Jan. 1992).

Russell LB, *Regulating the diffusion of hospital technologies,* 43. L. & CONTEMPORARY PROBLEMSp.26-42 (1979 Winter-Spring).

Salkever DS; Bice TW, *The impact of certificate-of need controls on hospital investment,* 54. THE MILBANK MEMORIAL FUND Q. HEALTH & SOC'Yp.185-214 (1976 Spring).

Salop, S.C,; Scheffman, D.T, *Raising Rivals' Costs,* 73. AM. ECONOMIC REV. (May 1983).

Samuel FE Jr, *Home health care: a proprietary perspective,* 3. HOME HEALTH REV.p.22-8 (1980 Mar).

Sanders CA, *A need for determination,* 297. NEW ENGLAND J. OF MED.p.1348-9 (1977 Dec 15).

Sanders CA, *Certificate of need law-a power grab in disguise,* AM. MED. NEWS, 1978 Jan 23, at 4.

Sands RJ, *CON in the 1990s: focusing on cost cutting and innovation,* 18. PROVIDERp.52, 50 (1992 Jan).

Saner RJ, *Certificate of need—is group practice next in line?,* 26. MED. GROUP MGMT.p.9-10, 12-3 (1979 Jul-Aug).

Saphier MD, *Health planning amendments will add to hospitals' certificate-of-need burdens,* 23. HOSP. F.p.47-8 (1980 Apr-May).

Sawada, Kristen, *Hawaii hospital consider merging,* PACIFICBUSINESNEWS, Aug, 02 2004.

Sawada, Kristen, *Maui split on need for new kihei hospital,* PACIFIC BUS. NEWS *(October 15, 2002) available at*http://pacific.bizjournals.com/pacific/stories/2004/10/18/story6.html

Saylor LJ, *Federal court grants summary judgment in Huron Valley case,* 10. HEALTH L. VIGILp.4-Mar (1987 Jan 16).

Saylor, Larry J, *Federal court grants summary judgment in Huron Valley case,* 10. HEALTH L. VIGIL p. 3-4.

Scanlon, William et al, *Medicaid long-term care: Successful state efforts to expand home services while limiting costs.* (Aug. 11, 1994).

Scarborough, C. Alabama Hospital Association, *No Place Like Home* (July 9, 2002).

Schmid, Ron, *State Certificate of Need,* 3. J. AM. HEALTH CARE ASS'N. p. 20-4 (1977 Jul).

Schmitz RL, *The voyage ahead. Commencement Address at the Chicago College of Osteopathic Medicine, June 3, 1979.* (1979 Jul-Sep).

Schneer EC; Fielding JE, *Quantifying the need for hospital beds,* 297. NEW ENGLAND J. OF MED.p.1065-8 (1977 Nov 10).

Schneller M, *[Consultant physician: liaison between patient, physician, hospital, insurance],* 114. REVUE MEDICALE DE LA SUISSE ROMANDEp. 125-6 (1994 Feb).

Schoenfeldt RC; Seale WB; Hale AW, *Survey alerts hospital to needs of consumers,* 68. HEALTH PROGRESSp.61-6 (1987 Sep).

Schramm, Carl J. and Renn, Steven C. *Hospital mergers, market concentration and the herfindahl-hirschman index* EMORY L. J. Vol. 33, no. 869 (1984) *available at* http://80-web.lexis-nexis.com

Schwartz JB, *Pennsylvania's new certificate-of-need law,* 4. HEALTH L. PROJECT LIBR. BULL.p.364-70 (1979 Nov-Dec).

Schwartz MD, *Possible cures for reducing demand for hospital care,* 3. J. OF CLINICAL ENGINEERINGp.52-4 (1978 Jan-Mar).

Schwartz RL, *Oklahoma court approves City of Faith certification: cite national constituency,* 4. HEALTH L. VIGILp. 1-Oct (1981 Apr 17).

Schwartz WB, *The regulation strategy for controlling hospital costs,* 305. NEW ENGLAND J. OF MED.p.1249-55 (1981 Nov 19).

Schwartz WB; Joskow PL, *Duplicated hospital facilities: How much can we save by consolidating them?,* 303. NEW ENGLAND J. OF MED.p.1449-57 (1980 Dec 18).

Schwarz MH, *Long term sickness certification problems,* 49. MEDICO-LEGAL J.p.37-41 (1981).

Schweiker RS, *Schweiker explains revisions by Senate in health law planning,* REV. - FEDERATION OF AM. HOSP, 1978 Oct, at 17-20.

Scott HD; Tierney JT, *Home care in a hectic environment,* 68. R.I. MED. J.p.465-7 (1985 Oct).

Scott HD; Tierney JT; Waters WJ; Williams DC; Donahue JX, *Certificate of need: a state perspective,* 70. R.I. MED. J.p.341-5 (1987 Aug).

Scott L, *2 Joplin, Mo, hospitals plan merger after talks with 3rd fail,* MOD. HEALTHCARE, 1994 Mar 28, at 15.

Scott L, *Iowa relaxes CON,* MOD. HEALTHCARE, 1997 May 26, at 28.

Scott L, *Missouri OKs controversial CON,* MOD. HEALTHCARE, 1995 Mar 13, at 11.

Scott, Lisa, *Turnabout in Nebraska: State's Repeal of CON Law a Return to Open Market,*, MOD. HEALTHCARE, 1997 Jun 30, at 40.

Scott, Lisa,, *Communities Strike Back: Residents Oppose Ceding Control to Outside Not-for-Profit Chains,*, MOD. HEALTHCARE, April 28, 1997.

Selby R, *A response to controlling physician oversupply through certificate of need,* 7. AM. J. OF L. & MED.p.183-5 (1981 Summer).

Senator Sanders, *A Bill to be entitled an act, available at* http://alisdb.legislature.state.al.us/acas/searchableinstruments/2004rs/bills/sb505.html.

Sensenig, A. L,; Heffler, S. K,; Donham, C. S, *Health Care Indicators,* 17. HEALTH CARE FINANCING REV. (Fall 1995).

Sexton, Christine, *Con funding woes could hinder expansions*, THE BUS. J, at 1-3.

Sexton, Christine, *Group liability plan may help nursing home*, JACKSONVILLE BUS. J, 01/28/2002.

Sexton, Christine, *Hospitals face costly legal fees over projects*, THE BUS. J, at p.1-2.

Sexton, Christine, *Hospital's growth challenged*, JACKSONVILLE BUS. J, 7/28/2004.

Sexton, Christine, *Legal showdown escalates in N.E. Fla. hospital battle: Stakes are high in legal showdown, available at* Bizjournals.com.

Sforza, Michelle, *Trade agreements & the corporate takeover of US healthcare: Trade rules affect you* (4/1/01), *available at* www.citizen.org/trade/wto/gats/health/articles.cfm?ID=6003.

Shactman, David; Altman, Stuart H.; Eliat, Efrat; Thorpe, Kenneth E.; Doonan, Michael, *The outlook for hospital spending: Rapid growth is likely to persist,* 22. HEALTH AFF. p. 12-26 (Nov/Dec 2003).

Shanholtz MI, *General procedures and criteria for certificate of need,* 101. VA. MED. MONTHLYp.484-5 (1974 Jun).

Shannon MA, *The new laws from a lawyer's viewpoint,* 25. MICH. HOSP.p.17-20 (1989 Feb).

Shannon, Margaret A, *MDPH and comparative CON reviews*, 20. MICH. HOSP. p. 7-10.

Shanor PL; Cook DA; Grayson C, *To CON or not to CON,* 87. J. OF THE MED. ASS'N OF GA.p.14 (1998 Jan).

Sheesley PG, *Changes in Tennessee Certificate of Need program,* TIMES, 1980 Mar, at 30-1.

Shepard, Scott *Psychiatric hospital gets new life at UT,* MEMPHIS BUS. J. *(2002) available at*http://memphis.bizjournals.com.

Shepard, Scott *Methodist to add 63 beds* MEMPHIS BUS. J. *(April 17, 2002) available at* http://memphis.bizjournals.com.

Shepard, Scott, *A tale of two cities: Baptist, Olive Branch end feud over Southaven*, MEMPHIS BUS. J, July 7, 2003.

Shepard, Scott, *Baptist expansion gets green light in DeSoto County*, MEMPHIS BUS. J, January 7, 2002.

Shepard, Scott, *Baptist to invest $175 million in DeSoto*, MEMPHIS BUS. J, September 20, 2002, at 2.

Shepard, Scott, *Bring back transplants: Le Bonheur assembling all-star surgical team*, MEMPHIS BUS. J, May 21, 2004.

Shepard, Scott, *Delta Medical Center to construct health care campus in Greenville*, MEMPHIS BUS. J, July 21, 2003.

Shepard, Scott, *Despite Baptist's protest, surgery center moves ahead*, MEMPHIS BUS. J, 10/14/2002, at 2.

Shepard, Scott, *Few pros can be cited for CON process*, MEMPHIS BUS. J, at 3.

Shepard, Scott, *Methodist plans surgery center in high-growth area*, MEMPHIS BUS. J, January 14, 2002.

Shepard, Scott, *New surgery center will make up lost capacity*, MEMPHIS BUS. J, 10/07/2002, at 2.

Shepard, Scott, *Primary medical ramps up with multi-specialty network*, MEMPHIS BUS. J *(February 8, 2002) available at* http://memphis.bizjournals.com/memphis/stories/2002/02/11/story4.html

Shepard, Scott, *Surgeons, patients to reap benefits from Baptist robot*, MEMPHIS BUS. J, 8/25/03, at 2 p.

Shigeoka JW; Stults BM, *Home oxygen therapy under Medicare. A primer*, 156. THE WESTERN J. OF MED.p.39-44 (1992 Jan).

Shih, Bruce John, *Certificate of need.*

Shinkman R, *Great flap in Montana. CON lawsuit latest weapon in Great Falls' turf battle*, MOD. HEALTHCARE, 1997 Sep 15, at 8.

Shortell SM; Hughes EF, *The effects of regulation, competition, and ownership on mortality rates among hospital inpatients*, 318. NEW ENGLAND J. OF MED.p.1100-7 (1988 Apr 28).

Shortell SM; Morrisey MA; Conrad DA, *Economic regulation and hospital behavior: the effects on medical staff organization and hospital-physician relationships*, 20 (1985 Dec).

Shortell SM; Morrison EM; Hughes SL; Friedman BS; Vitek JL, *Diversification of health care services: the effects of ownership, environment, and strategy*, 7. ADVANCES IN HEALTH ECONOMICS & HEALTH SERVICES RES. (1987).

Shriver K, *Ownership sectors fight for Va. hospital project*, MOD. HEALTHCARE, 1995 Jul 24, at 48-9.

Shriver K, *Turf wars erupt over subacute-care rules*, MOD. HEALTHCARE, 1996 Jan 22, at 39.

Siebenmark, Jerry, *New Wesley CFO got his start as management trainee at Neiman Marcus* (June 14, 2002), *available at* Bizjournals.com.

Siegal, B,; Weiss, A,; Lynch, D, *Setting New Jersey Hospital Rates: A Regulatory System Under Stress*, 14. U. PUGET SOUND L. REV. (1991).

Siegel T, *AHA's CON regulation testimony focuses on effective date, access, and procedures*, 3. HEALTH L. VIGILp.4-Mar (1980 May 2).

Silva, Chris, *D.C. begins its own probe into WellPoint's CareFirst bid, available at* Bizjournals.com.

Silva, Chris, *D.C. summit raises more questions than answers, available at* www.washington.bizjournals.com.

Silva, Chris, *Local collaboration brings kid's rehab center to D. C, available at* Bizjournals.com.

Silva, Chris, *MedStar Appeals Decision Allowing Cardiac Program* (July 19, 2002), *available at* Washington.bizjournals.com.

Silva, Chris, *Suburban's open-heart program nears approval*, WASHINGTON BUS. J, November 7, 2002.

Silva, Tricia Lynn, *Jason's Deli franchisee has scoop on new ice cream store concept* (Jul. 26, 2004), *available at* http://sanantonio.bizjournals.com/sanantonio/stories/2004/07/26/newscolumn2.html.

Simler SL, *Anti-blackmail rule eases CONs*, MOD. HEALTHCARE, 1979 Nov, at 54.

Simler SL, *Certificate-of-need data: much-questioned criteria*, MOD. HEALTHCARE, 1978 Mar, at 42.

Simler SL, *Chains fight for CONS; ads don't help much*, MOD. HEALTHCARE, 1981 Nov, at 28, 30.

Simler SL, *CON regs hand HSAs a 'loaded gun',* MOD. HEALTHCARE, 1980 Dec, at 31-2.

Simler SL, *Congress to try again on health plan,* MOD. HEALTHCARE, 1978 Dec, at 18-9.

Simler SL, *Harris signs notice of CON rules,* MOD. HEALTHCARE, 1980 Apr, at 12.

Simler SL, *HSA budget cuts could delay CON approvals, appropriateness reviews,* MOD. HEALTHCARE, 1980 May, at 1-Oct.

Simler SL, *HSAs misuse draft CON checklist,* MOD. HEALTHCARE, 1979 Nov, at 30.

Simler SL, *Planning bill amendment limits HSA inquiries to relevant' information,* MOD. HEALTHCARE, 1979 Jun, at 26.

Simler SL, *Planning units' authority left intact,* MOD. HEALTHCARE, 1979 Sep, at 14-5.

Simler SL, *Robert T. Jones and Health Systems Agency of South Florida attempt to hold line against expensive equipment,* MOD. HEALTHCARE, 1978 Feb, at 40-2.

Simler SL, *States face CON revision deadline,* MOD. HEALTHCARE, 1979 Dec, at 16.

Simpson J, *Conditions: a tool for effective certificate-of-need regulation,* 5. HEALTH L. PROJECT LIBR. BULL.p.231-40 (1980 Aug-Sep).

Simpson JB, *State certificate-of-need programs: the current status,* 75. AM. J. OF PUB. HEALTHp.1225-9 (1985 Oct).

Sinskey PE, *California courts disagree as to whether federal CON law preempts conflicting state statutes,* HEALTH CARE L.NEWS, 1986 Jul, at 15-6.

Skidmore, Sarah, *State process has hospitals hopping: Facilities crowded as expansion plans are put on hold,* FLA. TIMES - UNION, at p.1-6.

Sloan FA, *Government and the regulation of hospital care,* THE AMERICAN ECONOMIC REV, 1982 May, at 196-201.

Sloan FA; Shayne MW; Doyle MD, *Is there a rationale for regionalizing organ transplantation services?,* 14. J. OF HEALTH POLITICS, POL'Y & L.p.115-67 (1989 Spring).

Sloan FA; Valvona J; Perrin JM; Adamache KW, *Diffusion of surgical technology. An exploratory study,* 5. J. OF HEALTH ECONOMICSp.31-61 (1986 Mar).

Sloan, Frank A, *Regulation and the rising cost of hospital care,* 63. REV. OF ECONOMIC & STAT. p. 479-487 (Nov. 1981).

Sloan, Frank, *Rate Regulation as a Strategy for Hospital Cost Control: Evidence from the Last Decade,* 61. THE MILBANK MEMORIAL FUND Q. HEALTH & SOC'Y (1983).

Smith HL; Mick SS, *A theory of organizational response to hospital regulation: a reply,* 10. ACAD. OF MGMT. REV. p.332-6 (1985 Apr).

Smith MD, *Seeking common ground,* 29. HEALTH SYS. REV.p.33-4 (1996 Jan-Feb).

Smith, R, *Constitutional Law-Abstention & Abortion: Application of the Undue Burden Standard to Certificate of Need Regulations,* 21. U. ARK. LITTLE ROCK L. REV. (Winter 1999).

Smith, Terry. Alabama Hospital Association, *CON too Legalistic, Unfair to Smaller Hospitals* (Spring 1998).

Snider, Shane, *State eyes request for high-end MRI, available at* Bizjournals.com.

Snow C, *Exemption challenged. Petition claims S.C. merger OK ignored lack of local benefit from deal,* MOD. HEALTHCARE, 1997 Jul 7, at 19.

Snow, Charlotte,, *Miss. Rivalry Grows: Hospitals, Home Care Agencies at Odds Over State's CON Laws,,* MOD. HEALTHCARE, 1997 Apr 28, at 33.

Snow, Charolotte, *Columbia cleans house in Ky,* MOD. HEALTHCARE, at p. 60, 62.

Snow, John, *Hospices face competition,* BUS. J. SERVING JACKSONVILLE & NORTHEAST FLA, 9/1/03, at 3 p.

Snow, Stacey, *Cancer facilities find Lakeland to be inviting: Nonprofit and for-profit meeting needs*, BUS. J. TAMPA BAY, May 5, 2003.

Snow, Stacey, *Competition at heart of regional hospital battle*, BUS. J. OF TAMPA BAY, January 24, 2003, at 3 p.

Snow, Stacey, *CON update*, BUS. J. TAMPA BAY, May 12, 2003.

Snow, Stacey, *Groups lobby for changes to medical liability system*, BUS. J. OF TAMPA BAY, December 27, 2002, at 2 p.

Snow, Stacey, *Polk: Number of surgeries down at Lakeland Regional*, BUS. J. OF TAMPA BAY, 1/24/2003, at 2 p.

Snow, Stacey, *Sweeping denials for open-heart programs: Hospital leaders say need for programs will increase*, BUS. J. TAMPA BAY, Mar. 10, 2003.

Snow, Stacey, *Two cancer centers, one small city*, ORLANDO BUS. J, May 5, 2003.

Snyder, Dale, *Building Bureaucracy and invading patient privacy: Maryland's health care regulations* (Apr. 16, 1998).

Solheim, John *Innovators* THE BUS. PHOENIX J. (2004) *available at* http://phoenix.bizjournals.com

Solomon, Loel, *Rules of the game: how public policy affects local health care markets* HEALTH AFF. p. 140-148 (Jul./Aug. 1998).

Solomon, Loel, *Rules of the Game: How Public Policy Affects Local Health Care Markets,* 17. HEALTH AFF.p.140-8 (Jul-Aug 1998).

Solomon, Loel, *Rules of the game: how public policy affects local health care markets*, 17. HEALTH AFF. p. 140-148 (Jul/Aug 1998).

Somers AR; Somers HM, *A proposed framework for health and health care policies,* 14. INQUIRYp.115-70 (1977 Jun).

Somerville, Leigh, *Assisted Living Facilities tout their conveniences as battle for clients gets more intense*, BUS. J. SERVING THE GREATER TRIAD AREA, Feb. 3, 2003.

South Jersey Radiology Associates, P.A, *What's new: Latest technology PET/CT hybrid scanner available only at SJRA, available at* http://www.sjra.com/whatsnew.asp?intCategoryID=70&intArticleID=409.

Sperber, Marc N, *Short-sheeting the psychiatric bed: State-level strategies to curtail the unnecessary hospitalization of adolescents in for-profit mental health facilities* AM. J. L. AND MED. Vol. 18, no. 251 (1992) *available at* http://80-web.lexis.nexis.com

Spero, Barry, M. *Long-term care for the elderly: Managed care for the elderly: Obtaining cost effectiveness while enhancing quality* QUINNIPIAC HEALTH L. J. Vol. 1, no. 193 (1997) *available at* http://80-web.lexis-nexis.com

Spiegel AD; Hyman HH; Gary LR, *Issues and opportunities in the regulation of home health care,* 1. HEALTH POL'Y & EDUC. p. 237-53 (1980 Oct).

St. Louis Area Business Health Coalition, *St. Louis area hospitals: an industry overview* (1991).

St. Louis Area Business Health Coalition, *St. Louis area hospitals industry financial and statistical overview supplement.* (January 1998).

St. Louis Area Business Health Coalition, *St. Louis area hospitals industry financial and statistical overview supplement.* (December 1999).

State of Alaska, *Certificate of need & behavioral health planning unit* (5/15/04), *available at* http://www.chems.alaska.gov/CON_BHP/default.htm.

State of Maryland: Maryland Health Care Commission, *Guide to state regulations affecting freestanding ambulatory surgery providers in Maryland* (Mar. 28, 2004), *available at* http://www.mhcc.state.md.us/certificateofneed/study_report-_studyreport.htm.

State of Maryland: Maryland Healthcare Commission, *Certificate of need study reports* (Mar. 28, 2004), *available at* http://www.mhcc.state.md.us/certificateofneed/study_report-_studyreport.htm.

Steen, John, *Certificate of Need: A Review*, *available at* www.ahpanet.org.

Steen, John, *Community health planning and national public health performance standards* HEALTH PLAN. & POL'Yp.5 p. (1/16/2003).

Steen, John, *Healthcare reform: A Planner's Standards* HEALTH PLAN. TODAY p. 3, 4 (1st Quarter 2000).

Steen, John, *It's public health, stupid!* HEALTH PLAN. & POL'Yp.2 p.

Steen, John, *Managed care, regulatory oversight, and health planning: Challenges for a new age*, *available at* www.ahpanet.org.

Steen, John, *Regionalilzation for quality: Certificate of need and licensure standards*, *available at* www.ahpanet.org.

Steen, John, *Regulating in the public interest: The quality of nursing care*, *available at* www.ahpanet.org.

Steinberg EP, *The impact of regulation and payment innovations on acquisition of new imaging technologies*, 23. RADIOLOGIC CLINICS OF NORTH AMERICAp.381-9 (1985 Sep).

Steinberg EP; Sisk JE; Locke KE, *The diffusion of magnetic resonance imagers in the United States and worldwide*, 1. INTERNATIONAL J. OF TECHNOLOGY ASSESSMENT IN HEALTH CAREp.499-514 (1985).

Steinberg EP; Sisk JE; Locke KE, *X-ray CT and magnetic resonance imagers. Diffusion patterns and policy issues*, 313. NEW ENGLAND J. OF MED.p.859-64 (1985 Oct 3).

Steiner JE Jr; Kneen JW, *Senior housing developments raise legal issues for CFOs*, 41. HEALTHCARE FIN. MGMT.p.70, 72, 74-6 (1987 Dec).

Stella, Frank, *Michigan program reins in rising medical costs*, DETROIT NEWS, March 14, 2002.

Stephens, Joe, *Racketeering charges denied by defendants* (November 1, 1996).

Stephens, Laura L. *Nonprofit hospital mergers and section 7 of the Clayton act: Closing an antitrust loophole* B. U. L. REV. Vol. 75, no. 477 (1995) *available at* http://80-web.lexis-nexis.com

Stephenson P, *Q. A with Pam Stephenson*, 40. GA. HOSP. TODAYp.1, 4-5 (1996 Aug).

Stevens C, *Joint ventures: don't let the law take you by surprise*, 64. MED. ECONOMICSp.52-7, 61 (1987 Mar 30).

Steyer, Robert and Theresa Tighe, *Series: Missouri's Nursing Homes/Who Cares? Third of four parts: Overbuilding spawns glut of empty beds political favors, loopholes force though choices.*

Steyer, Robert, *Bypass: 'need' rule has loophole*, ST. LOUIS POST-DISPATCH, August 27, 1989.

Steyer, Robert, *Limits on spending many states require hospitals to prove need for costly equipment*, ST. LOUIS POST-DISPATCH.

Steyer, Robert, *Market for bypass surgery here to get even more crowded*, ST. LOUIS POST-DISPATCH.

Steyer, Robert, *Reprieve for health regulators*, ST. LOUIS POST-DISPATCH.

Steyer, Robert, *State guideline angers hospitals*, ST. LOUIS POST-DISPATCH.

Steyer, Robert, *State panel overrules staff, oks kidney-stone crusher*, ST. LOUIS POST-DISPATCH.

Steyer, Robert, *State's certificate-of-need rule for hospital attacked*, ST. LOUIS POST-DISPATCH, at 1-3.

Steyer, Robert, *States often ignore their own rules on bypass regulations*, ST. LOUIS POST-DISPATCH.

Steyer, Robert, *University hospital plans $22 million remodeling*, ST. LOUIS POST-DISPATCH, at 1-2.

Stout, Heidi J, *Local real estate market took its ups and downs*, BUS. J. PORTLAND, 7/28/04.

Stromberg, Clifford D. *Health law comes of age: Economics and ethics in a changing industry* YALE L. J. Vol. 92, no. 203 (1982) *available at* http://80-web.lexis-nexis.com

Strosberg MA; Padilla E, *Regulatory controls on capital-based medical technology,* 5. J. OF HEALTH & HUM. RESOURCES ADMIN.p.43-55 (1982 Summer).

Strugatch W, *Seminar stresses renovation over construction,* 58. HOSP.p.106, 108 (1984 Apr 1).

Stuart, Devin, *Mayo pulls at St. Luke's heartstrings: considers taking CON for its new hospital,* BUS. J. OF JACKSONVILLE, January 13, 2003.

Studnicki J, *Certification of need programs: regulation in search of the evaluation process,* 2. EVALUATIONp.94-6 (1975).

Stults HL Jr, *How to make certificate of need work for you,* 34. HOSP. FIN. MGMT.p.60-5 (1980 Jan).

Sturges BR, *Rhode Island's experience with budgets negotiated in advance,* 36. TRUSTEEp.28, 31-2 (1983 Sep).

Suddreth, Doug, *CON for adult care homes* HEALTH PLAN. TODAY p. 4, 6 (3rd Quarter 2001).

Sullivan A, *Washington struggle mirrors contention elsewhere,* EMERGENCY DEPARTMENT NEWS, 1981 Feb, at 3.

Sullivan PR; Damsgaard A; Rodkey GV, *A critique of the Massachusetts determination of need program,* 300. NEW ENGLAND J. OF MED. p. 794-5 (1979 Apr 5).

Swan JH; Estes CL, *Changes in aged populations served by home health agencies,* 2. J. OF AGING & HEALTHp.373-94 (1990 Aug).

Swan, James H, Ph.D,; Charlene Harrington, Ph.D,; Leslie Grant, Ph.D,; John Luehrs, Ph.D,; Steve Preston,, *Trends in Medicaid Nursing Home Reimbursement, 1978-89,,* 14. HEALTH CARE FINANCING REV. (Summer 1993).

Swan, James, Ph.D,; Charlene Harrington, Ph.D,, *Certificate of Need and Nursing Home Bed Capacity in States,,* 2. J. OF HEALTH & SOC. POL'Y p.87-105 (1990).

Swidler, Robert N. *Medical innovations and ethics: A State government perspective* ALB. L. REV. Vol. 57, no. 655 (1994) *available at* http://80-web.lexis-nexis.com

Sybert, Lucy, *St. John's Mercy plans $18.5 million expansion,* ST. LOUIS BUS. J, Jun 21, 2004.

Szalanski AM, *Free-standing emergency centers: a new frontier for dealers?,* 9. MPS MED. PRODUCTS SALESMAN p.1, 43-5 (1978 Oct).

Szerszen CA, *Regulation of medical technology: problems and proposals.* SOCIOECONOMIC ISSUES OF HEALTH p.109-32 (1981).

Tallon RW, *A vision of the challenges: changes in Medicare,* 39. OSTOMY/WOUND MGMT. p.1-Oct (1993 Nov-Dec).

Tanner, M. Cato, *Laboratory Failure: States are No Model for Health Care Reform.* INSTITUTE POL'Y ANALYSIS (Sep 23, 1993).

Tanner, Michael D, *Ending the CON Game* INTELLECTUAL AMMUNITION p. 1-2 (Jan./Feb. 1996).

Taravella S, *Market focus: Salt Lake City,* MOD. HEALTHCARE, 1988 Jan 1, at 46-8.

Taravella S, *New developer next door threatens plan for AIDS facility and residence in Harlem,* MOD. HEALTHCARE, 1989 Jul 7, at 86.

Taroni F, *Roemer's effect reconsidered,* 6. J. OF HEALTH SERVICES RES. & POL'Yp.56-8 (2001 Jan).

Tatge M, *NME used political maneuvers to get state's OK for hospital: documents,* MOD. HEALTHCARE, 1985 Apr 26, at 20.

Taylor KS, *Constructive change. Strong strategic plans can help hospitals keep facility plans in line,* 67.p.36-8 (1993 Aug 20).

Taylor M, *Benefis tries again. New competitor spurs Mont. system to seek further relief from merger rules,* MOD. HEALTHCARE, 2001 Aug 20, at 39-40.

Taylor M, *Systems duel over market control in Ala. Baptist, Tenet have CON approval to build cancer centers but are fighting each other in court,* MOD. HEALTHCARE, 1999 Nov 8, at 40.

Taylor, Brennen; Taylor, Ann, *Social work with transport disabled persons: A way finding perspective in health care,* SOCIAL WORK IN HEALTH CARE, at p. 3-19.

Taylor, Kathryn S, *Constructive change,* HEALTH FACILITIES MGMT, at p. 24-31.

Taylor, Mark, *Big brewings in a small town: Tenet could face competition in Missouri,* MOD. HEALTHCARE, at p. 20.

Taylor, Mark, *FTC, justice set to begin antitrust hearings,* MOD. HEALTHCARE, Jan. 29, 2003.

Taylor, S. L. et. al, *A Conceptual Choice Model for Hospital Services,* 7. J. OF MARKETING THEORY & PRAC. (Fall 1999).

Tedards WP Jr, *Assessing need in CON proceedings,* 35. NURSING HOMESp.3-Oct (1986 May-Jun).

Tennenbaum D, *Planning law deadlines threaten state programs,* 53. HOSP.p.75-7 (1979 Apr 16).

Terry, Ken, *Hospital hardball: Maine physicians are being pressured to pick sides in a nasty fight over economic credentialing* MED. ECONOMICS (August 9, 2002).

Terry, Ken, *Hospital hardball: Maine physicians are being pressured to pick sides in a nasty fight over economic credentialing* MED. ECONOMICS (August 9, 2002).

Texas Hospitals, *Project Review: Health Systems Agency/Texas Health Facilities Commission Involvement,* 34. TEX. HOSP. p. 14- 16 (1978 Aug).

Thamer, Mae, Ph.D,; Nancy F. Ray, M.S,; Christian Richard, M.S,; Joel W. Greer, Ph.D,; Brian C. Pearson,; Dennis Cotter, M.E,, *Excluded From Universal Coverage: ESRD Patients Not Covered by Medicare,,* 17. HEALTH CARE FINANCING REV. (Winter 1995).

The Bulletin of the American College of Physicians, *Health planning-unresolved questions,* THE BULL. OF THE AM. COLLEGE OF PHYSICIANS, at p. 18-20.

The Chattanoogan, *Governor names members of new state health board,* CHATTANOOGAN, July 26, 2002, at 2.

The Physician-Owned Group, *Physician-owned group: The Best strategy for success, available at* http://www.aafp.org/fpm/990500fm/38.html.

The State Journal-Register, *bill would alter hospital board review powers* HEALTH PLAN. TODAY p. 2, 8 (1st Quarter 2000).

Thill, Mark, *Certificates-of-need* (7/29/03), *available at* http://www.reillycomm.con/oc_to_0302.htm.

Thimangu, Patrick L, *Community Care adds 45 beds in $1.2 million renovation,* ST. LOUIS BUS. J, November 21-27, 2003.

Thimangu, Patrick L, *Hospital building projects top healthy $800 million,* ST. LOUIS BUS. J, 10/31/03.

Thimangu, Patrick L, *Kindred Plans $4 million long term-care hospital: 52-bed acute-care facility would be at St. Anthony's,* ST. LOUIS BUS. J, June 30, 2003.

Thomas, Richard K, *New health planning for the New Millennium* (1/16/2003), *available at* www.ahpanet.org/articles.html.

Thompson E, *Duking it out. Local hospitals fight back as physicians bring on competition with specialty facilities,* MOD. HEALTHCARE, 2000 Jul 17, at 3, 6, 9.

Thompson, Alvin J, *Certificate of need: A failed instrument,* 22. THE INTERNIST p. 9-10.

Thorpe, K.E.; Phelps, Charles, *Regulatory Intensity and Hospital Cost Growth,* 9. J. OF HEALTH ECONOMICS (1990).

Tieman, Jeff, *Hospitals file suit over Maine cancer center,* MOD. HEALTHCARE, May 7, 2003.

Tierney JT; Waters WJ; Rosenberg WH, *Certificate-of-need—no panacea but not without merit,* 3. J. OF PUB. HEALTH POL'Yp.178-81 (1982 Jun).

Tierney, John M,; William J. Waters,; Donald C. Williams,, *Controlling Physical Oversupply Through Certificate of Need,* 6. AM. J. OF L. & MED.p.335-60 (1980 Fall).

Tighe, Theresa, *Freeze on assisted living draws support, protests.*

Tilson JQ, *Commission on Hospitals and Health Care: five years of litigation. Part II,* 43. CONN. MED.p.453 (1979 Jul).

Tokarski C, *Debating the benefits of regulation,* MOD. HEALTHCARE, 1990 Aug 20, at 35-8.

Tokarski C, *Healthcare lobbying efforts turn to states,* MOD. HEALTHCARE, 1990 Jul 23, at 29-30, 38-40, 44.

Tonkel JR, *Implementing a good neighbor policy,* 23. HOSP. F.p.21-5 (1980 Apr-May).

Tortora, Andrea, *Heart hospital has more suitors: Health systems see chance to sway deal,* CINCINNATI BUS. COURIER, Dec. 12, 2003.

Tortora, Andrea, *Heart-only hospital in the works: Deaconess to team with Ohio Heart,* CHARLOTTE BUS. J, July 11, 2003.

Tortora, Andrea, *Quality might suffer in race for lucrative heart-care business,* BUS. COURIER, at 1-9.

Towler JN, *'47 varieties'. A survey of the use of Section 47 of the National Assistance Act 1948 in Bradford,* 102. PUB. HEALTHp.485-92 (1988 Sep).

Traska MR, *FHA's hospital program useful despite 'bum rap',* 60. HOSP.p.48, 53 (1986 Jun 20).

Traska MR, *Hospitals build more doctors' offices despite certificate-of-need uncertainties,* MOD. HEALTHCARE, 1978 Mar, at 46-9.

Traska MR, *HSAs to scrutinize Con applications for equipment,* MOD. HEALTHCARE, 1979 Jan, at 44, 46.

Traska MR, *Using global budgets in the United States,* 2. MANAGED CARE Q.p.45-9 (1994 Winter).

Trent GE, *Evolution of certificate of need: an administrator's role* CASE STUD. IN HEALTH ADMIN.p.18-22 (1978).

Trewyn, Phil, *Facilities authority still rubber-stamps projects: Democrats hoped change in statute would regulate hospital construction,* THE BUS. J. SERVING GREATER MILWAUKEE, June 23, 2003.

Trick, Dorothy, *What's inside their minds,* THE GREATER BATON ROUGE BUS. REP.COM, Aug. 13, 2002.

Tucker LR; Laric MV; McCann D, *The role of marketing research in securing a certificate of need for a new renal transplant facility,* 11. J. OF HEALTH CARE MARKETINGp.63-9 (1991 Jun).

Turner, Ben, *Mundy: Blue Cross Blue Shield in N.J. refunding $50 million; Pa. Blue Shield do same, available at* http://www.pahouse.com/pr/Mundy/120020904.html.

Tusler W Jr, *Could two-level process eliminate costly planning problems?,* 53. HOSP.p.85-90 (1979 Feb 16).

U.S. Department of Health and Human Services, *Medicare Hospital Building Costs* (August 30, 1991), *available at* www.hhs.gov.

Unger WJ, *New legislative changes may have effect on capital formation,* REV. - FEDERATION OF AM. HOSP, 1982 Sep-Oct, at 44-7.

Valaske, Martin J, *Certificate of Need,* 34. PATHOLOGIST p. 77 (1980 Feb).

Van Drake, Stephanie, *Growth sparks new health care facilities,* SOUTH FLA. BUS. J, Aug. 25, 2003.

Van Drake, Stephen, *Neonatal expansions approved,* SOUTH FLA. BUS. J, 12/19/03.

Vandewarter, Judy, *Officials spar over plan for hospital* (2/9/04), *available at* http://www.stltoday.com/stltoday/emaf.nsf/Popup?ReadForm&db=stltoday%5Cnews%5C.

VandeWater, Judith, *Hospital hearing draws crowd in O'Fallon, MO* (2/18/04), *available at* http://www.stltoday/emaf.nsf/Popup?ReadForm&db+stltoday%5Cbusiness%.

VandeWater, Judith, *Jewish agency may break ground for new kosher nursing complex by next year: $62.5 million project needs ok from state panel.*

Velasco, Anna, *Brookwood to expand surgical facilities*, BIRMINGHAM NEWS, Jun 19, 2004.

Velasco, Anna, *State Hospitals likely to keep certificate of need programs*, *available at* http://www.al.com/printer/printer.ssf?/base/living/1091613250179920.xml.

Velasco, Anna, *UAB expects Ok to buy site to build women's hospital*, BIRMINGHAM NEWS, 2/6/04.

Velasco, Anna, *UAB Medical West wins approval to build outpatient surgery center*, BIRMINGHAM NEWS, Jun 19, 2004.

Vester, S. Russell, *Community Hospitals Qualified in Heart Care*, CHARLOTTE BUS. J.

Vince Galloro, *Another heart war: Columbia, S.C, is competition battlefield*, MOD. HEALTHCARE, at p.30-31.

Virskus C; Sederburg W, *Public health committee chairs share their views on the reform process*, 25. MICH. HOSP.p.22, 24 (1989 Feb).

Vitaliano DF; Heshmat S, *Hospital cost containment regulations and the diffusion of the CAT scanner: a case study*, 9. J. OF HEALTH & HUM. RESOURCES ADMIN.p.185-99 (1986 Fall).

Vogel, Robert R, *Conditions for failure* (1/16/2003), *available at* www.ahpanet.org/articles.html.

Vollmer, Sabine, *Change could deliver new hospital beds*, TRIANGLE BUS. J, Mar. 10, 2003.

Vollmer, Sabine, *Changes could deliver new hospital beds*, TRIANGLE BUS. J, Mar. 10, 2003.

Vonderfecht, Dennis, *Tenn. CON law works*, MOD. HEALTHCARE, June 17, 2002, at p. 61.

Vraciu, Bob, *Rising Health Care Costs: What Will Solve the Problem?* (June 28, 2002), *available at* nashville.bizjournals.com.

Wagner M, *Developer expands legal battle to block opening of K.C. facility*, MOD. HEALTHCARE, 1992 Nov 23, at 22.

Wagner M, *Missouri governor wants to put CON decisions in different hands*, MOD. HEALTHCARE, 1992 Feb 10, at 30.

Wagner M, *St. Louis hospital cuts project size*, MOD. HEALTHCARE, 1993 Feb 22, at 17.

Wagner, Mary, *Keep unique design requirements in mind when planning for PET*, MOD. HEALTHCARE, November 30, 1992, at p. 35.

Waite, Mark, *Company gets hospital ok: Certificate of need goes to former clinic operator*, VIEW NEIGHBORHOOD NEWSPAPERS, July 26, 2002.

Waite, Mark, *New Company enters hospital fray*, VIEW NEIGHBORHOOD NEWSPAPERS, May 17, 2002.

Waldholz M, *Confusion stymies D.C. hospital's move*, 2. HEALTH CARE WK.p.4, 18 (1979 Jan 22).

Walker, Childs, *Medical hub plans possible expansion: Demands for health care prompt look into upgrade*, BALT. SUN, 2/20/04.

Walker, David Jr, *Regulatory, other hurdles complicate opening an ASC: Getting educated about the requirements and how to determine feasibility are necessary steps.* OPHTHALMOLOGY TIMES (Nov. 1, 2001).

Wall LH, *After CON—Colorado's experience*, 27. MICH. HOSP.p.13 (1991 Jan).

Wall MA, *Final CON rules hold to tight deadline for state compliance*, 3. HEALTH L. VIGILp.4-Mar (1980 Oct 31).

Ward R, *CON implications: a look into the crystal ball*, 25. MICH. HOSP.p.7-8, 11 (1989 Feb).

Ward RD, *Michigan's CON regulations: a closer look*, 27. MICH. HOSP.p.6-7, 9-11 (1991 Jan).

Warner DA, *Status report: health planning and capital expenditure regulation,* 9. HEALTH L. VIGILp.18-9 (1986 Aug 29).

Warner Kenneth E, *Effects of hospital cost containment on the development and use of medical technology,* 56. THE MILBANK MEMORIAL FUND Q. HEALTH & SOC'Yp.187-211 (1978 Spring).

Wasek Stephanie, *Medicine & Religion: A Contentious mix* OUTPATIENT SURGERY (7/31/03).

Washington, Michelle, *Angiography system OK's,* FAYETTEVILLE OBSERVER, April 25, 2002.

Washington, Michelle, *surgery bid submitted,* FAYETTEVILLE OBSERVER, April 22, 2002.

Wasley, T. Mackinac Institute for Public Policy, *Certificates of Need: Poor Health Care Policy* (Jun 7, 1993).

Watson, Bob, *Finalization of changes to certificate of need process coming soon,* JEFFERSON CITY NEWS TRIBUNE, Feb. 16, 2002.

Waxman, Henry A, *New health planning bill,* CONGRESSIONAL REC.

Weaver, Judith A, Esq. National Health Lawyers Association, *The Franchising of Long Term Care.*

Webster, Sarah A, *Law restricts number of surgical centers: Michigan Lawmakers consider modifying the rule that requires outpatient clinics prove they're needed,* DETROIT NEWS, at p.1-3.

Webster, Sarah A, *State rules pinch patient care: Thirty-year old law limits access to high-tech diagnostic tests, restricts hospital expansion,* DETROIT NEWS, at 1-6.

Wedel, Mark K. *California's legal implications for utilization review as a health care cost containment measure* SAN DIEGO JUSTICE J. Vol. 1, no. 415 (1993) *available at* http://80-web.lexis-nexis.com

Wedig, Gerard J.; Hassan, Mahmud; Sloan, Frank A, *Hospital investment decisions and the cost of capital,* 62. J. OF BUS. p. 517-537 (Oct. 1989).

Weingarten, Joseph P. Jr, *Cooperative ventures in a competitive environment: the influence of regulation on management,* 44. J. OF HEALTHCARE MGMT. p.1-11 (July 1994).

Weinstein SM, *Regulations governing home care programs,* 8. NITAp.361-2 (1985 Sep-Oct).

Weisbrod, Burton A, *The Health care quadrilemma: An Essay on technological change, insurance, quality of care, and cost containment,* 29. J. OF ECONOMIC LITERATURE p. 523-552 (June 1991).

Weissburg C, *Constraints on construction—revisited,* 20. HOSP. F.p.6-7, 34 (1977 Jul-Aug).

Weissburg C; Conn LC, *Health care and hospitals: things to come,* 25. HEALTH SYS. REV.p.42, 44-5 (1992 Jul-Aug).

Weissburg C; Mour AC, *Effect of scanners on nation's health bill remains undecided,* REV. - FEDERATION OF AM. HOSP, 1978 Apr, at 41-3.

Weissburg C; Stern KM, *Restrictive certificate-of-need conditions: do they survive beyond repeal of the law?,* 20. REV. (FEDERATION OF AM. HEALTH SYS.)p.56-7 (1987 Sep-Oct).

Weissman, Joel, Ph.D,, *Uncompensated Hospital Care: Will it be There If We Need It?,*, 276. JAMA (September 11, 1996).

Welch WP, *HMO enrollment: a study of market forces and regulations,* 8. J. OF HEALTH POLITICS, POL'Y & L.p.743-58 (1984 Winter).

Wellborn JL, *Future status of project review programs in health planning process remains uncertain,* REV. - FEDERATION OF AM. HOSP, 1984 Sep-Oct, at 44-6.

Wengel, Sheldon, *We Shall Overcome: And They Did* PROFILES IN HOSP. MARKETING p. 74 (1981 1st Quart).

Werronen HJ, *Health planning costs study indicates significant changes needed in system,* REV. - FEDERATION OF AM. HOSP, 1980 Aug, at 32-3.

Wessler J, *The Mount Sinai story. Down from the mountain and into the streets,* 16. HEALTH PAC BULL.p.3-Dec (1986 Jun).

Wheeler W, *Michigan's new CON reform package: major changes and implementation methods,* 25. MICH. HOSP.p.5-Dec (1989 Feb).

Wheeler, Walter S. III; Hochkammer, William O, *Public Health Code: a closer look at Article 17,* 15. MICH. HOSP. p. 18-20.

Wickizer, T. M, *The Effects of Utilization Review on Hospital Use and Expenditures: A Covariance Analysis,* 27 (April, 1992).

Wiener JM; Stevenson DG; Goldenson SM, *Controlling the supply of long-term care providers in thirteen states,* 10. J. OF AGING & SOC. POL'Yp.51-72 (1999).

Willemain TR, *A model for certification of need for long-term-care beds,* 12 (1977 Winter).

Willey EE, *Senate shepherd. Interview by Carl L. Shires,* 107. VA. MED.p.773-5 (1980 Nov).

Williams S, *Perspectives. Health planning faces new challenges,* 40. WASH. REP. ON MED. & HEALTH p. suppl 4 p. (1986 Feb 17).

Williamson, O.E, *Assessing Vertical Market Restrictions: Antitrust Ramifications of the Transaction Cost Approach,* 127. U. PA. L. REV. (1979).

Wilson TM, *Controlling health care costs: the certificate-of-need experience in Tennessee,* 8. J. OF HEALTH & HUM. RESOURCES ADMIN.p.126-46 (1985 Fall).

Wilson, L. D, *An Example of Hospital Utilization Review,* 150. THE WESTERN J. OF MED. (Jun 1989).

Wilson, Marty; Meeker, Robert, *CON competition steps up,* 21. MICH. HOSP. p. 38.

Wing, Kenneth R, *Health care reform in the year 2000: the view from the front of the classroom* AM. J. OF L. & MED. (Summer-Fall 2000).

Winter, Reni, *Nursing home plan hotly opposed,* THE SUN HERALD, August 8, 2001.

Wits, But, *Things you can do to stop spam before it gets to you* (Jul. 26, 2004), *available at* http://memphis.bizjournals.com/memphis/stories/2004/07/26/smallb2.html.

Wolfson, Lauretta Higgins, *State regulation of health facility planning: the economic theory and political realities of certificates of need* DEPAUL J. OF HEALTH CARE L. (Winter/Spring 2001).

Wood I Jr, *Legal planning constraints on new capital expenditures,* 12. HEALTH SERVICES MANAGERp.5-Apr (1979 Apr).

Woolhandler, Steffie, M.D, M.P.H.; David U. Himmelstein, M.D,, *Costs of Care and Administration at For-Profit and Other Hospitals in the United States* NEW ENGLAND J. OF MED. (Mar 13, 1997).

Woolhouse, Megan, *A $700 million treatment plan,* ATLANTA BUS. CHRON, Apr. 2, 2004.

Woolhouse, Megan, *Ambulatory care battle,* AM. CITY BUS. J, 2/13/04.

Woolhouse, Megan, *Dispute over Atlanta MRI center continuing,* ATLANTA BUS. CHRON, 3/26/04.

Woolhouse, Megan, *Hospitals use CON to fight outpatient centers,* ATLANTA BUS. J, 1/30/04.

Woolhouse, Megan, *Scanning service cited by state health officials,* ATLANTA BUS. CHRON, Jan. 16, 2004.

Woolhouse, Megan, *State's CON law being challenged,* ATLANTA BUS. CHRON, May 14, 2004.

Wooten, Jim, *Grady hospital must find ways to trim costs,* THE ATLANTA J.-CONST.

Worsing, Robert A, Patterson, Lorin E, Gibbens, Kimberly, *Opportunity at sunset: Missouri relaxes its certificate of need requirements for ambulatory surgery centers,* 99. MO. MED. p. 67-71.

Worthington NL; Tyson K; Chin M, *Prospective reimbursement in Maryland,* 6. TOPICS IN HEALTH CARE FINANCINGp.59-68 (1979 Fall).

Wronski, Richard, *Heart surgery plan faces a fight: 1 Elgin hospital balks at other's plea to expand,* CHICAGO TRIBUNE, Dec. 15, 2003.

Wronski, Richard, *Hospitals face off over procedure: One seeks to add open-heart work,* CHICAGO TRI BUNE, Dec. 16, 2003.

www.outpatientsurgery.net, *SUNY Optometrists move forward with ASC plans over MD objections* (3/4/02), *available at* www.outpatientsurgery.net.

Wysocki, Bernard Jr, *Regulation or competition? State battle over how to get reasonable, quality health care,* THE WALL STREET J. *A4 Tuesday (May 7, 2002)*

Yednak, Crystal, Bad news for new hospitals: State says firms don't show need, but talks to go on, CHICAGO TRIBUNE, Jun 19, 2004.

Yednak, Crystal, *Report rips 2 hospital projects: State staff calls plans inefficient,* CHICAGO TRIBUNE, Apr. 21, 2004.

Yednak, Crystal, *State rejects 2 hospital plans: Need in suburbs being questioned,* CHICAGO TRIBUNE, Apr. 22, 2004.

Yelland MJ; Hocking RB; Wright NF, *An improved workers' compensation and rehabilitation certificate,* 162. MED. J. OF AUSTL.p.554 (1995 May 15).

Young, David W, *Planning and controlling health capital: Attaining an appropriate balance between regulation and competition,* 48. MED. CARE REV. p. 261-293 (Fall 1991).

Young, Virginia, *Health agency gets senate reprieve,* ST. LOUIS POST-DISPATCH.

Young, Virginia, *Residential care law debated: Bill would lift ban on new facilities.*

Young, Virginia, *Senators fight to a draw over health bills.*

Yulsman T, *Birth pains for a new machine,* 92. SCI. DIG.p.21 (1984 Jul).

Zeik, Michael, *What Physicians Need to Know; New State CON Law,* 96. PA. MED.p.4-Dec (1993 Mar).

Zepf, Bill. M.D, *Integrating pet and CT for lung cancer staging,* AM. FAM. PHYSICIAN.

Zwanziger, J.; Melnick, G. A.; Bamezai, A, The Effect of Selective Contracting on Hospital Costs and Revenues, 35 (Oct 2000).

1991-92 in review: physicians, lobbyists work for good of all., 96. PA. MED.p.5-Dec (1993 Jan).

1996 Georgia General Assembly: a successful, defensive session, 40. GA. HOSP. TODAY p. 4, 6 (1996 Apr).

2 hospitals join up on Morristown cancer center, THE KNOXVILLE NEWS-SENTINEL, December 2, 2002.

52-bed hospital proposed: St Luke's announces plans to build Lee's Summit center, THE KAN. CITY STAR, February 22, 2002.

A complicated birth/bond act, five lawsuits, and a failed merger of three hospitals all played part in how Geisinger Medical Center came to be, THE TIMES LEADER, May 20, 2001.

A model for NHI in America., MOD. HEALTHCARE, 1979 Nov, at 3.

ACMC taking over virtual mobile paramedic units, PRESS OF ATLANTIC CITY, March 26, 2002.

Acquisition: Agreement in principle not enforceable under defraud, eighth circuit determines, 3. BNA s HEALTH L. REPORTER.

Acquisitions: FTC requires Columbia/HCA to divest outpatient surgical center in acquisition, 3. BNA s HEALTH L. REPORTER.

Acquisitions: Scaled-back purchase would resolve FTC concerns about psychiatric hospitals, 3. BNA s HEALTH L. REPORTER.

Ad Hoc Committee to Defend Health Care, For Our Patients, Not For Profits: A Call to action,, 278. JAMA (December 3, 1997,).

AGENCY FOR HEALTH CARE ADMINISTRATION, INTERIM REPORT OF THE FLORIDA CON WORKGROUP, (2001).

Agency officials give go ahead to allow creation of state's first for-profit hospital, BNA HEALTH CARE POL'Y REP., Apr. 8, 2002.

AHCA's Congressional Conference: health planning (H.R. 3917, S. 544)., 5. J. AM. HEALTH CARE ASS'N.p.7, 9-10, 12 (1979 Jul).

AHPA adopts proposal to streamline health planning., 10. HEALTH PLAN. & MANPOWER REP.sp.3 (1981 Mar 25).

Alabama: Emtala does not preempt state CON statute, court holds, 5. BNA S HEALTH L. REPORTER.

Alabama: State court reverses, remands CON case, sets aside approval of nursing home bed, 8. BNA S HEALTH L. REPORTER.

Alaska: Community hospital's restrictive policy illegally limits abortion rights, court rules, 6. BNA S HEALTH L. REPORTER.

Allegheny agrees to sell eight hospitals to Vanguard if bankruptcy court approves, BNA HEALTH CARE POL'Y REP., Aug 10, 1998.

Alliance for governmental action opposes Edward's for-profit cardiac center as unwarranted duplication of existing services, PR NEWSWIRE, August 23, 1999.

Alliance of competing hospitals fights proposed heart hospital's CON, 8. BNA S HEALTH L. REPORTER (Sep. 23, 1999).

Analysis: Detroit automakers oppose plan to build new hospitals in suburbs, fearing insurance premium increases, MORNING EDITION, Mar 23, 2004.

Anclote decision sharpens link between valuation and inurement, 7. BNA S HEALTH L. REPORTER.

Antitrust - implied repeal of the antitrust laws by the National Health Planning Act, 56. TUL. L. REV. p.749-803 (February 1982).

Antitrust and certificate of need: a doubtful prognosis, 69. IOWA L. REV. p.1451-1481 (July 1984).

Appeals court affirms state pick between competing CON proposals, 9. BNA S HEALTH L. REPORTER (Feb 17, 2000).

Appeals court again to hear coliseum case: state court may set October or November date to hear case on open-heart program, THE MACON TELEGRAPH, March 21, 2002.

appeals court reverses, remands denial of liver transplant certificate of need, 8. BNA S HEALTH L. REPORTER (Aug. 5, 1999).

Appeals court upholds state commission's grant of CON to Marriott nursing home, 8. BNA S HEALTH L. REPORTER (Mar. 18 1999).

Appropriateness review looms as next major battleground in health planning., REV. - FEDERATION OF AM. HOSP., 1980 Aug, at 13-8.

Arkansas nursing-home developer OK'd to build in Mississippi county, ADVOCATE, October 19, 1999.

As CON laws disappear, quality becomes more important in decisions, 23. HOSP. PEER REV. p. 197-201.

ASC regulation raises questions about certificate of need program, BNA HEALTH CARE POL'Y REP., Oct 28, 1996.

Assessing Need: area lawmaker says the uncontrolled expansion of medical projects is harming health care locally, and she wants to bring back an old law to rein them in, THE TIMES LEADER, April 8, 2001.

Atlanta hospital sues rival, claiming exclusionary contracts violate state law, 9. BNA S HEALTH L. REPORTER (June 15, 2000).

Audit says health planning board is inconsistent, ST. J.-REG., September 28, 2001.

Baptist gets ok to build surgery center, COMMERCIAL APPEAL, December 14, 2002.

Baptist makes golden move, MEMPHIS BUS. J., July 14, 2003.

Baptist opts not to appeal hospital's relocation: official says action would hurt community, THE KNOXVILLE NEWS-SENTINEL, November 8, 2002.

Baptist wins OK to build W. Knox hospital: State panel approves certificate despite opposition, THE KNOXVILLE NEWS-SENTINEL, December 16, 1999.

Baptist's bid for women's hospital OK'd, THE KNOXVILLE NEWS-SENTINEL, November 19, 1998.

Barnes-Jewish St. Peters opens outpatient surgery center, ST. LOUIS BUS. J., 7/11/03.

Bayhealth Medical Center Delaware bonds rated 'AA-' by Fitch IBCA, PR NEWSWIRE, April 30, 1999.

Beaumont wins 105 beds: prospect of bigger health system concerns rivals, DETROIT FREE PRESS, March 1, 2001.

Bed need formula creates presumption of sufficient beds., 24. J. OF HEALTH & HOSP. L.p.376-7 (1991 Dec).

Beds in nursing homes enough for now, state counted extra 3,318 beds in 2000: more facilities unlikely to be built, LEXINGTON HERALD-LEADER, April 3, 2002.

Bill seeks fast track for new digital hospital, BIRMINGHAM NEWS, August 8, 2001.

Bill to streamline health regulation, preserve oversight of spending signed, BNA HEALTH CARE POL'Y REP., May 27, 1996.

Bill would provide more equity, hospital, medical associations say, 10. BNA S HEALTH L. REPORTER (Apr. 26 2001).

Bill would repeal CON program (April 22, 2002).

BJC gerts state OK for new O'Fallon, Mo., hospital, ST. LOUIS BUS. J., Mar. 29, 2004.

BJC gets state OK for new O'Fallon, Mo., hospital, ST. LOUIS BUS. J., Mar. 29, 2004.

Blue Cross forces Dayton hospital to abide by HSA decision., 7. HEALTH PLAN. & MANPOWER REP.sp.9 (1978 Aug 2).

Board confident of nursing home ok, PANTAGRAPH, November 16, 2001.

Board wants to hear from public on lease of hospital, CHARLOTTE OBSERVER, Nov. 17, 1999.

Bon Secours moves ahead with its medical center plan: officials will offer campus setting on Princess Anne Road in Kempsville area, VIRGINIAN-PILOT, December 16, 1999.

Briefly construction news, MOD. HEALTHCARE, March 3, 2003, at p. 19.

Brooklyn bed need findings rebutted by hospital group over claim of 'excess' beds., 52. HOSP.p.23 (1978 Sep 16).

Bullitt might get diagnostic center in 2003, LEXINGTON HERALD-LEADER, February 25, 2002.

Bumps in rocky road to joint ventures for ancillary services being illuminated, 6. BNA S HEALTH L. REPORTER.

Calvani outlines FTC's concerns in health-care competition (Feb. 21,1986), *available at* www.ftc.gov/opa/predawn/f86/healthcare.htm.

Can health care affliction be treated?, BLADE, February 9, 1999.

Cancer center, children's hospital on agenda Thursday, POST-STANDARD, May 14, 2002.

Cancer-center rivalry takes new turn: both hospital groups vying to build a York County facility now have their own endorsements, PORTLAND PRESS HERALD, December 24, 2002.

Care center receives certificate of need: Sterling house, Quincy facility get state board's OK, J. STAR, August 20, 1999.

Carroll Co. hospital seeks $35 million expansion: 30 beds would be added, size of the ER doubled, THE SUN, May 4, 2001.

Case history: surgeons, hospital at odds: certificate of need is the key to case of surgeons vs. hospital, BOSTON GLOBE, May 16, 1999.

Catholic Hospital (A): an evaluation of the feasibility of two major metropolitan health centers sharing a computerized axial tomography system. CASE STUD. IN HEALTH ADMIN.p.117-25 (1983).

Center files to get bed space: High Point Hospital asks to buy licenses for 16 beds at AMOS, WINSTON SALEM J., March 12, 2002.

Central Maine Medical Center is approved for cardiac surgery center (November 27, 2000).

CEO explains merger of hospitals, BUFFALO NEWS, August 27, 1999.

Certificate of need futures: Bridge or barrier? HEALTH PLAN. TODAY p. 5-6 (2nd Quarter 2001).

Certificate of need laws., 37. CONN. MED.p.468-70 (1973 Sep).

Certificate of need not necessary to supply medical equipment to hospitals, 11. BNA S HEALTH L. REPORTER (Jan. 17, 2002).

Certificate of need process has served patients, system well: State should keep it, DETROIT FREE PRESS, January 27, 2002.

Certificate of Need Regulation and Entry: Evidence From the Dialysis Industry., 59. SOUTHERN ECONOMIC J.p.783 (April 1993).

Certificate of need revisions on the way., 11. MPS MED. PRODUCTS SALESMANp.29-30 (1980 Mar).

Certificate of need unnecessary for supplying equipment to hospitals, 11. BNA S HEALTH L. REPORTER (Dec 12, 2002).

Certificate of Need: Few alternatives seen as CON laws are threatened by rise of managed care, 6. BNA S HEALTH L. REPORTER.

Certificate of need: Florida city files lawsuit to block closing of hospital, 3. BNA S HEALTH L. REPORTER.

Certificate of need: Ninth circuit rejects antitrust challenge in CON denial attributed to lobbying drive, 7. BNA S HEALTH L. REPORTER.

Certificate of Need: Ohio law highlights sweeping changes for state CON programs, 4. BNA S HEALTH L. REPORTER.

CERTIFICATE OF NEED: REPUBLICAN LEGISLATURES ATTEMPTING CON ROLL-BACK, (1995).

Certificate of need: Town hall meeting HEALTH PLAN. TODAY p. 6, 8 (2nd Quarter 2001).

Certificate of needs hearing, FAYETTEVILLE OBSERVER, May 10, 2002.

'Certificate' rules reduce risks after surgery: study, THE GAZETTE, October 16., 2002.

Certificate-of-need laws., 288. NEW ENGLAND J. OF MED.p.1186-7 (1973 May 31).

Certificate-of-need program., 287. NEW ENGLAND J. OF MED.p.307 (1972 Aug 10).

Certificate-of-need requirements eliminated for most health facilities under new law, BNA HEALTH CARE POL'Y REP., July 13, 1998.

Challenge in Poughkeepsie is first to 'virtual mergers' in health care, 7. BNA S HEALTH L. REPORTER.

Chester county hospital taps into specialized care: officials plan to open a $12 million open-heart surgery center in 2001. The facility would limit the need to send patients elsewhere, PHILA. INQUIRER, June 8, 2000.

Chiles Signs health measures including facility manager background check bill, BNA HEALTH CARE POL'Y REP., June 29, 1998.

Circuit court rules planning board exceeded authority in promulgating emergency rule, 9. BNA S HEALTH L. REPORTER (Sep 28, 2000).

City of Faith dispute in State Supreme Court; moratorium set in Tulsa area., REV. - FEDERATION OF AM. HOSP., 1979 Feb, at 23.

City planners skeptical of hospital plan, THE OREGONIAN, December 13, 2002.

City says stay, hospitals say go, THE TAMPA TRIB., April 20, 2002.

Clinic proposes $700,000 expansion, COLUMBIAN, November 15, 2002.

Closings are bitter pill to swallow: business decision affects the health-care needs of pharmacies' customers, WINSTON SALEM J., May 29, 1999.

Collaboration will be key to medical efficiency in 90's, FRESNO BEE, November 2, 1992.

Columbia gets OK to build hospital, DAYTONA BEACH NEWS-J., August 3, 1999.

Comments and recommendations on the Department of Health, Education and Welfare's proposed resource standards concerning computed tomography: The Radiation Imaging Products Division of the National Electrical Manufacturers Association (NEMA)., 2. J. OF COMPUTED TOMOGRAPHYp.61-74 (1978 Mar).

Community can't afford huge richland heart project, THE ST., April 7, 2002.

Community Health Systems executes definitive agreement to acquire Salem, New Jersey hospital, BUS. WIRE, November 2, 2001.

Company planner raises some question about anti-trust FAH REV. p. 17 (Aug. 1980).

Competition endangers care system, hospital says, SEATTLE POST-INTELLIGENCER, April 27, 1998.

Competition is at the heart of a struggle: new surgery programs are cutting into established ones, quality of care is at issue, PHILA. INQUIRER, May 17, 1998.

CON applications in a traffic jam., 26. MED. WORLD NEWSp.24 (1985 Sep 9).

CON bill for outpatient surgery enacted into law by Gov. Easley, BNA HEALTH CARE POL'Y REP., July 9, 2001.

CON bill for outpatient surgery enacted into law by Gov. Easley, 10. BNA S HEALTH L. REPORTER (July 5, 2001).

CON committee member resignations delay decisions on health projects, BNA HEALTH CARE POL'Y REP., Sep. 30, 1996.

Conditional OK given for Brenner Tower, WINSTON SALEM J., July 1, 1999.

Conn. hospital expanding cardiac care (Apr. 23, 2004), *available at* http://news.yahoo.com/news?tmpl=story&cid=534&u=/ap/20040422/ap_on_he_me/cardiac_care....

CONs come back in context of state reform plans. American Hospital Association, State Issue Forum., 66. HOSP.p.44 (1992 Dec 20).

Conversions: State lawmakers give AGs more punch to regulate for-profit transactions, 6. BNA S HEALTH L. REPORTER.

Corrections, clarification (Nov. 24, 2003).

County hospital files to build PSL facility, STUART NEWS/PORT ST. LUCIE NEWS, March 15, 2002.

County needs 2nd hospital, officials say, WASHINGTON POST, June 13, 2002.

County to weigh nursing home plan, THE TIMES UNION, October 12, 1999.

Court affirms denial of new provider status exemption from routine cost limits for SNF, 10. BNA S HEALTH L. REPORTER (June 14, 2001).

Court approves transfer of operations for Puget Sound Hospital, PR NEWSWIRE, July 14, 2000.

Court order closes Mississippi hospital, ADVOCATE, January 2, 2000.

Court sides with mobile kidney stone breakers: ruling says providers don't need state approval to provide services, BIRMINGHAM NEWS (AL), November 26, 2002.

Court strikes down North Carolina certificate of need law, says hospitals are similar to businesses., MOD. HOSP., 1973 Mar, at 50 passim.

Court upholds CON for nursing home beds, dissent considers process anticompetitive, 9. BNA S HEALTH L. REPORTER (Oct. 5, 2000).

Crawford Long gets ready for a face lift, THE ATLANTA J.-CONST., November 30, 1999.

Credit-rating agencies and hospital lenders, 5. TOPICS IN HEALTH CARE FINANCINGp.55-64 (1978 Fall).

Critics blast health facilities proposal, TELEGRAPH HERALD, February 11, 2000.

Day surgery to find space at health center, THE HARTFORD COURANT, June 15, 2002.

DCH approves Emory cardiac catheterization expansion request. ATLANTA BUS. CHRON. (2002) available at http://atlanta.bizjournals.com.

Dean signs bill to continue state's expanded medicaid program, BNA HEALTH CARE POL'Y REP., Feb 26, 1996.

Delaware: State should consider changes to expand coverage, panel says, 6. BNA s HEALTH L. REPORTER.

Delays in California CON process add $25 million to costs., REV. - FEDERATION OF AM. HOSP., 1980 Sep-Oct, at 44-5.

Dems want to regulate hospital costs: call for limits on new construction, CAPITAL TIMES, May 29, 2002.

Denial of CON to retirement center upheld by Nebraska Supreme Court, 8. BNA s HEALTH L. REPORTER (Jan. 7, 1999).

Denial of MRI unit by Michigan agencies can't be challenged, 8. BNA s HEALTH L. REPORTER (Mar. 4, 1999).

Department of justice and federal trade commission statements of antitrust enforcement policy in health care, 5. BNA s HEALTH L. REPORTER.

Despite objections, district is expected to start preparations for Miramar hospital, THE MIAMI HERALD, May 21, 2002, at 10B.

Development of a master plan for a Medical Center CASE STUD. IN HEALTH ADMIN.p.104-8 (1983).

Diagnostic radiology guidelines: the Commonwealth of Massachusetts Department of Public Health., 2. RADIOLOGY MGMT.p.14-20 (1980 Spring).

Dialysis unit decision postponed, WATERTOWN DAILY TIMES, June 7, 2002.

Disabled adults await care: budget cuts freeze a statewide alternative to nursing homes, GREENSBORO NEWS & REC., October 11, 2001.

Distance to treatment center and mastectomy vs. Lumpectomy, NEWSWISE.

Distinguishing between cooperation and conspiracy. Swarthmore Radiation Oncology, Inc. v. Lapes., 11. HOSP. L. NEWSL.p.4-Jan (1994 Mar).

District of Columbia regulations broadening scope of CON law upheld., 24. J. OF HEALTH & HOSP. L.p.320 (1991 Oct).

District of Columbia: Panel recommends total restructuring of D.C. system to improve efficiency, 4. BNA s HEALTH L. REPORTER.

Divestiture: Columbia/HCA to divest hospital to resolve FTC's competitive concerns, 4. BNA s HEALTH L. REPORTER.

Divided third circuit upholds dismissal of CON case on state action grounds, 8. BNA s HEALTH L. REPORTER (Aug. 5, 1999).

Doctors battling for cancer center: Georgetown Memorial wants own site, THE SUN NEWS, Nov. 6, 1999.

Doctors' offices coming under CON MED. WORLD NEWS p. 11 (Aug. 21, 1978).

Doctors plan to build Horn Lake medical building with lower rents, COMMERCIAL APPEAL, December 8, 2001.

Doctors sue afterplans for surgery center blocked (Mar. 10, 2004), *available at* www.thestate.com/mld/thestate/news/local/8152109.htm?template=contentModules/printso....

DOH approves area hospital projects, BUS. REV., February 5, 2002.

Don't kill Missouri's health review agency.

Doubt raised on prospects for state ok of town of Tonawanda abortion facility, BUFFALO NEWS, April 18, 2002.

Dueling heart centers could be bad for health care, THE ST., March 17, 2002.

*Durham Regional Hospital to open LTAC DURHAM REGIONAL HOSP. TO OPEN LTAC (2002) available at*http://triangle.bizjournals.com

Durham, N.C. hospital continues to seek approval for new building, KNIGHT-RIDDER/TRIB. BUS. NEWS, July 10, 2002.

E.R. economics: health care: two hospitals aren't excited about the prospect of new competition, ORANGE COUNTY REG., June 11, 1996.

East Manatee to get hospital branch, BRADENTON HERALD, October 29, 1999.

End state's unwieldy medical rationing, DETROIT NEWS, March 1, 2002.

Enforcement: State activity on increase, approach more regulatory than feds, 4. BNA S HEALTH L. REPORTER.

Essent's Sharon hospital deal nears completion (7/28/2004), *available at* http://nashville.bizjournals.com/nashville/stories/2002/03/11/daily12.html?t=printable.

Exclusive contracts: Excluded anesthesiologist can't attack exclusive contract, peer review process, 7. BNA S HEALTH L. REPORTER.

Exempt status: IRS properly revoked exempt status of Florida hospital due to inurement, 7. BNA S HEALTH L. REPORTER.

Exemption denied: Surgical practice loses as court upholds CON program, MOD. HEALTHCARE, 9/20/2004, at 1 p.

Exemptions: Denial of MRI unit by Michigan agencies can't be challenged under antitrust law, 8. BNA S HEALTH L. REPORTER.

Expanding cardiac care, PITTSBURGH POST-GAZETTE, February 21, 1999.

FAH and AHA making separate studies of the planning laws FAH REV. p. 17-18 (Aug. 1980).

Fast track and public health and safety (6/6/02), *available at* www.citizen.org/trade/fasttrack/fthealth/articles.cfm?ID=7643.

Fast track endangers public health (6/6/02), *available at* www.citizen.org/trade/fasttrack/fthealth/articles.cfm?ID=4986.

Few alternatives seen as CON laws are threatened by rise of managed care, BNA HEALTH CARE POL'Y REP., Oct. 6 1997.

Few complaints result from demise of state's certificate-of-need program, BNA HEALTH CARE POL'Y REP., Aug 11, 1997.

Financial News: TriPath imaging (10/5/2004), *available at* http://www.80-web-lexis-nexis.com.ezproxy.umuc.edu/universe/document?_m=66c6a0123d2fcc....

Firm finds new site for hospital, THE MIAMI HERALD, June 15, 1984.

First certificate of need inventory released., 12. HEALTH PLAN. & MANPOWER REP.sp.6-May (1983 May 4).

Five W. VA. hospitals announce plans to study forming nonprofit alliance, BNA HEALTH CARE POL'Y REP., Apr. 14, 1997.

FLA. Facilities must report quality, price data, OUTPATIENT SURGERY MAG., 8/1/2004, at 1 p.

Florida: Auditors recommend CON changes to deal with long-term care shifts, 5. BNA S HEALTH L. REPORTER.

Florida: Budget plan estimates savings of $44.4 million from Medicaid managed care, 5. BNA S HEALTH L. REPORTER.

Florida: Civil penalty assessed against vencor over medicaid patients' discharge, 7. BNA S HEALTH L. REPORTER.

Florida: Columbia/HCA to close hospitals, keep CONs in exchange for dropping suit, 5. BNA S HEALTH L. REPORTER.

Florida: Governor signs background screening bill; allows deregulation measure to become law, 7. BNA S HEALTH L. REPORTER.

Florida: State officials seek to revoke hospital license following death, 3. BNA S HEALTH L. REPORTER.

Florida: State revokes license of destin hospital, citing failure to meet settlement terms, 4. BNA S HEALTH L. REPORTER.

Focus...Missouri Hospital Patterns, available at (www.Health.statemo.us/MonthlyVital Statistics).

For your information... August 10, 1987 FOR YOUR INFORMATION (Aug. 10, 1987).

For your information... June 22, 1989 FOR YOUR INFORMATION (June 22, 1989).

For your information... March 7, 1988 FOR YOUR INFORMATION (Mar. 7, 1988).

For your information... March 9, 1988 FOR YOUR INFORMATION (Mar. 9, 1988).

Ford urges national solution to U.S. healthcare, USA TODAY, Apr 7, 2004.

Forsyth Medical Center planning to replace ICU with updated unit if state oks request: hospital cam make more rooms private, WINSTON SALEM J., September 25, 2001.

fourth circuit court affirms HCFA refusal to pay costs for certificate of need, 8. BNA S HEALTH L. REPORTER (Apr. 15, 1999).

Frankfort, Ky., MOD. HEALTHCARE, Jan. 20, 2003, at p. 29.

Frankfort, Ky., MOD. HEALTHCARE, Jan. 20, 2003, at p. 29.

Frankfurt hospital to get $25,000, SOUTHERN ILLINOISAN, July 16, 2002.

Frankfurt hospitals electricity shut off, SOUTHERN ILLINOISAN, July 12, 2002.

Franklin county hospital possible, SOUTHERN ILLINOISAN, June 29, 2002.

Fraud and abuse: Group practices concerned about centralized location provision, 3. BNA S HEALTH L. REPORTER.

Frisbie Memorial Hospital's CON nears completion (March 19, 2001).

From our readers: allow transfer of unused hospital beds, DETROIT FREE PRESS (MI), December 10, 2002.

FTC and DOJ issue report on competition and health care, available at http://www.ftc.gov/opa/2004/7/healthcarerpt.html.

FTC Chairman Announces public hearings on health care and competition law and policy to begin in February 2003, available at http://www.ftc.gov/opa/2002/11/murishealthcare.html.

Garden View Care Center v. Missouri Health Facilities Review Committee, WEST'S REGIONAL REPORTER, 1996.

General assembly overrides veto of hospital purchase legislation, BNA HEALTH CARE POL'Y REP., July 28, 1997.

Georgia: Bill to eliminate hospital CON requirements unlikely to pass, 6. BNA S HEALTH L. REPORTER.

Georgia: Columbia/HCA won't pursue elimination of CON; will proceed on as-needed basis, 6. BNA S HEALTH L. REPORTER.

Georgia: Court finds state health planning agency exceeded powers in granting CON after move, 7. BNA S HEALTH L. REPORTER.

Georgia: Health agency cannot exempt facility from CON rules based on relocation, 3. BNA S HEALTH L. REPORTER.

Georgia: Hospital chain objects to designating long-term beds without CON review, 6. BNA S HEALTH L. REPORTER.

Georgia: Nursing home group sues state over medicaid payment freeze, BNA S HEALTH L. REPORTER.

Georgia: Vencor sues state health agency over policy on long-term care beds within hospitals, BNA S HEALTH L. REPORTER.

Gov. Bush signs nursing home, HMO contracting, other health bills, 8. BNA s HEALTH L. REPORTER.

Governor gets bill to expand youth psychiatric beds, THE SUN HERALD, March 29, 2001.

Governor gets' involved in CON dispute over Health Management Associates hospital, 8. BNA s HEALTH L. REPORTER (June 17, 1999).

Governor gets involved in CON dispute over Health Management Associates hospital, BNA HEALTH CARE POL'Y REP., June 21, 1999.

Governor shuts down health care spending, THE KY. POST, June 1, 2001.

Governor signs bill to eliminate waiting period for SCHIP coverage, BNA HEALTH CARE POL'Y REP., May 29, 2000.

Governor vetoes legislation to allow expansion of medicaid nursing home beds, BNA HEALTH CARE POL'Y REP., Apr. 27, 1998.

Governor's appointee comes under fire, ST. LOUIS TODAY, 8/12/2004, at 2 P.

Hawaii: State latest to adopt statute governing for-profit purchase of nonprofit hospitals, 7. BNA s HEALTH L. REPORTER.

HCA needs new hospital, THE BUS. J. KANSAS CITY, Jun 21, 2004.

HCA touts jobs, taxes for county: health care company defends hospital plan, WASHINGTON POST, August 11, 2002.

HCFA reviewing thousands of comments on proposed Stark II self-referral rule, BNA HEALTH CARE POL'Y REP., May 18, 1998.

Health access New Jersey. Position of the Medical Society of New Jersey., 87. N.J. MED.p.785-9 (1990 Oct).

Health board gives final approval to regulations revamping CON process, BNA HEALTH CARE POL'Y REP., Jan. 29, 1996.

Health board wants to simplify process, THE KAN. CITY STAR, August 3, 2001.

Health Care Alabama, Pros and CONS: Is There Still a Need for Certificate of Need? HEALTHCARE AL. (May-Jun 1992).

Health care choice: doctors have better plan for dialysis unit, WATERTOWN DAILY TIMES, June 5, 2002.

Health care conflict: Hatfield and McCoy continuum, THE MACON TELEGRAPH, February 9, 2002.

Health care conflict: who should decide what equipment is built, and where?: a move is afoot to eliminate the Certificates of Need that are now required to build or buy equipment or buildings in health care, ME. SUNDAY TELEGRAM, April 7, 2002.

Health care deregulation's only foe: cost, ROANOKE TIMES, January 20, 2001.

Health care isn't just a burden - it's a major economic opportunity, DENVER POST, July 20, 1991.

Health chief may reconsider heart center: the commissioner says he hopes CMMC will act on its own to change its policy on doctors' affiliations, PORTLAND PRESS HERALD, April 12, 2002.

Health dept. is target: hospital sues to obtain scanner, AM. MED. NEWS, April 2, 1982, at 1.

Health future predicted for nursing home industry., 16. MEDICAL PRODUCT SALESp.52, 55 (1985 Apr).

Health official can impose moratorium on nursing home CON application process, 10. BNA s HEALTH L. REPORTER (Aug. 30, 2001).

Health planning amendments—AHA's analysis., TIMES, 1980 Mar, at 26-9.

Health planning board had power but resistance brought down, STAR TRIB., April 14, 1991.

Health planning in action—accounts and anecdotes., 93. PUB. HEALTH REP.sp.24-30 (1978 Jan-Feb).

Health planning is still alive and well., 66. MED. ECONOMICSp.15 (1989 Nov 20).

Health systems agencies and state health planning and development agencies: proposed rulemaking., 43. FED. REG.p.11229-41 (1978 Mar 17).

Health-Care competition heating up in east Cooper, THE ST., December 19, 1999.

Health-care cost containment reviews shelved: legislation adjourns before extending law on wasteful spending, PITTSBURGH POST-GAZETTE, November 28, 1996.

Healthcare president works to license West Frankfort hospital, SOUTHERN ILLINOISAN, July 9, 2002.

Healthcare shortcomings, THE MACON TELEGRAPH, February 10, 2002.

Healthplan moratorium is extended: bans will stay in place despite their expiration, officials concerned about costs, LEXINGTON HERALD-LEADER, April 19, 2002.

HealthSouth argues digital hospital too far along to halt: lawsuit contends regulatory exemption unconstitutional, BIRMINGHAM NEWS (AL), October 29, 2002.

HealthTronics, Inc. acquires New Jersey Kidney Stone Treatment Center (Jan. 25, 2000), *available at* www.findarticles.com/cf_0/m0EIN/2000_Jan_25/58937891/p1/article.jhtml?term=%2....

Heart care a key service duplicated by local hospitals, THE TIMES LEADER, March 24, 2002.

Heart center in the works, MOD. HEALTHCARE, Feb. 3, 2003, at p. 24.

Heart department gets nod: after four failed attempts, Indian River memorial hospital gets initial approval for an open-heart surgery unit, VERO BEACH PRESS J., August 21, 2002.

Heart hospital vital to palmetto health's mission, THE ST., March 23, 2002.

High court declines to review four health law cases as term nears end, 9. BNA s HEALTH L. REPORTER (June 29, 2000).

high court will not hear antitrust challenge in denial of CON for kidney dialysis center, 8. BNA s HEALTH L. REPORTER (Mar. 4, 1999).

Hillsboro Providence has plans for new hospital along Cornell Road, THE OREGONIAN.

HMA wins CON approval, MOD. HEALTHCARE, Feb. 3, 2003, at p. 24.

Holder of certificate held not liable: Home was leased, operated by another, 9. BNA s HEALTH L. REPORTER (May 4, 2000).

Hospice is now ready to build, its officials say: with in-home care in place, permanent structure can proceed, CHARLOTTE OBSERVER, November 1, 2001.

Hospital acquisitions: States review oversight activity as non-profit hospital sales increase, 4. BNA s HEALTH L. REPORTER.

Hospital allowed to withdraw appeal of ruling approving rival's expansion plans, 10. BNA s HEALTH L. REPORTER (Dec. 13, 2001).

Hospital appealed CON denial., 59. HOSP. PROGRESSp.82 (1978 Nov).

Hospital approvals moving to new agency, NASHVILLE BUS. J., June 7, 2002.

Hospital asserts antitrust immunity as defense to false statements in Certificate of Need hearings. HEALTH CARE L. MON.p.25-7 (1999 Sep).

Hospital assets: District court rejects bankruptcy court on hospital assets subject to review, 6. BNA s HEALTH L. REPORTER.

Hospital attorneys withdraw challenges in case involving certificate of need, 9. BNA s HEALTH L. REPORTER (Jan. 27, 2000).

Hospital beds empty: capacity down but still far beyond need, DETROIT FREE PRESS, February 5, 2002.

Hospital board scandal trail leaders to bipartisan gift-giving, THE ILL. LEADER, 8/12/2004, at 3 p.

Hospital buildup vexing, ROCKY MOUNTAIN NEWS, September 10, 1995.

Hospital can expand heart center after surviving certificate of need challenge, 11. BNA S HEALTH L. REPORTER (Sep. 26, 2002).

Hospital cardiac care facility rejected again by regulators, 9. BNA S HEALTH L. REPORTER (June 8, 2000).

Hospital CON requirements bill unlikely to be enacted this year, BNA HEALTH CARE POL'Y REP., Mar. 24, 1997.

Hospital cost controls expire: law was designed to stop duplication of expensive services, PITTSBURGH POST-GAZETTE, December 19, 1996.

Hospital drops challenge to head program, ADVOCATE, October 27, 2001.

Hospital expansion deplored, BOSTON GLOBE, March 29, 1984.

Hospital expansion is delayed, WASH. POST, June 27, 1984.

Hospital expansion needs review.

Hospital eyes expansion, PHILA. DAILY NEWS, June 10, 1993.

Hospital files radiation center plan, THE UNION LEADER, August 2, 2002.

Hospital financial outlook is gloomy: Moody's saw little chance of improvement soon at not-for-profit institutions, patients could be affected, PHILA. INQUIRER, August 22, 2000.

Hospital free-for-all: general assembly: using political muscle to obtain open-heart surgery centers destroys regulatory system, THE SUN, April 12, 1999.

Hospital is given OK to relocate: Clark Regional plans to move to bypass, LEXINGTON HERALD-LEADER, December 31, 2002.

Hospital keeps hopes beating for unit: Indian River memorial hospital submits a bid for an open-heart surgery unit again, VERO BEACH PRESS J., July 4, 2002.

Hospital keeps hopes beating for unit: Indian River Memorial Hospital submits a bid for an open-heart surgery unit again, VERO BEACH PRESS J., July 4, 2002.

Hospital lease extension on agenda, CHARLOTTE OBSERVER, Nov. 15, 1999.

Hospital limits: certificate of need process needs to be defended, DETROIT FREE PRESS (MI), August 17, 1999.

Hospital maternity services urged, UNION NEWS, August 3, 1991.

Hospital merger approval nears, THE TIMES UNION, October 4, 2000.

Hospital plan: boost or threat?: specialty surgical hospital under consideration, but opponents fear revenue bleed from KMC, SPOKESMAN-REV..

Hospital plans for rehab center: High Point Regional must first get state approval to acquire beds from a Winston-Salem hospital, GREENSBORO NEWS & REC., March 8, 2002.

Hospital plans to double in size: Baptist-DeSoto wants to add 10-story tower, THE SUN HERALD, September 22, 2002.

Hospital plans to improve facility, BRADENTON HERALD, October 10, 1999.

Hospital playing politics, critics say: Englewood has edge in heart program bid, THE REC., July 15, 1999.

Hospital proposal rejected: company sought $57 million facility in Lee's Summit, THE KAN. CITY STAR, June 4, 2002.

Hospital reimbursement: Denial of medicare reimbursement for certificate and license affirmed, 7. BNA S HEALTH L. REPORTER.

Hospital relocations appealed: lawmaker out to block community, North Bay, THE TAMPA TRIB., July 17, 2002.

Hospital scanners need state okay in Massachusetts., 53. HOSP.p.17-8 (1979 Feb 1).

Hospital seeks to offer open=heart surgery, SEATTLE POST-INTELLIGENCER, September 6, 2002.

Hospital sues over CAT scanner denial., AM. MED. NEWS, 1982 Apr 9, at 6.

Hospital to be built in one phase, PRESS OF ATLANTIC CITY, March 14, 2001.

Hospital wars affect the entire community, BLADE, June 29, 1999.

Hospital with disputed CON closes: Governor's executive order overruled, BNA HEALTH CARE POL'Y REP., Jan. 10, 200.

Hospital with disputed CON closes: Governor's executive order overruled, 9. BNA s HEALTH L. REPORTER (Jan. 6, 2000).

Hospital withdraws maternity unit plan: state was to deny application, UNION NEWS, August 8, 1991.

Hospital within a hospital proposed, COLUMBUS LEDGER-ENQUIRER, June 13, 2002.

Hospital won't fill beds, turn profit, agency says: Manatee Memorial's request to move beds into a $40 million complex is questioned, SARASOTA HERALD-TRIB., June 23, 1999.

Hospitals agree to work as a team: Evergreen, Overlake form partnership on selected services, SEATTLE TIMES, September 6, 2002.

Hospital's beds bid denies, BRADENTON HERALD, June 22, 1999.

Hospitals' beef with for-profits ringing hollow, available at Bizjournals.com.

Hospitals can't be closed by legislative fiat, DENVER POST, July 16, 1993.

Hospitals delivering services differently forced by changes in the financing of health care, ST. J.-REG., April 21, 1996.

Hospitals denied approval to perform cardiac surgery, PHILADELPHIA INQUIRER, 2/12/04.

Hospitals expand cardiac care facilities, services, ST. LOUIS BUS. J., May 7, 2004.

Hospitals may win open-heart battle this year: An old General Assembly turf war may have a new outcome, BALT. BUS. J., Feb. 24, 2003.

Hospitals plan emergency room additions: Morehead Memorial Hospital hopes to have its expansion project completed by 2005 or 2006, GREENSBORO NEWS & REC., April 19, 2002.

Hospital's requests will test state officials, THE ST., October 4, 1999.

Hospital's sale approved: state agency backs deal with for-profit company, THE HARTFORD COURANT, March 28, 2002.

House OKs limit to hospital-spending checks: if signed into law, expenditure-review agency could die, ST. J.-REG., May 9, 2000.

House OK's limit to hospital-spending checks: if signed into law, expenditure review agency could die, J.-REG., April 11, 2000.

House panel to review basic health plan, certificate of need in legislative session, BNA HEALTH CARE POL'Y REP., Oct. 20, 1997.

III. Restructures health facilities board in wake of probe, MOD. PHYSICIAN.

Illinois health board needed, but its operations need review, PANTAGRAPH, December 21, 1999.

Illinois: State proposes tighter regulations for oversight of community hospital sales, 7. BNA s HEALTH L. REPORTER.

In pair of decisions, state high court approves one CON, strikes down another, 8. BNA s HEALTH L. REPORTER (Aug. 26, 1999).

Indian River's first psychiatric hospital gets OK, THE MIAMI HERALD, August 2, 1984.

Indiana: Certification of nursing home beds need not cover all beds at facility, 4. BNA s HEALTH L. REPORTER.

Indiana: Two new nursing home bills become law over governor's veto, 6. BNA s HEALTH L. REPORTER.

Industry calls for White House meeting about moratorium on medicare entry, BNA HEALTH CARE POL'Y REP., Sep. 29, 1997.

Inside the southside: hospital seeks to accommodate long-term stays, The Atlanta J.-Const., July 11, 2002.

Insurance coverage: Insurer has duty to defend against antitrust claims, 3. BNA s Health L. Reporter.

InteCardia Imaging opens a new cardiovascular diagnostic center and receives approval for another center in Tennessee, Bus. Wire, December 2, 1999.

Iowa: applying CON requirements to clinic unduly burdens rights, court decides, 6. BNA s Health L. Reporter.

IRS technical advice memo concludes hospital organization has charity tax status, 11. BNA s Health L. Reporter (Jan. 3, 2002).

Jackson eyes north Dade site, The Miami Herald, July 8, 2002, at 9G.

Jewish agency may break ground for new kosher nursing complex by next year: $62.5 million project needs OK from state panel, St. Louis Post-Dispatch, August 19, 1999.

John T. Finley, Inc. v. Missouri Health Facilities Review Committee, West's Regional Reporter, 1995.

Joint venture: Challenge to exemption denial offers clues on IRS whole hospital guidance, 6. BNA s Health L. Reporter.

Joint ventures: FTC staff clears Tenn. joint venture to operate new obstetrical hospital, 4. BNA s Health L. Reporter.

Judge delays SSM women's hospital,, St. Louis Bus. J., September 13,1999.

Judge will hear open-heart unit lawsuit, Birmingham News (AL), December 11, 2002.

Jurisdiction: Federal involvement with state planning does not warrant jurisdiction in dispute, 4. BNA s Health L. Reporter.

Keep health care healthy, The Ky. Post, January 4, 2001.

Kentucky: Doctor's office used for surgery must be licensed as surgical center, 3. BNA s Health L. Reporter.

Kentucky: Lawsuit alleges health reform was promoted by private interests, 3. BNA s Health L. Reporter.

Kentucky: Limited CON law exemption does not violate constitution, court holds, 5. BNA s Health L. Reporter.

Kentucky: Nursing service required certificate to treat patients in their homes, 3. BNA s Health L. Reporter.

Laconia surgery center dispute has snowball effect, Boston Globe, February 14, 1999.

Lapse of law could mean increase in nursing homes, Jefferson City News Trib., Jan. 2, 2003.

Lawmaker wants to halt health care spending surge, St. Paul Pioneer Press, April 7, 1993.

Lawmaker would revive state's certificate of need: Mundy eyes health cost reform, The Times Leader, October 7, 2000.

Lawmakers working to complete work on major medicaid program reforms, BNA Health Care Pol'y Rep., June 16, 1997.

Lawnwood shouldn't appeal hospital's certificate of need, Stuart News/Port St. Lucie News, February 26, 2002.

Legacy picks designer of new Vancouver hospital, Puget Sound Bus. J., 7/28/2004, at 1 p.

Legacy plans for sickest babies, The Oregonian, March 21, 2002.

Legacy wins ok to build hospital, Columbian, March 16, 2002.

Legal challenges delay nursing homes, The Sun Herald, December 19, 1999.

Legal crises limit growth of nursing homes, Bradenton Herald, February 23, 2001.

Legislation provides for health panel swap, Commercial Appeal, May 31, 2002.

Legislature approves bill for regulating hospital conversions to for-profit status, BNA Health Care Pol'y Rep., Jan. 19, 1998.

Legislature approves nursing home funding, Buffalo News, September 13, 2001.

Legislature backs hospital bill, BIRMINGHAM NEWS, September 11, 2001.

Legislatures to help Healthsouth bypass permit law, BIRMINGHAM NEWS, August 23, 2001.

Lenoir City working toward huge expansion: Town Creek project would add 265 acres, THE KNOXVILLE NEWS-SENTINEL, November 9, 2002.

Living with an allowance: Main hospitals review new capital-spending limits, MOD. HEALTHCARE, 9/6/2004, at 1 p.

Local open-heart unit would hurt patients, VERO BEACH PRESS J., February 16, 2002.

Louisiana: Lawmakers working to complete work on medicaid reforms, other bills, 6. BNA S HEALTH L. REPORTER.

Maine Coast Memorial Hospital certificate of need for expansion.

Maine to slow healthcare construction OUTPATIENT SURGERY.

Managed health care competition is becoming a scam, SAN JOSE MERCURY NEWS, February 17, 1993.

Martin Memorial South's emergency room to double in size with $5.1 million expansion, PALM BEACH POST, July 9, 2002.

Maryland: Appeals court upholds state commission's grant of CON to Marriott for nursing home, 8. BNA S HEALTH L. REPORTER.

Maryland: Court finds CON process improperly used to force update of projected cardiac needs, 7. BNA S HEALTH L. REPORTER.

Maryland: General assembly adjourns after passing patients' bill of rights, other legislation, 8. BNA S HEALTH L. REPORTER.

Maryland: Health planning commission, not courts, should decide nursing home CON question, 5. BNA S HEALTH L. REPORTER.

Maryland: Legislature passes 'patient access' law to limit ability to limit providers, 4. BNA S HEALTH L. REPORTER.

Maryland: Nursing home owner, not building owner, retains CON exemption, appeals court rules, 7. BNA S HEALTH L. REPORTER.

Maryland: State regulatory program reduces risk of federal antitrust action, GAO says, 3. BNA S HEALTH L. REPORTER.

Maryland: State will not mount challenge to formation of home health network, 4. BNA S HEALTH L. REPORTER.

Md. health care system a ticking time bomb, THE SUN, August 19, 2001.

Md. hospitals expanding to meet demand, WASHINGTON POST, December 5, 2002.

Medicaid program deficit prompts cuts in new facilities, eligibility, co-payments, BNA HEALTH CARE POLY'S REP., Jan. 27, 2003.

Medicaid program deficit prompts governor to reinstate CON moratorium, 12. BNA S HEALTH L. REPORTER (Jan. 23, 2003).

Medical boom causes alarm: officials are exploring whether the many expensive new services should be licensed, YORK DAILY REC., February 19, 1997.

Medical center may get face lift—$22.5 million project at BroMenn could being this August, J. STAR, May 24, 2001.

Medical Management of Osage Beach, Inc. v. Missouri Health Facilities Review Committee, WEST'S REGIONAL REPORTER, 1995.

Medical need, not politics, should direct DHS choice: the regulatory process ought to focus on costs and results, PORTLAND PRESS HERALD, April 19, 2002.

Medicare rural providers get special attention from congress in BBA refinement bill, BNA HEALTH CARE POL'Y REP., Dec. 13, 1999.

Mercy suggests a deal with dialysis doctors: state postpones approving either of two proposals, WATERTOWN DAILY NEWS, June 7, 2002.

Mergers/acquisitions... health care not-for-profits in Columbia, S.C., 71.p.25 (1997 Jun 20).

Mergers: Consolidation of two health systems will not adversely affect components, 5. BNA S HEALTH L. REPORTER.

Mergers: FTC authorizes staff to seek order blocking Michigan hospital acquisition, 3. BNA S HEALTH L. REPORTER.

Mergers: FTC official examines efficiency justifications of hospital mergers, 3. BNA S HEALTH L. REPORTER.

Mergers: FTC, Missouri AG seek to block hospital merger in Butler County, 7. BNA S HEALTH L. REPORTER.

Michigan court lifts ban on state issuing certificates., 52. HOSP.p.20 (1978 Oct 1).

Michigan Department of Public Health issues NMR certificate of need policies., 84. MICH. MED.p.210, 212 (1985 Apr).

Michigan: CON statutory goals must be met even if medical plan not yet adopted, 5. BNA S HEALTH L. REPORTER.

Michigan: One hospital wins expansion on remand; court upholds others' application denial, 6. BNA S HEALTH L. REPORTER.

Michigan: Site-specific CON not transferable; health department approval required, 5. BNA S HEALTH L. REPORTER.

Mid-America Georgian Gardens, Inc. v. Missouri Health Facilities Review Commission, WEST'S REGIONAL REPORTER, 1995.

Miramar hospital gets initial go-ahead, THE MIAMI HERALD, May 23, 2002, at 6B.

Mississippi: Disputed birthing center wins approval, but hospitals may challenge decision, 3. BNA S HEALTH L. REPORTER.

Mississippi: Exclusive hospital contract doesn't offend Mississippi law, 7. BNA S HEALTH L. REPORTER.

Mississippi: Governor gets involved in CON dispute over health management associates hospital, 8. BNA S HEALTH L. REPORTER.

Mississippi: Governor vetoes legislation to allow expansion of medicaid nursing home beds, 7. BNA S HEALTH L. REPORTER.

Mississippi: River Oaks hospital to appeal ruling blocking its plans for birthing center, 3. BNA S HEALTH L. REPORTER.

Mississippi: State supreme court reverses CON approval granted years ago for already-built hospital, 7. BNA S HEALTH L. REPORTER.

Missouri lifts restrictions on nursing home construction: critics say adding beds will spread customers, employees more thinly, ST. LOUIS POST-DISPATCH, January 2, 2003.

Missouri needs certificate of need.

Missouri: Per Capita Personal Health Care Expenditures, 1998, available at www.statehealthfacts.org.

MMC and SMMC propose cancer care center in York County (January 8, 2002).

MMC and SMMC files certificate of need for cancer center (May 28, 2002).

Mobile scanners are latest trend in service to hospitals., REV. - FEDERATION OF AM. HOSP., 1978 Mar, at 34-5.

Monopolization: Market share of 50-55 percent alone won't prove attempted monopolization, 6. BNA S HEALTH L. REPORTER.

Montana: AG approves joint venture between benefits, rival surgical center in Great Falls, Mon., 7. BNA S HEALTH L. REPORTER.

More health care services could come as state law expires, ERIE TIMES-NEWS, December 18, 1996.

More money available to HSA's; certificate of need regs amended., 31. EMPLOYEE BENEFIT PLAN REV. p. 38 (1977 Jun).

N.C. hospital plans for growth, THE SUN NEWS, July 30, 2001.

N.C. Memorial Hospital lobby construction delay will cost $500,000-y, *TRIANGLE BUS. J. (2002) available at* http://triangle.bizjournals.com.

Naperville facility loses first round for 'heart hospital': approval denies for $92 million medical project, ST. J.-REG., January 14, 2000.

Nashville hospitals face loss of patients, TENNESSEAN, 11/17/03.

Nebraska: Change in canonical sponsorship subject to review as acquisition, 4. BNA S HEALTH L. REPORTER.

Nebraska: Denial of CON to retirement center upheld by Nebraska supreme court, 8. BNA S HEALTH L. REPORTER.

Nebraska: State's CON law repealed except for certain long-term care projects, 6. BNA S HEALTH L. REPORTER.

Need for invasive cardiac center upheld: Court rejects certificate of need challenge, 10. BNA S HEALTH L. REPORTER (Nov. 8, 2001).

Neighbors say they're skeptical of mercy proposal, PORTLAND PRESS HERALD, November 30, 1999.

New Hampshire: Hospital tax exemption becomes law without Gov. Merrill's signature, 4. BNA S HEALTH L. REPORTER.

New Hanover County, N.C. hospital panel approves site for outpatient facility, KNIGHT-RIDDER/TRIB. BUS. NEWS, July 17, 2002.

New hospital campus advances: Baptist breaks ground at West Knox complex, THE KNOXVILLE NEWS-SENTINEL, September 26, 2001.

New hospital nearing approval, THE MIAMI HERALD, October 9, 1990.

New hospital plan takes shape: health company officials in town for public meeting, COLUMBUS LEDGER-ENQUIRER, November 20, 2002.

New hospitals: no exception to state's certificate of need process, DETROIT FREE PRESS (MI), December 7, 2002.

New Jersey SNFs oppose legislation favoring hospitals., 4. NAT'L REP. ON SUBACUTE CAREp.7-Jun (1996 Mar 27).

New Jersey: Certificate of need requirements eliminated for most health facilities under new law, 7. BNA S HEALTH L. REPORTER.

New Jersey: Health board gives final approval to rules revamping CON process, 5. BNA S HEALTH L. REPORTER.

New Jersey: Health department moratorium sticks for new cardiac services applications, 3. BNA S HEALTH L. REPORTER.

New Jersey: Health plan law adopted in 1992 does not invalidate 1993 CON rules, 4. BNA S HEALTH L. REPORTER.

New Jersey: Legislature approves bill regulating hospital conversions to for-profit status, 7. BNA S HEALTH L. REPORTER.

New Jersey: Proposed changes to CON program would result in licensing system, 4. BNA S HEALTH L. REPORTER.

New Jersey: Settlement reached in case involving 1993 revenue caps for hospitals, 3. BNA S HEALTH L. REPORTER.

New operating rooms sought, FAYETTEVILLE OBSERVER, April 12, 2002.

New state bureau to monitor managed care companies, PALM BEACH POST, November 23, 1998.

New York state consolidated laws.

New York: Gov. Pataki proposes easing regulatory rules for providers, 4. BNA S HEALTH L. REPORTER.

New York: Governor signs bill to provide money for hospitals, expand primary care, 3. BNA S HEALTH L. REPORTER.

NJ regs impose volume requirement for credentials, 23. HOSP. PEER REV. p. 204-5.

No certificate of need required for additional operating room., 24. J. OF HEALTH & HOSP. L.p.376 (1991 Dec).

No clues about new hospital's location in 400-page state application, SARASOTA HERALD-TRIB., April 30, 2002.

No need for CON program, BUS. J. SERVING METROPOLITAN KAN. CITY, May 5, 2003.

North Carolina judge recommends allowing $14 million hospital facility, KNIGHT-RIDDER/TRIB. BUS. NEWS, December 31, 2002.

North Carolina specialty hospital continues to seek authorization to build, KNIGHT-RIDDER/TRIB. BUS. NEWS, July 11, 2002.

Number of hospital services nearly triple since regulation lapsed, ERIE TIMES-NEWS, February 19, 1997.

Numbers, distribution are targets: planners take aim at physicians., AM. MED. NEWS, 1979 Jun 22, at 19.

Nursing beds OK's in Desoto County, COMMERCIAL APPEAL, October 28, 1999.

Nursing home adds care and conveniences, THE REC., February 17, 2002.

Nursing home aid may fall: state lawmakers not expected to be as generous as predecessors who granted $23 million subsidy, AKRON BEACON J., February 8, 2001.

Nursing home industry sues state challenging medicaid payment freeze, BNA HEALTH CARE POL'Y REP., Aug. 18, 1997.

Nursing home law penalizes consumers, THE KAN. CITY STAR, November 18, 1998.

Nursing home project revisited, THE TIMES UNION, June 26, 2002.

Nursing home, generic drug bills pass, expanded HMO liability fails in legislature, 10. BNA S HEALTH L. REPORTER (May 17, 2001).

Nursing homes: HCFA schedules first public session on nursing home quality regulation, 5. BNA S HEALTH L. REPORTER.

Nursing's solutions for the nursing shortage. NEV. RNFORMATIONp.16-8 (1990 Apr-May).

Ohio becomes first state to ban urgent care center construction., EMERGENCY DEPARTMENT NEWS, 1984 Feb, at 1, 6-7.

Ohio Department of Health halts SDS expansion., 7. SAME-DAY SURGERYp.117-9 (1983 Oct).

Ohio fuels Michigan's health-care discussion: are certificates of need still needed?, BLADE, March 18, 2002.

Ohio: 'An extraordinary glut of capacity', 23. HOSP. PEER REV. p. 205-6.

Ohio: General assembly extends state's certificate of need program, 3. BNA S HEALTH L. REPORTER.

Ohio: Open-heart facilities necessary for cardiac catheterization, 4. BNA S HEALTH L. REPORTER.

Ohio: State certificate-of-need program ends under bill signed by governor, 4. BNA S HEALTH L. REPORTER.

OK sought for hospital in Loudon, THE KNOXVILLE NEWS-SENTINEL, June 7, 2002.

Okla. health planners stymie healer's vision., 1. HEALTH CARE WK.p.3 (1978 May 1).

Open heart rivalry 'dangerous': St. Luke's in C.R. cites UI research to preempt Mercy, THE GAZETTE, October 30, 2002.

Opposition to CON for long-term care nursing facility is rejected by state court, 9. BNA S HEALTH L. REPORTER (Jan. 6, 2000).

Oral Roberts' City of Faith gives planning law a crucial test., REV. - FEDERATION OF AM. HOSP., 1978 Oct, at 28-31.

Orthopaedists, hospital battle over ASC project, AM. ACADEMY OF ORTHOP'DIC SURGEONS BULL., Feb 1999.

Our health system doesn't need wholesale reform, CAPITAL TIMES, March 23, 1994.

Outpatient center proposed in Largo: area hospitals oppose Howard plan, WASHINGTON POST, April 14, 1999.

Outpatient services: HCFA draft memo clarifies ASC medicare certification requirements, 3. BNA S HEALTH L. REPORTER.

Overlake, Evergreen launch broad health partnership with joint cardiac program as first initiative, PR Newswire, September 5, 2002.

Owensboro, KY doctor asks permission to build outpatient surgery center, Knight-Ridder/Trib. Bus. News, January 5, 2003.

Owners ask for larger nursing home.

Parkersburg, W.Va, hospitals vie for permission to start open heart surgery, Knight-Ridder/Trib. Bus. News, July 19, 2002.

Partial de-regulation of certificate of need.

Partnership: Health care entity will not be taxed on ambulatory surgical center revenues, 6. BNA s Health L. Reporter.

PA's in the 'wild, wild West for cardiac surgery', 23. Hosp. Peer Rev. p. 202-3.

Patton order paves way for Bullitt County health care center, Bus. First of Louisville (2002) available at http://louisville.bizjournals.com.

Pennsylvania Society of Physicians, 1991-92 in Review: Physicians, Lobbyists Work for the Good of All. Pa. Med. (Jan 1993).

Pennsylvania: AG convinces two hospitals to drop merger plans, but approves another, 4. BNA s Health L. Reporter.

Pennsylvania: Allegheny agrees to sell eight hospitals to vanguard if bankruptcy court approves, 7. BNA s Health L. Reporter.

Pennsylvania: attorney general sets $40 million as 'price' for antitrust waiver, 3. BNA s Health L. Reporter.

Pennsylvania: Nursing home need review process to focus on medicaid program needs, 6. BNA s Health L. Reporter.

Pennsylvania: State to replace CON program with licenses, provider approvals, 5. BNA s Health L. Reporter.

Pennsylvania: Unplanned demise of CON program has not caused upheaval in industry, 6. BNA s Health L. Reporter.

Perspectives. Another upset for health planning., 41. Med. & Healthp.suppl 4 p. (1987 Oct 5).

Perspectives. Congress ends federal health planning., 40. Med. & Healthp.suppl 4 p. (1986 Oct 6).

Perspectives. NMR challenges health planning., 38. Wash. Rep. on Med. & Healthp.suppl 4p (1984 Apr 2).

Perspectives. The state of health planning., 38. Wash. Rep. on Med. & Healthp.suppl 6p (1984 Oct 22).

Perspectives. Wakened FTC worries providers., 42. Med. & Healthp.suppl 4 p. (1988 Apr 4).

PET Outperforms CT in Cervical Cancer Detection Washington University School of Medicine, Medical Industry Today (Sept 2001).

Plan to close aging hospital worries official, residents: loss of emergency room tops official's concerns, Washington Post, June 27, 2002.

Planners approve medical school test tube baby clinics, 9. Health Plan. & Manpower Rep.sp.7 (1980 Jan 2).

Planning commission violated open meetings law in CON ruling, 8. BNA s Health L. Reporter (Apr 15, 1999).

Plans for cardiac center at N.H. hospital temporarily blocked by court ruling, 9. BNA s Health L. Reporter (May 25, 2000).

Plans for rehab hospital move ahead: phoenix city asked to annex land across U.S. 280 from Wal-Mart, Columbus Ledger-Enquirer, June 5, 2002.

Point/Counterpoint on CON Healthcare Alabama (Spring 1998).

Political evolution of federal health care regulation., 11. Health Aff.p.17-37 (1992 Winter).

Politicians disagree on hospital site in hazard area, LEXINGTON HERALD-LEADER, August 8, 1983.

Presby celebrates future hospital, CHARLOTTE BUS. J., June 25, 2002.

Price disclosure a part of package: Minnesota repeals certificate-of-need law., AM. MED. NEWS, 1982 Apr 9, at 7.

Private firms eye hospital transfer business, BALT. BUS. J., Mar, 3, 2003.

Procedures force hospital groups to focus on competition, THE UNION LEADER.

Professional planners skeptical of competition thrust FAH REV. p. 18 (Aug. 1980).

proposal's denial prompts lawsuit: Missouri rejected St. Luke's plans to build hospital, THE KAN. CITY STAR, July 3, 2002.

PSC recommends approval of power plants (7/28/2004), *available at* http://tamapbay.bizjournals.com/tampabay/stories/2002/11/18/daily17.html?t=printable.

Purchase of lithotripter requires CON when used for services other than originally stated purpose., 24. J. OF HEALTH & HOSP. L.p.320-1 (1991 Oct).

Put the state board on notice, CHI. TRIB., March 27, 2000.

Randolph business vie for nursing home beds: many adult care providers have approached Randolph towns, looking for support, GREENSBORO NEWS & REC., October 23, 1999.

Reform roundup: Taxing medicare hospital and physician benefits would raise $79 billion, CBO says, 4. BNA S HEALTH L. REPORTER.

Reforming Virginia's health-care regulation, ROANOKE TIMES, January 8, 2001.

Regulatory influences on the availability of angioplasty and bypass surgery., 317. NEW ENGLAND J. OF MED.p.1417-8 (1987 Nov 26).

Reimbursement: Fourth circuit affirms HCFA refusal to pay costs for certificate of need, 8. BNA S HEALTH L. REPORTER.

Rep. Edward J. Markey [D-MA], 52. HOSP.p.66 (1978 May 16).

Report suggests legislature authorize fines for hospitals failing to file CON reports, BNA HEALTH CARE POL'Y REP., Dec. 11, 2000.

Report: center would duplicate medical services, J. STAR, September 22, 1999.

Review denied: High court will not hear antitrust challenge in denial of CON for kidney dialysis center, 8. BNA S HEALTH L. REPORTER.

Review denied: ruling on peer review immunity among cases court declines to hear, 6. BNA S HEALTH L. REPORTER.

Revised justice/FTC enforcement guidelines for health care industry, 3. BNA S HEALTH L. REPORTER.

Rhode Island cost-cutters aim to restrict doctor population., 20. MED. WORLD NEWSp.24-5 (1979 Dec 24).

Rhode Island: Governor Almond vetoes conversion bill designed to block for-profit companies, 6. BNA S HEALTH L. REPORTER.

Rival cancer centers show need for plan: regional medical centers often do it better and cheaper, and state policy should reflect this, ME. SUNDAY TELEGRAM, December 1, 2002.

Rivalry behind hospitals' expansions: is growth healthy for rate-payers, BLADE, November 1, 1999.

Roundup: Government offers tradeoffs in negotiations over managed care safe harbor, 6. BNA S HEALTH L. REPORTER.

Roundup: Pneumonia upcoding, hospital discharges chief targets of government enforcement, 8. BNA S HEALTH L. REPORTER.

Ruling against 'virtual merger' puts other hospital deals in doubt, 9. BNA S HEALTH L. REPORTER (Apr. 20, 2000).

Rural Hospitals establish trade group to lobby for their unique legislative issues, BNA HEALTH CARE POL'Y REP., Jan. 26, 1998.

Russell hospital closer to reality, COLUMBUS LEDGER-ENQUIRER, November 26, 2002.

Rutland Regional Medical Center receives certificate of need for renovations (July 2, 2002).

Scanning the 'CAT' scene., 3. COST CONTAINMENTp.6-Mar (1981 Jul 14).

Second court reverses Fulton hospital approval, THE ATLANTA J.-CONST., November 15, 2002.

Senate extends life of state panel, THE KNOXVILLE NEWS-SENTINEL, May 11, 2001.

Senate fails to renew hospital law: the unintentional deregulation removes an impediment to spending by hospitals, YORK DAILY REC., November 30, 1996.

Services don't meet emergency needs, BRADENTON HERALD, July 8, 2002.

Several oppose new medical complex: OSF Saint Francis will dominate market, some people fear, J. STAR, July 23, 1999.

SGOH Acquisition Inc. v. Missouri Department of Mental Health, WEST'S REGIONAL REPORTER, 1996.

Should you add extended stay?, 16. OR MANAGER p. 20-2 (2000 Aug).

Small business seek insurance relief: state to be asked to rein in health care costs, DENVER POST, October 18, 2001.

SMRT chosen for Maine General certificate of need preparation (February 12, 2002).

SNFs challenge HCFA's latest exemption policy., 5. NAT'L REP. ON SUBACUTE CAREp.2-Jan (1997 Jan 22).

Some states center attention on certificate of need., REV. - FEDERATION OF AM. HOSP., 1979 Apr, at 36-7.

Some worry new hospital in Post Falls will bleed KMC: backers of surgical facility say competition will keep costs in check, SPOKESMAN-REV., March 4, 2002.

South Carolina: State's CON law doesn't prohibit duplication of underused facilities, 6. BNA S HEALTH L. REPORTER.

Speakers attack providence plans, THE OREGONIAN, November 8, 2002.

SSM get approval for women's hospital, available at Postnet. Com.

SSM Health Care seeks state OK for area's first women's hospital, ST. LOUIS POST-DISPATCH, October 26, 1999.

SSM Health Care seeks state OK for area's first women's hospital, ST. LOUIS POST-DISPATCH, October 27, 1999.

SSM Health Care v. Missouri Health Facilities Review Committee, WEST'S REGIONAL REPORTER.

St. Francis' plans for new center are targeted: new group's ads say medical complex would increase costs, J. STAR, August 5, 1999.

St. Joseph West celebrates expanded emergency room, ST. LOUIS POST-DISPATCH, May 17, 2002.

St. Luke's plans new campus: it sets sights again on Lee's Summit, THE KAN. CITY STAR, August 9, 2002.

St. Luke's will build $22M campus in Lee's Summit. THE BUS. J. OF KAN. CITY (2002) available at http://kansascity.bizjournals.com.

St. Mary's to build $19.2M facility: will focus on cancer treatment, women's health, THE KNOXVILLE NEWS-SENTINEL, November 20, 2002.

St. Raphael's wins CAT scanner in court., 43. CONN. MED.p.801-2 (1979 Dec).

Sta-Home stays exempt, founders get the bill, 11. BNA S HEALTH L. REPORTER (June 20, 2002).

State action doctrine: CA 11 rejects FTC's narrow definition of foresee ability in state action cases, 3. BNA S HEALTH L. REPORTER.

State action doctrine: Public hospital's exclusive contract is immune under state action doctrine, 5. BNA S HEALTH L. REPORTER.

State Action: Antitrust principles do not support claims of CON application interference, 6. BNA s HEALTH L. REPORTER.

State adopts law governing purchase of nonprofit hospitals by for-profits, BNA HEALTH CARE POL'Y REP., Aug, 10, 1998.

State agency approves plan of three hospitals to merge, BNA HEALTH CARE POL'Y REP., July 6, 1998.

State agency has approved 138 beds for new OBICI hospital, VIRGINIAN-PILOT, March 24, 2000.

State agency loosens review powers, THE ATLANTA J.-CONST., Dec. 22, 1999.

State approves hospital expansion: city panel OKs $20 million in bonds, GRAND FOLKS HERALD, March 16, 1994.

State board endorses regional hospital, PRESS OF ATLANTIC CITY, Nov. 5, 1999.

State clears way for Englewood heart surgery, THE REC., March 3, 2000.

State clears way for new hospital in Clark County, THE OREGONIAN, March 16, 2002.

State court finds CON holder unable to delegate responsibilities, 10. BNA s HEALTH L. REPORTER (July 12, 2001).

State court reverses, remands CON case, sets aside approval of nursing home beds, 8. BNA s HEALTH L. REPORTER (Jan. 14, 1999).

State delays decision on hospital regionalization, PRESS OF ATLANTIC CITY, August 21, 1999.

State eases restrictions on building hospitals, DAILY NEWS OF L.A. (CA), January 4, 1987.

State facilities planning board rejects proposed Edward Hospital heart facility, 9. BNA s HEALTH L. REPORTER (Jan 20, 2000).

State health authority denies request from Assurecare to set up network plan, BNA HEALTH CARE POL'Y REP., June 3, 1996.

State health commissioner did not err in denying COPN for liver transplant facility, 9. BNA s HEALTH L. REPORTER (Sep. 28, 2000).

State health officer denies CON for medical center, hospital may close, 8. BNA s HEALTH L. REPORTER (Dec. 2 1999).

State high court rules completion of ASC, issuance of license renders lawsuit moot, 11. BNA s HEALTH L. REPORTER (Sep. 26, 200).

State laws: Managed care regulation tops state activity, NCSL official says, 4. BNA s HEALTH L. REPORTER.

State Laws: NCSL state-by-state report details wide range of consumer protection laws, 8. BNA s HEALTH L. REPORTER.

State legislation: Managed care bills top state agendas in 1999; Legislation pending in every state, 7. BNA s HEALTH L. REPORTER.

State legislation: Managed care, children's health coverage top state legislatures' health care agendas, 7. BNA s HEALTH L. REPORTER.

State makes changes to health board: Legal issues: Edward's Plaintified proposal launched an investigation, HERALD NEWS, 8/12/2004, at 3 p.

State medical association targets corporate takeover of health industry, BNA HEALTH CARE POL'Y REP., Dec 22, 1997.

State nixes Presby's Hunterville plan (02/25/2002), *available at* http://charlotte.bizjournals.com/charlotte/stories/2002/02/25/daily39.html?t=printable.

state official describes plan for regulation of HMO's, 8. BNA s HEALTH L. REPORTER (Oct. 21, 1999).

State official urges lawmakers to support plan to regulate HMOs, BNA HEALTH CARE POL'Y REP., Oct 25, 1999.

State OKs move for hospital, THE KY. POST, January 1, 2003.

State OKs southern regional health system's LTACH, ATLANTA BUS. CHRON., November 6, 2002.

State proposes tighter regulations for oversight of community hospitals sales, BNA HEALTH CARE POL'Y REP., June 8, 1998.

State reaches agreement with provider to cover expanded medicaid population, BNA HEALTH CARE POL'Y REP., June 24, 1996.

State ready to announce decision on new hospital, THE OREGONIAN, March 12, 2002.

State regulation of MRIs appears to shift direction., 59. HOSP.p.105-6 (1985 Aug 16).

State regulators give final approval to creation of state's first for-profit hospital, 11. BNA S HEALTH L. REPORTER (Apr. 4, 2002).

State rejects bid for heart surgery program, THE MACON TELEGRAPH, Nov. 30, 1999.

State rejects expansion plan filed by the women's hospital, GREENSBORO NEWS & REC., October 30, 1999.

State says no to plan to expand hospital: but Charlotte Regional Medical officials say plans for a new campus aren't dead yet, SARASOTA HERALD-TRIB., June 15, 2002.

State should consider changes to expand coverage, panel says, BNA HEALTH CARE POL'Y REP., Jan. 20, 1997.

State Supreme Court upholds market share methodology used by state to grant CON, 9. BNA S HEALTH L. REPORTER (Jan. 6, 2000).

State to replace CON program with licenses, provider approvals, BNA HEALTH CARE POL'Y REP., Dec. 23, 1996.

Statement of the Kentucky Hospital Association in support of the Kentucky certificate of need program., KY. HOSP.S MAG., 1989, at 8.

State's highest court remands CONs issued for cardiac surgery at two hospitals, 9. BNA S HEALTH L. REPORTER (Jan. 13, 2000).

Strengthen health regulatory panel.

Stronger rules on hospitals should lead to lower costs: the new rules should help resolve a controversy in Lewiston, PORTLAND PRESS HERALD, April 15, 2002.

Summa to oppose surgery center: hospital officials argue that bath plan is too costly and unneeded AKRON BEACON J. (OH) (February 23, 1995).

Summary action: Court accepts no health cases for review as new term begins, 4. BNA S HEALTH L. REPORTER.

Sunrise Senior Living sells off more communities in $564 million deal.

Surgery center's approval appealed: Indian River medial center officials said the challenge by four South Florida hospitals was not a surprise, STUART NEWS/PORT ST. LUCIE NEWS, October 5, 2002.

'Surgicenters'—knifed by hospitals?, 21. MED. WORLD NEWSp.14, 19 (1980 Mar 3).

Tax-exempt bonds: Hospital's lease to private entity does not change county bonds' status, 3. BNA S HEALTH L. REPORTER.

Tenn. company will buy Martinsville hospital: sale attributed to possibility of needs-based construction laws discontinuation, ROANOKE TIMES, January 12, 2002.

The Columbia/HCA hospital sales: an opportunity to re-focus on community benefits., STATES OF HEALTH, 1998 Aug, at 8-Jan.

The CON game., 3. SUBACUTE CAREp.42 (1996 Nov-Dec).

The failure of diagnosis-related groups., 143. AM. J. OF PSYCHIATRYp.1317 (1986 Oct).

The high cost of a CON., REV. - FEDERATION OF AM. HOSP., 1980 Aug, at 12.

Three hospitals brave NMR marketplace in joint venture., 57. HOSP.p.40-2 (1983 Aug 1).

Time's run out on CON process, MEMPHIS BUS. J., September 27, 2002, at 2.

Too many beds: state is correct to bar hospital expansions, DETROIT FREE PRESS (MI), October 13, 1997.

Tort reform, quality of care featured in long-term care bill signed by Governor, BNA HEALTH CARE POL'Y REP., May 21, 2001.

Tort reform, quality of care featured in long-term care bill signed by Governor, 10. BNA S HEALTH L. REPORTER (May 24, 2001).

Trial court refuses to dismiss lawsuit over demise of competing surgical center, 11. BNA S HEALTH L. REPORTER (Aug. 29, 2002).

Two hospitals seek care units for long term: both hopefuls on Southside ATLANTA J. CONST. (July 2, 2002).

Two new dialysis centers panned: nation's largest dialysis company OK'd by state Department of Health, SPOKESMAN-REV., June 7, 2001.

U.S. plans to drop curbs on hospital purchase of CT scanners., 23. MED. WORLD NEWSp.26-7 (1982 Jul 5).

Unhealthy rivalry: hospitals' competition is killing us, PHILA. DAILY NEWS, February 25, 1990.

United States of America, ex rel. Sally A. Reagan, plaintiff, vs. East Texas medical center: Regional Healthcare System, et al., Defendants, available at http://80-web.lexis-nexis.com.ezproxy.umuc.edu/universe/printdoc.

Uniting a community through the Armenian nursing home, TODAY'S NURSING HOME, at p. 15-6.

University hospital adding 63 beds, COMMERCIAL APPEAL, April 18, 2002.

Unrelated business income: No tax stems from hospital involvement in rehabilitation medicine joint venture, 3. BNA S HEALTH L. REPORTER.

Vancouver hospital CEO retires, PUGET SOUND BUS. J. (2002) *available at* http://seattle.bizjournals.com.

Vermont to announce April 15 whether Assurecare will manage medicaid plan, BNA HEALTH CARE POL'Y REP., Apr. 1, 1996.

Vermont: Bill to halt Medicaid expansion sent to house-senate conference panel, 5. BNA S HEALTH L. REPORTER.

Vermont: Bill to streamline health regulation, preserve oversight of spending signed, 5. BNA S HEALTH L. REPORTER.

Vermont: Gov. Dean signs bill to continue state's expanded Medicaid program, 5. BNA S HEALTH L. REPORTER.

Vermont: Gov. Dean sketches modest initiatives, says more sweeping plan is not realistic, 4. BNA S HEALTH L. REPORTER.

Vermont: Home health agency seeking CON did not show consumer need, court rules, 7. BNA S HEALTH L. REPORTER.

Vermont: House to act on bill amended by senate to freeze coverage expansion program, 5. BNA S HEALTH L. REPORTER.

Vermont: State health authority denies request from assurecare to set up network plan, 5. BNA S HEALTH L. REPORTER.

Virginia hospital unneeded, board says, WASH. TIMES, December 4, 1998.

Virginia: Appeals court reverses, remands denial of liver transplant certificate of public need, 8. BNA S HEALTH L. REPORTER.

Virginia: Regulation of ASCs raises question about VA.'s certificate of need program, 5. BNA S HEALTH L. REPORTER.

'virtual merger' of Poughkeepsie hospitals ruled per se violation of state, federal law, 9. BNA S HEALTH L. REPORTER (Apr. 13, 2000).

Washington state approves both Clark County hospital proposal (7/28/2004), *available at* http://portland.bizjournals.com/portland/stories/2002/03/11/daily49.html?t=printable.

Washington: Affected competitor has standing to contest health dept. determination, 4. BNA S HEALTH L. REPORTER.

Washington: Health care committee to review legislation governing conversions, 6. BNA S HEALTH L. REPORTER.

Washington: House passes bill to stabilize individual health insurance market, 6. BNA S HEALTH L. REPORTER.

Waterbury, Conn. hospital restores services threatened with closure, KNIGHT-RIDDER/TRIB. BUS. NEWS, December 18, 1999.

We should stop the CON game, MEMPHIS BUS. J., January 21, 2002.

Well being: CON laws, THE PEORIA J. STAR, August 21, 2002.

Wells cancer center battle not serving public interest: a state health plan spelling out roles for medical centers and community hospitals is needed, PORTLAND PRESS HERALD, December 25, 2002.

Wenatchee hospital sues to keep competitor out, COLUMBIAN, October 16, 1996.

WFU health sciences wants three more dialysis centers (7/28/2004), *available at* http://triad.bizjournals.com/traid/stories/2002/10/28/daily5.html?t=printable.

WHAT IS EBCT?: EXECUTIVE SUMMARY (Nov. 29, 2000).

What's the Plan?: A Look at the State of Alabama's Health Planning Process HEALTHCARE ALABAMA (July 9, 2002).

CON CASE LAW
TABLE OF CASES – INDEXED BY CASE NAME

ABC Home Health Serv. v. Georgia Dep't of Medical Assistance, Court of Appeals of Georgia, (12/1/1993).

ABC Home Health Serv. v. Tennessee Health Facilities Comm'n, Supreme Court of Tennessee, at Nashville (12/19/1994).

Access Ctr. for Health v. Health Facilities Planning Bd., Appellate Court of Illinois, Second District, (9/17/1996).

ACSR Inc. v. Cabinet for Health Serv., Court of Appeals of Kentucky (8/25/2000).

Adams & Boyle P.C. v. Tennessee Dep't of Health, United States Court of Appeals for the Sixth Circuit (2/9/2001).

Adams & Boyle P.C. v. Tennessee Dep't of Health, United States Court of Appeals for the Sixth Circuit (2/9/2001).

Adventist Healthcare Midatlantic v. Suburban Hosp., Court of Appeals of Maryland (6/10/1998).

Agency for Health Care Admin. v. Mount Sinai Medical Ctr., Court of Appeal of Florida First District (4/17/1997).

Agency for Health Care Admin. v. Orlando Regional Healthcare Sys. Inc., Court of Appeal of Florida First District (5/6/1993).

Agency for Health Care Admin. v. University Hosp., Court of Appeal of Florida First District (4/16/1996).

Agency for Health Care Administration v. Mount Sinai Medical Center of Greater Miami, Florida District Court of Appeals (4/1/1997).

Aiken Regional Medical Center v. South Carolina Department of Health and Environmental Control, State of South Carolina Administrative Law Judge Division (5/9/2000).

Alabama Nursing Home Ass'n v. Alabama State Health Planning Agency, Court of Civil Appeals of Alabama (1/13/1989).

Alan D. Gordon v. Lewistown Hospital, United States District Court for the Middle District of Pennsylvania (7/11/2003).

Albany Surgical, P.C. v. Department of Community Health, Georgia Appeals Court (1/1/2002).

Albany Surgical, P.C. v. Dept. of Community Health, Court of Appeals of Georgia, Fourth Division (9/27/2002).

Allegheny County Inst. Dist. v. Department of Pub. Welfare, Commonwealth Court of Pennsylvania (12/5/1995).

American Medical (Cent.) Inc. v. Texas Health Facilities Com., Court of Appeals of Texas Third District, Austin, (10/2/1985).

Amisub v. Department of Health & Rehabilitative Services, Court of Appeal of Florida First District (4/30/1991).

Appeal of Behavior Science Inst. v., Supreme Court of New Hampshire (10/30/1981).

Appeal of Catholic Medical Center et al, Supreme Court of New Hampshire (8/7/1986).

Appeal of Catholic Medical Ctr. v., Supreme Court of New Hampshire (8/7/1986).

Appeal of Clipper Home v., Supreme Court of New Hampshire (8/29/1990).

Appeal of Courville (New Hampshire Health Serv. Planning & Review Bd.) v., Supreme Court of New Hampshire (11/7/1994).

Appeal of Lemire-Courville Assocs.v., Supreme Court of New Hampshire (8/5/1985).

Appeal of Nashua Brookside Hosp. v., Supreme Court of New Hampshire (12/23/1993).

Appeal of New England Heart Institute and Maine Medical Center, Supreme Court of New Hampshire (12/29/1999).

Appeal of New Hampshire Catholic Charities v., Supreme Court of New Hampshire (8/10/1988).

Appeal of Portsmouth Regional Hospital, Supreme Court of New Hampshire (5/6/2002).

Appeal of Psychiatric Insts. of Am. v., Supreme Court of New Hampshire (8/23/1989).

Appeal of Rehabilitation Assocs. v., Supreme Court of New Hampshire (4/7/1989).

Appeal of Salem Regional Medical Ctr. v., Supreme Court of New Hampshire (5/3/1991).

Arbor Health Care Co. v. Delaware Health Resources Bd., Superior Court of Delaware New Castle (5/20/1997).

Arbor Health Care Co. v. Jackson, Court of Appeals of Ohio Tenth Appellate District, Franklin County (5/14/1987).

Arbor Health Care Co. v. State, Court of Appeal of Florida First District (6/1/1995).

Arkansas Dep't of Human Services v. Hillsboro Manor Nursing Home Inc., Supreme Court of Arkansas (2/11/1991).

Arkansas Health Planning & Dev. Agency v. Hot Spring County Memorial Hospital, Supreme Court of Arkansas (2/9/1987).

Arkansas Health Services Agency and Arkansas Health Services Commission; Arkansas Health Care Association v. Desiderata, Inc., Supreme Court of Arkansas (1/22/1998).

Armstrong Surgical Ctr. Inc. v. Armstrong County Mem'l Hosp., United States Court of Appeals for the Third Circuit (6/26/2000).

Arnot-Ogden Memorial Hospital v. Guthrie Clinic Inc., Supreme Court of New York, Appellate Division, Third Department (7/17/1986).

Aroostook Home Care Agency Inc. v. Commissioner of Human Services, Supreme Judicial Court of Maine (12/30/1988).

Ashtabula County Med. Ctr. v. Thompson, United States District Court for the Northern District of Ohio (2/8/2002).

Ashtabula County Medical Center v. Tommy G. Thompson, United States Court of Appeals (12/19/2003).

Associated Home Health Agency Inc. v. State Dep't of Health & Rehabilitative Services, Court of Appeals of Florida First District (6/26/1984).

Associates in Obstetrics & Gynecology v. Upper Merion Township, United States District Court for the Eastern District of Pennsylvania (7/16/2003).

Associates in Radiation Oncology P.A. v. Siegel M.P.H., Superior Court of New Jersey Appellate Division, (3/8/1994).

Attala County Board of Supervisors d/b/a Attala Care Center v. Mississippi State Department of Health, Supreme Court of Mississippi (2/26/2004).

Attoma v. State Department of Social Welfare, Supreme Court, Appellate Division, Fourth Department (5/19/1966).

Auburn Med. Ctr. Inc. v. State Health Planning & De Agency, Court of Civil Appeals of Alabama (5/5/2000).

Auburn Med. Ctr. v. State Health Planning & Dev. Agency, Court of Civil Appeals of Alabama (5/11/2001).

Auburn Medical Center, Inc. v. East Alabama health Care Authority d/b/a East Alabama Medical Center, Court of Civil Appeals of Alabama (5/11/2001).

Auburn Medical Center, Inc. v. East Alabama Health Care Authority d/b/a East Alabama Medical Center, Court of Civil Appeals of Alabama (9/26/2003).

Auburn Medical Center, Inc. v. J. Elbert Peters, et al., United States District Court, M.D. Alabama, Northern Division (12/12/1996).

Auburn Medical Center, Inc. v. State Health Planning and Development Agency et al., Court of Civil Appeals of Alabama (5/11/2001).

Auburn Medical Center, Inc. v. State Health Planning and Development Agency et al., Supreme Court of Alabama (1/5/2001).

Auburn Medical Ctr. v. East Ala. Health Care Auth. ., Court of Civil Appeals of Alabama (12/19/1990).

Bakersfield Community Hosp. v. Department of Health, Court of Appeal of California, Fifth Appellate District, (12/29/1977).

Balsam v. Department of Health & Rehabilitative Services, Court of Appeals of Florida First District (3/31/1986).

Balsam v. Department of Health & Rehabilitative Services, Court of Appeals of Florida First District (6/13/1984).

Baptist Hospital Inc. v. Humana of Kentucky Inc., Court of Appeals of Kentucky (4/27/1984).

Baptist Hospital Inc. v. State Dep't of Health & Rehabilitative Services, Court of Appeals of Florida First district (12/23/1986).

Baptist Memorial Hospital-De Soto Inc. v. Mississippi Health Care Com. Civil Action, United States District Court for the Southern District of Mississippi (9/10/1985).

Baptist Memorial Hospital System v. Texas Health Facilities Com., Court of Appeals of Texas Third District, Austin, (10/2/1985).

Bath Memorial Hospital v. Maine Health Care Finance Com., United States Court of Appeals for the First Circuit (8/8/1988).

Bayonet Point Hospital Inc. v. Department of Health & Rehabilitative Services, Court of Appeals of Florida First District (6/25/1986).

Bayonet Point Regional Medical Center v. Department of Health & Rehabilitative Services, Court of Appeals of Florida First district (11/24/1987).

Beatrice Manor Inc. v. Department of Health, Supreme Court of Nebraska (2/1/1985).

Beebe Medical Ctr. v. Certificate of Need Appeals Bd., Superior Court of Delaware Kent, (8/31/1994).

Beechwood Restorative Care Center v. Laura E. Leeds, United States District Court for the Western District of New York (5/4/2004).

Benedictine Sisters Benevolent Asso. v. Pettersen, Supreme Court of Minnesota (12/5/1980).

Beverly Enterprises-Florida Inc.v. Department of Health & Rehabilitative Services, Court of Appeal of Florida First District (2/14/1990).

Beverly Enterprises-Florida inc v. Department of Health & Rehabilitative Services, Court of Appeals of Florida First district (2/4/1988).

Beverly Enters. v. Columbus Health Care, Nebraska Court of Appeals (12/28/1993).

Biloxi HMA Inc. v. Singing River Hosp., Supreme Court of Mississippi (7/29/1999).

Bio-Medical Applications Inc. v. Office of Community Medical Facilities etc., Court of Appeals of Florida First District (8/7/1997).

Bio-Medical Applications of Arlington Inc. v. Kenley, Circuit Court of Arlington County Virginia (6/4/1984).

Bio-Medical Applications of Arlington Inc. v. Kenley, Court of Appeals of Virginia (7/7/1987).

Bio-Medical Applications of Clearwater Inc. v. Department of Health & Rehabilitative Services etc., Court of Appeal of Florida Second District (2/23/1997).

Bio-Medical Applications of N.C. Inc. v. North Carolina Dep't of Human Resources Div. of Facility Serv. Certificate of Need Section, Court of Appeals of North Carolina (9/16/1999).

Bio-Medical Applications of the District of Columbia d/b/a/ Fresenius Medical Care North America v. District of Columbia Board of Appeals and Review, District of Columbia Court of Appeals (7/24/2003).

Blue Cross/Blue Shield Inc. v. Pouseman, Court of Appeals of Georgia, (6/17/1983).

Boca Raton Artificial Kidney Center Inc. v. Florida Dep't of Health & Rehabilitative Services, Court of Appeals of Florida First District (8/20/1985).

Boca Raton Artificial Kidney Ctr. v. Department of Health & Rehabilitative Serv., Court of Appeals of Florida First district (10/22/1987).

Boca Raton Artificial Kidney Ctr. v. Department of Health & Rehabilitative Serv., Court of Appeals of Florida First District (7/29/1986).

Boiling Springs Assisted Living v. South Carolina Department of Health and Environmental Control, State of South Carolina Administrative Law Judge Division (12/31/2001).

Boone County v. Apex of Arkansas Inc., Supreme Court of Arkansas (2/3/1986).

Boulware v. Department of Human Resources, Supreme Court of Nevada (5/27/1987).

Bradbury Memorial Nursing Home v. Tall Pines Manor Associates, Supreme Judicial Court of Maine (12/18/1984).

Bradford Hospital v. Donna E. Shalala, United States District Court, W.D. Pennsylvania (6/5/2000).

Brattleboro Memorial Hospital v. Department of Banking, Insurance, Securities and Health Care Administration, Supreme Court of Vermont (9/19/2001).

Britthaven Inc. v. North Carolina Dep't of Human Resources Div. of Facility Serv., Court of Appeals of North Carolina (4/4/1995).

Brookline v. Medical Area Service Corp., Appeals Court of Massachusetts, Suffolk (8/13/1979).

Brookwood Extended Care Centers Inc. v. State Dep't of Health & Rehabilitative Services, Court of Appeals of Florida First District (7/24/1984).

Brookwood-Jackson County Convalescent Center v. Department of Health & Rehabilitative Services, Court of Appeal of Florida First District (1/2/1992).

Brown Sch. Rehab. v. Ark. Dep't of Human Serv., Court of Appeals of Arkansas (3/6/2002).

Bureau of Community Medical Facilities Planning of Dep't of Health & Rehabilitative Services v. Samson, Court of Appeals of Florida First District (2/4/1977).

Burke Health Investors L.L.C. v. North Carolina Dep't of Human Resources Div. of Facility Serv. Certificate of Need Section, Court of Appeals of North Carolina (11/16/1999).

Cabinet for Human Resources v. Women's Health Serv., Court of Appeals of Kentucky (6/24/1994).

Cabinet for Human Resources Interim Office of Health Planning & Certification v. Jewish Hosp. Healthcare Serv., Court of Appeals of Kentucky (10/25/1996).

Cain v. Mississippi State Dep't of Health, Supreme Court of Mississippi (9/21/2000).

Cain v. Mississippi State Dep't of Health, Supreme Court of Mississippi (12/14/1995).

Canterbury Nursing Home Inc. v. Alabama State Health Planning & De Agency, Supreme Court of Alabama (1/28/1983).

Cape Fear Memorial Hosp. v. North Carolina Dep't of Human Resources, Court of Appeals of North Carolina (2/6/1996).

Capitol Hill Hosp. v. District of Columbia State Health Planning & Dev. Agency, District of Columbia Court of Appeals (11/20/1991).

Carle Found. v. Illinois Health Facilities Planning Bd., Appellate Court of Illinois, First District Fifth Division, (8/13/1999).

Carolina Orthopaedic Surgery Center v. South Carolina Department of Health and Environmental Control, State of South Carolina Administrative Law Judge Division (12/1/2000).

Carriage Hill-Cabin John Inc. v. Maryland Health Resources Planning Comm'n, Court of Special Appeals of Maryland (2/25/1999).

Carrolton Inc. v. Pine Manor Rest Home, United States District Court for the Eastern District of North Carolina Western Division (3/31/1997).

Carrolton Inc. v. Pine Manor Rest Home (In re Pine Manor Rest Home), United States Court of Appeals for the Fourth Circuit (11/24/1997).

Castle Nursing Home v. Donald L. Sullivan, United States Court of Appeals for the Sixth Circuit (8/9/2001).

Catawba Memorial Hosp. v. North Carolina Dep't of Human Resources, Court of Appeals of North Carolina (11/16/1993).

Cathedral Rock of Granite City v. Illinois Health Facilities Planning Bd., Appellate Court of Illinois, Fourth District, (12/9/1999).

Catholic Medical Ctr. v. Elliot Hosp., Supreme Court of New Hampshire (5/6/1988).

Catonsville Nursing Home v. Loveman, Court of Appeals of Maryland (5/15/1998).

Centennial Villas Inc. v. State, Court of Appeals of Washington, Division Two, (3/2/1987).

Central Florida Regional Hosp. Inc. v. Department of Health & Rehabilitative Services, Court of Appeal of Florida Fifth District, (1/6/1991).

Central Florida Regional Hospital v. Daytona Beach General Hospital, Court of Appeals of Florida First District (9/17/1985).

Central Maine Medical Center v. Kevin Concannon and Maine Medical Center, Superior Court of Maine (9/26/2000).

Central Pa. MRI L.P. v. Department of Health, Commonwealth Court of Pennsylvania (9/6/1994).

Changing Point Inc. v. Maryland Health Resources Planning Com., Court of Special Appeals of Maryland (5/6/1991).

Charleston Radiologists, P.A. v. South Carolina Department of Health and Environmental Control, State of South Carolina Administrative Law Judge Division (2/22/2001).

Charlotte-Mecklenburg Hospital Authority v. North Carolina Dep't of Human Resources, Court of Appeals of North Carolina (10/21/1986).

Charter Hosp. of Pasco Co. v. Department of Health & Rehabilitative Services, Court of Appeal of Florida First District (6/18/1990).

Charter Hospital of Bucks County Inc. v. Commonwealth Dep't of Health, Commonwealth Court of Pennsylvania (12/11/1987).

Charter Medical Corp. v. Mississippi Health Planning & Development Agency, Supreme Court of Mississippi (7/26/1978).

Charter Medical-Dallas Inc. v. Texas Health Facilities Com., Court of Appeals of Texas Third District, Austin, (7/20/1983).

Charter Medical-Fayette County Inc. v. Health Planning Agency Inc., Court of Appeals of Georgia, (12/5/1986).

Charter Medical of Cook County Inc. v. HCA Health Services of Midwest Inc., Appellate Court of Illinois, First District, Fourth Division, (6/29/1989).

Charter Medical-Southeast Inc. v. State Dep't of Health & Rehabilitative Services, Court of Appeals of Florida First District (7/29/1986).

Charter Pines Hospital Inc. v. North Carolina Dep't of Human Resources, Court of Appeals of North Carolina (11/4/1986).

Chatham County Hospital Authority v. St. Joseph's Hospital Inc., Court of Appeals of Georgia, (3/21/1986).

Chatham Orthopedic Surgery Center, LLC. v. Georgia Alliance of Community Hospitals, Inc., Court of Appeals of Georgia, Third District (4/15/2003).

Chattahoochee Valley Home Health Care Inc. v. Healthmaster Inc., Court of Appeals of Georgia, (3/3/1989).

Children's Hosp. & Med. Ctr. v. Department of Health, Court of Appeals of Washington, Division Two, (4/30/1999).

Christ Hosp. v. Department of Health & Senior Serv., Superior Court of New Jersey Appellate Division, (4/12/2000).

Christenbury Surgery Ctr. v. North Carolina, Court of Appeals of North Carolina (6/6/2000).

Christian Care Home Inc. v. State Certificate of Need Review Bd., Court of Appeals of Ohio Tenth Appellate District, Franklin County (5/26/1988).

Cincinnati Ambulatory Surgery Center v. Certificate of Need Review Bd., Court of Appeals of Ohio Tenth Appellate District, Franklin County (12/13/1988).

City of Cookeville, Tennessee v. William M. Humphrey, M.D., Court of Appeals of Tennessee, at Nashville (11/20/2002).

City of Cookeville, TN v. William M. Humphrey, M.D., Supreme Court of Tennessee, at Nashville (2/20/2004).

Clark v. Fancher, Court of Civil Appeals of Alabama (6/17/1994).

Clayton County Hosp. Auth. v. Webb, Court of Appeals of Georgia, (3/10/1993).

Cleveland Clinic Fla. Hosp. v. Agency for Health Care Admin., Court of Appeal of Florida First District (10/16/1996).

Clifton Springs Sanitarium Co., v. Axelrod, M.D. AS Commissioner of the Dept. of Health, Supreme Court, Appellate Division, Fourth Department (12/20/1985).

Coastal Care Centers Inc. v. Meeks, Court of Appeal of California, First Appellate District, Division Five, (8/7/1986).

Collier Medical Center Inc. v. State Dep't of Health & Rehabilitative Services, Court of Appeals of Florida First District (1/8/1985).

Colonial Management Group, L.P. v. State Health Planning and Development Agency et al., Court of Civil Appeals of Alabama (12/13/2002).

Colonial Management Group v. South Carolina Department of Health and Environmental Control, State of South Carolina Administrative Law Judge Division (8/7/2002).

Columbia Endoscopy Center v. South Carolina Department of Health and Environmental Control, State of South Carolina Administrative Law Judge Division (12/30/1994).

Commission for Health Economics Control v. Medical Consultants Imaging Co., Court of Appeals of Kentucky (12/24/1992).

Commission on Hospitals & Health Care v. Stamford Hospital, Supreme Court of Connecticut, (8/16/1988).

Commonwealth Dep't of Health v. Brownsville Golden Age Nursing Home Inc., Commonwealth Court of Pennsylvania (2/4/1987).

Commonwealth Dep't of Health v. Rehab Hosp. Services Corp., Commonwealth Court of Pennsylvania (6/12/1989).

Commonwealth of Kentucky v. Family Home Health Care, Inc., Court of Appeals of Kentucky (2/7/2003).

Community Care Center of Lemay v. Missouri Health Facilities Review Committee, Court of Appeals of Missouri, Western District (11/5/2002).

Community Care Centers Inc. v. Missouri Health Facilities Review Committee, Court of Appeals of Missouri Eastern District, Division Two, (5/19/1987).

Community Hospital of New Port Richey/University Psychiatric Center Inc. v. Department of Health & Rehabilitative Services, Court of Appeals of Florida First district (9/29/1987).

Community Psychiatric Centers Inc. v. Grant, United States Court of Appeals Ninth Circuit (12/28/1981).

Community Psychiatric Centers v. North Carolina Dep't of Human Resources Div. of Facility Services, Court of Appeals of North Carolina (7/16/1991).

Community Psychiatric Ctrs. v. Department of Health & Rehabilitative Serv., Court of Appeals of Florida First District (8/20/1985).

CON. Medical Personnel Pool v. Management Registry, Court of Appeals of Kentucky (3/12/1993).

Condell Hosp. v. Illinois Health Facilities Planning Bd., Supreme Court of Illinois, (9/29/1988).

Condell Hospital v. Health Facilities Planning Bd., Appellate Court of Illinois, First District Second Division, (9/29/1987).

County of Dodge on behalf of Memorial Hospital v. Department of Health, Supreme Court of Nebraska (9/21/1984).

Crestmont Cleveland Pshp. v. Ohio Dep't of Health, Court of Appeals of Ohio Tenth Appellate District, Franklin County (9/28/2000).

Crestmont Cleveland Pshp. v. State Dep't of Health, Court of Appeals of Ohio Tenth Appellate District, Franklin County (10/14/1999).

Delaware County Memorial Hospital v. Bowen, United States Court of Appeals for the Third Circuit (1/25/1989).

Delta Regional Med. Ctr. v. Mississippi State Dep't of Health, Supreme Court of Mississippi (12/16/1999).

Department of Community Health, Division of Health Planning v. Gwinnett Hospital System, Inc., Court of Appeals of Georgia, First Division (8/26/2003).

Department of Health and Rehabilitative Services v. University Community Hosp., Florida Supreme Court (1/8/1986).

Department of Health & Rehabilitative Serv. v. American Healthcorp of Vero Beach, Court of Appeals of Florida First District (6/18/1985).

Department of Health & Rehabilitative Services v. Florida Medical Center, Court of Appeal of Florida First District (4/9/1991).

Department of Health & Rehabilitative Services v. Johnson & Johnson Home Health Care Inc., Court of Appeals of Florida First District (3/8/1984).

Department of Health v. Columbia West Corp., Supreme Court of Nebraska (3/18/1988).

Department of Health v. Grand Island Health Care Inc., Supreme Court of Nebraska (8/1/1986).

Department of Health v. Lutheran Hospitals & Homes Soc., Supreme Court of Nebraska (12/11/1987).

Department of Health v. Manor Care Inc., Supreme Court of Nebraska (2/22/1991).

Department of Health v. Omaha Associates, Supreme Court of Nebraska (6/16/1989).

Department of Human Resources v. UHS of Colony, Supreme Court of Nevada (4/9/1987).

Dialysis Care of N.C. L.L.C. v. North Carolina HHS Div. of Facility Serv. Certificate of Need Section, Court of Appeals of North Carolina (5/2/2000).

Dianne J. Ford, M.D. v. Steven L. Stroup, M.D.; Radiation Oncology Associates; Nashville Memorial Health Systems, Inc.,, United States Court of Appeals for the Sixth Circuit (4/23/1997).

Dimensions Med. Ctr. v. Elmhurst Outpatient Surgery Ctr., Appellate Court of Illinois, Fourth District, (9/29/1999).

DISC Diagnostic Medical Imaging v. South Carolina Department of Health and Environmental Control, State of South Carolina Administrative Law Judge Division (10/25/1995).

DISC Diagnostic Medical Imaging v. South Carolina Department of Health and Environmental Control, State of South Carolina Administrative Law Judge Division (2/15/1996).

District of Columbia Hosp. Ass'n v. Barry, District of Columbia Court of Appeals (1/30/1991).

District of Columbia Hosp. Asso. v. Barry, District of Columbia Court of Appeals (9/16/1985).

Diversified Health Management Services Inc. v. Visiting Nurses Assoc., Supreme Court of Georgia, (6/27/1985).

Doctors Hospital Inc. v. Califano, United States District Court for the District of Columbia, (10/6/1978).

Doctors' Hospital of Prince George's County v. Maryland Health Resources Planning Com., Court of Special Appeals of Maryland (1/8/1986).

Doctors' Osteopathic Medical Center Inc. v. Department of Health & Rehabilitative Services, Court of Appeals of Florida First district (10/6/1986).

Doctors' Osteopathic Medical Center Inc. v. Department of Health & Rehabilitative Services, Court of Appeals of Florida First District (8/7/1984).

Dogwood Square Nursing Center Inc. v. State Health Planning Agency, Court of Appeals of Georgia, (10/28/1985).

Dogwood Square Nursing Center Inc. v. State Health Planning Agency, Supreme Court of Georgia, (2/18/1986).

Downriver Nursing Assoc. v. Department of Public Health, Court of Appeals of Michigan (4/7/1992).

Durant v. Humphreys County Memorial Hospital/Extended Care Facility, Supreme Court of Mississippi (9/18/1991).

East Tennessee Health Improv. Council Inc. v. Tennessee Health Facilities Com., Court of Appeals of Tennessee, Middle Section (9/18/1981).

Ebenezer Soc. v. Minnesota State Bd. of Health, Supreme Court of Minnesota (9/13/1974).

EBG Health Care III Inc. v. Missouri Health Facilities Review Comm., Court of Appeals of Missouri Western District (2/15/2000).

Edgehill Newport Inc. v. New England Alcoholism Treatment & Educ. Programs Inc., Superior Court of Rhode Island Providence (4/27/1983).

Edisto Surgery Center v. South Carolina Department of Health and Environmental Control, State of South Carolina Administrative Law Judge Division (7/2/1998).

Elaine L. Chao v. A-One Medical Services, Inc., United States Court of Appeals (10/6/2003).

Emergency Medical Transp. v. Tempe, Court of Appeals of Arizona, Division One, Department D, (5/19/1988).

Enez Balthazar v. Atlantic City Medical Center, United States District Court for the District of New Jersey (8/15/2003).

Ex parte Alabama State Health Planning Agency, Court of Civil Appeals of Alabama (3/15/1991).

Ex parte Beverly Enterprises-Alabama Inc., Supreme Court of Alabama (7/13/2001).

Ex parte Brookwood Health Serv. Inc., Supreme Court of Alabama (10/13/2000).

Ex parte Crestwood Hosp. & Nursing Home, Supreme Court of Alabama (9/8/1995).

Ex parte East State Healthcare Auth., Supreme Court of Alabama (1/5/2001).

Ex parte Forest Manor Inc., Supreme Court of Alabama (12/11/1998).

Ex parte Nursing Home of Dothan Inc., Supreme Court of Alabama (3/31/1989).

Ex parte Shelby Medical Center Inc., Supreme Court of Alabama (4/12/1990).

Ex parte State Health Planning and Development Agency v. LithoMedTech of Alabama, LLC, Supreme Court of Alabama (11/22/2002).

Ex parte State Health Planning & Dev. Agency, Court of Civil Appeals of Alabama (5/12/1998).

Ex parte State Health Planning & Dev. Agency, Court of Civil Appeals of Alabama (12/17/1986).

Ex parte State Health Planning & Dev. Agency, Court of Civil Appeals of Alabama (8/31/1983).

Ex parte Traylor Nursing Home Inc., Supreme Court of Alabama (9/30/1988).

Extendicare Inc. v. State Coordinating Council for Health Planning, Supreme Court of Kansas (3/1/1975).

Fairfax Surgical Center v. State Health Commissioner, Court of Appeals of Virginia (6/4/1991).

Fairhaven Corp. v. Tennessee Health Facilities Com., Court of Appeals of Tennessee, Middle Section (5/7/1976).

Fairview General Hosp. v. Fletcher, Court of Appeals of Ohio Tenth Appellate District, Franklin County (10/16/1990).

Fairview General Hosp. v. Fletcher, Court of Appeals of Ohio Tenth Appellate District, Franklin County (12/20/1990).

Fairview General Hosp. v. Fletcher, Supreme Court of Ohio (3/11/1992).

Famiglietti v. Brevard Medical Investors Ltd., Court of Appeals of Georgia (9/19/1990).

Farmworker Rights Org. v. Department of Health & Rehabilitative Serv., Court of Appeals of Florida First District (7/20/1982).

Farmworker Rights Org v. Department of Health & Rehabilitative Serv., District Court of Appeal of Florida First District (4/14/1983).

Federal Property Management Corp. v. Department of Health & Rehabilitative Services, Court of Appeals of Florida First District (1/20/1986).

Federal Property Management Corp. v. Health Care & Retirement Corp., Court of Appeals of Florida First District (12/21/1984).

Federal Property Management Corp. v. Richmond Healthcare Inc., Court of Appeal of Florida Fourth District (4/12/1989).

Federal Trade Commission v. Freeman Hospital and Tri-State Osteopathic Hospital Association, Inc., United States District Court, W.D. Missouri, Southwestern Division (6/9/1995).

Feiwel OSINA et al., v. City of Chicago, Appellate Court of Illinois (5/14/1975).

First American Home Care of South Carolina, Inc. v. South Carolina Department of Health and Environmental Control, State of South Carolina Administrative Law Judge Division (6/7/1996).

First American Home Care of South Carolina, Inc. v. South Carolina Department of Health and Environmental Control, State of South Carolina Administrative Law Judge Division (5/10/1996).

First Baptist Church of Crown Heights Center for Nursing & Rehabilitation, Inc. v. Antonia Novello, as Commissioner of Health of the Department of Health of the State of New York, Supreme Court, Kings County, New York (4/24/2001).

First Hosp. Corp. v. Department of Health & Rehabilitative Serv. Case No. -, Court of Appeal of Florida First District (9/12/1990).

First Hosp. Corp. v. Department of Health & Rehabilitative Services, Court of Appeal of Florida First District (8/21/1991).

Florida Convalescent Centers Inc. v. State Dep't of Health & Rehabilitative Services, Court of Appeals of Florida First District (2/8/1984).

Florida Hospital v. Department of Health & Rehabilitative Services, Court of Appeal of Florida First District (5/14/1987).

Florida Medical Center v. Department of Health & Rehabilitative Services, Court of Appeals of Florida First District (3/4/1986).

Florida Medical Center v. Department of Health & Rehabilitative Services, Court of Appeals of Florida First District (1/24/1985).

Florida Residential Treatment Centers Inc. v. Department of Health & Rehabilitative Services, Court of Appeal of Florida First District (11/14/1989).

Ford Hull-Mar Nursing Home Inc. v. Marr Knapp Crawfis & Assoc., Court of Appeals of Ohio Seventh Appellate District, Jefferson County (6/22/2000).

Forest Manor Inc. v. State Health Planning & Dev. Agency, Court of Civil Appeals of Alabama (5/1/1998).

Frene Valley Corp. v. Missouri Health Facilities Review Committee, Court of Appeals of Missouri Western District (10/29/1991).

Frye Reg'l Med. Ctr. Inc. v. Hunt, Supreme Court of North Carolina (2/5/1999).

Ft. Washington Community Hospital Inc. v. Southern Maryland Hospital Center, Court of Special Appeals of Maryland (3/5/1986).

FTC v. Hospital Bd. of Directors, United States Court of Appeals for the Eleventh Circuit (11/30/1994).

FTC v. University Health Inc., United States Court of Appeals for the Eleventh Circuit (7/26/1991).

G.M. Ambulance & Medical Supply Co. v. Canyon State Ambulance, Court of Appeals of Arizona, Division Two, Department A, (3/17/1987).

Garst v. Stoco Inc., United States District Court for the Eastern District of Arkansas (1/9/1985).

Gateway Hospital Corp. East v. Department of Health & Rehabilitative Services, District Court of Appeal of Florida First District (9/29/1982).

General Care Corp. v. Forehand, Court of Appeals of Florida First District (2/20/1976).

Genesis Center v. Financial and Insurance Services Commissioner, Court of Appeals of Michigan (9/18/2001).

George Washington University Medical Center v. District of Columbia Bd. of Appeals & Review, District of Columbia Court of Appeals (8/31/1987).

Georgia Department of Community Health v. Satilla Health Services, Inc., Court of Appeals of Georgia (3/17/2004).

Good Samaritan Hospital Inc. v. Department of Health & Rehabilitative Services, District Court of Appeal of the State of Florida Fourth District (3/26/1986).

Gooding v. Oklahoma ex rel. Oklahoma Welfare Commn., United States District Court for the Western District of Oklahoma (6/21/1977).

Governor v. Rehab Hospital Services Corp., Supreme Court of Arkansas (4/15/1985).

Gramercy Hill Enters. v. State, Supreme Court of Nebraska (12/11/1998).

Grandview Surgical Center Inc. v. Holy Spirit Hospital of Sisters of Christian Charity, Commonwealth Court of Pennsylvania (11/19/1987).

Grant Center Hospital Inc. v. Health Group of Jackson Inc., Supreme Court of Mississippi (5/25/1988).

Great Lakes Rehabilitation Hosp. v. Commonwealth Dep't of Health, Commonwealth Court of Pennsylvania (5/31/1991).

Greater St. Louis Health Systems Agency v. Teasdale, United States District Court for the Eastern District of Missouri (3/11/1980).

Greenbriar Convalescent Center Inc. v. Department of Public Health, Court of Appeals of Michigan (8/7/1981).

Greenbriar Nursing Home v. Pilley, Court of Appeal of Louisiana (7/2/1993).

Greenbriar Nursing Home v. Pilley, Supreme Court of Louisiana'- (5/23/1994).

Greenville Hospital System v. South Carolina Department of Health and Environmental Control, State of South Carolina Administrative Law Judge Division (6/29/1998).

Greenville Hospital System v. South Carolina Department of Health and Environmental Control, State of South Carolina Administrative Law Judge Division (6/4/1998).

Greenville Hospital System v. South Carolina Department of Health and Environmental Control, State of South Carolina Administrative Law Judge Division (2/8/2001).

Greenwood Manor v. Iowa Dep't of Pub. Health, Supreme Court of Iowa (4/3/2002).

Gulf Coast Health Care v. Agency for Health Care Admin., Court of Appeal of Florida First District (9/4/1996).

Gulf Coast Home Health Services Inc. v. Department of Health & Rehabilitative Services, Court of Appeal of Florida First District (3/2/1987).

Gulf Coast Home Health Services Inc. v. Department of Health & Rehabilitative Services, Court of Appeals of Florida First district (6/8/1988).

Gulf Coast Home Health Services Inc. v. Department of Health & Rehabilitative Services, Court of Appeals of Florida First district (9/11/1987).

Gulf Coast Home Health Services Inc. v. State Dep't of Health & Rehabilitative Services, Court of Appeal of Florida First District (9/11/1987).

Gulf Coast Hospital Inc. v. Department of Health & Rehabilitative Services, District Court of Appeal of Florida First District (12/16/1982).

Gulf Court Nursing Center v. Department of Health & Rehabilitative Services, Court of Appeal of Florida First District (2/14/1986).

Gulf Court Nursing Center v. Department of Health & Rehabilitative Services, Court of Appeals of Florida First District (8/20/1985).

Gummels v. North Carolina Dep't of Human Resources Div. of Facility Services, Court of Appeals of North Carolina (2/6/1190).

Gundry/Glass Hosp. v. Shalala, United States Court of Appeals for the Fourth Circuit (4/5/1999).

Gundry Glass Hosp. v. Shalala Civil, United States District Court for the District of Maryland (5/19/1998).

Gundry/Glass Hospital v. Donna E. Shalala, Secretary of Health and Human Services and Blue Cross and Blue Shield of Maryland; Health Care Financing Administration, United States Court of Appeals for the Fourth Circuit (4/5/1999).

Hale v. Petit Law Docket, Supreme Judicial Court of Maine (12/9/1981).

Harrisburg Hospital v. Thornburgh, United States District Court for the Middle District of Pennsylvania (6/25/1985).

Harrisburg Hospital v. Thornburgh Civil Action, United States District Court for the Middle District of Pennsylvania (8/27/1985).

HCA Crossroads Residential Centers Inc. v. North Carolina Dep't of Human Resources etc., Court of Appeals of North Carolina (6/19/1990).

HCA Crossroads Residential Ctrs. v. North Carolina Dep't of Human Resources etc., Supreme Court of North Carolina (12/5/1990).

HCA Health Serv. v. Roach, Supreme Court of Georgia (6/12/1995).

HCA Health Serv. v. Roach, Supreme Court of Georgia, (2/7/1994).

HCA Health Services Inc. v. Department of Health & Rehabilitative Services, Court of Appeal of Florida First District (5/13/1992).

HCA Health Services of Midwest Inc. v. Administrative Hearing Com., Court of Appeals of Missouri Eastern District, Division Two, (11/26/1985).

Health Care Management Inc. v. Department of Health & Rehabilitative Services, Court of Appeals of Florida First District (11/21/1985).

Health Care Medical Facility XXVI Partnership v. State Dep't of Health & Rehabilitative Services, Court of Appeals of Florida first district (9/24/1986).

Health Care & Retirement Corp. of America v. Tarpon Springs Hosp. Found., Court of Appeal of Florida First District (4/4/1996).

Health Care & Retirement Corp. v. Department of Health & Rehabilitative Services, Court of Appeal of Florida First District (3/29/1990).

Health Care & Retirement Corp. v. Department of Health & Rehabilitative Services, Court of Appeals of Florida First district (12/1/1987).

Health Care & Retirement Corp. v. Department of Health & Rehabilitative Services, Court of Appeals of Florida First District (5/14/1986).

Health Care & Retirement Corp. v. Department of Health & Rehabilitative Services, Court of Appeals of Florida First District (12/20/1984).

Health Facilities Research Inc. v. Bureau of Community Medical Facilities etc., Court of Appeals of Florida First District (12/14/1976).

Health Help Services Inc. v. State Health Planning Agency, Court of Appeals of Georgia, (3/28/1985).

Health Quest Corp. IV v. Department of Health & Rehabilitative Services, Court of Appeal of Florida (1/14/1992).

Health Quest Corp. v. Department of Health & Rehabilitative Services, Court of Appeals of Florida First district (8/2/1989).

Health Quest Corporation v. Department of Health and Rehabilitative Services, District Court of Appeal of Florida, First District (1/26/1990).

Health Quest Realty XII v. Department of Health & Rehabilitative Services, Court of Appeals of Florida First District (7/16/1985).

Health Services Management Inc. v. Missouri Health Facilities Review Committee, Court of Appeals of Missouri Western District (4/10/1990).

HealthAmerica Pennsylvania, Inc. v. Susquehanna Health System, United States District Court for the Middle District of Pennsylvania (7/21/2003).

Healthcare Services Group, Inc. v. Royal Healthcare of Middlesex, LLC., United States District Court for the District of New Jersey (8/13/2003).

Hedgework Brentwood Medical Services, Inc. v. South Carolina Department of Health and Environmental Control, State of South Carolina Administrative Law Judge Division (9/10/1996).

Heritage House v. Bailey, Court of Appeals of Indiana First District (6/12/1995).

Heritage of Yankton v. South Dakota Dep't of Health, Supreme Court of South Dakota (11/23/1988).

Hickory House Nursing Home Inc. v. Commonwealth Dep't of Health, Commonwealth Court of Pennsylvania (8/14/1985).

Hillsborough County Hospital Authority v. Tampa Heart Institute, Court of Appeals of Florida Second District (5/22/1985).

Hollingsworth v. Califano, United States District Court for the Northern District of Mississippi Greenville Division, (6/5/1997).

Holy Name Hosp. v. New Jersey Health Care Admin. Bd., Superior Court of New Jersey Appellate Division, (7/23/1992).

Home Health Professional Services Inc. v. Department of Health & Rehabilitative Services, Court of Appeals of Florida First District (1/11/1985).

Home Health Services Inc. v. South Carolina Dep't of Health & Environmental Control, Court of Appeals of South Carolina (4/24/1989).

Homewood v. State, Superior Court of Maine Kennebec County (3/4/1998).

Hospice of Palm Beach County, Inc. v. State of Florida, Agency for Health Care Administration, Court of Appeals of Florida, First District (4/26/2004).

Hospital Auth. v. State Health Planning Agency, Court of Appeals of Georgia, (11/19/1993).

Hospital Bldg. Co. v. Trustees of Rex Hospital, United States Court of Appeals for the Fourth Circuit (4/18/1986).

Hospital Bldg. Co. v. Trustees of Rex Hospital, United States Court of Appeals for the Fourth Circuit (10/19/1982).

Hospital Corp. of Am. v. Associates in Adolescent Psychiatry S.C., Court of Appeal of Florida Fourth District (9/23/1992).

Hospital Corp. of America v. FTC, United States Court of Appeals for the Seventh Circuit (12/18/1986).

Hospital Corp. of America v. Robinson, Court of Appeal of Louisiana (11/12/1986).

Hospital Corporation of America v. Federal Trade Commission, United States Court of Appeals, Seventh Circuit (12/18/1986).

Hospital Group of Western North Carolina Inc. v. North Carolina Dep't of Human Resources, Court of Appeals of North Carolina (8/6/1985).

Hospital of St. Raphael v. Commission on Hospitals & Health Care, Supreme Court of Connecticut (11/11/1980).

HTI Health Services Inc. v. Mississippi State Dep't of Health, Supreme Court of Mississippi (6/10/1992).

Humana Hosp. Corp. v. Oklahoma Health Planning Comm'n, Supreme Court of Oklahoma (5/28/1985).

Humana Hospital Corp. v. North Carolina Dep't of Human Resources Div. of Facility Services, Court of Appeals of North Carolina (7/1/1986).

Humana, Inc. & Plantation General Hospt. V. Department of Health and Rehabilitative Services, Court of Appeal of Florida First District (5/16/1985).

Humana Inc. v. Department of Health & Rehabilitative Services, Court of Appeals of Florida First District (5/16/1985).

Humana Inc. v. Department of Health & Rehabilitative Services, Court of Appeals of Florida fourth district (4/16/1986).

Humana Medical Corp. v. State Health Planning & Dev. Agency, Court of Civil Appeals of Alabama (8/22/1984).

Humana of Fla. Inc. v. Department of Health & Rehabilitative Serv., Court of Appeals of Florida First District (9/11/1986).

Humana of Florida Inc. v. Keller, Court of Appeals of Florida First District (4/2/1976).

Humana of Kentucky Inc.v. NKC Hospitals Inc., Supreme Court of Kentucky (3/31/1988).

Humana of Tennessee v. Tennessee Health Facilities Com., Supreme Court of Tennessee, (4/25/1977).

Humhosco Inc. v. Department of Health & Rehabilitative Serv., Court of Appeal of Florida First District (5/7/1990).

Humhosco Inc. v. Department of Health & Rehabilitative Serv., Court of Appeals of Florida First District (9/25/1985).

Huntington Manor of Murphy v. North Carolina Dep't of Human Resources etc., Court of Appeals of North Carolina (6/19/1990).

Huntsville Healthcare Ctr. Inc. v. Brown Health Serv. Inc., Court of Civil Appeals of Alabama (2/26/1999).

Huron Valley Hospital Inc. v. Michigan Dep't of Public Health, Court of Appeals of Michigan (9/4/1997).

Huron Valley Hospital Inc. v. Michigan State Health Facilities Com., Court of Appeals of Michigan (10/7/1981).

Huron Valley Hospital Inc. v. Pontiac, United States Court of Appeals for the Sixth Circuit (5/30/1986).

Huron Valley Hospital Inc. v. Pontiac, United States Court of Appeals for the Sixth Circuit (10/13/1989).

Huron Valley Hospital Inc. v. Pontiac, United States Court of Appeals Sixth Circuit (12/11/1981).

Huron Valley Hospital Inc. v. Pontiac, United States District Court for the Eastern District of Michigan (5/26/1988).

Huron Valley Hospital Inc. v. Pontiac, United States District Court for the Eastern District of Michigan, Southern Division, (12/18/1986).

Huron Valley Hospital Inc. v. Pontiac, United States District Court for the Eastern District of Michigan, Southern Division, (6/17/1985).

Huron Valley Hospital Inc. v. Pontiac, United States District Court for the Eastern District of Michigan, Southern Division, (3/2/1997).

Huron Valley Hospital Inc. v. Pontiac Civil Action, United States District Court for the Eastern District of Michigan, Southern Division' (4/30/1984).

IFIDA Health Care Group Ltd. v. Commonwealth Dep't of Health No., Commonwealth Court of Pennsylvania (9/15/1989).

IFIDA Health Care Group Ltd. v. Department of Health, Commonwealth Court of Pennsylvania (8/9/1991).

Image Trust Florence, Inc. v. South Carolina Department of Health and Environmental Control, State of South Carolina Administrative Law Judge Division (4/19/1996).

In re Adoption of Regulations Governing the State Health Plan, Supreme Court of New Jersey (2/28/1994).

In re Adoption of Regulations Governing the State Health Plan N.J.A.C., Superior Court of New Jersey Appellate Division, (2/10/1993).

In re Alexander Rand Alzheimer's Center, Court of Appeals of Ohio Tenth Appellate District, Franklin County (1/15/1991).

In re Appeal from Approval of Application of Wake Kidney Clinic P.A., Court of Appeals of North Carolina (5/19/1987).

In re Appeal of Banks, Supreme Court of Kansas (7/17/1981).

In re Application for Certificate of Need by HCA Health Serv., Supreme Court of Wyoming (10/3/1984).

In re Applications of Overlook Hospital, Superior Court of New Jersey Appellate Division, (3/3/1987).

In re AssureCare of Vt., Supreme Court of Vermont (11/1/1996).

In re Aultman Hosp., Court of Appeals of Ohio Tenth Appellate District, Franklin County (5/19/1992).

In re Beechmont, Court OF Appeals OF Ohio Tenth Appellate District, Franklin County (3/29/1996).

In re Bloomingdale Convalescent Center, Superior Court of New Jersey Appellate Division, (5/4/1989).

In re. Central Vermont Medical Center, Supreme Court of Vermont (12/16/2002).

In re Certificate of Need Application by Community Psychiatric Centers Inc. etc., Supreme Court of Kansas (1/13/1984).

In re Certificate of Need Application etc., Supreme Court of Kansas (7/17/1981).

In re Certificate of Need Application of Providence Hosp., Court of Appeals of Ohio Tenth Appellate District, Franklin County (4/19/1990).

In re Certificate of Need for Aston Park Hosp. Inc., Supreme Court of North Carolina (1/26/1973).

In re Certificate of Need of Arnold Walter Nursing Home, Superior Court of New Jersey Appellate Division, (11/23/1994).

In re Certification of Need Application of Chilton Memorial Hosp., Superior Court of New Jersey Appellate Division, (12/23/1993).

In re Change of Bed Category of Tieszen Memorial Home, Supreme Court of South Dakota (1/18/1984).

In re Christian Care Home Inc., Court of Appeals of Ohio Tenth Appellate District, Franklin County (6/6/1991).

In re Christian Care Home Inc., Court of Appeals of Ohio Tenth Appellate District, Franklin County (12/28/1989).

In re Cleveland Clinic Found., Court of Appeals of Ohio Tenth Appellate District, Franklin County (4/14/1994).

In re Continental Medical Sys., Court of Appeals of Ohio Tenth Appellate District, Franklin County (8/12/1993).

In re Cumberland Care Ctr., Court of Appeals of Ohio Tenth Appellate District, Franklin County (11/4/1997).

In re Deaconess Hosp., Court of Appeals of Ohio Tenth Appellate District, Franklin County (9/29/1992).

In re Deaconess Hosp., Court of Appeals of Ohio Tenth Appellate District, Franklin County (12/9/1993).

In re Denial of Request by Humana Hospital Corp. etc., Court of Appeals of North Carolina (1/7/1996).

In re Denial of Request for Declaratory Ruling by Total Care Inc., Court of Appeals of North Carolina (7/17/1990).

In re Dixon Health Care Ctr. Inc., Court of Appeals of Ohio Tenth Appellate District, Franklin County (7/11/1985).

In Re: Founder's Women's Health Center, Appellant-Appellant v. Ohio State Department of Health, Court of Appeals of Ohio, Tenth Appellate District, Franklin County (8/15/2002).

In re Good Samaritan Hosp., Court of Appeals of Ohio Tenth Appellate District, Franklin County (11/9/1995).

In re Good Samaritan Medical Center, Court of Appeals of Ohio Tenth Appellate District, Franklin County (1/10/1991).

In re Health Care & Retirement Corp. of America, Court of Appeals of North Carolina (2/2/1988).

In re Health Care & Retirement Corp. of America, Supreme Court of North Carolina (6/2/1988).

In re Healthco Facilities Inc., Court of Appeals of Ohio Tenth Appellate District, Franklin County (4/21/1992).

In re Heartland of Mentor, Court of Appeals of Ohio Tenth Appellate District, Franklin County (12/23/1993).

In re King Memorial Hospital Inc., United States Court of Appeals for the Eleventh Circuit (8/12/1985).

In re Labelle Nursing Center, Court of Appeals of Ohio Tenth Appellate District, Franklin County (8/30/1990).

In re Lima Mem. Hosp., Court of Appeals of Ohio Tenth Appellate District, Franklin County (5/23/1996).

In re Lorain Comm. Hosp., Court of Appeals Ninth Judicial District of Ohio (5/30/1984).

In re Mansfield Gen. Hosp., Court of Appeals of Ohio Tenth Appellate District, Franklin County (8/31/1993).

In re Mansfield Gen. Hosp., Supreme Court of Ohio (5/24/1995).

In re Mazal Health Care, Court of Appeals of Ohio Tenth Appellate District, Franklin County (1/9/1997).

In re Midwest Eye Ctr., Court of Appeals of Ohio Tenth Appellate District, Franklin County (5/30/1995).

In re National Church Residence Care Ctr., Court OF Appeals OF Ohio Tenth Appellate District, Franklin County (9/20/1994).

In re North Shore Radiology, Court of Appeals of Ohio Tenth Appellate District, Franklin County (10/20/1994).

In re North Shore Radiology, Court OF Appeals OF Ohio Tenth Appellate District, Franklin County (9/1/1994).

In re Pavilion, Court of Appeals of Ohio Tenth Appellate District, Franklin County (10/5/1993).

In re Professional Nurses Service, Supreme Court of Virginia (9/10/1998).

In re Review of Decision of Kansas Corp. Com. etc., Supreme Court of Kansas (2/19/1983).

In re Saltwell Nursing Home, Court of Appeals of Ohio Tenth Appellate District, Franklin County (4/27/1989).

In re Samaritan N. Health Ctr., Court of Appeals of Ohio Tenth Appellate District, Franklin County (5/12/1994).

In re St. John Medical Ctr., Court of Appeals of Ohio Tenth Appellate District, Franklin County (10/28/1993).

In re St. Louis South Park II Inc., United States Bankruptcy Court for the Western District of Missouri, Central Division, (2/23/1990).

In re St. Luke's Hosp., Supreme Court of South Dakota (10/21/1987).

In re Timken Mercy Medical Center, Supreme Court of Ohio (7/3/1991).

In re Valley Hosp., Superior Court of New Jersey Appellate Division, (4/20/1990).

In re VHA Diagnostic Services Inc., Supreme Court of Ohio (12/9/1992).

In re Wellesley Corp., Supreme Court of Ohio (7/10/1985).

In re Wilkesboro Ltd., Court of Appeals of North Carolina (1/5/1982).

In the matter of Beech Hill Civic Association, Inc. v. Elin M. Howe, Supreme Court, Appellate Division, Second Department (7/17/1994).

In the matter of certificate of need granted to St. Francis medical center, Superior Court of New Jersey, Appellate Division (11/8/1999).

In the matter of Fairfield Nursing Home v. Robert Whalen, Supreme Court, Appellate Division, Third Department (7/27/1978).

In the matter of Meadowbrook Nursing Home v. David Axelrod,as Commissioner of the Dept. of Heath, Supreme Court, Appellate Division, Third Department (7/16/1987).

In the matter of Sisters of Charity Hospital of Buffalo v. New York State Department of Health, Supreme Court, Appellate Division, Third Department (7/18/1991).

In the matter of the Town of Hempstead v. Commissioner, State of New York Office of Mental Retardation and Developmental Disabilities, Supreme Court, Appellate Division, Second Department (6/2/1986).

InMed Diagnostic Services, L.L.C. v. MedQuest Associates, Inc., Court of Appeals of South Carolina (3/22/2004).

Inverness Convalescent Ctr. v. Department of Health & Rehabilitative Serv., Court of Appeals of Florida First district (3/16/1989).

Inverness Convalescent Ctr. v. Department of Health & Rehabilitative Serv., Court of Appeals of Florida First district (8/26/1987).

Iowa State Dep't of Health v. Hertko, Supreme Court of Iowa (8/29/1979).

Iredell Memorial Hosp. v. North Carolina Dep't of Human Resources etc., Court of Appeals of North Carolina (8/6/1991).

Irvington General Hospital v. Department of Health, Superior Court of New Jersey Appellate Division, (5/2/1977).

Jackson HMA, Inc. v. Mississippi State Department of Health, Supreme Court of Mississippi (4/25/2002).

Jackson HMA, Inc. v. Mississippi State Dept. of Health, Supreme Court of Mississippi (7/25/2002).

Jackson Tennessee Hospital Company, LLC. v. West Tennessee Healthcare, Inc., United States District Court for the Western District of Tennessee, Eastern Division (2/27/2004).

James Allen Harper v. Public Service Commission of West Virginia, United States District Court for the Southern District of West Virginia (11/19/2003).

Jay Alexander Manor Inc. v. Antonia Novello, as Commissioner of Health of the State of New York, Supreme Court, Appellate Division, Third Department, New York (7/26/2001).

JDK Management Inc. v. Commonwealth Dep't of Public Welfare, Commonwealth Court of Pennsylvania (10/22/1986).

Jeannette Dist. Memorial Hosp. v. Department of Health, Commonwealth Court of Pennsylvania (7/12/1991).

Jeff Anderson Reg'l Med. Ctr. v. Miss. State Dep't of Health, Supreme Court of Mississippi (10/31/2001).

Jewish Hosp. v. Baptist Health Care Sys., Court of Appeals of Kentucky (7/21/1995).

John Ken Alzheimer's Center v. Ohio Certificate of Need Review Bd., Court of Appeals of Ohio Tenth Appellate District, Franklin County (10/24/1989).

John T. Finley Inc. v. Missouri Health Facilities Review Comm., Court of Appeals of Missouri Western District (5/9/1995).

Johns Hopkins Hospital Inc. v. Insurance Comm'r, Court of Appeals of Maryland (3/5/1985).

Johnston Ambulatory Surgical Associates, LTD. v. Patricia Nolan, in her capacity as Director of the Rhode Island Department of Health et al., Supreme Court of Rhode Island (7/12/2000).

Johnston Health Care Ctr. L.L.C. v. North Carolina Dep't of Human Resources Div. of Facility Serv. Certificate of Need Section, Court of Appeals of North Carolina (1/18/200).

Johnston-Willis Ltd. v. Kenley, Court of Appeals of Virginia (5/3/1988).

Kara Gedrich v. Fairfax County Department of Family Services, United States District Court for the Eastern District of Virginia, Alexandria Division (9/12/2003).

Koltis v. North Carolina Dep't of Human Resources Div. of Facility Serv. Certificate of Need Section, Court of Appeals of North Carolina (2/4/1997).

Kord's Ambulance Serv. v. Tucson, Court of Appeals of Arizona, Division Two, Department B, (6/16/1988).

Kottle v. Northwest Kidney Ctrs., United States Court of Appeals for the Ninth Circuit (7/18/1998).

La Moure v. State Health Council, Supreme Court of North Dakota (12/4/1973).

Lahey Clinic Foundation, Inc. v. Health Facilities Appeals Board, Supreme Judicial Court of Massachusetts, Suffolk (9/18/1978).

Lake East Hosp. v. Ohio Dep't of Health, Court of Appeals of Ohio Tenth Appellate District, Franklin County (10/6/1992).

Lake Otis Clinic Inc. v. Sisters of Providence, United States Court of Appeals for the Ninth Circuit (12/18/1990).

Lambright's Community Care Homes, Inc. v. South Carolina Department of Health and Environmental Control, State of South Carolina Administrative Law Judge Division (4/7/1997).

Lapid-Laurel, L.L.C. v. Zoning Board of Adjustment of the Township of Scotch Plains, United States Court of Appeals, Third Circuit (3/15/2002).

Laurel Mobile Health Services Ltd. v. Commonwealth Dep't of Health, Commonwealth Court of Pennsylvania (11/25/1988).

Lawnwood Medical Ctr. v. Agency for Health Care Admin., Court of Appeal of Florida First District (7/29/1996).

Lee Memorial Hosp. v. Department of Health & Rehabilitative Serv., Court of Appeal of Florida First District (5/9/1990).

Lee Memorial Hosp. v. Department of Health & Rehabilitative Serv., Court of Appeal of Florida First District (5/9/1990).

Lenoir Memorial Hosp. Inc. v. North Carolina Dep't of Human Resources etc., Court of Appeals of North Carolina (4/17/1990).

Liberty Mutual Insurance Company v. Open MRI of Morris & Essex, L.P., Superior Court of New Jersey, Law Division, Morris County (9/27/2002).

Life Care Centers of America, Inc., Appellant, v. Health Care and Retirement Corporation of American and Agency for Health Care Administration, Appellees., District Court of Appeal of Florida (4/23/1997).

Life Care Ctrs. of Am. v. Agency for Health Care Admin., Court of Appeal of Florida First District (6/12/1995).

Life Care Ctrs. of Am. v. Health Care & Retirement Corp. of Am., Court of Appeal of Florida First District (4/23/1997).

Life Care Ctrs. of Am. v. Sawgrass Care Ctr., Court of Appeal of Florida First District (12/9/1996).

Liljeberg Enterprises, Inc. v. Lifemark Hospitals, Inc., United States Court of Appeals (8/28/2002).

Liljeberg v. Health Services Acquisition Corp., Supreme Court of the United States (6/17/1988).

Living Centers-Southeast Inc. v. North Carolina HHS, Court of Appeals of North Carolina (7/5/2000).

Lloyd Noland Foundation, Inc. v. the City of Fairfield Healthcare Authority, Supreme Court of Alabama (2/22/2002).

The Long Term Care Foundation v. South Carolina Department of Health and Environmental Control, State of South Carolina Administrative Law Judge Division (7/14/1998).

Lonoke Nursing Home Inc. v. Wayne & Neil Bennett Family Partnership, Court of Appeals of Arkansas, Division 1 (11/28/1984).

Los Alamitos Gen. Hosp. Inc. v. Lackner, Court of Appeal of California, Second Appellate District, Division One, (11/17/1978).

Loveman v. Catonsville Nursing Home, Court of Special Appeals of Maryland (11/4/1996).

Loyd v. Georgia State Health Planning & Dev. Agency, Court of Appeals of Georgia, (10/25/1983).

Madarang v. Bermudes, United States Court of Appeals for the Ninth Circuit (11/9/1989).

Magnetic Resonance Technologies Ltd. Partnership v. Commissioner Maine Dep't of Human Serv., Supreme Judicial Court of Maine (1/19/1995).

Magnolia Hosp. v. Mississippi State Dep't of Health, Supreme Court of Mississippi (4/4/1990).

Manasota Osteopathic Gen. Hosp. v. State Dep't of Health & Rehabilitative Serv., Court of Appeal of Florida First District (4/6/1988).

Manor Care Inc. v. Department of Health & Rehabilitative Serv., Court of Appeal of Florida First District (10/3/1989).

Manor Healthcare Corp. v. Northwest Community Hospital, Appellate Court of Illinois, First District Third Division (11/28/1984).

Maple Leaf of Lee County Health Care v. Department of Health & Rehabilitative Serv., Court of Appeal of Florida First District (6/17/1992).

Marin Hospital Dist. v Department of Health, Court of Appeal, Second District, Division 3 (4/26/1979).

Marion Hospital Corporation, Appellee v. the Illinois Health Facilities Planning Board, Supreme Court of Illinois (9/19/2002).

Marlboro Park Hospital v. South Carolina Department of Health and Environmental Control, Court of Appeals of South Carolina (4/12/2004).

Marlboro Park Hospital v. South Carolina Department of Health and Environmental Control, State of South Carolina Administrative Law Judge Division (7/27/2000).

Marsh v. Finley, Superior Court of New Jersey Appellate Division, (6/15/1978).

Martin County Nursing Center, Inc. v Medco Centers, Inc., Court of Appeals of Indiana, First District (11/6/1982).

Martin Memorial Hosp. Ass'n v. Department of Health & Rehabilitative Services, Court of Appeal of Florida Fourth District (7/5/1991).

Martin v. Memorial Hosp., United States Court of Appeals for the Fifth Circuit (7/10/1996).

Maryland Gen. Hosp. v. Maryland Health Resources Planning Comm'n, Court of Special Appeals of Maryland (2/14/1995).

Maryland General Hospital, Inc. v. Tommy G. Thompson, United States Court of Appeals (10/9/2002).

Matter of Town of Gates v. Commissioner of NY State Office of Mental Retardation and Developmental Disabilities and Finger Lakes Developmental Disabilities Services Office, Supreme Court, Appellate Division, Fourth Department (12/31/1997).

McCoy Fla. SNF Trust v. State Dep't of Health & Rehabilitative Serv., Court of Appeal of Florida First District (12/17/1991).

McLeod Regional Medical Center v. South Carolina Department of Health and Environmental Control, State of South Carolina Administrative Law Judge Division (6/7/1996).

Md. Gen. Hosp. Inc. v. Thompson, United States District Court for the District of Maryland (6/27/2001).

Mechanicsburg Rehab Sys. v. Department of Health, Commonwealth Court of Pennsylvania (6/24/1994).

Medcor Inc. v. Finley, Superior Court of New Jersey Appellate Division, (5/22/1981).

Medical Arts Clinic P.C. v. Franciscan Initiatives, Supreme Court of North Dakota (5/9/1995).

Medical Center at Princeton v. the Township of Princeton Zoning Board of Adjustment, Superior Court of New Jersey (6/28/2001).

Medical Ctr. v. State Health Planning Agency, Court of Appeals of Georgia, (12/5/1995).

Medical Management v. Missouri Health Facilities Review Comm., Court of Appeals of Missouri Western District (6/6/1995).

Medivision of East Broward County Inc. v. Department of Health & Rehabilitative Services, Court of Appeals of Florida First District (5/15/1986).

Medstar Health v. Maryland Health Care Commission, Court of Appeals of Maryland (6/18/2003).

Melody Manor Convalescent Center v. Mississippi State Dep't of Health, Supreme Court of Mississippi (6/28/1989).

Members of the House of Representatives v., Supreme Court of Alabama (6/15/1992).

Memorial Health Sys. v. Halifax Hospice, Court of Appeal of Florida First District (2/26/1997).

Mercy Health Center Div. of Sisters of Mercy Health Corp. v. Iowa State Dep't of Health, Supreme Court of Iowa (10/17/1984).

Mercy Health Center Div. of Sisters of Mercy Health Corp. v. State Health Facilities Council, Supreme Court of Iowa (1/16/1995).

Mercy Hospital v. Commonwealth Dep't of Health, Commonwealth Court of Pennsylvania (9/21/1982).

Mercy Medical Ctr. Inc. v. Office of Health Policy, Court of Appeals of Oregon (7/14/1993).

Mercy Regional Health Sys. v. Department of Health NO. C.D. NO. C.D. Commonwealth Court of Pennsylvania, Commonwealth Court of Pennsylvania (7/12/1994).

Meridian Inc. v. Department of Health & Rehabilitative Services, Court of Appeals of Florida First district (9/12/1989).

Merle West Medical Center v. State Health Planning & Dev. Agency, Court of Appeals of Oregon (2/26/1988).

Merry Heart Nursing & Convalescent Home Inc. v. Dougherty, Superior Court of New Jersey Appellate Division, (12/4/1974).

Methodist Healthcare-Jackson Hospital v. Jackson-Madison County General Hospital District, Court of Appeals of Tennessee, at Nashville (5/22/2003).

Methodist Regional Hospital System Inc. v. State Dep't of Health & Rehabilitative Services, Court of Appeals of Florida first district (9/24/1986).

Metropolitan Ambulance Service Inc. v. Lexington-Fayette Urban County Government, United States Court of Appeals for the Sixth Circuit (12/17/1980).

Metropolitan Hospital v. Commonwealth Dep't of Health, Commonwealth Court of Pennsylvania (6/18/1987).

Metropolitan Hospital v. Thornburgh Civil Action, United States District Court for the Eastern District of Pennsylvania (6/11/1987).

Miami Jewish Home & Hosp. for the Aged v. Agency for Health Care Admin., Court of Appeal of Florida third district (8/8/1998).

Michigan Affiliated Healthcare Sys. v. Department of Pub. Health, Court of Appeals of Michigan (12/27/1994).

Mid-America Georgian Gardens v. Missouri Health Facilities Review Comm'n, Court of Appeals of Missouri (8/15/1995).

Millcreek Manor v. Department of Public Welfare, Commonwealth Court of Pennsylvania (11/6/2001).

Minnesota State Board of Health v. Governor's Certificate of Need Appeal Board, Supreme Court of Minnesota (1/17/1975).

Mississippi State Dep't of Health v. Golden Triangle Regional Medical Center, Supreme Court of Mississippi (6/17/1992).

Mississippi State Dep't of Health v. Mississippi Baptist Medical Ctr., Supreme Court of Mississippi (10/19/1995).

Mississippi State Dep't of Health v. Natchez Community Hosp., Supreme Court of Mississippi (7/29/1999).

Mississippi State Dep't of Health v. Southwest Mississippi Regional Medical Center, Supreme Court of Mississippi (5/3/1991).

Missouri Health Care Assoc. v. Missouri Health Facilities Review Committee, Court of Appeals of Missouri Western District (2/21/1989).

Missouri Health Facilities Review Committee v. Administrative Hearing Com., Supreme Court of Missouri (11/21/1985).

Mitchell Manor Convalescent Home Inc. v. Oklahoma Health Planning Comm'n, Court of Appeals of Oklahoma Division Two, (3/12/1991).

Monk & Excelsior Inc. v. Minnesota State Board of Health, Supreme Court of Minnesota (1/17/1975).

Monmouth Medical Ctr. v. State Dep't of Health, Superior Court of New Jersey Appellate Division, (3/31/1994).

Montana Health Sys. Agency v. Montana Bd. of Health & Envtl. Sciences, Supreme Court of Montana, (3/2/1980).

Morrisons Cove Home v. Department of Health, Commonwealth Court of Pennsylvania (6/17/1991).

Morristown Surgery Center, LLC v. Tennessee Health Facilities Commission, Court of Appeals of Tennessee, at Nashville (12/15/2003).

Morton F. Plant Hospital Assoc. v. State, Court of Appeals of Florida First District (7/9/1986).

Mount Royal Towers Inc. v. Alabama Board of Health, Supreme Court of Alabama (10/3/1980).

Mount Sinai Community Hosp. Ass'n v. Gorman, Superior Court OF Connecticut, Judicial District OF Hartford-New Britain, AT Hartford (3/4/1998).

Mt. Olive Home Health Care Agency Inc. v. N.C. Dep't of Human Resources, Court of Appeals of North Carolina (12/3/1985).

Multicare Health System d/b/a/ Tacoma General Allenmore Hospital v. Department of Health of the State of Washington, Court of Appeals of Washington, Division Two (9/30/2003).

Naples Community Hosp. v. Agency for Health Care Admin., Court of Appeal of Florida First District (1/31/1997).

Naples Community Hospital, Inc., Petitioner, v. State of Florida, Agency for Health Care Administration, and Big Cypress Medical Center, Inc., Respondents, District Court of Appeal of Florida (1/31/1997).

Naples Community Hospital Inc. v. Department of Health & Rehabilitative Services, Court of Appeals of Florida First District (1/18/1985).

National Gerimedical Hospital and Gerontology Center, Petitioner, v. Blue Cross of Kansas City and Blue Cross Association, Supreme Court of the United States (6/15/1981).

National Gerimedical Hospital & Gerontology v. Blue Cross of Kansas City, United States District Court for the Western District of Missouri Greenville Division, (11/2/1997).

National Health Corp. v. South Carolina Dep't of Health & Environmental Control, Court of Appeals of South Carolina (4/24/1989).

National Healthcorp L.P. v. Department of Health & Rehabilitative Services, Court of Appeal of Florida First District (12/22/1989).

National Nephrology Foundation v. Dougherty, Superior Court of New Jersey Appellate Division, (1/12/1976).

Nebraska Methodist Health Sys. v. Department of Health, Supreme Court of Nebraska (2/23/1996).

Neurosurgical Clinic & Allied Specialties Inc. v. State Health Planning & Resources Dev. Agency, Court of Appeals of Ohio Tenth Appellate District, Franklin County (1/5/1989).

New England Rehabilitation Hosp. Inc. v. Commission on Hosps. & Health Care, Superior Court of Connecticut, Judicial District of Hartford - New Britain, at Hartford (7/20/1992).

New England Rehabilitation Hosp. Inc. v. Commission on Hosps. & Health Care, Supreme Court of Connecticut, (6/22/1993).

New York v. St. Francis Hosp., United States District Court for the Southern District of New York, (4/10/2000).

NHC HealthCare Greenwood v. South Carolina Department of Health and Environmental Control, State of South Carolina Administrative Law Judge Division (6/11/1997).

NME Hospitals Inc. v. Department of Health & Rehabilitative Services, Court of Appeals of Florida First District (10/5/1986).

NME Hospitals Inc. v. Department of Health & Rehabilitative Services, Court of Appeals of Florida First District (6/24/1986).

North Carolina ex rel. Edmisten v. P.I.A. Asheville Inc., United States Court of Appeals for the Fourth Circuit (7/16/1984).

North Carolina ex rel. Morrow v. Califano, United States District Court for the Eastern District of North Carolina Raleigh Division (4/17/1978).

North Fulton Community Hospital Inc. v. State Health Planning & Dev. Agency, Court of Appeals of Georgia, (11/9/1983).

North Fulton Med. Ctr. v. Stephenson, Supreme Court of Georgia, (5/26/1998).

North Fulton Medical Ctr. v. Roach, Supreme Court of Georgia, (2/21/1994).

North Fulton Medical Ctr. v. Roach, Supreme Court of Georgia (2/20/1995).

North Memorial Medical Center v. Minnesota Dept. of Health, Court of Appeals of Minnesota (5/24/1988).

North Ridge General Hospital Inc. v. NME Hospitals Inc., Court of Appeals of Florida First District (11/15/1985).

Northbrook Residents Assoc. v. Iowa State Dep't of Health Office etc., Supreme Court of Iowa (11/12/1980).

Northern Virginia Community Hospital, LLC d/b/a Broadlands Regional Medical Center v. Robert B. Stroube, M.D., M.P.H., Circuit Court of Loudoun County, Virginia (10/3/2003).

Northside Hospital, Inc. v. McCord et al., Court of Appeals of Georgia (7/19/2000).

Nueces County Hospital Dist. v. Texas Health Facilities Com., Court of Civil Appeals of Texas Third District, Austin, (1/24/1997).

Convalescent Center Inc. v. Dougherty, Superior Court of New Jersey Appellate Division, (3/19/1975).

Nursing Home of Dothan Inc. v. Alabama State Health Planning & Dev. Agency, Court of Civil Appeals of Alabama (1/27/1988).

Oak Park Manor v. State Certificate of Need Review BD., Court of Appeals of Ohio Tenth Appellate District, Franklin County (10/3/1985).

Official Comm. of Unsecured Creditors of United Healthcare Sys. v. Medical Staff Local 1199J, United States Court of Appeals for the Third Circuit (12/29/1999).

Oficinas Medicas Inc. v. De Melecio, United States District Court for the District of Puerto Rico (3/12/1999).

Oklahoma Dept. of Health v. Medi-Plex Nursing Ctrs. Inc., Court of Appeals of Oklahoma Division Two, (2/8/1994).

Oklahoma Pioneer Inc. v. Carpenter, Supreme Court of Oklahoma (9/16/1980).

Olathe Community Hospital v. Kansas Corp. Com., Supreme Court of Kansas (10/22/1982).

Olathe Hospital Foundation Inc. v. Extendicare Inc., Supreme Court of Kansas (7/17/1975).

Omaha Health Facilities Inc. v. Department of Health, Supreme Court of Nebraska (4/27/1989).

On with Life v. State Health Facilities Council, Court of Appeals of Iowa (3/30/1995).

Oncology Therapies of Greenville, Inc. v. South Carolina Department of Health and Environmental Control, State of South Carolina Administrative Law Judge Division (6/6/1997).

Open MRI of Charlotte, Inc. v. South Carolina Department of Health and Environmental Control, State of South Carolina Administrative Law Judge Division (3/5/1999).

Oregon Health Care Ass'n v. Health Div., Court of Appeals of Oregon (6/25/1997).

Overlook Hospital v. Goldstein, Supreme Court of New Jersey (7/11/1985).

Overlook Medical Clinic v. Commonwealth Dep't of Health, Commonwealth Court of Pennsylvania (10/30/1989).

Overlook Medical Clinic v. Commonwealth Dep't of Health, Commonwealth Court of Pennsylvania (6/12/1989).

Page v. Capital Medical Center Inc., Court of Appeals of Florida First District (6/13/1997).

Palmetto General Hospital Inc. v. State Dep't of Health & Rehabilitative Services, Court of Appeals of Florida First District (5/24/1976).

Palmetto Richland Memorial Hospital v. South Carolina Department of Health and Environmental Control, State of South Carolina Administrative Law Judge Division (8/13/2002).

Paragon Health Network Inc. v. Thompson, United States Court of Appeals for the Seventh Circuit (6/5/2001).

Park City Hosp. v. Commission on Hosp. & Health Care, Appellate Court of Connecticut, (5/17/1988).

Paul Kimball Hospital Inc. v. Brick Township Hospital Inc., Supreme Court of New Jersey (6/24/1981).

Pennsylvania Dep't of Health v. North Hills Passavant Hosp., Commonwealth Court of Pennsylvania (4/10/1996).

Perini Services Inc. v. Maryland Health Resources Planning Com., Court of Special Appeals of Maryland (4/7/1986).

Phoebe Putney Mem. Hosp. v. Roach, Supreme Court of Georgia, (2/17/1997).

Physician Imaging Centers, Inc. v. South Carolina Department of Health and Environmental Control, State of South Carolina Administrative Law Judge Division (9/13/1995).

Physician Imaging Centers, Inc. v. South Carolina Department of Health and Environmental Control, State of South Carolina Administrative Law Judge Division (1/17/1996).

PIA Psychiatric Hospitals Inc. v. Missouri Health Facilities Review Committee, Court of Appeals of Missouri, Eastern District, Division Four, (3/10/1987).

PIA Psychiatric Hospitals Inc. v. Missouri Health Facilities Review Committee, Court of Appeals of Missouri, Western District, (11/25/1986).

Piedmont Medical Center v. South Carolina Department of Health and Environmental Control, State of South Carolina Administrative Law Judge Division (1/31/2002).

Piedmont Medical Center v. South Carolina Department of Health and Environmental Control, State of South Carolina Administrative Law Judge Division (6/22/2000).

Placentia-Linda Community Hosp. Inc. v. Zaretsky, Court of Appeal of California, Fourth Appellate District, Division Two, (6/2/1980).

Planned Parenthood v. Atchison, United States Court of Appeals for the Eighth Circuit (11/25/1997).

Platte County Medical Center Inc. v. Missouri Health Facilities Review Committee, Court of Appeals of Missouri Western District (8/11/1987).

Pontiac Osteopathic Hospital v. Department of Public Health, Court of Appeals of Michigan (11/19/1986).

Portland Surgery Center, LLC. v. Department of Human Services, Superior Court of Maine, Kennebec County (2/23/2004).

Potters Medical Center v. City Hospital Assoc., United States Court of Appeals for the Sixth Circuit (9/4/1986).

Powers v. Commonwealth Dep't of Health, Commonwealth Court of Pennsylvania (1/22/1990).

Powers v. Commonwealth Dep't of Health, Commonwealth Court of Pennsylvania (11/25/1988).

Pratt v. Board of County Comm'rs, Supreme Court of Kansas (7/14/1979).

Presbyterian Hospital North v. Texas Health Facilities Com., Court of Appeals of Texas Third District, Austin, (11/23/1983).

Presbyterian Medical Center v. Texas Health Facilities Com., Court of Appeals of Texas Third District, Austin, (10/2/1985).

Presbyterian-Orthopaedic Hosp. v. North Carolina DEP'T of Human Resources, Court of Appeals of North Carolina (6/4/1996).

Prime Lithotripter Operations, Inc., and Prime Medical Services, Inc. v. LithoMedTech of Alabama, LLC; State Health Planning and Development Agency v. LithoMedTech of Alabama, LLC; Prime Lithotripter Operations, Inc., and Prime Medical Services, Inc. v. Uroventure, LLC, et al., Court of Civil Appeals of Alabama (12/28/2001).

Princeton Community Hosp. v. State Health Planning, Supreme Court of Appeals of West Virginia (3/22/1985).

Professional Nurse Inc. v. State Dep't of Health & Rehabilitative Services, Court of Appeals of Florida First district (1/27/1988).

Providence Health System - Washington v. Tommy G. Thompson, United States Court of Appeals (12/17/2003).

Providence Hospital of Everett v. State of Washington, Department of Social & Health Services, and A.N. Shinpoch, Secretary of the Department of Social & Health Services, Thurston County Superior Court (4/13/1989).

Providence Hospital v. South Carolina Department of Health and Environmental Control, State of South Carolina Administrative Law Judge Division (9/11/2002).

Psychiatric Healthcare Corporation of Missouri d/b/a Lakeland Regional Hospital Respondent v. Department of Social Services, Court of Appeals of Missouri, Western District (4/1/2003).

Psychiatric Hospitals of Florida Inc.v. State Dep't of Health & Rehabilitative Services, Court of Appeals of Florida first district (10/16/1986).

Psychiatric Inst. of Am. v. Mediplex, Supreme Court of New Hampshire (12/4/1987).

Psychiatric Institutes of America Inc. v. Department of Health & Rehabilitative Services, Court of Appeals of Florida First District (7/17/1986).

Psychiatric Institutes of America Inc. v. Guissinger, Court of Appeal of Louisiana (12/28/1984).

Public Citizen, Inc., Oli, Chemcial, and Atomic Workers International Unione, AFL-CIO, National Consumer's League, National Urban Coalition, and Communities in Action Together petition to Department of Health, Education and Welfare, Department of Health, Education and Welfare (5/7/1975).

Public Health Dep't v. Rivergate Manor, Supreme Court of Michigan, (7/16/1996).

Public Health Trust v. Agency for Health Care Admin., Court of Appeal of Florida third district (1/5/2000).

Quintero v. Mora, United States District Court for the District of Puerto Rico, (9/26/1995).

Radiological Soc. of New Jersey v. New Jersey State Dep't of Health Hospital Rate Setting Com., Superior Court of New Jersey Appellate Division, (3/10/1986).

Ragsdale v. Turnock, United States Court of Appeals for the Seventh Circuit (3/10/1988).

Redbud Hosp. Dist. v. Heckler, United States District Court for the Northern District of California (5/12/1997).

Regional Dialysis of Anniston v. Northeast Alabama Kidney Clinic Inc., Court of Civil Appeals of Alabama (7/17/1985).

Rehab Hospital Services Corp. v. Delta-Hills Health Systems Agency Inc., Supreme Court of Arkansas (4/15/1985).

Rehab Hospital Services Corp. v. Health Systems Agency, Commonwealth Court of Pennsylvania (4/30/1984).

Renal Care of Illinois Inc. v. Health Facilities Planning Bd., Appellate Court of Illinois, First District, Fifth Division, (8/7/1987).

Research Ctr. v. Kamali'i, United States Court of Appeals for the Ninth Circuit (11/1/1993).

Retirement Villages v. North Carolina Dep't of Human Resources, Court of Appeals of North Carolina (11/19/1996).

RHPC Inc. v. Department of Health & Rehabilitative Serv., Court of Appeals of Florida First district (7/10/1987).

Richlands Medical Ass'n v. Commonwealth ex rel State Health Comm'r, Supreme Court of Virginia (11/27/1985).

Rivendell Children and Youth Center, a/k/a Rivendell of Tennessee, Inc., v. Tennessee Health Facilities Commission, Charter Medical of East Tennessee, Inc, and Peninsula Psychiatric Hospital, Court of Appeals of Tennessee, Middle Section (11/4/1987).

Riverside Hospital, Inc. d/b/a Riverside Regional Medical Center v. Robe B. Stroube, Circuit Court of Williamsburg and James City County, Virginia (3/17/2003).

Roanoke Memorial Hospitals v. Kenley, Court of Appeals of Virginia (1/6/1987).

Robert Packer Hosp. v. Department of Health, Commonwealth Court of Pennsylvania (9/7/1993).

Roberts Health Care v. State Health Planning & Dev. Agency, Supreme Court of Alabama (3/28/1997).

Robinson v. Kentucky Health Facilities, Court of Appeals of Kentucky (5/2/1980).

Roper Hospital, Inc. v. South Carolina Department of Health and Environmental Control, State of South Carolina Administrative Law Judge Division (9/5/2002).

Roper Hospital v. Coard of South Carolina Department of Health and Environmental Control and Francis Xavier Hospital, Supreme Court of South Carolina (12/3/1991).

Ross Gen. Hosp. Inc. v. Lackner, Court of Appeal of California, Second Appellate District, Division One, (7/28/1978).

Rowan Health Properties Inc. v. North Carolina Dep't of Human Resources Div. of Facility Services Certificate of Need Section, Court of Appeals of North Carolina (3/15/1988).

Rush City Hospital v. Sandstone Area Hospital, Supreme Court of Minnesota (11/24/1982).

Rush-Presbyterian-St. Luke's Medical Ctr. v. Hellenic Republic, United States Court of Appeals for the Seventh Circuit (11/23/1992).

Rutherford Hosp. Inc. v. RNH Pshp., United States Court of Appeals for the Fourth Circuit (2/5/1999).

Salud Para El Pueblo, et al. v. Department of Health of the Commonwealth of Puerto Rico, United States District Court, D. Puerto Rico (2/26/1997).

Samson v. Bureau of Community Medical Facilities Planning etc., Court of Appeals of Florida First District (10/24/1978).

San Bernardino Community Hospital v. Meeks, Court of Appeal of California, Fourth Appellate District, Division Two, (11/25/1986).

Sarasota County Public Hospital Bd. v. Department of Health & Rehabilitative Services, Court of Appeal of Florida Second District (10/11/1989).

Scott v. Ashland Healthcare Ctr., Supreme Court of Tennessee, Middle Section, at Nashville (7/9/2001).

Scott v. Consolidated Health Management Inc., Supreme Court of Arkansas (2/13/1989).

Shawnee Mission Medical Center v. Kansas Dep't of Health & Environment, Supreme Court of Kansas (7/13/1984).

Sheffield Towers Rehabilitation and Health Care Center v. Antonia Novello et al., Supreme Court, Nassau County (4/22/2002).

Shenango Valley Osteopathic Hospital v. Department of Health, Supreme Court of Pennsylvania (10/21/1982).

Shoolman v. Health Facilities Appeals Bd. (1980), Appeals Court of Massachusetts, Suffolk (12/11/1980).

Shoolman v. Health Facilities Appeals Bd. (1989), Supreme Judicial Court of Massachusettes, Suffolk (2/7/1989).

Sinai Hospital of Baltimore Inc. v. Maryland Health Resources Planning Com., Court of Appeals of Maryland (6/10/1986).

Sisters of Providence v. Department of Health & Social Serv., Supreme Court of Alaska, 648 P.2d 970 1982 Alas. LEXIS 334, (7/30/1982).

South Broward Hosp. Dist. v. Agency for Health Care Admin., Court of Appeal of Florida First District (10/27/1995).

South Broward Hospital Dist. v. Department of Health & Rehabilitative Services etc., Court of Appeal of Florida Fourth District (6/18/1980).

South Carolina Baptist Hospital v. South Carolina Dep't of Health & Environmental Control, Supreme Court of South Carolina (2/9/1987).

South Carolina Department of Health and Environmental Control v. Hawthorne Inn Assisted Living, State of South Carolina Administrative Law Judge Division (2/5/2002).

South Cent. Health Planning & Dev. v. Commissioner of Dep't of Admin., Supreme Court of Alaska, (5/15/1981).

South Miami Hospital, Inc. v. Agency for Health Care Administration and Variety Children's Hospital d/b/a Miami Children's Hospital, District Court of Appeals of Florida (6/1/1998).

South Shore Hospital, Inc. v. Tommy G. Thompson, United States Court of Appeals (10/16/2002).

South Shore Hospital v. Tommy G. Thompson, United States District Court, D. Massachusetts (1/3/2002).

Southern Chester County Medical Ctr. v. Commonwealth Dep't of Health, Commonwealth Court of Pennsylvania (6/24/1985).

Southern Maryland Hospital Center Inc. v. Ft. Washington Community Hospital Inc., Court of Appeals of Maryland (1/12/1987).

Southern Nev. Memorial Hosp. v. Department of Human Resources, Supreme Court of Nevada (8/27/1985).

Southwest Virginia Health Sys. Agency v. Kenley, Circuit Court of the CITY of Salem, Virginia (9/6/1985).

Sparks Regional Medical Center v. Arkansas Dep't of Human Services, Supreme Court of Arkansas (11/24/1986).

Speyer v. Barry, District of Columbia Court of Appeals (3/29/1991).

Springs Memorial Hospital v. South Carolina Department of Health and Environmental Control, State of South Carolina Administrative Law Judge Division (2/21/1997).

Springwood Assocs. v. Health Facilities Planning Bd., Appellate Court of Illinois, Fourth District, (3/3/1995).

SSM Health Care v. Missouri Health Facilities Review Comm., Supreme Court of Missouri (3/21/1995).

St. Dominic-Jackson Mem'l Hosp. v. Mississippi State Dep't of Health, Supreme Court of Mississippi (10/8/1998).

St. Francis Hosp. v. Appeals Bd. of Dep't of Health & Social Serv., Superior Court of Delaware New Castle (8/12/1993).

St. Francis Hospital Inc. v. Department of Health & Rehabilitative Services, Court of Appeal of Florida First District (12/20/1989).

St. Francis Parkside Lodge v. Department of Health & Rehabilitative Services, Court of Appeals of Florida First District (4/1/1986).

St. Francis/ St. George Hospital Inc. v. Blue Cross, Court of Appeals First Appellate District, Hamilton County Ohio (11/23/1983).

St. John's Home Health Agency v. Department of Health & Rehabilitative Services, Court of Appeals of Florida First district (6/23/1987).

St. Joseph Hosp. & Health Care Ctr. v. Department of Health, Supreme Court of Washington, (1/26/1995).

St. Joseph Hosp. Inc. v. Department of Health & Rehabilitative Services Case, Court of Appeal of Florida First District (4/12/1990).

St. Joseph Hospital v. Kevin Concannon, Superior Court of Maine (11/2/2001).

St. Joseph's Hill Infirmary Inc. v. Mandl, Court of Appeals of Missouri, Eastern District, Division Four, (5/22/1984).

St. Joseph's Hosp. Inc. v. Thunderbolt Health Care Inc, Court of Appeals of Georgia, (4/1/1999).

St. Joseph's Hosp. v. Hospital Auth. of Am., United States District Court for the Southern District of Georgia, Savannah Division, (7/18/1985).

St. Joseph's Hospital Inc. v. Hospital Corp. of America, United States Court of Appeals for the Eleventh Circuit (8/5/1986).

St. Joseph's Hospital & Medical Center v. Finley, Superior Court of New Jersey Appellate Division, (10/14/1977).

St. Joseph's Hospital v. Department of Health & Rehabilitative Services, Court of Appeals of Florida First district (12/21/1988).

St. Luke Hosp. v. Health Policy Bd., Court of Appeals of Kentucky (1/5/1996).

St. Luke's Hospital of Kansas City v. Missouri Health Facilities Review Committee, Circuit Court of Cole County (7/4/2002).

St. Mary's Hosp. v. State Health Planning & Dev. Tax Commr., Supreme Court of Appeals of West Virginia (12/15/1987).

Starks v. Kentucky Health Facilities, Court of Appeals of Kentucky (7/6/1984).

State Bd. of Health v. Virginia Hospital Ass'n, Court of Appeals of Virginia (8/6/1985).

State ex rel. Edmisten v. P.I.A. Asheville Inc., United States Court of Appeals for the Fourth Circuit (11/30/1983).

State ex rel. Greene Oaks v. Kilroy, Court of Appeals of Ohio Tenth Appellate District, Franklin County (9/22/1992).

State ex rel. Integrated Health Services v. Missouri Health Facilities Review Committee, Court of Appeals of Missouri Western District (8/27/1991).

State ex rel. Metzler v. Sisters of Charity of Leavenworth Health Services Corp., Supreme Court of Kansas (1/19/1980).

State ex rel. Missouri Health Care Assoc. v. Missouri Health Facilities Review Committee, Court of Appeals of Missouri (10/25/1988).

State ex rel. Parma Community Gen. Hosp. v. Kilroy, Court of Appeals of Ohio Tenth Appellate District, Franklin County (11/17/1992).

State ex rel. PIA Psychiatric Hosp. Inc. v. Ohio Certificate of Need Review Bd., Supreme Court of Ohio (5/15/1991).

State ex rel. Southwest Community Health Serv. v. Monroe, Supreme Court of New Mexico (2/23/1983).

State Health Commissioner v. Sentara Norfolk General Hospital, Supreme Court of Virginia (9/15/2000).

State Health Planning Agency v. Cribb Industries Inc., Court of Appeals of Georgia, (5/19/1992).

State Health Planning Agency v. Mobile Infirmary Ass'n, Court of Civil Appeals of Alabama (10/16/1992).

State Health Planning Agency v. Mobile Infirmary Assoc., Court of Civil Appeals of Alabama (9/7/1988).

State Health Planning and Development Agency and DeKalb Center for Healthcare, Inc. v. Baptist Health System, Inc., Court of Civic Appeals of Alabama (4/9/1999).

State Health Planning and Development Agency v. Forest Manor, Inc. Heritage Health Care center, Inc. v. Forest Manor, Inc., Court of Civic Appeals of Alabama (6/4/1999).

State Health Planning & De Agency v. Baptist Health Sys. Inc., Court of Civil Appeals of Alabama (4/9/1999).

State Health Planning & Dev. Agency v. Salem Hospital CA, Court of Appeals of Oregon (12/17/1986).

State Health Planning & Dev. Agency v. Ball Healthcare-Lowndes Inc., Court of Civil Appeals of Alabama (10/18/1996).

State Health Planning & Dev. Agency v. Baptist Medical Center, Court of Civil Appeals of Alabama (11/2/1983).

State Health Planning & Dev. Agency v. Forest Manor Inc., Court of Civil Appeals of Alabama (3/13/1998).

State Health Planning & Resource Dev. Admin v. Rivendell of Alabama, Court of Civil Appeals of Alabama (1/2/1985).

State Health Planning Review Bd. v. Piedmont Hospital Inc., Court of Appeals of Georgia, (2/6/1985).

State of New York v. Saint Francis Hospital, United States District Court for the Southern District of New York (10/28/2003).

Statewide Health Coordinating Council v. General Hospitals of Humana Inc., Supreme Court of Arkansas (12/12/1983).

Stewart v. Commonwealth Dep't of Health, Commonwealth Court of Pennsylvania (6/7/1991).

Stewart v. Commonwealth State Health Facility Hearing Bd., Commonwealth Court of Pennsylvania (7/12/1988).

Suburban Medical Center v. Olathe Community Hospital, Supreme Court of Kansas (7/14/1979).

Suburban Medical Hosp. Inc. v. Department of Health & Rehabilitative Services, Court of Appeal of Florida third district (5/26/1992).

Summit Neighborhood Association v. Rhode Island Department of Health, Superior Court of Rhode Island, Providence (5/27/2004).

Summit Villa Care Ctr. Inc. v. Ohio Dep't of Health, Court of Appeals of Ohio Tenth Appellate District, Franklin County (7/14/1992).

Surgical Care Center of Hammond, L.C. v. Hospital Service District No. 1 of Tangipahoa Parish, and Quorum Health Resources, Inc., United States Court of Appeals for the Fifth Circuit (8/27/1998).

Sussex Medical Investors, L.P. v. Delaware Health Resources Board, Superior Court of Delaware (4/8/1997).

Sylacauga Health Care Ctr. v. Alabama State Health Planning Agency, Court of Civil Appeals of Alabama (12/9/1994).

Tarabishi v. McAlester Regional Hosp., United States Court of Appeals for the Tenth Circuit (12/10/1991).

Tarabishi v. McAlester Regional Hospital, United States Court of Appeals for the Tenth Circuit (8/17/1987).

Tarpon Springs General Hospital v. Office of Community Medical Facilities etc., Court of Appeals of Florida First District (1/19/1997).

The Tennessee Department of Health v. Gary C. Boyle, M.D., Court of Appeals of Tennessee, at Nashville (12/19/2002).

Texas Health Facilities Com. v. Baptist General Convention, Court of Civil Appeals of Texas (10/19/1978).

Texas Health Facilities Com. v. Charter Medical-Dallas Inc., Supreme Court of Texas (2/15/1984).

Texas Health Facilities Com. v. El Paso Medical Surgical Assoc., Court of Civil Appeals of Texas Twelfth District, Tyler, (10/26/1978).

Texas Health Facilities Com. v. Nueces County Hospital Dist., Court of Civil Appeals of Texas Third District, Austin, (5/9/1997).

Texas Health Facilities Com. v. Presbyterian Hospital North, Supreme Court of Texas (5/29/1985).

Texas Health Facilities Com. v. West Texas Home Health Agency, Court of Civil Appeals of Texas Tenth District, Waco (9/27/1997).

Therapeutic Community Residence v. Minnesota Dep't of Health, Court of Appeals of Minnesota (6/19/1984).

Three Rivers Home Health Serv. Inc. v. Healthmaster Inc., Court of Appeals of Georgia, (10/16/1989).

Town of Hempstead v. Commissioner, State of New York Office of Mental Health, Supreme Court, Appellate Division, Second Department (1/24/1994).

Town of Hempstead v. Commissioner, State of New York Office of Mental Health and Pilgrim Psychiatric Center, Respondents, Supreme Court, Appellate Division, Fourth Department (2/1/1991).

Tri-County Hospice v. South Carolina Department of Health and Environmental Control, State of South Carolina Administrative Law Judge Division (12/18/1996).

Trident Medical Center, LLC v. South Carolina Department of Health and Environmental Control, State of South Carolina Administrative Law Judge Division (9/27/2000).

Tulsa Area Hosp. Council Inc. v. Oral Roberts Univ., Supreme Court of Oklahoma (3/24/1981).

Turro v. Department of Health & Rehabilitative Services, Court of Appeals of Florida First District (10/12/1984).

United Hosp. Ctr. v. Richardson, Supreme Court of Appeals of West Virginia (3/22/1985).

United States ex rel. Joslin v. Community Home Health Civil, United States District Court for the District of Maryland (11/17/1997).

United States of America, Et Al. v. East Texas Medical Center Regional Healthcare System, Et Al., United States District Court for the Southern District of Texas, Houston Division (3/4/2003).

United States of America v. East Texas Medical Center Regional Healthcare System, United States District Court for the Southern District of Texas, Houston Division (10/20/2002).

United States of America, v. East Texas Medical Center Regional Healthcare System, United States District Court for the Southern District of Texas, Houston Division (9/5/2002).

United States v. Ntshona, United States Court of Appeals for the Second Circuit (9/10/1998).

University Community Hosp. v. Department of Health & Rehabilitative Services, Court of Appeal of Florida First District (12/29/1992).

University Community Hospital v. Department of Health & Rehabilitative Services, Court of Appeal of Florida First District (1/12/1990).

University Community Hospital v. Department of Health & Rehabilitative Services, Court of Appeals of Florida Second district (5/16/1986).

University Community Hospital v. Department of Health & Rehabilitative Services, Court of Appeals of Florida Second district (5/22/1985).

University Medical Center Inc. v. Department of Health & Rehabilitative Services, Court of Appeals of Florida First District (2/13/1986).

University Medical Center Inc. v. Department of Health & Rehabilitative Services, Court of Appeals of Florida First District (8/20/1985).

University Medical Park Ltd. v. Department of Health & Rehabilitative Services, Court of Appeals of Florida Second district (1/28/1987).

University of Alabama Hospitals v. Alabama Renal Stone Institute Inc., Court of Civil Appeals of Alabama (4/1/1998).

University of Utah Medical Ctr. v. Bonneville County, Supreme Court of Idaho, (7/3/1974).

University Psychiatric Center Inc. v. Department of Health & Rehabilitative Services, Court of Appeal of Florida First District (4/20/1992).

Upjohn Healthcare Services Inc. v. Department of Health & Rehabilitative Services, Court of Appeals of Florida First District (7/22/1986).

Vantage Healthcare Corp. v. Agency for Health Care Admin., Court of Appeal of Florida First District (1/27/1997).

Vantage Healthcare Corporation, d/b/a Beverly Manor Rehabilitation and Specialty Care Center at Manatee County, Appellant, v. Agency for Health Care Administration and Manatee Springs Nursing Center, Inc., Appellees, District Court of Appeals of Florida (1/27/1997).

Vaughan Regional Medical Ctr. v. Smith, United States District Court for the Middle District of Alabama (12/5/1995).

Verdugo Hills Hospital Inc. v. Department of Health, Court of Appeal of California, Second Appellate District, Division Three, (4/26/1979).

W. A. Foote Mem. Hosp. v. Michigan Dep't of Pub. Health, Court of Appeals of Michigan, (5/12/1995).

Walgreen Co., et al. v. Carmen Feliciano De Melecio, Secretary of the Puerto Rico Department of Health, United States District Court, D. Puerto Rico (6/21/2000).

Walgreen Co. v. John V. Rullan, United States District Court for the District of Puerto Rico (9/8/2003).

Walterboro Community Hospital, Inc. v. South Carolina Department of Health and Environmental Control, State of South Carolina Administrative Law Judge Division (6/14/1996).

Watkins v. Restorative Care Center Inc., Court of Appeals of Washington, Division One, (3/30/1992).

Wausau Hospitals Inc. v. Department of Health & Social Services, Court of Appeals of Wisconsin (3/18/1980).

Wellmont Health System v. Tennessee Health Facilities Commission, Court of Appeals of Tennessee, at Nashville (1/29/2004).

West Bay Manor Co. v. Cuyahoga County Bd. of Revision, Supreme Court of Ohio (8/30/1995).

West Bloomfield Hosp. v. Certificate of Need Bd., Court of Appeals of Michigan, (5/16/1997).

West Bloomfield Hosp. v. Certificate of Need BD., Court of Appeals of Michigan (1/17/1995).

West Bloomfield Hosp. v. Certificate of Need Bd., Supreme Court of Michigan, (7/16/1996).

West County Care Center Inc. v. Missouri Health Facilities Review Committee, Court of Appeals of Missouri Western District (6/27/1989).

West-Mont Community Care v. Board of Health & Envtl. Sciences, Supreme Court of Montana, (7/30/1985).

West Side Deutscher Frauen Verein v. Tracy, Supreme Court of Ohio (4/2/1997).

West Virginia Health Care Cost Review Auth. v. Boone Mem. Hosp., Supreme Court of Appeals of West Virginia (4/24/1996).

Westchester General Hospital v. Department of Health & Rehabilitative Services, District Court of Appeal of Florida First District (9/8/1982).

Westchester General Hospital v. State Dep't of Health & Rehabilitative Services, Court of Appeals of Florida First District (3/22/1982).

Whitehall Boca v. Department of Health & Rehabilitative Services, Court of Appeals of Florida First District (9/5/1984).

Williamson v. Snow, Supreme Court of North Carolina (2/24/1954).

Wilmac Corp. v. Bowen, United States Court of Appeals for the Third Circuit (2/19/1987).

Women's Community Health Center Inc. v. Texas Health Facilities Com., United States Court of Appeals for the Fifth Circuit (9/15/1982).

Woodland Park Hospital Inc. v. Comprehensive Health Planning Authority, Court of Appeals of Oregon (12/22/1972).

Woods Serv. v. Department of Pub. Welfare, Commonwealth Court of Pennsylvania (8/1/1996).

Xun Imaging Assocs. v. Department of Health Div. of Need Review, Commonwealth Court of Pennsylvania (6/16/1994).

ANNOTATED CON CASE LAW
TABLE OF CASES – INDEXED BY LEGAL VENUE

Venue *Page*

FEDERAL

Supreme Court

Liljeberg v. Health Services Acquisition Corp., 486 U.S. 847 (U.S. 1988).

Abstract: Health Services Acquisition Corp. appealed for declaratory judgment for declaration of ownership of St. Jude Hospital. The District Court ruled in favor of Liljeberg. Health Services appealed on the grounds that the judge was associated with Liljeberg and the university and therefore had interest in the litigation. The Court of Appeals reversed and remanded the District Court's decision. During remand, the motion was denied again by the United States District Court of the Eastern District of Louisiana. Upon appeal, the Court of appeals, reversed and remanded the original judgment. A petition for writ of certiorari was filed, and the Supreme Court held that: (1) the judge violated statutes by not removing himself from the case, and (2) because of his failure to remove himself from the case, the violation of the statute require vacatur. Affirmed.

National Gerimedical Hospital and Gerontology Center v. Blue Cross of Kansas City and Blue Cross Association, 101 S. Ct. 2415 (U.S. 1981).

Abstract: Hospital went to the United States District Court for the Western District of Missouri to sue health care providers for violations of antitrust laws. Summary judgment was issued and the case was appealed and then affirmed by the Eight Circuit Court of Appeals where Certiorari was granted. Upon appeal, the Supreme Court held that: (1) providers funded by the National Health Planning and Resource Development Act were subject to antitrust laws, and (2) the Act is not so incompatible with the antitrust laws that is necessary to repeal the laws for each action taken during the health-care planning process. Reversed and remanded.

Courts of Appeals

First Circuit

South Shore Hospital, Inc. v. Tommy G. Thompson, 308 F.3d 91 (1st Cir. 2002).

Abstract: Department of Health and Human Services (DHHS) appeals from district court reversal of Provider Reimbursement Review Board of DHHS (PRRB) decision that plaintiff hospital did not qualify for "new provider" exemption. The court found that hospital from which the plaintiff purchased determination of need (DON) rights from operated as an equivalent of the plaintiff hospital. The court upheld the PRRB's decision to classify the plaintiff hospital as a "new provider."

Bath Memorial Hospital v. Maine Health Care Finance Commission, 853 F.2d 1007 (1st Cir. 1988).

Abstract: Hospitals appealed the United States District Court's decision to deem abstention appropriate and to dismiss the hospitals claim against the Maine Health Care Finance Commission (HCFC). The HCFC cross-appealed and the Court of Appeals held that: (1) because claim attacked the statute rather than requesting review of fact-specific regulatory decision making a Burford-type abstention was not appropriate, and (2) because the identical claims hospitals made in the state court could moot claims made in federal courts a Pullman-type claim could be appropriate. Vacated and remanded; cross appeal dismissed.

Second Circuit

United States v. Ntshona, 156 F.3d 318 (2d Cir. 1998).

Abstract: When Court found defendant guilty of Medicare fraud defendant appealed the judgment and sentence. The Court of Appeals held that: (1) victim's testimony was not too inflammatory to be permitted, (2) a list of 300 certificates of medical necessity was acceptable evidence, verbal testimony verifying this list was not necessary, and (3) the abuse of position of trust subjects doctor to sentencing enhancement. Affirmed.

Third Circuit

Lapid-Laurel, L.L.C. v. Zoning Board of Adjustment of the Township of Scotch Plains, 284 F.3d 442 (3d Cir. 2002).
Abstract: Developer appealed the U.S. District Court's affirmation of the township zoning board's denial of permission to build a 95-bed elderly care facility. The Court of Appeals held that: (1) in reviewing challenge, court is limited evidence presented to local land use board, (2) failure to separate developer's variance site plan applications did not bar adequate evidence from being submitted by the developer, (3) informal interaction between developer and local land authorities is not required by the Fair Housing Amendments Act (FHAA), (4) the burden of proof that accommodation is unreasonable falls to the defendant, (5) developer failed to rationalize size of the building on grounds of handicapped access, (6) evidence supported township's decision, and (7) disparate impact under FHAA was not established. Affirmed.

Armstrong Surgical Center Inc. v. Armstrong County Memorial Hospital, 185 F.3d 154 (3d Cir. 2000).
Abstract: Plaintiff appealed the dismissal of its complaint preventing a competing hospital and 19 of its physicians from establishing an ambulatory surgery center. The Court of Appeals held that the Noerr-Pennington doctrine protected actions of the physicians. Affirmed.

Official Commission of Unsecured Creditors of United Healthcare System v. Medical Staff Local 1199J, 200 F.3d 170 (3d Cir. 1999).
Abstract: Unsecured creditors committee appealed the Bankruptcy Court's finding that under the Worker Adjustment and Retraining Notification Act (WARN Act) debtor-hospital's employees were entitled to back pay. The Court of Appeals held that WARN Act requirements were not applicable to hospital for it did not constitute as an "employer" under the Acts stipulations. Reversed and remanded.

Delaware County Memorial Hospital v. Bowen, 871 F.2d 10 (3d Cir. 1989).
Abstract: Hospital appealed the court's decision to deny reimbursement for treatment of rehabilitation unit patients during those last two fiscal years. The Court of Appeals held that in order to eligible for rehabilitation 75% of the incoming population needed to require intensive rehabilitation, but the new bed rule does not recognize rehabilitation units if the its majority beds are not new. Affirmed.

Wilmac Corp. v. Bowen, 811 F.2d 809 (3d Cir. 1987).
Abstract: Health care provider sought judicial review of Pennsylvania's new amendment discontinuing reimbursement to Medicaid providers for construction costs of new additions to facilities. The Court of Appeals held that issue was not yet developed enough to receive judicial review. Vacated and remanded.

Fourth Circuit

Maryland General Hospital, Inc. v. Tommy G. Thompson, 308 F.3d 340 (4th Cir. 2002).
Abstract: Plaintiff hospital appeals from district court's upholding of DHHS decision denying "new provider" exemption to Medicare caps on reimbursement for routine services. The court held that plaintiff was considered a new provider notwithstanding purchase of certificate of need rights for skilled nursing facility beds. Provider refers to business institution providing services not the past and present ownership of assets of the institution. The court vacated the district court's order and remanded with instructions to enter judgment for plaintiff.

Gundry/Glass Hospital v. Donna E. Shalala, 1999 U.S. App. LEXIS 15418 (4th Cir. 1999).
Abstract: Plaintiffs sought injunctive relief that enjoined the Tennessee Health Department from enforcing the Tennessee Health Planning and Resource Development Act (THPRD Act of 1987) and instituting the state-court injunction that ordered the Center to stop performing abortions. The District Court granted injunctive relief on grounds that the THPRD Act of 1987 is unconstitutionally vague, and the State appealed. The Court of Appeals held that the Act was unconstitutionally vague but the time span of the injunction and efforts to

investigate merits of the injunction were not indicated, thus indicating merely a preliminary injunction rather than a permanent injunction. Affirmed and remanded with directions.

Gundry/Glass Hospital v. Shalala, 1999 U.S. App. LEXIS 6126 (4th Cir. 1999).
Abstract: Hospital appealed Blue Cross/Blue Shield's (BCBS) denial of reimbursement of costs incurred with the acquisition of a certificate of need (CON). The U.S. District Court affirmed the decision of BCBS, and met appeal. The Court of Appeals held that under the regulations of the Medicare Act only the allows reimbursement for interest expense that does not exceed the original capital expenditure, since the cost of obtaining the CON was nominal, the reimbursable interest expense relating to the CON could only be nominal. Affirmed.

Rutherford Hospital Inc. v. RNH Partnership, 168 F.3d 693 (4th Cir. 1999).
Abstract: Lessee's appealed the U.S. District Court's denial of its claim against the lessee's assertion that after the expiration of the leases the lessor did not have the adequate certification to operate the home. The Court of Appeals held that: (1) North Carolina law did not require a certificate of need to build and operate a nursing home, and therefore one was never issued, (2) lessor could continue to operate the home after expiration of the leases, and (3) bankruptcy court's order was not attacked by lessor. Affirmed.

Carrolton Inc. v. Pine Manor Rest Home (In re Pine Manor Rest Home), 1997 U.S. App. LEXIS 33323 (4th Cir. 1997).
Abstract: Pine Manor was a nursing home that was granted a certificate of need (CON) for the conversion of 30 beds and the construction of an additional 20 beds to its facility contingent on the fact that they would receive funding prior to December 15, 1993, else the CON would be rewarded to the plaintiffs. When Pine Manor secured funding for the construction of 50 beds, plaintiffs brought action against the defendants for breaching original settlement agreement by not following the conditions proscribed. Bankruptcy Court found in favor of the defendants and the District Court affirmed. Plaintiffs appealed and the Court of Appeals held that substantial evidence supports the District Court's decision. Affirmed.

Hospital Building. Co. v. Trustees of Rex Hospital, 791 F.2d 288 (4th Cir. 1986).
Abstract: Hospital appealed the Court of Appeals affirmation of the District Court dismissal of the hospital's action against another hospital for antitrust allegations and conspiring to block relocation of appellant. The Supreme Court reversed and the District Court held to its original decision, and upon appeal the court of appeals reversed and remanded and the District Court again ruled for defendant hospital. The Court of Appeals held that: (1) evidence supported the fact that defendant acted in good faith to prevent repeating health services, (2) defendant hospital intended to influence governmental action and therefore had immunity under the government influence doctrine, (3) notes taken at health planning council meeting were rightly not permitted, (4) no abuse of discretion was committed in limiting complainant's case.

North Carolina ex rel. Edmisten v. P.I.A. Asheville Inc., 740 F.2d 274 (4th Cir. 1984).
Abstract: State appealed the U.S. District court's decision to ruling for the defendants in granting them summary judgment in alleged antitrust violations. The Court of Appeals held that acquisition of all the psychiatric hospitals within the area is granted antitrust immunity implied under the National Health Planning and Resources Development Act. Affirmed.

State ex rel. Edmisten v. P.I.A. Asheville Inc., 722 F.2d 59 (4th Cir. 1983).
Abstract: Attorney General appealed the decision, affirmed by the Court of Appeals, of the U.S. District Court's ruling in favor of the defendants, a ruling determining that they were not in violation of antitrust laws. The Court of Appeals held that: (1) due to its acquisition of a certificate of need hospital did not have right to state action immunity, and (2) the application of antitrust laws was not repealed by the National Health Planning and Resources Development Act. Reversed and remanded.

Hospital Building Co. v. Trustees of Rex Hospital, 691 F.2d 678 (4th Cir. 1982).

Abstract: Operator of a 49-bed hospital appealed the dismissal by the U.S. District Court of its action against a private hospital, two of its officers, and a health planning officer for conspiring to block its expansion and maintaining their monopoly over the area. The Court of Appeals affirmed but the Supreme Court reversed and remanded. Respondents appealed. The Court of Appeals held that: (1) The Sherman Act was not violated if planning activities were undertaken in good faith and are in line with federal legislation, and (2) respondents' actions to prevent duplication of medical services rebuts alleged claims of monopolization. Affirmed in part and reversed and remanded in part.

Fifth Circuit

Surgical Care Center of Hammond, L.C. v. Hospital Service District No. 1 of Tangipahoa Parish, 153 F.3d 220 (5th Cir. 1998).

Abstract: Plaintiffs appealed the determination of the District Court that the defendant was entitled to antitrust law immunity. The Court of Appeals held that: (1) though defendant is a private actor it is still eligible for Parker Immunity; (2) exclusive nature of the contracts was not contradictory to Louisiana legislature; and (3) engaging in competitive practices is not in violation of Louisiana statute. Affirmed.

Martin v. Memorial Hospital, 86 F.3d 1391 (5th Cir. 1996).

Abstract: The municipal hospital and board members appealed the decision of the U.S. District Court's decision to deny a summary judgment motion granting immunity against the alleged antitrust claims brought forth by the plaintiff. The Court of Appeals held that: (1) the municipal hospital's exclusive contract with physician was eligible for state action immunity, (2) under collateral order doctrine, the District Court's opinion was appealable, and (3) all other decisions of the District Court were not within the jurisdiction of this Court to decide. Reversed and remanded, and all other appeals dismissed.

Women's Community Health Center Inc. v. Texas Health Facilities Commission, 685 F.2d 974 (5th Cir. 1982).

Abstract: Plaintiffs appealed the District Court's decision to dismiss action for declaratory and injunctive relief against the enforcement of certificate of need laws required by the Texas Health Planning Act. The Court of Appeals held that pending judicial proceedings of interest to the state would face interference by federal action and thus all federal action was dismissed. Affirmed.

Sixth Circuit

Ashtabula County Medical Center v. Tommy G. Thompson, 352 F.3d 1090(6th Cir. 2003).

Abstract: Secretary of Health and Human Services appeals District Court decision that Secretary's refusal to classify hospital, which purchased Certificates of Need for Skilled Nursing Facility beds to open a new facility, as a "new provider" was unreasonable. Hospital cross-appeals from District Court's failure to explicitly rule on its motion requesting costs and interest. Court of Appeals affirmed the District Court's decision and held that the term "provider" was not ambiguous and that the hospital is a "new provider" eligible for new provider exemption to the routine service cost limits. Court of Appeals remanded for District Court to determine costs and interest. Affirmed and remanded.

Castle Nursing Home v. Donald L. Sullivan, 2001 U.S. App. LEXIS 18655 (6th Cir. 2001).

Abstract: Plaintiff appealed the Bankruptcy Appellate Panel's affirmation of the Bankruptcy Court's decision to deem the debt owed to debtor dischargeable. The Court of Appeals held that: (1) only express trusts are eligible for being excepted from being dischargeable, no adequate proof indicated express trusts, and (2) proof indicated the debtor's breech of trust and violation of fiduciary duty. Affirmed.

Adams & Boyle P.C. v. Tennessee Department of Health, 3 Fed. Appx. 492 (6th Cir. 2001).

Abstract: State appealed the U.S. District Court's issuance of a temporary restraining order (TRO) on the

Tennessee License and certificate of need requirements governing the performance of abortions by private physician's offices. The Court of Appeals held that state raised issues were moot because they would be subject to later review. Affirmed.

Adams & Boyle P.C. v. Tennessee Department of Health, 4 Fed. Appx. 291 (6th Cir. 2001).
Abstract: State appealed the U.S. District Court's granting of an injunction on the Tennessee License and certificate of need requirements governing the performance of abortions by private physician's offices. The Court of Appeals held that: (1) granting preliminary injunction was within the District Court's jurisdiction and discretion, but (2) the accordance of plaintiff clinic party status was not supported by substantial evidence. Affirmed in part and reversed in part.

Dianne J. Ford, M.D. v. Steven L. Stroup, M.D., 1997 U.S. App. LEXIS 8692 (6th Cir. 1997).
Abstract: Plaintiffs appealed the U.S. District Court dismissal of its antitrust action against the defendant physician and practice group. The Court of Appeals held that: (1) evidence of significant barriers to market entry was lacking, and (2) defendants lacked the ability to control price structure and exhibit true monopoly behavior. Affirmed.

Huron Valley Hospital Inc. v. Pontiac, 887 F.2d 710 (6th Cir. 1989).
Abstract: Plaintiffs appealed the U.S. District Court dismissal of its action against the city and former officials to recover for alleged violations of due process in its efforts to obtain a certificate of need for the construction of a hospital. The Court of Appeals held that under Section 1983 plaintiff could not recover because it possessed adequate remedies. Affirmed.

Potters Medical Center v. City Hospital Association, 800 F.2d 568 (6th Cir. 1986).
Abstract: Plaintiffs appealed the U.S. District Court dismissal of its antitrust action against the hospital, its staff physician and attorney. The Court of Appeals held that: (1) no evidence indicated the capacity of the physician and attorney to conspire with hospital, but (2) court cannot reach antitrust determination without assessing the monopoly status of the hospital. Reversed and remanded.

Huron Valley Hospital Inc. v. Pontiac, 792 F.2d 563 (6th Cir. 1986).
Abstract: Former employees of the Michigan Department of Health appealed the U.S. District Court's finding for the plaintiff that asserted that city, state, and federal officials conspired in antitrust activities to prevent the plaintiff from gaining a certificate of need (CON) to construct a new hospital. The Court of Appeals held that: (1) under collateral order doctrine, the District Court's ruling denying summary judgment was appealable, (2) District Court's determination that defendants were not eligible for state action antitrust immunity is not appealable, (3) former employees' denial of CON was arbitrary and capricious and thus not entitled to immunity. Affirmed in part and dismissed in part.

Huron Valley Hospital Inc. v. Pontiac, 666 F.2d 1029 (6th Cir. 1981).
Abstract: Plaintiff appealed the U.S. District Court's finding for the defendants and dismissed the assertion that Department of Health, Education, and Welfare conspired in antitrust activities to prevent the plaintiff from gaining entry into hospital services marketplace. The Court of Appeals held that: (1) plaintiff had standing to bring action, (2) the National Health Planning and Resource Act of 1974 did not prevent consideration of antitrust allegations, (3) adjudication of antitrust claim was precluded due to a combination of prior administrative law. Vacated and remanded.

Metropolitan Ambulance Service Inc. v. Lexington-Fayette Urban County Government, 642 F.2d 452 (6th Cir. 1980).
Abstract: Decision without published opinion.

Seventh Circuit

Paragon Health Network Inc. v. Thompson, 251 F.3d 1141 (7th Cir. 2001).
Abstract: Plaintiff appealed the U.S. District Court's affirmation determining the non-eligibility of plaintiff for exemption from routine cost limits (RCLs) of Medicare and denying new provider status. The Court of Appeals held that: (1) denying new provider exemption (transferee) based on the transferor of certificate of need rights' operating history was not erroneous, and (2) using the same-cities-and-towns standard to indicate that the same population would be served by relocation was valid. Affirmed.

Rush-Presbyterian-St. Luke's Medical Center. v. Hellenic Republic, 980 F.2d 449 (7th Cir. 1992).
Abstract: The Greek government appealed the U.S. District Court's order that the Greek government pay the two unpaid bills in excess of $500,000 to hospital for provision of services related to the kidney transplant program. The Court of Appeals held that: (1) the reference to the $19,000 per hospitalization of a Greek patient cost was an estimation not a limitation to hospital costs, and (2) the performance of kidney transplants by hospital lacking the certificate of need to do so did not prevent the collection of bills. Affirmed.

Ragsdale v. Turnock, 841 F.2d 1358 (7th Cir. 1988).
Abstract: State appealed the U.S. District Court's granting of relief challenging the Illinois licensing scheme governing the provision of abortion service. The Court of Appeals held that: (1) plaintiffs had standing to bring action, (2) abortion decisions were being impacted by regulations, and (3) licensing regulations over physical plant were not in line with statute. Vacated in part and affirmed in part.

Hospital Corp. of America v. FTC, 807 F.2d 1381 (7th Cir. 1986).
Abstract: Hospital chain sought judiciary review against the Federal Trade Commission's determination that the acquisition of two hospital corporations violated the Clayton Act. The Court of Appeals held that: (1) substantial evidence indicated that acquisitions would foster consumer threatening collusive practices; (2) the executive powers of commission members were held in check by the President and therefore the commission was not in conflict with the constitution; and (3) requiring chain to provide information on its future acquisitions was within the commission's jurisdiction. Affirmed.

Eighth Circuit

Planned Parenthood v. Atchison, 126 F.3d 1042 (8th Cir. 1997).
Abstract: State appealed the U.S. District Court's ruling enjoining them from enforcing plaintiff's compliance with certificate of need (CON) regulations. The Court of Appeals held that: (1) enforcement of CON regulations was not an abuse of discretion by the District Court, (2) there were no issues in this case that would require abstention by the District Court, and (3) due to the fact that the burdens the plaintiff's project places on the right of access to abortion is unconstitutional, the District Court did not err in enforcing compliance with CON review process. Affirmed.

Ninth Circuit

Providence Health System - Washington v. Tommy G. Thompson, 353 F.3d 661 (9th Cir. 2003).
Abstract: Department of Health and Human Services (DHHS) appeals the district court's decision to deny plaintiff hospital's status as a "new provider." The court found that DHHS's belief that the purchase of certificate of need rights for new beds prevents the purchaser from being considered a "new provider" is reasonable and therefore entitled to deference. The court reversed the district court decision and issued summary judgment in favor of DHHS.

Kottle v. Northwest Kidney Centers, 146 F.3d 1056 (9th Cir. 1998).
Abstract: Denied applicant sued competitor after the Department of Health denied its application alleging

violation of antitrust law. The District Court dismissed the case. The Court of Appeals held that the competitor's actions were immune under Noerr-Pennington doctrine. Affirmed.

Lake Otis Clinic Inc. v. Sisters of Providence, 1990 U.S. App. LEXIS 22100 (9th Cir. 1990).
Abstract: Decision without published opinion.

Madarang v. Bermudes, 889 F.2d 251 (9th Cir. 1989).
Abstract: Dentist appealed to the District Court after it was denied a certificate of need. The District Court reversed the ruling. Upon appeal, the Court of Appeals held that: (1) Commonwealth did not violate equal protection clause, and (2) the dentist's procedural or substantive due process rights were not violated. Reversed.

Community Psychiatric Centers Inc. v. Grant, 664 F.2d 1148 (9th Cir. 1981).
Abstract: Competitor sought to prohibit hospital from building psychiatric unit until it underwent certificate of need proceedings and had gained a certificate of need. The District Court entered judgment. Upon appeal, the Court of Appeals held that competitor did not have the right to take action against the hospital, until the hospital had a certificate of need. Reversed in part, affirmed in part.

Tenth Circuit

Tarabishi v. McAlester Regional Hospital, 951 F.2d 1558 (10th Cir. 1991).
Abstract: Physician sued for antitrust action to the United States District Court for the Eastern District of Oklahoma after he was terminated from staffing privileges at hospital. The District Court ruled in favor of defendant in all claims except immunity. Upon appeal, the Court of Appeals held that: (1) hospital was not immune under the Local Government Antitrust Act of 1984, (2) the physician lacked evidence of monopolization, (3) physician lacked evidence to prove conspiracy of monopolization and conspiracy of restraint of trade. Affirmed.

Tarabishi v. McAlester Regional Hospital, 827 F.2d 648 (10th Cir. 1987).
Abstract: Doctor used his staffing privileges at hospital to apply for certificate of need. Hospital then terminated his staffing privileges. Doctor appealed to the United States District Court of Eastern Oklahoma arguing tortuous interference seeking injunctive relief and damages under civil right statutes. The Court ruled in favor of defendant. Upon appeal, the Court of appeals held that because the hospital was public, for purposes of civil rights action the hospitals decisions were state actions. Reversed and remanded.

Eleventh Circuit

FTC v. Hospital Board of Directors, 38 F.3d 1184 (11th Cir. 1994).
Abstract: Federal Trade Commission went to the District Court after hospital board's purposed purchase of private hospital. The District Court granted summary judgment to defendants. The Court of appeals held that: (1) "foreseeable anticompetitive effect" was expected when states were given power, and (2) board had state action immunity from federal antitrust laws. Affirmed

FTC v. University Health Inc., 938 F.2d 1206 (11th Cir. 1991).
Abstract: Federal Trade Commission sought a preliminary injunction from the District Court to keep a hospital from purchasing another. The Court did not grant the injunction, and the Commission appealed to the Court o Appeals. The Court of Appeals held that: (1) the Clayton act applied to non-profit hospitals, (2) Commission provided substantial evidence that the merging of the two hospitals would create less competition, and (3) the hospitals did not provide substantial evidence that merging the two hospitals would streamline efforts. Vacated and remanded.

St. Joseph's Hospital Inc. v. Hospital Corp. of America, 795 F.2d 948 (11th Cir. 1986).
Abstract: Hospital went to the District Court to bring action against competitors under Sherman Act. The case was dismissed. Upon appeal, the Court of Appeals held that: (1) hospitals had Noerr-Pennington immunity to use delay tactics against a competitor's application for certificate of need, (2) misrepresentation to governmental body did not have Noerr-Pennington immunity, and (3) hospital did not have sufficient evidence. Vacated and remanded.

In re King Memorial Hospital Inc., 767 F.2d 1508 (11th Cir. 1985).
Abstract: Motion was brought before the District Court to withdraw an adversary proceeding from the Bankruptcy Court. Motion was denied. Upon appeal, the Court of Appeals held that the District Court's motion could not be appealed as (1) a final order or (2) a collateral order exception. Dismissed.

Bankruptcy Courts

Carrolton Inc. v. Pine Manor Rest Home, 215 B.R. 341 (Bankr. E.D.N.C. 1997).
Abstract: Competitors filed suit objections to the North Carolina Office of Administrative Hearings after Department of Human Resources granted nursing home a CON for 90 beds. During hearing, loan agreements were reached so that the competitor would be granted a CON for 35 nursing beds, and nursing home would be granted a CON for 50- 30 by converting, and 20 by constructing. Competitors filed suit against nursing home for breaching settlement because nursing home secured conversion of 50 beds before the office of administrative hearings. An administrative law judge held that the loan commitment was not in breech of previous settlement. While appeal was pending, competitor also filed suit at the Bankruptcy Court seeking declaratory judgment concerning the nursing homes rights to its certificate of need. The nursing home filed for summary judgment, and it was granted. Upon appeal, the District Court held that: (1) Bankruptcy Court did not err in finding that nursing home did not forfeit its CON by signing an agreement that would convert 50 beds. Affirmed.

In re St. Louis South Park II Inc., 111 B.R. 260 (Bankr. W.D. Mo. 1990).
Abstract: Missouri Health Facilities Review Commission (MHFRC) held that a debtor's certificate of need was forfeited because it had failed to meet required capital expenditures. The Bankruptcy Court held that because the MHFRC did not know the debtor was going bankrupt and the MHFRC was not engaged in enforcing a regulation for protective purposes, the forfeiture is declared null and void. Ordered accordingly.

District Courts

Alabama

Vaughan Regional Medical Center. v. Smith, 6 F. Supp. 1142 (M.D. Ala. 1995).
Abstract: Competing hospital appealed to the District Court for declaratory judgment after the state agency approved a state license without considering federal statutes. The state agency moved to dismiss the case. The District Court held that state statutory schemes preempted federal statutes. Motion to dismiss the case is granted.

Arkansas

Garst v. Stoco Inc., 604 F. Supp. 326 (E.D. Ark. 1985).
Abstract: Two physicians went to the District Court, Eisele to sue hospitals for violating antitrust acts after they had opposed the physicians' certificates of need. The Court held that: (1) health agencies were governmental bodies that were protected from antitrust liability, and (2) the hospitals and employees were not liable under federal antitrust law. Motion granted.

California

Redbud Hospital District v. Heckler, 1984 U.S. Dist. LEXIS 24704 (N.D. Cal. 1997).

Abstract: Hospital appealed for injunction to District Court after the Secretary of the Department of Health and Human Services put a new amendment into effect called the Prospective Payment System and refused to grant the hospital a hearing concerning the system. The District Court held that the Secretary abused her discretion by ignoring Congressional mandates. Preliminary injunction granted.

District of Columbia

Doctors Hospital Inc. v. Califano, 459 F. Supp. 201 (D. D.C. 1978).

Abstract: Provider of Medicare services sought to obtain reimbursement for service rendered from the Secretary of Health, Education and Welfare. The Secretary filed a motion for summary judgment. The District Court held that: (1) money that was unpaid for more than a year should be reimbursable, (2) interest, legal and administrative fees should not be reimbursed, and (3) stipends for residents could not be determined. Motion of plaintiff granted in part, motion for defendant granted in part, and case remanded.

Georgia

St. Joseph's Hosp. v. Hospital Authority of America, 620 F. Supp. 814 (S.D. Ga. 1985).

Abstract: Hospital filed suit against competitor for antitrust violations after competitor appealed its certificate of need application. Competitor filed to dismiss suit on the grounds of failure to state a claim. The District Court held that there was insufficient evidence of concerted action. Motion granted.

Maryland

Maryland General Hospital Inc. v. Thompson, 155 F. Supp. 2d 459 (D. Md. 2001).

Abstract: Provider appealed to the District Court for judicial review after the Secretary of Health and Human Services denied its request for new provider exemption from Medicare payments. The Court held that the Secretary's ruling was reasonable and should be granted deference in this matter. Affirmed.

Gundry Glass Hospital v. Shalala Civil, 6 F. Supp. 2d 466 (D. Md. 1998).

Abstract: Hospital that had received certificate of need sought to reimburse interest cost of certificate from the Department of Health and Human Services. The District Court held that since the asset was intangible, the interest of the asset was not reimbursable. Defendant's motion granted.

United States ex rel. Joslin v. Community Home Health Civil, 984 F. Supp. 374 (D. Md. 1997).

Abstract: Plaintiff sued for qui tam action to recover Medicare payments to a home health care provider. The District Court held that: (1) provider was exempt from obtaining a certificate of need, (2) because of exemption, provider had not misled the government concerning state laws, (3) stock acquisition did not alter the providers status as exempt from CON, (4) although provider moved, they remained and served the same geographic area and therefore did not need to apply for CON, (5) sale of stock of corporation did not alter providers status as exempt from CON, and (6) provider was not liable under False Claims Act. Summary judgment for provider.

Massachusetts

South Shore Hospital v. Tommy G. Thompson, Vol. 2002 WL 69487 (D. Mass. 2002).

Abstract: Nursing facility appealed to the District Court after it was denied "new provider status". The defendant moved for summary judgment. The Court held that the nursing facility's purchase of a determination of need from a defunct facility did not qualify it for "new provider status". Summary judgment is granted.

Michigan

Huron Valley Hospital Inc. v. Pontiac, 466 F. Supp. 1301 (E.D. Mich. 1997).

Abstract: Nonprofit organization brought suit against defendants arguing violation of federal antitrust laws. The defendants filed for summary judgment. The District Court held that: (1) plaintiff had not yet exhausted all administrative remedies, (2) the plaintiff's complaints did qualify as violations of antitrust laws, and (3) however, those violations did not necessarily qualify as violation of federal antitrust laws. Summary judgment granted.

Huron Valley Hospital Inc. v. Pontiac, 686 F. Supp. 608 (E.D. Mich. 1988).
Abstract: Hospital appealed to the District Court after the state denied it a certificate of need. The state filed for summary judgment. The Court held that the hospital received appropriate state remedy. Summary judgment granted.

Huron Valley Hospital Inc. v. Pontiac, 650 F. Supp. 1325 (E.D. Mich. 1986).
Abstract: Hospital appealed to the District Court after it was denied certificate of need. The Court granted summary judgment to defendant holding that: (1) evidence of antitrust activity could not be proven among hospital and councils that were engaging in cooperation, and (2) hospitals and Michigan Department of Public Health did not enter into conspiracy with one another. Motions granted.

Huron Valley Hospital Inc. v. Pontiac, 612 F. Supp. 654 (E.D. Mich. 1985).
Abstract: Applicant for certificate of need appealed to the District Court holding that there was a conspiracy to prevent building of hospital. The defendants filed for summary judgment. The Court held that (1) statute of limitations did not bar antitrust claims, (2) applicants complaints were backed up by sufficient evidence to warrant examination of case, and (3) section of Local Government Antitrust Act would not be invoked in this case in order for applicant to receive damages from city defendants. Motions denied.

Huron Valley Hospital Inc. v. Pontiac Civil Action, 585 F. Supp. (E.D. Mich. 1984).
Abstract: After Department of Health reversed its initial decision to approve capital expenditure for a corporation, the corporation sough mandamus and brought antitrust action to the United States District Court for the Eastern District of Michigan. Summary judgment was granted concerning the antitrust issues. Upon appeal, the Court of appeals reversed and remanded the decision. During remand, the District Court held that: (1) Secretary's decision was subject to judicial review, and (2) writ was appropriate remedy. Writ issued.

Mississippi

Baptist Memorial Hospital-De Soto Inc. v. Mississippi Health Care Com. Civil Action , Jackson Division, 617 F. Supp. 686 1985 (S.D. Miss. 1985).
Abstract: Applicant that was granted conditional decision of intent to grant certificate of need brought action before the District Court, seeking action to enjoin settlement so unsuccessful applicant could receive certificate of need. The District Court held that: (1) applicant with condition decision had "property interest" that was protected under due process, and (2) relief could not be granted because of the Eleventh Amendment. Ordered accordingly.

Hollingsworth v. Califano, 477 F. Supp. 872 (N.D. Miss. 1979).
Abstract: Competitor appealed to the District Court after the Secretary of Health, Education and Welfare granted a certificate of need to another nursing home. The Court held that: (1) it lacked jurisdiction to rule, and (2) the competitor lacked standing to appeal. Vacated and remanded.

Missouri

Federal Trade Commission v. Freeman Hospital, 911 F.Supp. 1213 (W.D. Mo. 1995).
Abstract: The Federal Trade Commission sought to prohibit the consolidation of hospital by filing preliminary

injunction. The District Court held that: (1) the non-profit status of the hospital was relevant to the case, (2) aside from the FTC, no other party had voiced objection concerning the consolidation, (4) there was lack of evidence indicating anticompetitive effect of the consolidation. Motion denied.

Greater St. Louis Health Systems Agency v. Teasdale, 506 F. Supp. 23 (E.D. Mo. 1980).
Abstract: Plaintiff challenged the validity of provisions of certificate of need case law. The District Court held that: (1) declaratory judgment was denied because controversy would not exceed $10,000, (2) jurisdiction was not founded on proper act regulating commerce, (3) court had subject matter jurisdiction in federal but not state claims, (4) plaintiff's lacked standing to challenge certain certificate of need laws, (5) the definition of health system's agency varied in the law and the National Health Planning and Resources Development Act, (6) certain sections of law conflicted with Act. Injunctive and declaratory relief granted. Attorney's fees awarded to plaintiff.

National Gerimedical Hospital & Gerontology v. Blue Cross of Kansas City, 479 F. Supp. 1012 (W.D. Mo. 1997).
Abstract: Hospital brought antitrust violations against health care providers. Providers sought to dismiss the case. The District Court held that: (1) contracts between hospitals and health care providers were not exempt from federal antitrust laws, (2) health care providers were exempt from antitrust laws, and (3) state claims should be dismissed. Summary judgment granted.

New Jersey

Healthcare Services Group, Inc. v. Royal Healthcare of Middlesex, LLC., 276 F. Supp. 2d 255 (D. N.J. 2003).
Abstract: Plaintiff provider moves for summary judgment in breach of contract claim against defendant owner of certificate of need (CON). Both parties agreed that because defendant held the CON, defendant was legally responsible for management of the long-term care facility. Therefore, an agency relationship existed between defendant and defendant's contractor when contractor subcontracted with plaintiff to manage the facility. The court granted plaintiff's motion for summary judgment.

New York

Beechwood Restorative Care Center v. Laura E. Leeds, 2004 U.S. Dist. LEXIS 8906 (W.D.N.Y.. 2004).
Abstract: Plaintiffs allege that because plaintiffs' operating certificate was rescinded, plaintiffs could not transfer a certificate of need to a potential buyer thereby rendering the nursing home almost worthless as well as violating state statutes and regulations. Plaintiffs were not deprived of procedural due process. The Department of health did not revoke the facility's establishment approval, the plaintiffs had previously closed the facility. Under these circumstances, a new owner would have been required to obtain a new certificate of need to reopen the facility. Where a facility has ceased operations, new owners are required to follow the statutory approval process including the receipt of a determination that there is need for the facility.

New York v. St. Francis Hospital, 94 F. Supp. 2d 399 (S.D.N.Y. 2000).
Abstract: State sued two hospitals and petitioned to the District Court of injunctive relief on the grounds that the hospitals were violating the Sherman Act and state antitrust statutes. The hospitals filed for summary judgment, and the statue filed for summary judgment to deny the hospitals state-action immunity. The Court held that: (1) the two hospitals had engaged in violations of the Sherman Act, and (2) hospitals could not receive state-action immunity from antitrust liability. Summary judgment for the state granted.

North Carolina

North Carolina ex rel. Morrow v. Califano, 445 F. Supp. 532 (E.D.N.C. 1978).
Abstract: State brought suit against the Secretary of Health, Education and Welfare arguing that the provision by the National Health Planning and Resources Development Act that demanded a state is required to set up a

health planning agency and a certificate of need program to issue financial grants was not constitutional. The Three-Judge District Court held the requirement was valid. Summary judgment granted.

Ohio

Ashtabula County Medical Center v. Thompson, 191 F. Supp. 2d (N.D. Ohio 2002).

Abstract: Hospital appealed to the District Court for judicial review after the Secretary of Health and Human Services denied its request to be classified as a "new provider" since it had recently purchased a certificate of need from an unrelated provider. The Court held that: (1) hospital qualified as a "new provider", and (2) the Secretary's basis for denial was irrational. Review granted.

Oklahoma

Gooding v. Oklahoma ex rel. Oklahoma Welfare Commission, 436 F. Supp. 583 (W.D. Okla. 1977).

Abstract: Nursing home challenged the constitutionality of state statutes and the federal National Health Planning and Resources Development Act. The Three-Judge District Court held that the federal and state laws were constitutional. Dismissed.

Pennsylvania

Alan D. Gordon v. Lewistown Hospital, 272 F. Supp. 2d 393 (M.D. Pa. 2003).

Abstract: Plaintiff physician, an ophthalmologist, brings suit against defendant hospital alleging defendant violated sections 1 and 2 of the Sherman Act. Plaintiff alleges eight causes of actions: (Count I) a contract in restraint of trade; (Count II) illegal tying arrangement; (Count III) attempted monopolization; (Count IV) reciprocal dealing; (Count V) boycott; (Count VI) exclusive dealing; and, (Count VII and VIII) conspiracy to monopolize. Court granted summary judgment for defendants on Counts I, IV, V, VII, VIII. The court then granted plaintiffs motion for partial reconsideration and held that Count I was erroneously included in the motion for summary judgment. With respect to the remaining counts, the court held that in Count I (unreasonable restraint on trade) the restraints the defendant placed on plaintiff in "Conditions for Reappointment" were not unreasonable as they solely regulated competition. In Count II (Illegal Tying Arrangement), the court granted judgment in favor of defendants using a rule of reason analysis to determine that the Conditions of Reappointment were justified by pro-competitive motivations, which furthered competition in the market. For Count III (attempted monopolization) the court also granted judgment in favor of the defendant as plaintiff failed to show defendant's specific intent to monopolize. Judgment for defendant.

Bradford Hospital v. Donna E. Shalala, 108 F.Supp.2d 473 (W.D. Pa. 2000).

Abstract: Hospital appealed to the District Court after the Secretary of Department of Health and Human Services denied its request to redetermine hospital rate for Medicare reimbursement. The defendant filed for summary judgment and it was granted on the grounds that: (1) Administrator's ruling that the hospitals letter to a Medicare fiscal intermediary did not qualify as a request for redetermination was not arbitrary or capricious, and (2) equitable tolling was permitted and hospitals redeterminiation request was warranted. Plaintiff's motion granted, and defendant's motion denied.

Metropolitan Hospital v. Thornburgh Civil Action, 667 F. Supp. 208 (E.D. Pa. 1987).

Abstract: Osteopathic hospitals and members sued allopathic hospitals, District Court held that: (1) certificate of need program in Pennsylvania warranted the abstention of federal court ruling in favor of state action, (2) osteopathic hospitals had opportunities to discuss federal constitutional challenges and the state court review denial of certificate of need, and (3) state courts did not have jurisdiction over federal antitrust claims and so therefore antitrust claims are not subject to abstention.

Harrisburg Hospital v. Thornburgh Civil Action, 616 F. Supp. 699 (M.D. Pa. 1985).
Abstract: Decision published without opinion.

Harrisburg Hospital v. Thornburgh, 611 F. Supp. 900 (M.D. Pa. 1985).
Abstract: Corporation sought to challenge Pennsylvania legislation to allow medical center to bypass certificate of need law. The District Court held that: (1) corporation did not meet qualifications to act as intervener for the medical center, (2) the motion to intervene was filed in an untimely manner, and (3) grant was not warranted. Intervention denied.

Tennessee

Jackson Tennessee Hospital Company, LLC. v. West Tennessee Healthcare, Inc., 2004 U.S. Dist. LEXIS 4571 (W.D. Tenn. 2004).
Abstract: Plaintiff hospital company brought antitrust claim against the defendants, healthcare systems. Plaintiff alleges that defendants attempted to and succeeded in monopolizing a local health care region by, for example, using Certificate of Need to expand services and restrain plaintiff from doing so. Court dismissed the antitrust claim as defendants were immune from antitrust suit under state action doctrine. Other claims were dismissed without prejudice as the court decided not to exercise supplemental jurisdiction. Dismissed without prejudice.

Texas

United States of America v. East Texas Medical Center Regional Healthcare System, 274 F. Supp. 2d 824 (S.D. Tex. 2003).
Abstract: District Court order adopting magistrate judge's memorandum and recommendation and amended memorandum and recommendation. District Court notes that plaintiff, former hospital executive, has timely filed an objection to the amended memorandum and recommendation, but all are objections previously raised except that the recommendation is faulty as it requires plaintiff to prove injury to the government as a result of the Certificate of Need process. Court finds that plaintiff's objection is not timely and that if it was valid, it would not impact the recommendation's ultimate finding. Final Judgment.

United States of America v. East Texas Medical Center Regional Healthcare System, 274 F. Supp. 2d 824 (S.D. Tex. 2002).
Abstract: Plaintiff is a former executive director of a nonprofit hospital who alleges that she was wrongfully discharged by defendant healthcare system after she allegedly discovered Medicare fraud through false statements made by the hospital on annual cost reports. Plaintiff claims that the hospital was making a false statement on the cost report by saying that the hospital was in compliance with applicable Certificate of Need requirements as plaintiff claims that the hospital was not in compliance with CON financing requirements. Plaintiff brought suit under the qui tam provision of the False Claims Act. Defendant moved for summary judgment for lack of subject matter jurisdiction. The court granted the motion for summary judgment as: (1) plaintiff cannot prove that she was the original source of the evidence showing a False Claims Act violation, (2) plaintiff cannot prove conspiracy to defraud the government, and (3) plaintiff cannot prove that the government has suffered damaged by the alleged actions. Motion for summary judgment granted.

ALABAMA

Supreme Court of Alabama

Ex parte State Health Planning and Development Agency v. LithoMedTech of Alabama, LLC , 855 So. 2d 1098 (Ala. 2002).

Abstract: Alabama's State Health Planning and Development Agency (SHPDA) and Prime Medical Services petition for writ of certiorari in cases regarding the sale of mobile lithotripsy equipment to hospitals. SHPDA argues that the sale of mobile lithotripsy to a hospital is providing a health service, which is subject to state Certificate of Need regulations. Court of Civil Appeals held that the sale of medical equipment for use by hospitals and HMOs was not a "health service". Supreme Court of Alabama granted writ and affirmed the decision of the Court of Civil Appeals that only the healthcare facilities and HMOs providing health services must seek CON review. The Supreme Court also upholds the Court of Civil Appeals' decision not to give deference to SHPDA's interpretation. Affirmed.

Lloyd Noland Foundation, Inc. v. The City of Fairfield Healthcare Authority, 2002 WL 254104 (Ala. 2002).

Abstract: Seller of hospital appealed the Court's ruling for the buyer that seller did not have entitlement to the certificate of need (CON) for long-term acute care beds. The Supreme Court held that: (1) seller could apply for CON without buyer joining the applications, (2) the intermediate seller's obligations to sell beds and cooperate in their relicensure was an incorrect assumption by the buyer, (3) the lease agreement between intermediate and original seller for long-term acute care beds was valid evidence against the subsequent buyer, (4) the duty to renegotiate lease was the buyer's, (5) cooperation clause was breached when buyer intervened in CON process, and (6) misrepresentations in seller's applications for CON could not be challenged by the buyer. Reversed and remanded with directions.

Ex parte Beverly Enterprises-Alabama Inc., 812 So.2d 1189 (Ala. 2001).

Abstract: Two facilities applied to receive certificate of need from State Health Planning Agency. One was granted, while the other was refused by the Certificate of Need Review Board. Unsuccessful party appealed to the fair hearing officer who reversed and remanded the case. The successful bidder appealed to the Circuit Court which reversed the decision. The Court of Civil Appeals affirmed the decision by unpublished memorandum. The Supreme Court granted certiorari review and held that: (1) Circuit Court did not have authority to reweigh evidence in case and reinstate initial decision by CON Review Board, and (2) fair hearing officer's decision was not arbitrary or capricious and complied with applicable law. Reversed and remanded.

Auburn Medical Center, Inc. v. State Health Planning and Development Agency et al., 814 So.2d 260 (Ala. 2001).

Abstract: Alabama State Health Planning and Development Agency filed for writ of certiorari against the Court of Civil appeals' ruling for the petitioner in granting them declaratory relief against allegations of violating certificate of need rules. The Supreme Court held that amendments to the Act could not be applied to issues presented prior to institution of new rules. Reversed and remanded.

Ex parte East State Healthcare Auth., 814 So.2d 260 (Ala. 2001).

Abstract: Medical center appealed to the Montgomery Circuit Court after the CON review board denied their petition for declaratory relief. The Court upheld the Board's decision to dismiss. Upon appeal, the Court of Civil Appeals reversed and remanded. The State Health Planning and Development Agency then filed petitions for writ of certiorari to the Supreme Court. The Court held that: (1) prior to exhaustion of administrative remedies, decision about how certificate of need was handled could not be applied retrospectively. Reversed and remanded.

Ex parte Brookwood Health Services Inc., 781 So.2d 954 (Ala. 2000).
Abstract: Health care organization appealed to the Court of Civil Appeals for writ of mandamus after Montgomery Circuit Court ordered them to transfer their petition for judicial review to competitor. The Court of Civil Appeals denied the writ, and the organization appealed to the Supreme Court. The Court held that: (1) transferring petition was an abuse of discretion by the Court of Civil Appeals.

Ex parte Forest Manor Inc., 739 So.2d 20 (Ala. 1998).
Abstract: Unsuccessful applicant appealed to the Montgomery Circuit Court after they had been denied a certificate of need, and competitor had received one. Montgomery Circuit Court found in favor of unsuccessful applicant and set aside competitor's CON. The Court of Civil Appeals reversed and remanded. Upon further appeal, the Supreme Court held that: (1) a hearing concerning the granting or denial of CON is a "Contested case", (2) due process rights were violated due to the inadequate notice given by the State Health Planning and Development Agency. Reversed and remanded.

Roberts Health Care v. State Health Planning and Development Agency, 698 So.2d 106 (Ala. 1997).
Abstract: Joint venturers appealed to the Supreme Court after the Montgomery Circuit Court terminated its expired certificate of need. The Court held that the expiration of CON was delayed because one joint venturer was seeking declaration of ownership of CON and filing action against individual joint venturer. Reversed and Remanded.

Ex parte Crestwood Hospital and Nursing Home, 670 So.2d 45 (Ala. 1995).
Abstract: Successful applicant moved to dismiss on the grounds that competitor hospital had not yet exhausted all administrative remedies. The Circuit Court denied motion, and successful applicant petitioned for writ of certiorari to Supreme Court. The Court held that: (1) denied hospital failed to file notice of appeal and cost bond according to the Alabama Administrative Procedure Act which is needed prior to granting judicial review for failure to exhaust administrative remedies. Reversed and remanded.

Ex parte Virginia D. Condra Willis , 599 So.2d 1166 (Ala. 1992).
Abstract: House Resolution 384 requested the Supreme Court to give an advisory opinion concerning certificate of need exemption for nursing homes operated by the Department of Veterans' Affairs. The Court determined that the Dept. did not need to undergo the certificate of need process because they had already obtained all necessary federal government approval.

Ex parte Shelby Medical Center Inc., 564 So.2d 63 (Ala. 1990).
Abstract: Area hospitals appealed after State Health Planning and Development Agency granted certificate of need to hospital. The appeals were consolidated and the Circuit Court, Jefferson County reversed and vacated the Agency's decision. Upon appeal, the Court of Civil Appeals reversed. The area hospitals then petitioned for writ of certiorari. The Supreme Court held that: (1) Review Board of State Health Planning and Development Agency did not need to reach unanimous approval to approve certificate of need, (2) The Sunshine Act is not violated if the vote is by written ballot, and (3) the Agency's decision lacked substantial evidence in backing its decision, and clearly was in error for approving certificate of need. Reversed and remanded with directions.

Ex parte Nursing Home of Dothan Inc., 542 So.2d 940 (Ala. 1989).
Abstract: Nursing home appealed to the Court of Civil Appeals after the State Health Planning Agency denied its proposed amendment to state health plan and denied its application for certificate of need. The Court found in favor of the Agency. Upon appeal, the Supreme Court held that: (1) the process in which the Governor vetoed

the amendment was in accordance to the state and federal statutes, and (2) due process was administered fully by the Agency which met minimum standards in state statutes. Affirmed.

Ex parte Traylor Nursing Home Inc., 543 So.2d 1179 (Ala. 1988).
Abstract: After Statewide Health Coordinating Council adopted an amendment to state health plan, a nursing home went to the Circuit Court, Montgomery County requesting declaratory judgment and injunctive relief. The Circuit Court ruled in favor of the Council. Upon appeal, the Supreme Court held that: (1) the amendment did not violate the Administrative Procedures Act, rather it was a "rule" within the Act, (2) the Council acted as an "agency" in the Act, and (3) as an agency, the Council was required to follow the Act's procedures, which it failed to do. Reversed and remanded with instructions.

Canterbury Nursing Home Inc. v. Alabama State Health Planning and Development Agency, 425 So.2d 1103 (Ala. 1983).
Abstract: State Health Planning and Development Agency considered sale of nursing home stock a prohibited transfer of a certificate of need. The shareholders filed a counterclaim. The Agency won and sued for attorney fees. The Circuit Court, Montgomery County denied the motion for attorney fees. The Supreme Court held that the trial court was in error for not granting attorney fees to shareholders. Reversed and remanded.

Mount Royal Towers Inc. v. Alabama Board of Health, 388 So.2d 1209 (Ala. 1980).
Abstract: Facility appealed to the Circuit Court challenging constitutionality of Certificate of Need, after it had been denied CON. The Court ruled in favor of the Board of Health. Upon appeal, the Supreme Court held that: (1) due process was not violated by the Certificate of Need Act, and (2) individual rights and public welfare must be balanced when determining if legislation denies substantive due process. Reversed and Remanded.

Court of Civil Appeals

Colonial Management Group, L.P. v. State Health Planning and Development Agency et al., 853 So. 2d 972 (Ala. Civ. App. 2002).
Abstract: Appellant Colonial Management Group, L.P. appeals circuit court decision affirming State Health Planning and Development Agency's (SHPDA) decision to grant a certificate of need to Tuscaloosa Treatment Center Associates to operate a methadone clinic. The Court the decision because the appellant failed to show that the trial court's decision to affirm the SHPDA decision was arbitrary or capricious. Affirmed.

Prime Lithotripter Operations, Inc., v. LithoMedTech of Alabama, LLC, 2001 LEXIS 915 (Ala. Civ. App. 2001).
Abstract: Alabama State Health Planning and Development Agency (ASHPDA) appealed the court's order to enjoin ASHPDA from enforcing any certificate of need (CON) review on UroVenture's Proposal. The Court of Civil Appeals held that: (1) adoption of entities not expressly stated as requiring CON review under the law is outside of the jurisdiction of the ASHPDA, and (2) mobile lithotripsy units do not constitute as "new institutional health services" that require CON review. Affirmed.

Auburn Medical Center, Inc. v. East Alabama health Care Authority d/b/a East Alabama Medical Center, 2001 WL 499009 (Ala. Civ. App. 2001).
Abstract: Competitor appealed the trial court's decision to grant the medical center's request to render the grant of a competitor's certificate of need (CON) for operation of an acute-care hospital invalid and to issue a CON center's application for ambulatory surgery center in that area instead. The Court of Civil Appeals held that: (1) expiration of the competitor's CON was not nullified by prior federal litigation, but (2) center's CON application nullified the expiration period of the competitor's CON application. Reversed and remanded.

Auburn Medical Center, Inc. v. State Health Planning and Development Agency et al., 814 So.2d 263 (Ala. Civ. App. 2001).

Abstract: Medical center appealed the court's affirmation of the Certificate of Need Review Board to deny its petition for declaratory relief against allegations of violating certificate-of-need laws. The Court of Civil Appeals reversed and remanded and met a petition by Alabama State Health Planning and Development Agency for writ of certiorari. Upon reversal and remanding by the Supreme Court, the Court of Civil Appeals held that the decision to deny petition for declaratory relief was not reviewable due to medical center's lack of standing. Affirmed.

Auburn Medical Center Inc. v. State Health Planning and Development Agency, 814 So.2d 258 (Ala. Civ. App. 2000).

Abstract: Medical center filed petition for declaratory relief to CON review board arguing that there was violation of certificate of need rules. Review board denied petition and center appealed to the Montgomery Circuit Court. The Circuit Court granted petition, and upon appeal, the Court of Civil Appeals held that altering procedures did not make substantive changes to CON law. Reversed and remanded with instructions.

State Health Planning and Development Agency v. Forest Manor, Inc., 766 So.2d 25 (Ala. Civ. App. 1999).

Abstract: The Supreme Court reversed and remanded the judgment of the trial court and ordered it to set aside a certificate of need for Heritage Health Care. Upon remand, the Court of Civil Appeals reinstates judgment and remands it to the trial court.

State Health Planning and Development Agency v. Baptist Health System, Inc., 766 So.2d 176 (Ala. Civ. App. 1999).

Abstract: Provider appealed the court's decision to reverse the Alabama State Health Planning and Development Agency and Certificate of Need Review Board's granting of a certificate of need (CON) to the provider. The Court of Civil Appeals held that substantial evidence supported the Board's granting of CON to provider. Reversed and remanded for further proceedings.

Huntsville Healthcare Center. Inc. v. Brown Health Services Inc., 747 So.2d 330 (Ala. Civ. App. 1999).

Abstract: Court of Civil Appeals remands case back to the Certificate of Need Board on the grounds that although both Court and Board have jurisdiction, the Board has specialized expertise and therefore should review the case.

Forest Manor Inc. v. State Health Planning and Development Agency, 723 So.2d 75 (Ala. Civ. App. 1998).

Abstract: Five parties applied for certificates of need to the State Health Planning and Development Agency, the case was then appointed to an Administrative Law Judge. The ALJ recommended the approval of one party and the denied the challenger's. The State Health Planning and Development Agency's certificate of need review board did not rule with the ALJ and instead granted certificate of need to challenger. The fair hearing officer then overturned the board's ruling. Challenger petitioned to Montgomery Circuit for judicial review and the Circuit Court affirmed the fair hearing officer's ruling. The Court of Civil Appeals held that: (1) Montgomery County Circuit Court had jurisdiction to rule upon petition, (2) provisions in Alabama Administrative Procedure Act applied to judicial review, (3) fair hearing officer was final agency decision of Agency, and (4) fair hearing officer had substantial evidence and his decision was not arbitrary or capricious. Affirmed.

University of Alabama Hospitals v. Alabama Renal Stone Institute Inc., 518 So.2d 721 (Ala. Civ. App. 1998).

Abstract: Two hospitals received certificate of need exemption for equipment purchased for research purposes. The Circuit Court reversed the order on the grounds that the State Health Planning and Development Agency acted outside its scope of authority. Upon appeal, the Court of Civil Appeals held that: (1) Agency had statutory authority grant research exemption, and (2) state statute does not require certificate of need for research equipment. Reversed and rendered.

State Health Planning and Development Agency v. Forest Manor Inc., 739 So.2d 17 (Ala. Civ. App. 1998).
Abstract: Denied applicant appealed to the Montgomery County Circuit Court after the Certificate of Need Review Board granted a certificate of need (CON) to competitor. The Circuit Court ruled against the Board's decision to grant a CON. The Court of Civil Appeals held that denied applicant was given reasonable notice concerning hearing and its statutory and due process rights were not violated. Reversed and remanded.

State Health Planning and Development Agency v. Ball Healthcare-Lowndes Inc., 695 So.2d 6 (Ala. Civ. App. 1996).
Abstract: Denied applicant requested fair hearing after a certificate of need was denied and a competitor was approved by the state agency. Fair hearing officer reversed the decision of the state agency. Judicial review was sought. The Mobile Circuit Court granted preliminary injunction, and the agency appealed. The Court of Civil Appeals held that the fair hearing officer had the final decision. Affirmed.

Sylacauga Health Care Center v. Alabama State Health Planning Agency, 662 So.2d 265 (Ala. Civ. App. 1994).
Abstract: Health Care Providers appealed the decision of court to deny their petition for a writ certiorari. The Court of Civil Appeals affirms court. Application for rehearing overruled.

Clark v. Fancher, 662 So.2d 258 (Ala. Civ. App. 1994).
Abstract: Competitor appealed to the Montgomery Circuit Court after the Alabama State Health Planning Department Agency approved two certificates of need. The trial court affirmed the ruling, and the decision was appealed to the Court of Civil Appeals. The Court held that: (1) the Certificate of Need Review Board did not abuse authority in its ruling; (2) the Board's decision was based on substantial evidence; and (3) the trial court did not abuse discretion. Affirmed.

State Health Planning Agency v. Mobile Infirmary Association, 608 So.2d 1372 (Ala. Civ. App. 1992).
Abstract: Hospital appealed to the Mobile Circuit Court after the State Health Planning Agency denied its application to purchase new equipment. The Circuit Court reversed the Agency's decision, and the Agency appealed to the Court of Civil Appeals. The Court held that the Agency's decision was based on substantial evidence. Reversed and remanded with instructions.

Auburn Medical Center v. East Alabama Health Care Authority, 583 So.2d 1342 (Ala. Civ. App. 1990).
Abstract: Denied applicant appealed to the Circuit Court after the Board had granted certificate of need to competitor. The Court held bifurcated trial and reversed and remanded the Board's ruling. The Court of Civil Appeals held that the denied applicant did not exhaust all administrative remedies before turning to the Circuit Court and therefore the Circuit Court lacked jurisdiction to rule. Reversed and remanded.

Alabama Nursing Home Association v. Alabama State Health Planning Agency, 554 So.2d 1032 (Ala. Civ. App. 1989).
Abstract: Hospitals sought declaratory relief from the State Health Planning Agency which refused to make a ruling concerning the use of Medstone lithotripter. Hospitals then sought judicial review from the Circuit Court. The Court ruled in favor of hospitals. Agency appealed to the Court of Civil Appeals, which held that certificate of need (CON) approval was necessary before Medstone lithotripter could be used for a new procedure that had not been listed on previous CON. Reversed and remanded with instructions.

State Health Planning Agency v. Mobile Infirmary Association, 533 So.2d 255 (Ala. Civ. App. 1988).
Abstract: Nursing home appealed to Circuit Court for declaratory judgment concerning the ability to transfer and assign certificates of need. The Circuit Court held that it had no jurisdiction to rule upon the case. The Court of Civil appeals held that the court lacked jurisdiction on the grounds that the declaratory judgment had not been presented to administrative agency. Affirmed.

Nursing Home of Dothan Inc. v. Alabama State Health Planning and Development Agency, 542 So.2d 935 (Ala. Civ. App. 1988).
Abstract: Nursing home appealed to Circuit Court for declaratory judgment concerning the ability to transfer and assign certificates of need. The Circuit Court held that it had no jurisdiction to rule upon the case. The Court of Civil appeals held that the court lacked jurisdiction on the grounds that the declaratory judgment had not been presented to administrative agency. Affirmed.

Ex parte State Health Planning and Development Agency, 500 So.2d 1149 (Ala. Civ. App. 1986).
Abstract: The State Health Planning and Development Agency filed a writ of mandamus to move appeal of certificate of need proceedings to anther venue. The Court of Civil Appeals held that because the defendant filed its appeal in Jefferson County, the Jefferson County court did not abuse its discretion by denying the Agency's transfer appeal. Petition denied.

Regional Dialysis of Anniston v. Northeast Alabama Kidney Clinic Inc., 480 So.2d 1226 (Ala. Civ. App. 1985).
Abstract: A competitor appeals theAgency's decision to rehear an application for certificate of need. The Circuit Court found in favor of the competitor. The Agency appealed, and the Court of Civil appeals held that: (1) the Agency did not follow its adoptive procedures, and (2) lacking written presentation of evidence the Agency did not have grounds to reopen the case. Affirmed.

State Health Planning and Resource Development Administration Rivendell of Alabama, 469 So. 2d 613 (Ala. Civ. App. 1985).
Abstract: Denied applicant appealed to the Circuit Court after the State Health Planning and Resource Development Administration denied its application. The Circuit Court found in favor of the applicant. Upon appeal, the Court of Civil Appeals held that: (1) the Administration's ruling was not arbitrary or capricious, but (2) the evidence was meager and generalized. Reversed and remanded.

Humana Medical Corporation v. State Health Planning and Development Agency, 460 So.2d 1295 (Ala. Civ. App. 1984).
Abstract: Hospital appealed to the Circuit Court, Madison County after State Health Planning and Development Agency denied its application for certificate of need. The Circuit Court affirmed the ruling. Upon appeal, the Court of Civil Appeals held that: (1) the Agency's ruling was not arbitrary and capricious, (2) due process was not violated by the denial of CON, and (3) equal protection rights were not violated in an effort to determine if hospital had met statutory requirements. Affirmed.

State Health Planning and Development Agency v. Baptist Medical Center, 446 So.2d 619 (Ala. Civ. App. 1983).
Abstract: Six hospitals appealed to the Circuit Court, Montgomery County after the State Health Planning and Development Agency denied their certificates of need. The Agency then filed: (1) a petition to interplead all applicants, (2) enjoin pending appeals, and (3) consolidate all appeals into one court. Agency was granted permission to enjoin one action, but was denied right to interplead. Two hospitals moved to dismiss. Upon appeal, the Court of Civil Appeals granted writ of mandamus to consolidate all appeals to Circuit Court of

Montgomery County. Upon rehearing, Court held that consolidated appeal should continue to the Circuit Court. Motion to dismiss denied; writ of mandamus conditionally granted; application for rehearing denied.

Ex parte State Health Planning and Development Agency, 443 So.2d 1239 (Ala. Civ. App. 1983).
Abstract: Agency petitioned for writ of mandamus, prohibition and any other appropriate writ to the Court of Civil Appeals after a competitor filed an appeal when the Agency granted a certificate of need to another medical center. The Court held that: (1) the competitor lacked standing to appeal, and (2) proper jurisdiction for the competitors appeal is either the principle place of business of medical center or official residence of the Agency and its officials. Writs granted.

ALASKA

Supreme Court of Alaska

Sisters of Providence v. Department of Health and Social Services, 648 P.2d 970 (Alaska 1982).
Abstract: Hospital appealed the court's granting of summary judgment for the applicant in the Alaska Department of Health and Social Service's determination that the construction of the applicant's hospital had been "substantially implemented." The Supreme Court held that: (1) hospital possessed standing and was eligible for judicial review, (2) failing to adopt procedural regulations did not render the Department's decision invalid, (3) determining substantial implementation criteria was not invalid, and (4) public interest exception governing the awarding of attorney fees did not encompass the action. Affirmed in part, reversed in part, and remanded.

South Central Health Planning and Development v. Commissioner of Department of Administration, 628 P.2d 551 (Alaska 1981).
Abstract: Plaintiff appealed the court's denial of preliminary injunction and complaint against the construction of a skilled nursing addition to a home. The Supreme Court held that: (1) plaintiff had standing, (2) skilled nursing addition was a "health care facility" and therefore subject to certificate of need (CON) review, and (3) bill of sale indicating project cost was less than $25,000,000 did not deter requirement of CON review. Reversed and remanded.

ARIZONA

Arizona Court of Appeals

Kord's Ambulance Service v. Tucson, 757 P.2d 115 (Ariz. Ct. App. 1988).
Abstract: Ambulance service appealed the court's dismissal of its action against the city for allegedly operating unlicensed ambulance services. The Court of Appeals held that: (1) it was within the Department's discretion to file a cease and desist order, and therefore mandamus could not be filed, and (2) a 25% decrease in ambulance service calls was insufficient to evidence city's illegal operation of ambulance services. Affirmed.

Emergency Medical Transportation v. Tempe, 756 P.2d 929 (Ariz. Ct. App. 1988).
Abstract: Unsuccessful bidder for ambulance transportation service appealed the court's denial of its petition for special action relief. Upon accepting jurisdiction, the Court of Appeals denied relief and faced appeal. The Court of Appeals held that: (1) by entering into agreement, the city did not participate in unconstitutional

regulation of ambulance services, (2) it was within the Department's jurisdiction and regulatory authority to approve agreement; and (3) denial of attorney's fees was valid. Affirmed.

G.M. Ambulance & Medical Supply Company v. Canyon State Ambulance, 739 P.2d 203 (Ariz. Ct. App. 1987).
Abstract: Plaintiff appealed the court's ruling for a competing ambulance company that enjoined it from operating within competitor's territory. The Court of Appeals held that reliance on the State Health Department letter freed the plaintiff from liability for interference with contract. Affirmed.

ARKANSAS

Supreme Court of Arkansas

Arkansas Health Services Agency v. Desiderata, Inc., 958 S.W.2d 7 (Ark. 1998).
Abstract: An applicant filed to build a new 70-bed nursing home and was denied by both the Agency and the Health Services Commissions. Upon appeal, the trial court ruled in favor of the applicant. The Agency appealed, and the Supreme Court held that: (1) the Agency's rulings were based on substantial evidence, (2) the rulings were not arbitrary and capricious, and (3) the Equal Protection Clause was not violated. Reversed and remanded.

Arkansas Department of Human Services v. Hillsboro Manor Nursing Home Inc., 803 S.W.2d 891 (Ark. 1991).
Abstract: Nursing home appealed to the Circuit Court, Union County after the Department of Human Services refused to issue a license for more beds. The Department appealed after the Court ruled in favor of the nursing home. The Supreme Court held that: (1) DHS's decision was not made in an arbitrary and capricious manner, (2) nursing home did not need certificate of need to gain license, (3) license application process was still necessary despite the fact that there was no need for a certificate, and (4) licensure regulations applied to already licensed facilities. Reversed and remanded.

Scott v. Consolidated Health Management Inc., 764 S.W.2d 434 (Ark. 1989).
Abstract: Nursing home went to the Circuit Court, Pulaski County seeking writ of mandamus after the Health Planning and Development Agency to review its application to expand its facilities. The Agency appealed to the Supreme Court after writ was issued. The Supreme Court held that the nursing home was entitled to a review of its application. Affirmed.

Arkansas Health Planning and Development Agency v. Hot Spring County Memorial Hospital, 723 S.W.2d 363 (Ark. 1987).
Abstract: Hospital appealed to the Circuit Court after it was denied a certificate of need by the Arkansas Health Planning and Development Agency. The Circuit Court reversed the Agency's decision, and the Agency appealed. The Supreme Court held that the Agency's decision was not arbitrary and capricious, and was supported by substantial evidence. Reversed.

Sparks Regional Medical Center v. Arkansas Department of Human Services, 719 S.W.2d 434 (Ark. 1986).
Abstract: Competitor appealed and lost in the Circuit Court after the Department of Human Services granted a hospital's application to build a three-room outpatient surgery center. Upon appeal, the Supreme Court held that certain "shelled-in" outpatient operating rooms did not need to be counted when deciding whether to grant the certificate of need. Affirmed.

Boone County v. Apex of Arkansas Inc., 702 S.W.2d 795 (Ark. 1986).
Abstract: Nursing homes went to the Circuit Court seeking writ of mandamus after the Health Planning and Development Agency to act on its decision to grant certificates of need. The Agency appealed to the Supreme Court after writ was issued. The Supreme Court held that administrative review was in process and therefore writ should not be issued until procedure was completed. Reversed and remanded.

Governor v. Rehab Hospital Services Corporation, 688 S.W.2d 272 (Ark. 1985).
Abstract: Chancery Court issued an injunction against hospital because hospital had failed to request a review concerning a certificate of need in a timely manner. The Supreme Court held that the agency was not in error for allowing mail delivery time to be factored in addition to the 30-day limit stated in agency rules. Reversed.

Rehab Hospital Services Corporation v. Delta-Hills Health Systems Agency Inc., 687 S.W.2d 840 (Ark. 1985).
Abstract: Regional Health planning agency filed a motion for reconsideration, and a competitor appealed to the Circuit Court, Jackson County sought a declaratory judgment to void the motion. The competitor appealed after judgment was denied. The Supreme Court held that: (1) competitor did not follow through correct channel of appeals, (2) regional health planning agency was subject and violated Freedom of Information act by filing for rehearing, and (3) the agency's violation did not warrant a voiding of its motion. Affirmed.

Statewide Health Coordinating Council v. General Hospitals of Humana Inc., 660 S.W.2d 906 (Ark. 1983).
Abstract: Protestors appealed to the Circuit Court after a certificate of need was granted to build a 150-bed community hospital. The Circuit Court affirmed the Agency's decision, and the case was appealed. The Supreme Court held that the ruling did not comply with the State Health Plan's rules and since there were no exceptional conditions in the situation, deviation from the Plan could not be justified. Reversed.

CALIFORNIA

California Court of Appeal

San Bernardino Community Hospital v. Meeks, 187 Cal. App.3d 457 (Cal. Ct. App. 1986).
Abstract: Hospital builder and the California Office of Statewide Health Planning and Development moved for sanctions against the frivolousness of the appeal by hospital and expanding hospital challenging construction of hospital authorized by certificate of need. The Court of Appeal held that: (1) motions were timely because they need not be filed within the 15-day period for seeking rehearing and could be filed within the same period as motion for attorney fees or before issuance of remittitur, (2) Court of Appeal retains the power to award sanctions and discretionary costs prior to the issuance of remittitur, and (3) no conclusive evidence could establish that appeals taken by hospital and expanding hospital were solely for the purpose of delaying the construction of the new hospital. Denied.

Coastal Care Centers Inc. v. Meeks, 184 Cal. App.3d 85 (Cal. Ct. App. 1986).
Abstract: Coastal Care Centers, Inc. appealed decision to deny a preemptory writ of mandate that the California Office of Statewide Health Planning Development hold a hearing assessing the application for a certificate of need to construct a skilled nursing facility. The Court of Appeal held that: (1) competing provider did not have the authority to force the Office's compliance to federal regulations regarding the procedures for approving the establishment of new skilled nursing facilities, and (2) while the state health planning law does grant the right for "affected persons," in this case the competing facility, the right to request a public hearing prior to the granting of a certificate of need, the Office is not denied the discretion to refuse the request. Affirmed.

Placentia-Linda Community Hospital Inc. v. Zaretsky, 107 Cal. App.3d 850 (Cal. Ct. App. 1980).
Abstract: The hospital appeals the decision to deny the petition for the writ of mandate requiring California Director of Office of Statewide Health Planning and Development to grant a certificate of exemption to hospital from the requirement to attain a certificate of need to enable the relocation of beds from preexisting three-bed to two-bed rooms. The decision was pursuant to the first statute governing necessity for approval for remodeling or replacing existing licensed health facility. The Court of Appeal held that in construing the language of the first statute, which required approval of construction to build any new facility to replace any part of existing facility, to include "addition" or "expansion" was not inconsistent with purpose of Health Planning Act to stop or retard the cost of medical care in California to allow health care facilities to make relatively small capital expenditures. Reversed and remanded with directions.

Marin Hospital District v. Department of Health, 154 Cal. Rptr. 838 (Cal. Ct. App. 1979).
Abstract: California State Department of Health appealed a decision granting a peremptory writ ordering that the Department grant a certificate of exemption to the hospital district from the requirement to attain a certificate of need for the acquisition of a computerized tomographic full-body scanner. The Court of Appeal held that: (1) the Department's definition of the statutory term "financial obligation" was legally invalid and inconsistent than the statute by being more restrictive than the statute itself, (2) the statute granted exemption if hospital entered into contracts incurring a financial obligation prior to September 9, 1976, defined as the lesser of 10% of the project or $75,000, and where the project could not be terminated without significant economic loss, and (3) district lawyer's were not entitled to $1,500 in fees for their work on their case. Affirmed and modified.

Verdugo Hills Hospital Inc. v. Department of Health, 88 Cal. App.3d 957 (Cal. Ct. App. 1979).
Abstract: California State Department of Health and its director appealed the decision of the Court instructing that the Department grant a certificate of exemption to hospital from the requirement to attain a certificate of need for the lease-purchase of a computerized tomographic full-body scanner. The Court of Appeal held that: (1) the departmental regulation preventing the issuance of a certificate of exemption is legally invalid and, as a matter of law, the prevention of acquiring the scanner would cause the hospital to suffer "substantial economic loss," and (2) trial court did not err in awarding hospital attorney fees. Affirmed.

Los Alamitos General Hospital Inc. v. Lackner, 86 Cal. App.3d 417 (Cal. Ct. App. 1978).
Abstract: Post the denial of a "grandfather" exemption from California State Department of Health from approval of hospital expansion project, a petition for writ of administrative mandate filed by hospital instructing the Department grant certificate of exemption for new equipment and a full-body scanner was issued by the Court, and the Department appealed. The Court of Appeal held that: (1) the "substantial evidence test" was the appropriate standard of judicial review, and (2) evidence of the factual inclusion of specifically a full-body scanner in "project" seeking exemption could not be found, the gap between raw evidence and administrative decision was not bridged, and thus judicial review could not be performed. Reversed with directions.

Ross General Hospital Inc. v. Lackner, 83 Cal. App.3d 346 (Cal. Ct. App. 1978).
Abstract: California State Department of Health and its director appealed the decision of the Court instructing that the Department grant a certificate of exemption to hospital from the requirement to attain a certificate of need for the conversion of emergency room from "stand-by" to "basic" status. The Court of Appeal held that: (1) the departmental regulation preventing the issuance of a certificate of exemption was legally invalid, and (2) prior to September 9, 1976, hospital entered into binding contracts acquiring bulk material and property specifically necessary to pursue conversion project, thus under statutory "grandfather clause," commencement of project was exempt from obtaining certificate of need. Affirmed.

Bakersfield Community Hospital v. Department of Health, 77 Cal. App.3d 193 (Cal. Ct. App. 1977).

Abstract: California State Department of Health appealed the decision of the Court requiring that the Department determine the proposed relocation site of a hospital exempt from the requirement to attain a certificate of need for the relocation due to the fact that the relocation site was adjacent to existing facility. The Court of Appeal held that the proposed relocation was located three miles from existing hospital and therefore not "adjacent" therefrom. Reversed.

CONNECTICUT

Supreme Court of Connecticut

New England Rehabilitation Hospital Inc. v. Commission on Hospitals and Health Care, 627 A.2d 1257 (Conn. 1993).

Abstract: The Commission on Hospitals and Health Care denied the application for certificate of need to establish a rehabilitation facility. The applicants appealed to the Superior Court which held that: (1) although application was pending, the Commission could investigate need for rehabilitation facilities in the area, (2) additional opportunities for briefs and exceptions after changes in the Commission's opinion are not permitted, and (3) the Commission's decision was not arbitrary or unreasonable. Appeal is dismissed.

Commission on Hospitals and Health Care v. Stamford Hospital, 546 A.2d 257 (Conn. 1988).

Abstract: The Commission on Hospitals and Health Care called upon the Superior Court to stop a hospital from starting new programs relating to open heart surgery without a certificate of need. The Superior Court granted injunctive relief, and the hospital appealed to the Supreme Court. The Court held that: (1) the hospital did not err is using the deficiency letter procedure, (2) the ten-day limit for issuing deficiency letters will begin running from the date the hospital submits its full application, and (3) the Superior Court's rulings were not erroneous. Affirmed.

Hospital of St. Raphael v. Commission on Hospitals and Health Care, 438 A.2d 103 (Conn. 1980).

Abstract: The Superior Court reversed the Commission's ruling to deny a hospital a certificate of need for the purchase and operation of a computerized axial tomography scanner. The Commission appealed, and the Supreme Court held that: (1) the evidence substantiated the Commission's ruling, and (2) the Commission's ruling did not violate Equal Protection. Reversed and Remanded.

Connecticut Appellate Court

Park City Hospital v. Commission on Hospital and Health Care, 542 A.2d 326 (Conn. App. Ct. 1988).

Abstract: A competitor appealed the Commission's ruling to grant a certificate of need for an ambulatory surgical facility. The competitor first applied for stay pending decision of the appeal, and then withdrew its application. The Superior Court dismissed the case. The hospital appealed, the Appellate Court held that: (1) the lower court was correct in considering subject matter jurisdiction, (2) the hospital's withdrawal of application did not waive the court's right to investigate issues of aggrievement, or jurisdictional prerequisite, and (3) due process was not violated. No error.

Connecticut Superior Court

New England Rehabilitation Hospital Inc. v. Commission on Hospitals and Health Care, 622 A.2d 1067 (Conn. Super. Ct. 1992).

Abstract: Commission on Hospitals and Health Care filed and the Superior Court granted the motion to dismiss an appeal that had been filed by a consortium of health care providers that sought to review the Commission's decision to grant a certificate of need to build a rehabilitative hospital. The consortium appealed, and the Supreme Court ruled that: (1) the consortium lacked standing to challenge the ruling, and (2) the Commission's investigation was not proper and reasonable. Affirmed.

Mount Sinai Community Hospital Association v. Gorman, 1998 Conn. Super. LEXIS 601 (Conn. Super. Ct. 1998).
Abstract: The hospital sought an order of mandamus before the Superior Court in an effort to force the Commissioner of the Office of Health Care Access to hold a certificate of need hearing. The Court held that: (1) the hospital lacks standing to seek mandamus, and (2) there is no plain positive legal duty so mandamus cannot be ordered. Application is dismissed.

DELAWARE

Delaware Superior Court

Arbor Health Care Company v. Delaware Health Resources Board, 1997 Del. Super. LEXIS 232 (Del. Super. Ct. 1997).
Abstract: The Health Resources Board granted a certificate of need for a 140-bed nursing home. Competitor appealed to the Superior Court. The Court finds that the competitor has no standing to challenge ruling. Dismissed.

Sussex Medical Investors, L.P. v. Delaware Health Resources Board, 1997 Del. Super. LEXIS 334 (Del. Super. Ct. 1997).
Abstract: A hospital that was denied a certificate of need by the Health Resources Board appealed to the Superior Court. The Board filed a motion to dismiss. The Court granted the motion on the grounds that there is lack of evidence due to the failure for indispensable parties to join the suit. Motion to Dismiss granted.

Beebe Medical Center v. Certificate of Need Appeals Board, 1994 Del. Super. LEXIS 473, (Del. Super. Ct. 1994).
Abstract: The Bureau of Health, Planning and Resources Management denied certificates of need for two hospitals to establish catheterization services. The hospitals appealed to the Certificate of Appeals Board, and the Board approved one hospital, and denied another. The denied hospital appealed again to the Appeals Board, and the Board again affirmed the Bureau's findings. The denied hospital then appealed a third time to the Board. The Board then filed a motion to affirm before the Superior Court. The Court held that: (1) the appeal lacks merit due to insufficient evidence. Motion to Affirm is denied.

St. Francis Hospital v. Appeals Board of Department of Health and Social Services, 1993 Del. Super. LEXIS 230 (Del. Super. Ct. 1993).
Abstract: Competitor filed appeal against the Bureau of Health Planning and Resources Management that granted certificate of need to purchase radiation equipment to competition. The Superior Court held that the Bureau's ruling was supported by substantial evidence. Affirmed.

DISTRICT OF COLUMBIA

United States Court of Appeals for the District of Columbia

Bio-Medical Applications of the District of Columbia d/b/a/ *Fresenius Medical Care North America v. District of Columbia Board of Appeals and Review*, 829 A.3d 208 (D.C. 2003).

Abstract: Bio-Medical Applications of the District of Columbia appeals from a Board of Appeals decision to affirm a State Health Planning and Development Agency ("SHPDA") grant of a certificate of need to Capitol Dialysis to construct a kidney dialysis center. The Court of Appeals affirmed the decision as the SHPDA was not bound by a draft chapter for the Health Systems Plan, which did not project a need for kidney dialysis facilities, and therefore the Director of SHPDA did not act unreasonably in approving the certificate of need.. Affirmed.

Capitol Hill Hospital v. District of Columbia State Health Planning and Development Agency, 600 A.2d 793 (D.C. 1991).

Abstract: Citizens' group appealed to the Superior Court for equitable relief after the D.C. state health planning and development agency did not respond to its petition concerning alleged certificate of need violations by hospital's proposed closing of an acute inpatient services without certificate. The Superior Court issued a preliminary injunction that prohibited the hospital from closing the center without a certificate of need, the hospital appealed. The Court of Appeals held that: (1) administrative review and acquiescence is needed before an exception concerning certificate of need law made, (2) administrative review is needed regardless of whether capital expenditure would be involved, and (3) citizen's should have appealed to the Court of Appeals after the agency had failed to respond to the petition the first time. Ordered accordingly.

Speyer v. Barry, 588 A.2d 1147 (D.C. 1991).

Abstract: Residents went to the Superior Court when officials wanted to covert a home for the blind into a residential treatment center for emotionally disturbed children. Summary judgment was granted to the district on most claims, and residents appealed to the Court of Appeals. The Court held that: (1) in order to find out if manifest injustice occurred, it was necessary for the case to be remanded, and (2) residents had based on the Certificate of Need Act, and (3) the Mental Health Services Act did not supersede the Certificate of Need Act. Affirmed in part, reversed in part, vacated in part and remanded.

District of Columbia Hospital Association v. Barry, 586 A.2d 686 (D.C. 1991).

Abstract: The Superior Court heard a case brought by the District of Colombia Hospital Association which challenged the rules concerning certificate of need that were being promulgated by the State Health Planning and Development Agency. The Court found that the rules were valid and the Association appealed to the Court of Appeals. The Court held that the rules being promulgated did not exceed the authority that had been granted by the Certificate of Need Act. Affirmed.

George Washington University Medical Center v. District of Columbia Board of Appeals and Review, 530 A.2d 227 (D.C. 1987).

Abstract: Hospital appealed to the Court of Appeals when the Board of Appeals and Review had rejected its challenge to grant a certificate of need to competing hospital for a nuclear magnetic resonance scanner. The Court of Appeals held that the issue was not yet ripe because the hospital had not exhausted all administrative remedies and its own application for a certificate of need was still pending. Dismissed.

District of Columbia Hospital Association v. Barry, 498 A.2d 216 (D.C. 1985).

Abstract: The Superior Court determined that when the Health Planning and Development Agency failed to file a statement of basis and purposes for rules, they were violating rule-making provisions. The Court of Appeals held that they were not invalid because they were not supported by basis and purpose. Reversed in part and affirmed in part.

FLORIDA

Florida District Court of Appeal

Hospice of Palm Beach County, Inc. v. State of Florida, Agency for Health Care Administration, 2004 Fla. App. LEXIS 5652 (Fla. Dist. Ct. App. 2004).

Abstract: Appellant, Hospice of Palm Beach County, appeals an order of the appellee, Agency for Health Care Administration, that it lacks standing to initiate an administrative proceeding related to appellee's, Vitas Healthcare Corporation of Florida, purchase of a hospice. Appellant alleges that this purchase amounted to an illegal sale of a license and was an attempt to circumvent certificate of need laws regulating hospices. The Court of Appeals reversed the decision holding that standing was a question of law subject to de novo review, and appellant raised a factual question relating to the certificate of need issuance. Reversed and remanded.

Public Health Trust v. Agency for Health Care Administration, 751 So.2d 112 (Fla. Dist. Ct. App. 2000).

Abstract: Competitor appealed to the District Court of Appeal after the Agency for Health Care Administration dismissed its petition to appeal the awarding of a certificate of need. The Court held that because the competitor was in another district, it lacked standing to appeal. Affirmed.

Miami Jewish Home and Hospital for the Aged v. Agency for Health Care Administration, 710 So.2d 77 (Fla. Dist. Ct. App. 1998).

Abstract: Competitor appealed to the District Court of Appeal after the Agency for Health Care Administration approved a certificate of need for a home and hospital for the aged. The Court held that: (1) the administrative law judge did not abuse her power and properly used discretion to deny a motion to reopen hearing and to exclude irrelevant evidence, and (2) the Agency did not abuse discretion by denying competitors motion to remand cause to administrative judge in an effort to reopen the case. Affirmed.

South Miami Hospital, Inc. v. Agency For Health Care Administration and Variety Children's Hopital d/b/a Miami Children's Hospital, (Fla. Dist. Ct. App. 1998).

Abstract: Hospital was denied its application for certificate of need without section hearing by Department of Health and Rehabilitative Services. During appeal to the District Court of Appeals, hospital and Department of Health and Rehabilitative Services file joint motion for remand. The Court held that judicial economy is served by granting both parties petition. Reversed and remanded.

Bio-Medical Applications Inc. v. Office of Community Medical Facilities etc., 374 So.2d 88 (Fla. Dist. Ct. App. 1997).

Abstract: Health services provider appealed to the District Court of Appeal after the Department of Health and Rehabilitative Services denied its certificate of need application for ten-station chronic renal dialysis facility and a hearing for a teaching hospital. The Court held that the two applications were mutually exclusive and each had substantial interests that could be affected by the ruling of the other, and each was entitled to request hearing in proceedings of the other even if it was requested after a certificate of need had been granted. Reversed.

Page v. Capital Medical Center Inc., 371 So.2d 1087 (Fla. Dist. Ct. App. 1997).

Abstract: Applicant was denied certificate of need by the Bureau of Community Medical Facilities Planning and

State Hospital Advisory Council. The applicant appealed to the Circuit Court, which rendered declaratory judgment which ordered the Bureau to issue a certificate of need. On appeal, the District Court held that: (1) the Bureau's actions in this case were not ministerial, and (2) declaratory judgment by the trial judge cannot be sustained due to lack of substantial evidence indicating need for a hospital. Reversed.

Life Care Centers of America v. Health Care and Retirement Corporation of America, 692 So.2d 243 (Fla. Dist. Ct. App. 1997).

Abstract: Appeal to reverse the Agency for Health Care Administration's decision to approve a certificate of need for applicant A, and deny applicant B. The case was found in favor of the agency and applicant A. Applicant A then went to the District Court of Appeals in an effort to regain attorney fees. The Court ruled that applicant B's grounds for previous suit held no merit, and ruled in favor of Applicant A, awarding them attorney fees. Affirmed.

Life Care Centers of America, Inc. v. Health Care and Retirement Corporation of American and Agency for Health Care Administration, 692 So. 2d 243 (Fla. Dist. Ct. App. 1997).

Abstract: Competitor appeals to the District Court of Appeals after the Department of Health and Rehabilitative Services denied its application for certificate of need and approved another application. The Department files for attorney's fees on the grounds that the competitors claims are without merit. The Court holds that the competitor has no substantial evidence and its arguments are frivolous and meritless and grants the Department attorney fees. Remanded back to Department for determination of fees.

Agency for Health Care Administration v. Mount Sinai Medical Center, 690 So.2d 689 (Fla. Dist. Ct. App. 1997).

Abstract: Applicants denied a certificate of need for additional nursing home beds, in conjunction with the Agency for Health Care Administration filed for writ of mandamus for a comparative review of applications by an Administrative Law Judge. The District Court of Appeal held that: (1) the writ of mandamus would be considered an interlocutory relief pursuant, and (2) a formal required hearing would be required. Petition granted.

Agency for Health Care Administration v. Mount Sinai Medical Center of Greater Miami, 690 So.2d 689 (Fla. Dist. Ct. App. 1997).

Abstract: Applicants for nursing home and Agency for Health Care Administration petitioned for write of mandamus to the District Court of Appeals after Department of Health and Rehabilitative Services denied its application for certificate of need for nursing home beds. The Court held that: (1) decision by Department without administrative hearing is premature, (2) writ of mandamus is not adequate legal remedy, and (3) petition seeking relief is more appropriate. Petition for seeking relief is granted. Remanded with instructions.

Memorial Health System v. Halifax Hospice, 689 So.2d 373 (Fla. Dist. Ct. App. 1997).

Abstract: Hospice appealed to the Circuit Court against the Agency for Health Care Administration, arguing that an applicant must first obtain a certificate of need before it can be eligible for licensure. The Circuit Court issued a temporary injunction keeping the Administration from issuing a license. Applicant, who had not been named as party defendant, filed a motion to dissolve injunction. The Circuit Court struck down the motion and an appeal was filed with the District Court of Appeal. The Court held that the applicant had standing to issue the motion. Reversed and remanded with directions.

Bio-Medical Applications of Clearwater Inc. v. Department of Health a d Rehabilitative Services, 370 So.2d 19 (Fla. Dist. Ct. App. 1997).

Abstract: Applicant filed petition for review to the District Court of Appeals after the Department of Health and

Rehabilitative Services denied its application for a certificate of need and capital expenditure approval to install a kidney dialysis center. The Court ruled that the denial was a material error in procedure. Issuance of certificate of need set aside, matter remanded.

Naples Community Hospital, Inc. v. State of Florida, Agency for Health Care Administration, 687 So.2d 62 (Fla. Dist. Ct. App. 1997).
Abstract: Hospital filed petition to challenge intended denial of certificate of need by Department of Health and Rehabilitative Services. Competitor filed petition to intervene, and hospital filed requests for discovery. Competitor then filed for protective order but was denied by hearing officer. Intervener then appealed to the District Court of Appeals for review. Court held that requests for discovery were overbroad and much of the information requested was unnecessary. Order quashed. Remanded.

Vantage Healthcare Corporation, d/b/a *Beverly Manor Rehabilitation and Specialty Care Center at Manatee County v. Agency for Health Care Administration and Manatee Springs Nursing Center, Inc.*, 687 So.2d 306 (Fla. Dist. Ct. App. 1997).
Abstract: Competitor appealed to District Court of Appeal after the Department of Health and Rehabilitative Services denied its application for certificate of need and approved competitions certificate of need for community nursing home beds. The Court held that: (1) doctrine of equitable tolling did not hold, and (2) the Department could not violate own rule concerning filing applications in a timely manner. Reversed and remanded.

Tarpon Springs General Hospital v. Office of Community Medical Facilities, 366 So.2d 185 (Fla. Dist. Ct. App. 1997).
Abstract: Competitor appealed to the District Court of Appeals after the Department of Health and Rehabilitative Services denied its application for certificate of need to expand it facilities. The Court held that the Department's ruling was based on substantial evidence and was not arbitrary or capricious. Affirmed.

Life Care Centers of America v. Sawgrass Care Center, 683 So.2d 609 (Fla. Dist. Ct. App. 1996).
Abstract: Applicant appealed to the District Court of Appeal after the Agency for Health Care Administration denied their application for certificate of need. The Court held that based on mandate in the Administrative Procedure Act, the Agency was bound by statues to having rulings for each proposed finding of fact, hence the need for reversal and remand was obviated. Affirmed.

Cleveland Clinic Florida Hospital v. Agency for Health Care Administration, 679 So.2d 1237 (Fla. Dist. Ct. App. 1996).
Abstract: Before the Agency for Health Care Administration (ACHA) could rule on a hospitals application for a certificate of need to approve capital expenditures to relocate and rebuilt its hospital in the same health care service district but new location, competing hospitals filed with the Division of Administrative Hearings (DOAH) in order to alter the hearing to a comparative review. When the Agency agreed to this, the hospital filed a petition of review of the Division's decision and filed for a writ of mandate. The District Court of Appeal held that: the hospital was entitled to a non comparative review because relocation did not involve competition. DOAH's order quashed. AHCA's order reversed; remanded to DOAH.

Gulf Coast Health Care v. Agency for Health Care Administration, 679 So.2d 338 (Fla. Dist. Ct. App. 1996).
Abstract: Competitor petitioned for review of non-final orders to the District Court of Appeal after the Agency for Health Care Administration approved a an application for certificate of need to construct new replacement

facility on a different cite. The Court held that the competitors lacked standing to petition. Reversed and remanded.

Lawnwood Medical Center v. Agency for Health Care Administration, 678 So.2d 421 (Fla. Dist. Ct. App. 1996).
Abstract: A competitor appealed to the District Court of Appeal when the Agency for Health Care Administration approved for a certificate of need for the competition. The Court reversed the Agency's ruling, holding that after the hearing officer had made his decision, the Agency did not have power to consider new evidence or have additional findings. Reversed and remanded.

Agency for Health Care Administration v. University Hospital, 670 So.2d 1037 (Fla. Dist. Ct. App. 1996).
Abstract: The Agency for Health Care Administration appealed to the District Court of Appeal after the Division of Administrative Hearings invalidated rules concerning issuing hospital licenses. The Court held that the rules were permissible interpretations of statues. Reversed.

Health Care and Retirement Corporation of America v. Tarpon Springs Hospital Foundation, 671 So.2d 217 (Fla. Dist. Ct. App. 1996).
Abstract: Division of Administrative Hearings ruled that the rule concerning allowing certificate of need review of nursing home beds was invalid. Health care groups and hospitals appealed to the District Court of Appeal for review. The Court held the Division's ruling was based on substantial evidence. Affirmed.

South Broward Hospital District v. Agency for Health Care Administration, 661 So.2d 1279 (Fla. Dist. Ct. App. 1995).
Abstract: Hospital appealed to the District Court of Appeal after the Agency for Health Care Administration denied its request to modify its certificate of need by increasing the number of beds. The Court ruled in favor of the Agency holding that in order to add more beds, the hospital would need to undergo a certificate of need review. Affirmed.

Life Care Centers of America v. Agency for Health Care Administration, 656 So.2d 1329 (Fla. Dist. Ct. App. 1995).
Abstract: The Applicant appealed to the District Court of Appeal when the Agency for Health Care Administration denied its application for a certificate of need. The Court found in favor of the applicant, holding that: the applicant did not need to include total project costs as it was only possible to report 25% of total project costs. Reversed and remanded with instructions.

Arbor Health Care Company v. State, 654 So.2d 1020 (Fla. Dist. Ct. App. 1995).
Abstract: The District Court of Appeal set aside the Agency for Health Care Administration's decision to deny an applicant a certificate of need to build a nursing home. The Court held that what the Agency had defined as "capital projects" was not correctly defined. Therefore, the applicant's lack of disclosure concerning those projects should not be penalized. Order set aside; remanded.

Agency for Health Care Administration v. Orlando Regional Healthcare System Inc., 617 So.2d 385 (Fla. Dist. Ct. App. 1993).
Abstract: The Agency for Health Care Administration appealed to the District Court of Appeal when a non-final administrative order determined that in dealing with transferring certificate of needs, need criteria was inapplicable. The Court held that it was inapplicable because the Agency had reevaluated need criteria that had previously been established. Affirmed.

University Community Hospital v. Department of Health and Rehabilitative Services, 610 So.2d 1342 (Fla. Dist. Ct. App. 1992).

Abstract: Hospital appealed to the District Court of Appeal for review after the Agency for Health Care Administration directed that inventory of neonatal intensive care until included certain hospital beds. The Court held that a ruling based on estoppel could not be made until opposing hospitals were given for evidentiary hearing before the hearing examiner. Reversed and remanded.

Hospital Corporation of America v. Associates in Adolescent Psychiatry S.C., 605 So.2d 556 ((Fla. Dist. Ct. App. 1992).

Abstract: A hospital appealed to the District Court of Appeal when the Circuit Court ruled against them, because they had violated a 15- year oral agreement to operate a psychiatric care facility. The District Court held that the statute of frauds bars the enforcement of the oral agreement. Reversed.

Maple Leaf of Lee County Health Care v. Department of Health and Rehabilitative Services, 601 So. 2d 1238 (Fla. Dist. Ct. App. 1992).

Abstract: Applicant appealed to the District Court of Appeal after the Agency for Health Care Administration denied its certificate of need request for nursing home beds. The Court held that bed need is determined based on evidence given time of the trial. Affirmed in part and reversed in part and remanded.

Suburban Medical Hospital Inc. v. Department of Health and Rehabilitative Services, 600 So.2d 1195 (Fla. Dist. Ct. App. 1992).

Abstract: The applicant appealed to the District Court of Appeal when the Department of Health and Rehabilitative Services denied their application to convert a outpatient and ambulatory surgical center. The Court affirmed the decision, holding that the applicant did not demonstrate long-term or short-term financial viability. Affirmed

HCA Health Services Inc. v. Department of Health and Rehabilitative Services, 599 So.2d 211 (Fla. Dist. Ct. App. 1992).

Abstract: Competitors appealed to the District Court of Appeals to overturn the Department of Health and Rehabilitative Services decision to deny their petition. The Court held that based on governing statue, the competitors did not have standing to intervene in the administrative hearing and therefore the Department was correct in denying their petition to intervene. Affirmed.

University Psychiatric Center Inc. v. Department of Health and Rehabilitative Services, 597 So.2d 400 (Fla. Dist. Ct. App. 1992).

Abstract: The psychiatric center appealed to the District Court of Appeal when the Department of Health and Rehabilitation ruled that it lacked standing to revoke a hospital's license. The Court held that the case should be based on only facts from the petition, and not from matters outside of it. Reversed and remanded.

Health Quest Corporation IV v. Department of Health and Rehabilitative Services, 593 So.2d 533 (Fla. Dist. Ct. App. 1992).

Abstract: The applicant appealed to the District Court of Appeal when the Department of Health and Rehabilitative Services declared a certificate of need void because it had expired. The District Court held that: (1) due to governmental inaction, the holder of the certificate should have been granted an extension for the period of the project, and (2) by operation of law, any certificate that expires on Sunday should be extended to Monday. Reversed and remanded.

Brookwood-Jackson County Convalescent Center v. Department of Health and Rehabilitative Services, 591 So.2d 1085 (Fla. Dist. Ct. App. 1992).

Abstract: The applicant appealed to the District Court of Appeal when the Department of Health and Rehabilitative Services denied its request for a certificate of need to add additional bed. The Court held that the applicant was not the licensee and operator of the facility and therefore did not satisfy the statutory requirements. Affirmed.

McCoy Florida SNF Trust v. State Department of Health and Rehabilitative Services, 589 So.2d 351 (Fla. Dist. Ct. App. 1991).

Abstract: Applicant for a certificate of need withdrew their petition from the Department of Health and Rehabilitative Services. After its withdrawal, the Department still ruled upon the petition. The District Court of Appeals held that based on statues imposing time standard, the Department did not have jurisdiction to rule upon the decision after applicant had withdrawn its petition. Reversed and remanded.

First Hospital Corporation v. Department of Health and Rehabilitative Services, 589 So.2d 310 (Fla. Dist. Ct. App. 1991).

Abstract: After a hospital was denied its application for certificate of need, it appealed. A cross appeal was then filed by the competitor. The hearing officer then determined that the hospital that had been denied its certificate lacked standing to file to appeal. The Court ruled that the hearing officer's decision was harmless error on the grounds that the hospital was still able to participate in the hearings. Affirmed.

Martin Memorial Hospital Association v. Department of Health and Rehabilitative Services, 584 So.2d 39 (Fla. Dist. Ct. App. 1991).

Abstract: The hospital filed for review of non-final action to the District Court of Appeal after the Department of Health and Rehabilitative Services had rejected their preliminary letter to file for certificate of need. The Court held that the letter satisfied the statue that required programs to operate within certain cost guidelines. Reversed and remanded.

Amisub v. Department of Health and Rehabilitative Services, 577 So.2d 648 (Fla. Dist. Ct. App. 1991).

Abstract: Medical Center appealed to the District Court of Appeals when the Department of Health and Rehabilitative Services denied their petition to challenge an issuing of a certificate of need for a program in an adjoining district. The Court held that the Medical Center lack standing because it was not in the same district. Affirmed.

Department of Health and Rehabilitative Services v. Florida Medical Center, 578 So.2d 351 (Fla. Dist. Ct. App. 1991).

Abstract: Adult cardiac catheterization service providers challenged rule changed implemented by the Department of Health and Rehabilitative Services. Department of Administration, Division of Administrative Hearings found that the changes in rules were invalid. The Department challenged the ruling, and the District Court of appeal held that: (1) petition to review validity of rules was presented in a timely manner, (2) prior to adoption of rules public hearing is necessary, and (3) changes in the rules were material and excess of delegated legislative authority. Affirmed.

Central Florida Regional Hospital Inc. v. Department of Health and Rehabilitative Services, 582 So.2d 1193 (Fla. Dist. Ct. App. 1991).

Abstract: Hospital appealed to the District Court of Appeal when the Department of Health and Rehabilitative

Services denied its application for certificate of need (CON). The Court held that the Department had applied disparate standards to CON applicants who had challenged and those that had not been challenged. Reversed.

First Hospital Corporation v. Department of Health and Rehabilitative Services, 566 So.2d 917 (Fla. Dist. Ct. App. 1990).
Abstract: Department of Health and Rehabilitative Services dismissed petition to challenge approval of certificate of need. Competitor then sought review of order. The District Court held that it lacked standing because it was not in the same batching cycle as approved applicant. Affirmed.

Charter Hospital of Pasco County v. Department of Health and Rehabilitative Services, 563 So.2d 181 (Fla. Dist. Ct. App. 1990).
Abstract: Competitor appealed to the District Court of Appeal after the Department of Health and Rehabilitative Services had dismissed their petition to challenge the issuance of certificates of need. The District Court held that the competitor lacked standing. Affirmed.

Lee Memorial Hospital v. Department of Health and Rehabilitative Services, 560 So.2d 1367 (Fla. Dist. Ct. App. 1990).
Abstract: Hospital appealed to the District Court of Appeals after the Department of Health and Rehabilitative Services denied their petition for administrative hearing concerning the approval of certificate of need for a medical center to construct clinical and ancillary services building. The Court ruled that the hospital lacked standing on the grounds that they did not petition before the date that was specified on savings clause. Affirmed.

Humhosco Inc. v. Department of Health and Rehabilitative Services, 561 So.2d 388 (Fla. Dist. Ct. App. 1990).
Abstract: Applicant applied to the District Court of Appeal after the Department of Health and Rehabilitative Services denied its application for certificate of need. The Court held that the applicant did not comply with statutory laws: (1) the applicant lacked a letter of intent, and (2) the applicant lacked two years worth of audited financial statements for two years. Affirmed.

St. Joseph Hospital, Inc. v. Department of Health and Rehabilitative Services Case, 559 So.2d 595 (Fla. Dist. Ct. App. 1990).
Abstract: Competitor sought review from District Court of Appeal after the Department of Health and Rehabilitative Services had denied its application for certificate of need and had approved a competing applicant. The Court held that: (1) the competitor lacked standing because it did not apply for certificate of need in a timely manner, and (2) by failing to challenge the decision in a timely manner; the competitor forfeited its clear point of entry. Affirmed.

Health Care and Retirement Corporation v. Department of Health and Rehabilitative Services, 559 So.2d 665 (Fla. Dist. Ct. App. 1990).
Abstract: The applicant sough judicial review from the District Court of Appeals after the Department of Health and Rehabilitative Services had denied its certificate need for 20 additional beds. The Court held that the Department lacked substantial evidence to support its ruling. Reversed and remanded.

Beverly Enterprises-Florida, Inc. v. Department of Health and Rehabilitative Services, 573 So.2d 19 (Fla. Dist. Ct. App. 1990).
Abstract: Nursing home owner appealed to the District Court of Appeal after the Department of Health and Rehabilitative Services had denied their request for an expedited review after another nursing home had been

granted a similar request. The Court held that: (1) the owner legally was entitled to an expedited review, and (2) the Department was required to evaluate the merits of application. Reversed and remanded.

Health Quest Corporation v. Department of Health and Rehabilitative Services, 556 So.2d 456 (Fla. Dist. Ct. App. 1990).

Abstract: Health Quest appealed to the District Court of Appeals. The Court affirmed the decision of the Department of Health and Rehabilitative Services.

University Community Hospital v. Department of Health and Rehabilitative Services, 555 So.2d 922 (Fla. Dist. Ct. App. 1990).

Abstract: Hospital appealed to the District Court of Appeal after the Department of Health and Rehabilitative Services had denied its application for certificate of need. The Court held that the hearing officer was within law by operating discretion and determining that a second hearing was not necessary to decide upon hospital's application. Affirmed.

National Healthcorp L.P. v. Department of Health and Rehabilitative Services, 560 So.2d 1184 (Fla. Dist. Ct. App. 1989).

Abstract: Applicant appealed to the District Court of Appeal after the Department of Health and Rehabilitative Services had denied certificate of need without review of application. The Department argued that the applicant violated the non-rule policy stating that project costs could not exceed estimate project costs that were stated in letter of intent. The Court held that the non rule policy was invalid and could not be applied in this case because the applicants were the developer and operator. Reversed and remanded.

St. Francis Hospital Inc. v. Department of Health and Rehabilitative Services, 553 So.2d 1351 (Fla. Dist. Ct. App. 1989).

Abstract: Hospital appealed to the District Court of Appeal after the Department of Health and Rehabilitative Services had denied its application for certificate of need to convert beds. The Department argued that the applicant violated the non rule policy stating that project costs could not exceed estimate project costs that were stated in letter of intent. The Court held that the no rule policy was invalid. Reversed and remanded.

Florida Residential Treatment Centers Inc. v. Department of Health and Rehabilitative Services, 553 So.2d 229 (Fla. Dist. Ct. App. 1989).

Abstract: Hospital appealed to the District Court of appeals after the Department of Health and Rehabilitative Services denied its motion to intervene in an administrative hearing. The Court held that the hospital had standing due its preliminary approved certificate of need. Reversed and remanded.

Federal Property Management Corporation v. Richmond Healthcare Inc., 541 So.2d 757 (Fla. Dist. Ct. App. 1989).

Abstract: It was reasonable for appellant's agent to believe that the contract entered into between appellant and appellee to sell a certificate to the other party had been modified and therefore the deadline had been abandoned.

Sarasota County Public Hospital Board v. Department of Health and Rehabilitative Services, 553 So.2d 189 (Fla. Dist. Ct. App. 1989).

Abstract: Hospital appealed to the District Court of Appeals after the Department of Health and Rehabilitative Services dismissed its petition for comparative reviews of applications for certificate of need. The Court held that because the hospitals' applications were mutually exclusive it was necessary to have a comparative review. Reversed and remanded with instructions.

Manor Care Inc. v. Department of Health & Rehabilitative Services, 558 So.2d 26 (Fla. Dist. Ct. App. 1989).
Abstract: Health care providers appealed to the District Court of Appeals after the Department of Health and Rehabilitative Services denied their application for certificate of need to build a community nursing home. The Court held that the Department was correct in: (1) rejecting one provider's revisions as impermissible amendments, and (2) hearing officer correctly rejected another application as incomplete. Affirmed.

Meridian Inc. v. Department of Health and Rehabilitative Services, 548 So.2d 1169 (Fla. Dist. Ct. App. 1989).
Abstract: Applicants appealed to the District Court of Appeals after the Department of Health and Rehabilitative Services denied their certificate of need to construct additional nursing home beds. The Court held that when determining number of beds in the planning horizon fixed pool, it is incorrect to use the most recent estimates at the time of the hearing. Rather, the population estimates that are adopted by the Governor's office at the time of filing the application are appropriate. Affirmed.

Health Quest Corporation v. Department of Health and Rehabilitative Services, 548 So.2d 719 (Fla. Dist. Ct. App. 1989).
Abstract: The Department of Health and Rehabilitative Services properly denied corporation's request for a certificate of need because corporation failed to meet the conditions for the application of the controlling statute.

Inverness Convalescent Center v. Department of Health and Rehabilitative Services, 541 So.2d 677 (Fla. Dist. Ct. App. 1989).
Abstract: Nursing home appealed to the District Court of Appeals after the Department of Health and Rehabilitative Services denied its petition for formal administrative hearing. The Court held that: (1) the nursing home did not exercise its rights in a timely fashion after it had been denied its certificate of need, and (2) its untimely exercise of rights is inexcusable. Affirmed.

St. Joseph's Hospital v. Department of Health and Rehabilitative Services, 536 So.2d 346 (Fla. Dist. Ct. App. 1988).
Abstract: Hospital appealed to the District Court of Appeals after the Department of Health and Rehabilitative Services denied its application for certificate of need for transfer of 100 acute care beds. The Court held that the Department's decision was based on substantial evidence and was consistent with pertinent laws and rules.

Gulf Coast Home Health Services Inc. v. Department of Health & Rehabilitative Services, 527 So.2d 262 (Fla. Dist. Ct. App. 1988).
Abstract: Home health service agency appealed to the District Court of Appeals after the Department of Health and Rehabilitative Services denied its request for a certificate of need to operate additional health care subunits. The Court held that the subunits qualified as the equivalent of home health agencies and therefore the agency could not open subunits without a certificate of need review. Affirmed.

Manasota Osteopathic General Hospital v. State Department of Health and Rehabilitative Services, 523 So.2d 710 (Fla. Dist. Ct. App. 1988).
Abstract: Hospital appealed to the District Court of Appeals for judicial review after the Department of Health and Rehabilitative Services denied its application for certificate of need to build an osteopathic teaching hospital. The Court held that standing was only granted to osteopathic hospitals that had a minimal level of profitability. Affirmed.

Beverly Enterprises-Florida, Inc. v. Department of Health & Rehabilitative Services, 527 So.2d 218 (Fla. Dist. Ct. App. 1988).

Abstract: Nursing Home facilities appealed to the District Court of Appeals after the Department of Health and Rehabilitative Services denied their applications for certificates of need. The Court held that the facilities should have challenged the Department directly in their proceedings, and raised possible violations up during the trial, rather than in the appeal. Affirmed.

Professional Nurse Inc. v. State Department of Health and Rehabilitative Services, 519 So.2d 1061 (Fla. Dist. Ct. App. 1988).

Abstract: Applicant appealed to the District Court of Appeals after the Department of Health and Rehabilitative Services had denied its application The Court held that: (1) prohibition of introducing evidence was overly severe, and (2) applicant received hearing based on methodology formulated by hearing officer and should have received hearing based on valid methodology. Reversed and remanded.

Health Care and Retirement Corporation v. Department of Health and Rehabilitative Services, 516 So.2d 292 (Fla. Dist. Ct. App. 1987).

Abstract: Applicant appealed to the District Court of Appeals after the Department of Health and Rehabilitative Services denied application for a certificate of need to build a nursing home. The Court held that the Department's decision was arbitrary and capricious. Reversed and remanded.

Bayonet Point Regional Medical Center v. Department of Health and Rehabilitative Services, 516 So.2d 995 (Fla. Dist. Ct. App. 1987).

Abstract: Applicant appealed to the District Court of Appeals after the Department of Health and Rehabilitative Services denied its application for a certificate of need for a cardiac catheterization laboratory and an open-heart surgery service. The Court held that the Department's decision was arbitrary and capricious. Reversed and remanded.

Boca Raton Artificial Kidney Center v. Department of Health and Rehabilitative Services, 514 So.2d 1114 (Fla. Dist. Ct. App. 1987).

Abstract: Competitor appealed to the District Court of Appeals for court fees after the Department of Health and Rehabilitative Services granted a certificate of need for the operation of a free-standing hemodialysis facility. The Court held that (1) the challenge was moot by statute, and (2) that the awarding of a certificate of need to another party was not a gross enough abuse to warrant award of attorney's fees. Appeal dismissed.

Community Hospital of New Port Richey/University Psychiatric Center Inc. v. Department of Health and Rehabilitative Services, 520 So.2d 604 (Fla. Dist. Ct. App. 1987).

Abstract: Competitors appealed to the District Court of Appeals after the Department of Health and Rehabilitative Services granted certificate of need to a psychiatric center to build a freestanding psychiatric/ substance abuse hospital. The Court found the Department's decision was based on substantial evidence and was consistent with pertinent laws and rules.

Gulf Coast Home Health Services Inc. v. Department of Health and Rehabilitative Services, 515 So.2d 1009 (Fla. Dist. Ct. App. 1987).

Abstract: Applicant appealed for petition to intervene to the District Court of Appeals after the Department of Health and Rehabilitative Services had denied the petition. The Court held that the applicant was given a clear point of entry, however failed to take action within the 20 day prescribed period, which constituted a waiver or rights to administrative review. Affirmed.

Gulf Coast Home Health Services Inc. v. State Department of Health and Rehabilitative Services, 513 So.2d 704 (Fla. Dist. Ct. App. 1987).
Abstract: A home health service did not exhaust administrative remedies where it failed to await the agency's determination of its intervention actions regarding agency policy before seeking enforcement and injunctive relief from the circuit court.

Inverness Convalescent Center v. Department of Health and Rehabilitative Services, 512 So.2d 1011 (Fla. Dist. Ct. App. 1987).
Abstract: Applicants appealed to the District Court of Appeals after the Department of Health and Rehabilitative Services overturned the decision of the hearing officer who had granted a certificate of need to one applicant and denied the other. The Court ruled that the Department's decision to deny both applicants was wrong holding that: (1) proper remedy was to appeal grant of certificates of need prior to applicants, (2) the Department had not authority to go against the hearing officer's findings, and (3) the application that had been denied by the hearing officer was correctly denied by the Department. Affirmed in part, reversed in part, and remanded for further proceedings.

RHPC Inc. v. Department of Health and Rehabilitative Services, 509 So.2d 1267 (Fla. Dist. Ct. App. 1987).
Abstract: Applicant appealed to the District Court of Appeals after the Department of Health and Rehabilitative Services denied its application to reinstate its certificate of need application. The Court held that because the hospital had originally filed a dismissal, the Department did not have jurisdiction to reinstate the case.

St. John's Home Health Agency v. Department of Health and Rehabilitative Services, 509 So.2d 367 (Fla. Dist. Ct. App. 1987).
Abstract: Competitor appealed to the District Court of Appeals after the Department of Health and Rehabilitative Services approved certificates of need for two new competing Medicare certified home health care agencies. The Court held that it was correct for Medicaid and indigent patient need to be considered when applications were reviewed. Affirmed.

Florida Hospital v. Department of Health and Rehabilitative Services, 507 So.2d 696 (Fla. Dist. Ct. App. 1987).
Abstract: Competitor intervened concerning application for certificate of need to build ambulatory surgery center. Applicant voluntarily withdrew its application. Hearing officer denied motion to tax costs that competitor subsequently filed. The competitor appealed to the District Court of appeal for judicial review. The Court held that the hospital was not entitled to have costs taxed on the ground that all of the hearings were held in an administrative setting.

Gulf Coast Home Health Services Inc. v. Department of Health and Rehabilitative Services, 503 So.2d 415 (Fla. Dist. Ct. App. 1987).
Abstract: Home health care agency filed petition to enforce agency action and complaint for declaratory and injunctive relief to the Circuit Court after the Department of Health and Rehabilitative Services failed to take action regarding their petitions to intervene regarding a competitors' applications for certificates of need. The Circuit Court dismissed, and the agency appealed to the District Court of Appeal. The Court held that the untimely petitions made by the agency would not be granted judicial notice. Motion denied.

University Medical Park Ltd. v. Department of Health and Rehabilitative Services, 501 So.2d 692 (Fla. Dist. Ct. App. 1987).
Abstract: Applicant appealed to the District Court of Appeals after the Department of Health and Rehabilitative Services had denied an application for certificate of need to construct 130-bed acute care hospital. The Court

ruled that the Department had correctly weighed substantial evidence concerning competitive effect of proposed hospital. Affirmed.

Baptist Hospital Inc. v. State Department of Health and Rehabilitative Services, 500 So.2d 620 (Fla. Dist. Ct. App. 1986).

Abstract: Applicant appealed to the District Court of Appeals after the Department of Health and Rehabilitative Services ruled that it was not exempt from certificate of need review. The Court ruled that: (1) there was substantial change in services therefore a certificate of need review was necessary, and (2) a hospital in the same service area had standing to intervene. Affirmed.

Psychiatric Hospitals of Florida Inc. v. State Department of Health and Rehabilitative Services, 500 So.2d 190 (Fla. Dist. Ct. App. 1986).

Abstract: Applicant appealed to the District Court of Appeals after the Department of Health and Rehabilitative Services denied its right to have a certain number of beds in inventory. The Court held that: (1) existing licenses must conform to statue relating to specialty beds (2) applying specialty rules to current licenses is not retroactive, and (3) method of inventory by the Department was not arbitrary or capricious. Affirmed.

Doctors' Osteopathic Medical Center Inc. v. Department of Health and Rehabilitative Services, 498 So.2d 478 (Fla. Dist. Ct. App. 1986).

Abstract: Applicant appealed to the District Court of Appeals after the Department of Health and Rehabilitative Services disregarded the hearing officers finding that a 120- bed osteopathic facility was needed. The Court ruled that the Department ruling that there was only need for a 60 beds constituted gross abuse of power and its ruling was unsubstantiated by evidence. Reversed and remanded.

NME Hospitals Inc. v. Department of Health and Rehabilitative Services, 494 So.2d 256 (Fla. Dist. Ct. App. 1986).

Abstract: Applicant appealed to the District Court of Appeals for review after the Department of Health and Rehabilitative Services denied their application for certificate of need for cardiac catheterization laboratory. The Court held that: (1) the applicant was provided equal protection, and (2) the Department had acted properly in precluding applicant from demonstrating need outside of the proper methodology. Affirmed.

Health Care Medical Facility XXVI Partnership v. State Department of Health and Rehabilitative Services, 495 So.2d 803 (Fla. Dist. Ct. App. 1986).

Abstract: Applicant appealed to the District Court of Appeals after the Department of Health and Rehabilitative Services denied its application for certificate of need to construct nursing home. The Court ruled that: (1) the Department's ruling was made with substantial evidence, and (2) the ruling did not improperly depend on a competitor's application. Affirmed.

Humana of Florida Inc. v. Department of Health and Rehabilitative Services, 500 So.2d 186 (Fla. Dist. Ct. App. 1986).

Abstract: When the Department of Health and Rehabilitation preliminarily approved a certificate of need for an ambulatory surgical center, a competing hospital filed a petition for a formal hearing. An Intervener also filed a petition to intervene. The hospital voluntarily withdrew its petition, the hearing was cancelled and the application was approved. Intervener appealed to the District Court of Appeal, and the Court held that because the competing hospital and withdrew its petition, the intervener had no valid proceeding to intervene in. Affirmed.

Methodist Regional Hospital System Inc. v. State Department of Health and Rehabilitative Services, 497 So.2d 272 (Fla. Dist. Ct. App. 1986).

Abstract: Applicant was denied certificate of need by the Department of Health and Rehabilitative Service. The applicant then appealed to the District Court of Appeals after the Department denied its request for comparative review. The Court ruled that due to the change in rules for determining need for nursing home beds, the applicant was entitled to comparative hearing. Reversed and remanded.

Boca Raton Artificial Kidney Center v. Department of Health and Rehabilitative Services, 493 So.2d 1055 (Fla. Dist. Ct. App. 1986).

Abstract: Competitors filed petition for review of preliminary and intermediate agency action, or petition for writ of mandamus to the District Court of Appeals after the Department of Health and Rehabilitative Services approved applicant's certificate of need for an artificial kidney center. The Court remanded the case back to the Department. On remand, the Department again granted certificate of need to kidney center. The competitors appealed to the District Court of Appeal and again. The Court held that consideration of need data was incorrectly evaluated and should be determined within one year from date application. Reversed and remanded.

Charter Medical-Southeast Inc. v. State Department of Health and Rehabilitative Services, 495 So.2d 759 (Fla. Dist. Ct. App. 1986).

Abstract: Applicant appealed to the District Court of Appeals after the Department of Health and Rehabilitative Services denied their application for certificate of need to construct psychiatric hospital. The Court held that: (1) the Department had the authority to deny the hospital the certificate of need, (2) alternative method was not needed to determine whether there was need for the hospital. Affirmed.

Upjohn Healthcare Services Inc. v. Department of Health and Rehabilitative Services, 496 So.2d 147 (Fla. Dist. Ct. App. 1986).

Abstract: Applicant appealed to the District Court of Appeals after the Department of Health and Rehabilitative Services denied their application for certificate of need to qualify as a "home health agency". The Court held that: (1) hearing officer did not base his decision on the standards for a "home health agency" that were set in the county, (2) the Department's decision to accept the hearing officers gave the hearing officer undue authority, and (3) the Department acted in an arbitrary and capricious fashion. Reversed and remanded.

Psychiatric Institutes of America Inc. v. Department of Health and Rehabilitative Services, 491 So.2d 1199 (Fla. Dist. Ct. App. 1986).

Abstract: Competitor appealed to the Department of Health and Rehabilitative Services after the hearing officer had determined that: (1) the competitor had standing, and (2) the applicant should be granted certificate of need that was requested. The Department held that the competitor lacked standing and the certificate of need should still be granted to the applicant. The competitor appealed to the District Court of Appeal. The Court ruled that: (1) the competitor had standing, regardless of the difference in bed need methodology rules, (2) the erroneous determination by the Department did not warrant remand, and (3) hearing officer's orders were adequate. Affirmed.

Morton F. Plant Hospital Association v. State, 491 So.2d 586 (Fla. Dist. Ct. App. 1986).

Abstract: Applicant appealed to the District Court of Appeals after the Department of Health and Rehabilitative Services denied their application for certificate of need for a short-term psychiatric facility. The Department held that applicant did not demonstrate that converting current facilities would not be more cost efficient than building a new one. The Court agreed. Affirmed.

Bayonet Point Hospital Inc. v. Department of Health and Rehabilitative Services, 490 So.2d 1318 (Fla. Dist. Ct. App. 1986).

Abstract: Applicant appealed to the District Court of Appeals after the Department of Health and Rehabilitative Services denied its petition to amend rule concerning certificate of need standards for cardiac catheterization laboratories. The Court held that: (1) the Department was not legally obligated to reveal conclusions or findings of fact upon ruling, (2) the Department provided adequate reasons for denying the petition, and (3) hospital did not have a right to hearing on petition. Affirmed.

NME Hospitals Inc. v. Department of Health and Rehabilitative Services, 492 So.2d 379 (Fla. Dist. Ct. App. 1986).

Abstract: Competitors filed petition to contest the addition to a competing hospital and was denied hearing by the Department of Health and Rehabilitative Services. The competitors then appealed to the District Court of Appeals which affirmed the Department's ruling. A second appeal was filed, and a rehearing was held by the District Court. The Court ruled that: (1) fairness of proceedings was impaired by the Department's disregard to procedure concerning certificate of need, and (2) because hospital failed to follow appropriate procedure in filing out applications it lacks a clear point of entry. Reversed and remanded.

University Community Hospital v. Department of Health and Rehabilitative Services, 493 So.2d 2 (Fla. Dist. Ct. App. 1986).

Abstract: Hospital seeks recover litigation fees after the District Court of Appeals overturned the FL Department of Health and Rehabilitative Services denial of certificate of need for a cardiac catheterization laboratory and open heart surgery program. The Court held that the hospital was entitled to recover fees. So ordered.

Medivision of East Broward County Inc. v. Department of Health and Rehabilitative Services, 488 So.2d 886 (Fla. Dist. Ct. App. 1986).

Abstract: Applicant applied to receive certificate of need to build an ophthalmic ambulatory surgical center. Competitor intervened motioning to have the documents of the parent corporation of applicant to be reviewed. Department of Administrative Hearings granted the motion, and applicant filed for review of order. The District Court of Appeal held that: (1) the applicant was created by the parent corporation for the sole reason to apply for the certificate of need, and (2) therefore, the documents should be subject to discovery. Petition for review denied.

Health Care and Retirement Corporation v. Department of Health and Rehabilitative Services, 489 So.2d 789 (Fla. Dist. Ct. App. 1986).

Abstract: Applicants appealed to the District Court of Appeals after the Department of Health and Rehabilitative Services denied their applications for certificates of need for two 60-bed nursing homes. The Court held that: (1) patient census written by the Department lacked substantial evidence, (2) additional evidence did not have to be accepted by the Department after the formal hearing had been held, (3) bed need methodology is sufficient and there is no need to deviate from the methodology when making considering the applications, and (4) recommendations to applicants where not necessary because it had been demonstrated that no need existed. Affirmed in part, reversed in part, and remanded.

Humana Inc. v. Department of Health and Rehabilitative Services, 492 So.2d 388 (Fla. Dist. Ct. App. 1986).

Abstract: Applicant appealed to the District Court of Appeals after the Department of Health and Rehabilitative Services denied its application for certificate of need to operate a cardiac catheterization lab. The Court held that the 1982 and 1983 utilization data was insufficient information to justify a deviation from the mathematical formula that had been set forth to determine need. Affirmed.

St. Francis Parkside Lodge v. Department of Health and Rehabilitative Services, 486 So.2d 3 (Fla. Dist. Ct. App. 1986).

Abstract: Applicants appealed to the District Court of Appeals after the Department of Health and Rehabilitative Services denied their petitions to challenge ruling that granted a certificate of need to a competitor. The Court ruled that the applicants had sufficient standing based on the similar service area of applicants and competitor. Reversed.

Balsam v. Department of Health and Rehabilitative Services, 486 So.2d 1341 (Fla. Dist. Ct. App. 1986).

Abstract: After remand, Applicant again appealed to the District Court of Appeals after the FL Department of Health and Rehabilitative Services denied their certificate of need application for a short-term psychiatric and substance abuse hospital. The Court held that: (1) Department's ruling was arbitrary and capricious, and (2) applicant was incorrectly denied the right to present evidence due to the Department's failure to place sufficient weight upon the statues and rules. Reversed and remanded.

Good Samaritan Hospital Inc. v. Department of Health and Rehabilitative Services, 485 So.2d 871 (Fla. Dist. Ct. App. 1986).

Abstract: Hospital appealed to the District Court of Appeal concerning the Department of Health and Rehabilitative Services interpretation of Rule 10-5.08(1)(e). The Court holds that the Departments interpretation is not clearly erroneous and that it is fair and reasonable.

Florida Medical Center v. Department of Health and Rehabilitative Services, 484 So.2d 1292 (Fla. Dist. Ct. App. 1986).

Abstract: Applicant appealed to the District Court of Appeals after the Department of Health and Rehabilitative Services denied their petition for hearing to challenge the issuing of a certificate of need for a competitor. The Court held that: (1) the applicants had standing based on economic interest, (2) the Department's orders could be modified as long as intervening parties resolved its difficulties by executing stipulation, (3) hospital's that did not intervene in a timely manner in proceedings that led to final matter were not entitled to hearing, and (4) hospital's that did not intervene in a timely manner in proceedings prior to final order could intervene in the settlement of the final order. Affirmed in part, reversed in part and remanded.

Gulf Court Nursing Center v. Department of Health & Rehabilitative Services, 483 So.2d 700 (Fla. Dist. Ct. App. 1986).

Abstract: Corporation appealed to the District Court of Appeals after the Department of Health and Rehabilitative Services denied its application for a certificate of need and petition for comparative review. The Court held that: (1) the corporation should have been granted comparative review, and (2) the Department's reasoning for denying the corporation's application was erroneous. Reversed and remanded. Rehearing denied.

University Medical Center Inc. v. Department of Health and Rehabilitative Services, 483 So.2d 712 (Fla. Dist. Ct. App. 1986).

Abstract: Applicant appealed to the District Court of Appeals after the Administrative Hearing Officer denied its application for a comparative review with a second hospital that had been filed earlier. The Court held that the hospital failed to establish that both parties were in the same fixed pool of projected need. Affirmed.

Federal Property Management Corp. v. Department of Health and Rehabilitative Services, 482 So.2d 475 (Fla. Dist. Ct. App. 1986).

Abstract: Applicant appealed to the District Court of Appeals for review after the Department of Health and Rehabilitative Services denied their applications for certificate of need for an additional nursing home facility and beds. The Court held that: (1) discretion was abused when the bed need methodology was not used based on exceptional circumstances, and (2) the Department used incorrect numbers when applying the bed need methodology. Affirmed in part, reversed in part, and remanded.

Health Care Management Inc. v. Department of Health and Rehabilitative Services, 479 So.2d 193 (Fla. Dist. Ct. App. 1985).
Abstract: Applicant appealed to the District Court of Appeals seeking administrative review after the Department of Health and Rehabilitative Services denied their application for certificate of need to add 42 beds to a nursing home. The Court held that: (1) the Department's decision was based on substantial evidence, and (2) the Department's refusal examine additional evidence after ruling was not reversible error. Affirmed.

North Ridge General Hospital Inc. v. NME Hospitals Inc., 478 So.2d 1138 (Fla. Dist. Ct. App. 1985).
Abstract: Competitor appealed to the District Court of Appeals after the Department of Health and Rehabilitative Services approved a certificate of need to a competing hospital. The Court held that: (1) Competitor lacked standing, and (2) examination regarding utilization of facilities was properly evaluated during Department's hearing. Affirmed.

Humhosco Inc. v. Department of Health and Rehabilitative Services, 476 So.2d 258 (Fla. Dist. Ct. App. 1985).
Abstract: A hearing officer overruled a builder's challenge to the Department of Health and Rehabilitative Services concerning rules affecting the builder's application for certificate of need. The builder appealed to the District Court of Appeals. The Court held that: (1) there was no conflict between the statues and rules concerning certificate of need, (2) rules were not unconstitutional, (3) a rule that has more than one subject is not invalid, and (4) the Department's failure to prepare a proper economic impact statement does not render the rules invalid. Affirmed.

Central Florida Regional Hospital v. Daytona Beach General Hospital, 475 So.2d 974 (Fla. Dist. Ct. App. 1985).
Abstract: Competitor appealed to the District Court of Appeals after the Department of Health and Rehabilitative Services approved a certificate of need to open a new hospital and shift beds to new hospital and delicense 50 beds. The Court held that: (1) the Department's ruling was based on substantial evidence, and (2) the Department's deviation from rules is excusable because the rule does not apply to transfer of beds from one facility to another. Affirmed.

Boca Raton Artificial Kidney Center Inc. v. Florida Department of Health and Rehabilitative Services, 475 So.2d 260 (Fla. Dist. Ct. App. 1985).
Abstract: Applicant appealed to the District Court of Appeals after the Department of Health and Rehabilitative Services approved competitors' multiple petitions to challenge issuance of certificate of need, review of preliminary and intermediate agency action and writ of mandamus. The Court ruled that: (1) operation of center could not begin until after the administrative hearing and final approval of certificate of need, and (2) construction prior to approval of certificate of need could begin at applicant's own risk, special consideration would not be granted if construction began. Remanded for proceedings consistent with opinion.

Community Psychiatric Centers v. Department of Health and Rehabilitative Services, 474 So.2d 870 (Fla. Dist. Ct. App. 1985).
Abstract: Applicant appealed to the District Court of Appeals after the Department of Health and Rehabilitative Services dismissed its petition for a formal administrative hearing concerning the approval of a certificate of need for a competitor. The Court held that the applicant lacked standing because it had applied for a certificate of need as well, and was not an "affected person". Affirmed.

Gulf Court Nursing Center v. Department of Health and Rehabilitative Services, 483 So.2d 700 (Fla. Dist. Ct. App. 1985).

Abstract: Applicant appealed to the District Court of Appeals after the Department of Health and Rehabilitative Services denied its application for certificate of need to construct a nursing home facility and its denial of comparative review with other applications. The Court ruled: (1) the applicant should have been granted comparative review, and (2) denying the applicant on the grounds that projected need had been satisfied was incorrect. Reversed and remanded. Rehearing denied.

University Medical Center Inc. v. Department of Health and Rehabilitative Services, 483 So.2d 712 (Fla. Dist. Ct. App. 1985).

Abstract: Applicant appealed to the District Court of Appeals after the Department of Health and Rehabilitative Services denied its right to comparative review. The Court ruled that the applicant had not established the same fixed pool of projected need. Affirmed.

Department of Health and Rehabilitative Services v. American Healthcorp of Vero Beach, 471 So.2d 1312 (Fla. Dist. Ct. App. 1985).

Abstract: After the Department of Health and Rehabilitative Services failed to respond to corporation's application for certificate of need, corporation filed amended petition to the Circuit Court for writ of mandamus. The Department filed motion for rehearing and attached affidavits after Circuit Court granted summary judgment to corporation. The Circuit Court denied motion for rehearing and refused to rule on affidavits. The District Court held that: (1) writ of mandamus was not the correct remedy, (2) affidavits filed after summary judgment can be admitted at the discretion of trial court, and (3) all administrative remedies must be exhausted before legal action can be taken. Reversed; writ of mandamus dissolved.

University Community Hospital v. Department of Health and Rehabilitative Services, 472 So.2d 756 (Fla. Dist. Ct. App. 1985).

Abstract: Applicant appealed to the District Court of Appeals for review after the Department of Health and Rehabilitative Services denied its certificate of need application to create cardiac catheterization laboratories and open-heart surgery program. The Court held that: (1) the Department's ruling was arbitrary and capricious, and (2) there was substantial evidence to grant the applicant a certificate of need. Reversed and remanded.

Humana, Inc. v. Department of Health and Rehabilitative Services, 469 So.2d 889 (Fla. Dist. Ct. App. 1985).

Abstract: Hospitals went to the Division of Administrative Hearings to challenge the validity of rule that was adopted by the Department of Health and Rehabilitative Services. The Division upheld the rule. The hospitals appealed to the District Court of Appeals. The Court held that: (1) fairness was not impaired when an economic impact statement was used to adopt the rule, and (2) proper methodology was used by Department when adopting the rule. Affirmed.

Florida Medical Center v. Department of Health and Rehabilitative Services, 463 So.2d 380 (Fla. Dist. Ct. App. 1985).

Abstract: Applicant appealed to the District Court of Appeals for review after the Department of Health and Rehabilitative Services denied its application for certificate of need for nuclear magnetic resonance unit. The Court ruled that: (1) Department's ruling was not based on statutes or policy, and (2) Department lacked substantial evidence to back its claims of possible health hazards. Reversed and remanded with directions.

Naples Community Hospital Inc. v. Department of Health and Rehabilitative Services, 463 So.2d 375 (Fla. Dist. Ct. App. 1985).

Abstract: Intervener appealed to the Circuit Court after the Department of Health and Rehabilitative Services issued a certificate of need to a competing hospital. The Circuit Court denied the motion, and the intervener appealed to the District Court. The Court ruled that the intervener had standing based on its existing hospital and its application for a certificate of need in the same district. Reversed and remanded.

Home Health Professional Services Inc. v. Department of Health and Rehabilitative Services, 463 So.2d 345 (Fla. Dist. Ct. App. 1985).
Abstract: Applicant appealed to the District Court of Appeals after the Department of Health and Rehabilitative Services denied application to expand to different counties without a certificate of need review. The Court held that applicant could not expand to different counties without first holding the review because it was the Department's insure there would be no duplication of services. Affirmed.

Collier Medical Center Inc. v. State Department of Health and Rehabilitative Services, 462 So.2d 83 (Fla. Dist. Ct. App. 1985).
Abstract: Applicant appealed to the District Court of Appeals after the Department of Health and Rehabilitative Services denied its certificate of need proposal for a new hospital. The Court held that: (1) the Department had substantial evidence to deny the applicant, (2) existing hospitals in the area had standing to intervene, and (3) there was no error when the hearing officer denied the applicant's request to supplement its record after its hearing had closed. Affirmed.

Federal Property Management Corp. v. Health Care and Retirement Corporation, 462 So.2d 493 (Fla. Dist. Ct. App. 1984).
Abstract: Applicant appealed to the District Court of Appeals after the Department of Health and Rehabilitative Services denied its petition to intervene, The Court held that: (1) the applicant demonstrated standing to intervene, and (2) petition was not untimely. Reversed.

Health Care and Retirement Corporation. v. Department of Health & Rehabilitative Services, 463 So.2d 1175 (Fla. Dist. Ct. App. 1984).
Abstract: Applicant appealed to the District Court of Appeals after the Department of Health and Rehabilitative Services refused to review applications on the ground that they had not filed letters of intent with local health councils. The Court held that: (1) previously the Department had excused the rule because the health councils were not yet fully established, now the councils are established, the Department is permitted to enforce the rule, (2) the rule is authorized, and (3) the incomplete nature of the economic impact statement does not render agency rules invalid. Affirmed.

Turro v. Department of Health and Rehabilitative Services, 458 So.2d 345 (Fla. Dist. Ct. App. 1984).
Abstract: Applicant appealed to the District Court of Appeals after the Department of Health and Rehabilitative Services denied applications for certificates of need. The Court held that although the rule providing methodology was not formally effective until after the beginning of the hearing, it still could be applied in the case because the applicant aware of the possible amendment should have taken it into account when preparing its case. Affirmed.

Whitehall Boca v. Department of Health and Rehabilitative Services, 456 So.2d 928 (Fla. Dist. Ct. App. 1984).
Abstract: Two corporations were not entitled to separate administrative hearings and state agency's proposed rule was validly promulgated, because no error was shown with the informal hearing and the rule was sufficiently specific.

Doctors' Osteopathic Medical Center Inc. v. Department of Health and Rehabilitative Services, 459 So.2d 1063 (Fla. Dist. Ct. App. 1984).

Abstract: Applicant filed an emergency petition for writ of prohibition to the District Court of Appeals after the Department of Health and Rehabilitative Services granted a certificate of need to a competitor. The Court ruled that there were no substantial facts to evidence the issuance of a writ of prohibition. Order accordingly.

Brookwood Extended Care Centers Inc. v. State Department of Health and Rehabilitative Services, 453 So.2d 865 (Fla. Dist. Ct. App. 1984).

Abstract: Applicant appealed to the District Court of Appeals for review after the Department of Health and Rehabilitative Services denied its petition for revocation of its certificate of need for construction of a nursing home. The Court held that: (1) a published note of intent to revoke is deficient, and (2) the Department was error by denying hearing without allowing applicant to address allegations. Reversed and remanded.

Health Quest Realty XII v. Department of Health and Rehabilitative Services, 477 So.2d 576 (Fla. Dist. Ct. App. 1985).

Abstract: Applicant appealed to the District Court of Appeals after the Department of Health and Rehabilitative Services denied its application for certificate of need to build a nursing home. The Court held that: (1) the Department is not required to deviate from bed need methodology, and (2) any error by the Department during the hearing was harmless. Affirmed.

Humana Inc. v. Department of Health and Rehabilitative Services, 469 So.2d 889 (Fla. Dist. Ct. App. 1985).

Abstract: Hospitals appealed to the Division of Administrative Hearings concerning the validity of rules established by the Department of Health and Rehabilitative Services. The Hospitals appealed when the Division upheld the validity of the rules, the District Court of Appeal held that: (1) fairness was not impaired when the Department used the economic impact statement to adopt the rule, (2) the Department's rule was supported with substantial evidence and methodology. Affirmed.

Balsam v. Department of Health and Rehabilitative Services, 452 So.2d 976 (Fla. Dist. Ct. App. 1984).

Abstract: Applicant appealed hearing officer's decision that a moratorium on the receipt of certificate of need application is not subject to rule making procedures. The Court holds that the moratorium was consistently applied to applications and while it was in force and therefore should be subject to rule making procedures. Reversed.

Hillsborough County Hospital Authority v. Tampa Heart Institute, 472 So.2d 748 (Fla. Dist. Ct. App. 1985).

Abstract: Competitors appealed to the District Court of Appeals after the Department of Health and Rehabilitative Services denied one hospital the right to participate in hearings and denied the other the right to intervene in an applicant's certificate of need application for a new cardiac facility. The Court held that: (1) the Department lacked authority in penalizing the two competitors thus, (2) Department had no authority threatening the competitors to sanctions, and (3) the hearing officer did correctly deny on competitor petition to intervene on the grounds that it was untimely. Reversed and remanded for one competitor. Affirmed and remanded with instructions for intervener.

Associated Home Health Agency Inc. v. State Department of Health and Rehabilitative Services, 453 So.2d 104 (Fla. Dist. Ct. App. 1984).

Abstract: Provider of home health services appealed to the District Court of Appeals after the Department of Health and Rehabilitative Services rescinded its license. The Court held that: (1) Department failed to file a complaint and therefore the proceeding was fatally defective, and (2) competitor lacked standing to have hearing. Reversed.

Department of Health and Rehabilitative Services v. Johnson & Johnson Home Health Care Inc., 447 So.2d 361 (Fla. Dist. Ct. App. 1984).
Abstract: Applicant appealed to the District Court of Appeals after the FL Department of Health and Rehabilitative Services denied its certificate of need application. The Court ruled that the rule that sets a threshold requirement is invalid because it is arbitrary and violates a statue related to certificate of need applications. Affirmed.

Florida Convalescent Centers Inc. v. State Department of Health and Rehabilitative Services, 445 So.2d 631 (Fla. Dist. Ct. App. 1984).
Abstract: Applicant appealed to the District Court of Appeals for writ of prohibition after the Department of Health and Rehabilitative Services approved a certificate of need to a competitor pending a hearing they had requested. The Court held that the facts did not demonstrate that the Department was without jurisdiction to act. Petition denied.

Farmworker Rights Organization v. Department of Health and Rehabilitative Services, 430 So.2d 1 (Fla. Dist. Ct. App. 1983).
Abstract: Applicant appealed to the District Court of Appeals after the Department of Health and Rehabilitative Services and a hearing officer denied their petition for determination for invalidity. The Court ruled that: (1) the applicant had standing to challenge the ruling, (2) rules made by the Department were invalid exercise of delegated legislative authority because the did not contain specific criteria concerning low income and minority groups that is required to be in accordance with federal statutes. Reversed.

Gulf Coast Hospital Inc. v. Department of Health & Rehabilitative Services, 424 So.2d 86 (Fla. Dist. Ct. App. 1982).
Abstract: Applicant appealed to the District Court of Appeals after the Department of Health and Rehabilitative Services denied application for certificate of need to build an osteopathic hospital. The Court held that: (1) existing non osteopathic facilities should not assist in determining need for osteopathic facilities, and (2) there was a lack of substantial evidence to demonstrate need for the facility. Reversed and remanded.

Gateway Hospital Corporation East v. Department of Health and Rehabilitative Services, 420 So.2d 337 (Fla. Dist. Ct. App. 1982).
Abstract: Competitor appealed to the District Court of Appeals after the Department of Health and Rehabilitative Services approved certificate of need to competing hospital to purchase land. The Court held that: (1) the purchase of land was non competitive and competitor would not be substantially affected, and (2) the Department's decision was based on substantial evidence.

Westchester General Hospital v. Department of Health & Rehabilitative Services, 419 So.2d 705 (Fla. Dist. Ct. App. 1982).
Abstract: Hospital appealed to the District Court of Appeals after the Department of Health and Rehabilitative Services found that it had forfeited its grandfather exemption, so it would be required to obtain a certificate of need for a replacement hospital. The Court held that: (1) the Department erred in manipulating the findings of the hearing officer, (2) Department did not give timely notice to hospital that grandfather exemption had been repealed and therefore is equitably estopped from applying its rules against the hospital, and (3) Department ruled correctly concerning hospital's exceptions. Reversed and remanded.

Farmworker Rights Organization v. Department of Health and Rehabilitative Services, 417 So.2d 753 (Fla. Dist. Ct. App. 1982).

Abstract: Competitor appealed to the District Court of Appeals after the Department of Health and Rehabilitative Services denied its request for formal administrative proceeding concerning a certificate of need to construct an acute care hospital. The Court held that according to standing requirements in the Florida Home Builders applied to the procedures under the Administrative Procedure Act, and therefore the competitor had standing for the hearing. Reversed and remanded with direction.

Westchester General Hospital v. State Department of Health and Rehabilitative Services, 417 So.2d 261 (Fla. Dist. Ct. App. 1982).

Abstract: Hospitals consolidated their appeal to the District Court of Appeals concerning the validity of the rules established by the FL Department of Health and Rehabilitative Services. The Court held that the Department exercised invalid legislative power and failed to address economic impact statement rules' and how they would affect regulated hospitals. Affirmed.

South Broward Hospital District v. Department of Health and Rehabilitative Services, 385 So.2d 1094 (Fla. Dist. Ct. App. 1980).

Abstract: Hospital district petitioned to the District Court of Appeals for writ of prohibition or review after the Department of Health and Rehabilitative Services granted certificate of need to one applicant and had denied another. The hospital district wanted to determine whether the denied applicant had standing to contest. The Court held that: (1) if the two applications were mutually exclusive, then the denied applicant had standing, and (2) the question of mutually exclusive categories precludes the granting of writ of prohibition and review of non-final administrative action. Request relief denied.

Samson v. Bureau of Community Medical Facilities Planning, 363 So.2d 412 (Fla. Dist. Ct. App. 1978).

Abstract: Applicant petitioned for writ of certiorari to the District Court of Appeal after the Bureau of Community Medical Facilities Planning of State Department of Health and Rehabilitative Services denied its application for certificate of need for a 200-bed hospital. The Court ruled that the Bureau's failure to notify the applicant using written notification before its 90- day deadline indicated approval by the Bureau for the application. Reversed with directions.

Bureau of Community Medical Facilities Planning of Department of Health and Rehabilitative Services v. Samson, 341 So.2d 1071 (Fla. Dist. Ct. App. 1977).

Abstract: Florida Bureau of Community Medical Facilities Planning was not entitled to judicial review of administrative hearing officer's order requiring it to issue a certificate of need for hospital construction because there was no final agency action.

Health Facilities Research Inc. v. Bureau of Community Medical Facilities, 340 So.2d 125 (Fla. Dist. Ct. App. 1976).

Abstract: Hospital, as amicus curiae moved to dismiss a case where petitioners applied to review the validity of certain administrative actions which granted hospital a certificate of need. The Court held that: (1) as amicus curiae, the hospital lacked standing to dismiss the petition, and (2) petitions for review are dismissed. Petitions dismissed.

Palmetto General Hospital Inc. v. State Department of Health and Rehabilitative Services, 333 So.2d 531 (Fla. Dist. Ct. App. 1976).

Abstract: A private hospital appealed to the District Court after the Department of Health and Rehabilitative

Services found that they had no need federal participation in capital expenditure to add an additional 180 beds but hospital was exempt from the certificate of need statues for licensing purposes. The Court held that even though the hospital was exempt from certificate of need requirements, this fact did not affect whether or not federal participation in capital expenditures would or would not be approved without first demonstrating need for the construction.

Humana of Florida Inc. v. Keller, 329 So.2d 420 (Fla. Dist. Ct. App. 1976).
Abstract: Competitor appealed to the Circuit Court petitioning for declaratory and injunctive relief from a bureau under the jurisdiction of the Department of Health and Rehabilitative Services because they had not held a public hearing before approving a certificate of need for a new hospital that had 132 beds. The Circuit Court dismissed the complaint and the competitor appealed to the District Court of Appeal. The Court held that: (1) public hearing is mandatory according to the Health Facilities Planning Act, (2) expiration of 90 days from filing without notice, and lack of hearing does not constitute approval for certificate of need, and (3) the competitor correctly brought their grievance to the circuit court for hearing. Reversed.

General Care Corporation v. Forehand, 329 So.2d 49 (Fla. Dist. Ct. App. 1976).
Abstract: One applicant appealed to the Circuit Court petitioning for mandamus to review denial for certificate of need by Department of Health and Rehabilitative Services, while another applicant petitioned for declaratory judgment to review denial for certificate of need. The Circuit Court denied both applicants, and together the applicants consolidated their appeals and petitioned for rehearing to the District Court. The Court held that: (1) because of discretion that needed to be exercised, mandamus was the incorrect action, and (2) the first applicant could seek review in Circuit Court petitioning for declaratory judgment. Reversed and remanded.

GEORGIA

Supreme Court of Georgia

North Fulton Medical Center v. Stephenson, 501 S.E.2d (Ga. 1998).
Abstract: Georgia State Health Planning Agency (GSHPA) granted, under GSHPA's second relocation rule, a relocation certificate of need to hospital's outpatient surgery center; this faced administrative appeal by competitor, a decision that was affirmed. The competitor then sought and was denied mandamus relief by the Superior Court of Fulton County. The competitor appealed and outpatient center cross-appealed. The Supreme Court of Georgia held that: (1) GSHPA is only authorized to take action laws already passed by General Assembly and has no authority to legislate, thus the rule established by the GSHPA was invalid, (2) GSHPA is authorized only to adopt and implement rules that facilitate the administration of the State Health Planning Act's provisions including it's CON program, thus GSHPA acted beyond the scope of its administrative powers, and (3) the merits for mandamus action was reached, trial court did not err. Affirmed in part and reversed in part.

Phoebe Putney Memorial Hospital v. Roach, 480 S.E.2d 595 (Ga. 1997).
Abstract: Georgia State Health Planning Agency (GSHPA) and hospital appealed the decision of the Court, ruling for the unit's operator and prevented GSHPA to prohibit the operation of a mobile cardiac catheterization unit that was grandfathered under GSHPA at a new location without a certificate of need. The Supreme Court held that though the unit "grandfathered" under Georgia State Health Planning Act was exempt from obtaining certificate of need a certificate of need when it began operations in Vidalia it was required to obtain a certificate of need in order to relocate and operate in Albany. Reversed in part and dismissed in part.

HCA Health Services v. Roach, 458 S.E.2d 118 (Ga. 1995).
Abstract: Health care facility's competitor appealed the decision of the Court to deny competitor mandamus relief from Georgia State Health Planning Agency's (GSHPA) "grandfathering" facilities into the certificate of need (CON) program. Soon thereafter GSHPA issued a new rule exempting relocated "grandfathered" facilities from obtaining CON for new location. Additionally, the competitor filed a complaint challenging the validity of this new rule. The Supreme Court held that: (1) health facility was already in operation upon the establishment of the CON program therefore is eligible for "grandfather" exemption, (2) GSHPA does not have the authorization to grant exemption from CON for relocating, and (3) GSHPA does not have the authority to create legislature, therefore GSHPA's rule to grant exemption to relocating grandfathered facilities was unconstitutional. Affirmed in part and reversed in part.

North Fulton Medical Center v. Roach, 440 S.E.2d 18 (Ga. 1994).
Abstract: Hospital appealed the decision of the Court to dismiss the hospital's request for judicial review and request for mandamus challenging the Georgia State Health Planning Agency's (GSHPA) approval of relocation of competing facility. The Supreme Court held that: (1) GSHPA does not have the authorization to grant exemption from CON for relocating at its own discretion, (2) though hospital did not have certificate of need in the area of relocation, the hospital had standing as "aggrieved party," and (3) in efforts to challenge GSHPA hospital had exhausted administrative remedies. Reversed and remanded.

HCA Health Services v. Roach, 439 S.E.2d 494 (Ga. 1994).
Abstract: Health care facility's competitor appealed the decision of the Court to dismiss competitor's actions for mandamus and judicial relief from Georgia State Health Planning Agency's (GSHPA) declaration that the facility is: (1) an "ambulatory surgical center" operating prior to establishment of a certificate of need (CON) program and thus eligible for "grandfather" exemption, and (2) is exempt from CON requirements upon sale or relocation. The Court held that: (1) petition for judicial review was not filed within 30 days of Court's dismissal and therefore was untimely, (2) GSHPA does not have the authorization to determine whether to grandfather a particular facility, and (3) GSHPA does not have the authorization to grant exemption from CON for relocating. Dismissal of action for judicial review affirmed, and dismissal for mandamus reversed and remanded.

Dogwood Square Nursing Center Inc. v. State Health Planning Agency, 341 S.E.2d 432 (Ga. 1986).
Abstract: The certificate of need for construction of a nursing home was denied by the Georgia State Health Planning Agency. An action that was reversed by the Georgia State Health Planning Review Board, and the planning agency appealed this decision. The court ruled for the planning agency and a discretionary appeal was granted. The Supreme Court held that the review board exceeded its jurisdiction by deeming the "County Deficit Rule," by applying the rule to only a portion of the county rather than the whole, and thus the planning agency decision was the final decision. Affirmed.

Diversified Health Management Services Inc. v. Visiting Nurses Association, 330 S.E.2d 885 (Ga. 1985).
Abstract: Providers of health care services appealed the decision of the Court to dismiss the request to prohibit competitors' from agreements constituting illegal transfer of certificate of need. The Supreme Court held that only an "interested person" may have the standing to request enforcement of legal action, and plaintiffs did not qualify as "interested persons" and therefore lacked standing to impose action. Affirmed.

North Fulton Medical Center v. Roach, 453 S.E.2d 463 (Ga. 1995).
Abstract: Medical center appealed the decision of the court to dismiss their petitions for a judicial review considering the exemption of a competing hospital from obtaining a certificate of need to relocate its surgical facility. Supreme Court reversed and remanded and after the court again dismissed the petition, the medical center

appealed. The Supreme Court held that: (1) under the Administrative Procedure Act the medical center could not obtain a judicial review, and (2) the determination of the agency could be challenged by mandamus. Affirmed in part, reversed in part, and remanded.

Court of Appeals of Georgia

Georgia Department of Community Health v. Satilla Health Services, Inc., 2004 Ga. App. LEXIS 641 (Ga. Ct. App. 2004).

Abstract: Appellants, two hospitals and the Georgia Department of Community Health, appeal from a superior court decision to reverse a Health Planning Review Board decision to deny a certificate of need (CON) to appellee, a hospital, for an open-heart surgery service. The superior court found that the Health Planning Review Board decision was arbitrary and capricious and reversed the decision. The Court of Appeals of Georgia reversed the superior court decision as a need and impact exception to the CON regulations, which appellee attempted to invoke on the basis of geographic barriers, is a discretionary policy decision related to the health planning purpose of the Review Board. Reversed.

Department of Community Health, Division of Health Planning v. Gwinnett Hospital System, Inc., 586 S.E.2d 762 (Ga. Ct. App. 2003).

Abstract: Appellants, Georgia Department of Community Health ("Department") and a hospital system, appeal from two superior court decisions reversing the Department's grant of a certificate of need to the hospital system to combine and relocate two hospitals. Both superior courts reversed the decision on appeal by appellees, three Georgia hospitals, on the grounds that the decision was arbitrary and capricious, exceeded statutory authority, and was not supported by substantial evidence. The Court of Appeals reversed the superior courts' decisions holding that it was not arbitrary and capricious for the Department to find the hospital was a replacement facility and not a new facility. Reversed.

Albany Surgical, P.C. v. Department of Community Health, 572 S.E.2d 638 (Ga. Ct. App. 2002).

Abstract: Appeal seeking to declare invalid an administrative regulation which provides that an "ambulatory surgery center engaged only in the practice of general surgery does not qualify for the single specialty exemption for the Certificate of Need." The Dept. submitted the regulation to the legislative counsel before adopting it. The legislature did not act to correct it and so the court must presume that the regulation is consistent with the legislative intent of the statute. General surgery overlaps with several other surgical specialties. Since the purpose of CON is to avoid duplication, it is the job of the agency to determine where the overlap does not warrant exemption from CON.

Northside Hospital, Inc. v. McCord et al., 537 S.E.2d 697 (Ga. Ct. App. 2000).

Abstract: The authority and hospital appealed the court's decision to grant interlocutory injunctive relief to a radiation oncology service center from the hospital's declaration that the restrictive covenant in the sublease was unenforceable. The Court of Appeals held that: (1) no abuse in trial court's discretion was found in such a granting, and (2) evidence supported that the restrictive covenant was subject to scrutiny due to auxiliary restrictive covenants in employments agreements. Affirmed.

St. Joseph's Hospital Inc. v. Thunderbolt Health Care Inc., 517 S.E.2d 334 (Ga. Ct. App. 1999).

Abstract: The Georgia State Health Planning Agency (GSHPA) and hospital appealed, separately, the decision of the Court to reverse the review board decision to award the hospital a certificate of need (CON) to convert 13 general acute care beds to 11 skilled nursing beds. The court ruled in favor of a traditional nursing home facility who challenged the GSHPA after also requesting and being denied of a similar certificate of need to add 11 beds to its facility. The Court of Appeals held that: (1) sufficient evidence of the violation of rights of the facility due to the procedures of the GSHPA were not found, and thus it was improper for the court to reverse the decisions of the board while failing to make this required finding, and (2) the facility's contention that the hospital was providing services different from and outside of their own services thus warranting their own CON consideration was erroneous. Court ruled that "short-stay hospital" does not preclude the hospital from being categorized as a "skilled nursing" facility or "nursing home." Reversed.

Medical Center v. State Health Planning Agency, 464 S.E.2d 925 (Ga. Ct. App.1995).
Abstract: The medical center appealed the decision of the Court to affirm the review board decision to award the hospital a certificate of need (CON) to create new perinatal services. The Court of Appeals held that: (1) the board was required to apply the new perinatal services rule of substantial compliance, (2) the hospital met 4 of the 5 subparts necessary for compliance, thus indicating substantial compliance, and (3) the board is demanded to adhere to the CON standards and did not err in requiring compliance with the new standard. Affirmed.

ABC Home Health Services v. Georgia Department of Medical Assistance, 439 S.E.2d 696 (Ga. Ct. App. 1993).
Abstract: The department appealed the court decision requiring the department to review their denial of reimbursement to Medicaid provider. The Court of Appeals held that although the department granted reimbursement to the parent organization, the geographic location of the branch facility requesting financial support was not close enough to warrant sharing support. Failure of the provider to satisfy department regulations on branch facilities justified the denial of reimbursement. Reconsideration denied.

Hospital Authority v. State Health Planning Agency, 438 S.E.2d 912 (Ga. Ct. App. 1993).
Abstract: Hospitals' consolidated appeals challenged the decision of the court to affirm the denial of Gwinnett County application and reverse the denial of Cobb County application for certificates of need (CON) to provide open heart surgery services. The Court of Appeals held that substantial evidence was provided to indicate that either provision of CON would be detrimental to existing services. Both applications are to be denied. Affirmed in part and reversed in part.

Clayton County Hospital Authority v. Webb, 430 S.E.2d 89 (Ga. Ct. App. 1993).
Abstract: Hospital authority and affiliates appealed the decision of the court to grant the petition of the individual and hospital to disclose records of authority and affiliates. The Court of Appeals held that: (1) the Open Records Act declares all records of the authority and its affiliates to be public, (2) approval of the presiding official was required in order to gain access to records involving certificate of need proceedings, (3) despite being an uninvolved party in the certificate of need proceeding, in order for individual, when requesting documents purely on behalf of the hospital, to gain access to records prior approval is required, and (4) a signed contract by petitioners agreeing to not use information for "commercial purposes" discounts authority's and affiliate's grounds to refuse disclosure.

State Health Planning Agency v. Cribb Industries Inc., 419 S.E.2d 123 (Ga. Ct. App. 1992).
Abstract: Applicant appealed Georgia State Health Planning Review Board's affirmation of the Georgia State Health Planning Agency's decision to deny the application and reapplication for a certificate of need to build a nursing home. After the court's reversal of the board's decision the board applied for discretionary appeal. The Court of Appeals held that: (1) because the agency confirmed that the reapplication was complete, there was only a 90-day limit for any ruling on the reapplication, (2) despite applicant's withdrawal of request for delay in order to submit additional evidence, the 90-day time limit was not re-triggered, and (3) the board did not err in denial of application due to the fact that the applicant did not show adequate evidence that the new facility would not comply with the "County Deficit rule." Reversed.

Famiglietti v. Brevard Medical Investors Ltd., 397 S.E.2d 720 (Ga. Ct. App. 1990).
Abstract: Psychiatric hospital sought judicial review post the Georgia State Health Planning Review Board's affirmation of the Georgia State Health Planning Agency's decision to grant a certificate of need (CON) to add 24 adult psychiatric hospitals to a competing medical facility. Though one of the psychiatric hospital's claims of error was dismissed, the court dismissed the Board's decision based upon another of the psychiatric hospital's claims of error, this decision was appealed by the medical facility (applicant) and cross-appealed by the psychiatric facility. The Court of Appeals held that: (1) a reversal of the issuance of CON was not required even if the proposed addition did not equal the exact number of beds as deduced to constitute the area's need, and (2) when adding psychiatric beds to a general hospital, the hospital must show need for additional beds as a whole, but calculation of this need did not require using the institution specific formula. Affirmed in part and reversed in part.

Three Rivers Home Health Services Inc. v. Healthmaster Inc., 388 S.E.2d 7 (Ga. Ct. App. 1989).
Abstract: Appeals made by business competitors on the court ruling that granted joint motion to dismiss one competitor's action and grant the action of the other competitor for judicial review of declaratory ruling for the Georgia State Health Planning Agency (GSHPA) to exempt providers from certificate of need (CON) requirement. The Court of Appeals held that: (1) both parties had standing and therefore the right to seek judicial review of the rulings, and (2) both providers did not meet the requirements to be exempted from the statutory CON. Reversed in part and affirmed in part.

Chattahoochee Valley Home Health Care Inc. v. Healthmaster Inc., 381 S.E.2d 56 (Ga. Ct. App. 1989).
Abstract: Competitor petitioned for a discretionary appeal against the court's decision to dismiss the competitor's application for judicial review of administrative ruling and affirm the Georgia State Health Planning Agency's (GSHPA) decision to authorize that the corporation be exempt from obtaining a certificate of need for its new acquisitions of three home health agencies. The Court of Appeals held that: (1) competitor had standing and right to seek judicial review, and (2) Agency erred in allowing corporation to be exempt from filing for certificate of need as required by statute. Reversed.

Charter Medical-Fayette County Inc. v. Health Planning Agency Inc., 351 S.E.2d 547 (Ga. Ct. App. 1986).
Abstract: Applicant appealed the decision of the court to affirm the Georgia State Health Planning Agency's denial of the applicant's certificate of need application to build a hospital. The Court of Appeals held that: (1) court did not err in excluding evidence of the Health Planning Review Board's prior decisions, (2) board adhered to its own precedent, (3) equal protection and due process rights were not denied from the applicant, and (4) whether certificate of need should be granted is outside of the court's jurisdiction for failure of agency to issue decision within time as required by statute. Affirmed.

Chatham County Hospital Authority v. St. Joseph's Hospital Inc., 344 S.E.2d 463 (Ga. Ct. App. 1986).
Abstract: The Georgia State Health Planning Agency appealed the court's decision to accept and grant hospital's application for a certificate of need (CON) for providing cardiac surgery services using cardiac surgery rule as validation. The Court of Appeals held that: (1) CON for the provision of cardiac services were granted a two-year moratorium that was not considered in the cardiac surgery rule, (2) sufficient need for cardiac services were evidenced and therefore constituting the issuance of a CON. Affirmed.

Dogwood Square Nursing Center Inc. v. State Health Planning Agency, 336 S.E.2d 841 (Ga. Ct. App. 1985).
Abstract: Nursing home facility was granted a discretionary appeal after the court reversed the Georgia State Health Planning Review Board's reversal of the Georgia State Health Planning Agency's denial of the facility's

certificate of need application. The Court of Appeals held that the constitutionality of the Agency's authority granted by the statute needed to be resolved first by the Supreme Court. Transfer Ordered.

Health Help Services Inc. v. State Health Planning Agency, 329 S.E.2d 628 (Ga. Ct. App. 1985).
Abstract: Home health agency sought and was granted a discretionary appeal on the court's affirmation of the Georgia State Health Planning Review Board's decision to deny the agency's application for a certificate of need. The Court of Appeals held that: (1) trial court imposed a rule that was no longer in existence, but (2) since the rule had become effective again, no reversal was necessary. Affirmed.

State Health Planning Review Board. v. Piedmont Hospital Inc., 326 S.E.2d 814 (Ga. Ct. App. 1985).
Abstract: Two hospitals petitioned for a discretionary appeal granted by the trail court upon its reversal of the Georgia State Health Planning Review Board's decision to deny their separate applications for certificates of need to create cardiac surgery programs. The Court of Appeals held that they held no jurisdiction over this matter. Appeals dismissed.

North Fulton Community Hospital Inc. v. State Health Planning and Development Agency, 310 S.E.2d 764 (Ga. Ct. App. 1983).
Abstract: Applicant appealed the court's affirmation of the board's denial of the certificate of need for construction of a new hospital. The Court of Appeals held that: (1) alleged ex parte communications between board director and Georgia state assistant attorney general were not preserved by the applicant for appeal, (2) improper dual representation by the Georgia state assistant attorney general of both the Board and the Georgia State Health Planning Agency did not occur nor did it hinder applicant's ability to present the case in full, (3) applicant failed to evidence improper and prejudicial ex parte communications between the Board and the Georgia state assistant attorney general, and (4) a 6,000 page record substantiated the Board's decision. Affirmed.

Loyd v. Georgia State Health Planning and Development Agency, 310 S.E.2d 738 (Ga. Ct. App. 1983).
Abstract: Petitioners appealed the decision of the court to affirm the Georgia Health Planning and Development Agency's decision to dismiss the petition for judicial review on the issuance of a certificate of need pertaining to the construction of a new hospital on grounds that the petitioners did not have standing as required by the statute and for failing to name the review board as an indispensable party. The Court of Appeals held that: (1) claims of parties in appeal, under the new statutory law, are determined as no vested rights are involved, (2) the proper party respondent was GHPDA and the petitioners did not qualify for standing to petition them, and (3) to appeal to the review board from GHPDA's decision, petitioners had insufficient standing. Affirmed.

Blue Cross/Blue Shield Inc. v. Pouseman, 305 S.E.2d 855 (Ga. Ct. App. 1983).
Abstract: Insurer appealed the court decision to deem the insureds as eligible for coverage by satisfying "certificate of necessity" requirement. The Court of Appeals held that: (1) the letter from the insured's physician to the insurer gave sufficient evidence that the insured's medical condition warranted the "certificate of necessity" requirement, and (2) neither party was harmed by the trial court's jury charge and didn't require action. Affirmed.

IDAHO

Supreme Court of Idaho

University of Utah Medical Center v. Bonneville County, 529 P.2d 1304 (Idaho 1974).

Abstract: Medical center appealed the decision of the court to ruling for the defendants (the county and the Idaho Department of Public Assistance) in denying the center's request for reimbursement for medical care provided to indigents. The Supreme Court held that: (1) because no proper attempts by the medical center to obtain a certificate of need was ever made, the medical center did not have the authority to request reimbursement, but (2) the Department did not have the authority to limit payment for indigent patients to 20 days. Affirmed in part and reversed and remanded for further proceedings in part.

ILLINOIS

Supreme Court of Illinois

Marion Hospital Corporation v. The Illinois Health Facilities Planning Board, 746 N.E.2d 924 (Ill. 2002).

Abstract: Hospital competitor appeals certificate of need (CON) approval of orthopedic surgery center. Issue is whether the hospital's appeal was moot because the hospital untimely filed its complaint in the circuit court. Once a capital expenditure is approved by the Board and made by the CON holder, any question concerning the correctness of that expenditure is moot.

Condell Hospital v. Illinois Health Facilities Planning Board, 530 N.E.2d 217 (Ill. 1988).

Abstract: After health system agencies and area hospitals filed for and were denied rehearing in the granting of a certificate of need (CON) to a Medical school to build a hospital, hospitals filed for judicial review and agencies withdrew petitions. Court dismissed hospital's complaints and hospitals appealed. The Appellate Court reversed in part and remanded, and hospitals appealed again. The Supreme Court held that in order for finality regarding one party, parties needn't exhaust all administrative remedies. Affirmed and remanded.

Appellate Court of Illinois

Cathedral Rock of Granite City v. Illinois Health Facilities Planning Board, 720 N.E.2d 1113 (Ill. App. Ct. 1999).

Abstract: A competing nursing facility appealed the court's affirmation of the Illinois Health Facilities Planning Board's decision to grant a certificate of need for the construction of an 80-bed, long-term care nursing facility. The Appellate Court held that: (1) untimely submission of material to support the application was not reviewed the board, therefore the board's decision was not based on ex parte communication, (2) merely being competitors was not enough to constitute the competitor's protected due process, and (3) the manifest of evidence supported the Board's approval, thus the board's decision was not arbitrary and capricious. Affirmed.

Dimensions Medical Center v. Elmhurst Outpatient Surgery Center, 718 N.E.2d 249 (Ill. App. Ct. 1999).

Abstract: Medical care providers and the unsuccessful applicant for a certificate of need appealed the decision of the court that affirmed the Illinois Health Facilities Planning Board's decision to grant a certificate of need for the construction of an outpatient facility and an ambulatory surgical treatment center (ASTC) providing surgery services at the outpatient center. The Appellate Court held that: (1) due to the fact that the provider only performed pregnancy terminations, it lacked the standing to appeal, (2) by providing a full-range of ambulatory surgical services the other provider had standing to appeal, (3) the submission of a letter by the hospital post-board's decision was not in violation of any of the Board's rules or Administrative Procedure Act, and thus was fair, and (4) access to care would be improved with the building of a new ASTC and therefore the board's decision was fair and conventional.

Carle Found. v. Illinois Health Facilities Planning Board, 717 N.E.2d 447 (Ill. App. Ct. 1999).
Abstract: Operators of health care facilities appealed the decision of the court affirming the Illinois Health Facilities Planning Board's decision to issue a competing entity a certificate of need to build a ambulatory surgical treatment center. The Appellate Court held that: (1) the operator's requisite standing for challenging the board's decisions was not satisfied, and (2) there was not enough evidence against the Board's decision. Affirmed.

Access Center for Health v. Health Facilities Planning Board, 669 N.E.2d 668 (Ill. App. Ct. 1996).
Abstract: The health care provider appealed the court's decision to affirm the Board's denial of the provider's application for a certificate of necessity to construct an ambulatory surgical treatment center (ASTC). The Appellate Court held that: (1) by considering and relying the personal need of the hospital to relocate, a factor not intended by legislature, in weighing its review of the provider's application was not improper arbitration by the board, (2) by failing to consider relocation, the Board had not acted capriciously, (3) by opposing the recommendation of the Illinois Department of Public Health the Board had not acted capriciously, (4) the rights to claim the Board acted arbitrarily and capriciously based on insufficient required documentation were waived by the provider, (5) no violation of equal protection rights of provider was committed by the Board's rejection of the application, and (6) procedural due process was not violated by the Board's rejection of the application. Affirmed.

Springwood Associates v. Health Facilities Planning Board, 646 N.E.2d 1374 (Ill. App. Ct. 1995).
Abstract: The operator of a health center appealed the court's decision to uphold the Illinois Health Facilities Planning Board's granting of a certificate of need to the constructing an additional 28 beds to a nursing facility. The Appellate Court held that the Board's decision was not based upon adequate information required by its own regulations, and thus acted arbitrarily and capriciously. Reversed.

Charter Medical of Cook County Inc. v. HCA Health Services of Midwest Inc., 542 N.E.2d 82 (Ill. App. Ct. 1989).
Abstract: Psychiatric hospital and recent recipient of a certificate of need (CON) appealed the court's decision to affirm the awarding of the certificate of need to two other competing hospitals. The Appellate Court held that the Illinois Health Facilities Planning Board, in granting CONs to three hospitals and producing more beds than the projected bed need, was not in violation of the Planning Act. The Act compels the Board to consider other needs in addition to quantitative bed need, such as quality, availability and development. Affirmed.

Condell Hospital v. Health Facilities Planning Board, 515 N.E.2d 750 (Ill. App. Ct. 1987).
Abstract: After health system agencies and area hospitals filed for and were denied rehearing in the granting of a certificate of need (CON) to a Medical school to build a hospital, hospitals filed for judicial review and agencies withdrew petitions. Court dismissed hospital's complaints and hospitals appealed. The Appellate Court held that: (1) Board's decision to grant CON was final and therefore appealable, (2) administrative remedies had been exhausted by the hospitals, (3) hospitals evidenced requisite standing to challenge the board, (4) the untimely addition of another hospital was dismissed as party, and (5) the time period for seeking jurisdictional review provided by the limitation statutes were legally appropriate. Affirmed in part, reversed in part, and remanded.

Renal Care of Illinois Inc. v. Health Facilities Planning Board, 513 N.E.2d 32 (Ill. App. Ct. 1987).
Abstract: After seeking review and being denied a motion to stay the final decision of the final administrative decision of the Illinois Health Facilities Planning Board to grant the construction of a dialysis facility, the provider of renal care services filed for interlocutory appeal. The Appellate Court held that since the facility was already constructed and in operation the prohibition of construction of the facility was moot. Dismissed.

Manor Healthcare Corporation v. Northwest Community Hospital, 472 N.E.2d 492 (Ill. App. Ct. 1984).
Abstract: 151-bed Nursing home facility appealed the court's affirmation of the Illinois Health Facilities Planning Board's decision to grant the construction of a 200-bed nursing home within the same service area. The Appellate Court: (1) facility's requisite standing to seek judicial review was satisfied, (2) not enough evidence was supplied to reverse the grant of the certificate of need, and (3) adoption of the need determination planning area rule to conform with the Administrative Procedure Act was not required. Affirmed.

Feiwel OSINA et al., v. City of Chicago, 329 N.E.2d 498 (Ill. App. Ct. 1975).
Abstract: The owners of nursing homes and a bank appealed the decision of the court to uphold the zoning board's granting of a special use permit to construct a five-story building to be used as a nursing home. The Appellate Court held that: (1) the use of the words "manifest weight of the evidence" by the court was not controlling in the case, (2) plaintiffs provided sufficient evidence that they would be competent enough to meet the standards required by special permit, (3) residential character would not be retracted by the construction of the building, and (4) plaintiff possessed vested rights prior to zoning ordinance amendments and any withholding of permit would be unreasonable and arbitrary. Affirmed.

INDIANA

Court of Appeals of Indiana

Heritage House v. Bailey, 652 N.E.2d 69 (Ind. Ct. App. 1995).
Abstract: Nursing home requested certification as class action in a case that sought to declare the state's certificate of need (CON) program invalid concerning the requirement that all nursing homes participating in the Medicaid program have Medicaid certification for all beds. The Circuit Court, Washington County denied the certification of class action and entered summary judgment concerning the case. The nursing home appealed to the Court of Appeals, which held that: (1) other nursing homes were entitled to intervene as defendants, (2) class action was inappropriate in this matter, and (3) the CON program's authorization concerning Medicaid certification was supported by federal statue. Affirmed.

Martin County Nursing Center, Inc. v Medco Centers, Inc., 441 N.E. 2d 964 (Ind. Ct. App. 1982).
Abstract: Competitor appealed to the Circuit Court after certificate of need was granted to applicant. The Circuit Court reversed the ruling, and the applicant appealed to the Court of Appeals. The Court held that: (1) the hearing judge's decision was based on substantial evidence, and (2) the trail court did not have jurisdiction to reweigh evidence. Reversed.

IOWA

Supreme Court of Iowa

Greenwood Manor v. Iowa Department of Public Health, 641 N.W.2d 823 (Iowa 2002).
Abstract: A competitor appealed to the District Court when the State Health Facilities Council granted a certificate of need for a new facility. The District Court upheld the Council's ruling, and the competitor appealed to the Supreme Court. The Supreme Court held that: (1) the competitor lacked statutory right to appeal, (2) a contested hearing was not required for due process, and (3) evidence supported the Council's decision. Affirmed.

Mercy Health Center Division of Sisters of Mercy Health Corporation v. State Health Facilities Council, 360 N.W.2d 808 (Iowa 1995).

Abstract: The District Court reversed the decision of the Health Care Facilities council which denied the request to renovate an elderly care unit. The Council appealed and the Supreme Court held that: (1) the Council has the authority to examine cross subsidization of health dollars even thought it is not specifically listed under the statue governing certificate of need law, and (2) the Council's decision was not capricious or arbitrary and was sustained by substantial evidence. Reversed and remanded.

Mercy Health Center Division of Sisters of Mercy Health Corporation v. Iowa State Department of Health, 356 N.W.2d 200 (Iowa 1984).

Abstract: A health corporation appealed to the District Court after the Department of Health ruled that a project to establish a skilled nursing unit need to be reviewed for certificate of need purposes. The court reversed the decision of the Department, and an appeal was filed. The Supreme Court held that the health facility could not offer skilled nursing care under the designation of "temporary" while review was still pending.

Northbrook Residents Associates v. Iowa State Department of Health Office, 298 N.W.2d 330 (Iowa 1980).

Abstract: The District Court affirmed the ruling to grant certificates of need to two residential care facilities for mentally retarded adults. The residents association appealed to the Supreme Court which held that the association failed to: (1) indicate who its members were, (2) prove that it was a consumer, and (3) have establish standing in order to be able to challenge the ruling. Appeal dismissed.

Iowa State Department of Health v. Hertko, 282 N.W.2d 744 (Iowa 1979).

Abstract: A hospital appealed to the District Court, Polk County after it was prohibited by the State Department of Health (in conjunction with a competing hospital) from performing open heart surgery until it complied with certificate of need law. In the appeal, the hospital motioned to: (1) dismiss injunction, and (2) dismiss intervention petition made by county on the side of the Department and competitor. The District Court sustained these motions and ruled in favor of the hospital. In the appeal, the Supreme Court held that: (1) the trial court ruled correctly concerning the injunction, (2) the trial court incorrectly denied a hearing or trial to the Department and competitor, (3) the trail court incorrectly dismissed the intervention petition, and (4) the Agency's motion for discovery from hospital should have been granted. Affirmed in part, reversed in part and remanded.

Court of Appeals of Iowa

On with Life v. State Health Facilities Council, 532 N.W.2d 496 (Iowa Ct. App. 1995).

Abstract: The District Court , Polk County upheld the Council's position to deny an application for certificate of need to expand its facility. The facility appealed to the Court of Appeals which held that the Council's decision was not capricious or arbitrary and was sustained by substantial evidence. Affirmed.

KANSAS

Supreme Court of Kansas

Shawnee Mission Medical Center v. Kansas Department of Health and Environment, 685 P.2d 880 (Kan. 1984).

Abstract: Kansas Department of Health and Environment appealed the District Court's granting of relief to hospital to review the denial of a certificate of need for a freestanding alcoholism unit. The Supreme Court held that hospital had not provided cost containment evidence. Reversed.

In re Certificate of Need Application by Community Psychiatric Centers Inc. etc., 676 P.2d 107 (Kan. 1984).
Abstract: The Kansas Department of Health and Environment (KDHE) appealed the District Court's order granting of certificates of need to two psychiatric hospitals. The Supreme Court held that: (1) the error of reviewing concurrently the complete psychiatric hospital application with an incomplete psychiatric hospital application was harmless, and (2) KDHE's determinations to deny applications were supported by evidence. Reversed and remanded with instructions.

In re Review of Decision of Kansas Corporation Commission 659 P.2d 199 (Kan. 1983).
Abstract: Competitor appealed the District Court's affirmation of the Commission to issue a certificate of need (CON) to hospital for cancer treatment by radiation machine. The Supreme Court held that: (1) adequate evidence supporting the Commission's order was lacking, and (2) evidence supported that applicant failed to adequately assess the requirements for meeting "community need" and "cost containment" and would not be granted a certificate of need. Remanded with directions.

Olathe Community Hospital v. Kansas Corporation Commission, 652 P.2d 726 (Kan. 1982).
Abstract: Hospital filed a mandamus requesting determination of jurisdiction over reviewing applicable appeals against orders from the Secretary of the Kansas Department of Health and Environment (KDHE) in granting certificates of need pursuant to the Health Facilities Act. The Supreme Court held that all appeals from orders of the KDHE are under the jurisdiction of the district court and that the Kansas Corporation Commission lacked the jurisdiction to review these orders. Petition Granted.

In re Appeal of Banks, 630 P.2d 1131 (Kan. 1981).
Abstract: The Kansas Department of Health and Environment (KDHE) appealed the District Court's reversal of the Commission's affirmation of KDHE's decision to deny a certificate of need for a kidney dialysis center. The Supreme Court held that the Commission's assessment was validated by evidence that the proposed kidney dialysis center would not satisfy criteria of community need, financial feasibility, and cost containment. Reversed.

In re Certificate of Need Application etc., 630 P.2d 1136 (Kan. 1981).
Abstract: The Kansas Department of Health and Environment appealed the District Court's affirmation of the Kansas Corporation Commission's (KCC) issuance of a certificate of need to hospital for a six megavoltage linear accelerator. The Supreme Court held that: (1) as a final arbitrative tribunal, the KCC decision was appealable, and (2) substantial evidence supported KCC decision. Affirmed.

State ex rel. Metzler v. Sisters of Charity of Leavenworth Health Services Corporation, 605 P.2d 100 (Kan. 1980).
Abstract: State appealed the District Court's ruling to allow the hospital the right to implement a cardiac surgery unit without undergoing certificate of need (CON) review. The Supreme Court held that: (1) evidence indicated that project was less than the $150,000, the cutoff for requiring a CON; (2) the court did not err by excluding testimony of increased costs resulting from project implementation, and (3) certificate of architect could be admitted as evidence. Affirmed.

Pratt v. Board of County Commissioners, 597 P.2d 664 (Kan. 1979).
Abstract: Taxpayers appealed the District Court's ruling for the board of county commissioners in issuing general obligation bonds for construction of a new hospital. The Supreme Court held that: (1) the standing to challenge the validity of the certificate of need (CON) permitting injunctive relief prohibiting illegal levy of any tax, charge or assessment was evidenced by the taxpayers, (2) before election could be called and held on the

issuance of general obligation bonds it is required that the hospital obtain a CON, and (3) CON could not be extended for more than one year beyond initial approval period. Reversed with directions.

Suburban Medical Center v. Olathe Community Hospital, 597 P.2d 654 (Kan. 1979).
Abstract: Medical center appealed the District Court's affirmation of the decision of the statewide health coordinating council to grant a certificate of need (CON) to a community hospital for expansion. The Supreme Court held that though evidence supported the fact that project met requirements necessary for issuance of CON, but due to the fact that the majority of council members participated in ex parte communication and considered extra record evidence renders their approval invalid. Decision of council vacated and District Court's judgment reversed in part and affirmed in part.

Olathe Hospital Foundation Inc. v. Extendicare Inc., 539 P.2d 1 (Kan. 1975).
Abstract: Operators appealed the District Court's affirmation of the appeals panel's granting of a certificate of need for construction of a new hospital. The Supreme Court held that: (1) application was complete, (2) collateral attack on the panel's decision based on the composition of panel was inappropriate, (3) rejecting testimony was not an abuse of discretion by the court, and (4) though the panel's deliberation session was contrary to the "open public meetings" Act, it was not enough violation to render the panel's decision invalid. Affirmed.

Extendicare Inc. v. State Coordinating Council for Health Planning, 532 P.2d 1119 (Kan. 1975).
Abstract: Foreign Corporation, Physicians, and Physician association appealed the District Court's affirmation of an order stating that under the Regional Health Programs Act they lacked the statutory rights to appeal the health planning agency's decision to grant a certificate of need to a medical center. The Supreme Court held that though the foreign corporation did possess a certificate of need for a construction of a competing hospital, all appellants were not health facilities and thus lacked standing to appeal. Affirmed.

KENTUCKY

Supreme Court of Kentucky

Humana of Kentucky Inc. v. North Kansas City Hospitals Inc., 751 S.W.2d 369 (Ky. 1988).
Abstract: Trial court dismissed request for a writ of mandamus compelling State Health Planning Council to prohibit competitor's pediatric services until proper certification, a decision which was later reversed by the Court of Appeals. Upon review, the Supreme Court held that it was within the hospital's rights, due to its standing, to request for hearing to assess whether the competing hospital's certificate of need (CON) was enough to encompass pediatric services and, if not, to encourage the assessment of the issuance of additional CONs.

Court of Appeals of Kentucky

Commonwealth of Kentucky v. Family Home Health Care, Inc., 98 S.W.3d 524 (Ky. Ct. App. 2003).
Abstract: Appeal from a judgment reversing a final decision of the Cabinet. The Cabinet had affirmed an advisory opinion issued by the certificate of need office. That opinion allowed a healthcare provider to draw blood in conjunction with its license to provide mobile IV services. Competitor claimed that this procedure exceeded the scope of the healthcare provider's license. The Court finds that the procedure was a legitimate function of the healthcare provider's license and rules in favor of the Cabinet.

ACSR Inc. v. Cabinet for Health Services, 32 S.W.3d 96 (Ky. Ct. App. 2000).
Abstract: Operator of existing facility appealed the court's affirmation of the Administrative Law Judge's (ALJ) approval of the Cabinet for Health services acceptance of the application for a certificate of need to establish an adult day care health program. The Court of Appeals held that: (1) the Cabinet did not exceed it's authority in establishing presumptions of need for the proposed facility for which no rules, standards, and review criteria are indicated in the State health plan, and (2) as emergency regulations, the cabinet properly enacted these rules. Affirmed.

Cabinet for Human Resources Interim Office of Health Planning and Certification v. Jewish Hospital Healthcare Services, 932 S.W.2d 388 (Ky. Ct. App. 1996).
Abstract: The interim office appealed the court's reversal of the office's decision to require a certificate of need (CON) for the addition of a sixth cardiac catheterization lab in hospital. The Court of Appeals held that the addition was not an "addition of hospital service" and therefore did not require a CON. Affirmed.

St. Luke Hospital v. Health Policy Board., 913 S.W.2d 1 (Ky. Ct. App. 1996).
Abstract: Hospital appealed the Court's ruling that seeking exemption from certificate of need (CON) laws for its neonatal care facility was unconstitutional. The Court of Appeals held that the exemption was not a constitutional violation under the time-limited statutory exemption from CON and the fact that the neonatal facility cost less than $600,000. Reversed.

Jewish Hospital v. Baptist Health Care System, 902 S.W.2d 844 (Ky. Ct. App. 1995).
Abstract: Hospital appealed the court's upholding of the interim office's granting of another hospital's application for a certificate of need (CON) to add operating rooms. The Court of Appeals held that CON hearings only needed to be held at the request of affected person to satisfy due process. A regulation allowing the withdrawal of such requests did not conflict with the statute and did not violate the affected person's rights to due process. Affirmed.

Certificate of Need Medical Personnel Pool v. Management Registry, 869 S.W.2d 42 (Ky. Ct. App. 1993).
Abstract: The Commission for Health Economics Control in Kentucky (CHECK) and competing nursing service appealed the court's reversal of CHECK's requiring a nursing service to obtain certificate of need (CON) before providing private duty nursing services. The Court of Appeals held that CHECK did not err by enforcing CON laws on the nursing service and a CON was indeed necessary. Reversed with directions.

Commission for Health Economics Control v. Medical Consultants Imaging Company, 844 S.W.2d 437 (Ky. Ct. App. 1992).
Abstract: Commission appealed the court's reversal of its decision to require a certificate of need (CON) for establishing a mobile single photon emission computed tomography (SPECT) unit. The Court of Appeals held that the SPECT unit did not require a CON because it was not an establishment of the "health facility." Affirmed.

Starks v. Kentucky Health Facilities, 684 S.W.2d 5 (Ky. Ct. App. 1984).
Abstract: Resident appealed the Court's affirmation of the state agency's issuance of a certificate of need (CON) to the construction of a new hospital. The Court of Appeals held that the applicant met the criteria for the issuance of the CON. Affirmed.

Cabinet for Human Resources v. Women's Health Services, 878 S.W.2d 806 (Ky. Ct. App. 1994).
Abstract: The Cabinet for Human Resources appealed the court's dismissal of their complaint enjoining Women's Health Services, a unlicensed ambulatory surgery center that required a certificate of need (CON) for its operations, from operating without proper certification. The Court of Appeals held that substantial evidence indicating that Women's Health Services operated primarily as an ambulatory surgery center was presented and thus indicated the requiring of a CON. Reversed and remanded.

Baptist Hospital Inc. v. Humana of Kentucky Inc., 672 S.W.2d 669 (Ky. Ct. App. 1984).
Abstract: Hospital appealed the Court's affirmation of the Health Facilities and Health Services Certificate of Need and Licensure Board's approval of a certificate of need to build a second hospital. The Court of Appeals held that: (1) the proper subject of an appeal was the issue of fact of whether the Board's decision was consistent with the State Health Plan, not the declaratory judgment, and (2) administrative remedies were not exhausted and therefore it could not seek relief in courts. Affirmed.

Robinson v. Kentucky Health Facilities, 600 S.W.2d 491 (Ky. Ct. App. 1980).
Abstract: License holder appealed the Court's upholding of the Health Facilities and Health Services Certificate of Need and Licensure Board's decision to deny the holder relicensure. The Court of Appeals held that by denying the opportunity to review evidence entered by the hearing officer and enter exceptions with the Board, the holder's rights of due process was violated. Reversed and remanded.

LOUISIANA

Supreme Court of Louisiana

Greenbriar Nursing Home v. Pilley, 637 So.2d 429 (La. 1994).
Abstract: Certificate of need (CON) holders for nursing homes applied for supervisory/remedial writs after District court granted the same writs to the Department of Health and Hospitals and affirmed their decision of exception of no right of action on the issue of the CON review for a third party. The Supreme Court granted rights and remanded to the Court of Appeals which held reversed the decision of the Supreme Court. The Supreme Court then held that the right to seek judicial review belonged to the nursing homes and granted them certiorari. Court of Appeal judgment reversed, exception of no right of action overruled, and remanded.

Court of Appeal of Louisiana

Greenbriar Nursing Home v. Pilley, 623 So.2d 94 (La. Ct. App. 1993).
Abstract: Certificate of need (CON) holders for nursing homes applied for supervisory/remedial writs after District court granted the same writs to the Department of Health and Hospitals and affirmed their decision of exception of no right of action on the issue of the CON review for a third party. The Supreme Court granted rights and remanded to the Court of Appeals which held holders could not challenge the third party's CON review due to their lack of standing. Reversed.

Hospital Corporation of America v. Robinson, 499 So.2d 246 (La. Ct. App. 1986).
Abstract: After Hospital and Hospital Corporations denial of a certificate of need for the construction of a new 166-bed hospital first by the Louisiana Department of Health and Human Resources (LDHHR) that was affirmed upon a fair hearing and a re-hearing, and then upon another appeal in which a second hospital intervened, the District Court also affirmed LDHHR's denial. The Hospital appealed again and the Court of Appeal

held that: (1) timely notice of denial by LDDHR was issued, (2) LDHHR was not required to render a decision after 45 days because motion for summary judgment was not "fair hearing", (3) failure of the hearing officer to admit 1990 population projections into evidence was a harmless error, and (4) hearing officer's findings were supported by substantial evidence. Affirmed.

Psychiatric Institutes of America Inc. v. Guissinger, 464 So.2d 7 (La. Ct. App. 1984).
Abstract: Opponent health agency appealed the District Court's dismissal of its challenge of the state-designated planning agency's authorization of providing another health care provider federal reimbursement for its capital expenditures. The Court of Appeal held that the Secretary of the Department of Health could enter into reimbursement agreements with states, and since opponent participated in the review process and public hearings, it had standing to make allegations against the agency. Reversed and remanded.

MAINE

Supreme Judicial Court of Maine

Magnetic Resonance Technologies Ltd. Partnership v. Commissioner Maine Department of Human Services, 652 A.2d 655 (Me. 1995).
Abstract: The partnership appealed the Court's affirmation of the Commissioner of Department of Human Service's denial of an application for a certificate of need (CON) for a mobile magnetic resonance imaging (MRI) machine. The Supreme Judicial Court held that: (1) Commissioner did not err in remanding the application due to lack of information, (2) despite the submission of an amended application, the initial application was not improperly considered, (3) the one-and-a-half-month delay in rendering a decision did not violate the partnership's procedural rights, (4) failing to discuss the division staff analysis was not an error on the Commissioner's part, and (5) Commissioner's decision was substantiated by lack of requisite evidence in record that proved satisfaction of public need and economic feasibility. Affirmed.

Aroostook Home Care Agency Inc. v. Commissioner of Human Services, 552 A.2d 538 (Me. 1988).
Abstract: Appellant took action against the Court's affirmation of the Maine Commissioner of Health Services decision to issue to certificate of need (CON) for a proprietary home health agency to establish branch offices in a statewide project. The Supreme Judicial Court held that: (1) substantial evidence indicated that public need would be addressed by the installment of the project, and (2) approving a single CON for all five-phases was within the Commissioner's jurisdiction. Affirmed.

Bradbury Memorial Nursing Home v. Tall Pines Manor Associates, 485 A.2d 634 (Me. 1984).
Abstract: Nursing Home appealed the decision of the Court in affirming the Maine Department of Human Services' awarding of a certificate of need (CON) for the construction of a nursing home. The Supreme Judicial Court held that the Department's failure to render decisions on any of the competing applications within the 150-day review period was not enough to render its issuance of CON invalid. Affirmed.

Hale v. Petit Law Docket, 438 A.2d 226 (Me. 1981).
Abstract: Second Applicants appealed the Court's affirmation of the Commissioner of Department of Human Services' decision to grant a certificate of need for the construction of a nursing home to the first applicants while denying issuance to the second applicants. The Supreme Judicial Court held that: (1) Administrative Procedure Act did not apply, (2) procedures were provided adequately, (3) evidence of being prejudiced by lack of cross-

examination was not substantially presented by second applicants, (4) right to appellate review was forfeited due to second applicants failure to properly raise issue, (5) Commissioner's letter served as sufficient notice of the grounds upon which the decision was based and thus second applicants qualified for judicial review, (6) department utilized no improper criteria in rendering a decision, and (7) by denying motion to consider additional evidence, the Court did not abuse its discretion. Affirmed.

Superior Court of Maine

Portland Surgery Center, LLC. v. Department of Human Services, 2004 Me. Super. LEXIS 47 (Me. Super. Ct. 2004).

Abstract: Ambulatory surgery center alleges that the Department has refused to timely act on its certificate of need (CON) application and asks the Court to issue an order requiring the Dept. to make a decision. The date the Department deems a CON application complete is the date the statutory time table begins. The Department's decision was due 180 days from the date it certified that the application was complete.

St. Joseph Hospital v. Kevin Concannon, 2001 WL 1715945 (Me. Super. Ct. 2001).

Abstract: The Central Maine Medical Center petitioned for court to order a determination by the Maine Department of Human Services on its application for a certificate of need for a cardiac surgery center. The motion for an expedited hearing was granted and the petition will also be granted, in part, after the record and evidential submissions have been reviewed.

Central Maine Medical Center v. Kevin Concannon, 2000 WL 33671789 (Me. Super. Ct. 2000).

Abstract: The Central Maine Medical Center petitioned for court to order a determination by the Maine Department of Human Services on its application for a certificate of need (CON) for a cardiac surgery center. The motion for an expedited hearing was granted and the petition will also be granted, in part, after the record and evidential submissions have been reviewed.

Homewood v. State, 1998 Me. Super. LEXIS 48, (Me. Super. Ct. 1998).

Abstract: The petitioner filed action for judicial review on the Department's denial of relief under the Specialty Facility Exemption under the Department's Principles of Reimbursement. The Court held that the commissioner did not indicate clear standards of distinguishing a facility from being a specialty facility from a regular facility and thus did not have grounds to deny relief. Reversed, appeal sustained, Department decision vacated, and remanded.

MARYLAND

Court of Appeals of Maryland

Medstar Health v. Maryland Health Care Commission, 827 A.2d 83 (Md. 2003).

Abstract: Hospital challenged regulation amendment claiming that the regulation conflicted with the commission's statutory authority and violated the Commerce Clause of the U.S. Constitution. The amendment placed a cap on the number of open heart operations that a hospital may perform. This amendment is contrary to the Commission's own policies of promoting a small number of high volume programs rather than a large number of lower volume programs. The amendment is unlawful.

Adventist Healthcare Midatlantic v. Suburban Hospital, 711 A.2d 158 (Md. 1998).
Abstract: Opposing hospital and Commission appealed the Court's reversal of the Maryland Health Resources Planning Commission's denial of a certificate of need (CON) for the commencement of open heart surgery services. The Court of Special Appeals and the Court of Appeals held that: (1) applications were properly denied, and (2) the contested CON case proceedings were inappropriate for the establishing of new need projections in state health plan. Reversed and remanded.

Catonsville Nursing Home v. Loveman, 709 A.2d 749 (Md. 1998).
Abstract: Tenant and commission appealed the court's ruling that the right to seek approval over the beds operating as a convalescent center belonged to the landlord. The Court of Appeals held that: (1) certificate of need exemptions for projects completed before June 1, 1978 is granted to the person or entity exempted, and (2) rights to exemption were abandoned/waived by landlord. Reversed and remanded with directions.

Southern Maryland Hospital Center Inc. v. Ft. Washington Community Hospital Inc., 519 A.2d 727 (Md. 1987).
Abstract: Objecting hospitals appealed the affirmation of the Court of Maryland State Health Resources Commission's issuance of a "conditional" certificate of need (CON) to a hospital for constructing an addition to its 308 bed facility, a decision that was reversed by the Court of Special Appeals and was granted certiorari. The Court of Appeals affirmed certiorari and held that the Commission exceeded the scope of its jurisdiction in granting the CON. Affirmed.

Johns Hopkins Hospital Inc. v. Insurance Commissioner, 488 A.2d 942 (Md. 1985).
Abstract: Hospital appealed the court's affirmation of the Insurance Commissioner's approval of an insurance plan designed to encourage "low-cost" hospital usage for non-emergency in-patient care. The Court of Special Appeals, the Court of Appeals held that the Insurance Commissioner was acting within the scope of his jurisdiction as appointed to him by the Health Services Cost Review Commission or the Maryland Health Services Planning Commission. Affirmed.

Court of Special Appeals of Maryland

Carriage Hill-Cabin John Inc. v. Maryland Health Resources Planning Commission, 724 A.2d 745 (Md. Ct. Spec. App. 1999).
Abstract: Provider appealed the court's affirmation of the Maryland Health Resources Planning Commission's decision to award certificate of need (CON) to competitor for developing new nursing home beds while denying the provider's application. The Court of Special Appeals held that: (1) the court only had jurisdiction to review the Commission's decision, (2) Commission adequately considered and addressed hearing officer's findings in rendering a decision, (3) Commission properly assessed "more effective alternatives," (4) county health department's position was adequately weighed into the CON decision, and (5) inappropriate sale of CON was not involved in corporate reorganization. Affirmed.

Loveman v. Catonsville Nursing Home, 691 A.2d 693 (Md. Ct. Spec. App. 1996).
Abstract: Owner appealed the dismissal of its action for declaratory judgment by the court against nursing home operator's right to certificate of need (CON) only by virtue of lease. The Court of Special Appeals held that it did not have the jurisdiction to decide status of CON. Jurisdiction remained with Maryland Health Resources Planning Commission. Affirmed.

Maryland General Hospital v. Maryland Health Resources Planning Commission, 653 A.2d 1029 (Md. Ct. Spec. App. 1995).

Abstract: Unsuccessful applicants appealed the court's affirmation of the Maryland Health Resources Planning Commission's decision to award certificate of need to establish an open-heart surgery and coronary angiography unit to competitors while rejecting appellant's application. The Court of Special Appeals held that: (1) consideration of documents provided by successful applicant's accountants did not need to be taken into account, (2) not ordering agency to take additional evidence was not an error by the court, and (3) Commission's decision was supported by substantial evidence. Affirmed.

Changing Point Inc. v. Maryland Health Resources Planning Commission, 589 A.2d 502 (Md. Ct. Spec. App. 1991).

Abstract: Competitor appealed the court's affirmation of the Maryland Health Resources Planning Commission's decision to allow the construction of a new addiction treatment facility. The Court of Special Appeals held that: (1) evidence established need, and (2) no financial control or interest over the facility would belong to physicians involved in settlement agreements that would repay amounts overbilled. Affirmed.

Sinai Hospital of Baltimore Inc. v. Maryland Health Resources Planning Commission, 509 A.2d 1202 (Md. Ct. Spec. App. 1986).

Abstract: Two hospitals appealed the court's affirmation of the Maryland Health Resources Planning Commission's denial of their separate applications for certificates of need to perform open-heart surgery. The Court of Appeals held that Commission's decision was supported by evidence. Affirmed.

Perini Services Inc. v. Maryland Health Resources Planning Commission, 506 A.2d 1207 (Md. Ct. Spec. App. 1986).

Abstract: Nursing home appealed the court's affirmation of the Maryland Health Resources Planning Commission's denial of their application of a certificate of need to build a nursing home and adult day care center. The Court of Special Appeals held that: (1) Commission's determination that proposal was inconsistent to government health plan was supported by evidence, (2) consistency with health plan did not indicate need, and (3) Commission did not unconstitutionally create new criteria by using present and future data in the review process. Affirmed.

Ft. Washington Community Hospital Inc. v. Southern Maryland Hospital Center, 505 A.2d 117 (Md. Ct. Spec. App. 1986).

Abstract: Objecting hospitals appealed the court's affirmation of the Maryland Health Resources Planning Commission's issuance of a "conditional" certificate of need (CON) for constructing an addition to 208-bed facility. The Court of Special Appeals held that: (1) for a single commissioner to be designated to act as a "committee" for the review application was valid, (2) commissioner's decision was in conflict with statutory mandate by failing to assess specific capital expenditures that would occur under the CON, and (3) Commission's decision to grant CON was not supported by substantial evidence. Reversed and remanded.

Doctors' Hospital of Prince George's County v. Maryland Health Resources Planning Commission, 501 A.2d 1324 (Md. Ct. Spec. App. 1986).

Abstract: Hospital appealed the court's affirmation of the Maryland Health Resources Planning Commission's denial of their application of a certificate of need (CON) to increase its bed capacity. The Court of Special Appeals held that: (1) substantial evidence supported the Commission's decision, (2) Commission did not engage in illegal delay of rendering CON decision, (3) hospital was not subject to arbitrary discrimination; and (4) "review by ambush" method was not used by Commission. Affirmed.

MASSACHUSETTS

Supreme Judicial Court of Massachusetts

Shoolman v. Health Facilities Appeals Board, 533 N.E. 2d 632 (Mass. 1989).

Abstract: Taxpayer groups appealed the affirmation of the court on the decision of the Massachusetts Health Facilities Appeals Board to grant certificate of need for the hospital's construction of three additional buildings. The Supreme Judicial Court held that: (1) the "hotel floors" that was excluded from the proposal was valid, (2) bed need determination was valid, and (3) a defective notice was not grounds for reversal. Affirmed.

Lahey Clinic Foundation, Inc. v. Health Facilities Appeals Board, 380 N.E. 2d 675 (Mass. 1978).

Abstract: When the Health Facilities Appeals Board dismissed Corporation's appeal from the department's approval of increases in gross square feet and cost, Corporation, which enjoyed a "determination of need" (DON), filed for declaratory relief. Taxpayers called for enforcement of DON and town and Board intervened. The court dismissed all proceedings before the Board, and faced appeals. The Supreme Judicial court held that: (1) the Board' jurisdiction over the department's claim that action was an extension of DON was not conclusive, (2) court judge erred in prematurely dismissing proceedings before the board, (3) taxpayers failed to exhaust administrative remedies and thus were not entitled to judicial review, (4) Supreme Judicial Court will grant declaratory relief, despite failure to exhaust administrative remedies, and (5) the approval of increase in cost and gross square footage did not create a new DON. Reversed and Remanded.

Appeals Court of Massachusetts

Shoolman v. Health Facilities Appeals Board, 314 N.E.2d 742 (Mass. App. Ct. 1980).

Abstract: Taxpayers appealed the affirmations of the Superior Court and Massachusetts Health Facilities Appeals Board of the Department of Public Health's granting of a determination of need (DON) to a hospital for construction of a new ambulatory care center. The Appeals Court held that: (1) subject matter jurisdiction over the matter belonged to the trial court, (2) taxpayers possessed standing requisite for filing action, and (3) DON determination did not require a regional study. Modified and affirmed as modified.

Brookline v. Medical Area Service Corporation, (Mass. App. Ct. 1979).

Abstract: Plaintiff's appealed the court's granting of the defendant's motion to dismiss action to enjoin construction of a total energy plant and to impose a determination of need. The Appeals Court held that: (1) total energy plant was not a "part of a health care facility" and therefore not subject to statutory prohibition, and (2) order issued that dismissal vacated and replaced with a judgment determining that prior regulatory approval was not required by the total energy plant. Affirmed as modified.

MICHIGAN

Supreme Court of Michigan

Public Health Department v. Rivergate Manor, 550 N.W.2d 515 (Mich. 1996).
Abstract: The defendant appealed the Court's granting of superintending control of the Michigan Department of Public Health over the Michigan Certificate of Need Board in granting modifications over the certificate of need issued for the construction of a nursing home. The Supreme Court held that: (1) jurisdiction remained the circuit court's, (2) it was within the scope of the Board's jurisdiction to modify the certificate, (3) Board was not in compliance with the Administrative Procedure Act, and (4) the prevention from licensing in what may have been an over-bedded area provided substantial evidence for the Department's actions to be without laches or estoppel. Affirmed.

West Bloomfield Hospital v. Certificate of Need Board, 550 N.W.2d 223 (Mich. 1996).
Abstract: Hospitals appealed the Court's affirmation of the denials of the certificates by the Michigan Department of Public Health and Certificate of Need Board. The Court of Appeals reversed and ordered circuit court to award certificates of need, against which the Department and Board appealed. The Supreme Court held that it was not necessary for the Department to wait for the state medical facilities plan to be in effect in order to review hospitals' applications. Reversed and remanded to the Court of Appeals.

Court of Appeals of Michigan

Genesis Center v. Financial and Insurance Services Commissioner, 633 N.W.2d 834 (Mich. Ct. App. 2001).
Abstract: Owners appealed the Court's granting of a summary disposition in favor of the Commissioner after a non-profit corporation denied request to become a participating provider. The Court of Appeals held that: (1) administrative remedies were not exhausted, (2) therefore, court lacked jurisdiction over the matter, and (3) no actual controversy was presented in the claim. Affirmed.

Huron Valley Hospital Inc. v. Michigan Department of Public Health, 284 N.W.2d 758 (Mich. Ct. App. 1997).
Abstract: Hospital appealed the court order that prevented the Michigan Department of Health from granting the hospital any application for certificate of need for acute care hospital by dissolving an injunction. The Court of Appeals held that by dissolving the injunction was not an abuse of the trial court's discretion. Affirmed.

West Bloomfield Hospital v. Certificate of Need Board, 567 N.W.2d 1 (Mich. Ct. App. 1997).
Abstract: The Michigan Department of Public Health and the Michigan Certificate of Need Board appealed the Court of Appeals' reversal of the circuit Court's decision to affirm the denials of certificates of need by the Department and the Board. The Supreme Court then ruled to reverse the ruling and remanded. The Court of Appeals held that: (1) using the acute-care-bed-need methodology to determine future need could be excused, (2) the Attorney General was not acting with prejudicial conflict by representing both the Department and the Board, and (3) except one hospital, all evidence supported the Board and Department's denial of the certificates. Affirmed in part, reversed in part, and remanded.

W.A. Foote Memorial Hospital v. Michigan Department of Public Health, 534 N.W.2d 206 (Mich. Ct. App. 1995).
Abstract: The Michigan Department of Public Health appealed the Court's order to prevent the department from applying new promulgated standards to hospitals' applications for certificates of need (CON) for open heart surgery units, denied Department's request for summary disposition, and granted the motion for the second hospital to intervene. The Court of Appeals held that: (1) Circuit Court lacked subject matter over jurisdiction because hospitals failed to exhaust all administrative remedies,(2) under old CON regulations, when

hospitals submitted their applications, hospitals did not possess the vested rights to have their applications reviewed so due process was not violated, (3) it was not in the Circuit Court's jurisdiction to grant hospital the right to intervene, and (4) entitlement to writ of mandamus was denied to both hospitals. Reversed.

West Bloomfield Hospital v. Certificate of Need Board, 528 N.W.2d 744 (Mich. Ct. App. 1995).
Abstract: Various hospitals appealed the Court's decision to affirm the Board's granting of one certificate of need (CON) and denial of all other applicants, after the Department had denied all applications. The Court of Appeals held that the Department was improperly acting outside of its jurisdictional scope and failing to utilize the health facilities plan as required when granting CONs. Reversed and remanded.

Michigan Affiliated Healthcare System v. Department of Public Health, 531 N.W.2d 722 (Mich. Ct. App. 1994).
Abstract: The plaintiff appealed the Court's decision to dismiss the action of the plaintiff to challenge the decision of the Michigan Department of Public Health in granting a certificate of need (CON) to hospital for cardiac catheterization and open-heart surgical services. The Court of Appeals held that: (1) as competitors, the hospitals did not have standing to challenge Department's decision, (2) under the taxpayer's suit, the hospitals lacked standing, and (3) under constitutional provision for administrative agencies, the hospitals lacked standing as well. Affirmed.

Downriver Nursing Association v. Department of Public Health, 484 N.W.2d 748 (Mich. Ct. App. 1992).
Abstract: Certificate of need holders appealed the Court's decision to grant summary disposition to the Michigan Department of Public Health (MDPH) after their denial of the holders request to amend the certificate. The Court of Appeals held that: (1) the protective due process rights included the certificate of need process, but (2) MDPH's denial of amendment was not overstepping hospitals' due process rights. Affirmed.

Pontiac Osteopathic Hospital v. Department of Public Health, 403 N.W.2d 82 (Mich. Ct. App. 1986).
Abstract: Plaintiffs appealed the Court's decision to grant the Michigan Department of Public Health (MDPH) summary disposition in their denial of the plaintiff's application for a certificate of need to construct an acute care hospital and challenged the MDPH's acceptance of another facility's application. The Court of Appeals held that: (1) plaintiffs lacked standing to challenge MDPH's acceptance of the other applicant, and (2) the Certificate of Need Board was an appropriate forum for the plaintiff's complaints on the denial of their application. Affirmed.

Huron Valley Hospital Inc. v. Michigan State Health Facilities Commission, 312 N.W.2d 422 (Mich. Ct. App. 1981).
Abstract: The Michigan Health Commission appealed the court's reversal of their decision to deny the application of a nonprofit corporation the certificate of need to build a hospital and ordered the Department to issue to certificate. The Court of Appeals held that: (1) Department's evaluation improperly used unpromulgated criteria and was in violation of statute procedures, (2) rights of due process was denied due to Department's failure to grant comparative hearings to both applicants, and (3) court was not in err to issue an order to grant certificate of need. Affirmed.

Greenbriar Convalescent Center Inc. v. Department of Public Health, 310 N.W.2d 812 (Mich. Ct. App. 1981).
Abstract: Michigan Department of Public Health appealed the granting of declaratory relief to a nursing home operator and owner by the Court. The operator and owner in response applied for dismissal of this motion. The Court of Appeals held that: (1) under the Administrative Procedures Act the trial court did not have jurisdiction over the determination of the Department over the proposed addition to a nursing home, and (2) the federal Social Security Act exempted the Department's decision from review. Reversed and remanded.

MINNESOTA

Supreme Court of Minnesota

Benedictine Sisters Benevolent Association v. Pettersen, 299 N.W.2d 738 (Minn. 1980).
Abstract: Commissioner of health appealed the order and writ of mandamus from the Court deciding to grant the applicant a certificate of need primarily due to the fact that the commissioner did not render a decision within the 30-day period specified by the statute. The Supreme Court held that the time period requirement in the statute is directory only and the commissioner's decision still holds whether or not it was made in that time frame. Reversed.

Minnesota State Board of Health v. Governor's Certificate of Need Appeal Board, 230 N.W.2d 176 (Minn. 1975).
Abstract: Nursing homes appealed the Court's decision to reverse the orders to the Minnesota State Board of Health (MSBH) of the Certificate of Need Appeal Board (CONAP) to issue certificates of need to nursing homes. The Supreme Court held that MSBH did not have adequate standing to petition for review on decisions of the CONAP in district court. Reversed.

Monk & Excelsior Inc. v. Minnesota State Board of Health, 225 N.W.2d 821 (Minn. 1975).
Abstract: Builders of nursing home appealed the Court's decision ordering them to obtain a certificate of need (CON) for nursing home. The Supreme Court held that substantial commitment and activity in project commencement were undertaking prior to the CON act and therefore the project was exempt from CON review. Reversed and remanded.

Ebenezer Society v. Minnesota State Board of Health, 223 N.W.2d 385 (Minn. 1974).
Abstract: The Minnesota Board of Health issued a writ requesting a change of venue to Hennepin County. The Supreme Court held that: (1) despite the filing time being outside the time allotted for appeal, the writ was filed in a timely matter, and (2) since actions were made against a "public officer" in a county wherein officer's offices are located, and the Board is deemed to be a "public officer," venue change is allowed under the venue statute. Writ issued and order staying proceedings discharged.

Court of Appeals of Minnesota

North Memorial Medical Center v. Minnesota Department of Health, 423 N.W. 2d 737 (Minn. Ct. App. 1988).
Abstract: Hospitals appealed the Commissioner of Department of Health's decision to deny its application for license to extend its service area. The Court of Appeals held that on grounds that application would duplicate services and cause deleterious competition the commissioner was not in err in denying the application. Affirmed.

Therapeutic Community Residence v. Minnesota Department of Health, 351 N.W.2d 647 (Minn. Ct. App. 1984).
Abstract: Applicant appealed the hearing examiner's affirmation of the Minnesota Commissioner of Department of Health's decision to deny a certificate of need (CON) for construction of an eight-bed facility for the mentally retarded. The Court of Appeals held that there was unsubstantial evidence to support examiner's findings. Reversed.

Rush City Hospital v. Sandstone Area Hospital, 326 N.W.2d 638 (Minn. Ct. App. 1982).
Abstract: Area hospital appealed the Court's decision to grant competing hospital's motion for declaratory judgment on the exemption of hospital from having to obtain a certificate of need (CON) for the establishment of a

satellite hospital facility. The Supreme Court held that exemption laws, though validly passed, were not yet effective and hence subject to local statutes governing certificate of approval of special laws. Reversed.

MISSISSIPPI

Supreme Court of Mississippi

Attala County Board of Supervisors d/b/a Attala Care Center v. Mississippi State Department of Health, 867 So.2d 1019 (Miss. 2004).

Abstract: Competitor appeals certificate of need (CON) approval for construction of nursing home. Where competing applicants apply for the same CON, the commission rates the applicants on a point scale. Competitor alleges that the Commission acted arbitrarily and capriciously when evaluating the applicants' CON applications. Appellate court finds that the Commission's decision was supported by substantial evidence.

Jackson HMA, Inc. v. Mississippi State Department of Health, 822 So.2d 968 (Miss. 2002).

Abstract: Competitor appeals certificate of need (CON) approval for construction of medical office building. Competitor alleges that the Department should have evaluated the application in accordance with the criteria appropriate to ambulatory surgery centers (ASC) because one of the building's tenants will be an ASC. The court does not have the authority to determine whether there is a need for a particular service. The court may only determine whether the Department's decision was supported by substantial evidence. The Department's decision was based on the 1999 State Health Plan and the CON Review Manual general criteria. Therefore, the decision was not arbitrary and capricious and supported by substantial evidence. The Department's decision must be upheld.

Jeff Anderson Regional Medical Center v. Mississippi State Department of Health, 798 So.2d 1264 (Miss. 2001).

Abstract: Competitor sought judicial review at the Chancery Court, Hinds County after the Department of Health granted another hospital a certificate of need (CON)for a new cardiac hospital. The Court affirmed the ruling and the competitor appealed to the Supreme Court. The Court held that: (1) the Department of Health based its decision on substantial evidence, and specifically (2) the cost-containment purposes of CON laws were taken into consideration when ruling. Affirmed.

Cain v. Mississippi State Department of Health, 767 So.2d 207 (Miss. 2000).

Abstract: Denied applicant appealed to the Chancery Court, Hinds County after certificate of need (CON) was granted to competitor. The Chancery Court, Hinds County affirmed the decision, and the denied applicant appealed tot eh Supreme Court. The Court held that: (1) the Department of Health's ruling was not arbitrary and capricious, and (2) a statute permitted the ruling. Affirmed.

Delta Regional Medical Center v. Mississippi State Department of Health, 759 So.2d 1174 (Miss. 1999).

Abstract: Denied applicants appealed to the Chancery Court, Hinds County after certificate of need was granted to competitor for cardiac catheterization. The applicants appealed again after the Chancery Court affirmed. The Supreme Court held that: (1) denied parties did not prove that the Department was in error, (2) it is appropriate to use market share methodology in determining the minimum permissible population served by the hospital, and (2) the Department was not arbitrary and capricious when ruling and had demonstrated in its decision process impact on existing providers and need for services in the area had been considered before ruling. Affirmed.

Biloxi HMA Inc. v. Singing River Hospital, 743 So.2d 979 (Miss. 1999).
Abstract: Denied applicant appealed to the Chancery Court, Hinds County after certificate of need was granted to competitor for ambulatory surgical center. The approved applicant after the Chancery Court reversed and remanded the ruling. The Supreme Court held that: (1) was supported by substantial evidence, (2) was not arbitrary and capricious, (3) had administrative authority to rule, and (4) did not violate statutory or constitutional rights. Reversed and rendered.

Mississippi State Department of Health v. Natchez Community Hospital, 743 So.2d 973 (Miss. 1999).
Abstract: Denied applicant appealed to the Chancery Court, Hinds County after certificate of need was granted to physician establishing a freestanding ambulatory surgery center. The physician and the Department of Health appealed after the Chancery Court reversed its decision. The Supreme Court held that the Department of Health's decision lacked substantial evidence to support need. Affirmed.

St. Dominic-Jackson Memorial Hospital v. Mississippi State Department of Health, 728 So.2d 81 (Miss. 1998).
Abstract: Competitors appealed to the Chancery Court, Hinds County after certificate of need was granted to competitor to build a medical center. The competitors appealed to the Supreme Court after the ruling was affirmed. The Court held that the Department of Health lacked substantial evidence to support need. Reversed, rendered, and remanded.

Cain v. Mississippi State Department of Health, 666 So.2d 506 (Miss. 1995).
Abstract: Denied applicant appealed to the Chancery Court, Hinds County after certificate of need was granted to competitor. The denied applicant appealed to the Supreme Court after the ruling was affirmed. The Court held that: (1) substantial evidence supported the ruling, and (2) the ruling was not arbitrary or capricious. Affirmed.

Mississippi State Department of Health v. Mississippi Baptist Medical Center, 663 So.2d 563 (Miss. 1995).
Abstract: Competitor appealed to the Chancery Court, Hinds County after certificate of need (CON) was granted to hospital for construction of an obstetrical unit. The hospital appealed after the Chancery Court reversed the ruling. The Supreme Court held that: (1) the chancellor's decision did not exceed the proper scope of review, (2) the condition that the hospital was required to maintain a 25% Medicaid services rate had not viable methods of enforcement and was completely unsupported by evidence, and (3) the decision to grant the CON lacked substantial evidence. Affirmed.

Mississippi State Department of Health v. Golden Triangle Regional Medical Center, 603 So.2d 854 (Miss. 1992).
Abstract: Applicant appealed to the Chancery Court, Lowndes County after it was denied a certificate of need to establish a cardiac catheterization service. The state appealed after the Chancery Court reversed the state's decision. The Supreme Court held that market share analysis to determine if the applicant could satisfy population requirements was not an abuse of discretion. Reversed and remanded.

HTI Health Services Inc. v. Mississippi State Department of Health, 603 So.2d 848 (Miss. 1992).
Abstract: Denied applicant appealed to the Chancery Court, Hinds County after the Department of Health denied its application to establish adult cardiac catheterization services. The Chancery Court transferred the case tot eh Chancery Court, Warren County. The applicant appealed tot eh Supreme Court after the Chancery Court, Warren County affirmed the Department's ruling. The Supreme Court held that: (1) hospital did not demonstrate minimum population base criterion, (2) the Department had statutory authority to rule based on market share methodology, and (3) the use of market share methodology wax not arbitrary and capricious. Affirmed.

Durant v. Humphreys County Memorial Hospital/Extended Care Facility, 587 So.2d 244 (1991).
Abstract: City residents went to the Holmes County Chancery Court seeking to enjoin administrative authorization and construction of a nursing home. The residents appealed to the Supreme Court after the Chancery Court denied relief. The Supreme Court held that: (1) there were not statutes or regulations indicating that each city resident should receive notice of the hospital's certificate of need application, (2) statutory criteria were not violated in issuing the certificate, (3) the district did not abuse discretion by denying injunctive relief, and (4) the Chancery Court had authority to grant injunctive relief. Affirmed.

Mississippi State Department of Health v. Southwest Mississippi Regional Medical Center, 580 So.2d 1238 (Miss. 1991).
Abstract: Hospital appealed to the Chancery Court, Pike County after the state health officer denied its application for certificate of need to offer cardiac catheterization services. The state appealed after the Court reversed its decision. The Supreme Court held that: (1) the state officer did make his decision in an arbitrary or capricious manner. Reversed and rendered.

Magnolia Hospital v. Mississippi State Department of Health, 559 So.2d 1042 (Miss. 1990).
Abstract: Hospital appealed to the Chancery Court, Hinds County after the Department of Health denied its application for certificate of need to establish an open heart/cardiovascular surgery unit. The hospital appealed to the Supreme Court after the Chancery Court affirmed the ruling. The Supreme Court held that the Court's ruling was supported by substantial evidence. Affirmed.

Melody Manor Convalescent Center v. Mississippi State Department of Health, 546 So.2d 972 (Miss. 1989).
Abstract: Competitor appealed to the Chancery Court, Hinds County after certificate of need was granted to hospital to expand extended care facility. The competitor appealed to the Supreme Court after the Chancery Court Affirmed the ruling. The Supreme Court held that the decision: (1) was not arbitrary or capricious, and (2) the ruling was supported by substantial evidence. Affirmed.

Grant Center Hospital Inc. v. Health Group of Jackson Inc., 528 So.2d 804 (Miss. 1988).
Abstract: Health care provider's application was remanded for comparative hearing. The provider was granted a certificate of need to construct 60-bed freestanding psychiatric hospital for children and adolescents. The competitor appealed to the Chancery Court, Hinds County and the order was reversed. Upon appeal, the Supreme Court held that applications should be evaluated based on the state health plan that was in effect when the application was submitted. Reversed and remanded.

Charter Medical Corporation v. Mississippi Health Planning and Development Agency, 362 So.2d 180 (Miss. 1978).
Abstract: Operator of hospital filed suit to the Chancery Court, Hinds County after it was denied a certificate of need to obtain computerized axial tomography body scanner. The suit was dismissed and the operator of hospital appealed to the Supreme Court. The Supreme Court held that the hospital had stated claim for relief in suit. Reversed and remanded.

MISSOURI

Supreme Court of Missouri

SSM Health Care v. Missouri Health Facilities Review Commission, 894 S.W.2d 674 (Mo. 1995).
Abstract: Operator of hospital appealed to the Circuit Court, Cole County after the Missouri Health Facilities Review Committee ruled that it was necessary for them to obtain a certificate of need (CON) for an outpatient radiation therapy service. The Circuit Court affirmed the Committee's ruling. Upon appeal, the Supreme Court held that: (1) the service was not qualified as a "health care facility" and thus did not need a CON, (2) equipment is valued t its cot to hospital as opposed to its original purchase price, (3) cost of private commercial building and land does not factor into evaluating if the hospital had meet the $600,000 capital expenditure minimum that would subject it to CON law, and (4) the radiation therapy services were not on hospital grounds and were owned by an outside entity. Reversed.

Missouri Health Facilities Review Committee v. Administrative Hearing Commission, 700 S.W.2d 445 (Mo. 1985).
Abstract: Medical corporation appealed the Administrative Hearing Commission after the Committee denied its certificate of need application. The Administration granted a certificate of need to corporation. Upon appeal, the Circuit Court, Green County reversed the Commissions ruling. The corporation then appealed to the Court of Appeals, which affirmed the Circuit Court's ruling. The case transferred to the Supreme Court which held that: (1) committee had standing to contest ruling, (2) inadequacy of health commissions ruling does not warrant the granting of a certificate of need, and (3) appeal to Administrative Heating Commission is appropriate recourse for medical corporation. Circuit Court affirmed. Remanded to Administrative Hearing Commission.

Court of Appeals of Missouri

Community Care Center of Lemay v. Missouri Health Facilities Review Committee, 92 S.W.3d 232 (Mo. Ct. App. 2002).
Abstract: Competitor appeals from dismissal of petition seeking a declaration that a certificate of need (CON) issued by the Commission was null and void. Competitor alleges that CON applicant did not meet the statutory requirements for a replacement CON. Appellants brought their action as taxpayers. The court finds that competitor failed to demonstrate a direct expenditure of funds or a pecuniary loss attributable to the Commission's CON approval. The Commission's decision is upheld.

EBG Health Care III Inc. v. Missouri Health Facilities Review Commission, 12 S.W.3d 354 (Mo. Ct. App. 2000).
Abstract: Nursing home facility appealed to the Circuit Court, Cole County after the Administrative Hearing Commission denied its request for certificate of need to transfer beds to a new facility. The Commission appealed after the Circuit Court reversed its ruling. The Court of Appeals held that: (1) facilities request required certificate of need approval, (2) statutory moratorium barred option of transferring beds to another facility, (3) exception to moratorium could not be made based on the grounds that the facility had inadequate design, and (4) nursing home lacked standing to challenge the regulation concerning moratorium. Reversed.

Mid-America Georgian Gardens v. Missouri Health Facilities Review Commission, 908 S.W.2d 715 (Mo. Ct. App. 1995).
Abstract: Competitor appealed to the Circuit Court, Cole County for declaratory and injunctive relief after state agency granted site change for approved certificate of need of nursing home. The competitor appealed after the Circuit Court granted summary judgment. The Court of Appeals held that the competitor did not have standing to challenge the certificate of need, or site change. Affirmed.

Medical Management v. Missouri Health Facilities Review Commission, 904 S.W.2d 291 (Mo. Ct. App. 1995).
Abstract: Competitors appealed to the Circuit Court, Morgan County for administrative hearing after commission granted a certificate of need to build a new facility. Competitors appealed to the Court of Appeals after the Circuit Court dismissed on the grounds of lack of subject matter jurisdiction. The Court of Appeals held that the operators lacked standing to seek remedy. Affirmed.

John T. Finley Inc. v. Missouri Health Facilities Review Commission, 904 S.W.2d 1 (Mo. Ct. App. 1995).
Abstract: Competitors appealed to the circuit court after review committee granted a certificate of need to replace intermediate care facility beds to skilled nursing facility beds. The Circuit Court dismissed the action and the competitors appealed to the Court of Appeals. The Court held that the competitors lacked taxpayer standing. Affirmed.

Frene Valley Corporation v. Missouri Health Facilities Review Committee, 818 S.W.2d 665 (Mo. Ct. App. 1991).
Abstract: Nursing homes appealed to the Circuit Court, Cole County for declaratory relief, injunctive relief and judicial review after the Review Committee granted a certificate of need to construct and operate a skilled nursing facility. The petition was dismissed and the nursing homes appealed to the Court of Appeals. The Court held that: (1) the nursing homes had standing, and (2) with the establishment of a nursing facility, the hospital district is not exceeding its powers. Affirmed.

State ex rel. Integrated Health Services v. Missouri Health Facilities Review Committee, 814 S.W.2d 677 (Mo. Ct. App. 1991).
Abstract: Competitors filed petition of certiorari, declaratory judgment, injunction and administrative review to the Circuit Court, Cole County after review committee granted a certificate of need to facility. The Circuit Court dismissed the petition and the competitors appealed. The Court of Appeals held that the competitors lacked standing. Affirmed.

Health Services Management Inc. v. Missouri Health Facilities Review Committee, 791 S.W.2d 732 (Mo. Ct. App. 1990).
Abstract: Applicants appealed the Circuit Court after they were denied certificates of need (CON). The Circuit Court granted summary judgment, and the Committee appealed to the Court of Appeals. The Court held that the Committee's failure to issue decision in a timely manner (underneath 130 days) closed the matter as administrative proceeding and indicated approval of CON. Affirmed.

West County Care Center Inc. v. Missouri Health Facilities Review Committee, 773 S.W.2d 474 (Mo. Ct. App. 1989).
Abstract: Competitor filed petition for writ of prohibition to the Circuit Court, Cole County after Committee deferred decision of another facility beyond statutory time limit. The competitor appealed after the Circuit Court dismissed the petition. The Court of Appeals held that the competitor lacked standing. Affirmed.

Missouri Health Care Associates v. Missouri Health Facilities Review Committee, 777 S.W.2d 241 (Mo. Ct. App. 1989).
Abstract: Providers appealed to the Circuit Court, Cole County after Committee ruled that applicant was not subject to certificate of need law. The Circuit Court found that the providers lacked standing. Upon appeal, the Court of Appeals also held that the providers lacked standing. Affirmed.

State ex rel. Missouri Health Care Associates v. Missouri Health Facilities Review Committee, 8 S.W.2d 559 (Mo. Ct. App. 1988).

Abstract: Health care association petitioned for writ of prohibition to the circuit court after a competing hospital applied for certificate of need and requested extension on time limit. The writ of prohibition was issued and the Review Committee appealed. The Court of Appeals held that: (1) the Committee had standing to challenge, and (2) the Committee could not extend time limit because of statutory deadline. Affirmed.

Platte County Medical Center Inc. v. Missouri Health Facilities Review Committee, 734 S.W.2d 608 (Mo. Ct. App. 1987).
Abstract: Denied applicant appealed to the Circuit Court, Cole County after Committee denied its application for certificate of need (CON). The Circuit Court granted the application and the Committee appealed to the Court of Appeals. The Court held that Committee's failure to issue decision in a timely manner (under 120 days) indicated approval of CON. Affirmed.

Community Care Centers Inc. v. Missouri Health Facilities Review Committee, 735 S.W.2d 13 (Mo. Ct. App. 1987).
Abstract: Competitor sought judicial review at the Circuit Court, Cole County after Committee granted certificate to nursing home. Upon dismissal of the case, the competitor appealed the Court of Appeals. The Court held that: (1) competitor lacked standing, and (2) the state statute that ruled that competitor lacked standing overruled the federal statute that allowed judicial review. Affirmed.

PIA Psychiatric Hospitals Inc. v. Missouri Health Facilities Review Committee, 729 S.W.2d 491 (Mo. Ct. App. 1987).
Abstract: Provider sought declaratory judgment action at the circuit court after the Committee denied its application to build an adolescent psychiatric hospital 125 days after it was filed. The Circuit Court granted summary judgment. Upon appeal, the Court of Appeals held that: (1) rules that were promulgated by Committee in attempt to suspend time period indicated in statute were abrogated by statute; and (2) failure of Committee to rule in a timely manner indicated approval of application.

PIA Psychiatric Hospitals Inc. v. Missouri Health Facilities Review Committee, 724 S.W.2d 524 (Mo. Ct. App. 1986).
Abstract: Competitors petitioned for review to the circuit court, after the Committee approved a certificate of need (CON) to construct an adolescent psychiatric hospital and residential treatment center. The Circuit Court denied the review and the competitors appealed. The Court of Appeals held that competitor that sought similar CON at the same time lacked standing. Affirmed.

HCA Health Services of Midwest Inc. v. Administrative Hearing Committee, 702 S.W.2d 884 (Mo. Ct. App. 1985).
Abstract: Competitor appealed to the circuit court after Committee granted certificate of need to another hospital. The Circuit Court dismissed the challenge and the competitor appealed to the Court of Appeals. The Court held that: (1) competitor lacked standing to challenge, and (2) if two applications are not mutually exclusive then comparative review is not required.

St. Joseph's Hill Infirmary Inc. v. Mandl, 682 S.W.2d 821 (Mo. Ct. App. 1984).
Abstract: Competitor appealed at the Circuit Court, Jefferson County after Committee granted certificate of need to another hospital. The Circuit Court reversed the Committee's ruling. Upon appeal, the Court of Appeals held that the competitor lacked standing to file the petition. Reversed and petition dismissed.

MONTANA

Supreme Court of Montana

West-Mont Community Care v. Board of Health & Environmental Sciences, 703 P.2d 850 (Mont. 1985).

Abstract: Competitor appealed to the First Judicial District Court after the Board of Health and Environmental Science granted a certificate of need to a home health care agency. The competitor appealed again after the District Court affirmed the ruling. The Supreme Court held that: (1) Board's decision was supported by substantial evidence, and (2) new federal rules concerning certificate of need did not impede the agencies ability to have a fair hearing. Affirmed.

Montana Health Systems Agency v. Montana Board of Health & Environmental Sciences, 612 P.2d 1275 (Mont. 1980).

Abstract: Hospital appealed to the Supreme Court after the District Court denied its motion to change venue for a recently approved petition for certificate of need. The Supreme Court held that: Administrative Procedure Act directed that petition should be filed where petitioner lived or had his principal place of business or where principal office was maintained. Affirmed.
Nebraska

Supreme Court of Nebraska

Gramercy Hill Enterprises v. State, 587 N.W.2d 378 (Neb. 1998).

Abstract: The center appealed the affirmation of the District Court of the Nebraska Department of Health's decision to deny its application for a certificate of need (CON) to add 60 skilled nursing beds to its current facility. The Supreme Court held that: (1) substantial evidence that the project would be less costly than alternatives and financially feasible was not presented; (2) center did not possess the grounds to challenge the constitutionality of the Health Care Certificate of Need Act and require issuance of CON at the same time; and (3) substantial evidence to make equal protection claims was not provided by the center. Affirmed.

Nebraska Methodist Health System v. Department of Health, 543 N.W.2d 466 (Neb. 1996).

Abstract: Health care company appealed the District Court's dismissal of its petition for review of a certificate of need determination by the Nebraska Department of Health (NDOH). The Supreme Court held that the requirement that the Attorney General provide personal jurisdiction over the state agency was not waived due to the NDOH's general appearance. Affirmed.

Department of Health v. Manor Care Inc., 465 N.W.2d 764 (Neb. 1991).

Abstract: The Nebraska Department of Health and competitors appealed the District Court's affirmation of the Nebraska Certificate of Need Appeal Panel's granting of a certificate of need (CON) to build a 120-bed nursing home. The Supreme Court held that: (1) the comparison between existing beds and projected need for beds was not considered, and (2) the issuance of CON was supported by substantial evidence. Affirmed.

Department of Health v. Omaha Associates, 441 N.W.2d 579 (Neb. 1989).

Abstract: The Nebraska Department of Health appealed the District Court's affirmation of the decision to award a certificate of need for purchase and lease of nursing home. The Supreme Court held that applicant qualified for a certificate by satisfying all criteria for issuance. Affirmed.

Omaha Health Facilities Inc. v. Department of Health, 439 N.W.2d 78 (Neb. 1989).

Abstract: Applicant appealed the affirmation of the Court of the certificate of need review panel's decision to deny application of a certificate of need (CON) to build a skilled nursing care facility. The Supreme Court held that the failure of the Department of Health (DOH) to use the 10% add-on in regulations determining need for facilities was not dire to the issuance of the CON, and did not render the DOH's decision invalid. Affirmed.

Department of Health v. Columbia West Corp., 420 N.W.2d 314 (Neb. 1988).
Abstract: State appealed the Court's affirmation of the certificate of need review panel's decision to issue a certificate of need for corporation to purchase an intermediate-care nursing home facility. The Supreme Court held that the result in the purchase of the facility would be a less costly care than other alternatives and corporation provided substantial evidence that adequate cash flow could be maintained throughout the life of the asset. Affirmed.

Department of Health v. Lutheran Hospitals & Homes Society, 416 N.W.2d 222 (Neb. 1987).
Abstract: The Nebraska Department of Health appealed the District Court's affirmation of the appeal panel's reversal of the trial court's affirmation of the Certificate of Need Review committee's denial of a hospital's application for certificate of need (CON). The Supreme Court held that the need for radiation therapy in the service area and the lack of significant impact to other service areas were grounds that warranted approval of the Hospital's application. Affirmed.

Department of Health v. Grand Island Health Care Inc., 391 N.W.2d 582 (Neb. 1986).
Abstract: Nebraska Department of Health appealed the District Court's affirmation of granting a certificate of need to establish a nursing home facility. The Supreme Court held that: (1) by showing that only small portions of the service area were being served by existing facilities, the applicant demonstrated need, and (2) because alternative methods for satisfying this need were not likely to be installed, applicant demonstrated that project was the most efficient method to address the service area's need. Affirmed.

Beatrice Manor Inc. v. Department of Health, 362 N.W.2d 45 (Neb. 1985).
Abstract: The Nebraska Department of Health appealed the District Court's reversal of the appeal panel's denial of a certificate of need for constructing a 23-bed addition to a health facility serving the elderly. The Supreme Court held that due to the 68.6-bed ratio criteria that the appeal panel based the rejection upon, the Court erred in not considering this evidence in support of denying the application. Reversed and remanded with directions.

County of Dodge on behalf of Memorial Hospital v. Department of Health, 355 N.W.2d 775 (Neb. 1984).
Abstract: Hospital appealed the appeal panel's affirmation of the Nebraska Department of Health's (NDOH) ruling that a certificate of need could only be awarded for the purchase of nuclear medicine equipment and not the lease of the equipment. The District Court reversed this decision to be met by the appeal from NDOH. The Supreme Court held that though it is within the jurisdiction of the NDOH to consider the project's derivative cost to taxpayers, evidence supporting the NDOH's decision to permit only purchase is not supported. In fact, Court found that it was more cost advantageous to lease. Affirmed.

Nebraska Court of Appeals

Beverly Enterprises v. Columbus Health Care, 510 N.W.2d 569 (Neb. Ct. App. 1993).
Abstract: The decisions to deny and grant certificates of need (CON) to nursing homes were petitioned for review. The Certificate of Need Review Committee's decision to grant CONs was affirmed for one hospital and reversed for another by the District Court. Upon appeal from the second hospital, the Court of Appeals held that: (1) substantial evidence that it would be serving currently underserved was not presented by the second hospital; (2) request for judicial review was a right exercisable by the second hospital, and (3) evidence supported the decision to award CON to the first hospital. Affirmed.

NEVADA

Supreme Court of Nevada

Boulware v. Department of Human Resources, 737 P.2d 502 (Nev. 1987).

Abstract: First Judicial District Court entered injunction prohibiting physician from acquiring magnetic resonance imaging machine or constructing facility for machine without certificate of need. On appeal, the Supreme Court held that statue was not meant for equipment used by private physicians. Reversed and remanded.

Department of Human Resources v. UHS of Colony, 735 P.2d 319 (Nev. 1987).

Abstract: The Eight Judicial District Court granted petition to health care provider after Department of Human Resources argued that a certificate of need was needed to acquire a magnetic resonance imaging machine. Upon appeal, the Supreme Court held that: (1) judicial review was proper remedy for provider, but (2) provider's facilities qualified as "health facility" and therefore was subject to certificate of need laws. Reversed and remanded.

Southern Nevada Memorial Hospital v. Department of Human Resources, 705 P.2d 139 (Nev. 1985).

Abstract: The Eight Judicial District Court remanded issue back to Department of Human Resources after the Department had issued and then rescinded certificates of need for multiple hospitals. The Supreme Court held that due to the fact that the Department had already issued letters of approval within which were specified time tables that threatened loss of authorization for project if not completed on time the Department is estopped from vacating its first decision. Reversed and remanded.

NEW HAMPSHIRE

Supreme Court of New Hampshire

Appeal of New England Heart Institute and Maine Medical Center, 746 A.2d 990 (N.H. 1999).

Abstract: Petitioners appealed the Health Services Planning and Review Board's (HSPRB) rejection of their motion for reconsideration of the granting of certificates of need (CON) to respondents. The Court of Appeals held that HSPRB's granting of CON lacked sufficient evidence indicating sufficient need. Remanded.

Appeal of Courville, 649 A.2d 1233 (N.H. 1994).

Abstract: Nursing home appealed to the Supreme Court after New Hampshire State Health Service Planning and Review Board (HSPRB) denied its request for extensions of expiration date of certificate of need and an extension for completing the nursing home. The Court held that: (1) nursing home did not issue petition in a timely manner, (2) nursing home lacked substantial cause for extension, and (3) HSPRB's consideration of certain information violated Administrative Procedure Act, however material prejudice was correct by rehearing. Affirmed.

Appeal of Nashua Brookside Hospital, 636 A.2d 57 (N.H. 1993).

Abstract: Competitors consolidated and appealed to the Supreme Court after the State Health Service Planning and Review Board (HSPRB) granted certificates of need to hospitals to convert beds. The Court held that: (1)

the HSPRB's decisions were based on improper and limited findings; and(2) the HSPRB could not grant certificates of need without applications to obtain certificates. Reversed.

Appeal of Salem Regional Medical Center, 590 A.2d 602 (N.H. 1991).
Abstract: Town did not demonstrate over- concentration of facilities in a manner which would lead to alteration of nature and character of area. Confirmed.

Appeal of Clipper Home, 579 A.2d 808 (N.H. 1990).
Abstract: Applicant petitioned for relief from conditions to the Supreme Court after the State Health Services Planning and Review Board (HSPRB) established conditions concerning Medicaid reimbursement rates. The Court held that: (1) the HSPRB did not usurp the authority granted to the Bureau of Provider Audits, (2) the HSPRB had statutory authority to establish the conditions, and (3) the HSPRB did not have statutory power to exercise discretion or grant relief to applicant because of the unforeseen and uncontrollable labor costs. Affirmed.

Appeal of Psychiatric Institutes of America, 564 A.2d 818 (N.H. 1989).
Abstract: Two applicants and competitor appealed to the Supreme Court after the State Health Services Planning and Review Board (HSPRB) denied their applications and approved the remaining applicant.. The Court held that: (1) the petitioners had standing; (2) HSPRB had discretion to use state health plan provision; (3) remand would be needed to see if the applicant had fulfilled the provision; (4) HSPRB did not err in treating hearing as reconsideration of prior ruling; (5) the three applicants should have been considered separately. Affirmed in part, remanded in part and vacated in part.

Appeal of Rehabilitation Associations, 556 A.2d 1183 (N.H. 1989).
Abstract: Applicant appealed to the Supreme Court after the State Health Services Planning and Review Board denied its application to build an acute physical rehabilitation center. The Court held that: (1) applicant did not need to apply for certificate of need because changing the site of the center did not substantially change the "nature" of the project, and (2) applicant submitted the proper forms and did not commence construction in an untimely manner. Appeal granted.

Appeal of New Hampshire Catholic Charities, 546 A.2d 1085 (N.H. 1988).
Abstract: Denied applicant appealed to the Supreme Court after the State Health Services Planning and Review Board (HSPRB) approved a certificate of need for its competitor. The Court held that: (1) the HSPRB considered evidence that was unreasonable and arbitrary, (2) the HSPRB's failure to consider predetermined bed need before approval of CON was unlawful. Reversed and remanded.

Catholic Medical Center v. Elliot Hospital, 543 A.2d 901 (N.H. 1988).
Abstract: Competing hospital appealed to the State Health Services Planning and Review Board after a hospital announced plans to provide left heart catheterization services without a certificate of need. The competing hospital and intervener petitioned to the Superior Court after the Board ruled that a certificate of need (CON) was unnecessary. The Superior Court ruled in favor of the competing hospital and intervener, but did not grant injunctive relief. The two plaintiffs then appealed to the Supreme Court which held that: (1) hospitals procedure did not qualify as "new institutional health service" and thus did not need a CON, (2) CON, according to statute, did not need to be obtained before offering of procedure began. Reversed and remanded.

Psychiatric Institute of America v. Mediplex, 536 A.2d 169 (N.H. 1989).
Abstract: Applicant filed a petition for declaratory hearing to the Superior Court in order to determine if it was

prohibited to issue certificate of need for specialty care beds. The Court did not rule, but approved an interlocutory transfer. The Supreme Court held that applicants ruling for certificate of need transpired before the moratorium of issuing certificates and before the passing of a statutory amendment. Therefore, the rules that applied at the time of ruling should also be applied at the time of reconsideration. Remanded.

Appeal of Catholic Medical Center, 515 A.2d 1205 (N.H. 1986).
Abstract: Applicant appealed to the Supreme Court for reconsideration hearing after the State Health Services Planning and Review Board granted certificate of need to competitor. The Court held that: (1) although formal notice of reconsideration hearing was not given to all initial applicants, competitor's certificate of need was still valid, and (2) lack of formal notice concerning reconsideration hearing did not violate due process rights of applicants. Affirmed.

Appeal of Lemire-Courville Associates, 499 A.2d 1328 (N.H. 1985).
Abstract: Two unsuccessful applicants appealed to the Supreme Court after the Department of Health and Welfare (DHW) approved a competitor's application for certificate of need. The Court held that: the DHW had substantial evidence for ruling, (2) the DHW correctly applied administrative criteria, (3) the DHW's evaluation was not in error, (4) the two unsuccessful applicants had contradictory findings and therefore remand was required. Affirmed in part, Remanded in part.

Appeal of Behavior Science Institute, 436 A.2d 1329 (N.H. 1981).
Abstract: Applicant appealed to the Supreme Court after the Department of Health and Welfare (DHW) retracted its approval of a certificate of need. The Court held that (1) the DHW's procedures for approval and retraction were ambiguous and inconsistent, (2) additional applicant in the process should have been given "competing" applicant status, and (3) hearing held by Commissioner of DHW was in error because the Commissioner lacked authority to hold it. Reversed and remanded.

NEW JERSEY

Supreme Court of New Jersey

In re Adoption of Regulations Governing the State Health Plan, 637 A.2d 1246 (N.J. 1994).
Abstract: Hospital sought judicial review for standards of review for certificate of need established by Department of Health. The Supreme Court affirmed the Superior Courts decision that the regulations were invalid. The Supreme Court held that: (1) legislature could restrict authority of Department, and (2) safeguards that had previously been established were deemed enough to satisfy due process. Affirmed.

Paul Kimball Hospital Inc. v. Brick Township Hospital Inc., 432 A.2d 36 (N.J. 1981).
Abstract: Trial Court found that that amendment exempting certain nonprofit corporations from necessity of approval of certificate of need was unconstitutional. The Superior Court affirmed, and the case was taken to the Supreme Court. The Court held that: (1) effect of amendment was not dependent upon date of passage of amendment (2) equal protection criteria was in amendment, and (3) state constitutional interdiction against special legislation was not violated. Reversed.

Superior Court of New Jersey

Medical Center at Princeton v. The Township of Princeton Zoning Board of Adjustment, 778 A.2d 482 (N.J. Super. Ct. App. Div. 2001).

Abstract: Hospital appealed to the Superior Court after the township's zoning board denied the use of variances. The Superior Court remanded the issue, but the validity of the ordinance was upheld. During Cross Appeals, the Superior Court held: (1) location is an appropriate factor for beneficial use analysis in variance applications, (2) each proposed use must be examined to determine benefit, and (3) ordinance was valid when applied to the hospital. Affirmed as modified and remanded.

Christ Hospital v. Department of Health and Senior Services, 748 A.2d 1156 (N.J. Super. Ct. App. Div. 2000).

Abstract: Hospital sought review with Superior Court after the Department of Health and Senior Services did not renew its license to operate a cardiac catheterization facility. Interveners were permitted to act as respondents. The Court held that: (1) Department violated Administrative Procedures Act by refusing a hearing, and (2) at no point did the hospital waive its right to such an administrative hearing. Reversed and remanded.

In the Matter of Certificate of Need Granted to St. Francis Medical Center, 25 N.J. Super. 423 (N.J. Super. Ct. App. Div. 1999).

Abstract: Medical center went to the Superior Court to challenge the Department of Health and Senior Services decision to permit a hospital and medical center to convert open beds into voluntary psychiatric admission. The Court held that the Department's decision was supported with evidence and was not arbitrary or capricious. Affirmed.

In re Certificate of Need of Arnold Walter Nursing Home, 649 A.2d 1319 (N.J. Super. Ct. App. Div. 1994).

Abstract: Unsuccessful applicant appealed the Commission of Health's approval for certificates of need for two competitors. Applicant also motioned for hearing for denial of its own application and motioned for consolidation. The Superior Court held that the Commission lacked substantial evidence for its ruling. Reversed and remanded.

Monmouth Medical Center v. State Department of Health, 639 A.2d 1129 (N.J. Super. Ct. App. Div. 1994).

Abstract: Hospitals appealed the State Department of Health and Health Care Administration Board's decision to impose moratoria concerning certificate of need for cardiac catheterization and surgery services. The Superior Court held that: (1) amendment in Health Care Facilities Planning Act prohibits Department from issuing regulations that implement any information from the State Health Plan, but the Department is permitted to issue regulations that do not implement such information, (2) regulations established by the Department were not arbitrary or capricious, and (3) alleged conflict of interest by member of the Health Care Administration Board was not required to remove herself from ruling because the matter did not affect her affiliated health care provider directly. Affirmed.

Associates in Radiation Oncology P.A. v. Siegel M.P.H., 639 A.2d 729 (N.J. Super. Ct. App. Div. 1994).

Abstract: Competing facility appealed to the Superior Court after the Acting Commissioner of Health had ruled that a certificate of need was not need to construct and install radiation equipment at a hospital. The Court held that: (1) the facility had standing, (2) remand was needed to discover more information concerning equipment, (3) Commissioner failed to address potentially pertinent certificates. Remanded.

In re Certification of Need Application of Chilton Memorial Hospital, 635 A.2d 986 (N.J. Super. Ct. App. Div. 1993).

Abstract: Competitor appealed to the Superior Court after the Acting Commissioner granted certificate of need to establish radiation therapy services for hospital. The Court held that the Acting Commissioner laced discretion and the hospital need to apply for new application. Reversed and Remanded.

In re Adoption of Regulations Governing the State Health Plan N.J.A.C., 621 A.2d 484 (N.J. Super. Ct. App. Div. 1993).

Abstract: Hospital association sough judicial review and challenged the validity of regulations to the Superior Court after the Department of Health adopted regulations concerning certificate of need. The Court held that: (1) it is constitutional to add amendments to the Health Care Cost Reduction Act and Health Care Facilities Planning Act, and (2) amendments must comply with regulations or else they are invalid. So ordered.

Holy Name Hospital v. New Jersey Health Care Administrative Board, 609 A.2d 1305 (N.J. Super. Ct. App. Div. 1992).

Abstract: Hospital appealed to Administrative Law Judge after Commissioner of Health denied its application for certificate of need for magnetic resonance imaging facility. Judge and Health Care Administration Board all affirmed the Commissioners denial. The Superior Court held that: (1) the Commissioner's decision lacked substantial evidence, and 2) equal standards for sufficiency are required for denying and granting certificate of need. Reversed and remanded with instructions.

In re Valley Hospital, 573 A.2d 203 (N.J. Super. Ct. App. Div. 1990).

Abstract: Competitor appealed to Superior Court after the Commissioner of Health granted a certificate of need to hospital to establish new cardiac surgery facility. The Court held that: (1) competitor had standing, (2) Commissioner's ruling lacked substantial evidence, and (3) Competing hospital lacked status to be granted trial-type hearing. Affirmed in part and remanded.

In re Bloomingdale Convalescent Center, 558 A.2d 19 (N.J. Super. Ct. App. Div. 1989).

Abstract: Borough appealed to the Superior Court after the Health Commissioner issued a certificate of need for establishing a nursing home. The Court held that the Commissioner did not comply with procedural requirements. Reversed and remanded with instructions.

In re Applications of Overlook Hospital, 521 A.2d 1350 (N.J. Super. Ct. App. Div. 1987).

Abstract: Order that required approved applicant hospital to submit to the discovery requests of denied applicant hospitals was not proper because the discovery would cause significant delays that would prejudice the public interest.

Radiological Society of New Jersey v. New Jersey State Department of Health Hospital Rate Setting Commission, 506 A.2d 755 (N.J. Super. Ct. App. Div. 1986).

Abstract: The Superior Court heard appeal concerning the rule that the Hospital Rate Setting Commission set stating that certificate of need would have be obtained prior to reimbursement for computerized tomography scanning and magnetic resonance imaging services. The Court held that: (1) regulation complied with Health Care Facilities Planning Act, and (2) regulation did not affect physician private practice. Affirmed.

Medcor Inc. v. Finley, 430 A.2d 964 (N.J. Super. Ct. App. Div. 1981).

Abstract: Health care services vendor appealed to the Superior Court after the State Commissioner of Health denied it a hearing to determine if its mobile "multiphasic health testing" services were subject to the Health Care Facilities Planning Act. The Court held that the vendor operated a "facility" and therefore was subject to the Health Care Facilities Planning Act and a hearing was not required. Affirmed.

Marsh v. Finley, 389 A.2d 490 (N.J. Super. Ct. App. Div. 1981).
Abstract: Physician appealed to the Superior Court after Commissioner of Health ruled that if his computerized axial tomography equipment would be subject to certificate of need review in the Health Care Facilities Planning Act. The Court held that the Health Care Facilities Planning Act does not regulated private physicians. Reversed.

St. Joseph's Hospital v. Finley, 379 A.2d 467 (N.J. Super. Ct. App. Div. 1977).
Abstract: Hospital appealed to the Superior Court after the Health Care Administration Board denied its application to establish a cardiac surgery program at its facility. The Court held that: (1) the Board's decision was based on substantial evidence, (2) the Board did not over extend authority to adopt new regulations, (3) hospital was subject to new regulations after it was obvious that there was an absence of prejudicial reliance on prior determination, and (4) there was no evidence indicating that the Board improperly used licensing standards. Affirmed.

Irvington General Hospital v. Department of Health, 374 A.2d 49 (N.J. Super. Ct. App. Div. 1977).
Abstract: Hospital appealed to the Superior Court after the Health Care Administration Board denied its certificate of need and dismissed its proceeding in lieu of prerogative writs. The Court held that: (1) bed need statistics cannot be the sole basis to reject an application, (2) judiciary lacked authority to direct the Governor in removing officials, and lacks jurisdiction to remove the officials directly, (3) officials were immune to suit due to the fact that all actions were administrative action or inaction of a judicial nature, and (4) applications for different types of beds should be considered separately.

National Nephrology Foundation v. Dougherty, 351 A.2d 392 (N.J. Super. Ct. App. Div. 1976).
Abstract: Hospital appealed to the Superior Court after the Commissioner of Health denied its application for certificate of need and approved a competitor's application for an intermediate renal dialysis facility. The Court held that the Commissioner had substantial evidence for both rulings. Affirmed.

Cooper River Convalescent Center Inc. v. Dougherty, 336 A.2d 35 (N.J. Super. Ct. App. Div. 1975).
Abstract: Nursing appealed to the Superior Court after the Health Care Administration Board denied its application for certificate of need. The Court held that the moratorium was properly applied and when it lapses, then the application should again be reviewed. Reversed and remanded.

Merry Heart Nursing & Convalescent Home Inc. v. Dougherty, 330 A.2d 370 (N.J. Super. Ct. App. Div. 1974).
Abstract: Operator of private nursing home appealed to the Superior Court after the Health Care Administration Board ruled that testimony should be heard regarding the updated state plan for health care services. The Court held that: (1) agency did not have to file for formal amendment procedures before they were used, (2) due process was not violated if the testimony was used, (3) certificate of need (CON) requirement is not invalidated by the use of police power, (4) all administrative remedies did not have to be used before turning to the court; and (5) there is not an unlawful abdication of Legislature if the Commissioner of Health issues CON. Affirmed.

NEW MEXICO

Supreme Court of New Mexico

State ex rel. Southwest Community Health Services v. Monroe, 659 P.2d 315 (N.M. 1983).

Abstract: Applicant that was granted certificate of need sued for writ of prohibition after intervener petitioned for administrative appeal. The District Court granted writ, and the State appealed to the Supreme Court. The Court held that statute applied to certificate o need review because although application had been filed before the statute was enacted, application was not complete until after the date of enact ion. Writ set aside and cause remanded.

NEW YORK

Supreme Court of New York, Appellate Division

Sheffield Towers Rehabilitation and Health Care Center v. Antonia Novello et al., 741 N.Y.S.2d 103 (N.Y. App. Div. 2002).

Abstract: Nursing home promoter appealed to the Supreme Court, Nassau County seeking injunction of moratorium concerning new homes. Agencies appealed after the Supreme Court, Nassau County granted injunctive relief. The Supreme Court, Appellate Division held that: (1) moratorium was issued with discretion, and (2) project was subject to moratorium. Reversed.

Jay Alexander Manor Inc. v. Antonia Novello, as Commissioner of Health of the State of New York, 285 A.2d 951 (N.Y. App. Div. 2001).

Abstract: After Commissioner of Health imposed temporary moratorium, construction company initiated Article 78. The Supreme Court, Albany County redirected to Supreme Court Appellate Decision. The Court held that the Commissioner of Health did not abuse authority.

First Baptist Church of Crown Heights Center for Nursing & Rehabilitation, Inc. v. Antonia Novello, as Commissioner of Health of the Department of Health of the State of New York, 728 N.Y.S.2d 881 (N.Y. App. Div. 2001).

Abstract: Corporations initiated Article 78 after Department of Health stalled on processing their applications. The Supreme Court held that: (1) moratorium could not be declared until the Department had promulgated new methodology, (2) due process rights were violated by the Department of Health, and (3) moratorium is subject to the State Administrative Procedure Act. Petitions granted.

Matter of Town of Gates v. Commissioner of NY State Office of Mental Retardation and Developmental Disabilities and Finger Lakes Developmental Disabilities Services Office, 667 N.Y.S.2d 568 (N.Y. App. Div. 1997).

Abstract: Article 78 was initiated after town objected to the Commissioner of the Office of Mental Retardation and Developmental Disabilities ruling to establish a residential facility for developmentally disabled adults. The Supreme Court, Monroe County rejected the town's objections, and the town appealed. The Supreme Court, Appellate Division held that: (1) the Commissions ruling was based on substantial evidence, and (2) town did not demonstrate over- concentration of facilities in a manner which would lead to alteration of nature and character of area. Confirmed.

Town of Hempstead v. Commissioner, State of New York Office of Mental Health, 606 N.Y.S.2d 756 (N.Y. App. Div. 1994).

Abstract: After Commissioner of State Office of Mental Health approved a community residence facility, town went to Supreme Court, Appellate Division to seek review. The Court held that: (1) Commissioner demonstrated need of facility, and (2) town did not demonstrate over- concentration of facilities in a manner which would lead to alteration of nature and character of area. Confirmed.

In the matter of Beech Hill Civic Association, Inc. v. Elin M. Howe, 613 N.Y.S.2d 694 (N.Y. App. Div. 1994).

Abstract: Article 78 was initiated after Commissioner of Mental Health approved community residence facility. The Supreme Court held that the Commissioner properly considered need for the county. Determination confirmed.

In the matter of Sisters of Charity Hospital of Buffalo v. New York State Department of Health, 175 A.2d. 419 (N.Y. App. Div. 1991).

Abstract: Article 78 was initiated by applicant after Commissioner of Health denied its application. The Supreme Court held that the Commissioner's ruling was not arbitrary or capricious. Determination confirmed.

Town of Hempstead v. Commissioner, State of New York Office of Mental Health and Pilgrim Psychiatric Center, 565 N.Y.S.2d 938 (N.Y. App. Div. 1991).

Abstract: Article 78 was initiated after Commissioner of Office of Mental Health approved community residential facility. The Supreme Court, Nassau County and Supreme Court, Appellate Division found that the Commissioner's decision was based on substantial evidence. Determination confirmed and petition dismissed.

In the matter of Meadowbrook Nursing Home v. David Axelrod, as Commissioner of the Dept. of Heath, 517 N.Y.S.2d 625 (N.Y. App. Div. 1987).

Abstract: After nursing home was denied by the State Commissioner its application to expand its facility, it brought action to annul the determination to the Supreme Court, Special Term. The Supreme Court, Special Term ordered that the case be evaluated solely on its financial feasibility. Upon appeal, the Supreme Court, Appellate Division annulled the decision on the grounds that the need to test in regulation was improper. The Commissioner upheld the initial ruling, and the nursing home appealed to the Supreme Court, Appellate Division. The Court held that the Commissioner's ruling was arbitrary and capricious. Determination annulled.

Arnot-Ogden Memorial Hospital v. Guthrie Clinic Inc., 122 A.2d 413 (N.Y. App. Div. 1986).

Abstract: Hospitals complained to the Supreme Court, Special Term after physicians did not obtain certificate of need to operated clinic. The Supreme Court, Special Term approved of the physicians' motion to dismiss. The Supreme Court, Appellate Division held that the hospital did not have standing to sue the physicians. Affirmed.

In the matter of the Town of Hempstead v. Commissioner, State of New York Office of Mental Retardation and Developmental Disabilities, 503 N.Y.S.2d 98 (N.Y. App. Div. 1986).

Abstract: Article 78 was initiated after a community residence facility was approved by the Commissioner of New York State Office of Mental Retardation and Developmental disabilities. The Supreme Court held that the ruling was appropriate. Determination confirmed.

Clifton Springs Sanitarium Company, v. Axelrod, M.D. as Commissioner of the Department of Health, 497 N.Y.2d 949 (N.Y. App. Div. 1985).

Abstract: The Commissioner and the State Department of Health charged hospital with operating a Cat scanner without a certificate of need (CON). The hospital petitioned for reviews, and the case was moved from the

Supreme Court, Monroe County to the Supreme Court, Appellate Division. The Court held that: (1) conclusion that the trailer was apart of hospital services was unsubstantiated, (2) private physicians did not need a certificate of need to operate equipment, (3) statutes concerning CON allowed hospitals to assist in helping private physicians to start private cat scanning service. Determination annulled.

In the matter of Fairfield Nursing Home v. Robert Whalen, 407 N.Y.S.2d 923 (N.Y. App. Div. 1978).
Abstract: Commissioner of Health denied application to construct nursing care facilities. Article 78 was initiated and the Supreme Court at Special Term transferred to the Supreme Court, Appellate Division, which held that the "needs" formulation that was applied was arbitrary. Petition granted, determination annulled and matter remitted for further proceedings.

Attoma v. State Department of Social Welfare, 270 N.Y.S.2d 167 (N.Y. App. Div. 1966).
Abstract: Private nursing home appealed to the Supreme Court after the State Department of Welfare did not process its application pursuant to the law existing prior to October 1, 1964. The Supreme Court ruled in favor of the nursing home. Upon appeal, the Supreme Court, Appellate Division held that statute was constitutional. Judgment reversed and petition dismissed.

NORTH CAROLINA

Supreme Court of North Carolina

Frye Regional Medical Center Inc. v. Hunt, 510 S.E.2d 159 (N.C. 1999).
Abstract: An existing open heart surgery program challenged the governor's amendment to the State Medical Facilities Plan (SMFP) stating that any new open-heart surgery programs were not needed. The Superior Court ruled for the hospital and suspending the amendment and reinstating provisions in place during prior SMFP, and the state appealed. After the Court of Appeals' granting of a discretionary review petition, the Supreme Court held that it was within the scope of the governor's jurisdiction and approval process to amend the SMFP. Reversed.

HCA Crossroads Residential Ctrs. v. North Carolina Department of Human Resources etc., 398 S.E.2d 466 (N.C. 1990).
Abstract: Applicants appealed the decision of the North Carolina Department of Human Resources denial of their application for a certificate of need (CON) for construction of chemical dependency treatment facilities. The Court of Appeals held that in their failure to render a decision on the application in a timely manner, the Department lost subject matter jurisdiction over all decisions except for issuing the CON. Vacated and remanded.

In re Health Care and Retirement Corporation of America, 370 S.E.2d 220 (N.C. 1988).
Abstract: Applicant petitioned for discretionary review of the decision to deny their application for certificate of need (CON) for construction of a retirement home. The Court of Appeals ordered that the application for CON is to be denied. Denied.

In re Certificate of Need for Aston Park Hospital Inc., 193 S.E.2d 729 (N.C. 1973).
Abstract: Commission appealed the Court's decision to reverse the commission's denial of a certificate of need (CON) to the hospital for building a new facility. The Supreme Court held that substantial evidence indicating

that the implementation of the project would meet unmet need, and failure to grant CON would institute a monopoly and violate the hospital's rights to due process all of which are contrary to the Constitution. Affirmed.

Williamson v. Snow, 80 S.E.2d 262 (N.C. 1954).
Abstract: Plaintiff appealed the Superior Court's granting of the action taken by the Board of County Commissioners and ex officio enjoining the issuance of bonds for the construction of a hospital and nurses home by the governing body of Hospital District. The Supreme Court held that the Court properly delegated the Commission the power to determine whether sufficient need existed for the proposed hospital district and to determine whether the creation of the hospital district in order to meet need was advisable. Affirmed.

Court of Appeals of North Carolina

Living Centers-Southeast Inc. v. North Carolina HHS, 532 S.E.2d 192 (N.C. Ct. App. 2000).
Abstract: Applicants appealed the decision of the North Carolina Department of Human Resources denial of their application for a certificate of need (CON) for construction of a 110 bed nursing facility, while awarding CON to a competitor. The Court of Appeals held that: (1) unsuccessful applicants are allotted a hearing in which they may present evidence pertinent in their applications, (2) in a contested CON case involving two or more applicants a full adjudicatory hearing is most appropriate, and (3) a review of the Department's full initial decision was necessary prior to rendering any judgment by the Administrative Law Judge. Remanded.

Christenbury Surgery Center v. North Carolina, 531 S.E.2d 219 (N.C. Ct. App. 2000).
Abstract: When the hospital appealed the Department's decision that the surgical facility obtain both a certificate of need (CON) and a license for every location, the court ruled to affirm the license requirement and to reverse the CON requirement, and the Department appealed. The Court of Appeals held that the facility's different locations did not constitute as establishing a "new institutional health service" and therefore was not subject to obtaining a CON. Affirmed.

Dialysis Care of North Carolina L.L.C. v. North Carolina HHS Division of Facility Services, Certificate of Need Section, 529 S.E.2d 257 (N.C. Ct. App. 2000).
Abstract: Provider appealed the North Carolina Department of Health and Human Services' issuance of a certificate of need for a competing dialysis facility. The Court of Appeals held that: (1) adequate funding for the facility was established, (2) application was not amended by the bank employee's testimony, (3) additional documentation of funding was permissible, and (4) applicants properly demonstrated need. Affirmed.

Johnston Health Care Center L.L.C. v. North Carolina Department of Human Resources Division of Facility Services, Certificate of Need Section, 524 S.E.2d 352 (N.C. Ct. App. 2000).
Abstract: Applicant appealed the North Carolina Department of Health and Human Services denial of its application for certificate of need while accepting its competitor's application. The Court of Appeals held that: (1) competitor provided evidence indicated financial feasibility, (2) amendments to its initial pre-hearing statement were permitted, and (3) applicant failed to provide evidence of financial feasibility. Affirmed.

Burke Health Investors L.L.C. v. North Carolina Department of Human Resources Division of Facility Services, Certificate of Need Section, 522 S.E.2d 96 (N.C. Ct. App. 1999).
Abstract: Applicant appealed the North Carolina Department of Health and Human Services' decision to deny their certificate of need (CON) application for constructing a nursing facility. The Court of Appeals held that: (1) by non indicating the typographical and transcriptional errors in comments the application could not be successfully amended, (2) a Medicaid rate exceeding the rates of private patients did not warrant a rejection of

the application, (3) evidence established financial feasibility, (4) application was not rendered non-conforming due to its conditions to approval, and (5) both applications were weighed adequately. Affirmed.

Bio-Medical Applications of North Carolina Inc. v. North Carolina Department of Human Resources Division of Facility Services, Certificate of Need Section, 523 S.E.2d 677 (N.C. Ct. App. 1999).
Abstract: Competitor appealed the Administrative Law Judge's affirmation of the North Carolina Department of Health and Human Services' issuance of a certificate of need (CON) to establish a new dialysis center and a home training teaching patients how to do self-dialysis. The Court of Appeals held that: (1) all criteria for issuing CON were evidenced and met, and (2) Director did not have to disqualify herself from participating in the final agency decision. Affirmed.

Koltis v. North Carolina Department of Human Resources Division of Facility Services, Certificate of Need Section, 480 S.E.2d 702 (N.C. Ct. App. 1997).
Abstract: Facility appealed the North Carolina Department of Health and Human Services' decision to allow a physician and professional corporations to provide oncology service center without requiring a certificate of need (CON). The Court of Appeals held that: (1) accounting records evidenced grandfather clause and warranted exemption from CON, and (2) though they did not involve actual services, contracts evidenced grandfather clause. Affirmed.

Retirement Villages v. North Carolina Department of Human Resources, 477 S.E.2d 697 (N.C. Ct. App. 1996).
Abstract: Nursing home appealed the Department of Health and Human Services' decision to deny their certificate of need (CON) application for expanding services while awarding it to the expansion of a competing a nursing facility. The Court of Appeals held that: (1) if applicants themselves do not submit financial information, the CON application can still be approved, (2) successful applicant did not evidence financial feasibility of project, (3) computing patient origin was not clearly stated by the successful applicant, and (4) clear definition of the types of services to be provided was not adequately stated by the successful applicant. Affirmed in part, reversed in part, and remanded.

Presbyterian-Orthopaedic Hospital v. North Carolina Department of Human Resources, 470 S.E.2d 831 (N.C. Ct. App. 1996).
Abstract: Hospital appealed the North Carolina Department of Health and Human Resources' decision to deny their certificate of need (CON) application for creating a rehabilitation unit while awarding another competing hospital a CON and conditionally approving a third hospital's application to downsize beds. The Court of Appeals held that: (1) due to insufficient staff proposed for the project, the petitioner's application was properly denied, (2) financial feasibility of the decrease in beds prevented summary judgment and required hearing, (3) changing management company after its application was complete and review for competing applications were under was not a permissible amendment to respondent's application. Affirmed in part, reversed in part, and remanded in part.

Cape Fear Memorial Hospital v. North Carolina Department of Human Resources, 466 S.E.2d 299 (N.C. Ct. App. 1996).
Abstract: Hospital appealed the Administrative Law Judge's upholding of the North Carolina Department of Health and Human Resource's decision to require a certificate of need (CON) for their proposed image intensifier upgrade to their cardiac catheterization equipment. The Court of Appeals held that: (1) the upgrade did not constitute "cardiac catheterization equipment" and thus would not require a CON, and (2) total cost was below $2 million statutory limit and thus would also be exempt from CON requirements. Reversed and remanded.

Britthaven Inc. v. North Carolina Department of Human Resources Division of Facility Services, 455 S.E.2d 455 (N.C. Ct. App. 1995).

Abstract: When the North Carolina Department of Health and Human Resources decided to deny the nursing facility's application for certificate of need application for expanding number of nursing and home-for-aged beds, the nursing home appealed. Due to alleged misrepresented information in plaintiff's application, another successful applicant moved for cross-assignment. The Court of Appeals held that: (1) the applicant was not allotted the right to a new proceeding by administrative law judge while beginning a contested case challenging Department's decision, (2) Department simply based on finding the competing applicant's project less costly and most effective did not warrant a determination that the plaintiff's application was non-conforming per statutory criteria, and (3) subcounty analysis performed by Department was supported by evidence. Affirmed.

Catawba Memorial Hospital v. North Carolina Department of Human Resources, 436 S.E.2d 390 (N.C. Ct. App. 1993).

Abstract: Hospital appealed the agency decision to deny its request for declaratory ruling after the North Carolina Department of Health and Human Resources determined that the proposed development of a heart surgery facility required a certificate of need (CON). Superior court affirmed agency decision and declared the hospital's petition as moot. Upon appeals by all parties, the Court of Appeals held that: (1) denial of request for declaratory hearing was supported by good cause, and (2) res judicata barred hospital from seeking declaratory hearing due to the fact that final agency decision on CON was a judicial decision. Reversed in part and affirmed in part.

Iredell Memorial Hospital v. North Carolina Department of Human Resources, 406 S.E.2d 304 (N.Y. Ct. App. 1991).

Abstract: Unsuccessful applicant appealed the North Carolina Department of Health and Human Resources' decision to deny their certificate of need application for operating an ambulatory surgical facility. The Court of Appeals held that statute only allowed direct review from contested cases gone to hearing, and since consideration for contested case hearing for both applications was rejected prior to hearing, the court did not have jurisdiction to make a determination. Dismissed.

Community Psychiatric Centers v. North Carolina Department of Human Resources Division of Facility Services, 405 S.E.2d 769 (N.Y. Ct. App. 1991).

Abstract: Petitioner appealed the administrative law judge's granting of the North Carolina Department of Health and Human Resources' request for dismissal of the petitioner's request for a contested case hearing over the denial of their certificate of need. The Court of Appeals held that it did not have jurisdiction to review issue due to the fact that petitioner was not a "party in a contested case hearing." Appeal dismissed.

In re Denial of Request for Declaratory Ruling by Total Care Inc., 393 S.E.2d 338 (N.C. Ct. App. 1990).

Abstract: North Carolina Department of Health and Human Resources' appealed the Superior Court's determination that obtaining a certificate of need (CON) before opening new branch offices was not required to be obtained by the health care agency. The Court of Appeals held that establishing new branch offices in area which it is already serving did not constitute establishing a new home health agency, and thus did not require a CON. Affirmed.

HCA Crossroads Residential Centers Inc. v. North Carolina Department of Human Resources, 392 S.E.2d 398 (N.C. Ct. App. 1990).

Abstract: Hospital appealed the Department of Health and Human Resources' denial their motion to intervene in cases reviewing two organizations' application for certificate of need for developing chemical dependency treatment facilities. The Court of Appeals held that hospital did not possess the standing to make jurisdictional appeal due to it being not a party to the contested cases. Dismissed.

Huntington Manor of Murphy v. North Carolina Department of Human Resources, 393 S.E.2d 104 (N.C. Ct. App. 1990).

Abstract: Unsuccessful applicant appealed the Secretary of North Carolina Department of Health and Human Resources' decision to deny their certificate of need (CON) application for development of a 30-bed nursing home facility. The Court of Appeals held that: (1) court possessed subject-matter jurisdiction over appeal due to the timely receipt of applicant's petition for contested case, and (2) the determination that CON application was non-conforming was an error by the Secretary. Reversed and remanded.

Lenoir Memorial Hospital Inc. v. North Carolina Department of Human Resources etc., 390 S.E.2d 448 (N.C. Ct. App. 1990).

Abstract: Hospital appealed the North Carolina Department of Health and Human Resources' decision to deny their certificate of need application for the conversion of unused acute care beds to psychiatric beds. The Court of Appeals held that: (1) in wrongly calculating the number of beds made available per year and failing to consider the conversion's positive impact to health care costs, the Department acted arbitrarily and capriciously, and (2) failure to consider service area's need for psychiatric beds was a Department error. Reversed and remanded.

Gummels v. North Carolina Department of Human Resources Division of Facility Services, 388 S.E.2d 223 (N.C. Ct. App. 1990).

Abstract: Partnership petitioned for judicial review of the North Carolina Department of Health and Human Resources' decision to deny their certificate of need (CON) application for nursing home beds due to the fact that it was untimely. Competing applicants and intended recipients of CON moved to intervene and the Superior Court granted the motion to intervene and denied the partnership's petition for judicial review. Upon appeal, the Court of Appeals held that: (1) second applicant had the standing to intervene due to its interest in the outcome of the proceeding, and (2) residence within the county where petition was filed was not evidenced. Affirmed.

Rowan Health Properties Inc. v. North Carolina Department of Human Resources Division of Facility Services, Certificate of Need Section, 365 S.E.2d 635 (N.C. Ct. App. 1988).

Abstract: Applicant petitioned for judicial review of the North Carolina Department of Health and Human Resources' decision to deny their certificate of need application for operating a long-term health care facility. The Court of Appeals held that in never being a party to contested case hearing, the applicant did not have the standing to petition for judicial review. Dismissed.

In re Health Care and Retirement Corporation of America, 364 S.E.2d 150 (N.C. Ct. App. 1988).

Abstract: Unsuccessful applicant appealed the North Carolina Department of Health and Human Resources' decision to approve a competing facility's application for certificate of need application for construction of nursing home facility. The Court of Appeals held that: (1) successful applicant possession of a suitable project site, community support and financial feasibility were all adequately demonstrated by the analyst's evidence, and (2) all witnesses of the successful applicant were qualified to provide expert testimony. Affirmed.

In re Appeal from Approval of Application of Wake Kidney Clinic P.A., 355 S.E.2d 788 (N.C. Ct. App. 1987).

Abstract: Competing agency appealed the agency's finalization of the North Carolina Department of Health and Human Resources' decision to grant a certificate of need (CON) to a professional medical association to establish renal dialysis facility. The Court of Appeals held that: (1) hearing officer is not limited to the consideration of evidence made before the CON section, and can consider updated matters before section in making final decision, (2) in-state and out-of-state financial information were proper amendments and were adequately considered, (3) evidence supported need for proposed facility, (4) proposed facility was the least costly and most effective solution, and (5) financial feasibility of proposed project was financially feasible. Affirmed.

Charter Pines Hospital Inc. v. North Carolina Department of Human Resources, 349 S.E.2d 639 (N.C. Ct. App. 1986).

Abstract: Hospital appealed the Court's affirmation of the North Carolina Department of Health and Human Resources' decision to deny their certificate of need application for construction of new psychiatric unit. The Court of Appeals held that: (1) the Department did not improperly create new review criteria by requesting letters supporting proposed facility, (2) need for proposed facility was evidenced, (3) despite conflicting testimony concerning application of state medical facilities planning, enough evidence supported bed need conclusions, and (4) Department decision was not arbitrary or capricious in denying application. Affirmed.

Charlotte-Mecklenburg Hospital Authority v. North Carolina Department of Human Resources, 349 S.E.2d 291 (N.C. Ct. App. 1986).

Abstract: When the North Carolina Department of Health and Human Resources' issued certificate of need to competing hospital, Hospital appealed. The Court of Appeals held that hospital did not exhaust administrative remedies in superior court on issue thus was not entitled to hearing in Court of Appeals. Dismissed.

Humana Hospital Corporation v. North Carolina Department of Human Resources Division of Facility Services, 345 S.E.2d 235 (N.C. Ct. App. 1986).

Abstract: Unsuccessful applicant appealed the North Carolina Department of Health and Human Resources' decision to reject hearing officer's recommendations to approve and to approve, with certain conditions, a competing facility's application for certificate of need (CON) application for 160 acute-care hospital beds. The Court of Appeals held that: (1) determining how many beds out of the twenty should be transferred between facilities was not within the Department's jurisdiction,(2) making adjustments in applications for CON was within the Department's jurisdiction, (3) up-to date addition to application regarding policy of indigent admissions was properly added, and (4) substantial evidence supports Department's decisions. Affirmed in part, reversed in part, and remanded.

In re Denial of Request by Humana Hospital Corp., 338 S.E.2d 139 (N.C. Ct. App. 1996).

Abstract: Applicant appealed the Superior Courts affirmation of the Department to deny their application for a certificate of need (CON) to construct a new hospital. The Court of Appeals held that: (1) due the nearly identical nature of a second application considered during the court proceedings, all reasons to deny the first application is moot, and (2) despite its request for hearing and administrative appeal, the applicant was entitled to no priority status. Affirmed.

Mt. Olive Home Health Care Agency Inc. v. North Carolina Department of Human Resources, 336 S.E.2d 625 (N.C. Ct. App. 1985).

Abstract: Existing service provider appealed the North Carolina Department of Human Resources Division of Facility Services granting of a certificate of need (CON) to a proposed home health care agency. The Court of Appeals held that: (1) exclusion of expert witness testimony due to failure to properly identify them was valid, and (2) the Department's decision to grant the CON was supported by sufficient evidence. Affirmed.

Hospital Group of Western North Carolina Inc. v. North Carolina Department of Human Resources, 332 S.E.2d 748 (N.C. Ct. App. 1985).

Abstract: Applicant appealed the North Carolina Department of Human Resources' decision to deny their application for a certificate of need (CON) to construct a new psychiatric hospital. The Court of Appeals held that: (1) it was not within the scope of the agency's jurisdiction to decide the statute's constitutionality and thus was not properly before the Court of Appeals, and (2) Department acted properly in denying the CON. Affirmed.

In re Wilkesboro Ltd., 285 S.E.2d 626 (N.C. Ct. App. 1982).

Abstract: Petitioner appealed the Court's denial of their request for judicial review of the decision of the North Carolina Department of Human Resources' decision to deny their request for reconsideration of their application for certificate of need (CON) under CON law. The Court of Appeals held that as a "person aggrieved" by being within two miles of a site chosen for the construction of a nursing home that was deemed a "grandfather exemption" the petitioner was entitled to a judicial review hearing determining whether or not the respondent's project did in fact begin construction prior to January 1, 1980 as well as a and a "final agency decision," a letter stating the Department's reasons for denying petitioner's request for reconsideration. Vacated and remanded.

NORTH DAKOTA

Supreme Court of North Dakota

Medical Arts Clinic P.C. v. Franciscan Initiatives, 531 N.W.2d 289 (N.D. 1995).

Abstract: Competitor and hearing officer appealed the Court's decision to enjoin the officer from issuing and enforcing a discovery order on the applicant to discover the sanctions against hospital, and to impose the disclosure of information allegedly protected by trade secret privilege. The Supreme Court held that: (1) it is within the scope of the officer's authority to make initial administrative discovery which included those protected by trade secret privilege claims, (2) officer's resolution on trade secret claims are subject to appeal by judicial review and, in some circumstances, writ of prohibition once all administrative remedies are exhausted, and (3) the abuse of discretion standard limits the scope of officer's judicial authority over trade secret claims. Reversed and Remanded.

La Moure v. State Health Council, 213 N.W.2d 869 (N.D. 1973).

Abstract: Plaintiffs appealed the Court's decision to quash their filing of a writ of mandamus that ordered the North Dakota Health Council and Department of Health to grant a certificate of need (CON) or state reasons for denying such license for the operation of hospital for long term care. The Supreme Court held that projects proposed in the hospital's long term operation constituted as "construction" and no construction or expansion of a hospital or like facility can occur without obtaining a CON required by statute. Applicant was compliant with the prior law, and it was not within the Department's jurisdiction to hold compliance with new law not yet taken effect as grounds for rejection of application. Order reversed and action remanded.

OHIO

Supreme Court of Ohio

West Side Deutscher Frauen Verein v. Tracy, 676 N.E.2d 895 (Ohio 1997).
Abstract: The nursing home operator appealed the affirmation of the Court in favor of the Ohio Certificate of Need Review Board's decision to deny application for exemption from real property tax for its new addition. The Supreme Court held that all years in which the facility addition was not licensed are not exempt from taxation. Affirmed

West Bay Manor Co. v. Cuyahoga County Bd. of Revision, 653 N.E.2d 379 (Ohio 1995).
Abstract: Taxpayer appealed the Board of Tax Appeals (BTA) rejection of nursing home's valuation and used the County Board of Revision valuation instead. The Supreme Court held that the BTA did not act outside of the scope of its discretion in upholding the County Board of Revision valuation. Affirmed.

In re Mansfield Gen. Hosp., 648 N.E.2d 1346 (Ohio 1995).
Abstract: When the Court reversed and remanded the Ohio State Certificate of Need Review Board's decision in denying a certificate of need (CON) to Hospital for cardiac catheterization services the motion to certify record was allowed. The Supreme Court held that a hospital will be denied a CON application for high-risk cardiac catheterization services if the hospital lacks on-site open-heart surgery capabilities. Reversed.

In re VHA Diagnostic Services Inc., 602 N.E.2d 647 (Ohio 1992).
Abstract: The Ohio Department of Health (DOH) appealed the Court's affirmation of the Ohio State Certificate of Need Review Board's decision to grant applicant's certificate of need (CON) due to the fact that the DOH failed to render a decision within the statute allotted 90-day time period upon receipt of application. The Supreme Court held that: (1) since application met all statutory requirements for completeness the CON would be granted by operation of law, (2) CON issuance could not be prevented by change in ownership of application, and (3) merits of application would not be allowed to be litigated by the DOH. Affirmed.

Fairview General Hosp. v. Fletcher, 586 N.E.2d 80 (Ohio 1992).
Abstract: The hospital appealed the Court of Appeal's affirmation of trial court's determination that the proposed re-designation of a hospital level was not subject to certificate of need review and law. The Supreme Court held that the Court of Appeals had jurisdiction on this matter. Affirmed.

State ex rel. PIA Psychiatric Hosp. Inc. v. Ohio Certificate of Need Review Board, 573 N.E.2d 14 (Ohio 1991).
Abstract: After being denied one writ of mandamus and granted limited writ of mandamus on another enjoining the issuance of a certificate of need (CON) for the construction of child adolescent psychiatric, psychiatric facility appealed. The Supreme Court held that: (1) the former "Certificate of Need Law" allowing the automatic adoption provision did not apply to Ohio Certificate of Need Review Board (CONRB) review of application, (2) CONRB was required to issue independent decisions on latter applications but, on CONRB's final decision, applicants were afforded remedy by way of appeal, and (3) entitlement to limited writ was bestowed on one applicant and denied to the other. Affirmed.

In re Timken Mercy Medical Center, 572 N.E.2d 673 (Ohio 1991).
Abstract: The application for a certificate of need (CON) by hospital for an open heart unit was denied by the Ohio State Department of Health, whose decision was reversed by the Certificate of Need Review Board (CONRB)and affirmed by trial Court and Court of Appeals. The Supreme Court held that the CONRB had jurisdiction not only to determine Department's abuse of discretion but to determine if need existed for pro-

posed project, therefore the CONRB did not act outside of the scope of its authority in awarding the CON. Affirmed.

In re Wellesley Corp., 480 N.E.2d 461 (Ohio 1985).
Abstract: Applicants appealed the Court's decision to affirm the Ohio State Health Planning Development Agency's (OSHPDA) denial of a certificate of need for the construction of a new psychiatric facility. This decision was affirmed by the Court of Appeals and the motion to certify the record was entertained. The Supreme Court held that sufficient evidence was provided in support of OSHPDA's decision. Affirmed.

Ohio Court of Appeals

Crestmont Cleveland Partnership v. Ohio Department of Health, 746 N.E.2d 222 (Ohio Ct. App. 2000).
Abstract: Nursing home owners appealed the Court's granting of non-State defendant's motion to dismiss the Nursing home owner's appeal for injunctive relief seeking declaration of ownership of certificate of need (CON) for nursing home and prevention of the State from changing said ownership. The Court denied the State's similar motion to dismiss appeal as moot. This decision was affirmed by the Court of Appeals on part of the non-State defendants and reversed on part of the State defendants. Owner amended complaint and appealed when Court dismissed the new complaint. The Court of Appeals held that: (1) motion to dismiss the case after remand was not barred by res judicata or law of the case, (2) motion to dismiss still applied even with amendments to the complaint, and (3) there was insufficient evidence to show the requisite standing of owners to seek injunctive relief. Affirmed.

Ford Hull-Mar Nursing Home Inc. v. Marr Knapp Crawfish & Assoc., 740 N.E.2d 729 (Ohio Ct. App. 2000).
Abstract: Upon a dispute over payment of an expansion project commissioned by the nursing home to the architectural firm, the nursing home appealed the Court's decision to affirm the arbitrator's ruling for the architectural firm and for finding the nursing home liable for $81,000.00 plus costs. The Court of Appeals held that: (1) in awarding $81,000.00 when the Appellee sought the amount of $129,147.90 was not an abuse of discretion on the arbitrator's part due to the fact that Appellee included the claim based upon quantum meruit, (2) Court did consider non-claims of the Appellant by admitting testimony based on the Appellant's allegations and thus rights to due process was not violated and the Court's decision was not arbitrary and capricious. Affirmed.

Crestmont Cleveland Partnership v. State Department of Health, 1999 Ohio App. LEXIS 4825, (Ohio Ct. App. 1999).
Abstract: Members of the partnership filed a motion for reconsideration of the Court's dismissal of the partnership's request for injunctive relief relating from a certificate of need (CON). The Court of Appeals held that trial court declined jurisdiction over part of the matter due to jurisdictional priority rule, therefore appellant's claim against trial court's dismissal is moot. Motion denied.

In re Cumberland Care Center, 704 N.E.2d 1275 (Ohio Ct. App. 1997).
Abstract: Operator of nursing home appealed the Ohio Certificate of Need Review Board's affirmation of the Director of Ohio Department of Health's decision to deny the certificate of need (CON) application for a new 83-bed nursing home facility. The Court of Appeals held that denial of CON was warranted by evidence indicating that new facility was not financially feasible. Affirmed.

In re Mazal Health Care, 691 N.E.2d 338 (Ohio Ct. App. 1997).
Abstract: Administrator of nursing home appealed the decision of the Ohio State Department of Health (OSDH) to grant a certificate of need (CON) to the construction of a new nursing home. The Court of Appeals held that: (1) grant of CON was adequately supported by evidence, (2) there was no abuse of discretion by the OSDH

despite its consideration of evidence submitted after the hearing, and (3) hearing examiner did not violate the administrator's right to due process. Affirmed.

In re Lima Memorial Hospital, 675 N.E.2d 1320 (Ohio Ct. App. 1996).
Abstract: The Ohio Certificate of Need Review Board appealed the Court of Appeals decision to reverse and remand its decision to grant certificate of need (CON) to hospital applicants. Upon remand, the board denied the CON and the court entertained applicant appeal and ruled in favor of the applicant with remand. The board granted CON on remand and the Ohio Department of Health (ODH) appealed. The Court of Appeals held that: (1) no res judicata or collateral effect was applicable because the ODH's decision to deny second CON application was quasi-judicial; (2) per Court of Appeal's prior determination, whether the 800 catheterizations requirement had been met was the sole issue before the board; (3) Board's granting of CON was invalid due to the invalid vote of an ineligible Senator replacing a board member; and (4) ODH Director's prior denial of CON as final order could not be resurrected by the statutory "deemer" provision. Reversed and remanded.

In re Beechmont, 1996 Ohio App. LEXIS 1314 (Ohio Ct. App. 1996).
Abstract: Objecting facility appealed the Ohio Certificate of Need Review Board's decision to grant a certificate of need for the relocation of beds from three nursing homes to a newly-constructed one. The Court of Appeals held that: (1) though the application was altered in that one of the three nursing homes was replaced by a fourth nursing home, the application may be amended as long as the site of reviewable activity remains the same, and (2) substantial evidence indicated need and that the project was the least costly method to address the need. Affirmed.

In re Good Samaritan Hospital, 668 N.E.2d 974 (Ohio Ct. App. 1995).
Abstract: Hospital appealed the granting by Ohio Certificate of Need Review of a joint application for certificate of need to two other hospitals. The Court of Appeals held that: (1) because application was amended prior to the end of the review period, it could not be accepted by operation of law within the time frame allotted the director by the statute, and (2) review board did not consider merits for joint application therefore merits could not be placed before the appellate court. Reversed and remanded.

In re Midwest Eye Center, 661 N.E.2d 774 (Ohio Ct. App. 1995).
Abstract: Plaintiffs appealed the Ohio Certificate of Need Review Board's affirmation of the Director of Ohio Department of Health's reviewability determination. The Court of Appeals held that under certificate of need laws, outpatient surgery services were not deemed a "reviewable activity." Reversed and remanded.

In re Samaritan North Health Center, 641 N.E.2d 1134 1994 (Ohio Ct. App. 1994).
Abstract: Labor council appealed the dismissal of the council's notice of appeal and request for adjudication by the Ohio Certificate of Need Review Board (OCONRB) when a hospital was granted a certificate of need for establishment of an ambulatory care center by the Director of Ohio Department of Health (ODH). The Court of Appeals held that the council did not have standing as an "affected person" and therefore did not have the authority to request adjudication. Affirmed.

In re Cleveland Clinic Foundation, 640 N.E.2d 900 1994 (Ohio Ct. App. 1994).
Abstract: Opponent appealed the awarding of a certificate of need to applicant for reclassification of applicant/medical clinic's beds by the Ohio Certificate of Need Review Board (OCONRB) upon approval of the Ohio Department of Health (ODH). The Court of Appeals held that: (1) modification of original denial of application was within the jurisdiction of the ODH, and (2) failure to achieve majority of votes in the OCONRB to adopt the ODH's order was not sufficient. Reversed and remanded.

In re North Shore Radiology, 1994 Ohio App. LEXIS 4751(Ohio Ct. App. 1994).
Abstract: The plaintiff appealed for reconsideration of the Ohio Certificate of Need Review Board's (OCONRB) order that the plaintiff must obtain a certificate of need (CON) for its magnetic resonance imaging (MRI) unit. The Court of Appeals held that: (1) OCONRB did adequately assess all assignments of error, and (2) substantiated evidence supports that the cost of the lease was more than $1 million, and therefore subject to CON jurisdiction. Reconsideration denied.

In re National Church Residence Care Center, 1994 Ohio App. LEXIS 4218 (Ohio Ct. App. 1994).
Abstract: Applicant appealed the decision of the Ohio Certificate of Need Review Board's (OCONRB) affirmation of the Director Ohio Department of Health's decision to deny its application for a certificate of need (CON) for the construction of a 100-bed nursing home, while awarding it to two other applicants. The Court of Appeals held that: (1) no preferential ranking system is instituted by state statute for CON applications and therefore the Director did not err in reviewing application in conjunction with other applications, and (2) substantial evidence indicated financial feasibility of both applicants and therefore OCONRB did not err in decision to grant CON. Affirmed.

In re North Shore Radiology, 1994 Ohio App. LEXIS 3821 (Ohio Ct. App. 1994).
Abstract: Objector appealed the decision of the Ohio Certificate of Need Review Board to order review over the Ohio Department of Health's determination that the proposed magnetic resonance unit was not subject to certificate of need (CON) regulation. The Court of Appeals held that substantial evidence indicated that facility was indeed a free-standing center and the project cost $1million dollars or more thus rendering the applicant subject to CON laws. Affirmed.

In re Deaconess Hospital, 1993 Ohio App. LEXIS 5850 (Ohio Ct. App. 1993).
Abstract: Applicant appealed the decision of the Ohio Certificate of Need Review Board's order to deny their application for certificate of need. The Court of Appeals held that the review officer properly assessed the evidence and facts pertinent to the review criteria in making her determination. Affirmed.

In re Pavilion, 1993 Ohio App. LEXIS 4874 (Ohio Ct. App. 1993).
Abstract: Nursing home appealed the decision of the Ohio Department of Health to grant a competitor, in full, both applications for certificates of need for additional beds while only partially granting their application. The Court of Appeals held that: (1) Ohio Certificate of Need Review Board did not err in calculating the bed need for the service area, and (2) appellee did not fail in showing sufficient need for its project and would be cost effective in meeting that need. Affirmed.

In re Heartland of Mentor, 634 N.E.2d 260 (Ohio Ct. App. 1993).
Abstract: Competitor appealed the Ohio Certificate of Need Review Board's (OCONRB) affirmation of the Ohio Department of Health's (ODH) granting of a certificate of need for the conversion of rest home beds to nursing home beds. The Court of Appeals held that in determining that the proposal sufficiently met the statute's minimum requirements for application the Director of the ODH and the OCONRB were acting within the scope of their discretion. Affirmed.

In re St. John Medical Center, 632 N.E.2d 595 (Ohio Ct. App. 1993).
Abstract: A religiously sponsored hospital appealed the denial of its application for Certificate of Need by the Ohio Certificate of Need Review Board. The Court of Appeals held that the appellant's right to pursue its religious mission was not considered. Reversed and remanded.

In re Mansfield General Hospital, 628 N.E.2d 93 (Ohio Ct. App. 1993).
Abstract: Hospital appealed the denial of its application for a certificate of need for cardiac catheterization services by the Ohio Certificate of Need Review Board. The Court of Appeals held that the application was not reviewable under statute specifications. Reversed and remanded.

In re Continental Medical Systems, 627 N.E.2d 1018 (Ohio Ct. App. 1993).
Abstract: Plaintiff appealed the Ohio Certificate of Need Review Board's denial of a certificate of need (CON) for a new facility providing rehabilitative care. The Court of Appeals held that: (1) decision was rendered within the statute specified time frame and thus adopted, (2) examiner's conclusion of CON issuance was supported by substantial evidence, and (3) because the letter did not constitute part of the record of appeal the appeal would not be abandoned. Motion to dismiss overruled; reversed and remanded with instructions.

In re Deaconess Hospital, 613 N.E.2d 1049 (Ohio Ct. App. 1992).
Abstract: Appeals were taken against the Ohio Certificate of Need Review Board's (OCONRB) reversal of the Ohio Department of Health's (ODH) decision to grant separate certificates of need (CON) to hospital recategorizing medical/surgical beds to skilled nursing beds. The Court of Appeals held that: (1) hearing examiner improperly excluded pertinent evidence and relied solely on statistical data, (2) it was necessary to consider availability of medical/surgical beds within nursing homes, (3) hearing examiner was in err by delaying information regarding discharged patients from hospital beds in nursing by solely considering statistical information, and (4) ODH's authority to grant CONs was not voided by Public Health Council's failure, within the six month period, to promulgate rules. Reversed and remanded.

Summit Villa Care Center. Inc. v. Ohio Department of Health, 612 N.E.2d 377 (Ohio Ct. App. 1992).
Abstract: Nursing home appealed the denial of a certificate of need for the relocation of 30 long-term beds from another facility by the Ohio Certificate of Need Review Board. The Court Appeals held that: (1) qualification as an existing health care facility of the nursing home from which the beds were to be relocated was not shown; (2) there was no estoppel of the Department of Health's (DOH) decision due to the miscommunication between DOH and applicant that the facility was indeed a licensed facility; and (3) sufficient evidence to establish need for proposed bed was not presented. Affirmed.

In re Aultman Hospital, 608 N.E.2d 1104 (Ohio Ct. App. 1992).
Abstract: Hospital appealed the Ohio Certificate of Need Review Board's verification of the Ohio Department of Health's determination that the implementation of Level III neonatal and obstetrical services is a reviewable activity. The Court of Appeals held that proposed implementation required certificate of need review. Affirmed.

In re Healthco Facilities Inc., 607 N.E.2d 503 (Ohio Ct. App. 1992).
Abstract: Upon appeal the trial court decision reversed the Ohio Certificate of Need Review Board's decision to dismiss the appeal of the health care provider against the decision of the Ohio Department of Health to grant a certificate of need to the construction of a new long-term care facility. The court's ruling was then reversed and remanded by the Court of Appeals, which on remand dismissed the appeal. The provider appealed again and the Court of Appeals held that: (1) compliance of the notice to appeal with statutory requirements was evidenced, (2) administrative requirements were not under jurisdiction, and (3) unspecified maximum capital expenditures for authorized projects were stated clearly in notice of appeal. Reversed and remanded.

State ex rel. Parma Community General Hospital v. Kilroy, 1992 Ohio App. LEXIS 5870 (Ohio Ct. App. 1992).
Abstract: Hospital filed a mandamus requesting the granting of a certificate of need to hospital and file notice to

all related parties in order to commence the thirty-day appeal period. The Court of Appeals held that hospital did not have the standing to file writ. Writ denied.

Lake East Hospital v. Ohio Department of Health, 1992 Ohio App. LEXIS 5194 (Ohio Ct. App. 1992).
Abstract: Hospital and the Ohio Department of Health (ODH) appealed the decision of the Ohio Certificate of Need Review Board's (OCONRB) decision to reverse the ODH granting of a certificate of need to the appellant. The Court of Appeals held that: (1) hearing officer erred by limiting consideration solely to the twelve-week studies and failed to consider hearing examiner's report of the testimony presented at the hearing, but (2) OCONRB's interpretation of the Ohio Administrative Code was valid and congruent with the Ohio Revised Code. Order reversed and remanded.

State ex rel. Greene Oaks v. Kilroy, 1992 Ohio App. LEXIS 4880 (Ohio Ct. App. 1992).
Abstract: Hospital filed a mandamus to order the Ohio Department of Health to issue a certificate of need for conversion of 18 rest home beds to nursing beds. The Court of Appeals held that hospital did not have clear legal right and standing to file writ. Writ denied.

In re Christian Care Home Inc., 599 N.E.2d 342 (Ohio Ct. App. 1991).
Abstract: When long-term care facility appealed the Ohio Certificate of Need Review Board's (OCONRB) decision to deny request for additional beds the court dismissed appeal, which was reversed and remanded by the Court of Appeals. On remand the court again ruled for the Board and the facility appealed again. Upon appeal the Court of Appeals reversed and remanded and the court remanded to the OCONRB which on remand held its original decision and was appealed. The Court of Appeals held that: (1) OCONRB's denial of facility request was based upon reliable evidence, and (2) rights of the facility to due process were not violated by the OCONRB's appointment of a new hearing officer to oversee the case. Affirmed.

In re Alexander Rand Alzheimer's Center, 594 N.E.2d 119 (Ohio Ct. App. 1991).
Abstract: Applicant appealed the decision of the Ohio Certificate of Need Review Board to deny their application for certificate of need in establishing a nursing home facility. The Court of Appeals held that in determining application the date application was declared complete rather than the date application was filed was to be considered. Affirmed.

In re Good Samaritan Medical Center, 572 N.E.2d 849 (Ohio Ct. App. 1991).
Abstract: Applicant appealed the decision of the Ohio Certificate of Need Review Board to deny their application for certificate of need (CON) in establishing a cardiac catheterization service. The Court of Appeals held that: (1) when the completed form was submitted rather than when the agency mailed a notice of completeness is deemed to be the start of the statute required 90-day period for rendering a decision; (2) due to the Ohio Department of Health's (ODH) failure to render a decision in a timely matter, a CON was granted by operation of law; and (3)when the date of decision was mailed by Director of ODH the appeal period begins. Affirmed.

Fairview General Hospital v. Fletcher, 591 N.E.2d 1312 (Ohio Ct. App. 1990).
Abstract: Competitor hospital appealed the court's denial of its motion to intervene in the hospital petition to seek exemption from certificate of need law in its request to be redesignated a level III perinatal services provider. The Court of Appeals held that: (1) the court's denial was final and could be appealed; (2) competitor hospital did not have the right to intervene; (3) the denial of intervention was not the court's abuse of discretion; and (4) no reasonable cause for appeal was presented and therefore attorney fees would be awarded. Affirmed.

Fairview General Hospital v. Fletcher, 1990 Ohio App. LEXIS 5756 (Ohio Ct. App. 1990).

Abstract: Director of the Ohio Department of Health appealed the court's ruling in favor of the appellee declaring that Ohio certificate of need laws were not applicable for a re-designation of the level of its neonatal intensive care unit. The Court of Appeals held that: (1) trial court erred in that failing to recognize that administrative remedies were not exhausted and therefore facility was not eligible for declaratory relief; (2) director's ruling was final and binding and not subject to attack in the trial court; (3) not enough substantial evidence deeming the change in status level non-reviewable was presented. Reversed and remanded with instructions.

In re Labelle Nursing Center, 1990 Ohio App. LEXIS 3852 (Ohio Ct. App. 1990).
Abstract: Nursing appealed the affirmation of the Ohio Certificate of Need Review Board's decision to affirm the Director of the Ohio Department of Health's decision to deny appellant's application for a certificate of need (CON) for 100 beds for care of Alzheimer's patients. The Court of Appeals held that applicant failed to include a written affiliation agreement with hospital or university, a requisite by statute in order for CON to be issued. Affirmed.

In re Certificate of Need Application of Providence Hospital, 587 N.E.2d 326 (Ohio Ct. App. 1990).
Abstract: The Ohio Department of Health appealed the court's reversal of the Ohio Certificate of Need Review Board's (OCONRB) decision to deny applicant a certificate of need (CON). The Court of Appeals held that: (1) it was within the OCONRB's jurisdiction to independently review evidence and from such evidence draw its own conclusions, (2) substantial supported the lack of need for the obstetric unit, (3) if less than 90% of population in the service area was within 30 minutes of travel time of existing facilities does not require a granting of a CON. Motions to dismiss overruled; reversed and remanded.

John Ken Alzheimer's Center v. Ohio Certificate of Need Review Board, 583 N.E.2d 337 (Ohio Ct. App. 1989).
Abstract: Applicant appealed the denial of a certificate of need by the Ohio Certificate of Need Review Board (OCONRB) to construct a facility providing care for Alzheimer's patients. The Court of Appeals held that the OCONRB's decision to deny application was still a pending issue before the 10th circuit court of appeals and therefore court lacked jurisdiction to consider appeal. Appeal Dismissed.

In re Christian Care Home Inc., 581 N.E.2d 1157 (Ohio Ct. App. 1989).
Abstract: Upon remand the Court affirmed its original order to dismiss the appeal of a long-term care facility against the Ohio Certificate of Need Review Board's (OCONRB) denial to grant a certificate of need for additional beds. In response the facility appealed and the Court of Appeals held that: (1) Department of Health evidenced the requisite standing to file objection with Board to report of hearing examiner; (2) in order to rebut insufficient need the facility had to evidence need by not only indicating a waiting list for beds in its own facility, but (3) OCONRB erred in failing to consider expert testimony testifying that actual bed occupancy rate that was in excess to the stat's desired minimum rate. Reversed and remanded.

In re Saltwell Nursing Home, 1989 Ohio App. LEXIS 1655 (Ohio Ct. App. 1989).
Abstract: Ohio Department of Health appealed the Court's decision to sustain a motion to dismiss filed by nursing home (Saltwell) from an appeal by the center (Netwick) against the trial court's decision to reject Saltwell's application for a certificate of need and accept Netwick's application. The Court of Appeals held that trial court's decision was final and appealable and thus the appeal was properly before the court. The Court erred in dismissing appeal on the grounds that the appeal was taken from a non-final order. Reversed and remanded.

Neurosurgical Clinic & Allied Specialties Inc. v. State Health Planning & Resources Development Agency, 1989 Ohio App. LEXIS 12 (Ohio Ct. App. 1989).
Abstract: Clinic appealed the court's affirmation of State Health Planning and Development Agency's (SHPDA)

refusal to reconsider the determination of the director of health that the clinic's ownership of a Tomographic Scanner (CT) was subject to certificate of need (CON) review. The Court of Appeals held that substantial evidence supported the court's affirmation of the SHPDA's decision to subject clinic's CT ownership to CON review. Affirmed.

Cincinnati Ambulatory Surgery Center v. Certificate of Need Review Board, 574 N.E.2d 529 (Ohio Ct. App. 1988).

Abstract: Facility appealed the Board's reversal of the Department's decision to grant a certificate of need (CON) for an ambulatory surgical facility. The Court reversed and appeals were made by competing hospital. The Court of Appeals held that: (1) certificate of need application was incomplete and could not be approved; (2) only when specified address satisfied conditions of approval could a CON decision be final; and (3) request of the competing hospital was within required statute time frame. Reversed and remanded.

Christian Care Home Inc. v. State Certificate of Need Review Board, 548 N.E.2d 981 (Ohio Ct. App. 1988).

Abstract: Facility appealed the court's dismissal of its appeal against the Ohio Certificate of Need Review Board's (OCONRB) decision to deny facility's request to amend its certificate of need by adding additional beds for the facility. The Court of Appeals held that: (1) facility could appeal the OCONRB's decision because it was quasi-judicial, and (2) the remanded decision of the OCONRB to the Director of Ohio Department of Health was final and could also be appealed. Reversed and Remanded.

Arbor Health Care Co. v. Jackson, 530 N.E.2d 928 (Ohio Ct. App. 1987).

Abstract: The applicant appealed the court granting of the defendant's motion to dismiss the applicant's motion for declaratory relief. The Court of Appeals held that: (1) adequate administrative remedy was taken by the applicant, and (2) the court did not abuse its discretion by declaring the applicant's action as moot. Affirmed.

Oak Park Manor v. State Certificate of Need Review Board, 500 N.E.2d 895 (Ohio Ct. App. 1985).

Abstract: Facility appealed the Court's affirmation of the Ohio Certificate of Need Review Board's (OCONRB) decision to deny its application for a certificate of need. The Court of Appeals held that: (1) OCONRB's decision was arbitrary and capricious and not based on sufficient evidence, and (2) no substantial evidence indicated the OCONRB's denial as pertaining to preferential treatment of another facility. Reversed and Remanded.

In re Dixon Health Care Center Inc., 1985 Ohio App. LEXIS 6861 (Ohio Ct. App. 1985).

Abstract: Intervener appealed the court's affirmation of the Ohio Certificate of Need Review Board's overruling its motion to dismiss an appeal from the determination of the certificate of need (CON) proceedings, and sustaining of appellee's motion to dismiss. The Court of Appeals held that that Board had jurisdiction over the case and did not err in refusing to hear the merits of the appeal. Affirmed.

In re Lorain Community Hospital, 1984 Ohio App. LEXIS 10279 (Ohio Ct. App. 1984).

Abstract: Hospital filed and was denied certificate of need for a cardiac catheterization laboratory by the Development Agency and the Certificate of Need Review Board. The hospital then appealed to the Lorain County Court of Common Pleas. The County Court dismissed the case on the grounds that it lacked jurisdiction. Upon appeals, the Court affirmed the ruling of the County Court. Affirmed.

St. Francis/St. George Hospital Inc. v. Blue Cross, 1983 Ohio App. LEXIS 14684 (Ohio Ct. App. 1983).

Abstract: Competitor sued after discovering a hospital had expanded its total number of acute care bed without receiving approval from the Health Care Planning Agency. The hospital petitioned for summary judgment. Trial

Court granted summary judgment. Upon appeal, the Court of Appeals held that there was no genuine issue of material fact. Affirmed.

OKLAHOMA

Supreme Court of Oklahoma

Humana Hospital Corp. v. Oklahoma Health Planning Commission, 705 P.2d 175 (Okla. 1985).
Abstract: The Oklahoma Health Planning Commission (OHPC) appealed the district court's reversal of the trial court's decision to deny the hospital's application for a certificate of need (CON) to build a 125-bed hospital, a decision that the court of appeals affirmed. The Supreme Court held that OHPC's decision complied with applicable laws and was not capricious or arbitrary. Appeals Court Opinion vacated; trial court judgment reversed; and OHPC order affirmed.

Tulsa Area Hospital Council Inc. v. Oral Roberts University, 626 P.2d 316 (Okla. 1981).
Abstract: Commission appealed the order by the District Court to remand the granting of a certificate of need (CON) to university for construction of a holistic medicine hospital. The Supreme Court held that: (1) the granting of the CON was substantiated by evidence, and (2) no violation of establishment clause was committed by the Commission's granting of the CON. Reversed.

Oklahoma Pioneer Inc. v. Carpenter, 617 P.2d 210 (Okla. 1980).
Abstract: Competitor appealed the decision of the court to affirm the Oklahoma Commissioner of Health's granting of a certificate of need (CON) for the expansion of a nursing home. The Supreme Court held that issuing the CON was abuse of discretion and exceeded the judicial scope of agency's authority.. Reversed and remanded.

Oklahoma Court of Appeals

Oklahoma Department of Health v. Medi-Plex Nursing Centers, Inc., 875 P.2d 437 (Okla. Ct. App. 1994).
Abstract: Competitor appealed the District Court's affirmation of the Oklahoma State Department of Health's issuance of a certificate of need (CON) for expansion of an existing nursing home. The Court of Appeals held that awarding a CON complied with applicable laws and that the allowance of replacing, changing parts, or constructing onto an existing facility was not arbitrary or capricious. Affirmed.

Mitchell Manor Convalescent Home Inc. v. Oklahoma Health Planning Commission, 808 P.2d 998 (Okla. Ct. App. 1991).
Abstract: Opponents appealed the court's dismissal of their petition for review of the Oklahoma Health Planning Commission's granting of a certificate of need for the construction of a nursing home facility. The Court of Appeals held that bringing the action in the county of the opponent's was not necessary. Vacated and remanded.

OREGON

Court of Appeals of Oregon

Oregon Health Care Association v. Health Division, 941 P.2d 593 (Or. Ct. App. 1997).

Abstract: When Association of Health Division requested that the Oregon Health Board reconsider the issuance of certificate of need to construct a skilled nursing facility, the Board subpoenaed facilities belonging to the association who failed to appear in this matter. The association and its facilities made motions against the subpoenas only to have motions denied by the Board. The association and its facilities then appealed to the court to determine jurisdiction to review orders. The Court of Appeals held that the court did have jurisdiction by provisions in the Administrative Procedure Act. Motion granted and jurisdiction determined in the Court of Appeals.

Mercy Medical Center, Inc. v. Office of Health Policy, 855 P.2d 1156 (Or. Ct. App. 1993).

Abstract: Hospital requested judicial review of the Oregon Office of Health Policy's decision to exempt a competitor from requiring a certificate of need in providing magnetic resonance imaging services. The Court of Appeals held that it held no jurisdiction in this matter and did not possess the authority to determine whether or not the minimum financial threshold requiring certificate of need was exceeded by the project. Petition dismissed.

Merle West Medical Center v. State Health Planning & Development Agency, 764 P.2d 613 (Or. Ct. App. 1988).

Abstract: The Oregon State Health Planning and Development Agency appealed the court's reversal of its decision to impress certificate of need review upon the conversion of a number of medical center's acute beds to skilled nursing facility's beds. The Court of Appeals held that the conversion was not judicially reviewable by the court. Reversed and remanded.

State Health Planning & Development Agency v. Salem Hospital CA, 730 P.2d 589 (Or. Ct. App. 1986).

Abstract: The Oregon State Health Planning and Development Agency appealed the Board's reversal of their order of the applicant to provide psychiatric services at their current facility rather than constructing a new unit. The Court of Appeals held that the Board's decision was properly based on the interpretation of the in-patient bed capacity rules, determining that accommodating an additional psychiatric facility would cause the existing unit to exceed its capacity. Affirmed.

Woodland Park Hospital Inc. v. Comprehensive Health Planning Authority, 504 P.2d 753 (Or. Ct. App. 1972).

Abstract: Competing hospital appealed the Oregon Comprehensive Health Planning Authority's decision to award a certificate of need for relocation of hospital. The Court of Appeals held that construction of the hospital was reasonably necessary in light of physician referrals that the "defined population" would be essentially the same as the hospital at its original location. Affirmed.

PENNSYLVANIA

Supreme Court of Pennsylvania

Shenango Valley Osteopathic Hospital v. Department of Health, 451 A.2d 434 (Pa. 1982).
Abstract: The Pennsylvania Department of Health (DOH) appealed the court's order granting hospital special relief from the litigation involved in the DOH's ruling that a certificate of need was required in order for the hospital to acquire a tomography scanner. The Supreme Court held that: (1) the Court possessed the jurisdiction to act over the Hospital's constitutional challenge to the Health Care Facilities Act, and (2) due to the hospital's lack of candor in supplying information to the DOH in its acquisition and disrupting the delivery of health services by interrupting the administration of the Health Care Facilities act, the hospital shall not be granted special relief after filing petition for review. Vacated and Remanded.

Commonwealth Court of Pennsylvania

Millcreek Manor v. Department of Public Welfare, 796 A.2d 1020 (Pa. Commw. Ct. 2001).
Abstract: Nursing home appealed the Pennsylvania State Health Facility Hearing Board's affirmation of the Pennsylvania Department of Public Welfare's (DPW) denial of the nursing home's expansion request. The Court held that: (1) the Officer's disallowance of the nursing home's challenge of the validity of the DPW's decision was in err, and (2) nursing home's right to due process were violated. Vacated and remanded.

Woods Services v. Department of Public Welfare, 681 A.2d 238 (Pa. Commw. Ct. 1996).
Abstract: When the Department of Public Welfare (DPW) refused to act on the organization's application for licensing the intermediate care facility, the non-profit organizations petitioned for judicial review and both parties moved for summary judgment. The Court ruled for the organizations and required DPW to act on the application. Petitioner's motion granted and respondent's motion denied.

Pennsylvania Department of Health v. North Hills Passavant Hospital, 674 A.2d 1141 Pa. Commw. Ct. 1996).
Abstract: The Facility and the Pennsylvania Department of Health (DOH) appealed the Pennsylvania State Health Facility Hearing Board's (HFHB) reversal of the DOH's denial of a hospital's certificate of need (CON) application to provide an open heart surgery facility. The Court held that: (1) HFHB acted outside of its scope of authority in reversing the denial in challenging the need formula; (2) HFHB acted outside of its scope of authority in challenging the need formula and replacing the formula with an adult population based need calculation; and (3) DOH's utilization of the original need formula, based on total population, was not in error. Reversed.

Allegheny County Institution District v. Department of Public Welfare, 668 A.2d 252 (Pa. Commw. Ct. 1995).
Abstract: County Institution District appealed the Pennsylvania Department of Public Welfare's (DPW) decision to deny reimbursement to the district for medical costs that exceeded DPW's operating costs ceilings and for interest and depreciation expenses outside of DPW's per-bed limit. The Court held that: (1) DPW's regulations for calculating amount of assistance provided to the public nursing home care was not in conflict with DPW statute authorizing the authority to make such computations; (2) DPW's regulations for calculating and setting per-bed limit for assistance in depreciation and interest was not in conflict with the federal Social Security Act; and (3) DPW's regulations remain valid even if inflation, differences in construction costs between large and small facilities, and different costs associated with different geographic areas were not taken into consideration. Affirmed.

Central Pa. MRI L.P. v. Department of Health, 648 A.2d 91 (Pa. Commw. Ct. 1994).

Abstract: The competing facility moved to quash the health care facilities' appeal for review of the nonreviewability determination under the Health Care Facilities Act regarding six magnetic resonance imaging centers to be operated by competing facility. The Court held that the health care facilities did not have sufficient standing nor the authority to issue such a petition. Motion to quash petition granted.

Mercy Regional Health System v. Department of Health, 645 A.2d 924 (Pa. Commw. Ct. 1994).
Abstract: When Pennsylvania State Health Facility Hearing Board (HFHB) affirmed the Pennsylvania Department of Health's (DOH) grant of certificate of need (CON) to a surgical center, the Regional Health System petitioned for review. The Court held that: (1) 2 of 3 votes from HFHB members was adequate majority to affirm the DOH, (2) due to improper ex parte communications between CON applicant and DOH after the commencement of the hearing, the DOH's decision was invalid, (3) the hearing provided by the DOH was not applicable to the requirements of administrative agency law, and (4) HFHB needed to make its own findings in light of the fact that substantial evidence scope of review pursuant regulations conflicted with the Health Care Facilities act. Vacated and remanded.

Mechanicsburg Rehabilitation System v. Department of Health, 645 A.2d 372 (Pa. Commw. Ct. 1994).
Abstract: A rehabilitation facility appealed the Pennsylvania State Health Facility Hearing Board's affirmation of the Pennsylvania Department of Health (DOH) to grant a certificate of need (CON) to construct another rehabilitation facility. The Court held that: (1) the requisite "bright-line" test for granting CON was not met by the eighty-five percent occupancy level, and (2) failure to establish factual findings of the State Health Plan's need methodologies by the DOH needed to be remanded. Vacated and remanded.

Xun Imaging Associates v. Department of Health Division of Need Review, 644 A.2d 255 (Pa. Commw. Ct. 1994).
Abstract: Diagnostic facility appealed the court's decision to deny their petition to intervene in the reviewability determination concerning the proposed purchase of diagnostic equipment by a doctor. The Court held that: (1) no pending reviewability existed for the facility to intervene in, and (2) denying the petition to intervene is an adjudicationary act and thus can be appealed. Affirmed.

Robert Packer Hospital v. Department of Health, 631 A.2d 813 (Pa. Commw. Ct. 1993).
Abstract: Medical Facilities' competitors appealed the Pennsylvania State Health Facility Hearing Board's (HFHB) affirmation of the Pennsylvania Department of Health (DOH) to grant a certificate of need (CON) to institute invasive cardiology services. The Court held that: (1) the DOH should use the prior state health plan in effect at the time rather than the current plan in evaluating its decision, and (2) in deciding that CON met criteria of new state health plan, the scope of the HFHB's authority was exceeded. Vacated and remanded.

IFIDA Health Care Group Ltd. v. Department of Health, 596 A.2d 1174(Pa. Commw. Ct. 1991).
Abstract: Health Care Group made consolidated appeals on the Pennsylvania State Health Facility Hearing Board's affirmation of the Pennsylvania Department of Health (DOH) decision to grant a certificate of need (CON) for the construction of nursing homes. The Court held that: (1) in rejecting "hierarchal group clustering" planning formula for determining bed location and in using "by-county" allocation in its stead, the DOH was not acting arbitrarily and capriciously, (2) exhibits not presented at the first public hearings and the planning analysts' irrelevant testimony were properly excluded from DOH hearings, and (3) a de facto amendment to the State Health Plan was not necessary in the application of the "by-county" allocation method. Affirmed.

Jeannette District Memorial Hospital v. Department of Health, 595 A.2d 677 (Pa. Commw. Ct. 1991).
Abstract: Hospital appealed the Pennsylvania State Health Facility Hearing Board's affirmation of the Pennsylva-

nia Department of Health (DOH) decision to grant a certificate of need (CON) for the construction of a freestanding ambulatory surgery center. The Court held that: (1) sufficient evidence had to be made by the ambulatory surgery center that the project would be providing a better less costly alternative to inpatient surgery and that in obtaining a CON it would not increase the total community cost of health care, and (2) DOH's decision relied on not only the ambulatory surgery center evidence but third-party reimbursement evidence, and thus was not arbitrary and capricious. Affirmed.

Morrisons Cove Home v. Department of Health, 593 A.2d 925 (Pa. Commw. Ct. 1991
Abstract: The Pennsylvania State Health Facility Hearing Board's affirmation of the Pennsylvania Department of Health (DOH) decision to grant a certificate of need (CON) for the construction of a nursing home was appealed. The Court held that: (1) by considering occupancy rate of existing nursing homes in addition to table of projected nursing home bed need, was an allowable determination by the DOH of need, (2) DOH did not err in relying on the sufficient evidence was made in determining the level of rehabilitation services were permissible at a skilled nursing facility, (3) accepting the proposed percentage of Medicare patients based on applicant's prior experience as evidence was within the DOH's discretionary authority; (4) deciding the sufficiency of the proposed facility's contribution to the medically underserved groups was within the DOH's discretionary authority; and (5) in excluding the recently approved average occupancy rate or existing nursing home beds computation from its decision and relying only on existing beds was not an abuse of discretion. Affirmed.

Stewart v. Commonwealth Department of Health, 593 A.2d 14 (Pa. Commw. Ct. 1991).
Abstract: Objector appealed the Pennsylvania State Health Facility Hearing Board's (HFHB) denial of an appeal of the Pennsylvania Department of Health's (DOH) decision to grant a certificate of need (CON) for the construction of a long-term care facility as an extension of a continuing care retirement community. This decision was reversed and remanded, but soon thereafter, the HFHB affirmed the decision of the DOH to grant the CON. In a petition for review by the Objector, the Court held that: (1) quashing the motion to appeal was an interlocutory order and could not be appealed; (2) as a member of the public to be served by the proposed project, the objector had sufficient requisite standing; and (3) evidence for the economic feasibility of the facility, substantial need for the facility, and the fact that the facility would have a sliding scale restricting the use of beds to community residents only was established. Appeal quashed in part; order affirmed.

Great Lakes Rehabilitation Hospital v. Commonwealth Department of Health, 592 A.2d 769 (Pa. Commw. Ct. 1991).
Abstract: Competing hospitals sought to challenge the Pennsylvania Department of Health's (DOH) standards for a determination of non-reviewability. The Court held that hospitals lacked standing to challenge and prevent the DOH from issuing determinations of non-reviewability. Dismissed.

Powers v. Commonwealth Department of Health, 570 A.2d 1350 (Pa. Commw. Ct. 1990).
Abstract: The Pennsylvania Department of Health (DOH) and corporation moved to quash the appeal made by competitors against the DOH's decision to deem nonreviewability and exemption of a proposed radiation therapy center from the certificate of need (CON) process. The Court held that there was insufficient evidence to provide competitors the standing to appeal the DOH's decision. Motion to quash granted; petition dismissed.

Overlook Medical Clinic v. Commonwealth Department of Health, 565 A.2d 834 (Pa. Commw. Ct. 1989).
Abstract: When the Pennsylvania State Health Facility Hearing Board deemed that the operator lacked standing to challenge the awarding of a certificate of need (CON) to the competitor the operator petitioned for review. The Court held that the operator did in fact have standing and could challenge the CON granting, and on further consideration, the court held that within 15 days following the publication of notice that the competitor's

CON application was completed, no written objections needed to be filed by the operator in order to be a party to appeal. Reversed and remanded.

IFIDA Health Care Group Ltd. v. Commonwealth Department of Health, 564 A.2d 535 (Pa. Commw. Ct. 1989).
Abstract: Competitor appealed the dismissal of their appeal of the grant of application for certificate of need (CON) by the Pennsylvania State Health Facility Hearing Board. The Court held that the competitor did in fact have standing to file for appeal despite the fact that the competitor did not file written objections within 15 days of publication of notice that CON application was completed by health care operator. Reversed and remanded.

Commonwealth Department of Health v. Rehab Hospital Services Corp., 561 A.2d 342(Pa. Commw. Ct. 1989).
Abstract: The Pennsylvania Department of Health (DOH) sought review of the Pennsylvania State Health Facility Hearing Board's (HFHB) reversal of their decision to award certificate of need to hospital. The Court held that: (1) the HFHB still had jurisdiction to review the DOH's grant despite the fact that CON was issued pursuant to "settlement agreement," (2) right to object to hospital corporation's standing was waived due to the fact that issued was not raised in a timely fashion, (3) if a "settlement agreement" is reached two years after the DOH's decision to deny hospital's CON, the DOH does not have authority to grant CON pursuant to the agreement, and (4) the Court possessed jurisdiction in the case and thus the HFHB's decision could be reviewed. Affirmed.

Overlook Medical Clinic v. Commonwealth Department of Health, 560 A.2d 268 (Pa. Commw. Ct. 1989).
Abstract: When the Pennsylvania State Health Facility Hearing Board deemed that the operator lacked standing to challenge the awarding of a certificate of need (CON) to the competitor the operator petitioned for review. The Court held that the operator did in fact have standing and could challenge the CON granting, despite the fact that operator's initial objections did not contain specifics. Reversed and remanded.

Powers v. Commonwealth Department of Health, 550 A.2d 857 (Pa. Commw. Ct. 1988).
Abstract: Program and other respondents filed objections and moved to quash physician and cancer treatment facility's petition seeking declaratory and injunctive relief against the Pennsylvania Department of Health's (DOH) determination of the program's "non-reviewability" and exemption from obtaining a certificate of need. The Court held that there was insufficient evidence to provide the facility the standing to challenge the DOH's decision. Preliminary objection sustained and motion to quash granted.

Laurel Mobile Health Services Ltd. v. Commonwealth Department of Health, 550 A.2d 616 (Pa. Commw. Ct. 1988).
Abstract: The successor to a certificate of need (CON) for a computerized tomography scanner for two hospitals appealed the Pennsylvania Department of Health's (DOH) exemption of a hospital from requiring a certificate of need (CON) for a computerized tomography scanner. The appealed was dismissed by the DOH and the successor and the hospital petitioned and cross-petitioned for review. The Court denied the successor the motion to quash the hospital's cross petition to consolidate the case and held that: (1) DOH's decision for exemption was a violation of the Health Care Facilities Act, (2) hospital should not have requested a grant of "determination of Non-reviewability" and should have proceeded to obtain a certificate of need, (3) successor had standing to appeal, and (4) it was prohibited by the hospital to presume that because the successor applied for a CON it could not challenge the hospital's acquisition of the scanner. Reversed.

Stewart v. Commonwealth State Health Facility Hearing Bd., 543 A.2d 1290 (Pa. Commw. Ct. 1988).
Abstract: Citizens requested judicial review from the Pennsylvania State Health Facility Hearing Board's decision to quash their appeal against the Department of Health's (DOH) granting of a certificate of need (CON) to

the construction of a long-term care facility. The Court held that the DOH's inability indicate mailing date on citizen's copy of the decision abolished the time limitation applicable to the citizen's appeal. Reversed and remanded.

Charter Hospital of Bucks County, Inc. v. Commonwealth Department of Health, 534 A.2d 1125 (Pa. Commw. Ct. 1987).
Abstract: Hospital appealed the Pennsylvania State Health Facility Hearing Board's affirmation of the Pennsylvania Department of Health decision to hold that the hospital's project was subject to a certificate of need (CON) review. The Court held that: (1) there were no statutes or regulations that exempted nonrecipient health care facilities from the CON review, and (2) the exclusionary provision is not inconsistent with the Pennsylvania Health Care Facilities Act and did not call for unlawful delegation of legislative authority. Affirmed.

Grandview Surgical Center Inc. v. Holy Spirit Hospital of Sisters of Christian Charity, 533 A.2d 796 (Pa. Commw. Ct. 1987).
Abstract: Hospital and the Pennsylvania Department of Health (DOH) appealed the Pennsylvania State Health Facility Hearing Board's reversal of the DOH's decision to grant the hospital a certificate of need (CON) to construct a free-standing ambulatory surgical center. The appeals were consolidated that the Court held that: (1) the CON memorandum in assessing the hospital's application was applied correctly by the DOH, (2) deciding the CON a exception to the state health plan was within DOH jurisdiction; and (3) application was consistent with the state health plan as required by the Health Care Facilities Act. Reversed and remanded.

Metropolitan Hospital v. Commonwealth Department of Health, 527 A.2d 1067 (Pa. Commw. Ct. 1987).
Abstract: When the Pennsylvania State Health Facility Hearing Board affirmed the Pennsylvania Department of Health's (DOH) decision to deny the hospital's application for certificate of need (CON), hospital petitioned for review. The Court held that denial was proper action for the DOH. Affirmed.

Commonwealth Department of Health v. Brownsville Golden Age Nursing Home, Inc., 520 A.2d 926 (Pa. Commw. Ct. 1987).
Abstract: The Pennsylvania Department of Health (DOH) petitioned for judicial review of Pennsylvania State Health Facility Hearing Board's (HFHB) order to lift the suspension on a skilled nursing facility imposed by the DOH and failure to revoke the facility's license. The Court held that: (1) rights of due process were denied the DOH, (2) HFHB decision that DOH did not prove serious violations to health care regulations, was arbitrary and capricious, and (3) revocation of the facility's license without consideration of plan of correction is within the DOH's jurisdiction. HFHB decision vacated; matter remanded with directions.

JDK Management, Inc. v. Commonwealth Department of Public Welfare, 516 A.2d 810 (Pa. Commw. Ct. 1986).
Abstract: Petitioner appealed decision of the Pennsylvania Department of Public Welfare (DPW), for purpose of calculating reimbursements, to omit certain costs. The Court held that: (1) DPW erred in disallowance of construction supervision fee, (2) certificate of need (CON) development fee was a related party cost and could not be disallowed, and (3) in calculating medical assistance reimbursements, CON development fee must be included. Affirmed in part and reversed in part.

Hickory House Nursing Home, Inc. v. Commonwealth Department of Health, 496 A.2d 921 (Pa. Commw. Ct. 1985).
Abstract: When the Pennsylvania Department of Health (DOH) granted the nursing home's application for certificate of need (CON), a competing nursing home petitioned for review. The Court held that the DOH and

applicant supporters entered in illicit ex parte communications violating statutory prohibition Reversed and remanded.

Southern Chester County Medical Center v. Commonwealth Department of Health, 494 A.2d 885 (Pa. Commw. Ct. 1985).
Abstract: Medical center appealed the Pennsylvania State Health Facility Hearing Board's reversal of the Pennsylvania Department of Health's (DOH) decision to grant the proposed addition of beds to medical center was non-reviewable. The Court held that: (1) determination for appeal of the DOH's decision was an adjudication and the Court rather than the Board has jurisdiction over this matter, and (2) because the health systems agency is serving the area of the proposed project, they have standing to opposed the DOH's determination. Remanded.

Rehab Hospital Services Corp. v. Health Systems Agency, 475 A.2d 883 (Pa. Commw. Ct. 1984).
Abstract: The Facility and the Pennsylvania Department of Health (DOH) appealed the Pennsylvania State Health Facility Hearing Board's reversal of the Secretary of the DOH's granting of a certificate of need (CON) to prospective health provider. The appeals were consolidated that the Court held that the Secretary did not err in finding that the rehabilitation center would be less costly financially feasible alternative to providing rehabilitation services to the area and thus warranted a CON. Reversed and remanded with directions.

Mercy Hospital v. Commonwealth Department of Health, 450 A.2d 761 (Pa. Commw. Ct. 1982).
Abstract: Hospital petitioned for judicial review of the Pennsylvania State Health Facility Hearing Board's affirmation of the Pennsylvania Department of Health determination that the hospital's proposal for the new addition of a rehabilitation unit was subject to certificate of need review. The Court held that hospital petitioned prematurely. Motion to quash appeal granted.

RHODE ISLAND

Supreme Court of Rhode Island

Johnston Ambulatory Surgical Associates, LTD. v. Patricia Nolan, in her capacity as Director of the Rhode Island Department of Health, 755 A.2d 799 (R.I. 2000).
Abstract: Applicant appealed and petitioned for writ of certiorari on the Court's affirmation of the Rhode Island Department of Health's rejection of application of certificate of need (CON) to establish a free standing surgical center. After consolidating petitions the Supreme Court held that: (1) no special treatment to recommend the health services to approve application was obligated by the Department director, and (2) precluding the grant of second CON application was the doctrine of administrative finality. Petitions denied and dismissed.

Superior Court of Rhode Island

Summit Neighborhood Association v. Rhode Island Department of Health, 2004 R.I. Super. LEXIS 98 (R.I. Super. Ct. 2004).
Abstract: Neighborhood association appeals a certificate of need (CON) approval allowing Miriam Hospital the ability to reorganize and renovate its surgical department. Appellant alleges that the Rhode Island Department of Health (DOH) was acting without statutory authority when it granted the CON. The Court finds that the DOH's decision was supported by substantial evidence and that the CON approval was not an abuse of discretion.

Edgehill Newport, Inc. v. New England Alcoholism Treatment & Education Programs, Inc., 1983 R.I. Super. LEXIS 50 (R.I. Super. Ct. 1983).

Abstract: Plaintiff appealed the Rhode Island Department of Health's decision to grant "grandfathered" exemption to the defendant from obtaining a certificate of need (CON). The Court held that the defendant did take sufficient substantial activity and project commencements before July 1, 1980, when CON first came into effect, and therefore is eligible for the grandfather exemption. Affirmed.

SOUTH CAROLINA

Supreme Court of South Carolina

Roper Hospital v. Board of South Carolina Department of Health and Environmental Control, 410 S.E. 2d 558 (S.C. 1991).

Abstract: A hospital appealed the South Carolina Board of Health and Environmental Control's (BHEC) decision to deny them a certificate of need to build a new hospital. The Richland County Circuit ruled in favor of the hospital and BHEC appealed. The Supreme Court found that BHEC's decision had been made based on substantial evidence and was neither arbitrary nor capricious. Reversed

South Carolina Baptist Hospital v. South Carolina Department of Health & Environmental Control, 353 S.E.2d 277 (S.C. 1987).

Abstract: Four hospitals appealed to the South Carolina Board of Health and Environmental Control (BHEC) after being denied certificates of need (CON) by the Department of Health and Environmental Control (DHEC). The BHEC remanded the case back to the DHEC. The hospitals appealed to the Common Pleas Court were the judge decided in favor of the hospitals and directed the DHEC to issue CONs to all four hospitals. The Department appealed to the Supreme Court on grounds that the BHEC's interlocutory decision to remand was not subject to judicial review. The court found this reasoning to be sound. The court found it premature to decide upon the merits of this dispute when it appeared that the DHEC had not yet had time to examine the merits of the case. Reversed and remanded.

South Carolina Court of Appeals

Marlboro Park Hospital v. South Carolina Department of Health and Environmental Control, 595 S.E.2d 851 (S.C. Ct. App. 2004).

Abstract: Competitor appeals from certificate of need (CON) approval for outpatient clinic reversing and Administrative Law Judge's (ALJ) decision denying the CON. The Department's erred in using a de novo standard of review and that the ALJ's decision was supported by substantial evidence. The Court reinstates the ALJ's decision denying the CON.

National Health Corp. v. South Carolina Department of Health & Environmental Control, 380 S.E.2d 841 (S.C. Ct. App. 1989).

Abstract: The appellant sought judicial review for the decision of the South Carolina Department of Health and Environmental Control (DHEC) to grant a certificate of need to another corporation. The Court of Common Pleas affirmed the DHEC's decision. The appellant claimed that the DHEC's decisions were: (1) a violation of constitutional or statutory law, (2) affected by error of law, and (3) contrary to substantial evidence and erroneous, arbitrary and capricious. The Court of Appeals did not find these three claims to hold. Judicial review denied. Affirmed.

Home Health Services, Inc. v. South Carolina Department of Health & Environmental Control, 379 S.E.2d 734 (S.C. Ct. App. 1989).

Abstract: After the South Carolina Department of Health and Environmental Control (DHEC) granted a certificate of need to a home health service agency, a competitor brought action to seek judicial review of the decision. The Common Pleas court granted the DHEC's motion for dismissal. The competitor appealed to the Court of Appeals claiming that it was a "person adversely affected" by the ruling and sought to obtain judicial review of the DHEC's decision. The Court held that since the competitor did not seek "party" status during the DHEC proceedings, it lacked standing to seek judicial review. Affirmed.

SOUTH DAKOTA

Supreme Court of South Dakota

Heritage of Yankton v. South Dakota Department of Health, 432 N.W.2d 68 (S.D. 1988).

Abstract: The Circuit Court of the First Judicial Circuit, Yankton County affirmed the South Dakota Department of Health's(DOH) decision to deny an application for an addition and renovation of an existing nursing home. The nursing home appealed on the grounds that (1) there was a need for additional nursing home beds, (2) the DOH acted arbitrarily and capriciously in denying the application, and (3) the DOH did not provide valid reasons for rejecting new information that had been submitted at the rehearing. The Supreme Court found the grounds to be unsubstantiated. Affirmed.

In re St. Luke's Hospital, 414 N.W.2d 297 (S.D. 1987).

Abstract: The Circuit Court reversed and remanded the South Dakota Department of Health's (DOH) decision to grant a certificate of need to an applicant who sought to purchase advance cancer treatment equipment that was brought forth by a competitor. The Hospital appealed the ruling holding that the DOH's decision to grant the request was neither arbitrary nor capricious. The Supreme Court found that the DOH's decision was consistent with the guidelines. Reversed and remanded.

In re Change of Bed Category of Tieszen Memorial Home, 343 N.W.2d 97 (S.D. 1984).

Abstract: The Circuit Court found that it was not necessary for a nursing home to obtain a certificate of need to create a permanent change in bed categories. The South Dakota Department of Health appealed. The Supreme Court found in favor of the nursing home because the change in bed categories would not affect the capital expenditure. Affirmed.

TENNESSEE

Supreme Court of Tennessee

Scott v. Ashland Healthcare Center, 49 S.W.3d 281 (Tenn. 2001).

Abstract: The Circuit Court granted summary judgment to nursing home operator, nursing home builder, and wholly-owned subsidiary of builder after beneficiary brought wrongful death action against them. The beneficiary appealed to the Court of Appeals which affirmed the decision. Appealing to the Supreme Court, the beneficiary argued that the nursing home was negligent in providing care for the deceased, and should be held liable. The Supreme Court found that the nursing home as the holder of the certificate of need was (1) responsible for initiating operation of the facility, and (2) that duty could not be delegable. Therefore the decision of summary judgment was incorrect and is reversed and remanded.

ABC Home Health Serv. v. Tennessee Health Facilities Commission, 891 S.W.2d 213 (Tenn. 1994).
Abstract: The Tennessee Health Facilities Commission denied ABC's request for a certificate of need in order to relocate two of its parent offices. ABC then filed a petition for judicial review and was denied. In the appeal, the Davidson County Chancery Court affirmed the Commissions ruling. ABC then went to the Court of Appeals claiming that the county court had acted arbitrarily and capriciously in denying its application. The Court found no evidence of such actions. Affirmed.

Humana of Tennessee v. Tennessee Health Facilities Commission, 551 S.W.2d 664 (Tenn. 1977).
Abstract: A competitor appealed to the Supreme Court concerning the decision of the Tennessee Health Facilities Commission (HFC) to grant a certificate of need to a rival hospital that sought to construct a 65-bed specialty care hospital in the area. The competitor held that there was substantive or procedural error in the HFC's decision. The Supreme Court held that there was no indication of error Affirmed.

Tennessee Court of Appeals

Wellmont Health System v. Tennessee Health Facilities Commission, 2004 Tenn. App. LEXIS 71 (Tenn. Ct. App. 2004).
Abstract: An Administrative Law Judge vacated a certificate of need (CON) on the grounds that a Tennessee Health Facilities Commission (HFC) member had a conflict of interest. At issue is whether HFC members have a duty to recuse themselves from CON proceedings with which they have a conflict of interest. A HFC rule requires members who have a conflict of interest with any project to recuse himself or herself from the deliberations and vote. A competitor's failure to petition the HFC for recusal does not act as a waiver of the conflict of interest. The member's vote is void. However, the decision of the HFC is final and not subject to reconsideration.

Morristown Surgery Center, LLC v. Tennessee Health Facilities Commission, 2003 Tenn. App. LEXIS 879 (Tenn. Ct. App. 2003).
Abstract: Competitor appeals from an Administrative Law Judge's denial of a petition for a contested case hearing. Competitor alleges that because the Commission reviewed both CON applications simultaneously, it automatically converted the petitions into competing petitions. The Court finds that the only effect of the simultaneous review is to consider two applications in the same session. The Commission has discretion whether to approve one, both or none. The court cannot review an agency decision de novo or substitute its judgment for that of the agency. The ALJ was appropriate to dismiss competitor's petition.

Methodist Healthcare-Jackson Hospital v. Jackson-Madison County General Hospital District, 129 S.W.3d 57 (Tenn. Ct. App. 2003).
Abstract: Competitor appeals certificate of need (CON) approval. Competitor alleges that the Administrative Law Judge (ALJ) did not have jurisdiction to enter a final order because of pending conflict of interest issues. The Court finds that those issues were separate and distinct from the ones facing the ALJ and that the ALJ had jurisdiction to enter the final order. The Commission is prohibited by statute from reconsidering a decision to approve or deny a CON application. However, a member had a disqualifying conflict of interest in the proceed-

ing rendering the vote void. The case is remanded to the Commission for reconsideration of competitor's CON application.

The Tennessee Department of Health v. Gary C. Boyle, M.D., 2002 Tenn. App. LEXIS 894 Tenn. Ct. App. 2002).
Abstract: At issue is whether a Tennessee statute requiring a private clinic that performs a "substantial number" of abortions to obtain a certificate of need is constitutional. The Court finds that the statute is unconstitutionally vague because it fails to give fair notice of its requirements and encourages arbitrary and discriminatory enforcement. The statute is also an undue burden on a woman's right to privacy.

Rivendell Children and Youth Center, a/k/a *Rivendell of Tennessee, Inc., v. Tennessee Health Facilities Commission*, 1987 Tenn. App. LEXIS 3044 (Tenn. Ct. App. 1987).
Abstract: Rivendell Children and Youth Center appealed a Tennessee Health Facilities Commission (HFC) decision to deny their application for a certificate of need. Rivendell filed a petition, but then voluntarily withdrew it. A few months later, they again filed petition. The HFC moved to dismiss the petition because it was filed after the 60 day period. The Chancery Court ruled in favor of Rivendell and the case was appealed to the Court of Appeals. The court held that: the statute that the Chancery Court had based its decision on, was not valid in this case. Reversed and Remanded.

East Tennessee Health Improvement Council Inc. v. Tennessee Health Facilities Commission, 626 S.W.2d 272 (Tenn. Ct. App. 1981).
Abstract: Agency was denied by the Chancery Court, Davidson County for its petition requesting judicial review of decision of Tennessee State Health Facilities Commission to grant hospital a certificate of need for the addition of 100 beds. In the appeal the agency held that it was an "aggrieved person" and therefore had the right to request judicial review. The Court of Appeals found that it did not classify as such and therefore did not have proper standing to seek judicial review. Affirmed.

Fairhaven Corp. v. Tennessee Health Facilities Commission, 566 S.W.2d 885 (Tenn. Ct. App. 1976).
Abstract: After being denied its application for certificate of need to expand its facilities, the nursing home sought a writ of certiorari through the Davidson County Chancery Court. The petition was dismissed. The nursing home then appealed to the Court of Appeals. The court ruled that because the request did not fall into the 30-day time limitation, the court did not have jurisdiction to grant its request. Affirmed.

TEXAS

Supreme Court of Texas

Texas Health Facilities Commission v. Presbyterian Hospital North, 690 S.W.2d 564 (Tex. 1985).
Abstract: After judicial review, the Texas Health Facilities Commission (HFC) denied the request of an applicant for a certificate of need (CON) to build a new hospital. The 250th District Court affirmed the HFC's decision, and the applicant appealed to the Austin Court of Appeals where the case was reversed and remanded. The HFC was also granted its request for a writ of error. The Supreme Court found that the HFC's facts to deny the CON did not satisfy statutory requirements. Affirms in part. Remands the case back to the HFC.

Texas Health Facilities Commission v. Charter Medical-Dallas Inc., 665 S.W.2d 446 (Tex. 1984).
Abstract: The Texas Health Facilities Commission (HFC) granted certificate of needs to two hospitals and denied another. The 250th Judicial District Court upheld the decision, and upon appeal with the Austin Court

of Appeals, the decision was reversed and remanded with instructions. The Supreme Court then heard the appeal upon the basis that the HFC's decisions had been arbitrary and capricious. The Court found the HFC's findings to be supported by substantial evidence. Reversed.

Texas Court of Appeals

Presbyterian Medical Center v. Texas Health Facilities Commission, 698 S.W.2d 247 (Tex. App. 1985).
Abstract: The hospital appealed to the 345th Judicial District Court when the Texas Health Facilities Commission adjudicated a contested case concerning the certificate of need program. After the Court affirmed the order, the hospital appealed. The Court of Appeals ruled that because agency and governing statutes were abolished while the appeal was pending, then the appeal was moot. Appeal dismissed.

American Medical Center, Inc. v. Texas Health Facilities Commission, 697 S.W.2d 533 (Tex. App. 1985).
Abstract: The 201st Judicial District Court upheld the Texas Health Facilities Commission's ruling of a contested case concerning certificate of need. In the subsequent appeal, the Court of Appeals deemed the appeal to be moot on the grounds that the agency was already abolished. Appeal dismissed.

Baptist Memorial Hospital System v. Texas Health Facilities Commission, 697 S.W.2d 531 (Tex. App. 1985).
Abstract: A hospital appealed against the Texas Health Facilities Commission's ruling of a contested case concerning certificate of need. The 261st Judicial District Court deemed the appeal to be moot on the ground that the agency was already abolished. Appeal dismissed.

Presbyterian Hospital North v. Texas Health Facilities Commission, 664 S.W.2d 391 (Tex. App. 1983).
Abstract: Applicants appealed to the 250th Judicial District Court after a request for a certificate of need was denied by the Texas Health Facilities Commission (HFC). The Court affirmed the HFC's decision, so a second appeal was sent to the Court of Appeals. The Court of Appeals found that the HFC's facts (1) were opinions, (2) did not support its own conclusion, and (3) are invalid concerning the applicants ability to be less costly and more effective. Reversed, remanded with instructions.

Charter Medical-Dallas, Inc. v. Texas Health Facilities Commission, 656 S.W.2d 928 (Tex. App. 1983).
Abstract: Charter Medical appealed to the 250th Judicial District Court after a request for a certificate need was denied. The court sustained the Texas Health Facilities Commission (HFC) ruling, and Charter appealed to the Court of Appeals. The Court of Appeals found the HFC's findings to be arbitrary and capricious, lacking supporting evidence. Reversed and Remanded.

Texas Health Facilities Commission v. West Texas Home Health Agency, 588 S.W.2d 655 (Tex. App. 1979).
Abstract: A hospital operated "work rooms" without obtaining prior approval by the Texas Health Facilities Commission (HFC) and was ordered to close its offices. The 126th District Court ruled to set aside the HFC's order. The HFC appealed to the Court of Civil Appeals on the grounds that (1) the trial court did not have jurisdiction, (2) it had found violations concerning the hospital, and (3) the HFC's rules did not exempt the hospital from obtaining a certificate of need. The Court disagreed on all three counts. Affirmed.

Texas Health Facilities Commission v. Nueces County Hospital District, 581 S.W.2d 768 (Tex. App. 1979).
Abstract: The 53rd District Court reversed the order issued by the Texas Health Facilities Commission (HFC) denying the hospital a certificate of need to authorize the purchase and installation of a body scanner. The HFC appealed to the Court of Civil Appeals. The Court found the HFC's evidence arbitrary and capricious. Affirmed.

Nueces County Hospital District v. Texas Health Facilities Commission, 576 S.W.2d 908 (Tex. App. 1979).
Abstract: The Texas State Health Facilities Commission (HFC) granted a certificate of need for a body scanner for one hospital, but denied a similar application by the country hospital district. The 53rd District Court upheld the HFC's ruling. The district appealed to the Court of Civil Appeals. The Court found that (1) there was supporting evidence for the HFC's decision, (2) there was no abuse of discretion, and (3) there was no reversible error done by previous courts. Affirmed.

Texas Health Facilities Commission v. Baptist General Convention, 573 S.W.2d 575 (Tex. App. 1978).
Abstract: The 201st District Court overturned the Texas Health Facilities Commission's (HFC) decision to deny a hospital a certificate of need. The HFC appealed to the Court of Civil Appeals. The Court found that: (1) the HFC's conclusions were unsubstantiated, (2) prior to determination of need, the hospital was not required to designate use for shelled space, (3) it is the HFC's responsibility to establish a rule concerning shelled space and inform hospitals to submission of applications, and (4) because of the aforementioned statements, the HFC's decision to deny application was arbitrary and capricious. District Court Affirmed.

Texas Health Facilities Commission v. El Paso Medical Surgical Associates, 573 S.W.2d 291 (Tex. App. 1978).
Abstract: The 126th District Court overturned the Texas Health Facilities Commission's (HFC) decision to deny the application of an association of physicians that sought to transfer ownership of a certificate of need and relocate. The HFC appealed and the Court of Civil Appeals held that: (1) the HFC's ruling was not arbitrary or capricious, (2) nor was the HFC's failure to follow its established holding which authorized transfer and relocation arbitrary or capricious. District Court reversed; HFC affirmed.

VERMONT

Supreme Court of Vermont

In re Central Vermont Medical Center, 816 A.2d 531 (Vt. 2002).
Abstract: Appeal from certificate of need application denial for a renovation and expansion of Central Vermont Hospital. The Commissioner found that the hospital's application did not meet the general and mandatory criteria. The challenging party must show a "compelling indication of error" to overcome the presumption that the Agency's decision is correct. The hospital was given adequate notice that it would have to demonstrate need for the expansion. The Commissioner provided adequate justification for the decision and the findings were based on substantial evidence in the record.

Brattleboro Memorial Hospital v. Department of Banking, Insurance, Securities and Health Care Administration, 782 A.2d 1217 (Vt. 2001).
Abstract: Hospital appealed to the Supreme Court after the Health Care Administration ruled that it required a certificate of need (CON) to have a mobile magnetic resonance imaging service. The Court held that: (1) "new institutional health service" status was not granted solely on the grounds that there was an annual operating expense in excess of $300,000, and (2) therefore, a CON should be required based on those grounds. Reversed and remanded.

In re Professional Nurses Service, 719 A. 2d 894 (Vt. 1998).
Abstract: Nursing Company appealed to the Supreme Court after the Health Care Administration denied its application for certificate of need. The Court held that: (1) Health Resources Management Plan directed Administration to demonstrate need for certification based on high costs or gaps in service, (2) Department was not

required issue recommendation on need, and (3) nursing company's charge of discrimination against the Department was not subject to review. Affirmed.

In re AssureCare of Vermont, 686 A.2d 959 (Vt. 1996).
Abstract: Health care organization appealed to the Supreme Court after the Health Care Authority (HCA) denied its application for certificate of need to operate as an HMO. The Court held that: (1) HCA did not abuse discretion and create new criterion, (2) delayed notice about criterion did not hurt the organization, (3) HCA did not abuse discretion by evaluating with its own predictions concerning success of failure of the venture, (4) statues did not authorize HCA to examine availability of resources when ruling, and (5) HCA's failure to act in an timely manner did not automatically warrant relief. Affirmed.

VIRGINIA

Supreme Court of Virginia

State Health Commissioner v. Sentara Norfolk General Hospital, 534 S.E. 325 (Va. 2000).
Abstract: Application for an additional liver transplant program was denied by the health commissioner, the Circuit Court, and City of Norfolk. The applicant then appealed to the Court of Appeals, Overton where the decision was reversed. Upon appeal, the Supreme Court held that: (1) by complying with the state medical facilities plan does not assure approval of certificate of public need (COPN), (2) Commissioner did not abuse discretion by applying a lighter standard for denying COPN, and (3) decision was based on substantial evidence. Reversed. Dismissal of petition for appeal reinstated.

Richlands Medical Association v. Commonwealth ex rel State Health Commissioner, 337 S.E.2d 737 (Va. 1985).
Abstract: State Health Commissioner appealed for writ of mandamus to the Circuit Court of the city of Richmond after the hearing examiner overturned its denial of certificate of need to applicant. The Circuit Court granted writ. Applicant appealed to the Supreme Court which held that the Commissioner that was granted discretion and judgment could not be subject to review by mandamus. Reversed, write vacated, and petition dismissed.

Virginia Court of Appeals

Fairfax Surgical Center v. State Health Commissioner, 405 S.E. 2d 430 (Va. Ct. App. 1991).
Abstract: Hospital appealed to the Circuit Court, Fairfax County after the State Health Commissioner ruled that it was necessary for them to obtain a certificate of need (CON) before they could construct an additional out-patient room. The Circuit Court affirmed the ruling, and the hospital appealed to the Court of Appeals. The Court held that a CON was not necessary because it was not an additional bed or an extension for project requiring review. Reversed.

Johnston-Willis Ltd. v. Kenley, 369 S.E.2d 1 (Va. Ct. App. 1988).
Abstract: Hospital appealed to the Circuit Court, Chesterfield County after the State Health Commissioner denied its application for certificate of need to add obstetrical beds and to reorganize its outpatient surgery program. The Circuit Court affirmed the denial to add beds, but reversed the reorganization ruling. The Court of Appeals held that: (1) decision to deny was supported by substantial evidence, (2) under the State Health Plan the hospital did not fit appropriate criteria to receive certificate, (3) statistical methodologies were appropriate to evaluate need, and (4)federal minimum occupancy standards could be applied in determining need. Affirmed.

Bio-Medical Applications of Arlington, Inc. v. Kenley, 358 S.E.2d 722 (Va. Ct. App. 1987).
Abstract: Competitor appealed to the Circuit Court, City of Salem after the Commissioner of Health approved a certificate of need (CON) for additional radiation therapy services. The competitor appealed after the Circuit Court affirmed the ruling. The Court of Appeals held that: (1) Commissioner had authority to discern if CON would be "consistent" to the State Health Plan, (2) the issuing of CON was consistent to the State Health Plan, and (3) the trail court did not err in determining that the Commissioner's ruling was based on substantial evidence. Affirmed.

Roanoke Memorial Hospitals v. Kenley, 352 S.E.2d 525 (Va. Ct. App. 1987).
Abstract: Competitor appealed to the Circuit Court, City of Salem after the Commissioner of Health approved a certificate of need (CON) for additional radiation therapy services. The competitor appealed after the Circuit Court affirmed the ruling. The Court of Appeals held that: (1) Commissioner had authority to discern if CON would be "consistent" to the State Health Plan, (2) the issuing of CON was consistent to the State Health Plan, and (3) the trail court did not err in determining that the Commissioner's ruling was based on substantial evidence. Affirmed.

State Board of Health v. Virginia Hospital Association, 332 S.E.2d 793 (Va. Ct. App. 1985).
Abstract: Hospital appealed for injunctive and declaratory relief to the Circuit Court, City of Richmond because the Board of Health adopted regulations that were not according to law. The Circuit Court granted relief, and the Board appealed to the Court of Appeals. The Court held that the Board's regulation concerning the extension time beyond 120 days to determine final ruling was invalid. Affirmed.

Virginia Circuit Court

Riverside Hospital, Inc. d/b/a *Riverside Regional Medical Center v. Robe B. Stroube*, 61 Va. Cir. 331(Va. Cir. Ct. 2003).
Abstract: Appeal from Certificate of Public Need (COPN) application denial for mobile MRI unit. The Commissioner was appropriate in denying the COPN application. The healthcare provider's application was inconsistent with the State Medical Facilities Plan criteria. The provider's application was also not the least costly of competing applications.

Northern Virginia Community Hospital, LLC d/b/a *Broadlands Regional Medical Center v. Robert B. Stroube*, M.D., M.P.H., 63 Va. Cir. 196 (Va. Cir. Ct. 2003).
Abstract: Appeal from Certificate of Need (CON) application denial for the replacement of two hospitals with one larger hospital. The Commissioner is required to consider the recommendation and the reasons of the CON agency. Here, the Agency never gave any reasons on which the Commissioner could rely. The case must be remanded with instructions to the CON agency to provide a formal recommendation with reasons for that recommendation.

Southwest Virginia Health System Agency v. Kenley, 5 Va. Cir. 270 (Va. Cir. Ct. 1985).
Abstract: Three hospitals filed a notice of appeal, and cross bill to the Circuit Court after the State Health Commissioner approved a certificate of need for a competitor. The Court held that: (1) notice of appeal was filed in untimely manner, and so is dismissed, (2) the cross bill raises questions that are not appropriate in this case, so it is dismissed, (3) Commissioner did not err in his ruling. Affirmed.

Bio-Medical Applications of Arlington, Inc. v. Kenley, 5 Va. Cir. 159 (Va. Cir. Ct. 1984).
Abstract: Facility appealed for injunctive relief to the Circuit Court of Arlington County after it was denied a

certificate of need (CON) to expand its facilities and a competitor was granted a CON. The Court held that (1) there was substantial evidence to support the ruling, and (2) a fair comparative review was held. Motion denied. Washington

Supreme Court of Washington

St. Joseph Hospital & Health Care Center v. Department of Health, 887 P.2d 891 (Wash 1995).

Abstract: Competitor filed for and was denied hearing by the Department of Health (DOH). The applicant filed for administrative appeal after being denied its application. The case was remanded and the applicant was granted a conditional certificate of need. Competitor filed a petition for review to the Superior Court. The Superior Court remanded the proceedings on the grounds that the competitor was denied procedural due process. The Supreme Court held that: (1) the competitor had standing, (2) DOH was in error for failing to notify competitor concerning the reopening review of application, and (3) validity of a regulation can only be challenged at the time of its adoption. Affirmed.

Washington Court of Appeals

Multicare Health System d/b/a/ *Tacoma General Allenmore Hospital v. Department of Health of the State of Washington*,77 P.3d 363(Wash. Ct. App. 2003).

Abstract: Issue is whether the relocation of beds to a new facility requires a certificate of need. A license shall only be issued for the premises and that a license shall not be transferable except with the Department of Health's (DOH) approval. When a healthcare provider wants to bring new premises under an existing license, it must obtain a new license or amend the old one that includes a new license. To obtain a license the applicant must follow DOH regulations.

Children's Hospital & Medical Center v. Department of Health, 975 P.2d 567 (Wash. Ct. App. 1999).

Abstract: A children's hospital appealed to the Superior Court after the Department of Health ruled that a neighboring hospital could perform pediatric open heart surgeries without a Certificate of Need (CON). The case was dismissed. Upon appeal, the Court of Appeals held that: (1) pediatric open heart surgery qualifies as "specialized inpatient pediatric services" and therefore is subject to CON law, and (2) the Superior Court's ruling was arbitrary and capricious. Reversed.

Watkins v. Restorative Care Center Inc., 831 P.2d 1085 (Wash. Ct. App. 1992).

Abstract: Lessor appealed to the Superior Court after the lessee reduced number of nursing home beds in operation. The Superior Court found in favor of the lessor, and the lesse appealed to the Court of Appeals. The Court held that the lessee did not violate regulatory agreement or breach lease by reducing number of beds. Affirmed in part, remanded in part.

Centennial Villas Inc. v. State, 733 P.2d 564 (Wash. Ct. App. 1987).

Abstract: Nursing homes and hospitals with certificates of need (CON) appealed to the Superior Court for declaratory and injunctive relief after the Department of Social and Health Services ruled that they need to undergo a second CON review. The Superior Court granted summary judgment. The Department appealed, the cases were consolidated and the Court of Appeals held that supplying new and additional services qualified as "new health care facility" status and had to obtain a second certificate of need review. Reversed.

Washington Superior Court

Providence Hospital of Everett v. State of Washington, 112 Wash.2d 353 (Wash. Super. Ct. 1989).
Abstract: Applicant appealed to the Thurston County Superior Court after the Department of Social Health Services (DSHS) denied its application to provide obstetrical services. The Superior Court affirmed the DSHS's ruling, and the applicant appealed to the Supreme Court. The Court held that the DSHS's decision was not arbitrary and capricious. Affirmed.

WEST VIRGINIA

West Virginia Supreme Court of Appeals

West Virginia Health Care Cost Review Authority v. Boone Memorial Hospital, 472 S.E.2d 411 (W. Va. 1996).
Abstract: Hospital appealed to Office of Hearings and Appeals (OHA) after the Health Care Cost Review Authority (HCCRA) ruled that certificate of need was require to switch from computer tomography to stationary machine on hospital premises, operated by outside company. The OHA reversed the ruling and the HCCRA appealed, the circuit court ruled in favor of the HCCRA, and hospital appealed. The Supreme Court held that: (1) statutes concerning case were ambiguous, (2) HCCRA had legislative authority to interpret statute, and (3) HCCRA's rulings would be sustained. Affirmed.

St. Mary's Hospital v. State Health Planning & Development Tax Commissioner, 364 S.E.2d 805 (W. Va. 1987).
Abstract: Competitor appealed to Tax Department after the West Virginia State Health Planning and Development Agency (SHPDA) approved an applicant's certificate of need to build a hospital. The Tax Department affirmed the ruling and competitor turned to circuit court for review of administrative decisions. Circuit court affirmed, and competitor appealed to the Supreme Court. The Court ruled that the SHPDA's ruling lacked substantial evidence and its findings were made in conclusory fashion and therefore were inadequate. Reversed and remanded.

United Hospital Center v. Richardson, 328 S.E.2d 195 (W. Va. 1985).
Abstract: Hospitals petitioned for writ of mandamus to Supreme Court after West Virginia Public Health Planning Agency (PHPA) did not respond within 15 days of receiving the applications. The Court held that the PHPA must comply to statutes. Writ granted.

Princeton Community Hospital v. State Health Planning, 328 S.E.2d 164 (W. Va. 1985).
Abstract: Hospitals appealed to Tax Department after the State Health Planning and Development Agency (SHPDA) denied their applications to add acute care beds. Tax Department affirmed its ruling, and the hospitals appealed to the Circuit Court. The Circuit Court reversed the ruling and the SHPDA appealed to the Supreme Court. The Court held that: (1) bed need methodology was applied erroneously, (2) inconsistent findings by hospitals' and State Health plan were not an abuse of discretion. Circuit Court ruling reversed.

WISCONSIN

Wisconsin Court of Appeals

Wausau Hospitals Inc. v. Department of Health & Social Services, 291 N.W.2d (Wis. Ct. App. 1980).
Abstract: Hospital appealed to circuit court after Department of Health and Social Services (DHSS) ruled that all hospitals that wished to resume elective open heart surgery and performing the surgery at a new facility needed to obtain a certificate of need. The Circuit Court ruled in favor of the hospital, and DHSS appealed to the Court of Appeals. The Court held that because of transition provisions, hospital's did not need to apply for certificate of need. Orders affirmed.

WYOMING

Supreme Court of Wyoming

In re Application for Certificate of Need by HCA Health Services, 689 P.2d 108 (Wyo. 1984).
Abstract: Hospital filed for administrative review after the State Certificate of Need Review Board (CONRB) granted a certificate of need to competitor. The hearing officer stayed the appeal pending judicial resolution as to whether or not CONRB had authority to resolve the issue. The Supreme Court held that CONRB according to federal and state statues was obligated to provide administrative hearings to affected persons. Reversed and remanded.

CON CASE LAW
ORGANIZED BY UNDERLYING CAUSE OF ACTION

Classified List of Causes of Action for CON

Listed below is Health Capital Consultants' standard list of causes of action applicable to Certificate of Need case law. Causes of action printed in **bold** are broader in scope than causes of action printed in normal typeface. When a case is decided on more than one issue of law, each cause of action is listed in order of importance to the decision.

CAUSES OF ACTION

1. **Antitrust**
   a. Applicability of Noerr-Pennington doctrine- Defense which protects those who attempt to use the power of the government to further private interests. (*See* Noerr, 365 U.S. at 145.)

2. **Constitutional Challenge**
   a. Equal Protection violation
   b. Procedural Due Process violation

3. **Statutory Violation**
   a. Violation of Administrative Procedures Act
   b. CON board exceeded statutory authority when establishing rules, standards, and/or criteria
   c. Violation of state law during CON proceedings
   d. Defining statutory term

4. **Regulatory Violation**
   a. Violation of CON board's internal/administrative rules
   b. CON board's internal/administrative rules are arbitrary
   c. Defining regulatory term

5. **Validity of CON Board Decision**
   a. CON board decision was arbitrary
   b. Reconsideration of previous CON decision

6. **Public Need Challenge**
   a. Temporary Restraining Order (TRO) on CON requirements
   b. Injunction on CON requirements
   c. Establishment/challenge to new need requirements for state health plan
   d. Defining state health plan term
   e. Applicability of need criteria to applicant
   f. Applicability of need criteria to transfer of CON

7. **Miscellaneous**
   a. Court's denial of petition for judicial review was arbitrary
   b. Failure to obtain CON

CON Case Law
Organized by Underlying Cause of Action

I. ANTITRUST

1. Antitrust, "Jackson Tennessee Hospital Company, LLC. v. West Tennessee Healthcare, Inc.", United States District Court for the Western District of Tennessee, Eastern Division, (2/27/2004).
2. Antitrust, "Alan D. Gordon v. Lewistown Hospital", United States District Court for the Middle District of Pennsylvania, (7/11/2003).
3. Antitrust, "New York v. St. Francis Hosp.", United States District Court for the Southern District of New York, (4/10/2000).
4. Antitrust, 3. Statutory Violation, "Surgical Care Center of Hammond, L.C. v. Hospital Service District No. 1 of Tangipahoa Parish, and Quorum Health Resources, Inc.", United States Court of Appeals for the Fifth Circuit, (8/27/1998).
5. Antitrust, 1.a. Applicability of Pennington-Pennington Doctrine, "Kottle v. Northwest Kidney Ctrs.", United States Court of Appeals For the Ninth Circuit, (7/18/1998).
6. Antitrust, "Dianne J. Ford, M.D. v. Steven L. Stroup, M.D.; Radiation Oncology Associates; Nashville Memorial Health Systems, Inc.," United States Court of Appeals for the Sixth Circuit, (4/23/1997).
7. Antitrust, 3.a. Violation of Administrative Procedures Act, 3. Statutory Violation, 4. Regulatory Violation, "Huron Valley Hospital Inc. v. Pontiac Ci", United States District Court For the Eastern District of Michigan, Southern Division, (3/2/1997).
8. Antitrust, "Martin v. Memorial Hosp.", United States Court of Appeals For the Fifth Circuit, (7/10/1996).
9. Antitrust, 5. Validity of CON Board Decision, "FTC v. Hospital Bd. of Directors", United States Court of Appeals for the Eleventh Circuit, (11/30/1994).
10. Antitrust, 3. Statutory Violation, 5. Validity of CON Board Decision, "Tarabishi v. McAlester Regional Hosp.", United States Court of Appeals For the Tenth Circuit, (12/10/1991).
11. Antitrust, "Hospital Corp. of America v. FTC", United States Court of Appeals For the Seventh Circuit, (12/18/1986).
12. Antitrust, "Huron Valley Hospital Inc. v. Pontiac", United States District Court For the Eastern District of Michigan, Southern Division, (12/18/1986).
13. Antitrust, "Potters Medical Center v. City Hospital Assoc.", United States Court of Appeals for the Sixth Circuit, (9/4/1986).
14. Antitrust, 5.a. CON Board Decision Arbitrary 5. Validity of CON Board Decision "Huron Valley Hospital Inc. v. Pontiac", United States Court of Appeals For the Sixth Circuit, (5/30/1986).
15. Antitrust, "Hospital Bldg. Co. v. Trustees of Rex Hospital", United States Court of Appeals For the Fourth Circuit, (4/18/1986).
16. Antitrust, "St. Joseph's Hosp. v. Hospital Auth. of Am.", United States District Court For the Southern District of Georgia, Savannah Division, (7/18/1985).
17. Antitrust, 3. Statutory Violation, "Huron Valley Hospital Inc. v. Pontiac", United States District Court For the Eastern District of Michigan, Southern Division, (6/17/1985).
18. Antitrust, "Gars v. Stoco Inc.", United States District Court For the Eastern District of Arkansas, (1/9/1985).
19. Antitrust, 3. Statutory Violation, "North Carolina ex reel. Edmisten v. P.I.A. Asheville Inc.", United States Court of Appeals For the Fourth Circuit, (7/16/1984).

20. Antitrust, 5. Validity of CON Board Decision, "Huron Valley Hospital Inc. v. Pontiac Civil Action", United States District Court For the Eastern District of Michigan, Southern Division', (4/30/1984).
21. Antitrust, "State ex rel. Edmisten v. P.I.A. Asheville Inc.", United States Court of Appeals For the Fourth Circuit, (11/30/1983).
22. Antitrust, "Hospital Bldg. Co. v. Trustees of Rex Hospital", United States Court of Appeals For the Fourth Circuit, (10/19/1982).
23. Antitrust, 5.a. CON Board Decision Arbitrary, 5. Validity of CON Board Decision, "Gateway Hospital Corp. East v. Department of Health & Rehabilitative Services", District Court of Appeal of Florida First District, (9/29/1982).
24. Antitrust, "Huron Valley Hospital Inc. v. Pontiac", United States Court of Appeals Sixth Circuit, (12/11/1981).
25. Antitrust, "National Geri medical Hospital and Gerontology Center, Petitioner, v. Blue Cross of Kansas City and Blue Cross Association", Supreme Court of the United States, (6/15/1981).
26. Antitrust, "National Geri medical Hospital & Gerontology v. Blue Cross of Kansas City", United States District Court For the Western District of Missouri Greenville Division, (11/2/1979).

I A. Applicability of Noerr-Pennington Doctrine

2. Applicability of Noerr-Pennington Doctrine, 1. Antitrust, "Armstrong Surgical Ctr. Inc. v. Armstrong County Mem'l Hosp.", United States Court of Appeals For the Third Circuit, (6/26/2000).
3. Applicability of No err-Pennington Doctrine, 1. Antitrust, "St. Joseph's Hospital Inc. v. Hospital Corp. of America", United States Court of Appeals For the Eleventh Circuit, (8/5/1986).

II. CONSTITUTIONAL CHALLENGE

1. Constitutional Challenge, "Walgreen Co. v. John V. Rullan", United States District Court for the District of Puerto Rico, (9/8/2003).
2. Constitutional Challenge, 7. Miscellaneous, "The Tennessee Department of Health v. Gary C. Boyle, M.D.", Court of Appeals of Tennessee, at Nashville, (12/19/2002).
3. Constitutional Challenge, 3. Statutory Violation, "Oficinas Medicas Inc. v. De Melecio", United States District Court for the District of Puerto Rico, (3/12/1999).
4. Constitutional Challenge, 6.e. Applicability of Need Criteria to Applicant, "Salad Para El Pueblo, et al. v. Department of Health of the Commonwealth of Puerto Rico", United States District Court, D. Puerto Rico, (2/26/1997).
5. Constitutional Challenge, 6.e. Applicability of Need Criteria to Applicant, "St. Luke Hosp. v. Health Policy Bd.", Court of Appeals of Kentucky, (1/5/1996).
6. Constitutional Challenge, 5.a. CON Board Decision Arbitrary, 5. Validity of CON Board Decision, "Quintero v. Mora", United States District Court for the District of Puerto Rico, (9/26/1995).
7. Constitutional Challenge, 3. Statutory Violation, 5.a. CON Board Decision Arbitrary, 5. Validity of CON Board Decision, "National Health Corp. v. South Carolina Dep't of Health & Environmental Control", Court of Appeals of South Carolina, (4/24/1989).
8. Constitutional Challenge, 3.b. CON Board Exceeded Rulemaking Authority, "Emergency Medical Transp. v. Tempe", Court of Appeals of Arizona, Division One, Department D, (5/19/1988).
9. Constitutional Challenge, 1. Antitrust, 5. Validity of CON Board Decision, "Metropolitan Hospital v. Thornburgh Civil Action", United States District Court For the Eastern District of Pennsylvania, (6/11/1987).
10. Constitutional Challenge, "Dogwood Square Nursing Center Inc. v. State Health Planning Agency", Court of Appeals of Georgia, (10/28/1985).
11. Constitutional Challenge, 5. Validity of CON Board Decision, "Hospital Group of Western North Carolina Inc. v. North Carolina Dep't of Human Resources", Court of Appeals of North Carolina, (8/6/1985).

12. Constitutional Challenge, 3. Statutory Violation, 6.e. Applicability of Need Criteria to Applicant, "Shenango Valley Osteopathic Hospital v. Department of Health", Supreme Court of Pennsylvania, (10/21/1982).
13. Constitutional Challenge, 5.a. CON Board Decision Arbitrary, 5. Validity of CON Board Decision, "Tulsa Area Hosp. Council Inc. v. Oral Roberts Univ.", Supreme Court of Oklahoma, (3/24/1981).
14. Constitutional Challenge, "Gooding v. Oklahoma ex rel. Oklahoma Welfare Commn." United States District Court For the Western District of Oklahoma , (6/21/1977).
15. Constitutional Challenge, "Attoma v. State Department of Social Welfare", Supreme Court, Appellate Division, Fourth Department, (5/19/1966).

II A. Equal Protection Violation

1. Equal Protection Violation, 2.b. Procedural Due Process Violation, 2. Constitutional Challenge, "Madarang v. Bermudes", United States Court of Appeals For the Ninth Circuit, (11/9/1989).
2. Equal Protection Violation, 2. Constitutional Challenge, 6.e. Applicability of Need Criteria to Applicant, 5. Validity of CON Board Decision, "NME Hospitals Inc. v. Department of Health & Rehabilitative Services", Court of Appeals of Florida First District, (10/5/1986).
3. Equal Protection Violation, 2. Constitutional Challenge, 6.e. Applicability of Need Criteria to Applicant, "Paul Kimball Hospital Inc. v. Brick Township Hospital Inc.", Supreme Court of New Jersey, (6/24/1981).

II B. PROCEDURAL DUE PROCESS VIOLATION

1. Procedural Due Process Violation, 2. Constitutional Challenge, 6.f. Applicability of Need Criteria to Transfer of CON, "Beechwood Restorative Care Center v. Laura E. Leeds", United States District Court for the Western District of New York, (5/4/2004).
2. Procedural Due Process Violation, 2. Constitutional Challenge, "St. Luke's Hospital of Kansas City v. Missouri Health Facilities Review Committee", Circuit Court of Cole County, (7/4/2002).
3. Procedural Due Process Violation, 2. Constitutional Challenge, 7. Miscellaneous, "Ford Hull-Mar Nursing Home Inc. v. Marr Knapp Crawfis & Assoc.", Court of Appeals of Ohio Seventh Appellate District, Jefferson County, (6/22/2000).
4. Procedural Due Process Violation, 2. Constitutional Challenge, "Ex parte Forest Manor Inc.", Supreme Court of Alabama, (12/11/1998).
5. Procedural Due Process Violation, 2. Constitutional Challenge, 3. Statutory Violation, "State Health Planning & Dev. Agency v. Forest Manor Inc.", Court of Civil Appeals of Alabama, (3/13/1998).
6. Procedural Due Process Violation, 2. Constitutional Challenge, 3. Statutory Violation, "Auburn Medical Center, Inc. v. J. Elbert Peters, et al.", United States District Court, M.D. Alabama, Northern Division, (12/12/1996).
7. Procedural Due Process Violation, 2. Constitutional Challenge, 3. Statutory Violation, "Jewish Hosp. v. Baptist Health Care Sys." Court of Appeals of Kentucky , (7/21/1995).
8. Procedural Due Process Violation, 2. Constitutional Challenge, "Downriver Nursing Assoc. v. Department of Public Health", Court of Appeals of Michigan, (4/7/1992).
9. Procedural Due Process Violation, 2. Constitutional Challenge, "Huron Valley Hospital Inc. v. Pontiac", United States Court of Appeals for the Sixth Circuit, (10/13/1989).
10. Procedural Due Process Violation, 2. Constitutional Challenge, "Park City Hosp. v. Commission on Hosp. & Health Care", Appellate Court of Connecticut, (5/17/1988).
11. Procedural Due Process Violation, 2. Constitutional Challenge, 5.a. CON Board Decision Arbitrary, 5. Validity of CON Board Decision, 4. Regulatory Violation, "Commonwealth Dep't of Health v. Brownsville Golden Age Nursing Home Inc.", Commonwealth Court of Pennsylvania, (2/4/1987).

12. Procedural Due Process Violation, 5. Validity of CON Board Decision, 7. Miscellaneous, "Turro v. Department of Health & Rehabilitative Services", Court of Appeals of Florida First District, (10/12/1984).
13. Procedural Due Process Violation, 2. Constitutional Challenge, "Brookwood Extended Care Centers Inc. v. State Dep't of Health & Rehabilitative Services", Court of Appeals of Florida First District, (7/24/1984).
14. Procedural Due Process Violation, 2. Constitutional Challenge, "Mount Royal Towers Inc. v. Alabama Board of Health", Supreme Court of Alabama, (10/3/1980).
15. Procedural Due Process Violation, 2. Constitutional Challenge, "Robinson v. Kentucky Health Facilities", Court of Appeals of Kentucky, (5/2/1980).

II. STATUATORY VIOLATION

1. Statutory Violation, "Hospice of Palm Beach County, Inc. v. State of Florida, Agency for Health Care Administration", Court of Appeals of Florida, First District, (4/26/2004).
2. Statutory Violation, 5. Validity of CON Board Decision, "Methodist Healthcare-Jackson Hospital v. Jackson-Madison County General Hospital District", Court of Appeals of Tennessee, at Nashville, (5/22/2003).
3. Statutory Violation, "United States of America v. East Texas Medical Center Regional Healthcare System", United States District Court for the Southern District of Texas, Houston Division, (10/20/2002).
4. Statutory Violation, 6.e. Applicability of Need Criteria to Applicant, 7. Miscellaneous, "Lipid-Laurel, L.L.C. v. Zoning Board of Adjustment of the Township of Scotch Plains", United States Court of Appeals, Third Circuit, (3/15/2002).
5. Statutory Violation, "Auburn Medical Center, Inc. v. East Alabama health Care Authority d/b/a East Alabama Medical Center", Court of Civil Appeals of Alabama, (5/11/2001).
6. Statutory Violation, "Auburn Medical Center, Inc. v. State Health Planning and Development Agency et al.", Court of Civil Appeals of Alabama, (5/11/2001).
7. Statutory Violation, 4. Regulatory Violation, "Central Maine Medical Center v. Kevin Concannon and Maine Medical Center", Superior Court of Maine, (9/26/2000).
8. Statutory Violation, 5.a. CON Board Decision Arbitrary, 5. Validity of CON Board Decision, 6. Public Need Challenge, "Matter of Town of Gates v. Commissioner of NY State Office of Mental Retardation and Developmental Disabilities and Finger Lakes Developmental Disabilities Services Office", Supreme Court, Appellate Division, Fourth Department, (12/31/1997).
9. Statutory Violation, "Vaughan Regional Medical Ctr. v. Smith", United States District Court for the Middle District of Alabama, (12/5/1995).
10. Statutory Violation, "In re Good Samaritan Hosp.", Court of Appeals of Ohio Tenth Appellate District, Franklin County, (11/9/1995).
11. Statutory Violation, 5.a. CON Board Decision Arbitrary, 5. Validity of CON Board Decision, "In re National Church Residence Care Ctr.", Court OF Appeals OF Ohio Tenth Appellate District, Franklin County, (9/20/1994).
12. Statutory Violation, 3.b. CON Board Exceeded Rulemaking Authority, 4.a. Violation of CON, Board's Internal Rules 4. Regulatory Violation 5. Validity of CON Board Decision "Monmouth Medical Ctr. v. State Dep't of Health", Superior Court of New Jersey Appellate Division, (3/31/1994).
13. Statutory Violation, 3.a. Violation of Administrative Procedures Act, "Catawba Memorial Hosp. v. North Carolina Dep't of Human Resources", Court of Appeals of North Carolina, (11/16/1993).
14. Statutory Violation, "In re Mansfield Gen. Hosp.", Court of Appeals of Ohio Tenth Appellate District, Franklin County, (8/31/1993).

15. Statutory Violation, 5.a. CON Board Decision Arbitrary, 5. Validity of CON Board Decision. "In re Continental Medical Sys." Court of Appeals of Ohio Tenth Appellate District, Franklin County, (8/12/1993).
16. Statutory Violation. "Hospital Corp. of Am. v. Associates in Adolescent Psychiatry S.C.", Court of Appeal of Florida Fourth District, (9/23/1992).
17. Statutory Violation. "In re Health co Facilities Inc.", Court of Appeals of Ohio Tenth Appellate District, Franklin County, (4/21/1992).
18. Statutory Violation. "Health Quest Corp. IV v. Department of Health & Rehabilitative Services", Court of Appeal of Florida, (1/14/1992).
19. Statutory Violation, 3.c. Violation of State Law During CON Proceedings, 5. Validity of CON Board Decision. "McCoy Fla. SNF Trust v. State Dep't of Health & Rehabilitative Serv.", Court of Appeal of Florida First District, (12/17/1991).
20. Statutory Violation. "Ire dell Memorial Hosp. v. North Carolina Dep't of Human Resources etc.", Court of Appeals of North Carolina, (8/6/1991).
21. Statutory Violation. "Martin Memorial Hosp. Ass'n v. Department of Health & Rehabilitative Services", Court of Appeal of Florida Fourth District, (7/5/1991).
22. Statutory Violation. "Spryer v. Barry", District of Columbia Court of Appeals, (3/29/1991).
23. Statutory Violation, 5. Validity of CON Board Decision. "In re Labelle Nursing Center", Court of Appeals of Ohio Tenth Appellate District, Franklin County, (8/30/1990).
24. Statutory Violation, 5. Validity of CON Board Decision. "Lee Memorial Hosp. v. Department of Health & Rehabilitative Serv.", Court of Appeal of Florida First District, (5/9/1990).
25. Statutory Violation, 4. Regulatory Violation. "Hummock Inc. v. Department of Health & Rehabilitative Serv.", Court of Appeal of Florida First District, (5/7/1990).
26. Statutory Violation. "Health Quest Corp. v. Department of Health & Rehabilitative Services", Court of Appeals of Florida First district, (8/2/1989).
27. Statutory Violation, 2.b. Procedural Due Process Violation, 2. Constitutional Challenge. "Ex parte Nursing Home of Dothan Inc.", Supreme Court of Alabama, (3/31/1989).
28. Statutory Violation. "Cincinnati Ambulatory Surgery Center v. Certificate of Need Review Bd.", Court of Appeals of Ohio Tenth Appellate District, Franklin County, (12/13/1988).
29. Statutory Violation. "Laurel Mobile Health Services Ltd. v. Commonwealth Dep't of Health", Commonwealth Court of Pennsylvania, (11/25/1988).
30. Statutory Violation. "Bath Memorial Hospital v. Maine Health Care Finance Com.", United States Court of Appeals For the First Circuit, (8/8/1988).
31. Statutory Violation. "Liljeberg v. Health Services Acquisition Corp.", Supreme Court of the United States, (6/17/1988).
32. Statutory Violation, 7. Miscellaneous. "Tarbush v. McAlester Regional Hospital", United States Court of Appeals for the Tenth Circuit, (8/17/1987).
33. Statutory Violation. "Community Care Centers Inc. v. Missouri Health Facilities Review Committee", Court of Appeals of Missouri Eastern District, Division Two, (5/19/1987).
34. Statutory Violation, 4. Regulatory Violation, 5.a. CON Board Decision Arbitrary, 5. Validity of CON Board Decision. "Psychiatric Hospitals of Florida Inc. v. State Dep't of Health & Rehabilitative Services", Court of Appeals of Florida first district, (10/16/1986).
35. Statutory Violation. "Coastal Care Centers Inc. v. Meeks", Court of Appeal of California, First Appellate District, Division Five, (8/7/1986).
36. Statutory Violation, 5. Validity of CON Board Decision. "In the matter of the Town of Hempstead v. Commissioner, State of New York Office of Mental Retardation and Developmental Disabilities", Supreme Court, Appellate Division, Second Department, (6/2/1986).

37. Statutory Violation. "Hickory House Nursing Home Inc. v. Commonwealth Dep't of Health", Commonwealth Court of Pennsylvania, (8/14/1985).
38. Statutory Violation, 5.a. CON Board Decision Arbitrary, 5. Validity of CON Board Decision. "Texas Health Facilities Com. v. Presbyterian Hospital North", Supreme Court of Texas, (5/29/1985).
39. Statutory Violation, 3.a. Violation of Administrative Procedures Act. "In re Application for Certificate of Need by HCA Health Serv.", Supreme Court of Wyoming, (10/3/1984).
40. Statutory Violation. "Lloyd v. Georgia State Health Planning & Dev. Agency", Court of Appeals of Georgia, (10/25/1983).
41. Statutory Violation. "State ex reel. Southwest Community Health Serv. v. Monroe", Supreme Court of New Mexico, (2/23/1983).
42. Statutory Violation, 2. Constitutional Challenge. "North Carolina ex rel. Morrow v. Califano", United States District Court For the Eastern District of North Carolina Raleigh Division, (4/17/1978).
43. Statutory Violation, 4. Regulatory Violation. "Humana of Florida Inc. v. Keller", Court of Appeals of Florida First District, (4/2/1976).
44. Statutory Violation. "Extend care Inc. v. State Coordinating Council for Health Planning", Supreme Court of Kansas, (3/1/1975).
45. Statutory Violation. "Ebenezer Soc. v. Minnesota State Bd. of Health", Supreme Court of Minnesota, (9/13/1974).

III A. Violation of Administrative Procedures Act

46. Violation of Administrative Procedures Act, 3. Statutory Violation, 5. Validity of CON Board Decision. "United States of America, Et Al. v. East Texas Medical Center Regional Healthcare System, Et Al.", United States District Court for the Southern District of Texas, Houston Division, (3/4/2003).
47. Violation of Administrative Procedures Act, 3. Statutory Violation, 5. Validity of CON Board Decision. "Marion Hospital Corporation, Appellee v. The Illinois Health Facilities Planning Board", Supreme Court of Illinois, (9/19/2002).
48. Violation of Administrative Procedures Act, 3. Statutory Violation, 2.b. Procedural Due Process Violation, 2. Constitutional Challenge, 5.a. CON Board Decision Arbitrary, 5. Validity of CON Board Decision. "Greenwood Manor v. Iowa Dep't of Pub. Health", Supreme Court of Iowa, (4/3/2002).
49. Violation of Administrative Procedures Act, 3. Statutory Violation. "Genesis Center v. Financial and Insurance Services Commissioner", Court of Appeals of Michigan, (9/18/2001).
50. Violation of Administrative Procedures Act, 3. Statutory Violation. "Ex parte East State Healthcare Auth.", Supreme Court of Alabama, (1/5/2001).
51. Violation of Administrative Procedures Act, 3. Statutory Violation. "Living Centers-Southeast Inc. v. North Carolina HHS", Court of Appeals of North Carolina, (7/5/2000).
52. Violation of Administrative Procedures Act, 3. Statutory Violation. "Christ Hosp. v. Department of Health & Senior Serv.", Superior Court of New Jersey Appellate Division, (4/12/2000).
53. Violation of Administrative Procedures Act, 3. Statutory Violation, 5. Validity of CON Board Decision. "Public Health Trust v. Agency for Health Care Admin." Court of Appeal of Florida third district, (1/5/2000).
54. Violation of Administrative Procedures Act, 3. Statutory Violation, 5.a. CON Board Decision Arbitrary, 5. Validity of CON Board Decision. "Dimensions Med. Ctr. v. Elmhurst Outpatient Surgery Ctr.", Appellate Court of Illinois, Fourth District, (9/29/1999).
55. Violation of Administrative Procedures Act, 3. Statutory Violation, 5.a. CON Board Decision Arbitrary, 5. Validity of CON Board Decision. "Forest Manor Inc. v. State Health Planning & Dev. Agency", Court of Civil Appeals of Alabama, (5/1/1998).

56. Violation of Administrative Procedures Act, 3. Statutory Violation. "Mount Sinai Community Hosp. Ass'n v. Gorman", Superior Court OF Connecticut, Judicial District OF Hartford-New Britain, AT Hartford, (3/4/1998).
57. Violation of Administrative Procedures Act, 3. Statutory Violation. "Oregon Health Care Ass'n v. Health Div.", Court of Appeals of Oregon, (6/25/1997).
58. Violation of Administrative Procedures Act, 3. Statutory Violation. "Life Care Ctrs. of Am. v. Sawgrass Care Ctr.", Court of Appeal of Florida First District, (12/9/1996).
59. Violation of Administrative Procedures Act, 3. Statutory Violation. "Gulf Coast Health Care v. Agency for Health Care Admin." Court of Appeal of Florida First District , (9/4/1996).
60. Violation of Administrative Procedures Act, 3. Statutory Violation. "Ex parte Crestwood Hosp. & Nursing Home", Supreme Court of Alabama, (9/8/1995).
61. Violation of Administrative Procedures Act, 3. Statutory Violation. "Mid-America Georgian Gardens v. Missouri Health Facilities Review Comm'n", Court of Appeals of Missouri, (8/15/1995).
62. Violation of Administrative Procedures Act, 3. Statutory Violation, 2.b. Procedural Due Process Violation, 2. Constitutional Challenge. "W. A. Foote Mem. Hosp. v. Michigan Dep't of Pub. Health", Court of Appeals of Michigan, (5/12/1995).
63. Violation of Administrative Procedures Act, 3. Statutory Violation. "North Fulton Medical Ctr. v. Roach", Supreme Court of Georgia, (2/20/1995).
64. Violation of Administrative Procedures Act, 3. Statutory Violation, 5. Validity of CON Board Decision. "St. Joseph Hosp. & Health Care Ctr. v. Department of Health", Supreme Court of Washington, (1/26/1995).
65. Violation of Administrative Procedures Act, 3. Statutory Violation, 2. Constitutional Challenge. "Michigan Affiliated Healthcare Sys. v. Department of Pub. Health", Court of Appeals of Michigan, (12/27/1994).
66. Violation of Administrative Procedures Act, 3. Statutory Violation. "Greenbriar Nursing Home v. Pilley", Court of Appeal of Louisiana, (7/2/1993).
67. Violation of Administrative Procedures Act ,3. Statutory Violation. "State ex rel. Parma Community Gen. Hosp. v. Kilroy", Court of Appeals of Ohio Tenth Appellate District, Franklin County, (11/17/1992).
68. Violation of Administrative Procedures Act, 3. Statutory Violation. "State ex rel. Greene Oaks v. Kilroy", Court of Appeals of Ohio Tenth Appellate District, Franklin County, (9/22/1992).
69. Violation of Administrative Procedures Act, 3. Statutory Violation, 5.a. CON Board Decision Arbitrary, 5. Validity of CON Board Decision. "New England Rehabilitation Hosp. Inc. v. Commission on Hosps. & Health Care", Superior Court of Connecticut, Judicial District of Hartford - New Britain, at Hartford, (7/20/1992).
70. Violation of Administrative Procedures Act, 3. Statutory Violation. "HCA Health Services Inc. v. Department of Health & Rehabilitative Services", Court of Appeal of Florida First District, (5/13/1992).
71. Violation of Administrative Procedures Act, 3. Statutory Violation. "Frene Valley Corp. v. Missouri Health Facilities Review Committee", Court of Appeals of Missouri Western District, (10/29/1991).
72. Violation of Administrative Procedures Act, 3. Statutory Violation, 6.e. Applicability of Need Criteria to Applicant, 5. Validity of CON Board Decision. "Stewart v. Commonwealth Dep't of Health", Commonwealth Court of Pennsylvania, (6/7/1991).
73. Violation of Administrative Procedures Act, 3. Statutory Violation. "HCA Crossroads Residential Ctrs. v. North Carolina Dep't of Human Resources etc.", Supreme Court of North Carolina, (12/5/1990).
74. Violation of Administrative Procedures Act, 3. Statutory Violation. "HCA Crossroads Residential Centers Inc. v. North Carolina Dep't of Human Resources etc.", Court of Appeals of North Carolina, (6/19/1990).

75. Violation of Administrative Procedures Act, 3. Statutory Violation. "St. Joseph Hosp. Inc. v. Department of Health & Rehabilitative Services Case", Court of Appeal of Florida First District, (4/12/1990).
76. Violation of Administrative Procedures Act, 3. Statutory Violation. "Florida Residential Treatment Centers Inc. v. Department of Health & Rehabilitative Services", Court of Appeal of Florida First District, (11/14/1989).
77. Violation of Administrative Procedures Act, 3. Statutory Violation, 6.e. Applicability of Need Criteria to Applicant. "Three Rivers Home Health Serv. Inc. v. Healthmaster Inc.", Court of Appeals of Georgia, (10/16/1989).
78. Violation of Administrative Procedures Act, 3. Statutory Violation. "Overlook Medical Clinic v. Commonwealth Dep't of Health", Commonwealth Court of Pennsylvania, (6/12/1989).
79. Violation of Administrative Procedures Act, 3. Statutory Violation, 5. Validity of CON Board Decision. "State ex rel. Missouri Health Care Asso. v. Missouri Health Facilities Review Committee", Court of Appeals of Missouri, (10/25/1988).
80. Violation of Administrative Procedures Act, 3. Statutory Violation, 5.a. CON Board Decision Arbitrary, 5. Validity of CON Board Decision. "Ex parte Traylor Nursing Home Inc.", Supreme Court of Alabama, (9/30/1988).
81. Violation of Administrative Procedures Act, 3. Statutory Violation. "Minnesota Osteopathic Gen. Hosp. v. State Dep't of Health & Rehabilitative Serv.", Court of Appeal of Florida First District, (4/6/1988).
82. Violation of Administrative Procedures Act, 3. Statutory Violation. "Rowan Health Properties Inc. v. North Carolina Dep't of Human Resources Div. of Facility Services Certificate of Need Section", Court of Appeals of North Carolina, (3/15/1988).
83. Violation of Administrative Procedures Act, 3. Statutory Violation, 4.b. CON Board's Internal Rules Arbitrary, 4. Regulatory Violation. "Ragsdale v. Turlock", United States Court of Appeals For the Seventh Circuit, (3/10/1988).
84. Violation of Administrative Procedures Act, 3. Statutory Violation, 6.b. Injunction on CON Requirements. "Gulf Coast Home Health Services Inc. v. State Dep't of Health & Rehabilitative Services", Court of Appeal of Florida First District, (9/11/1987).
85. Violation of Administrative Procedures Act, 3. Statutory Violation. "George Washington University Medical Center v. District of Columbia Bd. of Appeals & Review", District of Columbia Court of Appeals, (8/31/1987).
86. Violation of Administrative Procedures Act, 3. Statutory Violation, 4. Regulatory Violation, 7. Miscellaneous. "San Bernardino Community Hospital v. Meeks", Court of Appeal of California, Fourth Appellate District, Division Two, (11/25/1986).
87. Violation of Administrative Procedures Act, 3. Statutory Violation. "PIA Psychiatric Hospitals Inc. v. Missouri Health Facilities Review Committee", Court of Appeals of Missouri, Western District, (11/25/1986).
88. Violation of Administrative Procedures Act, 3. Statutory Violation. "Pontiac Osteopathic Hospital v. Department of Public Health", Court of Appeals of Michigan, (11/19/1986).
89. Violation of Administrative Procedures Act, 3. Statutory Violation. "Methodist Regional Hospital System Inc. v. State Dep't of Health & Rehabilitative Services", Court of Appeals of Florida first district, (9/24/1986).
90. Violation of Administrative Procedures Act, 3. Statutory Violation, 6.e. Applicability of Need Criteria to Applicant, 6. Public Need Challenge, 5.a. CON Board Decision Arbitrary, 5. Validity of CON Board Decision. "Psychiatric Institutes of America Inc. v. Department of Health & Rehabilitative Services", Court of Appeals of Florida First District, (7/17/1986).
91. Violation of Administrative Procedures Act, 3. Statutory Violation. "St. Francis Parkside Lodge v. Department of Health & Rehabilitative Services", Court of Appeals of Florida First District, (4/1/1986).

92. Violation of Administrative Procedures Act, 3. Statutory Violation. "Florida Medical Center v. Department of Health & Rehabilitative Services", Court of Appeals of Florida First District, (3/4/1986).
93. Violation of Administrative Procedures Act, 3. Statutory Violation, 5. Validity of CON Board Decision. "HCA Health Services of Midwest Inc. v. Administrative Hearing Com.", Court of Appeals of Missouri Eastern District, Division Two, (11/26/1985).
94. Violation of Administrative Procedures Act, 3. Statutory Violation, 5. Validity of CON Board Decision. "Missouri Health Facilities Review Committee v. Administrative Hearing Com.", Supreme Court of Missouri, (11/21/1985).
95. Violation of Administrative Procedures Act, 3. Statutory Violation, 5.a. CON Board Decision Arbitrary, 5. Validity of CON Board Decision. "North Ridge General Hospital Inc. v. NME Hospitals Inc.", Court of Appeals of Florida First District, (11/15/1985).
96. Violation of Administrative Procedures Act, 3. Statutory Violation, 5.a. CON Board Decision Arbitrary, 5. Validity of CON Board Decision. "Southwest Virginia Health Sys. Agency v. Kenley", Circuit Court of the CITY of Salem, Virginia, (9/6/1985).
97. Violation of Administrative Procedures Act, 3. Statutory Violation, 4. Regulatory Violation. "Harrisburg Hospital v. Thornburgh", United States District Court for the Middle District of Pennsylvania, (6/25/1985).
98. Violation of Administrative Procedures Act, 3. Statutory Violation, 5. Validity of CON Board Decision. "Southern Chester County Medical Ctr. v. Commonwealth Dep't of Health", Commonwealth Court of Pennsylvania, (6/24/1985).
99. Violation of Administrative Procedures Act, 3. Statutory Violation, 5. Validity of CON Board Decision. "Rehab Hospital Services Corp. v. Delta-Hills Health Systems Agency Inc.", Supreme Court of Arkansas, (4/15/1985).
100. Violation of Administrative Procedures Act, 3. Statutory Violation. "Naples Community Hospital Inc. v. Department of Health & Rehabilitative Services", Court of Appeals of Florida First District, (1/18/1985).
101. Violation of Administrative Procedures Act, 3. Statutory Violation. "Psychiatric Institutes of America Inc. v. Guissinger", Court of Appeal of Louisiana, (12/28/1984).
102. Violation of Administrative Procedures Act, 3. Statutory Violation. "Federal Property Management Corp. v. Health Care & Retirement Corp.", Court of Appeals of Florida First District, (12/21/1984).
103. Violation of Administrative Procedures Act, 3. Statutory Violation, 5. Validity of CON Board Decision. "Westchester General Hospital v. Department of Health & Rehabilitative Services", District Court of Appeal of Florida First District, (9/8/1982).
104. Violation of Administrative Procedures Act, 3. Statutory Violation, 6.e. Applicability of Need Criteria to Applicant, 5.a. CON Board Decision Arbitrary, 5. Validity of CON Board Decision. "Sisters of Providence v. Department of Health & Social Serv.", Supreme Court of Alaska, (7/30/1982).
105. Violation of Administrative Procedures Act, 3. Statutory Violation. "Farmworker Rights Org. v. Department of Health & Rehabilitative Serv.", Court of Appeals of Florida First District, (7/20/1982).
106. Violation of Administrative Procedures Act, 3. Statutory Violation, 4. Regulatory Violation, 5.a. CON Board Decision Arbitrary, 5. Validity of CON Board Decision. "Hale v. Petit Law Docket", Supreme Judicial Court of Maine, (12/9/1981).
107. Violation of Administrative Procedures Act, 3. Statutory Violation, 7.b. Failure to Obtain CON, 4.c. Defining Regulatory Term, 4. Regulatory Violation, 3.e. Defining Statutory Term, 3. Statutory Violation. "South Cent. Health Planning & Divvy. Commissioner of Dep't of Admin." Supreme Court of Alaska, (5/15/1981).
108. Violation of Administrative Procedures Act, 3. Statutory Violation, 6. Public Need Challenge. "Shoolman v. Health Facilities Appeals Bd. (1980)", Appeals Court of Massachusetts, Suffolk, (12/11/1980).

109. Violation of Administrative Procedures Act, 3. Statutory Violation, 7. Miscellaneous. "Northbrook Residents Assoc. v. Iowa State Dep't of Health Office etc.", Supreme Court of Iowa, (11/12/1980).
110. Violation of Administrative Procedures Act, 3. Statutory Violation. "South Broward Hospital Dist. v. Department of Health & Rehabilitative Services etc.", Court of Appeal of Florida Fourth District, (6/18/1980).
111. Violation of Administrative Procedures Act, 3. Statutory Violation. "Montana Health Sys. Agency v. Montana Bd. of Health & Evil. Sciences", Supreme Court of Montana, (3/2/1980).
112. Violation of Administrative Procedures Act, 3. Statutory Violation. "Health Facilities Research Inc. v. Bureau of Community Medical Facilities etc.", Court of Appeals of Florida First District, (12/14/1976).
113. Violation of Administrative Procedures Act, 3. Statutory Violation. "Minnesota State Board of Health v. Governor's Certificate of Need Appeal Board", Supreme Court of Minnesota, (1/17/1975).

III B. CON Board Exceeded Rulemaking Authority

114. CON Board Exceeded Rulemaking Authority, 3. Statutory Violation, 5.a. CON Board Decision Arbitrary, 5. Validity of CON Board Decision. "Summit Neighborhood Association v. Rhode Island Department of Health", Superior Court of Rhode Island, Providence, (5/27/2004).
115. CON Board Exceeded Rulemaking Authority, 3. Statutory Violation, 2. Constitutional Challenge. "Med star Health v. Maryland Health Care Commission", Court of Appeals of Maryland, (6/18/2003).
116. CON Board Exceeded Rulemaking Authority, 4.c. Defining Regulatory Term. "Albany Surgical, P.C. v. Department of Community Health", Georgia Appeals Court, (1/1/2002).
117. CON Board Exceeded Rulemaking Authority, 3. Statutory Violation, 7.b. Failure to Obtain CON, 6.e. Applicability of Need Criteria to Applicant, 4.c. Defining Regulatory Term, 3.e. Defining Statutory Term. "Prime Lithographer Operations, Inc., and Prime Medical Services, Inc. v. LithoMedTech of Alabama, LLC; State Health Planning and Development Agency v. LithoMedTech of Alabama, LLC; Prime Lithotripter Operations, Inc., and Prime Medical Services, Inc. v. Uroventure, LLC, et al.", Court of Civil Appeals of Alabama, (12/28/2001).
118. CON Board Exceeded Rulemaking Authority, 4.a. Violation of CON Board's Internal Rules. "ACSR Inc. v. Cabinet for Health Serv.", Court of Appeals of Kentucky, (8/25/2000).
119. CON Board Exceeded Rulemaking Authority, 3. Statutory Violation. "North Fulton Med. Ctr. v. Stephenson", Supreme Court of Georgia, (5/26/1998).
120. CON Board Exceeded Rulemaking Authority, 3. Statutory Violation. "University of Alabama Hospitals. Alabama Renal Stone Institute Inc.", Court of Civil Appeals of Alabama, (4/1/1998).
121. CON Board Exceeded Rulemaking Authority, 3. Statutory Violation, 4.a. Violation of CON Board's Internal Rules, 4. Regulatory Violation, 5.a. CON Board Decision Arbitrary, 5. Validity of CON Board Decision. "In re Assure Care of Vt.", Supreme Court of Vermont, (11/1/1996).
122. CON Board Exceeded Rulemaking Authority, 3. Statutory Violation, 5. Validity of CON Board Decision. "West Virginia Health Care Cost Review Auth. v. Boone Memo. Hosp.", Supreme Court of Appeals of West Virginia, (4/24/1996).
123. CON Board Exceeded Rulemaking Authority, 5. Validity of CON Board Decision. "Agency for Health Care Admin. v. University Hosp.", Court of Appeal of Florida First District, (4/16/1996).
124. CON Board Exceeded Rulemaking Authority, 6.c. Establishment Challenge to New Need Requirements, 6.e. Applicability of Need Criteria to Applicant, 6. Public Need Challenge, 5. Validity of CON Board Decision. "Pennsylvania Dep't of Health v. North Hills Passavant Hosp.", Commonwealth Court of Pennsylvania, (4/10/1996).
125. CON Board Exceeded Rulemaking Authority. "Allegheny County Inst. Dist. v. Department of Pub. Welfare", Commonwealth Court of Pennsylvania, (12/5/1995).

126. CON Board Exceeded Rulemaking Authority, 3. Statutory Violation, 4. Regulatory Violation, 5. Validity of CON Board Decision. "West Bloomfield Hosp. v. Certificate of Need BD.", Court of Appeals of Michigan, (1/17/1995).
127. CON Board Exceeded Rulemaking Authority, 5.a. CON Board Decision Arbitrary, 5. Validity of CON Board Decision. "Clark v. Fancier", Court of Civil Appeals of Alabama, (6/17/1994).
128. CON Board Exceeded Rulemaking Authority, 3.a. Violation of Administrative Procedures Act, 3. Statutory Violation. "North Fulton Medical Ctr. v. Roach", Supreme Court of Georgia, (2/21/1994).
129. CON Board Exceeded Rulemaking Authority, 3. Statutory Violation. "District of Columbia Hosp. Ass'n v. Barry", District of Columbia Court of Appeals, (1/30/1991).
130. CON Board Exceeded Rulemaking Authority, 3. Statutory Violation. "Appeal of Clipper Home v." Supreme Court of New Hampshire , (8/29/1990).
131. CON Board Exceeded Rulemaking Authority, 5.a. CON Board Decision Arbitrary, 5. Validity of CON Board Decision. "Charter Medical-Southeast Inc. v. State Dep't of Health & Rehabilitative Services", Court of Appeals of Florida First District, (7/29/1986).
132. CON Board Exceeded Rulemaking Authority, 3. Statutory Violation, 5.a. CON Board Decision Arbitrary, 5. Validity of CON Board Decision. "Ft. Washington Community Hospital Inc. v. Southern Maryland Hospital Center", Court of Special Appeals of Maryland, (3/5/1986).
133. CON Board Exceeded Rulemaking Authority, 5. Validity of CON Board Decision. "Dogwood Square Nursing Center Inc. v. State Health Planning Agency", Supreme Court of Georgia, (2/18/1986).
134. CON Board Exceeded Rulemaking Authority, 3. Statutory Violation. "District of Columbia Hosp. Assoc. v. Barry", District of Columbia Court of Appeals, (9/16/1985).
135. CON Board Exceeded Rulemaking Authority, 3. Statutory Violation. "State Bd. of Health v. Virginia Hospital Ass'n", Court of Appeals of Virginia, (8/6/1985).
136. CON Board Exceeded Rulemaking Authority, 3. Statutory Violation. "Humana, Inc. & Plantation General Hospital v. Department of Health and Rehabilitative Services", Court of Appeal of Florida First District, (5/16/1985).
137. CON Board Exceeded Rulemaking Authority, 3. Statutory Violation. "Humana Inc. v. Department of Health & Rehabilitative Services", Court of Appeals of Florida First District, (5/16/1985).
138. CON Board Exceeded Rulemaking Authority, 3. Statutory Violation. "Whitehall Boca v. Department of Health & Rehabilitative Services", Court of Appeals of Florida First District, (9/5/1984).
139. CON Board Exceeded Rulemaking Authority, 5. Validity of CON Board Decision. "Florida Convalescent Centers Inc. v. State Dep't of Health & Rehabilitative Services", Court of Appeals of Florida First District, (2/8/1984).
140. CON Board Exceeded Rulemaking Authority, 3. Statutory Violation. "Farmworker Rights Org v. Department of Health & Rehabilitative Serv.", District Court of Appeal of Florida First District, (4/14/1983).
141. CON Board Exceeded Rulemaking Authority, 3. Statutory Violation, 6.e. Applicability of Need Criteria to Applicant, 5. Validity of CON Board Decision. "Westchester General Hospital v. State Dep't of Health & Rehabilitative Services", Court of Appeals of Florida First District, (3/22/1982).
142. CON Board Exceeded Rulemaking Authority, 5.a. CON Board Decision Arbitrary, 5. Validity of CON Board Decision. "Oklahoma Pioneer Inc. v. Carpenter", Supreme Court of Oklahoma, (9/16/1980).
143. CON Board Exceeded Rulemaking Authority, 3. Statutory Violation, 3.a. Violation of Administrative Procedures Act. "Lacey Clinic Foundation, Inc. v. Health Facilities Appeals Board", Supreme Judicial Court of Massachusetts, Suffolk, (9/18/1978).

III C. Violation of State Law During CON Proceedings

144. Violation of State Law During CON Proceedings, 7. Miscellaneous. "Lloyd Noland Foundation, Inc. v. The City of Fairfield Healthcare Authority", Supreme Court of Alabama, (2/22/2002).
145. Violation of State Law During CON Proceedings, 3. Statutory Violation, 4. Regulatory Violation, 5.a. CON Board Decision Arbitrary, 5. Validity of CON Board Decision. "Medical Ctr. v. State Health Planning Agency", Court of Appeals of Georgia, (12/5/1995).
146. Violation of State Law During CON Proceedings, 3. Statutory Violation, 4. Regulatory Violation, 5. Validity of CON Board Decision. "In re VHA Diagnostic Services Inc.", Supreme Court of Ohio, (12/9/1992).
147. Violation of State Law During CON Proceedings, 3. Statutory Violation, 5.a. CON Board Decision Arbitrary. "Charter Medical of Cook County Inc. v. HCA Health Services of Midwest Inc.", Appellate Court of Illinois, First District, Fourth Division, (6/29/1989).
148. Violation of State Law During CON Proceedings, 3. Statutory Violation, 5. Validity of CON Board Decision. "Chattahoochee Valley Home Health Care Inc. v. Healthmaster Inc.", Court of Appeals of Georgia, (3/3/1989).
149. Violation of State Law During CON Proceedings, 3. Statutory Violation. "Rivendell Children and Youth Center, a/k/a Rivendell of Tennessee, Inc., v. Tennessee Health Facilities Commission, Charter Medical of East Tennessee, Inc, and Peninsula Psychiatric Hospital", Court of Appeals of Tennessee, Middle Section, (11/4/1987).
150. Violation of State Law During CON Proceedings, 3. Statutory Violation. "Bulwark v. Department of Human Resources", Supreme Court of Nevada, (5/27/1987).
151. Violation of State Law During CON Proceedings, 3. Statutory Violation, 5. Validity of CON Board Decision. "Southern Maryland Hospital Center Inc. v. Ft. Washington Community Hospital Inc.", Court of Appeals of Maryland, (1/12/1987).
152. Violation of State Law During CON Proceedings, 3. Statutory Violation, 5. Validity of CON Board Decision. "Benedictine Sisters Benevolent Assoc. v. Pettersen", Supreme Court of Minnesota, (12/5/1980).

III D. Defining Statutory Term

153. Defining Statutory Term, 3. Statutory Violation, 7. Miscellaneous. "Official Comm. of Unsecured Creditors of United Healthcare Sys. v. Medical Staff Local 1199J", United States Court of Appeals For the Third Circuit, (12/29/1999).
154. Defining Statutory Term. "In re Good Samaritan Medical Center", Court of Appeals of Ohio Tenth Appellate District, Franklin County, (1/10/1991).
155. Defining Statutory Term, 3. Statutory Violation, 6.e. Applicability of Need Criteria to Applicant. "Marin Hospital Dist. v Department of Health", Court of Appeal, Second District, Division 3, (4/26/1979).

III. REGULATORY VIOLATION

1. Regulatory Violation. "Auburn Medical Center, Inc. v. East Alabama Health Care Authority d/b/a East Alabama Medical Center", Court of Civil Appeals of Alabama, (9/26/2003).
2. Regulatory Violation, 3. Statutory Violation. "St. Joseph Hospital v. Kevin Concannon", Superior Court of Maine, (11/2/2001).
3. Regulatory Violation, 5. Validity of CON Board Decision. "Health Care & Retirement Corp. of America v. Tarpon Springs Hosp. Found." Court of Appeal of Florida First District , (4/4/1996).
4. Regulatory Violation, 3. Statutory Violation. "Nebraska Methodist Health Sys. v. Department of Health", Supreme Court of Nebraska, (2/23/1996).
5. Regulatory Violation, 3. Statutory Violation, 2. Constitutional Challenge. "In re Adoption of Regulations

Governing the State Health Plan N.J.A.C.", Superior Court of New Jersey Appellate Division, (2/10/1993).

6. Regulatory Violation, 3. Statutory Violation, 5. Validity of CON Board Decision, 6.e. Applicability of Need Criteria to Applicant. "State Health Planning Agency v. Crib Industries Inc.", Court of Appeals of Georgia, (5/19/1992).
7. Regulatory Violation. "Watkins v. Restorative Care Center Inc.", Court of Appeals of Washington, Division One, (3/30/1992).
8. Regulatory Violation, 3. Statutory Violation, 5. Validity of CON Board Decision, 6.b. Injunction on CON Requirements. "Durant v. Humphrey's County Memorial Hospital/Extended Care Facility", Supreme Court of Mississippi, (9/18/1991).
9. Regulatory Violation, 3. Statutory Violation. "Beverly Enterprises-Florida Inc. v. Department of Health & Rehabilitative Services", Court of Appeal of Florida First District, (2/14/1990).
10. Regulatory Violation, 3.a. Violation of Administrative Procedures Act, 3. Statutory Violation. "IFIDA Health Care Group Ltd. v. Commonwealth Dep't of Health No.", Commonwealth Court of Pennsylvania, (9/15/1989).
11. Regulatory Violation. "Appeal of Psychiatric Insets. Of Am. v." Supreme Court of New Hampshire , (8/23/1989).
12. Regulatory Violation, 3. Statutory Violation. "West County Care Center Inc. v. Missouri Health Facilities Review Committee", Court of Appeals of Missouri Western District, (6/27/1989).
13. Regulatory Violation, 3. Statutory Violation. "Inverness Convalescent Ctr. v. Department of Health & Rehabilitative Serv.", Court of Appeals of Florida First district, (3/16/1989).
14. Regulatory Violation. "Gulf Coast Home Health Services Inc. v. Department of Health & Rehabilitative Services", Court of Appeals of Florida First district, (9/11/1987).
15. Regulatory Violation. "Charlotte-Mecklenburg Hospital Authority v. North Carolina Dep't of Human Resources", Court of Appeals of North Carolina, (10/21/1986).
16. Regulatory Violation, 3. Statutory Violation. "Boone County v. Apex of Arkansas Inc.", Supreme Court of Arkansas, (2/3/1986).
17. Regulatory Violation, 3. Statutory Violation, 7. Miscellaneous. "Presbyterian Medical Center v. Texas Health Facilities Com.", Court of Appeals of Texas Third District, Austin, (10/2/1985).
18. Regulatory Violation, 3. Statutory Violation, 2. Constitutional Challenge. "Hummock Inc. v. Department of Health & Rehabilitative Serv.", Court of Appeals of Florida First District, (9/25/1985).
19. Regulatory Violation. "Johns Hopkins Hospital Inc. v. Insurance Comm'r", Court of Appeals of Maryland, (3/5/1985).
20. Regulatory Violation. "Health Care & Retirement Corp. v. Department of Health & Rehabilitative Services", Court of Appeals of Florida First District, (12/20/1984).
21. Regulatory Violation, 3. Statutory Violation, 3.a. Violation of Administrative Procedures Act. "Associated Home Health Agency Inc. v. State Dep't of Health & Rehabilitative Services", Court of Appeals of Florida First District, (6/26/1984).
22. Regulatory Violation. "Balsam v. Department of Health & Rehabilitative Services", Court of Appeals of Florida First District, (6/13/1984).
23. Regulatory Violation, 3.b. CON Board Exceeded Rulemaking Authority, 3. Statutory Violation. "Vertigo Hills Hospital Inc. v. Department of Health", Court of Appeal of California, Second Appellate District, Division Three, (4/26/1979).

IV A. Violation of CON Board's Internal Rules

24. Violation of CON Board's Internal Rules, 4. Regulatory Violation, 5. Validity of CON Board Decision, 3. Statutory Violation. "Portland Surgery Center, LLC. v. Department of Human Services", Superior Court of Maine, Kennebec County, (2/23/2004).

25. Violation of CON Board's Internal Rules, 4. Regulatory Violation, 5. Validity of CON Board Decision. "Elmont Health System v. Tennessee Health Facilities Commission", Court of Appeals of Tennessee, at Nashville, (1/29/2004).
26. Violation of CON Board's Internal Rules. "Auburn Med. Ctr. v. State Health Planning & Dev. Agency", Court of Civil Appeals of Alabama, (5/11/2001).
27. Violation of CON Board's Internal Rules, 4. Regulatory Violation. "Auburn Medical Center, Inc. v. State Health Planning and Development Agency et al.", Supreme Court of Alabama, (1/5/2001).
28. Violation of CON Board's Internal Rules 4. Regulatory Violation. "Auburn Med. Ctr. Inc. v. State Health Planning & De Agency", Court of Civil Appeals of Alabama, (5/5/2000).
29. Violation of CON Board's Internal Rules, 4. Regulatory Violation. "Bio-Medical Applications Inc. v. Office of Community Medical Facilities etc.", Court of Appeals of Florida First District, (8/7/1997).
30. Violation of CON Board's Internal Rules. "Agency for Health Care Admin. v. Mount Sinai Medical Ctr.", Court of Appeal of Florida First District, (4/17/1997).
31. Violation of CON Board's Internal Rules, 5. Validity of CON Board Decision. "Bio-Medical Applications of Clearwater Inc. v. Department of Health & Rehabilitative Services etc.", Court of Appeal of Florida Second District, (2/23/1997).
32. Violation of CON Board's Internal Rules, 4. Regulatory Violation, 3.a. Violation of Administrative Procedures Act, 3. Statutory Violation. "Vantage Healthcare Corp. v. Agency for Health Care Admin." Court of Appeal of Florida First District , (1/27/1997).
33. Violation of CON Board's Internal Rules, 4. Regulatory Violation, 3. Statutory Violation. "Vantage Healthcare Corporation, d/b/a Beverly Manor Rehabilitation and Specialty Care Center at Manatee County, Appellant, v. Agency for Health Care Administration and Manatee Springs Nursing Center, Inc., Apples", District Court of Appeals of Florida, (1/27/1997).
34. Violation of CON Board's Internal Rules, 4. Regulatory Violation, 5. Validity of CON Board Decision. "In re Alexander Rand Alzheimer's Center", Court of Appeals of Ohio Tenth Appellate District, Franklin County, (1/15/1991).
35. Violation of CON Board's Internal Rules, 4. Regulatory Violation. "Health Services Management Inc. v. Missouri Health Facilities Review Committee", Court of Appeals of Missouri Western District, (4/10/1990).
36. Violation of CON Board's Internal Rules, 4.b. CON Board's Internal Rules Arbitrary, 4. Regulatory Violation, 5. Validity of CON Board Decision. "St. Francis Hospital Inc. v. Department of Health & Rehabilitative Services", Court of Appeal of Florida First District, (12/20/1989).
37. Violation of CON Board's Internal Rules, 4. Regulatory Violation. "Commonwealth Dep't of Health v. Rehab Hosp. Services Corp.", Commonwealth Court of Pennsylvania, (6/12/1989).
38. Violation of CON Board's Internal Rules, 4. Regulatory Violation, 5. Validity of CON Board Decision. "In re Bloomingdale Convalescent Center", Superior Court of New Jersey Appellate Division, (5/4/1989).
39. Violation of CON Board's Internal Rules. "Commission on Hospitals & Health Care v. Stamford Hospital", Supreme Court of Connecticut, (8/16/1988).
40. Violation of CON Board's Internal Rules, 4. Regulatory Violation. "Stewart v. Commonwealth State Health Facility Hearing Bd.", Commonwealth Court of Pennsylvania, (7/12/1988).
41. Violation of CON Board's Internal Rules, 4. Regulatory Violation, 3. Statutory Violation. "Platte County Medical Center Inc. v. Missouri Health Facilities Review Committee", Court of Appeals of Missouri Western District, (8/11/1987).
42. Violation of CON Board's Internal Rules, 4. Regulatory Violation, 5.a. CON Board Decision Arbitrary, 5. Validity of CON Board Decision. "Hospital Corp. of America v. Robinson", Court of Appeal of Louisiana, (11/12/1986).

43. Violation of CON Board's Internal Rules, 4. Regulatory Violation, 5. Validity of CON Board Decision. "NME Hospitals Inc. v. Department of Health & Rehabilitative Services", Court of Appeals of Florida First District, (6/24/1986).
44. Violation of CON Board's Internal Rules, 4. Regulatory Violation, 5. Validity of CON Board Decision. "Appeal of Lemire-Courville Assoc.", Supreme Court of New Hampshire, (8/5/1985).
45. Violation of CON Board's Internal Rules, 4. Regulatory Violation, 5.b. Reconsideration of Previous CON Decision, 5. Validity of CON Board Decision. "Regional Dialysis of Anniston v. Northeast Alabama Kidney Clinic Inc.", Court of Civil Appeals of Alabama, (7/17/1985).
46. Violation of CON Board's Internal Rules, 4. Regulatory Violation, 3.a. Violation of Administrative Procedures Act, 3. Statutory Violation. "United Hosp. Ctr. v. Richardson", Supreme Court of Appeals of West Virginia, (3/22/1985).
47. Violation of CON Board's Internal Rules, 4. Regulatory Violation, 5. Validity of CON Board Decision. "Bradbury Memorial Nursing Home v. Tall Pines Manor Associates", Supreme Judicial Court of Maine, (12/18/1984).
48. Violation of CON Board's Internal Rules, 4. Regulatory Violation, 3. Statutory Violation. "Samson v. Bureau of Community Medical Facilities Planning etc.", Court of Appeals of Florida First District, (10/24/1978).

IV B. CON Board's Internal Rules Arbitrary

49. CON Board's Internal Rules Arbitrary, 4. Regulatory Violation, 2.b. Procedural Due Process Violation, 2. Constitutional Challenge. "In re Adoption of Regulations Governing the State Health Plan", Supreme Court of New Jersey, (2/28/1994).
50. CON Board's Internal Rules Arbitrary, 4. Regulatory Violation. "Great Lakes Rehabilitation Hosp. v. Commonwealth Dep't of Health", Commonwealth Court of Pennsylvania, (5/31/1991).
51. CON Board's Internal Rules Arbitrary, 4. Regulatory Violation, 3.b. CON Board Exceeded Rulemaking Authority, 3. Statutory Violation. "Department of Health & Rehabilitative Services v. Florida Medical Center", Court of Appeal of Florida First District, (4/9/1991).
52. CON Board's Internal Rules Arbitrary, 4. Regulatory Violation. "National Healthcare L.P. v. Department of Health & Rehabilitative Services", Court of Appeal of Florida First District, (12/22/1989).
53. CON Board's Internal Rules Arbitrary, 6. Public Need Challenge, 5. Validity of CON Board Decision. "Professional Nurse Inc. v. State Dep't of Health & Rehabilitative Services", Court of Appeals of Florida First district, (1/27/1988).
54. CON Board's Internal Rules Arbitrary, 4.a. Violation of CON Board's Internal Rules, 4. Regulatory Violation, 3. Statutory Violation. "PIA Psychiatric Hospitals Inc. v. Missouri Health Facilities Review Committee", Court of Appeals of Missouri, Eastern District, Division Four, (3/10/1987).
55. CON Board's Internal Rules Arbitrary, 4. Regulatory Violation. "Radiological Soc. of New Jersey v. New Jersey State Dep't of Health Hospital Rate Setting Com.", Superior Court of New Jersey Appellate Division, (3/10/1986).
56. CON Board's Internal Rules Arbitrary, 3. Statutory Violation. "Department of Health & Rehabilitative Services v. Johnson & Johnson Home Health Care Inc.", Court of Appeals of Florida First District, (3/8/1984).
57. CON Board's Internal Rules Arbitrary, 4.a. Violation of CON Board's Internal Rules, 3.b. CON Board Exceeded Rulemaking Authority. "Appeal of Behavior Science Inst. v." Supreme Court of New Hampshire, (10/30/1981).
58. CON Board's Internal Rules Arbitrary, 6.e. Applicability of Need Criteria to Applicant."Ross Gen. Hosp. Inc. v. Locker", Court of Appeal of California, Second Appellate District, Division One, (7/28/1978).

IV C. Defining Regulatory Term

59. Defining Regulatory Term, 4. Regulatory Violation. "Ashtabula County Medical Center v. Tommy G. Thompson", United States Court of Appeals, (12/19/2003).
60. Defining Regulatory Term, 4. Regulatory Violation, 3.e. Defining Statutory Term, 3. Statutory Violation. "Providence Health System - Washington v. Tommy G. Thompson", United States Court of Appeals, (12/17/2003).
61. Defining Regulatory Term, 4. Regulatory Violation, 3.e. Defining Statutory Term, 3. Statutory Violation. "South Shore Hospital, Inc. v. Tommy G. Thompson", United States Court of Appeals, (10/16/2002).
62. Defining Regulatory Term, 3.b. CON Board Exceeded Rulemaking Authority. "Albany Surgical, P.C. v. Dept. of Community Health", Court of Appeals of Georgia, Fourth Division, (9/27/2002).
63. Defining Regulatory Term, 4. Regulatory Violation, 5.a. CON Board Decision Arbitrary. "Ashtabula County Med. Ctr. v. Thompson", United States District Court for the Northern District of Ohio, (2/8/2002).
64. Defining Regulatory Term, 4. Regulatory Violation, 3.e. Defining Statutory Term, 3. Statutory Violation. "South Shore Hospital v. Tommy G. Thompson", United States District Court, D. Massachusetts, (1/3/2002).
65. Defining Regulatory Term, 4. Regulatory Violation, 3. Statutory Violation. "Brattleboro Memorial Hospital v. Department of Banking, Insurance, Securities and Health Care Administration", Supreme Court of Vermont, (9/19/2001).
66. Defining Regulatory Term, 4. Regulatory Violation, 3. Statutory Violation. "Cabinet for Human Resources Interim Office of Health Planning & Certification v. Jewish Hosp. Healthcare Serv.", Court of Appeals of Kentucky, (10/25/1996).
67. Defining Regulatory Term, 4. Regulatory Violation, 3. Statutory Violation, 6.e. Applicability of Need Criteria to Applicant. "Cape Fear Memorial Hosp. v. North Carolina Dep't of Human Resources", Court of Appeals of North Carolina, (2/6/1996).
68. Defining Regulatory Term, 4. Regulatory Violation. "Arbor Health Care Co. v. State", Court of Appeal of Florida First District, (6/1/1995).
69. Defining Regulatory Term, 6.e. Applicability of Need Criteria to Applicant, 7.b. Failure to Obtain CON. "In re Midwest Eye Ctr.", Court of Appeals of Ohio Tenth Appellate District, Franklin County, (5/30/1995).
70. Defining Regulatory Term, 4. Regulatory Violation, 3.e. Defining Statutory Term, 3. Statutory Violation, 6.e. Applicability of Need Criteria to Applicant. "SSM Health Care v. Missouri Health Facilities Review Comm.", Supreme Court of Missouri, (3/21/1995).
71. Defining Regulatory Term. "Commission for Health Economics Control v. Medical Consultants Imaging Co.", Court of Appeals of Kentucky, (12/24/1992).
72. Defining Regulatory Term. "Overlook Medical Clinic v. Commonwealth Dep't of Health", Commonwealth Court of Pennsylvania, (10/30/1989).
73. Defining Regulatory Term, 6.e. Applicability of Need Criteria to Applicant. "Appeal of Rehabilitation Assocs. V." Supreme Court of New Hampshire , (4/7/1989).
74. Defining Regulatory Term, 4. Regulatory Violation, 3.e. Defining Statutory Term, 3. Statutory Violation, 6. Public Need Challenge. "Schoolman v. Health Facilities Appeals Bd. (1989)", Supreme Judicial Court of Massachusetts, Suffolk, (2/7/1989).
75. Defining Regulatory Term, 6.e. Applicability of Need Criteria to Applicant. "Alabama Nursing Home Ass'n v. Alabama State Health Planning Agency", Court of Civil Appeals of Alabama, (1/13/1989).
76. Defining Regulatory Term, 4. Regulatory Violation, 3.e. Defining Statutory Term, 3. Statutory Violation. "Department of Human Resources v. UHS of Colony", Supreme Court of Nevada, (4/9/1987).

77. Defining Regulatory Term, 4. Regulatory Violation, 3.e. Defining Statutory Term, 3. Statutory Violation. "Centennial Villas Inc. v. State", Court of Appeals of Washington, Division Two, (3/2/1987).
78. Defining Regulatory Term, 4. Regulatory Violation, 3.e. Defining Statutory Term, 3. Statutory Violation. "Mercy Health Center Div. Of Sisters of Mercy Health Corp. v. Iowa State Dep't of Health", Supreme Court of Iowa, (10/17/1984).
79. Defining Regulatory Term, 4. Regulatory Violation, 3. Statutory Violation. "Brookline v. Medical Area Service Corp.", Appeals Court of Massachusetts, Suffolk, (8/13/1979).
80. Defining Regulatory Term, 4. Regulatory Violation, 3.e. Defining Statutory Term, 3. Statutory Violation, 3.a. Violation of Administrative Procedures Act. "Los Alamitos Gen. Hosp. Inc. v. Lackner", Court of Appeal of California, Second Appellate District, Division One, (11/17/1978).
81. Defining Regulatory Term. "Bakersfield Community Hosp. v. Department of Health", Court of Appeal of California, Fifth Appellate District, (12/29/1977).
82. Defining Regulatory Term, 4. Regulatory Violation, 3.e. Defining Statutory Term, 3. Statutory Violation. "La Moore v. State Health Council", Supreme Court of North Dakota, (12/4/1973).

IV. VALIDITY OF CON BOARD DECISION

1. Validity of CON Board Decision, 2.b. Procedural Due Process Violation, 2. Constitutional Challenge. "Mill creek Manor v. Department of Public Welfare", Commonwealth Court of Pennsylvania, (11/6/2001).
2. Validity of CON Board Decision. "Md. Gen. Hosp. Inc. v. Thompson", United States District Court for the District of Maryland, (6/27/2001).
3. Validity of CON Board Decision, 2.b. Procedural Due Process Violation, 2. Constitutional Challenge, 3.a. Violation of Administrative Procedures Act, 3. Statutory Violation. "First Baptist Church of Crown Heights Center for Nursing & Rehabilitation, Inc. v. Antonia Novello, as Commissioner of Health of the Department of Health of the State of New York", Supreme Court, Kings County, New York, (4/24/2001).
4. Validity of CON Board Decision. "Johnston Ambulatory Surgical Associates, LTD. v. Patricia Nolan, in her capacity as Director of the Rhode Island Department of Health et al.", Supreme Court of Rhode Island, (7/12/2000).
5. Validity of CON Board Decision. "Carle Found. v. Illinois Health Facilities Planning Bd.", Appellate Court of Illinois, First District Fifth Division, (8/13/1999).
6. Validity of CON Board Decision. "United States v. Nashua", United States Court of Appeals for the Second Circuit, (9/10/1998).
7. Validity of CON Board Decision. "Arbor Health Care Co. v. Delaware Health Resources Bd.", Superior Court of Delaware New Castle, (5/20/1997).
8. Validity of CON Board Decision, 5.b. Reconsideration of Previous CON Decision. "Agency for Health Care Administration, Life mark Hospitals of Florida, Baptist Hospital of Miami, St. Anne's Nursing Center, St. Anne's Residence, Inc., Florida Convalescent Associates, and Cedars Health-Care Group, Ltd., Petitioners, v. Mount Sinai Medical Center of Greater Miami, Marco Healthcare Investors, Inc., Brookwood Extended Care Center of Homestead, Beverly Enterprises-Florida, Arbor Health Care Company, Meadowbrook Healthcare Services of North Carolina, Marriott Senior Living Services, Miami Beach Healthcare Group, Ltd., and Kendall Healthcare Group, Ltd. Respondants." , Florida District Court of Appeals , (4/1/1997).
9. Validity of CON Board Decision, 7. Miscellaneous. "Naples Community Hosp. v. Agency for Health Care Admin." Court of Appeal of Florida First District , (1/31/1997).
10. Validity of CON Board Decision, 7. Miscellaneous. "Naples Community Hospital, Inc., Petitioner, v.

State of Florida, Agency for Health Care Administration, and Big Cypress Medical Center, Inc., Respondents", District Court of Appeal of Florida, (1/31/1997).

11. Validity of CON Board Decision. "Woods Serv. v. Department of Pub. Welfare", Commonwealth Court of Pennsylvania, (8/1/1996).
12. Validity of CON Board Decision. "Lawn wood Medical Ctr. v. Agency for Health Care Admin." Court of Appeal of Florida First District , (7/29/1996).
13. Validity of CON Board Decision. "West Bloomfield Hosp. v. Certificate of Need Bd.", Supreme Court of Michigan, (7/16/1996).
14. Validity of CON Board Decision. "First American Home Care of South Carolina, Inc. v. South Carolina Department of Health and Environmental Control", State of South Carolina Administrative Law Judge Division, (6/7/1996).
15. Validity of CON Board Decision, 3.a. Violation of Administrative Procedures Act, 3. Statutory Violation. "Appeal of Courville (New Hampshire Health Serv. Planning & Review Bd.) V." Supreme Court of New Hampshire , (11/7/1994).
16. Validity of CON Board Decision. "Beebe Medical Ctr. v. Certificate of Need Appeals Bd.", Superior Court of Delaware Kent, (8/31/1994).
17. Validity of CON Board Decision, 3.c. Violation of State Law During CON Proceedings, 3. Statutory Violation. "Mercy Regional Health Sys. v. Department of Health NO. C.D. NO. C.D. Commonwealth Court of Pennsylvania", Commonwealth Court of Pennsylvania, (7/12/1994).
18. Validity of CON Board Decision. "Greenbriar Nursing Home v. Pilley", Supreme Court of Louisiana'-, (5/23/1994).
19. Validity of CON Board Decision. "In re Cleveland Clinic Found." Court of Appeals of Ohio Tenth Appellate District, Franklin County , (4/14/1994).
20. Validity of CON Board Decision, 5.a. CON Board Decision Arbitrary, 4.a. Violation of CON Board's Internal Rules. "Appeal of Nashua Brookside Hosp. v." Supreme Court of New Hampshire , (12/23/1993).
21. Validity of CON Board Decision. "In re St. John Medical Ctr.", Court of Appeals of Ohio Tenth Appellate District, Franklin County, (10/28/1993).
22. Validity of CON Board Decision. "University Community Hosp. v. Department of Health & Rehabilitative Services", Court of Appeal of Florida First District, (12/29/1992).
23. Validity of CON Board Decision, 3.b. CON Board Exceeded Rulemaking Authority, 3. Statutory Violation. "Lake East Hosp. v. Ohio Dep't of Health", Court of Appeals of Ohio Tenth Appellate District, Franklin County, (10/6/1992).
24. Validity of CON Board Decision. "First Hosp. Corp. v. Department of Health & Rehabilitative Services", Court of Appeal of Florida First District, (8/21/1991).
25. Validity of CON Board Decision. "Am sub v. Department of Health & Rehabilitative Services", Court of Appeal of Florida First District, (4/30/1991).
26. Validity of CON Board Decision, 4. Regulatory Violation, 3. Statutory Violation, 3.a. Violation of Administrative Procedures Act. "Fairview General Hosp. v. Fletcher", Court of Appeals of Ohio Tenth Appellate District, Franklin County, (12/20/1990).
27. Validity of CON Board Decision. "Huntington Manor of Murphy v. North Carolina Dep't of Human Resources etc.", Court of Appeals of North Carolina, (6/19/1990).
28. Validity of CON Board Decision. "In re Saltwell Nursing Home", Court of Appeals of Ohio Tenth Appellate District, Franklin County, (4/27/1989).
29. Validity of CON Board Decision, 4. Regulatory Violation. "Connell Hosp. v. Illinois Health Facilities Planning Bd.", Supreme Court of Illinois, (9/29/1988).

30. Validity of CON Board Decision. "Christian Care Home Inc. v. State Certificate of Need Review Bd.", Court of Appeals of Ohio Tenth Appellate District, Franklin County, (5/26/1988).
31. Validity of CON Board Decision. "Huron Valley Hospital Inc. v. Pontiac", United States District Court for the Eastern District of Michigan, (5/26/1988).
32. Validity of CON Board Decision. "North Memorial Medical Center v. Minnesota Dept. of Health", Court of Appeals of Minnesota, (5/24/1988).
33. Validity of CON Board Decision, 4. Regulatory Violation, 3. Statutory Violation. "Condell Hospital v. Health Facilities Planning Bd.", Appellate Court of Illinois, First District Second Division, (9/29/1987).
34. Validity of CON Board Decision. "Metropolitan Hospital v. Commonwealth Dep't of Health", Commonwealth Court of Pennsylvania, (6/18/1987).
35. Validity of CON Board Decision. "Florida Hospital v. Department of Health & Rehabilitative Services", Court of Appeal of Florida First District, (5/14/1987).
36. Validity of CON Board Decision, 2.b. Procedural Due Process Violation, 2. Constitutional Challenge. "Appeal of Catholic Medical Center et al", Supreme Court of New Hampshire, (8/7/1986).
37. Validity of CON Board Decision, 2.a. Equal Protection Violation, 2. Constitutional Challenge. "Appeal of Catholic Medical Ctr. v." Supreme Court of New Hampshire , (8/7/1986).
38. Validity of CON Board Decision. "Medivision of East Broward County Inc. v. Department of Health & Rehabilitative Services", Court of Appeals of Florida First District, (5/15/1986).
39. Validity of CON Board Decision. "Southern Nev. Memorial Hosp. v. Department of Human Resources", Supreme Court of Nevada, (8/27/1985).
40. Validity of CON Board Decision. "Community Psychiatric Cars. v. Department of Health & Rehabilitative Serv.", Court of Appeals of Florida First District, (8/20/1985).
41. Validity of CON Board Decision. "In re Dixon Health Care Ctr. Inc.", Court of Appeals of Ohio Tenth Appellate District, Franklin County, (7/11/1985).
42. Validity of CON Board Decision. "In re Wellesley Corp.", Supreme Court of Ohio, (7/10/1985).
43. Validity of CON Board Decision. "Department of Health & Rehabilitative Serv. v. American Healthcare of Vero Beach", Court of Appeals of Florida First District, (6/18/1985).
44. Validity of CON Board Decision. "Hillsborough County Hospital Authority v. Tampa Heart Institute", Court of Appeals of Florida second District, (5/22/1985).
45. Validity of CON Board Decision, 4. Regulatory Violation, 3. Statutory Violation. "Governor v. Rehab Hospital Services Corp.", Supreme Court of Arkansas, (4/15/1985).
46. Validity of CON Board Decision. "State Health Planning Review Bd. v. Piedmont Hospital Inc.", Court of Appeals of Georgia, (2/6/1985).
47. Validity of CON Board Decision. "Baptist Hospital Inc. v. Humana of Kentucky Inc.", Court of Appeals of Kentucky, (4/27/1984).
48. Validity of CON Board Decision. "Cooper River Convalescent Center Inc. v. Dougherty", Superior Court of New Jersey Appellate Division, (3/19/1975).
49. Validity of CON Board Decision, 3.a. Violation of Administrative Procedures Act, 3. Statutory Violation, 4. Regulatory Violation. "Gummels v. North Carolina Dep't of Human Resources Div. of Facility Services", Court of Appeals of North Carolina, (2/6/1190).

V A. CON Board Decision Arbitrary

50. CON Board Decision Arbitrary, 5. Validity of CON Board Decision. "Georgia Department of Community Health v. Stella Health Services, Inc.", Court of Appeals of Georgia, (3/17/2004).
51. CON Board Decision Arbitrary. "Attalla County Board of Supervisors d/b/a Attala Care Center v. Mississippi State Department of Health", Supreme Court of Mississippi, (2/26/2004).
52. CON Board Decision Arbitrary, 5. Validity of CON Board Decision. "Morristown Surgery Center, LLC v. Tennessee Health Facilities Commission", Court of Appeals of Tennessee, at Nashville, (12/15/2003).

53. CON Board Decision Arbitrary, 5. Validity of CON Board Decision. "Northern Virginia Community Hospital, LLC d/b/a Broad lands Regional Medical Center v. Robert B. Stroube, M.D., M.P.H.", Circuit Court of Loudoun County, Virginia, (10/3/2003).
54. CON Board Decision Arbitrary, 5. Validity of CON Board Decision. "Department of Community Health, Division of Health Planning v. Ginned Hospital System, Inc.", Court of Appeals of Georgia, First Division, (8/26/2003).
55. CON Board Decision Arbitrary, 5. Validity of CON Board Decision. "In re. Central Vermont Medical Center", Supreme Court of Vermont, (12/16/2002).
56. CON Board Decision Arbitrary, 5. Validity of CON Board Decision. "Jackson HMA, Inc. v. Mississippi State Dept. of Health", Supreme Court of Mississippi, (7/25/2002).
57. CON Board Decision Arbitrary, 5. Validity of CON Board Decision, 3.c. Violation of State Law During CON Proceedings. "Jeff Anderson Regal Med. Ctr. v. Miss. State Dep't of Health", Supreme Court of Mississippi, (10/31/2001).
58. CON Board Decision Arbitrary, 5. Validity of CON Board Decision, 3. Statutory Violation. "Jay Alexander Manor Inc. v. Antonia Novello, as Commissioner of Health of the State of New York", Supreme Court, Appellate Division, Third Department, New York, (7/26/2001).
59. CON Board Decision Arbitrary, 5. Validity of CON Board Decision, 3. Statutory Violation. "Ex parte Beverly Enterprises-Alabama Inc.", Supreme Court of Alabama, (7/13/2001).
60. CON Board Decision Arbitrary, 3.b. CON Board Exceeded Rulemaking Authority. "Cain v. Mississippi State Dep't of Health", Supreme Court of Mississippi, (9/21/2000).
61. CON Board Decision Arbitrary, 5. Validity of CON Board Decision. "Delta Regional Med. Ctr. v. Mississippi State Dep't of Health", Supreme Court of Mississippi, (12/16/1999).
62. CON Board Decision Arbitrary, 5. Validity of CON Board Decision, 2.b. Procedural Due Process Violation, 2. Constitutional Challenge. "Cathedral Rock of Granite City v. Illinois Health Facilities Planning Bd.", Appellate Court of Illinois, Fourth District, (12/9/1999).
63. CON Board Decision Arbitrary, 5. Validity of CON Board Decision. "Burke Health Investors L.L.C. v. North Carolina Dep't of Human Resources Div. Of Facility Serv. Certificate of Need Section", Court of Appeals of North Carolina, (11/16/1999).
64. CON Board Decision Arbitrary, 5. Validity of CON Board Decision. "In the matter of certificate of need granted to sty. Francis medical center", Superior Court of New Jersey, Appellate Division, (11/8/1999).
65. CON Board Decision Arbitrary, 3.b. CON Board Exceeded Rulemaking Authority, 3. Statutory Violation, 2. Constitutional Challenge. "Biloxi HMA Inc. v. Singing River Hosp.", Supreme Court of Mississippi, (7/29/1999).
66. CON Board Decision Arbitrary, 5. Validity of CON Board Decision. "Mississippi State Dep't of Health v. Natchez Community Hosp.", Supreme Court of Mississippi, (7/29/1999).
67. CON Board Decision Arbitrary, 5. Validity of CON Board Decision. "State Health Planning and Development Agency and Decal Center for Healthcare, Inc. v. Baptist Health System, Inc.", Court of Civic Appeals of Alabama, (4/9/1999).
68. CON Board Decision Arbitrary, 5. Validity of CON Board Decision. "State Health Planning & De Agency v. Baptist Health Sys. Inc.", Court of Civil Appeals of Alabama, (4/9/1999).
69. CON Board Decision Arbitrary, 5. Validity of CON Board Decision, 4.c. Defining Regulatory Term, 3.e. Defining Statutory Term. "St. Joseph's Hosp. Inc. v. Thunderbolt Health Care Inc", Court of Appeals of Georgia, (4/1/1999).
70. CON Board Decision Arbitrary, 5. Validity of CON Board Decision. "Carriage Hill-Cabin John Inc. v. Maryland Health Resources Planning Common", Court of Special Appeals of Maryland, (2/25/1999).
71. CON Board Decision Arbitrary, 2. Constitutional Challenge. "Gramercy Hill Enters. v. State", Supreme Court of Nebraska, (12/11/1998).

72. CON Board Decision Arbitrary, 5. Validity of CON Board Decision. "St. Dominic-Jackson Mom's Hosp. v. Mississippi State Dep't of Health", Supreme Court of Mississippi, (10/8/1998).
73. CON Board Decision Arbitrary, 5. Validity of CON Board Decision, 2.a. Equal Protection Violation, 2. Constitutional Challenge. "Arkansas Health Services Agency and Arkansas Health Services Commission; Arkansas Health Care Association v. Desiderata, Inc.", Supreme Court of Arkansas, (1/22/1998).
74. CON Board Decision Arbitrary, 5. Validity of CON Board Decision, 2. Constitutional Challenge. "Planned Parenthood v. Atchison", United States Court of Appeals For the Eighth Circuit, (11/25/1997).
75. CON Board Decision Arbitrary, 5. Validity of CON Board Decision. "Texas Health Facilities Com. v. Nieces County Hospital Dist.", Court of Civil Appeals of Texas Third District, Austin, (5/9/1997).
76. CON Board Decision Arbitrary, 5. Validity of CON Board Decision. "Life Care Centers of America, Inc., Appellant, v. Health Care and Retirement Corporation of American and Agency for Health Care Administration, Applees." District Court of Appeal of Florida , (4/23/1997).
77. CON Board Decision Arbitrary, 5. Validity of CON Board Decision. "Nueces County Hospital Dist. v. Texas Health Facilities Com.", Court of Civil Appeals of Texas Third District, Austin, (1/24/1997).
78. CON Board Decision Arbitrary, 5. Validity of CON Board Decision. "Tarpon Springs General Hospital v. Office of Community Medical Facilities etc.", Court of Appeals of Florida First District, (1/19/1997).
79. CON Board Decision Arbitrary, 5. Validity of CON Board Decision. "In re Mazola Health Care", Court of Appeals of Ohio Tenth Appellate District, Franklin County, (1/9/1997).
80. CON Board Decision Arbitrary, 5. Validity of CON Board Decision, 2. Constitutional Challenge, 2.a. Equal Protection Violation, 2.b. Procedural Due Process Violation. "Access Ctr. for Health v. Health Facilities Planning Bd.", Appellate Court of Illinois, Second District, (9/17/1996).
81. CON Board Decision Arbitrary, 5. Validity of CON Board Decision. "Public Health Dep't v. Rivergate Manor", Supreme Court of Michigan, (7/16/1996).
82. CON Board Decision Arbitrary, 5. Validity of CON Board Decision. "Cain v. Mississippi State Dep't of Health", Supreme Court of Mississippi, (12/14/1995).
83. CON Board Decision Arbitrary, 5. Validity of CON Board Decision, 6.e. Applicability of Need Criteria to Applicant, 6. Public Need Challenge, 3.d. CON Law Arbitrary. "Mississippi State Dep't of Health v. Mississippi Baptist Medical Ctr.", Supreme Court of Mississippi, (10/19/1995).
84. CON Board Decision Arbitrary, 5. Validity of CON Board Decision. "West Bay Manor Co. v. Cuyahoga County Bd. of Revision", Supreme Court of Ohio, (8/30/1995).
85. CON Board Decision Arbitrary, 5. Validity of CON Board Decision, 3.a. Violation of Administrative Procedures Act, 3. Statutory Violation. "Medical Arts Clinic P.C. v. Franciscan Initiatives", Supreme Court of North Dakota, (5/9/1995).
86. CON Board Decision Arbitrary. "Britt haven Inc. v. North Carolina Dep't of Human Resources Div. Of Facility Serv.", Court of Appeals of North Carolina, (4/4/1995).
87. CON Board Decision Arbitrary, 5. Validity of CON Board Decision. "On with Life v. State Health Facilities Council", Court of Appeals of Iowa, (3/30/1995).
88. CON Board Decision Arbitrary, 5. Validity of CON Board Decision "Springwood Assocs. v. Health Facilities Planning Bd.", Appellate Court of Illinois, Fourth District, (3/3/1995).
89. CON Board Decision Arbitrary, 5. Validity of CON Board Decision. "Maryland Gen. Hosp. v. Maryland Health Resources Planning Common", Court of Special Appeals of Maryland, (2/14/1995).
90. CON Board Decision Arbitrary, 5. Validity of CON Board Decision, 2.b. Procedural Due Process Violation, 2. Constitutional Challenge, 6.e. Applicability of Need Criteria to Applicant, 6. Public Need Challenge. "Magnetic Resonance Technologies Ltd. Partnership v. Commissioner Maine Dep't of Human Serv.", Supreme Judicial Court of Maine, (1/19/1995).
91. CON Board Decision Arbitrary, 5. Validity of CON Board Decision. "Mercy Health Center Div. of Sisters of Mercy Health Corp. v. State Health Facilities Council", Supreme Court of Iowa, (1/16/1995).

92. CON Board Decision Arbitrary, 5. Validity of CON Board Decision. "In re Certificate of Need of Arnold Walter Nursing Home", Superior Court of New Jersey Appellate Division, (11/23/1994).
93. CON Board Decision Arbitrary, 5. Validity of CON Board Decision. "Oklahoma Dept. of Health v. Medi-Plex Nursing Cars. Inc.", Court of Appeals of Oklahoma Division Two, (2/8/1994).
94. CON Board Decision Arbitrary, 5. Validity of CON Board Decision. "In re Heartland of Mentor", Court of Appeals of Ohio Tenth Appellate District, Franklin County, (12/23/1993).
95. CON Board Decision Arbitrary, 4.c. Defining Regulatory Term. "In re Certification of Need Application of Chilton Memorial Hosp.", Superior Court of New Jersey Appellate Division, (12/23/1993).
96. CON Board Decision Arbitrary, 5. Validity of CON Board Decision. "In re Deaconess Hosp.", Court of Appeals of Ohio Tenth Appellate District, Franklin County, (12/9/1993).
97. CON Board Decision Arbitrary, 5. Validity of CON Board Decision. "Hospital Auth. v. State Health Planning Agency", Court of Appeals of Georgia, (11/19/1993).
98. CON Board Decision Arbitrary, 5. Validity of CON Board Decision. "St. Francis Hosp. v. Appeals Bd. of Dep't of Health & Social Serv.", Superior Court of Delaware New Castle, (8/12/1993).
99. CON Board Decision Arbitrary, 5. Validity of CON Board Decision. "State Health Planning Agency v. Mobile Infirmary Ass'n", Court of Civil Appeals of Alabama, (10/16/1992).
100. CON Board Decision Arbitrary, 5. Validity of CON Board Decision. "Holy Name Hosp. v. New Jersey Health Care Admin. Bd.", Superior Court of New Jersey Appellate Division, (7/23/1992).
101. CON Board Decision Arbitrary, 5. Validity of CON Board Decision. "University Psychiatric Center Inc. v. Department of Health & Rehabilitative Services", Court of Appeal of Florida First District, (4/20/1992).
102. CON Board Decision Arbitrary, 7. Miscellaneous. "Brook wood-Jackson County Convalescent Center v. Department of Health & Rehabilitative Services", Court of Appeal of Florida First District, (1/2/1992).
103. CON Board Decision Arbitrary, 5. Validity of CON Board Decision. "Roper Hospital v. Board of South Carolina Department of Health and Environmental Control and Francis Xavier Hospital", Supreme Court of South Carolina, (12/3/1991).
104. CON Board Decision Arbitrary, 5. Validity of CON Board Decision. "IFIDA Health Care Group Ltd. v. Department of Health", Commonwealth Court of Pennsylvania, (8/9/1991).
105. CON Board Decision Arbitrary, 5. Validity of CON Board Decision. "In the matter of Sisters of Charity Hospital of Buffalo v. New York State Department Of Health", Supreme Court, Appellate Division, Third Department, (7/18/1991).
106. CON Board Decision Arbitrary, 5. Validity of CON Board Decision, 6. Public Need Challenge. "In re Timken Mercy Medical Center", Supreme Court of Ohio, (7/3/1991).
107. CON Board Decision Arbitrary, 5. Validity of CON Board Decision, 2.b. Procedural Due Process Violation, Constitutional Challenge. "In re Christian Care Home Inc.", Court of Appeals of Ohio Tenth Appellate District, Franklin County, (6/6/1991).
108. CON Board Decision Arbitrary, 5. Validity of CON Board Decision. "Mississippi State Dep't of Health v. Southwest Mississippi Regional Medical Center", Supreme Court of Mississippi, (5/3/1991).
109. CON Board Decision Arbitrary, 6.e. Applicability of Need Criteria to Applicant, 5. Validity of CON Board Decision. "Arkansas Dep't of Human Services v. Hillsboro Manor Nursing Home Inc.", Supreme Court of Arkansas, (2/11/1991).
110. CON Board Decision Arbitrary, 5. Validity of CON Board Decision. "Town of Hempstead v. Commissioner, State of New York Office of Mental Health and Pilgrim Psychiatric Center, Respondents", Supreme Court, Appellate Division, Fourth Department, (2/1/1991).
111. CON Board Decision Arbitrary, 5. Validity of CON Board Decision. "Central Florida Regional Hosp. Inc. v. Department of Health & Rehabilitative Services", Court of Appeal of Florida Fifth District, (1/6/1991).

112. CON Board Decision Arbitrary. "Charter Hosp. of Pasco Co. v. Department of Health & Rehabilitative Services", Court of Appeal of Florida First District, (6/18/1990).
113. CON Board Decision Arbitrary, 5. Validity of CON Board Decision. "In re Valley Hosp.", Superior Court of New Jersey Appellate Division, (4/20/1990).
114. CON Board Decision Arbitrary, 5. Validity of CON Board Decision. "Lenoir Memorial Hosp. Inc. v. North Carolina Dep't of Human Resources etc.", Court of Appeals of North Carolina, (4/17/1990).
115. CON Board Decision Arbitrary, 5. Validity of CON Board Decision, 3. Statutory Violation. "Ex parte Shelby Medical Center Inc.", Supreme Court of Alabama, (4/12/1990).
116. CON Board Decision Arbitrary, 5. Validity of CON Board Decision. "Magnolia Hosp. v. Mississippi State Dep't of Health", Supreme Court of Mississippi, (4/4/1990).
117. CON Board Decision Arbitrary, 5. Validity of CON Board Decision. "Health Care & Retirement Corp. v. Department of Health & Rehabilitative Services", Court of Appeal of Florida First District, (3/29/1990).
118. CON Board Decision Arbitrary, 5. Validity of CON Board Decision. "Powers v. Commonwealth Dep't of Health", Commonwealth Court of Pennsylvania, (1/22/1990).
119. CON Board Decision Arbitrary, 5. Validity of CON Board Decision. "University Community Hospital v. Department of Health & Rehabilitative Services", Court of Appeal of Florida First District, (1/12/1990).
120. CON Board Decision Arbitrary, 5. Validity of CON Board Decision. "Manor Care Inc. v. Department of Health & Rehabilitative Serv.", Court of Appeal of Florida First District, (10/3/1989).
121. CON Board Decision Arbitrary, 5. Validity of CON Board Decision. "Melody Manor Convalescent Center v. Mississippi State Dep't of Health", Supreme Court of Mississippi, (6/28/1989).
122. CON Board Decision Arbitrary, 5. Validity of CON Board Decision. "Providence Hospital of Everett v. State of Washington, Department of Social & Health Services, and A.N. Shinto, Secretary of the Department of Social & Health Services", Thurston County Superior Court, (4/13/1989).
123. CON Board Decision Arbitrary, 5. Validity of CON Board Decision, 4. Regulatory Violation, 3. Statutory Violation. "St. Joseph's Hospital v. Department of Health & Rehabilitative Services", Court of Appeals of Florida First district, (12/21/1988).
124. CON Board Decision Arbitrary, 5. Validity of CON Board Decision. "Powers v. Commonwealth Dep't of Health", Commonwealth Court of Pennsylvania, (11/25/1988).
125. CON Board Decision Arbitrary, 3.c. Violation of State Law During CON Proceedings, 5. Validity of CON Board Decision. "Appeal of New Hampshire Catholic Charities v." Supreme Court of New Hampshire , (8/10/1988).
126. CON Board Decision Arbitrary, 5. Validity of CON Board Decision. "Department of Health v. Columbia West Corp.", Supreme Court of Nebraska, (3/18/1988).
127. CON Board Decision Arbitrary, 5. Validity of CON Board Decision. "St. Mary's Hosp. v. State Health Planning & Dev. Tax Comer." Supreme Court of Appeals of West Virginia , (12/15/1987).
128. CON Board Decision Arbitrary, 5. Validity of CON Board Decision. "Health Care & Retirement Corp. v. Department of Health & Rehabilitative Services", Court of Appeals of Florida First district, (12/1/1987).
129. CON Board Decision Arbitrary. "Bayonet Point Regional Medical Center v. Department of Health & Rehabilitative Services", Court of Appeals of Florida First district, (11/24/1987).
130. CON Board Decision Arbitrary, 5. Validity of CON Board Decision. "In re St. Luke's Hosp.", Supreme Court of South Dakota, (10/21/1987).

131. CON Board Decision Arbitrary, 5. Validity of CON Board Decision. "Community Hospital of New Port Richey/University Psychiatric Center Inc. v. Department of Health & Rehabilitative Services", Court of Appeals of Florida First district, (9/29/1987).
132. CON Board Decision Arbitrary, 5. Validity of CON Board Decision. "Inverness Convalescent Ctr. v. Department of Health & Rehabilitative Serv.", Court of Appeals of Florida First district, (8/26/1987).
133. CON Board Decision Arbitrary, 5. Validity of CON Board Decision. "In the matter of Meadow brook Nursing Home v. David Axelrod, as Commissioner of the Dept. of Heath", Supreme Court, Appellate Division, Third Department, (7/16/1987).
134. CON Board Decision Arbitrary, 5. Validity of CON Board Decision. "Arkansas Health Planning & Dev. Agency v. Hot Spring County Memorial Hospital", Supreme Court of Arkansas, (2/9/1987).
135. CON Board Decision Arbitrary, 5. Validity of CON Board Decision. "University Medical Park Ltd. v. Department of Health & Rehabilitative Services", Court of Appeals of Florida Second district, (1/28/1987).
136. CON Board Decision Arbitrary, 5. Validity of CON Board Decision, 2.a. Equal Protection Violation, 2.b. Procedural Due Process Violation, 2. Constitutional Challenge, 4.a. Violation of CON Board's Internal Rules, 3. Statutory Violation. "Charter Medical-Fayette County Inc. v. Health Planning Agency Inc.", Court of Appeals of Georgia, (12/5/1986).
137. CON Board Decision Arbitrary, 5. Validity of CON Board Decision, 6.e. Applicability of Need Criteria to Applicant. "Charter Pines Hospital Inc. v. North Carolina Dep't of Human Resources", Court of Appeals of North Carolina, (11/4/1986).
138. CON Board Decision Arbitrary, 5. Validity of CON Board Decision, 3.b. CON Board Exceeded Rulemaking Authority. "Doctors' Osteopathic Medical Center Inc. v. Department of Health & Rehabilitative Services", Court of Appeals of Florida First district, (10/6/1986).
139. CON Board Decision Arbitrary, 5. Validity of CON Board Decision. "Health Care Medical Facility XXVI Partnership v. State Dep't of Health & Rehabilitative Services", Court of Appeals of Florida first district, (9/24/1986).
140. CON Board Decision Arbitrary, 5. Validity of CON Board Decision. "Upjohn Healthcare Services Inc. v. Department of Health & Rehabilitative Services", Court of Appeals of Florida First District, (7/22/1986).
141. CON Board Decision Arbitrary, 5. Validity of CON Board Decision. "Humana Hospital Corp. v. North Carolina Dep't of Human Resources Div. of Facility Services", Court of Appeals of North Carolina, (7/1/1986).
142. CON Board Decision Arbitrary, 6.c. Establishment Challenge to New Need Requirements. "Bayonet Point Hospital Inc. v. Department of Health & Rehabilitative Services", Court of Appeals of Florida First District, (6/25/1986).
143. CON Board Decision Arbitrary, 5. Validity of CON Board Decision. "Sinai Hospital of Baltimore Inc. v. Maryland Health Resources Planning Com.", Court of Appeals of Maryland, (6/10/1986).
144. CON Board Decision Arbitrary, 5. Validity of CON Board Decision, 6. Public Need Challenge, 6.e. Applicability of Need Criteria to Applicant. "Health Care & Retirement Corp. v. Department of Health & Rehabilitative Services", Court of Appeals of Florida First District, (5/14/1986).
145. CON Board Decision Arbitrary, 5. Validity of CON Board Decision, 6.e. Applicability of Need Criteria to Applicant, 6. Public Need Challenge, 2. Constitutional Challenge. "Perini Services Inc. v. Maryland Health Resources Planning Com.", Court of Special Appeals of Maryland, (4/7/1986).
146. CON Board Decision Arbitrary, 5. Validity of CON Board Decision. "Balsam v. Department of Health & Rehabilitative Services", Court of Appeals of Florida First District, (3/31/1986).
147. CON Board Decision Arbitrary, 5. Validity of CON Board Decision. "Good Samaritan Hospital Inc. v. Department of Health & Rehabilitative Services", District Court of Appeal of the State of Florida Fourth District, (3/26/1986).

148. CON Board Decision Arbitrary, 5. Validity of CON Board Decision. "Gulf Court Nursing Center v. Department of Health & Rehabilitative Services", Court of Appeal of Florida First District, (2/14/1986).
149. CON Board Decision Arbitrary, 5. Validity of CON Board Decision, 6.e. Applicability of Need Criteria to Applicant, 6. Public Need Challenge. "Federal Property Management Corp. v. Department of Health & Rehabilitative Services", Court of Appeals of Florida First District, (1/20/1986).
150. CON Board Decision Arbitrary, 4. Regulatory Violation, 5. Validity of CON Board Decision. "Doctors' Hospital of Prince George's County v. Maryland Health Resources Planning Com.", Court of Special Appeals of Maryland, (1/8/1986).
151. CON Board Decision Arbitrary, 5. Validity of CON Board Decision. "Mt. Olive Home Health Care Agency Inc. v. N.C. Dep't of Human Resources", Court of Appeals of North Carolina, (12/3/1985).
152. CON Board Decision Arbitrary, 5. Validity of CON Board Decision. "Richland's Medical Ass'n v. Commonwealth ex rel State Health Comm'r", Supreme Court of Virginia, (11/27/1985).
153. CON Board Decision Arbitrary, 5. Validity of CON Board Decision. "Health Care Management Inc. v. Department of Health & Rehabilitative Services", Court of Appeals of Florida First District, (11/21/1985).
154. CON Board Decision Arbitrary, 5. Validity of CON Board Decision. "Oak Park Manor v. State Certificate of Need Review BD.", Court of Appeals of Ohio Tenth Appellate District, Franklin County, (10/3/1985).
155. CON Board Decision Arbitrary, 5. Validity of CON Board Decision, 4.a. Violation of CON Board's Internal Rules. "Central Florida Regional Hospital v. Daytona Beach General Hospital", Court of Appeals of Florida First District, (9/17/1985).
156. CON Board Decision Arbitrary, 5. Validity of CON Board Decision, 6.e. Applicability of Need Criteria to Applicant, 6. Public Need Challenge. "Gulf Court Nursing Center v. Department of Health & Rehabilitative Services", Court of Appeals of Florida First District, (8/20/1985).
157. CON Board Decision Arbitrary, 5. Validity of CON Board Decision. "West-Mont Community Care v. Board of Health & Evil. Sciences", Supreme Court of Montana, (7/30/1985).
158. CON Board Decision Arbitrary, 5. Validity of CON Board Decision. "Humana Hosp. Corp. v. Oklahoma Health Planning Common", Supreme Court of Oklahoma, (5/28/1985).
159. CON Board Decision Arbitrary, 5. Validity of CON Board Decision. "University Community Hospital v. Department of Health & Rehabilitative Services", Court of Appeals of Florida Second district, (5/22/1985).
160. CON Board Decision Arbitrary, 5. Validity of CON Board Decision. "Florida Medical Center v. Department of Health & Rehabilitative Services", Court of Appeals of Florida First District, (1/24/1985).
161. CON Board Decision Arbitrary, 5. Validity of CON Board Decision. "Collier Medical Center Inc. v. State Dep't of Health & Rehabilitative Services", Court of Appeals of Florida First District, (1/8/1985).
162. CON Board Decision Arbitrary, 5. Validity of CON Board Decision. "State Health Planning & Resource Dev. Admen. Rivendell of ALABAMA", Court of Civil Appeals of Alabama, (1/2/1985).
163. CON Board Decision Arbitrary, 5. Validity of CON Board Decision, 3.c. Violation of State Law During CON Proceedings, 3. Statutory Violation. "Manor Healthcare Corp. v. Northwest Community Hospital", Appellate Court of Illinois, First District Third Division, (11/28/1984).
164. CON Board Decision Arbitrary, 5. Validity of CON Board Decision. "County of Dodge on behalf of Memorial Hospital v. Department of Health", Supreme Court of Nebraska, (9/21/1984).
165. CON Board Decision Arbitrary, 5. Validity of CON Board Decision, 2.b. Procedural Due Process Violation, 2.a. Equal Protection Violation, 2. Constitutional Challenge. "Humana Medical Corp. v. State Health Planning & Dev. Agency", Court of Civil Appeals of Alabama, (8/22/1984).
166. CON Board Decision Arbitrary, 5. Validity of CON Board Decision. "Doctors' Osteopathic Medical Center Inc. v. Department of Health & Rehabilitative Services", Court of Appeals of Florida First District, (8/7/1984).

167. CON Board Decision Arbitrary, 5. Validity of CON Board Decision. "Therapeutic Community Residence v. Minnesota Dep't of Health", Court of Appeals of Minnesota, (6/19/1984).
168. CON Board Decision Arbitrary. "Bio-Medical Applications of Arlington Inc. v. Kenly", Circuit Court of Arlington County Virginia, (6/4/1984).
169. CON Board Decision Arbitrary, 5. Validity of CON Board Decision. "Texas Health Facilities Com. v. Charter Medical-Dallas Inc.", Supreme Court of Texas, (2/15/1984).
170. CON Board Decision Arbitrary, 5. Validity of CON Board Decision. "In re Certificate of Need Application by Community Psychiatric Centers Inc. etc.", Supreme Court of Kansas, (1/13/1984).
171. CON Board Decision Arbitrary, 5. Validity of CON Board Decision. "Presbyterian Hospital North v. Texas Health Facilities Com.", Court of Appeals of Texas Third District, Austin, (11/23/1983).
172. CON Board Decision Arbitrary, 5. Validity of CON Board Decision, 7. Miscellaneous. "North Fulton Community Hospital Inc. v. State Health Planning & Dev. Agency", Court of Appeals of Georgia, (11/9/1983).
173. CON Board Decision Arbitrary, 5. Validity of CON Board Decision. "Charter Medical-Dallas Inc. v. Texas Health Facilities Com.", Court of Appeals of Texas Third District, Austin, (7/20/1983).
174. CON Board Decision Arbitrary, 5. Validity of CON Board Decision, 3.a. Violation of Administrative Procedures Act, 3. Statutory Violation. "In re Certificate of Need Application etc.", Supreme Court of Kansas, (7/17/1981).
175. CON Board Decision Arbitrary, 5. Validity of CON Board Decision, 2.a. Equal Protection Violation, 2. Constitutional Challenge. "Hospital of St. Raphael v. Commission on Hospitals & Health Care", Supreme Court of Connecticut, (11/11/1980).
176. CON Board Decision Arbitrary, 5. Validity of CON Board Decision, 3.b. CON Board Exceeded Rulemaking Authority, 3. Statutory Violation. "St. Joseph's Hospital & Medical Center v. Finley", Superior Court of New Jersey Appellate Division, (10/14/1977).
177. CON Board Decision Arbitrary, 5. Validity of CON Board Decision. "Humana of Tennessee v. Tennessee Health Facilities Com.", Supreme Court of Tennessee, (4/25/1977).
178. CON Board Decision Arbitrary, 5. Validity of CON Board Decision. "National Nephrology Foundation v. Dougherty", Superior Court of New Jersey Appellate Division, (1/12/1976).
179. CON Board Decision Arbitrary, 5. Validity of CON Board Decision, 3.a. Violation of Administrative Procedures Act, 3. Statutory Violation. "Olathe Hospital Foundation Inc. v. Extend care Inc.", Supreme Court of Kansas, (7/17/1975).

V B. Reconsideration of Previous CON Decision

180. Reconsideration of Previous CON Decision, 6. Public Need Challenge, 6.e. Applicability of Need Criteria to Applicant, 5. Validity of CON Board Decision. "Appeal of New England Heart Institute and Maine Medical Center", Supreme Court of New Hampshire, (12/29/1999).
181. Reconsideration of Previous CON Decision. "State Health Planning and Development Agency v. Forest Manor, Inc. Heritage Health Care center, Inc. v. Forest Manor, Inc.", Court of Civic Appeals of Alabama, (6/4/1999).
182. Reconsideration of Previous CON Decision, 5. Validity of CON Board Decision, 3. Statutory Violation. "In re Lima Memo. Hosp.", Court of Appeals of Ohio Tenth Appellate District, Franklin County, (5/23/1996).
183. Reconsideration of Previous CON Decision. "Central Pa. MRI L.P. v. Department of Health", Commonwealth Court of Pennsylvania, (9/6/1994).
184. Reconsideration of Previous CON Decision, 5. Validity of CON Board Decision. "ABC Home Health Serv. v. Georgia Dep't of Medical Assistance", Court of Appeals of Georgia, (12/1/1993).
185. Reconsideration of Previous CON Decision. "Scott v. Consolidated Health Management Inc.", Supreme Court of Arkansas, (2/13/1989).

186. Reconsideration of Previous CON Decision. "RHPC Inc. v. Department of Health & Rehabilitative Serv.", Court of Appeals of Florida First district, (7/10/1987).
187. Reconsideration of Previous CON Decision, 3.c. Violation of State Law During CON Proceedings, 3. Statutory Violation, 2.b. Procedural Due Process Violation, 2. Constitutional Challenge, 5. Validity of CON Board Decision. "Huron Valley Hospital Inc. v. Michigan State Health Facilities Com.", Court of Appeals of Michigan, (10/7/1981).

V. PUBLIC NEED CHALLENGE

1. Public Need Challenge, 5.a. CON Board Decision Arbitrary. "Bio-Medical Applications of the District of Columbia d/b/a/ Fresenius Medical Care North America v. District of Columbia Board of Appeals and Review", District of Columbia Court of Appeals, (7/24/2003).
2. Public Need Challenge, 6.e. Applicability of Need Criteria to Applicant, 3.d. CON Law Arbitrary, 3. Statutory Violation. "Medical Center at Princeton v. The Township of Princeton Zoning Board of Adjustment", Superior Court of New Jersey, (6/28/2001).
3. Public Need Challenge. "Frye Reg'l Med. Ctr. Inc. v. Hunt", Supreme Court of North Carolina, (2/5/1999).
4. Public Need Challenge, 5. Validity of CON Board Decision. "In re Professional Nurses Service", Supreme Court of Virginia, (9/10/1998).
5. Public Need Challenge, 6.c. Establishment Challenge to New Need Requirements. "Adventist Healthcare Midatlantic v. Suburban Hosp.", Court of Appeals of Maryland, (6/10/1998).
6. Public Need Challenge. "Page v. Capital Medical Center Inc.", Court of Appeals of Florida First District, (6/13/1997).
7. Public Need Challenge, 5.a. CON Board Decision Arbitrary, 5. Validity of CON Board Decision ."West Bloomfield Hosp. v. Certificate of Need Bd.", Court of Appeals of Michigan, (5/16/1997).
8. Public Need Challenge, 4.a. Violation of CON Board's Internal Rules, 4. Regulatory Violation, 5. Validity of CON Board Decision. "Hedgework Brentwood Medical Services, Inc. v. South Carolina Department of Health and Environmental Control" State of South Carolina Administrative Law Judge Division, (9/10/1996).
9. Public Need Challenge. "In re Mansfield Gen. Hosp.", Supreme Court of Ohio, (5/24/1995).
10. Public Need Challenge, 5.a. CON Board Decision Arbitrary, 5. Validity of CON Board Decision, 2. Constitutional Challenge. "Columbia Endoscopy Center v. South Carolina Department of Health and Environmental Control", State of South Carolina Administrative Law Judge Division, (12/30/1994).
11. Public Need Challenge, 4.a. Violation of CON Board's Internal Rules, 4. Regulatory Violation, 5.a. CON Board Decision Arbitrary, 5. Validity of CON Board Decision. "New England Rehabilitation Hosp. Inc. v. Commission on Hosps. & Health Care", Supreme Court of Connecticut, (6/22/1993).
12. Public Need Challenge. "Maple Leaf of Lee County Health Care v. Department of Health & Rehabilitative Serv.", Court of Appeal of Florida First District, (6/17/1992).
13. Public Need Challenge, 5.a. CON Board Decision Arbitrary, 5. Validity of CON Board Decision. "Mississippi State Dep't of Health v. Golden Triangle Regional Medical Center", Supreme Court of Mississippi, (6/17/1992).
14. Public Need Challenge, 6.e. Applicability of Need Criteria to Applicant. "Changing Point Inc. v. Maryland Health Resources Planning Com.", Court of Special Appeals of Maryland, (5/6/1991).
15. Public Need Challenge. "Appeal of Salem Regional Medical Ctr. v." Supreme Court of New Hampshire, (5/3/1991).
16. Public Need Challenge, 6.e. Applicability of Need Criteria to Applicant. "Famiglietti v. Brevard Medical Investors Ltd.", Court of Appeals of Georgia, (9/19/1990).

17. Public Need Challenge, 5.a. CON Board Decision Arbitrary, 5. Validity of CON Board Decision. "In re Certificate of Need Application of Providence Hosp.", Court of Appeals of Ohio Tenth Appellate District, Franklin County, (4/19/1990).
18. Public Need Challenge, 5. Validity of CON Board Decision. "Meridian Inc. v. Department of Health & Rehabilitative Services", Court of Appeals of Florida First district, (9/12/1989).
19. Public Need Challenge. "Grant Center Hospital Inc. v. Health Group of Jackson Inc.", Supreme Court of Mississippi, (5/25/1988).
20. Public Need Challenge, 5. Validity of CON Board Decision. "Williamson v. Snow", Supreme Court of North Carolina, (2/24/1954).

VI A. TEMPORARY RESTRAINING ORDER ON CON REQUIREMENTS

21. Temporary Restraining Order on CON Requirements. "Adams & Boyle P.C. v. Tennessee Dep't of Health", United States Court of Appeals for the Sixth Circuit, (2/9/2001).
22. Temporary Restraining Order on CON Requirements, 5.a. CON Board Decision Arbitrary, 5. Validity of CON Board Decision. "Redbud Hosp. Dist. v. Heckler", United States District Court for the Northern District of California, (5/12/1997).
23. Temporary Restraining Order on CON Requirements. "G.M. Ambulance & Medical Supply Co. v. Canyon State Ambulance", Court of Appeals of Arizona, Division Two, Department A, (3/17/1987).

VI B. Injunction on CON Requirements

24. Injunction on CON Requirements. "Adams & Boyle P.C. v. Tennessee Dep't of Health", United States Court of Appeals for the Sixth Circuit, (2/9/2001).
25. Injunction on CON Requirements. "Crestmont Cleveland Pshp. v. Ohio Dep't of Health", Court of Appeals of Ohio Tenth Appellate District, Franklin County, (9/28/2000).
26. Injunction on CON Requirements, 5.a. CON Board Decision Arbitrary, 5. Validity of CON Board Decision. "Northside Hospital, Inc. v. McCord et al.", Court of Appeals of Georgia, (7/19/2000).
27. Injunction on CON Requirements, 7. Miscellaneous. "Crestmont Cleveland Pshp. v. State Dep't of Health", Court of Appeals of Ohio Tenth Appellate District, Franklin County, (10/14/1999).
28. Injunction on CON Requirements, 2. Constitutional Challenge. "Gundry/Glass Hospital v. Donna E. Shalala, Secretary of Health and Human Services and Blue Cross and Blue Shield of Maryland; Health Care Financing Administration", United States Court of Appeals for the Fourth Circuit, (4/5/1999).
29. Injunction on CON Requirements, 7.a. Court's Denial of Judicial Review Arbitrary. "Huron Valley Hospital Inc. v. Michigan Dep't of Public Health", Court of Appeals of Michigan, (9/4/1997).
30. Injunction on CON Requirements. "Memorial Health Sys. v. Halifax Hospice", Court of Appeal of Florida First District, (2/26/1997).
31. Injunction on CON Requirements, 5. Validity of CON Board Decision. "State Health Planning & Dev. Agency v. Ball Healthcare-Lowndes Inc.", Court of Civil Appeals of Alabama, (10/18/1996).
32. Injunction on CON Requirements, 1. Antitrust. "Federal Trade Commission v. Freeman Hospital and Tri-State Osteopathic Hospital Association, Inc.", United States District Court, W.D. Missouri, Southwestern Division, (6/9/1995).
33. Injunction on CON Requirements, 6.e. Applicability of Need Criteria to Applicant. "Capitol Hill Hosp. v. District of Columbia State Health Planning & Dev. Agency", District of Columbia Court of Appeals, (11/20/1991).
34. Injunction on CON Requirements, 3.a. Violation of Administrative Procedures Act, 3. Statutory Violation. "State ex rel. Integrated Health Services v. Missouri Health Facilities Review Committee", Court of Appeals of Missouri Western District, (8/27/1991).

35. Injunction on CON Requirements, 1. Antitrust, 6.e. Applicability of Need Criteria to Applicant. "FTC v. University Health Inc.", United States Court of Appeals For the Eleventh Circuit, (7/26/1991).
36. Injunction on CON Requirements. "Renal Care of Illinois Inc. v. Health Facilities Planning Bd.", Appellate Court of Illinois, First District, Fifth Division, (8/7/1987).
37. Injunction on CON Requirements, 4. Regulatory Violation, 3. Statutory Violation. "Gulf Coast Home Health Services Inc. v. Department of Health & Rehabilitative Services", Court of Appeal of Florida First District, (3/2/1987).
38. Injunction on CON Requirements, 2. Constitutional Challenge, 7. Miscellaneous. "Baptist Memorial Hospital-De Soto Inc. v. Mississippi Health Care Com. Civil Action", United States District Court For the Southern District of Mississippi, (9/10/1985).
39. Injunction on CON Requirements. "Women's Community Health Center Inc. v. Texas Health Facilities Com.", United States Court of Appeals For the Fifth Circuit, (9/15/1982).
40. Injunction on CON Requirements. "Community Psychiatric Centers Inc. v. Grant", United States Court of Appeals Ninth Circuit, (12/28/1981).
41. Injunction on CON Requirements, 3.a. Violation of Administrative Procedures Act, 3. Statutory Violation, 3.e. Defining Statutory Term. "Greater St. Louis Health Systems Agency v. Teasdale", United States District Court For the Eastern District of Missouri, (3/11/1980).

VI C. Establishment Challenge to New Need Requirements

42. Establishment Challenge to New Need Requirements, 6. Public Need Challenge, 6.e. Applicability of Need Criteria to Applicant, 3.b. CON Board Exceeded Rulemaking Authority, 3. Statutory Violation. "Robert Packer Hosp. v. Department of Health", Commonwealth Court of Pennsylvania, (9/7/1993).
43. Establishment Challenge to New Need Requirements, 6.e. Applicability of Need Criteria to Applicant, 6. Public Need Challenge. "In the matter of Fairfield Nursing Home v. Robert Whalen", Supreme Court, Appellate Division, Third Department, (7/27/1978).
44. Establishment Challenge to New Need Requirements, 6. Public Need Challenge, 7. Miscellaneous. "Public Citizen, Inc., Oli, Chemical, and Atomic Workers International Union, AFL-CIO, National Consumer's League, National Urban Coalition, and Communities in Action Together petition to Department of Health, Education and Welfare", Department of Health, Education and Welfare, (5/7/1975).
45. Establishment Challenge to New Need Requirements, 6. Public Need Challenge, 2.b. Procedural Due Process Violation, 3.a. Violation of Administrative Procedures Act, 3. Statutory Violation, 3.c. Violation of State Law During CON Proceedings, 5. Validity of CON Board Decision. "Merry Heart Nursing & Convalescent Home Inc. v. Dougherty", Superior Court of New Jersey Appellate Division, (12/4/1974).

VI D. Defining State Health Plan Term

46. Defining State Health Plan Term, 4.c. Defining Regulatory Term, 3.b. CON Board Exceeded Rulemaking Authority. "HCA Health Serv. v. Roach", Supreme Court of Georgia, (2/7/1994).
47. Defining State Health Plan Term, 6. Public Need Challenge, 6.c. Establishment Challenge to New Need Requirements, 4. Regulatory Violation. "Delaware County Memorial Hospital v. Bowen", United States Court of Appeals For the Third Circuit, (1/25/1989).
48. Defining State Health Plan Term, 4.c. Defining Regulatory Term, 4. Regulatory Violation, 3.e. Defining Statutory Term, 3. Statutory Violation. "Woodland Park Hospital Inc. v. Comprehensive Health Planning Authority", Court of Appeals of Oregon, (12/22/1972).

VI E. Applicability of Need Criteria to Applicant

49. Applicability of Need Criteria to Applicant, 5. Validity of CON Board Decision. "Riverside Hospital, Inc. d/b/a Riverside Regional Medical Center v. Robe B. Stroube", Circuit Court of Williamsburg and James City County, Virginia, (3/17/2003).
50. Applicability of Need Criteria to Applicant. "Commonwealth of Kentucky v. Family Home Health Care, Inc.", Court of Appeals of Kentucky, (2/7/2003).
51. Applicability of Need Criteria to Applicant, 6.d. Defining State Health Plan Term, 4.c. Defining Regulatory Term, 4. Regulatory Violation. "Ex parte State Health Planning and Development Agency v. LithoMedTech of Alabama, LLC", Supreme Court of Alabama, (11/22/2002).
52. Applicability of Need Criteria to Applicant, 5.a. CON Board Decision Arbitrary, 5. Validity of CON Board Decision. "Community Care Center of Lemma v. Missouri Health Facilities Review Committee", Court of Appeals of Missouri, Western District, (11/5/2002).
53. Applicability of Need Criteria to Applicant, 6.d. Defining State Health Plan Term, 4.c. Defining Regulatory Term, 4. Regulatory Violation, 3.e. Defining Statutory Term, 3. Statutory Violation. "Maryland General Hospital, Inc. v. Tommy G. Thompson", United States Court of Appeals, (10/9/2002).
54. Applicability of Need Criteria to Applicant, 6. Public Need Challenge, 5.a. CON Board Decision Arbitrary, 5. Validity of CON Board Decision. "Jackson HMA, Inc. v. Mississippi State Department of Health", Supreme Court of Mississippi, (4/25/2002).
55. Applicability of Need Criteria to Applicant, 5.a. CON Board Decision Arbitrary, 5. Validity of CON Board Decision. "Sheffield Towers Rehabilitation and Health Care Center v. Antonia Novello et al.", Supreme Court, Nassau County, (4/22/2002).
56. Applicability of Need Criteria to Applicant, 6. Public Need Challenge, 5. Validity of CON Board Decision. "Paragon Health Network Inc. v. Thompson", United States Court of Appeals for the Seventh Circuit, (6/5/2001).
57. Applicability of Need Criteria to Applicant, 6. Public Need Challenge, 5.a. CON Board Decision Arbitrary, 5. Validity of CON Board Decision. "State Health Commissioner v. Sentara Norfolk General Hospital", Supreme Court of Virginia, (9/15/2000).
58. Applicability of Need Criteria to Applicant, 4.c. Defining Regulatory Term, 4. Regulatory Violation. "Christenbury Surgery Ctr. v. North Carolina" Court of Appeals of North Carolina, (6/6/2000).
59. Applicability of Need Criteria to Applicant, 5.a. CON Board Decision Arbitrary, 5. Validity of CON Board Decision. "Dialysis Care of N.C. L.L.C. v. North Carolina HHS Div. of Facility Serv. Certificate of Need Section", Court of Appeals of North Carolina, (5/2/2000).
60. Applicability of Need Criteria to Applicant, 3. Statutory Violation. "EBG Health Care III Inc. v. Missouri Health Facilities Review Comm.", Court of Appeals of Missouri Western District, (2/15/2000).
61. Applicability of Need Criteria to Applicant. "Bio-Medical Applications of N.C. Inc. v. North Carolina Dep't of Human Resources Div. Of Facility Serv. Certificate of Need Section", Court of Appeals of North Carolina, (9/16/1999).
62. Applicability of Need Criteria to Applicant, 3. Statutory Violation. "Catonsville Nursing Home v. Loveman", Court of Appeals of Maryland, (5/15/1998).
63. Applicability of Need Criteria to Applicant, 3. Statutory Violation., "United States ex rel. Joslin v. Community Home Health Civil", United States District Court For the District of Maryland, (11/17/1997).
64. Applicability of Need Criteria to Applicant, 5.a. CON Board Decision Arbitrary, 5. Validity of CON Board Decision. "In re Cumberland Care Ctr.", Court of Appeals of Ohio Tenth Appellate District, Franklin County, (11/4/1997).

65. Applicability of Need Criteria to Applicant, 7.b. Failure to Obtain CON, 5. Validity of CON Board Decision. "Phoebe Putney Mem. Hosp. v. Roach", Supreme Court of Georgia, (2/17/1997).
66. Applicability of Need Criteria to Applicant, 5. Validity of CON Board Decision. "Retirement Villages v. North Carolina Dep't of Human Resources", Court of Appeals of North Carolina, (11/19/1996).
67. Applicability of Need Criteria to Applicant. "Cleveland Clinic Fla. Hosp. v. Agency for Health Care Admin." Court of Appeal of Florida First District , (10/16/1996).
68. Applicability of Need Criteria to Applicant, 6. Public Need Challenge. "McLeod Regional Medical Center v. South Carolina Department of Health and Environmental Control", State of South Carolina Administrative Law Judge Division, (6/7/1996).
69. Applicability of Need Criteria to Applicant, 5.a. CON Board Decision Arbitrary, 5. Validity of CON Board Decision. "Presbyterian-Orthopaedic Hosp. v. North Carolina Dep't of Human Resources", Court of Appeals of North Carolina, (6/4/1996).
70. Applicability of Need Criteria to Applicant, 6. Public Need Challenge, 5. Validity of CON Board Decision. "In re Beechmont", Court OF Appeals OF Ohio Tenth Appellate District, Franklin County, (3/29/1996).
71. Applicability of Need Criteria to Applicant, 5. Validity of CON Board Decision. "Life Care Ctrs. of Am. v. Agency for Health Care Admin." Court of Appeal of Florida First District , (6/12/1995).
72. Applicability of Need Criteria to Applicant, 3.b. CON Board Exceeded Rulemaking Authority, 2. Constitutional Challenge. "HCA Health Serv. v. Roach", Supreme Court of Georgia, (6/12/1995).
73. Applicability of Need Criteria to Applicant, 7.b. Failure to Obtain CON. "In re North Shore Radiology", Court of Appeals of Ohio Tenth Appellate District, Franklin County, (10/20/1994).
74. Applicability of Need Criteria to Applicant, 7.b. Failure to Obtain CON. "In re North Shore Radiology", Court OF Appeals OF Ohio Tenth Appellate District, Franklin County, (9/1/1994).
75. Applicability of Need Criteria to Applicant, 6.c. Establishment Challenge to New Need Requirements, 6. Public Need Challenge, 5. Validity of CON Board Decision. "Mechanicsburg Rehab Sys. v. Department of Health", Commonwealth Court of Pennsylvania, (6/24/1994).
76. Applicability of Need Criteria to Applicant, 7.b. Failure to Obtain CON. "Cabinet for Human Resources v. Women's Health Serv.", Court of Appeals of Kentucky, (6/24/1994).
77. Applicability of Need Criteria to Applicant. "Associates in Radiation Oncology P.A. v. Siegel M.P.H.", Superior Court of New Jersey Appellate Division, (3/8/1994).
78. Applicability of Need Criteria to Applicant. "Town of Hempstead v. Commissioner, State of New York Office of Mental Health", Supreme Court, Appellate Division, Second Department, (1/24/1994).
79. Applicability of Need Criteria to Applicant, 5.a. CON Board Decision Arbitrary. "Beverly Enters. v. Columbus Health Care", Nebraska Court of Appeals, (12/28/1993).
80. Applicability of Need Criteria to Applicant, 6. Public Need Challenge, 5. Validity of CON Board Decision. "In re Pavilion", Court of Appeals of Ohio Tenth Appellate District, Franklin County, (10/5/1993).
81. Applicability of Need Criteria to Applicant. "Mercy Medical Ctr. Inc. v. Office of Health Policy", Court of Appeals of Oregon, (7/14/1993).
82. Applicability of Need Criteria to Applicant, 4. Regulatory Violation, 3.c. Violation of State Law During CON Proceedings, 3. Statutory Violation, 5. Validity of CON Board Decision. "In re Deaconess Hosp.", Court of Appeals of Ohio Tenth Appellate District, Franklin County, (9/29/1992).
83. Applicability of Need Criteria to Applicant, 5. Validity of CON Board Decision. "Summit Villa Care Ctr. Inc. v. Ohio Dep't of Health", Court of Appeals of Ohio Tenth Appellate District, Franklin County, (7/14/1992).
84. Applicability of Need Criteria to Applicant, 3.b. CON Board Exceeded Rulemaking Authority, 3. Statutory Violation, 5.a. CON Board Decision Arbitrary, 5. Validity of CON Board Decision. "HTI Health Services Inc. v. Mississippi State Dep't of Health", Supreme Court of Mississippi, (6/10/1992).

85. Applicability of Need Criteria to Applicant, 5. Validity of CON Board Decision. "Suburban Medical Hosp. Inc. v. Department of Health & Rehabilitative Services", Court of Appeal of Florida third district, (5/26/1992).
86. Applicability of Need Criteria to Applicant. "Fairview General Hosp. v. Fletcher", Supreme Court of Ohio, (3/11/1992).
87. Applicability of Need Criteria to Applicant, 5.a. CON Board Decision Arbitrary, 5. Validity of CON Board Decision. "Jeannette Dist. Memorial Hosp. v. Department of Health", Commonwealth Court of Pennsylvania, (7/12/1991).
88. Applicability of Need Criteria to Applicant, 5.a. CON Board Decision Arbitrary, 5. Validity of CON Board Decision. "Morrisons Cove Home v. Department of Health", Commonwealth Court of Pennsylvania, (6/17/1991).
89. Applicability of Need Criteria to Applicant, 5. Validity of CON Board Decision. "State ex rel. PIA Psychiatric Hosp. Inc. v. Ohio Certificate of Need Review Bd.", Supreme Court of Ohio, (5/15/1991).
90. Applicability of Need Criteria to Applicant, 5.a. CON Board Decision Arbitrary, 5. Validity of CON Board Decision. "Department of Health v. Manor Care Inc.", Supreme Court of Nebraska, (2/22/1991).
91. Applicability of Need Criteria to Applicant, 5. Validity of CON Board Decisio.n "In re Christian Care Home Inc.", Court of Appeals of Ohio Tenth Appellate District, Franklin County, (12/28/1989).
92. Applicability of Need Criteria to Applicant, 5. Validity of CON Board Decision. "Department of Health v. Omaha Associates", Supreme Court of Nebraska, (6/16/1989).
93. Applicability of Need Criteria to Applicant, 5. Validity of CON Board Decision. "Omaha Health Facilities Inc. v. Department of Health", Supreme Court of Nebraska, (4/27/1989).
94. Applicability of Need Criteria to Applicant, 3.a. Violation of Administrative Procedures Act, 3. Statutory Violation. "Missouri Health Care Assoc. v. Missouri Health Facilities Review Committee", Court of Appeals of Missouri Western District, (2/21/1989).
95. Applicability of Need Criteria to Applicant, 4. Regulatory Violation. "Aroostook Home Care Agency Inc. v. Commissioner of Human Services", Supreme Judicial Court of Maine, (12/30/1988).
96. Applicability of Need Criteria to Applicant, 6. Public Need Challenge, 5.a. CON Board Decision Arbitrary, 5. Validity of CON Board Decision. "Heritage of Yankton v. South Dakota Dep't of Health", Supreme Court of South Dakota, (11/23/1988).
97. Applicability of Need Criteria to Applicant. "Gulf Coast Home Health Services Inc. v. Department of Health & Rehabilitative Services", Court of Appeals of Florida First district, (6/8/1988).
98. Applicability of Need Criteria to Applicant 6. Public Need Challenge 5.a. CON Board Decision Arbitrary 5. Validity of CON Board Decision "Johnston-Willis Ltd. v. Kenley", Court of Appeals of Virginia, (5/3/1988).
99. Applicability of Need Criteria to Applicant, 7.b. Failure to Obtain CON, 6.b. Injunction on CON Requirements, 6. Public Need Challenge. "Humana of Kentucky Inc. v. NKC Hospitals Inc.", Supreme Court of Kentucky, (3/31/1988).
100. Applicability of Need Criteria to Applicant. "In re Health Care & Retirement Corp. of America", Court of Appeals of North Carolina, (2/2/1988).
101. Applicability of Need Criteria to Applicant. "Department of Health v. Lutheran Hospitals & Homes Soc.", Supreme Court of Nebraska, (12/11/1987).
102. Applicability of Need Criteria to Applicant, 5.a. CON Board Decision Arbitrary, 5. Validity of CON Board Decision, 3. Statutory Violation. "Grandview Surgical Center Inc. v. Holy Spirit Hospital of Sisters of Christian Charity", Commonwealth Court of Pennsylvania, (11/19/1987).
103. Applicability of Need Criteria to Applicant, 5.a. CON Board Decision Arbitrary. "Bio-Medical Applications of Arlington Inc. v. Kenley", Court of Appeals of Virginia, (7/7/1987).

104. Applicability of Need Criteria to Applicant, 5.a. CON Board Decision Arbitrary, 5. Validity of CON Board Decision. "St. John's Home Health Agency v. Department of Health & Rehabilitative Services", Court of Appeals of Florida First district, (6/23/1987).
105. Applicability of Need Criteria to Applicant, 5. Validity of CON Board Decision. "In re Appeal from Approval of Application of Wake Kidney Clinic P.A.", Court of Appeals of North Carolina, (5/19/1987).
106. Applicability of Need Criteria to Applicant, 5.a. CON Board Decision Arbitrary, 5. Validity of CON Board Decision. "Roanoke Memorial Hospitals v. Kenley", Court of Appeals of Virginia, (1/6/1987).
107. Applicability of Need Criteria to Applicant. "Baptist Hospital Inc. v. State Dep't of Health & Rehabilitative Services", Court of Appeals of Florida First district, (12/23/1986).
108. Applicability of Need Criteria to Applicant, 5.a. CON Board Decision Arbitrary, 5. Validity of CON Board Decision. "State Health Planning & Dev. Agency v. Salem Hospital CA", Court of Appeals of Oregon, (12/17/1986).
109. Applicability of Need Criteria to Applicant. "Sparks Regional Medical Center v. Arkansas Dep't of Human Services", Supreme Court of Arkansas, (11/24/1986).
110. Applicability of Need Criteria to Applicant, 6. Public Need Challenge. "Department of Health v. Grand Island Health Care Inc.", Supreme Court of Nebraska, (8/1/1986).
111. Applicability of Need Criteria to Applicant, 6. Public Need Challenge, 4.a. Violation of CON Board's Internal Rules, 4. Regulatory Violation. "Boca Raton Artificial Kidney Ctr. v. Department of Health & Rehabilitative Serv.", Court of Appeals of Florida First District, (7/29/1986).
112. Applicability of Need Criteria to Applicant, 6. Public Need Challenge, 5. Validity of CON Board Decision. "Morton F. Plant Hospital Assoc. v. State", Court of Appeals of Florida First District, (7/9/1986).
113. Applicability of Need Criteria to Applicant, 6. Public Need Challenge. "Humana Inc. v. Department of Health & Rehabilitative Services", Court of Appeals of Florida fourth district, (4/16/1986).
114. Applicability of Need Criteria to Applicant. "Chatham County Hospital Authority v. St. Joseph's Hospital Inc.", Court of Appeals of Georgia, (3/21/1986).
115. Applicability of Need Criteria to Applicant, 5. Validity of CON Board Decision. "University Medical Center Inc. v. Department of Health & Rehabilitative Services", Court of Appeals of Florida First District, (2/13/1986).
116. Applicability of Need Criteria to Applicant. "Boca Raton Artificial Kidney Center Inc. v. Florida Dep't of Health & Rehabilitative Services", Court of Appeals of Florida First District, (8/20/1985).
117. Applicability of Need Criteria to Applicant. "University Medical Center Inc. v. Department of Health & Rehabilitative Services", Court of Appeals of Florida First District, (8/20/1985).
118. Applicability of Need Criteria to Applicant, 5. Validity of CON Board Decision. "Health Quest Realty XII v. Department of Health & Rehabilitative Services", Court of Appeals of Florida First District, (7/16/1985).
119. Applicability of Need Criteria to Applicant, 6. Public Need Challenge, 5.a. CON Board Decision Arbitrary, 5. Validity of CON Board Decision. "Princeton Community Hosp. v. State Health Planning", Supreme Court of Appeals of West Virginia, (3/22/1985).
120. Applicability of Need Criteria to Applicant, 5.a. CON Board Decision Arbitrary, 5. Validity of CON Board Decision. "Shawnee Mission Medical Center v. Kansas Dep't of Health & Environment", Supreme Court of Kansas, (7/13/1984).
121. Applicability of Need Criteria to Applicant. "Starks v. Kentucky Health Facilities", Court of Appeals of Kentucky, (7/6/1984).
122. Applicability of Need Criteria to Applicant, 6. Public Need Challenge, 5. Validity of CON Board Decision. "Rehab Hospital Services Corp. v. Health Systems Agency", Commonwealth Court of Pennsylvania, (4/30/1984).

123. Applicability of Need Criteria to Applicant, 6. Public Need Challenge, 5.a. CON Board Decision Arbitrary, 5. Validity of CON Board Decision. "Statewide Health Coordinating Council v. General Hospitals of Humana Inc.", Supreme Court of Arkansas, (12/12/1983).
124. Applicability of Need Criteria to Applicant. "Edgehill Newport Inc. v. New England Alcoholism Treatment & Educ. Programs Inc.", Superior Court of Rhode Island Providence, (4/27/1983).
125. Applicability of Need Criteria to Applicant, 6.d. Defining State Health Plan Term, 5.a. CON Board Decision Arbitrary, 5. Validity of CON Board Decision. "In re Review of Decision of Kansas Corp. Com. etc.", Supreme Court of Kansas, (2/19/1983).
126. Applicability of Need Criteria to Applicant, 6. Public Need Challenge. "Gulf Coast Hospital Inc. v. Department of Health & Rehabilitative Services", District Court of Appeal of Florida First District, (12/16/1982).
127. Applicability of Need Criteria to Applicant. "Rush City Hospital v. Sandstone Area Hospital", Supreme Court of Minnesota, (11/24/1982).
128. Applicability of Need Criteria to Applicant, 3. Statutory Violation. "In re Wilkesboro Ltd.", Court of Appeals of North Carolina, (1/5/1982).
129. Applicability of Need Criteria to Applicant, 5.a. CON Board Decision Arbitrary, 5. Validity of CON Board Decision. "In re Appeal of Banks", Supreme Court of Kansas, (7/17/1981).
130. Applicability of Need Criteria to Applicant, 4.c. Defining Regulatory Term, 4. Regulatory Violation, 3.e. Defining Statutory Term, 3. Statutory Violation. "Placentia-Linda Community Hosp. Inc. v. Zaretsky", Court of Appeal of California, Fourth Appellate District, Division Two, (6/2/1980).
131. Applicability of Need Criteria to Applicant. "Wausau Hospitals Inc. v. Department of Health & Social Services", Court of Appeals of Wisconsin, (3/18/1980).
132. Applicability of Need Criteria to Applicant, 7.b. Failure to Obtain CON, 5. Validity of CON Board Decision. "State ex rel. Metzler v. Sisters of Charity of Leavenworth Health Services Corp.", Supreme Court of Kansas, (1/19/1980).
133. Applicability of Need Criteria to Applicant, 5.a. CON Board Decision Arbitrary, 5. Validity of CON Board Decision, 4.a. Violation of CON Board's Internal Rule,s 4. Regulatory Violation, 3.c. Violation of State Law During CON Proceedings, 3. Statutory Violation. "Suburban Medical Center v. Olathe Community Hospital", Supreme Court of Kansas, (7/14/1979).
134. Applicability of Need Criteria to Applicant, 5.a. CON Board Decision Arbitrary, 5. Validity of CON Board Decision. "Texas Health Facilities Com. v. Baptist General Convention", Court of Civil Appeals of Texas, (10/19/1978).
135. Applicability of Need Criteria to Applicant, 7. Miscellaneous. "Irvington General Hospital v. Department of Health", Superior Court of New Jersey Appellate Division, (5/2/1977).
136. Applicability of Need Criteria to Applicant, 7.b. Failure to Obtain CON, 6. Public Need Challenge. "Palmetto General Hospital Inc. v. State Dep't of Health & Rehabilitative Services", Court of Appeals of Florida First District, (5/24/1976).
137. Applicability of Need Criteria to Applicant, 4. Regulatory Violation, 3. Statutory Violation. "Monk & Excelsior Inc. v. Minnesota State Board of Health", Supreme Court of Minnesota, (1/17/1975).
138. Applicability of Need Criteria to Applicant, 1. Antitrust, 2.b. Procedural Due Process, Violation, 2. Constitutional Challenge. "In re Certificate of Need for Aston Park Hosp. Inc.", Supreme Court of North Carolina, (1/26/1973).
139. Applicability of Need Criteria to Applicant, 5.a. CON Board Decision Arbitrary, 5. Validity of CON Board Decision. "Johnston Health Care Ctr. L.L.C. v. North Carolina Dep't of Human Resources Div. Of Facility Serv. Certificate of Need Section", Court of Appeals of North Carolina, (1/18/200).

VI F. Applicability of Need Criteria to Transfer of CON

140. Applicability of Need Criteria to Transfer of CON, 7. Miscellaneous. "Multicare Health System d/b/a/ Tacoma General Allenmore Hospital v. Department of Health of the State of Washington", Court of Appeals of Washington, Division Two, (9/30/2003).
141. Applicability of Need Criteria to Transfer of CON. "Agency for Health Care Admin. v. Orlando Regional Healthcare Sys. Inc.", Court of Appeal of Florida First District, (5/6/1993).
142. Applicability of Need Criteria to Transfer of CON. "Federal Property Management Corp. v. Richmond Healthcare Inc.", Court of Appeal of Florida Fourth District, (4/12/1989).
143. Applicability of Need Criteria to Transfer of CON, 3.a. Violation of Administrative Procedures Act, 3. Statutory Violation. "State Health Planning Agency v. Mobile Infirmary Assoc.", Court of Civil Appeals of Alabama, (9/7/1988).
144. Applicability of Need Criteria to Transfer of CON, 3.a. Violation of Administrative Procedures Act, 3. Statutory Violation. "Nursing Home of Dothan Inc. v. Alabama State Health Planning & Dev. Agency", Court of Civil Appeals of Alabama, (1/27/1988).
145. Applicability of Need Criteria to Transfer of CON, 7. Miscellaneous. "Diversified Health Management Services Inc. v. Visiting Nurses Assoc.", Supreme Court of Georgia, (6/27/1985).
146. Applicability of Need Criteria to Transfer of CON, 5.a. CON Board Decision Arbitrary, 5. Validity of CON Board Decision. "Texas Health Facilities Com. v. El Paso Medical Surgical Assoc.", Court of Civil Appeals of Texas Twelfth District, Tyler, (10/26/1978).

VI. MICELLANEOUS

1. Miscellaneous. "Healthcare Services Group, Inc. v. Royal Healthcare of Middlesex, LLC." United States District Court for the District of New Jersey , (8/13/2003).
2. Miscellaneous. "Colonial Management Group, L.P. v. State Health Planning and Development Agency et al.", Court of Civil Appeals of Alabama, (12/13/2002).
3. Miscellaneous. "Castle Nursing Home v. Donald L. Sullivan", United States Court of Appeals for the Sixth Circuit, (8/9/2001).
4. Miscellaneous. "Scott v. Ashland Healthcare Ctr.", Supreme Court of Tennessee, Middlesection, at Nashville, (7/9/2001).
5. Miscellaneous. "Ex parte Brookwood Health Serv. Inc.", Supreme Court of Alabama, (10/13/2000).
6. Miscellaneous. "Walgreen Co., et al. v. Carmen Feliciano De Melecio, Secretary of the Puerto Rico Department of Health", United States District Court, D. Puerto Rico, (6/21/2000).
7. Miscellaneous. "Bradford Hospital v. Donna E. Shalala", United States District Court, W.D. Pennsylvania, (6/5/2000).
8. Miscellaneous. "Gundry/Glass Hosp. v. Shalala", United States Court of Appeals for the Fourth Circuit, (4/5/1999).
9. Miscellaneous. "Huntsville Healthcare Ctr. Inc. v. Brown Health Serv. Inc.", Court of Civil Appeals of Alabama, (2/26/1999).
10. Miscellaneous. "South Miami Hospital, Inc. v. Agency For Health Care Administration and Variety Children's Hospital d/b/a Miami Children's Hospital", District Court of Appeals of Florida, (6/1/1998).
11. Miscellaneous. "Gundry Glass Hosp. v. Shalala Civil", United States District Court For the District of Maryland, (5/19/1998).
12. Miscellaneous, 5. Validity of CON Board Decision. "Homewood v. State", Superior Court of Maine Kennebec County, (3/4/1998).
13. Miscellaneous. "Carrolton Inc. v. Pine Manor Rest Home (In re Pine Manor Rest Home)", United States Court of Appeals for the Fourth Circuit, (11/24/1997).

14. Miscellaneous. "Life Care Ctrs. of Am. v. Health Care & Retirement Corp. of Am.", Court of Appeal of Florida First District, (4/23/1997).
15. Miscellaneous. "Sussex Medical Investors, L.P. v. Delaware Health Resources Board", Superior Court of Delaware, (4/8/1997).
16. Miscellaneous. "West Side Deutscher Frauen Verein v. Tracy", Supreme Court of Ohio, (4/2/1997).
17. Miscellaneous. "Carrolton Inc. v. Pine Manor Rest Home", United States District Court for the Eastern District of North Carolina Western Division, (3/31/1997).
18. Miscellaneous. "Roberts Health Care v. State Health Planning & Dev. Agency", Supreme Court of Alabama, (3/28/1997).
19. Miscellaneous. "Loveman v. Catonsville Nursing home", Court of Special Appeals of Maryland, (11/4/1996).
20. Miscellaneous. "In re Denial of Request by Humana Hospital Corp. etc.", Court of Appeals of North Carolina, (1/7/1996).
21. Miscellaneous. "Heritage House v. Bailey", Court of Appeals of Indiana First District, (6/12/1995).
22. Miscellaneous. "Medical Management v. Missouri Health Facilities Review Comm.", Court of Appeals of Missouri Western District, (6/6/1995).
23. Miscellaneous, 5. Validity of CON Board Decision. "John T. Finley Inc. v. Missouri Health Facilities Review Comm.", Court of Appeals of Missouri Western District, (5/9/1995).
24. Miscellaneous. "Sylacauga Health Care Ctr. v. Alabama State Health Planning Agency", Court of Civil Appeals of Alabama, (12/9/1994).
25. Miscellaneous. "In re Samaritan N. Health Ctr.", Court of Appeals of Ohio Tenth Appellate District, Franklin County, (5/12/1994).
26. Miscellaneous. "Clayton County Hosp. Auth. v. Webb", Court of Appeals of Georgia, (3/10/1993).
27. Miscellaneous. "Rush-Presbyterian-St. Luke's Medical Ctr. v. Hellenic Republic", United States Court of Appeals For the Seventh Circuit, (11/23/1992).
28. Miscellaneous. "Mitchell Manor Convalescent HomeInc. v. Oklahoma Health Planning Comm'n", Court of Appeals of Oklahoma Division Two, (3/12/1991).
29. Miscellaneous. "Auburn Medical Ctr. v. East Ala. Health Care Auth.", Court of Civil Appeals of Alabama, (12/19/1990).
30. Miscellaneous, 5. Validity of CON Board Decision. "First Hosp. Corp. v. Department of Health & Rehabilitative Serv. Case No. -", Court of Appeal of Florida First District, (9/12/1990).
31. Miscellaneous. "Lee Memorial Hosp. v. Department of Health & Rehabilitative Serv.", Court of Appeal of Florida First District, (5/9/1990).
32. Miscellaneous. "In re St. Louis South Park II Inc.", United States Bankruptcy Court For the Western District of Missouri, Central Division, (2/23/1990).
33. Miscellaneous, 5. Validity of CON Board Decision. "John Ken Alzheimer's Center v. Ohio Certificate of Need Review Bd.", Court of Appeals of Ohio Tenth Appellate District, Franklin County, (10/24/1989).
34. Miscellaneous. "Sarasota County Public Hospital Bd. v. Department of Health & Rehabilitative Services", Court of Appeal of Florida Second District, (10/11/1989).
35. Miscellaneous. "Home Health Services Inc. v. South Carolina Dep't of Health & Environmental Control", Court of Appeals of South Carolina, (4/24/1989).
36. Miscellaneous, 5.b. Reconsideration of Previous CON Decision. "Beverly Enterprises-Florida inch. Department of Health & Rehabilitative Services", Court of Appeals of Florida first district, (2/4/1988).
37. Miscellaneous. "Boca Raton Artificial Kidney Ctr. v. Department of Health & Rehabilitative Serv.", Court of Appeals of Florida First district, (10/22/1987).
38. Miscellaneous. "Arbor Health Care Co. v. Jackson", Court of Appeals of Ohio Tenth Appellate District, Franklin County, (5/14/1987).

39. Miscellaneous. "In re Applications of Overlook Hospital", Superior Court of New Jersey Appellate Division, (3/3/1987).
40. Miscellaneous. "Wilma Corp. v. Bowen", United States Court of Appeals for the Third Circuit, (2/19/1987).
41. Miscellaneous. "JDK Management Inc. v. Commonwealth Dep't of Public Welfare", Commonwealth Court of Pennsylvania, (10/22/1986).
42. Miscellaneous. "Humana of Fla. Inc. v. Department of Health & Rehabilitative Serv.", Court of Appeals of Florida First District, (9/11/1986).
43. Miscellaneous. "University Community Hospital v. Department of Health & Rehabilitative Services", Court of Appeals of Florida second district, (5/16/1986).
44. Miscellaneous, 5. Validity of CON Board Decision. "American Medical (Cent.) Inc. v. Texas Health Facilities Com.", Court of Appeals of Texas Third District, Austin, (10/2/1985).
45. Miscellaneous. "Baptist Memorial Hospital System v. Texas Health Facilities Com.", Court of Appeals of Texas Third District, Austin, (10/2/1985).
46. Miscellaneous. "In re King Memorial Hospital Inc.", United States Court of Appeals For the Eleventh Circuit, (8/12/1985).
47. Miscellaneous, 7.a. Court's Denial of Judicial Review Arbitrary. "Health Help Services Inc. v. State Health Planning Agency", Court of Appeals of Georgia, (3/28/1985).
48. Miscellaneous. "Beatrice Manor Inc. v. Department of Health", Supreme Court of Nebraska, (2/1/1985).
49. Miscellaneous. "In re Lorain Comm. Hosp.", Court of Appeals Ninth Judicial District of Ohio, (5/30/1984).
50. Miscellaneous. "St. Joseph's Hill Infirmary Inc. v. Mandy", Court of Appeals of Missouri, Eastern District, Division Four, (5/22/1984).
51. Miscellaneous. "State Health Planning & Dev. Agency v. Baptist Medical Center", Court of Civil Appeals of Alabama, (11/2/1983).
52. Miscellaneous. "Ex parte State Health Planning & Dev. Agency", Court of Civil Appeals of Alabama, (8/31/1983).
53. Miscellaneous. "Canterbury Nursing Home Inc. v. Alabama State Health Planning & De Agency", Supreme Court of Alabama, (1/28/1983).
54. Miscellaneous. "Olathe Community Hospital v. Kansas Corp. Com.", Supreme Court of Kansas, (10/22/1982).
55. Miscellaneous. "East Tennessee Health Improv. Council Inc. v. Tennessee Health Facilities Com.", Court of Appeals of Tennessee, Middle Section, (9/18/1981).
56. Miscellaneous, 5. Validity of CON Board Decision. "Greenbriar Convalescent Center Inc. v. Department of Public Health", Court of Appeals of Michigan, (8/7/1981).
57. Miscellaneous. "Hollingsworth v. Califano", United States District Court For the Northern District of Mississippi Greenville Division, (6/5/1979).
58. Miscellaneous. "Doctors Hospital Inc. v. Califano", United States District Court for the District of Columbia, (10/6/1978).
59. Miscellaneous. "Fairhaven Corp. v. Tennessee Health Facilities Com.", Court of Appeals of Tennessee, Middle Section, (5/7/1976).
60. Miscellaneous, 6.b. Injunction on CON Requirements. "General Care Corp. v. Forehand", Court of Appeals of Florida First District, (2/20/1976).
61. Miscellaneous. "Fidel OSINA et al., v. City of Chicago", Appellate Court of Illinois, (5/14/1975).

VII A. Court's Denial of Judicial Review Arbitrary

62. Court's Denial of Judicial Review Arbitrary, 7. Miscellaneous. "Marlboro Park Hospital v. South Carolina Department of Health and Environmental Control", Court of Appeals of South Carolina, (4/12/2004).

63. Court's Denial of Judicial Review Arbitrary, 5. Validity of CON Board Decision. "Miami Jewish Home & Hosp. for the Aged v. Agency for Health Care Admin." Court of Appeal of Florida third district, (8/8/1998).
64. Court's Denial of Judicial Review Arbitrary. "ABC Home Health Serv. v. Tennessee Health Facilities Comm'n", Supreme Court of Tennessee, at Nashville, (12/19/1994).
65. Court's Denial of Judicial Review Arbitrary. "Xun Imaging Assocs. v. Department of Health Div. of Need Review", Commonwealth Court of Pennsylvania, (6/16/1994).
66. Court's Denial of Judicial Review Arbitrary. "Community Psychiatric Centers v. North Carolina Dep't of Human Resources Div. of Facility Services", Court of Appeals of North Carolina, (7/16/1991).
67. Court's Denial of Judicial Review Arbitrary. "Fairview General Hosp. v. Fletcher", Court of Appeals of Ohio Tenth Appellate District, Franklin County, (10/16/1990).
68. Court's Denial of Judicial Review Arbitrary, 5.b. Reconsideration of Previous CON Decision. "Merle West Medical Center v. State Health Planning & Dev. Agency", Court of Appeals of Oregon, (2/26/1988).
69. Court's Denial of Judicial Review Arbitrary. "South Carolina Baptist Hospital v. South Carolina Dep't of Health & Environmental Control", Supreme Court of South Carolina, (2/9/1987).
70. Court's Denial of Judicial Review Arbitrary. "Ex parte State Health Planning & Dev. Agency", Court of Civil Appeals of Alabama, (12/17/1986).
71. Court's Denial of Judicial Review Arbitrary, 7. Miscellaneous. "Lonoke Nursing Home Inc. v. Wayne & Neil Bennett Family Partnership", Court of Appeals of Arkansas, Division 1, (11/28/1984).
72. Court's Denial of Judicial Review Arbitrary, 7. Miscellaneous. "Martin County Nursing Center, Inc. v Medco Centers, Inc.", Court of Appeals of Indiana, First District, (11/6/1982).
73. Court's Denial of Judicial Review Arbitrary. "Charter Medical Corp. v. Mississippi Health Planning & Development Agency", Supreme Court of Mississippi, (7/26/1978).
74. Court's Denial of Judicial Review Arbitrary. "Bureau of Community Medical Facilities Planning of Dep't of Health & Rehabilitative Services v. Samson", Court of Appeals of Florida First District, (2/4/1977).

VII B. Failure to Obtain CON

75. Failure to Obtain CON, 6.d. Defining State Health Plan Term, 4.c. Defining Regulatory Term,4. Regulatory Violation, 3. Statutory Violation. "Children's Hosp. & Med. Ctr. v. Department of Health", Court of Appeals of Washington, Division Two, (4/30/1999).
76. Failure to Obtain CON, 6.e. Applicability of Need Criteria to Applicant, 7. Miscellaneous. "Rutherford Hosp. Inc. v. RNH Pshp.", United States Court of Appeals For the Fourth Circuit, (2/5/1999).
77. Failure to Obtain CON. "Texas Health Facilities Com. v. West Texas Home Health Agency", Court of Civil Appeals of Texas Tenth District, Waco, (9/27/1997).
78. Failure to Obtain CON. "Kilties v. North Carolina Dep't of Human Resources Div. Of Facility Serv. Certificate of Need Section", Court of Appeals of North Carolina, (2/4/1997).
79. Failure to Obtain CON, 6.e. Applicability of Need Criteria to Applicant. "South Broward Hosp. Dist. v. Agency for Health Care Admin." Court of Appeal of Florida First District , (10/27/1995).
80. Failure to Obtain CON, 6.e. Applicability of Need Criteria to Applicant. "CoN. Medical Personnel Pool v. Management Registry", Court of Appeals of Kentucky, (3/12/1993).
81. Failure to Obtain CON, 7. Miscellaneous. "Ex parte Virginia D. Contra Willis", Supreme Court of Alabama, (6/15/1992).
82. Failure to Obtain CON. "In re Aultman Hosp.", Court of Appeals of Ohio Tenth Appellate District, Franklin County, (5/19/1992).
83. Failure to Obtain CON, 6.e. Applicability of Need Criteria to Applicant. "Fairfax Surgical Center v. State Health Commissioner", Court of Appeals of Virginia, (6/4/1991).

84. Failure to Obtain CON. "In re Denial of Request for Declaratory Ruling by Total Care Inc.", Court of Appeals of North Carolina, (7/17/1990).
85. Failure to Obtain CON, 6.e. Applicability of Need Criteria to Applicant, 5. Validity of CON Board Decision. "Neurosurgical Clinic & Allied Specialties Inc. v. State Health Planning & Resources Dev. Agency", Court of Appeals of Ohio Tenth Appellate District, Franklin County, (1/5/1989).
86. Failure to Obtain CON, 6. Public Need Challenge. "Kurd's Ambulance Serv. v. Tucson", Court of Appeals of Arizona, Division Two, Department B, (6/16/1988).
87. Failure to Obtain CON, 4.c. Defining Regulatory Term, 4. Regulatory Violation, 3.e. Defining Statutory Term, 3. Statutory Violation. "Catholic Medical Ctr. v. Elliot Hosp.", Supreme Court of New Hampshire, (5/6/1988).
88. Failure to Obtain CON, 6.e. Applicability of Need Criteria to Applicant. "Charter Hospital of Bucks County Inc. v. Commonwealth Dep't of Health", Commonwealth Court of Pennsylvania, (12/11/1987).
89. Failure to Obtain CON, 6.e. Applicability of Need Criteria to Applicant. "Psychiatric Inst. of Am. v. Mediplex", Supreme Court of New Hampshire, (12/4/1987).
90. Failure to Obtain CON, 3. Statutory Violation. "Arnot-Ogden Memorial Hospital v. Guthrie Clinic Inc.", Supreme Court of New York, Appellate Division, Third Department, (7/17/1986).
91. Failure to Obtain CON, 6.e. Applicability of Need Criteria to Applicant. "Clifton Springs Sanitarium Co., v. Axelrod, M.D. AS Commissioner of the Dept. of Health", Supreme Court, Appellate Division, Fourth Department, (12/20/1985).
92. Failure to Obtain CON. "Home Health Professional Services Inc. v. Department of Health & Rehabilitative Services", Court of Appeals of Florida First District, (1/11/1985).
93. Failure to Obtain CON. "In re Change of Bed Category of Tieszen Memorial Home", Supreme Court of South Dakota, (1/18/1984).
94. Failure to Obtain CON. "St. Francis/sty. George Hospital Inc. v. Blue Cross", Court of Appeals First Appellate District, Hamilton County Ohio, (11/23/1983).
95. Failure to Obtain CON, 6.e. Applicability of Need Criteria to Applicant. "Mercy Hospital v. Commonwealth Dep't of Health", Commonwealth Court of Pennsylvania, (9/21/1982).
96. Failure to Obtain CON, 5. Validity of CON Board Decision, 4.c. Defining Regulatory Term, 4. Regulatory Violation, 3.e. Defining Statutory Term, 3. Statutory Violation. "Medcor Inc. v. Finley" Superior Court of New Jersey Appellate Division, (5/22/1981).
97. Failure to Obtain CON, 6.b. Injunction on CON Requirements, 7.a. Court's Denial of Judicial Review Arbitrary. "Iowa State Dep't of Health v. Hertko", Supreme Court of Iowa, (8/29/1979).
98. Failure to Obtain CON, 7. Miscellaneous. "Pratt v. Board of County Comm'rs", Supreme Court of Kansas, (7/14/1979).
99. Failure to Obtain CON, 3. Statutory Violation. "Marsh v. Finley", Superior Court of New Jersey Appellate Division, (6/15/1978).
100. Failure to Obtain CON, 3.b. CON Board Exceeded Rulemaking Authority, 3. Statutory Violation. "University of Utah Medical Ctr. v. Bonneville County", Supreme Court of Idaho, (7/3/1974).

CON CASE LAW
TABLE OF CASES – INDEXED BY CLASSIFICATION OF REGULATED ASSET

The following certificate of need cases are sorted based on equipment, facility, or service classification.

I. EQUIPMENT

I A. Computerized Tomography (CT)

Neurosurgical Clinic & Allied Specialties Inc. v. State Health Planning & Resources Dev. Agency, Court of Appeals of Ohio Tenth Appellate District, Franklin County, (1/5/1989).

Laurel Mobile Health Services Ltd. v. Commonwealth Dep't of Health, Commonwealth Court of Pennsylvania, (11/25/1988).

Radiological Soc. of New Jersey v. New Jersey State Dep't of Health Hospital Rate Setting Com., Superior Court of New Jersey Appellate Division, (3/10/1986).

Verdugo Hills Hospital Inc. v. Department of Health, Court of Appeal of California, Second Appellate District, Division Three, (4/26/1979).

Marin Hospital Dist. v Department of Health, Court of Appeal, Second District, Division 3, (4/26/1979).

Marsh v. Finley, Superior Court of New Jersey Appellate Division, (6/15/1978).

I B. Equipment

Auburn Medical Center, Inc. v. East Alabama Health Care Authority d/b/a East Alabama Medical Center, Court of Civil Appeals of Alabama, (9/26/2003).

In re North Shore Radiology, Court of Appeals of Ohio Tenth Appellate District, Franklin County, (10/20/1994).

In re North Shore Radiology, Court OF Appeals OF Ohio Tenth Appellate District, Franklin County, (9/1/1994).

Associates in Radiation Oncology P.A. v. Siegel M.P.H., Superior Court of New Jersey Appellate Division, (3/8/1994).

Commission for Health Economics Control v. Medical Consultants Imaging Co., Court of Appeals of Kentucky, (12/24/1992).

Department of Human Resources v. UHS of Colony, Supreme Court of Nevada, (4/9/1987).

In re Certificate of Need Application etc., Supreme Court of Kansas, (7/17/1981).

I C. Linear Accelerator

McLeod Regional Medical Center v. South Carolina Department of Health and Environmental Control, State of South Carolina Administrative Law Judge Division, (6/7/1996).

I D. Magnetic Resonance Imaging (MRI)

Magnetic Resonance Technologies Ltd. Partnership v. Commissioner Maine Dep't of Human Serv., Supreme Judicial Court of Maine, (1/19/1995).

Central Pa. MRI L.P. v. Department of Health, Commonwealth Court of Pennsylvania, (9/6/1994).

Boulware v. Department of Human Resources, Supreme Court of Nevada, (5/27/1987).

II. FACILITIES

II A. Adult Day Care

ACSR Inc. v. Cabinet for Health Service, Court of Appeals of Kentucky, (8/25/2000).

II B. Ambulatory Surgery Center

Alan D. Gordon v. Lewistown Hospital, United States District Court for the Middle District of Pennsylvania, (7/11/2003).

Albany Surgical, P.C. v. Department of Community Health, Georgia Appeals Court, (1/1/2002).

Columbia Endoscopy Center v. South Carolina Department of Health and Environmental Control, State of South Carolina Administrative Law Judge Division, (12/30/1994).

Portland Surgery Center, LLC. v. Department of Human Services, Superior Court of Maine, Kennebec County, (2/23/2004).

Morristown Surgery Center, LLC v. Tennessee Health Facilities Commission, Court of Appeals of Tennessee, at Nashville, (12/15/2003).

Albany Surgical, P.C. v. Dept. of Community Health, Court of Appeals of Georgia, Fourth Division, (9/27/2002).

Johnston Ambulatory Surgical Associates, LTD. v. Patricia Nolan, in her capacity as Director of the Rhode Island Department of Health et al., Supreme Court of Rhode Island, (7/12/2000).

Armstrong Surgical Ctr. Inc. v. Armstrong County Memorial Hosp., United States Court of Appeals For the Third Circuit, (6/26/2000).

Carle Found. v. Illinois Health Facilities Planning Board, Appellate Court of Illinois, First District Fifth Division, (8/13/1999).

Biloxi HMA Inc. v. Singing River Hosp., Supreme Court of Mississippi, (7/29/1999).

Surgical Care Center of Hammond, L.C. v. Hospital Service District No. 1 of Tangipahoa Parish, and Quorum Health Resources, Inc., United States Court of Appeals for the Fifth Circuit, (8/27/1998).

Adventist Healthcare Midatlantic v. Suburban Hosp., Court of Appeals of Maryland, (6/10/1998).

Access Ctr. for Health v. Health Facilities Planning Bd., Appellate Court of Illinois, Second District, (9/17/1996).

Cabinet for Human Resources v. Women's Health Services, Court of Appeals of Kentucky, (6/24/1994).

In re Samaritan N. Health Ctr., Court of Appeals of Ohio Tenth Appellate District, Franklin County, (5/12/1994).

Cincinnati Ambulatory Surgery Center v. Certificate of Need Review Bd., Court of Appeals of Ohio Tenth Appellate District, Franklin County, (12/13/1988).

Arnot-Ogden Memorial Hospital v. Guthrie Clinic Inc., Supreme Court of New York, Appellate Division, Third Department, (7/17/1986).

Medivision of East Broward County Inc. v. Department of Health & Rehabilitative Services, Court of Appeals of Florida First District, (5/15/1986).

II C. Assisted Living

Cathedral Rock of Granite City v. Illinois Health Facilities Planning Bd., Appellate Court of Illinois, Fourth District, (12/9/1999).

II D. Cancer Treatment Facility

Powers v. Commonwealth Dep't of Health, Commonwealth Court of Pennsylvania, (1/22/1990).

Powers v. Commonwealth Dep't of Health, Commonwealth Court of Pennsylvania, (11/25/1988).

II E. Clinic

The Tennessee Department of Health v. Gary C. Boyle, M.D., Court of Appeals of Tennessee, at Nashville, (12/19/2002).

In re Cleveland Clinic Found., Court of Appeals of Ohio Tenth Appellate District, Franklin County, (4/14/1994).

Overlook Medical Clinic v. Commonwealth Dep't of Health, Commonwealth Court of Pennsylvania, (10/30/1989).

Overlook Medical Clinic v. Commonwealth Dep't of Health, Commonwealth Court of Pennsylvania, (6/12/1989).

II F. Dentist Offices

Madarang v. Bermudes, United States Court of Appeals For the Ninth Circuit, (11/9/1989).

II G. Drug and Alcohol Treatment Facility

Changing Point Inc. v. Maryland Health Resources Planning Com., Court of Special Appeals of Maryland, (5/6/1991).

HCA Crossroads Residential Ctrs. v. North Carolina Dep't of Human Resources etc., Supreme Court of North Carolina, (12/5/1990).

II H. Hospitals

Patient Tower, (5/31/2004).

Summit Neighborhood Association v. Rhode Island Department of Health, Superior Court of Rhode Island, Providence, (5/27/2004).

Marlboro Park Hospital v. South Carolina Department of Health and Environmental Control, Court of Appeals of South Carolina, (4/12/2004).

Georgia Department of Community Health v. Satilla Health Services, Inc., Court of Appeals of Georgia, (3/17/2004).

Jackson Tennessee Hospital Company, LLC. v. West Tennessee Healthcare, Inc., United States District Court for the Western District of Tennessee, Eastern Division, (2/27/2004).

Ashtabula County Medical Center v. Tommy G. Thompson, United States Court of Appeals, (12/19/2003).

Providence Health System - Washington v. Tommy G. Thompson, United States Court of Appeals, (12/17/2003).

Northern Virginia Community Hospital, LLC d/b/a *Broadlands Regional Medical Center v. Robert B. Stroube*, M.D., M.P.H., Circuit Court of Loudoun County, Virginia, (10/3/2003).

Multicare Health System d/b/a/ *Tacoma General Allenmore Hospital v. Department of Health of the State of Washington*, Court of Appeals of Washington, Division Two, (9/30/2003).

Department of Community Health, *Division of Health Planning v. Gwinnett Hospital System, Inc.*, Court of Appeals of Georgia, First Division, (8/26/2003).

Medstar Health v. Maryland Health Care Commission, Court of Appeals of Maryland, (6/18/2003).

Methodist Healthcare-Jackson Hospital v. Jackson-Madison County General Hospital District, Court of Appeals of Tennessee, at Nashville, (5/22/2003).

Riverside Hospital, Inc. d/b/a Riverside Regional Medical Center v. Robe B. Stroube, Circuit Court of Williamsburg and James City County, Virginia, (3/17/2003).

United States of America, Et Al. v. East Texas Medical Center Regional Healthcare System, Et Al., United States District Court for the Southern District of Texas, Houston Division, (3/4/2003).

In re. Central Vermont Medical Center, Supreme Court of Vermont, (12/16/2002).

United States of America v. East Texas Medical Center Regional Healthcare System, United States District Court for the Southern District of Texas, Houston Division, (10/20/2002).

South Shore Hospital, Inc. v. Tommy G. Thompson, United States Court of Appeals, (10/16/2002).

Marion Hospital Corporation, Appellee v. The Illinois Health Facilities Planning Board, Supreme Court of Illinois, (/19/2002).

Jackson HMA, Inc. v. Mississippi State Dept. of Health, Supreme Court of Mississippi, (7/25/2002).

St. Luke's Hospital of Kansas City v. Missouri Health Facilities Review Committee, Circuit Court of Cole County, (7/4/2002).

Lloyd Noland Foundation, Inc. v. The City of Fairfield Healthcare Authority, Supreme Court of Alabama, (2/22/2002).

Ashtabula County Med. Ctr. v. Thompson, United States District Court for the Northern District of Ohio, (2/8/2002).

South Shore Hospital v. Tommy G. Thompson, United States District Court, D. Massachusetts, (1/3/200).

St. Joseph Hospital v. Kevin Concannon, Superior Court of Maine, (11/2/2001).

Jeff Anderson Reg'l Med. Ctr. v. Miss. State Dep't of Health, Supreme Court of Mississippi, (10/31/2001).

Brattleboro Memorial Hospital v. Department of Banking, Insurance, Securities and Health Care Administration, Supreme Court of Vermont, (9/19/2001).

Medical Center at Princeton v. The Township of Princeton Zoning Board of Adjustment, Superior Court of New Jersey, (6/28/2001).

Md. Gen. Hosp. Inc. v. Thompson, United States District Court for the District of Maryland, (6/27/2001).

Auburn Med. Ctr. v. State Health Planning & Dev. Agency, Court of Civil Appeals of Alabama, (5/11/2001).

Auburn Medical Center, Inc. v. East Alabama health Care Authority d/b/a East Alabama Medical Center, Court of Civil Appeals of Alabama, (5/11/2001).

Auburn Medical Center, Inc. v. State Health Planning and Development Agency et al., Court of Civil Appeals of Alabama, (5/11/2001).

Ex parte East State Healthcare Auth., Supreme Court of Alabama, (1/5/2001).

Central Maine Medical Center v. Kevin Concannon and Maine Medical Center, Superior Court of Maine, (9/26/2000).

Northside Hospital, Inc. v. McCord et al., Court of Appeals of Georgia, (7/19/2000).

Christenbury Surgery Ctr. v. North Carolina, Court of Appeals of North Carolina, (/6/2000).

Bradford Hospital v. Donna E. Shalala, United States District Court, W.D. Pennsylvania, (6/5/2000).

Auburn Med. Ctr. Inc. v. State Health Planning & De Agency, Court of Civil Appeals of Alabama, (5/5/2000).

Christ Hosp. v. Department of Health & Senior Serv., Superior Court of New Jersey Appellate Division, (4/12/2000).

New York v. St. Francis Hosp., United States District Court for the Southern District of New York, (4/10/2000).

Appeal of New England Heart Institute and Maine Medical Center, Supreme Court of New Hampshire, (12/29/1999).

Delta Regional Med. Ctr. v. Mississippi State Dep't of Health", Supreme Court of Mississippi, (12/16/1999).

In the Matter of Certificate of Need Granted to St. Francis Medical Center, Superior Court of New Jersey, Appellate Division, (11/8/1999).

Dimensions Med. Ctr. v. Elmhurst Outpatient Surgery Ctr., Appellate Court of Illinois, Fourth District, (9/29/1999).

Mississippi State Dep't of Health v. Natchez Community Hosp., Supreme Court of Mississippi, (7/29/1999).

Children's Hosp. & Med. Ctr. v. Department of Health, Court of Appeals of Washington, Division Two, (4/30/1999).

Gundry/Glass Hosp. v. Shalala", United States Court of Appeals for the Fourth Circuit, (4/5/1999).

Gundry/Glass Hospital v. Donna E. Shalala, Secretary of Health and Human Services and Blue Cross and Blue Shield of Maryland; Health Care Financing Administration, United States Court of Appeals for the Fourth Circuit, (4/5/1999).

St. Joseph's Hosp. Inc. v. Thunderbolt Health Care Inc., Court of Appeals of Georgia, (4/1/1999).

Frye Reg'l Med. Ctr. Inc. v. Hunt, Supreme Court of North Carolina, (2/5/1999).

St. Dominic-Jackson Mem'l Hosp. v. Mississippi State Dep't of Health, Supreme Court of Mississippi, (10/8/1998).

South Miami Hospital, Inc. v. Agency For Health Care Administration and Variety Children's Hospital d/b/a Miami Children's Hospital, District Court of Appeals of Florida, (6/1/1998).

North Fulton Med. Ctr. v. Stephenson, Supreme Court of Georgia, (5/26/1998).

Gundry Glass Hosp. v. Shalala Civil, United States District Court For the District of Maryland, (5/19/1998).

University of Alabama Hospitals v. Alabama Renal Stone Institute Inc., Court of Civil Appeals of Alabama, (4/1/1998).

Mount Sinai Community Hosp. Ass'n v. Gorman, Superior Court OF Connecticut, Judicial District OF Hartford-New Britain, AT Hartford, (3/4/1998).

Texas Health Facilities Com. v. West Texas Home Health Agency, Court of Civil Appeals of Texas Tenth District, Waco, (9/27/1997).

Huron Valley Hospital Inc. v. Michigan Dep't of Public Health, Court of Appeals of Michigan, (9/4/1997).

West Bloomfield Hosp. v. Certificate of Need Bd., Court of Appeals of Michigan, (5/16/1997).

Redbud Hosp. Dist. v. Heckler, United States District Court for the Northern District of California, (5/12/1997).

Texas Health Facilities Com. v. Nueces County Hospital Dist., Court of Civil Appeals of Texas Third District, Austin, (5/9/1997).

Sussex Medical Investors, L.P. v. Delaware Health Resources Board, Superior Court of Delaware, (4/8/1997).

Huron Valley Hospital Inc. v. Pontiac Ci, United States District Court For the Eastern District of Michigan, Southern Division, (3/2/1997).

Phoebe Putney Mem. Hosp. v. Roach, Supreme Court of Georgia, (2/17/1997).

Naples Community Hosp. v. Agency for Health Care Admin., Court of Appeal of Florida First District, (1/31/1997).

Naples Community Hospital, Inc., Petitioner, v. State of Florida, Agency for Health Care Administration, and Big Cypress Medical Center, Inc., Respondents, District Court of Appeal of Florida, (1/31/1997).

Nueces County Hospital Dist. v. Texas Health Facilities Com., Court of Civil Appeals of Texas Third District, Austin, (1/24/1997).

Tarpon Springs General Hospital v. Office of Community Medical Facilities etc., Court of Appeals of Florida First District, (1/19/1997).

Auburn Medical Center, Inc. v. J. Elbert Peters, et al., United States District Court, M.D. Alabama, Northern Division, (12/12/1996).

Cabinet for Human Resources Interim Office of Health Planning & Certification v. Jewish Hosp. Healthcare Serv., Court of Appeals of Kentucky, (10/25/1996).

Cleveland Clinic Fla. Hosp. v. Agency for Health Care Admin., Court of Appeal of Florida First District, (10/16/1996).

Lawnwood Medical Ctr. v. Agency for Health Care Admin., Court of Appeal of Florida First District, (7/29/1996).

West Bloomfield Hosp. v. Certificate of Need Bd., Supreme Court of Michigan, (7/16/1996).

Martin v. Memorial Hosp., United States Court of Appeals for the Fifth Circuit, (7/10/1996).

Presbyterian-Orthopaedic Hosp. v. North Carolina Dep't of Human Resources, Court of Appeals of North Carolina, (6/4/1996).

In re Lima Mem. Hosp., Court of Appeals of Ohio Tenth Appellate District, Franklin County, (5/23/1996).

West Virginia Health Care Cost Review Auth. v. Boone Mem. Hosp., Supreme Court of Appeals of West Virginia, (4/24/1996).

Agency for Health Care Admin. v. University Hosp., Court of Appeal of Florida First District, (4/16/1996).

Pennsylvania Dep't of Health v. North Hills Passavant Hosp., Commonwealth Court of Pennsylvania, (4/10/1996).

Nebraska Methodist Health Sys. v. Department of Health, Supreme Court of Nebraska, (2/23/1996).

Cape Fear Memorial Hosp. v. North Carolina Dep't of Human Resources, Court of Appeals of North Carolina, (2/6/1996).

In re Denial of Request by Humana Hospital Corp. etc., Court of Appeals of North Carolina, (1/7/1996).

St. Luke Hosp. v. Health Policy Bd., Court of Appeals of Kentucky, (1/5/1996).

Medical Ctr. v. State Health Planning Agency, Court of Appeals of Georgia, (12/5/1995).

Vaughan Regional Medical Ctr. v. Smith, United States District Court for the Middle District of Alabama, (12/5/1995).

In re Good Samaritan Hosp., Court of Appeals of Ohio Tenth Appellate District, Franklin County, (11/9/1995).

South Broward Hosp. Dist. v. Agency for Health Care Admin., Court of Appeal of Florida First District, (10/27/1995.

Mississippi State Dep't of Health v. Mississippi Baptist Medical Ctr., Supreme Court of Mississippi, (10/19/1995).

Ex parte Crestwood Hosp. & Nursing Home, Supreme Court of Alabama, (9/8/1995).

Mid-America Georgian Gardens v. Missouri Health Facilities Review Comm'n, Court of Appeals of Missouri, (8/15/1995).

Jewish Hosp. v. Baptist Health Care Sys., Court of Appeals of Kentucky, (7/21/1995).

HCA Health Serv. v. Roach, Supreme Court of Georgia, (6/12/1995).

Federal Trade Commission v. Freeman Hospital and Tri-State Osteopathic Hospital Association, Inc., United States District Court, W.D. Missouri, Southwestern Division, (6/9/1995).

In re Mansfield Gen. Hosp., Supreme Court of Ohio, (5/24/1995).

W. A. Foote Mem. Hosp. v. Michigan Dep't of Pub. Health, Court of Appeals of Michigan, (5/12/1995).

Medical Arts Clinic P.C. v. Franciscan Initiatives, Supreme Court of North Dakota, (5/9/1995).

SSM Health Care v. Missouri Health Facilities Review Comm., Supreme Court of Missouri, (3/21/1995).

North Fulton Medical Ctr. v. Roach, Supreme Court of Georgia, (2/20/1995).

Maryland Gen. Hosp. v. Maryland Health Resources Planning Comm'n, Court of Special Appeals of Maryland, (2/14/1995).

St. Joseph Hosp. & Health Care Ctr. v. Department of Health, Supreme Court of Washington, (1/26/1995).

West Bloomfield Hosp. v. Certificate of Need BD., Court of Appeals of Michigan, (1/17/1995).

Mercy Health Center Div. of Sisters of Mercy Health Corp. v. State Health Facilities Council, Supreme Court of Iowa, (1/16/1995).

Michigan Affiliated Healthcare Sys. v. Department of Pub. Health, Court of Appeals of Michigan, (12/27/1994).

FTC v. Hospital Bd. of Directors, United States Court of Appeals for the Eleventh Circuit, (11/30/1994).

Beebe Medical Ctr. v. Certificate of Need Appeals Bd., Superior Court of Delaware Kent, (8/31/1994).

Mercy Regional Health Sys. v. Department of Health NO. C.D. NO. C.D. Commonwealth Court of Pennsylvania, Commonwealth Court of Pennsylvania (7/12/1994).

Monmouth Medical Ctr. v. State Dep't of Health, Superior Court of New Jersey Appellate Division, (3/31/1994).

In re Adoption of Regulations Governing the State Health Plan, Supreme Court of New Jersey, (2/28/1994).

North Fulton Medical Ctr. v. Roach, Supreme Court of Georgia, (2/21/1994).

HCA Health Serv. v. Roach, Supreme Court of Georgia, (2/7/1994).

In re Certification of Need Application of Chilton Memorial Hosp., Superior Court of New Jersey Appellate Division, (12/23/1993).

Appeal of Nashua Brookside Hosp. v. Supreme Court of New Hampshire, (12/23/1993).

In re Deaconess Hosp., Court of Appeals of Ohio Tenth Appellate District, Franklin County, (12/9/1993).

Hospital Auth. v. State Health Planning Agency, Court of Appeals of Georgia, (11/19/1993).

Catawba Memorial Hosp. v. North Carolina Dep't of Human Resources, Court of Appeals of North Carolina, (11/16/1993).

In re St. John Medical Ctr., Court of Appeals of Ohio Tenth Appellate District, Franklin County, (10/28/1993).

Robert Packer Hosp. v. Department of Health, Commonwealth Court of Pennsylvania, (9/7/1993).

In re Mansfield Gen. Hosp., Court of Appeals of Ohio Tenth Appellate District, Franklin County, (8/31/1993).

St. Francis Hosp. v. Appeals Bd. of Dep't of Health & Social Serv., Superior Court of Delaware New Castle, (8/12/1993).

Mercy Medical Ctr. Inc. v. Office of Health Policy, Court of Appeals of Oregon, (7/14/1993).

New England Rehabilitation Hosp. Inc. v. Commission on Hosps. & Health Care, Supreme Court of Connecticut, (6/22/1993).

Clayton County Hosp. Auth. v. Webb, Court of Appeals of Georgia, (3/10/1993).

In re Adoption of Regulations Governing the State Health Plan N.J.A.C., Superior Court of New Jersey Appellate Division, (2/10/1993).

University Community Hosp. v. Department of Health & Rehabilitative Services, Court of Appeal of Florida First District, (12/29/1992).

Rush-Presbyterian-St. Luke's Medical Ctr. v. Hellenic Republic, United States Court of Appeals For the Seventh Circuit, (11/23/1992).

State ex rel. Parma Community Gen. Hosp. v. Kilroy, Court of Appeals of Ohio Tenth Appellate District, Franklin County, (11/17/1992).

State Health Planning Agency v. Mobile Infirmary Ass'n, Court of Civil Appeals of Alabama, (10/16/1992).

Lake East Hosp. v. Ohio Dep't of Health, Court of Appeals of Ohio Tenth Appellate District, Franklin County, (10/6/1992).

In re Deaconess Hosp., Court of Appeals of Ohio Tenth Appellate District, Franklin County, (9/29/1992).

Hospital Corp. of Am. v. Associates in Adolescent Psychiatry S.C., Court of Appeal of Florida Fourth District, (9/23/1992).

State ex rel. Greene Oaks v. Kilroy, Court of Appeals of Ohio Tenth Appellate District, Franklin County, (9/22/1992).

Holy Name Hosp. v. New Jersey Health Care Admin. Bd., Superior Court of New Jersey Appellate Division, (7/23/1992).

New England Rehabilitation Hosp. Inc. v. Commission on Hosps. & Health Care, Superior Court of Connecticut, Judicial District of Hartford - New Britain, at Hartford, (7/20/1992).

Mississippi State Dep't of Health v. Golden Triangle Regional Medical Center, Supreme Court of Mississippi, (6/17/1992).

HTI Health Services Inc. v. Mississippi State Dep't of Health, Supreme Court of Mississippi, (6/10/1992).

Suburban Medical Hosp. Inc. v. Department of Health & Rehabilitative Services, Court of Appeal of Florida Third District, (5/26/1992).

In re Aultman Hosp., Court of Appeals of Ohio Tenth Appellate District, Franklin County, (5/19/1992).

HCA Health Services Inc. v. Department of Health & Rehabilitative Services, Court of Appeal of Florida First District, (5/13/1992).

University Psychiatric Center Inc. v. Department of Health & Rehabilitative Services, Court of Appeal of Florida First District, (4/20/1992).

Tarabishi v. McAlester Regional Hosp., United States Court of Appeals for the Tenth Circuit, (12/10/1991).

Roper Hospital v. Board of South Carolina Department of Health and Environmental Control and Francis Xavier Hospital, Supreme Court of South Carolina, (12/3/1991).

Capitol Hill Hosp. v. District of Columbia State Health Planning & Dev. Agency, District of Columbia Court of Appeals, (11/20/1991).

First Hosp. Corp. v. Department of Health & Rehabilitative Services, Court of Appeal of Florida First District, (8/21/1991).

Iredell Memorial Hosp. v. North Carolina Dep't of Human Resources etc., Court of Appeals of North Carolina, (8/6/1991).

FTC v. University Health Inc., United States Court of Appeals for the Eleventh Circuit, (7/26/1991).

In the matter of Sisters of Charity Hospital of Buffalo v. New York State Department of Health, Supreme Court, Appellate Division, Third Department, (7/18/1991).

Community Psychiatric Centers v. North Carolina Dep't of Human Resources Div. of Facility Services, Court of Appeals of North Carolina, (7/16/1991).

Jeannette Dist. Memorial Hosp. v. Department of Health, Commonwealth Court of Pennsylvania, (7/12/1991).

Martin Memorial Hosp. Ass'n v. Department of Health & Rehabilitative Services, Court of Appeal of Florida Fourth District, (7/5/1991).

In re Timken Mercy Medical Center, Supreme Court of Ohio, (7/3/1991).

Fairfax Surgical Center v. State Health Commissioner, Court of Appeals of Virginia, (6/4/1991).

Great Lakes Rehabilitation Hosp. v. Commonwealth Dep't of Health, Commonwealth Court of Pennsylvania, (5/31/1991).

State ex rel. PIA Psychiatric Hosp. Inc. v. Ohio Certificate of Need Review Bd., Supreme Court of Ohio, (5/15/1991).

Mississippi State Dep't of Health v. Southwest Mississippi Regional Medical Center, Supreme Court of Mississippi, (5/3/1991).

Amisub v. Department of Health & Rehabilitative Services, Court of Appeal of Florida First District, (4/30/1991).

District of Columbia Hosp. Ass'n v. Barry, District of Columbia Court of Appeals, (1/30/1991).

In re Good Samaritan Medical Center, Court of Appeals of Ohio Tenth Appellate District, Franklin County, (1/10/1991).

Central Florida Regional Hosp. Inc. v. Department of Health & Rehabilitative Services, Court of Appeal of Florida Fifth District, (1/6/1991).

Fairview General Hosp. v. Fletcher, Court of Appeals of Ohio Tenth Appellate District, Franklin County, (12/20/1990).

Auburn Medical Ctr. v. East Ala. Health Care Auth., Court of Civil Appeals of Alabama, (12/19/1990).

Fairview General Hosp. v. Fletcher, Court of Appeals of Ohio Tenth Appellate District, Franklin County, (10/16/1990).

Famiglietti v. Brevard Medical Investors Ltd., Court of Appeals of Georgia, (9/19/1990).

First Hosp. Corp. v. Department of Health & Rehabilitative Serv. Case No., Court of Appeal of Florida First District, (9/12/1990).

HCA Crossroads Residential Centers Inc. v. North Carolina Dep't of Human Resources etc., Court of Appeals of North Carolina, (6/19/1990).

Charter Hosp. of Pasco Co. v. Department of Health & Rehabilitative Services, Court of Appeal of Florida First District, (6/18/1990).

Lee Memorial Hosp. v. Department of Health & Rehabilitative Serv., Court of Appeal of Florida First District, (5/9/1990).

Lee Memorial Hosp. v. Department of Health & Rehabilitative Serv., Court of Appeal of Florida First District, (5/9/1990).

In re Valley Hosp., Superior Court of New Jersey Appellate Division, (4/20/1990).

In re Certificate of Need Application of Providence Hosp., Court of Appeals of Ohio Tenth Appellate District, Franklin County, (4/19/1990).

Lenoir Memorial Hosp. Inc. v. North Carolina Dep't of Human Resources etc., Court of Appeals of North Carolina, (4/17/1990).

St. Joseph Hosp. Inc. v. Department of Health & Rehabilitative Services Case, Court of Appeal of Florida First District, (4/12/1990).

Ex parte Shelby Medical Center Inc., Supreme Court of Alabama, (4/12/1990).

Magnolia Hosp. v. Mississippi State Dep't of Health, Supreme Court of Mississippi, (4/4/1990).

University Community Hospital v. Department of Health & Rehabilitative Services, Court of Appeal of Florida First District, (1/12/1990).

National Healthcorp L.P. v. Department of Health & Rehabilitative Services, Court of Appeal of Florida First District, (12/22/1989).

St. Francis Hospital Inc. v. Department of Health & Rehabilitative Services, Court of Appeal of Florida First District, (12/20/1989).

Florida Residential Treatment Centers Inc. v. Department of Health & Rehabilitative Services, Court of Appeal of Florida First District, (11/14/1989).

Huron Valley Hospital Inc. v. Pontiac, United States Court of Appeals for the Sixth Circuit, (10/13/1989).

Sarasota County Public Hospital Bd. v. Department of Health & Rehabilitative Services, Court of Appeal of Florida Second District, (10/11/1989).

Appeal of Psychiatric Institutes of Am. v. Supreme Court of New Hampshire, (8/23/1989).

Charter Medical of Cook County Inc. v. HCA Health Services of Midwest Inc., Appellate Court of Illinois, First District, Fourth Division, (6/29/1989).

Melody Manor Convalescent Center v. Mississippi State Dep't of Health, Supreme Court of Mississippi, (6/28/1989).

Commonwealth Dep't of Health v. Rehab Hosp. Services Corp., Commonwealth Court of Pennsylvania, (6/12/1989).

National Health Corp. v. South Carolina Dep't of Health & Environmental Control, Court of Appeals of South Carolina, (4/24/1989).

Providence Hospital of Everett v. State of Washington, Department of Social & Health Services, and A.N. Shinpoch, Secretary of the Department of Social & Health Services, Thurston County Superior Court, (4/13/1989).

Shoolman v. Health Facilities Appeals Bd. (1989), Supreme Judicial Court of Massachusetts, Suffolk, (2/7/1989).

Delaware County Memorial Hospital v. Bowen, United States Court of Appeals for the Third Circuit, (1/25/1989).

St. Joseph's Hospital v. Department of Health & Rehabilitative Services, Court of Appeals of Florida First District, (12/21/1988).

State ex rel. Missouri Health Care Assoc. v. Missouri Health Facilities Review Committee, Court of Appeals of Missouri, (10/25/1988).

Condell Hosp. v. Illinois Health Facilities Planning Bd., Supreme Court of Illinois, (9/29/1988).

Commission on Hospitals & Health Care v. Stamford Hospital, Supreme Court of Connecticut, (8/16/1988).

Bath Memorial Hospital v. Maine Health Care Finance Com., United States Court of Appeals For the First Circuit, (8/8/1988).

Liljeberg v. Health Services Acquisition Corp., Supreme Court of the United States, (6/17/1988).

Huron Valley Hospital Inc. v. Pontiac, United States District Court for the Eastern District of Michigan, (5/26/1988).

Grant Center Hospital Inc. v. Health Group of Jackson Inc., Supreme Court of Mississippi, (5/25/1988).

North Memorial Medical Center v. Minnesota Dept. of Health, Court of Appeals of Minnesota, (5/24/1988).

Park City Hosp. v. Commission on Hosp. & Health Care, Appellate Court of Connecticut, (5/17/1988).

Catholic Medical Ctr. v. Elliot Hosp., Supreme Court of New Hampshire, (5/6/1988).

Johnston-Willis Ltd. v. Kenley, Court of Appeals of Virginia, (5/3/1988).

Manasota Osteopathic Gen. Hosp. v. State Dep't of Health & Rehabilitative Serv., Court of Appeal of Florida First District, (4/6/1988).

Humana of Kentucky Inc.v. NKC Hospitals Inc., Supreme Court of Kentucky, (3/31/1988).

Merle West Medical Center v. State Health Planning & Dev. Agency, Court of Appeals of Oregon, (2/26/1988).

St. Mary's Hosp. v. State Health Planning & Dev. Tax Commissioner, Supreme Court of Appeals of West Virginia, (12/15/1987).

Charter Hospital of Bucks County Inc. v. Commonwealth Dep't of Health, Commonwealth Court of Pennsylvania, (12/11/1987).

Bayonet Point Regional Medical Center v. Department of Health & Rehabilitative Services, Court of Appeals of Florida First District, (11/24/1987).

Grandview Surgical Center Inc. v. Holy Spirit Hospital of Sisters of Christian Charity, Commonwealth Court of Pennsylvania, (11/19/1987).

In re St. Luke's Hosp., Supreme Court of South Dakota, (10/21/1987).

Condell Hospital v. Health Facilities Planning Bd., Appellate Court of Illinois, First District Second Division, (9/29/1987).

Community Hospital of New Port Richey/University Psychiatric Center Inc. v. Department of Health & Rehabilitative Services, Court of Appeals of Florida First District, (9/29/1987).

George Washington University Medical Center v. District of Columbia Bd. of Appeals & Review, District of Columbia Court of Appeals, (8/31/1987).

Tarabishi v. McAlester Regional Hospital, United States Court of Appeals for the Tenth Circuit, (8/17/1987).

Platte County Medical Center Inc. v. Missouri Health Facilities Review Committee, Court of Appeals of Missouri Westerm District, (8/11/1987).

Metropolitan Hospital v. Commonwealth Dep't of Health, Commonwealth Court of Pennsylvania, (6/18/1987).

Metropolitan Hospital v. Thornburgh Civil Action, United States District Court For the Eastern District of Pennsylvania, (6/11/1987).

PIA Psychiatric Hospitals Inc. v. Missouri Health Facilities Review Committee, Court of Appeals of Missouri, Eastern District, Division Four, (3/10/1987).

In re Applications of Overlook Hospital, Superior Court of New Jersey Appellate Division, (3/3/1987).

Arkansas Health Planning & Dev. Agency v. Hot Spring County Memorial Hospital, Supreme Court of Arkansas, (2/9/1987).

South Carolina Baptist Hospital v. South Carolina Dep't of Health & Environmental Control, Supreme Court of South Carolina, (2/9/1987).

University Medical Park Ltd. v. Department of Health & Rehabilitative Services, Court of Appeals of Florida Second District, (1/28/1987).

Southern Maryland Hospital Center Inc. v. Ft. Washington Community Hospital Inc., Court of Appeals of Maryland, (1/12/1987).

Roanoke Memorial Hospitals v. Kenley, Court of Appeals of Virginia, (1/6/1987).

Baptist Hospital Inc. v. State Dep't of Health & Rehabilitative Services, Court of Appeals of Florida First District, (12/23/1986).

Hospital Corp. of America v. FTC, United States Court of Appeals for the Seventh Circuit, (12/18/1986).

Huron Valley Hospital Inc. v. Pontiac, United States District Court For the Eastern District of Michigan, Southern Division, (12/18/1986).

State Health Planning & Dev. Agency v. Salem Hospital CA, Court of Appeals of Oregon, (12/17/1986).

Charter Medical-Fayette County Inc. v. Health Planning Agency Inc., Court of Appeals of Georgia, (12/5/1986).

San Bernardino Community Hospital v. Meeks, Court of Appeal of California, Fourth Appellate District, Division Two, (11/25/1986).

PIA Psychiatric Hospitals Inc. v. Missouri Health Facilities Review Committee, Court of Appeals of Missouri Western District, (11/25/1986

Sparks Regional Medical Center v. Arkansas Dep't of Human Services, Supreme Court of Arkansas, (11/24/1986).

Pontiac Osteopathic Hospital v. Department of Public Health, Court of Appeals of Michigan, (11/19/1986).

Hospital Corp. of America v. Robinson, Court of Appeal of Louisiana, (11/12/1986).

Charter Pines Hospital Inc. v. North Carolina Dep't of Human Resources, Court of Appeals of North Carolina, (11/4/1986).

Charlotte-Mecklenburg Hospital Authority v. North Carolina Dep't of Human Resources, Court of Appeals of North Carolina, (10/21/1986).

Psychiatric Hospitals of Florida Inc.v. State Dep't of Health & Rehabilitative Services, Court of Appeals of Florida First District, (10/16/1986).

Doctors' Osteopathic Medical Center Inc. v. Department of Health & Rehabilitative Services, Court of Appeals of Florida First District, (10/6/1986).

NME Hospitals Inc. v. Department of Health & Rehabilitative Services, Court of Appeals of Florida First District, (10/5/1986).

Methodist Regional Hospital System Inc. v. State Dep't of Health & Rehabilitative Services, Court of Appeals of Florida First District, (9/24/1986).

Humana of Fla. Inc. v. Department of Health & Rehabilitative Serv., Court of Appeals of Florida First District, (9/11/1986).

Potters Medical Center v. City Hospital Assoc., United States Court of Appeals for the Sixth Circuit, (9/4/1986).

St. Joseph's Hospital Inc. v. Hospital Corp. of America, United States Court of Appeals For the Eleventh Circuit, (8/5/1986).

Charter Medical-Southeast Inc. v. State Dep't of Health & Rehabilitative Services, Court of Appeals of Florida First District, (7/29/1986).

Psychiatric Institutes of America Inc. v. Department of Health & Rehabilitative Services, Court of Appeals of Florida First District, (7/17/1986).

Morton F. Plant Hospital Assoc. v. State, Court of Appeals of Florida First District, (7/9/1986).

Humana Hospital Corp. v. North Carolina Dep't of Human Resources Div. of Facility Services, Court of Appeals of North Carolina, (7/1/1986).

NME Hospitals Inc. v. Department of Health & Rehabilitative Services, Court of Appeals of Florida First District, (6/24/1986).

Sinai Hospital of Baltimore Inc. v. Maryland Health Resources Planning Com., Court of Appeals of Maryland, (6/10/1986).

Huron Valley Hospital Inc. v. Pontiac, United States Court of Appeals for the Sixth Circuit, (5/30/1986).

University Community Hospital v. Department of Health & Rehabilitative Services, Court of Appeals of Florida Second District, (5/16/1986).

Hospital Bldg. Co. v. Trustees of Rex Hospital, United States Court of Appeals For the Fourth Circuit, (4/18/1986).

Humana Inc. v. Department of Health & Rehabilitative Services, Court of Appeals of Florida Fourth District, (4/16/1986).

Balsam v. Department of Health & Rehabilitative Services, Court of Appeals of Florida First District, (3/31/1986).

Good Samaritan Hospital Inc. v. Department of Health & Rehabilitative Services, District Court of Appeal of the State of Florida Fourth District, (3/26/1986).

Chatham County Hospital Authority v. St. Joseph's Hospital Inc., Court of Appeals of Georgia, (3/21/1986).

Ft. Washington Community Hospital Inc. v. Southern Maryland Hospital Center, Court of Special Appeals of Maryland, (3/5/1986).

Florida Medical Center v. Department of Health & Rehabilitative Services, Court of Appeals of Florida First District, (3/4/1986).

University Medical Center Inc. v. Department of Health & Rehabilitative Services, Court of Appeals of Florida First District, (2/13/1986).

Doctors' Hospital of Prince George's County v. Maryland Health Resources Planning Com., Court of Special Appeals of Maryland, (1/8/1986).

Clifton Springs Sanitarium Co., v. Axelrod, M.D. as Commissioner of the Dept. of Health, Supreme Court, Appellate Division, Fourth Department, (12/20/1985).

HCA Health Services of Midwest Inc. v. Administrative Hearing Com., Court of Appeals of Missouri Eastern District, Division Two, (11/26/1985).

North Ridge General Hospital Inc. v. NME Hospitals Inc., Court of Appeals of Florida First District, (11/15/1985).

Baptist Memorial Hospital System v. Texas Health Facilities Comm., Court of Appeals of Texas Third District, Austin, (10/2/1985).

Presbyterian Medical Center v. Texas Health Facilities Comm., Court of Appeals of Texas Third District, Austin, (10/2/1985).

Central Florida Regional Hospital v. Daytona Beach General Hospital, Court of Appeals of Florida First District, (9/17/1985).

District of Columbia Hosp. Assoc. v. Barry, District of Columbia Court of Appeals, (9/16/1985).

Baptist Memorial Hospital-De Soto Inc. v. Mississippi Health Care Comm. Civil Action, United States District Court For the Southern District of Mississippi, (9/10/1985).

Southwest Virginia Health Sys. Agency v. Kenley, Circuit Court of the City of Salem, Virginia, (9/6/1985).

Southern Nev. Memorial Hosp. v. Department of Human Resources, Supreme Court of Nevada, (8/27/1985).

Community Psychiatric Ctrs. v. Department of Health & Rehabilitative Serv., Court of Appeals of Florida First District, (8/20/1985).

University Medical Center Inc. v. Department of Health & Rehabilitative Services, Court of Appeals of Florida First District, (8/20/1985).

In re King Memorial Hospital Inc., United States Court of Appeals for the Eleventh Circuit, (8/12/1985).

Hospital Group of Western North Carolina Inc. v. North Carolina Dep't of Human Resources, Court of Appeals of North Carolina, (8/6/1985).

State Bd. of Health v. Virginia Hospital Ass'n, Court of Appeals of Virginia, (8/6/1985).

St. Joseph's Hosp. v. Hospital Auth. of Am., United States District Court For the Southern District of Georgia, Savannah Division, (7/18/1985).

In re Wellesley Corp., Supreme Court of Ohio, (7/10/1985).

Harrisburg Hospital v. Thornburgh, United States District Court for the Middle District of Pennsylvania, (6/25/1985).

Southern Chester County Medical Ctr. v. Commonwealth Dep't of Health, Commonwealth Court of Pennsylvania, (6/24/1985).

Huron Valley Hospital Inc. v. Pontiac, United States District Court For the Eastern District of Michigan, Southern Division, (6/17/1985).

Texas Health Facilities Comm. v. Presbyterian Hospital North, Supreme Court of Texas, (5/29/1985).

Humana Hosp. Corp. v. Oklahoma Health Planning Comm'n, Supreme Court of Oklahoma, (5/28/1985).

University Community Hospital v. Department of Health & Rehabilitative Services, Court of Appeals of Florida Second District, (5/22/1985).

Hillsborough County Hospital Authority v. Tampa Heart Institute, Court of Appeals of Florida Second District, (5/22/1985).

Humana, Inc. & Plantation General Hosp. v. Department of Health and Rehabilitative Services, Court of Appeal of Florida First District, (5/16/1985).

Humana Inc. v. Department of Health & Rehabilitative Services, Court of Appeals of Florida First District, (5/16/1985).

Governor v. Rehab Hospital Services Corp., Supreme Court of Arkansas, (4/15/1985).

Rehab Hospital Services Corp. v. Delta-Hills Health Systems Agency Inc., Supreme Court of Arkansas, (4/15/1985).

Princeton Community Hosp. v. State Health Planning, Supreme Court of Appeals of West Virginia, (3/22/1985).

United Hosp. Ctr. v. Richardson, Supreme Court of Appeals of West Virginia, (3/22/1985).

Johns Hopkins Hospital Inc. v. Insurance Commissioner, Court of Appeals of Maryland, (3/5/1985).

State Health Planning Review Bd. v. Piedmont Hospital Inc., Court of Appeals of Georgia, (2/6/1985).

Florida Medical Center v. Department of Health & Rehabilitative Services, Court of Appeals of Florida First District, (1/24/1985).

Naples Community Hospital Inc. v. Department of Health & Rehabilitative Services, Court of Appeals of Florida First District, (1/18/1985).

Collier Medical Center Inc. v. State Dep't of Health & Rehabilitative Services, Court of Appeals of Florida First District, (1/8/1985).

Mercy Health Center Div. of Sisters of Mercy Health Corp. v. Iowa State Dep't of Health, Supreme Court of Iowa, (10/17/1984).

In re Application for Certificate of Need by HCA Health Serv., Supreme Court of Wyoming, (10/3/1984).

County of Dodge on Behalf of Memorial Hospital v. Department of Health, Supreme Court of Nebraska, (9/21/1984).

Humana Medical Corp. v. State Health Planning & Dev. Agency, Court of Civil Appeals of Alabama, (8/22/1984).

Doctors' Osteopathic Medical Center Inc. v. Department of Health & Rehabilitative Services, Court of Appeals of Florida First District, (8/7/1984).

North Carolina ex rel. Edmisten v. P.I.A. Asheville Inc., United States Court of Appeals For the Fourth Circuit, (7/16/1984).

Shawnee Mission Medical Center v. Kansas Dep't of Health & Environment, Supreme Court of Kansas, (7/13/1984).

Starks v. Kentucky Health Facilities, Court of Appeals of Kentucky, (7/6/1984).

In re Lorain Comm. Hosp., Court of Appeals Ninth Judicial District of Ohio, (5/30/1984).

St. Joseph's Hill Infirmary Inc. v. Mandl, Court of Appeals of Missouri, Eastern District, Division Four, (5/22/1984).

Huron Valley Hospital Inc. v. Pontiac Civil Action, United States District Court For the Eastern District of Michigan, Southern Division, (4/30/1984).

Baptist Hospital Inc. v. Humana of Kentucky Inc., Court of Appeals of Kentucky, (4/27/1984).

Texas Health Facilities Com. v. Charter Medical-Dallas Inc., Supreme Court of Texas, (2/15/1984).

In re Certificate of Need Application by Community Psychiatric Centers Inc. etc., Supreme Court of Kansas, (1/13/1984).

Statewide Health Coordinating Council v. General Hospitals of Humana Inc., Supreme Court of Arkansas, (12/12/1983).

Presbyterian Hospital North v. Texas Health Facilities Comm., Court of Appeals of Texas Third District, Austin, (11/23/1983).

St. Francis/St. George Hospital Inc. v. Blue Cross, Court of Appeals First Appellate District, Hamilton County Ohio, (11/23/1983).

North Fulton Community Hospital Inc. v. State Health Planning & Dev. Agency, Court of Appeals of Georgia, (11/9/1983).

State Health Planning & Dev. Agency v. Baptist Medical Center, Court of Civil Appeals of Alabama, (11/2/1983).

Loyd v. Georgia State Health Planning & Dev. Agency, Court of Appeals of Georgia, (10/25/1983).

Ex parte State Health Planning & Dev. Agency, Court of Civil Appeals of Alabama, (8/31/1983).

Charter Medical-Dallas Inc. v. Texas Health Facilities Comm., Court of Appeals of Texas Third District, Austin, (7/20/1983).

Farmworker Rights Org v. Department of Health & Rehabilitative Serv., District Court of Appeal of Florida First District, (4/14/1983).

In re Review of Decision of Kansas Corp. Comm. etc., Supreme Court of Kansas, (2/19/1983).

Gulf Coast Hospital Inc. v. Department of Health & Rehabilitative Services, District Court of Appeal of Florida First District, (12/16/1982).

Rush City Hospital v. Sandstone Area Hospital, Supreme Court of Minnesota, (11/24/1982).

Olathe Community Hospital v. Kansas Corp. Comm., Supreme Court of Kansas, (10/22/1982).

Shenango Valley Osteopathic Hospital v. Department of Health, Supreme Court of Pennsylvania, (10/21/1982).

Hospital Bldg. Co. v. Trustees of Rex Hospital, United States Court of Appeals For the Fourth Circuit, (10/19/1982).

Gateway Hospital Corp. East v. Department of Health & Rehabilitative Services, District Court of Appeal of Florida First District, (9/29/1982).

Mercy Hospital v. Commonwealth Dep't of Health, Commonwealth Court of Pennsylvania, (9/21/1982).

Westchester General Hospital v. Department of Health & Rehabilitative Services, District Court of Appeal of Florida First District, (9/8/1982).

Sisters of Providence v. Department of Health & Social Serv., Supreme Court of Alaska, (7/30/1982).

Farmworker Rights Org. v. Department of Health & Rehabilitative Serv., Court of Appeals of Florida First District, (7/20/1982).

Westchester General Hospital v. State Dep't of Health & Rehabilitative Services, Court of Appeals of Florida First District, (3/22/1982).

Community Psychiatric Centers Inc. v. Grant, United States Court of Appeals Ninth Circuit, (12/28/1981).

Huron Valley Hospital Inc. v. Pontiac, United States Court of Appeals Sixth Circuit, (12/11/1981).

Huron Valley Hospital Inc. v. Michigan State Health Facilities Comm., Court of Appeals of Michigan, (10/7/1981).

East Tennessee Health Improv. Council Inc. v. Tennessee Health Facilities Comm., Court of Appeals of Tennessee, Middle Section, (9/18/1981).

Paul Kimball Hospital Inc. v. Brick Township Hospital Inc., Supreme Court of New Jersey, (6/24/1981).

National Gerimedical Hospital and Gerontology Center, Petitioner, v. Blue Cross of Kansas City and Blue Cross Association, Supreme Court of the United States, (6/15/1981).

Tulsa Area Hosp. Council Inc. v. Oral Roberts Univ., Supreme Court of Oklahoma, (3/24/1981).

Shoolman v. Health Facilities Appeals Bd., Appeals Court of Massachusetts, Suffolk, (12/11/1980).

Hospital of St. Raphael v. Commission on Hospitals & Health Care, Supreme Court of Connecticut, (11/11/1980).

South Broward Hospital Dist. v. Department of Health & Rehabilitative Services etc., Court of Appeal of Florida Fourth District, (6/18/1980).

Placentia-Linda Community Hosp. Inc. v. Zaretsky, Court of Appeal of California, Fourth Appellate District, Division Two, (6/2/1980).

Wausau Hospitals Inc. v. Department of Health & Social Services, Court of Appeals of Wisconsin, (3/18/1980).

Greater St. Louis Health Systems Agency v. Teasdale, United States District Court For the Eastern District of Missouri, (3/11/1980).

Montana Health Sys. Agency v. Montana Bd. of Health & Environmental. Sciences, Supreme Court of Montana, (3/2/1980).

State ex rel. Metzler v. Sisters of Charity of Leavenworth Health Services Corp., Supreme Court of Kansas, (1/19/1980).

National Gerimedical Hospital & Gerontology v. Blue Cross of Kansas City, United States District Court For the Western District of Missouri Greenville Division, (11/2/1979).

Iowa State Dep't of Health v. Hertko, Supreme Court of Iowa, (8/29/1979).

Pratt v. Board of County Commissioners, Supreme Court of Kansas, (7/14/1979).

Suburban Medical Center v. Olathe Community Hospital, Supreme Court of Kansas, (7/14/1979).

Los Alamitos Gen. Hosp. Inc. v. Lackner, Court of Appeal of California, Second Appellate District, Division One, (11/17/1978).

Samson v. Bureau of Community Medical Facilities Planning etc., Court of Appeals of Florida First District, (10/24/1978).

Texas Health Facilities Com. v. Baptist General Convention, Court of Civil Appeals of Texas, (10/19/1978).

Doctors Hospital Inc. v. Califano, United States District Court for the District of Columbia, (10/6/1978).

Ross Gen. Hosp. Inc. v. Lackner, Court of Appeal of California, Second Appellate District, Division One, (7/28/1978).

Charter Medical Corp. v. Mississippi Health Planning & Development Agency, Supreme Court of Mississippi, (7/26/1978).

Bakersfield Community Hosp. v. Department of Health, Court of Appeal of California, Fifth Appellate District, (12/29/1977).

St. Joseph's Hospital & Medical Center v. Finley, Superior Court of New Jersey Appellate Division, (10/14/1977).

Irvington General Hospital v. Department of Health, Superior Court of New Jersey Appellate Division, (5/2/1977).

Humana of Tennessee v. Tennessee Health Facilities Comm., Supreme Court of Tennessee, (4/25/1977).

Bureau of Community Medical Facilities Planning of Dep't of Health & Rehabilitative Services v. Samson, Court of Appeals of Florida First District, (2/4/1977).

Health Facilities Research Inc. v. Bureau of Community Medical Facilities etc., Court of Appeals of Florida First District, (12/14/1976).

Palmetto General Hospital Inc. v. State Dep't of Health & Rehabilitative Services, Court of Appeals of Florida First District, (5/24/1976).

Humana of Florida Inc. v. Keller, Court of Appeals of Florida First District, (4/2/1976).

Olathe Hospital Foundation Inc. v. Extendicare Inc., Supreme Court of Kansas, (7/17/1975).

Public Citizen, Inc., Oli, Chemcial, and Atomic Workers International Unione, AFL-CIO, National Consumer's League, National Urban Coalition, and Communities in Action Together Petition to Department of Health, Education and Welfare, Department of Health, Education and Welfare, (5/7/1975).

Extendicare Inc. v. State Coordinating Council for Health Planning, Supreme Court of Kansas, (3/1/1975).

University of Utah Medical Ctr. v. Bonneville County, Supreme Court of Idaho, (7/3/1974).

La Moure v. State Health Council, Supreme Court of North Dakota, (12/4/1973).

In re Certificate of Need for Aston Park Hosp. Inc., Supreme Court of North Carolina, (1/26/1973).

Woodland Park Hospital Inc. v. Comprehensive Health Planning Authority, Court of Appeals of Oregon, (12/22/1972).

Williamson v. Snow, Supreme Court of North Carolina, (2/24/1954).

II I. Intermediate Care Facility

Woods Serv. v. Department of Pub. Welfare, Commonwealth Court of Pennsylvania, (8/1/1996).

II J. Kidney Dialysis Center

Bio-Medical Applications of the District of Columbia d/b/a/ Fresenius Medical Care North America v. District of Columbia Board of Appeals and Review, District of Columbia Court of Appeals, (7/24/2003).

Dialysis Care of N.C. L.L.C. v. North Carolina HHS Div. of Facility Serv. Certificate of Need Section, Court of Appeals of North Carolina, (5/2/2000).

Bio-Medical Applications of N.C. Inc. v. North Carolina Dep't of Human Resources Div. of Facility Serv. Certificate of Need Section, Court of Appeals of North Carolina, (9/16/1999).

Bio-Medical Applications Inc. v. Office of Community Medical Facilities etc., Court of Appeals of Florida First District, (8/7/1997).

Bio-Medical Applications of Clearwater Inc. v. Department of Health & Rehabilitative Services etc., Court of Appeal of Florida Second District, (2/23/1997).

Boca Raton Artificial Kidney Ctr. v. Department of Health & Rehabilitative Serv., Court of Appeals of Florida First District, (10/22/1987).

Renal Care of Illinois Inc. v. Health Facilities Planning Bd., Appellate Court of Illinois, First District, Fifth Division, (8/7/1987).

In re Appeal from Approval of Application of Wake Kidney Clinic P.A., Court of Appeals of North Carolina, (5/19/1987).

Boca Raton Artificial Kidney Ctr. v. Department of Health & Rehabilitative Serv., Court of Appeals of Florida First District, (7/29/1986).

Boca Raton Artificial Kidney Center Inc. v. Florida Dep't of Health & Rehabilitative Services, Court of Appeals of Florida First District, (8/20/1985).

Regional Dialysis of Anniston v. Northeast Alabama Kidney Clinic Inc., Court of Civil Appeals of Alabama, (7/17/1985).

In re Appeal of Banks, Supreme Court of Kansas, (7/17/1981).

National Nephrology Foundation v. Dougherty, Superior Court of New Jersey Appellate Division, (1/12/1976).

II K. Laboratories

Bayonet Point Hospital Inc. v. Department of Health & Rehabilitative Services, Court of Appeals of Florida First District, (6/25/1986).

II L. Long Term Care

Healthcare Services Group, Inc. v. Royal Healthcare of Middlesex, LLC., United States District Court for the District of New Jersey, (8/13/2003).

Matter of Town of Gates v. Commissioner of NY State Office of Mental Retardation and Developmental Disabilities and Finger Lakes Developmental Disabilities Services Office, Supreme Court, Appellate Division, Fourth Department, (12/31/1997).

Oregon Health Care Ass'n v. Health Div., Court of Appeals of Oregon, (6/25/1997).

In re Healthco Facilities Inc., Court of Appeals of Ohio Tenth Appellate District, Franklin County, (4/21/1992).

Stewart v. Commonwealth Dep't of Health, Commonwealth Court of Pennsylvania, (6/7/1991).

In re Christian Care Home Inc., Court of Appeals of Ohio Tenth Appellate District, Franklin County, (6/6/1991).

In re Christian Care Home Inc., Court of Appeals of Ohio Tenth Appellate District, Franklin County, (12/28/1989).

Omaha Health Facilities Inc. v. Department of Health, Supreme Court of Nebraska, (4/27/1989).

Stewart v. Commonwealth State Health Facility Hearing Bd., Commonwealth Court of Pennsylvania, (7/12/1988).

Rowan Health Properties Inc. v. North Carolina Dep't of Human Resources Div. of Facility Services Certificate of Need Section, Court of Appeals of North Carolina, (3/15/1988).

In the matter of the Town of Hempstead v. Commissioner, State of New York Office of Mental Retardation and Developmental Disabilities, Supreme Court, Appellate Division, Second Department, (6/2/1986).

Northbrook Residents Assoc. v. Iowa State Dep't of Health Office etc., Supreme Court of Iowa, (11/12/1980).

II M. Medical Office Buildings

Jackson HMA, Inc. v. Mississippi State Department of Health, Supreme Court of Mississippi, (4/25/2002).

Oficinas Medicas Inc. v. De Melecio, United States District Court for the District of Puerto Rico, (3/12/1999).

II N. Methadone Clinic

Colonial Management Group, L.P. v. State Health Planning and Development Agency et al., Court of Civil Appeals of Alabama, (12/13/2002).

II O. Nursing Homes

Beechwood Restorative Care Center v. Laura E. Leeds, United States District Court for the Western District of New York, (5/4/2004).

Attala County Board of Supervisors d/b/a Attala Care Center v. Mississippi State Department of Health, Supreme Court of Mississippi, (2/26/2004).

Community Care Center of Lemay v. Missouri Health Facilities Review Committee, Court of Appeals of Missouri, Western District, (11/5/2002).

Sheffield Towers Rehabilitation and Health Care Center v. Antonia Novello et al., Supreme Court, Nassau County, (4/22/2002).

Greenwood Manor v. Iowa Dep't of Pub. Health, Supreme Court of Iowa, (4/3/2002).

Lapid-Laurel, L.L.C. v. Zoning Board of Adjustment of the Township of Scotch Plains, United States Court of Appeals, Third Circuit, (3/15/2002).

Millcreek Manor v. Department of Public Welfare, Commonwealth Court of Pennsylvania, (11/6/2001).

Castle Nursing Home v. Donald L. Sullivan, United States Court of Appeals for the Sixth Circuit, (8/9/2001).

Ex parte Beverly Enterprises-Alabama Inc., Supreme Court of Alabama, (7/13/2001).

Scott v. Ashland Healthcare Ctr., Supreme Court of Tennessee, Middlesection, at Nashville, (7/9/2001).

First Baptist Church of Crown Heights Center for Nursing & Rehabilitation, Inc. v. Antonia Novello, as Commissioner of Health of the Department of Health of the State of New York, Supreme Court, Kings County, New York, (4/24/2001).

Crestmont Cleveland Partnership v. Ohio Dep't of Health, Court of Appeals of Ohio Tenth Appellate District, Franklin County, (9/28/2000).

Living Centers-Southeast Inc. v. North Carolina HHS, Court of Appeals of North Carolina, (7/5/2000).

Ford Hull-Mar Nursing Home Inc. v. Marr Knapp Crawfis & Assoc., Court of Appeals of Ohio Seventh Appellate District, Jefferson County, (6/22/2000).

EBG Health Care III Inc. v. Missouri Health Facilities Review Comm., Court of Appeals of Missouri Western District, (2/15/2000).

Carriage Hill-Cabin John Inc. v. Maryland Health Resources Planning Commission, Court of Special Appeals of Maryland, (2/25/1999).

Rutherford Hosp. Inc. v. RNH Partnership, United States Court of Appeals for the Fourth Circuit, (2/5/1999).

Ex parte Forest Manor Inc., Supreme Court of Alabama, (12/11/1998).

Miami Jewish Home & Hosp. for the Aged v. Agency for Health Care Admin., Court of Appeal of Florida Third District, (8/8/1998).

Catonsville Nursing Home v. Loveman, Court of Appeals of Maryland, (5/15/1998).

Forest Manor Inc. v. State Health Planning & Dev. Agency, Court of Civil Appeals of Alabama, (5/1/1998).

Arkansas Health Services Agency and Arkansas Health Services Commission, Arkansas Health Care Association v. Desiderata, Inc., Supreme Court of Arkansas, (1/22/1998).

Carrolton Inc. v. Pine Manor Rest Home (In re Pine Manor Rest Home), United States Court of Appeals for the Fourth Circuit, (11/24/1997).

In re Cumberland Care Ctr., Court of Appeals of Ohio Tenth Appellate District, Franklin County, (11/4/1997).

Arbor Health Care Co. v. Delaware Health Resources Bd., Superior Court of Delaware New Castle, (5/20/1997).

Agency for Health Care Admin. v. Mount Sinai Medical Ctr., Court of Appeal of Florida First District, (4/17/1997).

West Side Deutscher Frauen Verein v. Tracy, Supreme Court of Ohio, (4/2/1997).

Agency for Health Care Administration, Lifemark Hospitals of Florida, Baptist Hospital of Miami, St. Anne's Nursing Center, St. Anne's Residence, Inc., Florida Convalescent Associates, and Cedars Health-Care Group, Ltd., Petitioners, v. Mount Sinai Medical Center of Greater Miami, Marco Healthcare Investors, Inc., Brookwood Extended Care Center of Homestead, Beverly Enterprises-Florida, Arbor Health Care Company, Meadowbrook Healthcare Services of North Carolina, Marriott Senior Living Services, Miami Beach Healthcare Group, Ltd., and Kendall Healthcare Group, Ltd. Respondants, Florida District Court of Appeals, (4/1/1997).

Carrolton Inc. v. Pine Manor Rest Home, United States District Court for the Eastern District of North Carolina Western Division, (3/31/1997).

Vantage Healthcare Corporation, d/b/a Beverly Manor Rehabilitation and Specialty Care Center at Manatee County, Appellant, v. Agency for Health Care Administration and Manatee Springs Nursing Center, Inc., Appellees, District Court of Appeals of Florida, (1/27/1997).

In re Mazal Health Care, Court of Appeals of Ohio Tenth Appellate District, Franklin County, (1/9/1997).

Retirement Villages v. North Carolina Dep't of Human Resources, Court of Appeals of North Carolina, (11/19/1996).

Loveman v. Catonsville Nursing Home, Court of Special Appeals of Maryland, (11/4/1996).

Public Health Dep't v. Rivergate Manor, Supreme Court of Michigan, (7/16/1996).

Health Care & Retirement Corp. of America v. Tarpon Springs Hosp. Found., Court of Appeal of Florida First District, (4/4/1996).

In re Beechmont, Court of Appeals of Ohio Tenth Appellate District, Franklin County, (3/29/1996).

West Bay Manor Co. v. Cuyahoga County Bd. of Revision, Supreme Court of Ohio, (8/30/1995).

Heritage House v. Bailey, Court of Appeals of Indiana First District, (6/12/1995).

Arbor Health Care Co. v. State, Court of Appeal of Florida First District, (6/1/1995).

Britthaven Inc. v. North Carolina Dep't of Human Resources Div. of Facility Serv., Court of Appeals of North Carolina, (4/4/1995).

Springwood Assocs. v. Health Facilities Planning Bd., Appellate Court of Illinois, Fourth District, (3/3/1995).

In re Certificate of Need of Arnold Walter Nursing Home, Superior Court of New Jersey Appellate Division, (11/23/1994).

Appeal of Courville (New Hampshire Health Serv. Planning & Review Bd.) v. Supreme Court of New Hampshire, (11/7/1994).

In re National Church Residence Care Ctr., Court of Appeals of Ohio Tenth Appellate District, Franklin County, (9/20/1994).

Greenbriar Nursing Home v. Pilley, Supreme Court of Louisiana, (5/23/1994).

Oklahoma Dept. of Health v. Medi-Plex Nursing Ctrs. Inc., Court of Appeals of Oklahoma Division Two, (2/8/1994).

Beverly Enters. v. Columbus Health Care, Nebraska Court of Appeals, (12/28/1993).

In re Heartland of Mentor, Court of Appeals of Ohio Tenth Appellate District, Franklin County, (12/23/1993).

In re Pavilion, Court of Appeals of Ohio Tenth Appellate District, Franklin County, (10/5/1993).

Greenbriar Nursing Home v. Pilley, Court of Appeal of Louisiana, (7/2/1993).

Summit Villa Care Ctr. Inc. v. Ohio Dep't of Health, Court of Appeals of Ohio Tenth Appellate District, Franklin County, (7/14/1992).

Maple Leaf of Lee County Health Care v. Department of Health & Rehabilitative Serv., Court of Appeal of Florida First District, (6/17/1992).

Ex parte Virginia D. Condra Willis, Supreme Court of Alabama, (6/15/1992).

State Health Planning Agency v. Cribb Industries Inc., Court of Appeals of Georgia, (5/19/1992).

Watkins v. Restorative Care Center Inc., Court of Appeals of Washington, Division One, (3/30/1992).

Frene Valley Corp. v. Missouri Health Facilities Review Committee, Court of Appeals of Missouri Western District, (10/29/1991).

Durant v. Humphreys County Memorial Hospital/Extended Care Facility, Supreme Court of Mississippi, (9/18/1991).

IFIDA Health Care Group Ltd. v. Department of Health, Commonwealth Court of Pennsylvania, (8/9/1991).

Morrisons Cove Home v. Department of Health, Commonwealth Court of Pennsylvania, (6/17/1991).

Mitchell Manor Convalescent HomeInc. v. Oklahoma Health Planning Commission, Court of Appeals of Oklahoma Division Two, (3/12/1991).

Department of Health v. Manor Care Inc., Supreme Court of Nebraska, (2/22/1991).

Arkansas Dep't of Human Services v. Hillsboro Manor Nursing Home Inc., Supreme Court of Arkansas, (2/11/1991).

In re Alexander Rand Alzheimer's Center, Court of Appeals of Ohio Tenth Appellate District, Franklin County, (1/15/1991).

In re Labelle Nursing Center, Court of Appeals of Ohio Tenth Appellate District, Franklin County, (8/30/1990).

Huntington Manor of Murphy v. North Carolina Dep't of Human Resources etc., Court of Appeals of North Carolina, (6/19/1990).

Health Care & Retirement Corp. v. Department of Health & Rehabilitative Services, Court of Appeal of Florida First District, (3/29/1990).

Beverly Enterprises-Florida Inc. v. Department of Health & Rehabilitative Services, Court of Appeal of Florida First District, (2/14/1990).

Gummels v. North Carolina Dep't of Human Resources Div. of Facility Services, Court of Appeals of North Carolina, (2/6/1990).

John Ken Alzheimer's Center v. Ohio Certificate of Need Review Bd., Court of Appeals of Ohio Tenth Appellate District, Franklin County, (10/24/1989).

Manor Care Inc. v. Department of Health & Rehabilitative Serv., Court of Appeal of Florida First District, (10/3/1989).

Meridian Inc. v. Department of Health & Rehabilitative Services, Court of Appeals of Florida First District, (9/12/1989).

Department of Health v. Omaha Associates, Supreme Court of Nebraska, (6/16/1989).

In re Bloomingdale Convalescent Center, Superior Court of New Jersey Appellate Division, (5/4/1989).

In re Saltwell Nursing Home, Court of Appeals of Ohio Tenth Appellate District, Franklin County, (4/27/1989).

Ex parte Nursing Home of Dothan Inc., Supreme Court of Alabama, (3/31/1989).

Inverness Convalescent Ctr. v. Department of Health & Rehabilitative Serv., Court of Appeals of Florida First District, (3/16/1989).

Scott v. Consolidated Health Management Inc., Supreme Court of Arkansas, (2/13/1989).

Heritage of Yankton v. South Dakota Dep't of Health, Supreme Court of South Dakota, (11/23/1988).

Ex parte Traylor Nursing Home Inc., Supreme Court of Alabama, (9/30/1988).

State Health Planning Agency v. Mobile Infirmary Assoc., Court of Civil Appeals of Alabama, (9/7/1988).

In re Health Care & Retirement Corp. of America, Supreme Court of North Carolina, (6/2/1988).

Christian Care Home Inc. v. State Certificate of Need Review Bd., Court of Appeals of Ohio Tenth Appellate District, Franklin County, (5/26/1988).

Department of Health v. Columbia West Corp., Supreme Court of Nebraska, (3/18/1988).

Beverly Enterprises-Florida Inc. v. Department of Health & Rehabilitative Services, Court of Appeals of Florida First District, (2/4/1988).

In re Health Care & Retirement Corp. of America, Court of Appeals of North Carolina, (2/2/1988).

Nursing Home of Dothan Inc. v. Alabama State Health Planning & Dev. Agency, Court of Civil Appeals of Alabama, (1/27/1988).

Health Care & Retirement Corp. v. Department of Health & Rehabilitative Services, Court of Appeals of Florida First District, (12/1/1987).

Inverness Convalescent Ctr. v. Department of Health & Rehabilitative Serv., Court of Appeals of Florida First District, (8/26/1987).

In the matter of Meadowbrook Nursing Home v. David Axelrod,as Commissioner of the Dept. of Heath, Supreme Court, Appellate Division, Third Department, (7/16/1987).

Community Care Centers Inc. v. Missouri Health Facilities Review Committee, Court of Appeals of Missouri Eastern District, Division Two, (5/19/1987).

Centennial Villas Inc. v. State, Court of Appeals of Washington, Division Two, (3/2/1987).

Commonwealth Dep't of Health v. Brownsville Golden Age Nursing Home Inc., Commonwealth Court of Pennsylvania, (2/4/1987).

Health Care Medical Facility XXVI Partnership v. State Dep't of Health & Rehabilitative Services, Court of Appeals of Florida First District, (9/24/1986).

Coastal Care Centers Inc. v. Meeks, Court of Appeal of California, First Appellate District, Division Five, (8/7/1986).

Department of Health v. Grand Island Health Care Inc., Supreme Court of Nebraska, (8/1/1986).

Health Care & Retirement Corp. v. Department of Health & Rehabilitative Services, Court of Appeals of Florida First District, (5/14/1986).

Perini Services Inc. v. Maryland Health Resources Planning Comm., Court of Special Appeals of Maryland, (4/7/1986).

Dogwood Square Nursing Center Inc. v. State Health Planning Agency, Supreme Court of Georgia, (2/18/1986).

Gulf Court Nursing Center v. Department of Health & Rehabilitative Services, Court of Appeal of Florida First District, (2/14/1986).

Boone County v. Apex of Arkansas Inc., Supreme Court of Arkansas, (2/3/1986).

Federal Property Management Corp. v. Department of Health & Rehabilitative Services, Court of Appeals of Florida First District, (1/20/1986).

Health Care Management Inc. v. Department of Health & Rehabilitative Services, Court of Appeals of Florida First District, (11/21/1985).

Dogwood Square Nursing Center Inc. v. State Health Planning Agency, Court of Appeals of Georgia, (10/28/1985).

Gulf Court Nursing Center v. Department of Health & Rehabilitative Services, Court of Appeals of Florida First District, (8/20/1985).

Hickory House Nursing Home Inc. v. Commonwealth Dep't of Health, Commonwealth Court of Pennsylvania, (8/14/1985).

Health Quest Realty XII v. Department of Health & Rehabilitative Services, Court of Appeals of Florida First District, (7/16/1985).

Beatrice Manor Inc. v. Department of Health, Supreme Court of Nebraska, (2/1/1985).

Health Care & Retirement Corp. v. Department of Health & Rehabilitative Services, Court of Appeals of Florida First District, (12/20/1984).

Bradbury Memorial Nursing Home v. Tall Pines Manor Associates, Supreme Judicial Court of Maine, (12/18/1984).

Manor Healthcare Corp. v. Northwest Community Hospital, Appellate Court of Illinois, First District Third Division, (11/28/1984).

Lonoke Nursing Home Inc. v. Wayne & Neil Bennett Family Partnership, Court of Appeals of Arkansas, Division 1, (11/28/1984).

Brookwood Extended Care Centers Inc. v. State Dep't of Health & Rehabilitative Services, Court of Appeals of Florida First District, (7/24/1984).

Florida Convalescent Centers Inc. v. State Dep't of Health & Rehabilitative Services, Court of Appeals of Florida First District, (2/8/1984).

In re Change of Bed Category of Tieszen Memorial Home, Supreme Court of South Dakota, (1/18/1984).

Canterbury Nursing Home Inc. v. Alabama State Health Planning & De Agency, Supreme Court of Alabama, (1/28/1983).

Martin County Nursing Center, Inc. v Medco Centers, Inc., Court of Appeals of Indiana, First District, (11/6/1982).

Hale v. Petit Law Docket, Supreme Judicial Court of Maine, (12/9/1981).

Greenbriar Convalescent Center Inc. v. Department of Public Health, Court of Appeals of Michigan, (8/7/1981).

South Cent. Health Planning & Dev. v. Commissioner of Dep't of Admin., Supreme Court of Alaska, (5/15/1981).

Oklahoma Pioneer Inc. v. Carpenter, Supreme Court of Oklahoma, (9/16/1980).

Hollingsworth v. Califano, United States District Court for the Northern District of Mississippi Greenville Division, (6/5/1979).

In the matter of Fairfield Nursing Home v. Robert Whalen, Supreme Court, Appellate Division, Third Department, (7/27/1978).

Gooding v. Oklahoma ex rel. Oklahoma Welfare Commission, United States District Court for the Western District of Oklahoma, (6/21/1977).

Fairhaven Corp. v. Tennessee Health Facilities Com., Court of Appeals of Tennessee, Middle Section, (5/7/1976).

Feiwel OSINA et al., v. City of Chicago, Appellate Court of Illinois, (5/14/1975).

Cooper River Convalescent Center Inc. v. Dougherty, Superior Court of New Jersey Appellate Division, (3/19/1975).

Minnesota State Board of Health v. Governor's Certificate of Need Appeal Board, Supreme Court of Minnesota, (1/17/1975).

Monk & Excelsior Inc. v. Minnesota State Board of Health, Supreme Court of Minnesota, (1/17/1975).

Merry Heart Nursing & Convalescent Home Inc. v. Dougherty, Superior Court of New Jersey Appellate Division, (12/4/1974).

Attoma v. State Department of Social Welfare, Supreme Court, Appellate Division, Fourth Department, (5/19/1966).

In re Professional Nurses Service, Supreme Court of Virginia, (9/10/1998).

CON Medical Personnel Pool v. Management Registry, Court of Appeals of Kentucky, (3/12/1993).

Professional Nurse Inc. v. State Dep't of Health & Rehabilitative Services, Court of Appeals of Florida First District, (1/27/1988).

II P. Physician Group

Dianne J. Ford, M.D. v. Steven L. Stroup, M.D.; Radiation Oncology Associates; Nashville Memorial Health Systems, Inc., United States Court of Appeals for the Sixth Circuit, (4/23/1997).

Garst v. Stoco Inc., United States District Court For the Eastern District of Arkansas, (1/9/1985).

Texas Health Facilities Com. v. El Paso Medical Surgical Assoc., Court of Civil Appeals of Texas Twelfth District, Tyler, (10/26/1978).

II Q. Physician Offices

Adams & Boyle P.C. v. Tennessee Dep't of Health, United States Court of Appeals for the Sixth Circuit, (2/9/2001).

II R. Rehabilitative Care Facility

Mechanicsburg Rehab Sys. v. Department of Health, Commonwealth Court of Pennsylvania, (6/24/1994).

In re Continental Medical Sys., Court of Appeals of Ohio Tenth Appellate District, Franklin County, (8/12/1993).

Rehab Hospital Services Corp. v. Health Systems Agency, Commonwealth Court of Pennsylvania, (4/30/1984).

II S. Residential Treatment Center

Town of Hempstead v. Commissioner, State of New York Office of Mental Health, Supreme Court, Appellate Division, Second Department, (1/24/1994).

Speyer v. Barry, District of Columbia Court of Appeals, (3/29/1991).

Town of Hempstead v. Commissioner, State of New York Office of Mental Health and Pilgrim Psychiatric Center, Respondents, Supreme Court, Appellate Division, Fourth Department, (2/1/1991).

Rivendell Children and Youth Center, a/k/a Rivendell of Tennessee, Inc., v. Tennessee Health Facilities Commission, Charter Medical of East Tennessee, Inc, and Peninsula Psychiatric Hospital, Court of Appeals of Tennessee, Middle Section, (11/4/1987).

Therapeutic Community Residence v. Minnesota Dep't of Health, Court of Appeals of Minnesota, (6/19/1984).

II T. Skilled Nursing

Maryland General Hospital, Inc. v. Tommy G. Thompson, United States Court of Appeals, (10/9/2002).

Gramercy Hill Enters. v. State, Supreme Court of Nebraska, (12/11/1998).

John T. Finley Inc. v. Missouri Health Facilities Review Comm., Court of Appeals of Missouri Western District, (5/9/1995).

McCoy Fla. SNF Trust v. State Dep't of Health & Rehabilitative Serv., Court of Appeal of Florida First District, (12/17/1991).

I. SERVICE

III A. Ambulance Service

Kord's Ambulance Service v. Tucson, Court of Appeals of Arizona, Division Two, Department B, (6/16/1988).

Emergency Medical Transportation v. Tempe, Court of Appeals of Arizona, Division One, Department D, (5/19/1988).

Florida Hospital v. Department of Health & Rehabilitative Services, Court of Appeal of Florida First District, (5/14/1987).

G.M. Ambulance & Medical Supply Co. v. Canyon State Ambulance, Court of Appeals of Arizona, Division Two, Department A, (3/17/1987).

III B. Cardiac Catheterization

Christ Hosp. v. Department of Health & Senior Services, Superior Court of New Jersey Appellate Division, (4/12/2000).

Delta Regional Med. Ctr. v. Mississippi State Dep't of Health, Supreme Court of Mississippi, (12/16/1999).

Phoebe Putney Memorial Hosp. v. Roach, Supreme Court of Georgia, (2/17/1997).

Cabinet for Human Resources Interim Office of Health Planning & Certification v. Jewish Hosp. Healthcare Services, Court of Appeals of Kentucky, (10/25/1996).

Cape Fear Memorial Hosp. v. North Carolina Dep't of Human Resources, Court of Appeals of North Carolina, (2/6/1996).

In re Mansfield Gen. Hospital, Supreme Court of Ohio, (5/24/1995).

Michigan Affiliated Healthcare Sys. v. Department of Pub. Health, Court of Appeals of Michigan, (12/27/1994).

Monmouth Medical Ctr. v. State Dep't of Health, Superior Court of New Jersey Appellate Division, (3/31/1994).

In re Mansfield Gen. Hosp., Court of Appeals of Ohio Tenth Appellate District, Franklin County, (8/31/1993).

Mississippi State Dep't of Health v. Golden Triangle Regional Medical Center, Supreme Court of Mississippi, (6/17/1992).

Mississippi State Dep't of Health v. Southwest Mississippi Regional Medical Center, Supreme Court of Mississippi, (5/3/1991).

Department of Health & Rehabilitative Services v. Florida Medical Center, Court of Appeal of Florida First District, (4/9/1991).

In re Good Samaritan Medical Center, Court of Appeals of Ohio Tenth Appellate District, Franklin County, (1/10/1991).

Catholic Medical Ctr. v. Elliot Hosp., Supreme Court of New Hampshire, (5/6/1988).

Bayonet Point Regional Medical Center v. Department of Health & Rehabilitative Services, Court of Appeals of Florida First District, (11/24/1987).

NME Hospitals Inc. v. Department of Health & Rehabilitative Services, Court of Appeals of Florida First District, (10/5/1986).

Bayonet Point Hospital Inc. v. Department of Health & Rehabilitative Services, Court of Appeals of Florida First District, (6/25/1986).

University Community Hospital v. Department of Health & Rehabilitative Services, Court of Appeals of Florida Second District, (5/16/1986).

Humana Inc. v. Department of Health & Rehabilitative Services, Court of Appeals of Florida Fourth District, (4/16/1986).

University Community Hospital v. Department of Health & Rehabilitative Services, Court of Appeals of Florida Second District, (5/22/1985).

III C. Dialysis

Bio-Medical Applications of the District of Columbia d/b/a/ Fresenius Medical Care North America v. District of Columbia Board of Appeals and Review, District of Columbia Court of Appeals, (7/24/2003).

Dialysis Care of N.C. L.L.C. v. North Carolina HHS Div. of Facility Serv. Certificate of Need Section, Court of Appeals of North Carolina, (5/2/2000).

Bio-Medical Applications of N.C. Inc. v. North Carolina Dep't of Human Resources Div. of Facility Serv. Certificate of Need Section, Court of Appeals of North Carolina, (9/16/1999).

Bio-Medical Applications Inc. v. Office of Community Medical Facilities etc., Court of Appeals of Florida First District, (8/7/1997).

Bio-Medical Applications of Clearwater Inc. v. Department of Health & Rehabilitative Services etc., Court of Appeal of Florida Second District, (2/23/1997).

Boca Raton Artificial Kidney Ctr. v. Department of Health & Rehabilitative Serv., Court of Appeals of Florida First District, (10/22/1987).

Renal Care of Illinois Inc. v. Health Facilities Planning Bd., Appellate Court of Illinois, First District, Fifth Division, (8/7/1987).

In re Appeal from Approval of Application of Wake Kidney Clinic P.A., Court of Appeals of North Carolina, (5/19/1987).

Boca Raton Artificial Kidney Ctr. v. Department of Health & Rehabilitative Serv., Court of Appeals of Florida First District, (7/29/1986).

Boca Raton Artificial Kidney Center Inc. v. Florida Dep't of Health & Rehabilitative Services, Court of Appeals of Florida First District, (8/20/1985).

Regional Dialysis of Anniston v. Northeast Alabama Kidney Clinic Inc., Court of Civil Appeals of Alabama, (7/17/1985).

In re Appeal of Banks, Supreme Court of Kansas, (7/17/1981).

National Nephrology Foundation v. Dougherty, Superior Court of New Jersey Appellate Division, (1/12/1976).

III D. Endoscopy

Columbia Endoscopy Center v. South Carolina Department of Health and Environmental Control, State of South Carolina Administrative Law Judge Division, (12/30/1994).

III E. Home Health

United States ex rel. Joslin v. Community Home Health Civil, United States District Court For the District of Maryland, (11/17/1997).

Hedgework Brentwood Medical Services, Inc. v. South Carolina Department of Health and Environmental Control, State of South Carolina Administrative Law Judge Division, (9/10/1996).

Gulf Coast Health Care v. Agency for Health Care Admin., Court of Appeal of Florida First District, (9/4/1996).

First American Home Care of South Carolina, Inc. v. South Carolina Department of Health and Environmental Control, State of South Carolina Administrative Law Judge Division, (6/7/1996).

ABC Home Health Serv. v. Tennessee Health Facilities Comm'n, Supreme Court of Tennessee, at Nashville, (12/19/1994).

ABC Home Health Serv. v. Georgia Dep't of Medical Assistance, Court of Appeals of Georgia, (12/1/1993).

In re Denial of Request for Declaratory Ruling by Total Care Inc., Court of Appeals of North Carolina, (7/17/1990).

Three Rivers Home Health Serv. Inc. v. Healthmaster Inc., Court of Appeals of Georgia, (10/16/1989).

Home Health Services Inc. v. South Carolina Dep't of Health & Environmental Control, Court of Appeals of South Carolina, (4/24/1989).

Chattahoochee Valley Home Health Care Inc. v. Healthmaster Inc., Court of Appeals of Georgia, (3/3/1989).

Aroostook Home Care Agency Inc. v. Commissioner of Human Services, Supreme Judicial Court of Maine, (12/30/1988).

Gulf Coast Home Health Services Inc. v. Department of Health & Rehabilitative Services, Court of Appeals of Florida First District, (6/8/1988).

Gulf Coast Home Health Services Inc. v. State Dep't of Health & Rehabilitative Services, Court of Appeal of Florida First District, (9/11/1987).

Gulf Coast Home Health Services Inc. v. Department of Health & Rehabilitative Services, Court of Appeals of Florida First District, (9/11/1987).

Gulf Coast Home Health Services Inc. v. Department of Health & Rehabilitative Services, Court of Appeal of Florida First District, (3/2/1987).

Upjohn Healthcare Services Inc. v. Department of Health & Rehabilitative Services, Court of Appeals of Florida First District, (7/22/1986).

Mt. Olive Home Health Care Agency Inc. v. N.C. Dep't of Human Resources, Court of Appeals of North Carolina, (12/3/1985).

West-Mont Community Care v. Board of Health & Envtl. Sciences, Supreme Court of Montana, (7/30/1985).

Health Help Services Inc. v. State Health Planning Agency, Court of Appeals of Georgia, (3/28/1985).

Home Health Professional Services Inc. v. Department of Health & Rehabilitative Services, Court of Appeals of Florida First District, (1/11/1985).

Associated Home Health Agency Inc. v. State Dep't of Health & Rehabilitative Services, Court of Appeals of Florida First District, (6/26/1984).

III F. Hospice

Hospice of Palm Beach County, Inc. v. State of Florida, Agency for Health Care Administration, Court of Appeals of Florida, First District, (4/26/2004).

Memorial Health Sys. v. Halifax Hospice, Court of Appeal of Florida First District, (2/26/1997).

Fairview General Hosp. v. Fletcher, Supreme Court of Ohio, (/11/1992).

St. John's Home Health Agency v. Department of Health & Rehabilitative Services, Court of Appeals of Florida First District, (6/23/1987).

III G. Imaging

Xun Imaging Assocs. v. Department of Health Div. of Need Review, Commonwealth Court of Pennsylvania, (6/16/1994).

III H. Lithotripsy

Ex parte State Health Planning and Development Agency v. LithoMedTech of Alabama, LLC, Supreme Court of Alabama, (11/22/2002).

Prime Lithotripter Operations, Inc., and Prime Medical Services, Inc. v. LithoMedTech of Alabama, LLC; State

Health Planning and Development Agency v. LithoMedTech of Alabama, LLC; Prime Lithotripter Operations, Inc., and Prime Medical Services, Inc. v. Uroventure, LLC, et al., Court of Civil Appeals of Alabama, (12/28/2001).

Alabama Nursing Home Ass'n v. Alabama State Health Planning Agency, Court of Civil Appeals of Alabama, (1/13/1989).

III I. Mobile Health Testing Service

Medcor Inc. v. Finley, Superior Court of New Jersey Appellate Division, (5/22/1981).

III J. Mobile IV Service

Commonwealth of Kentucky v. Family Home Health Care, Inc., Court of Appeals of Kentucky, (2/7/2003).

III K. Neonatal

St. Luke Hosp. v. Health Policy Board, Court of Appeals of Kentucky, (1/5/1996).

University Community Hosp. v. Department of Health & Rehabilitative Services, Court of Appeal of Florida First District, (12/29/1992).

In re Aultman Hosp., Court of Appeals of Ohio Tenth Appellate District, Franklin County, (5/19/1992).

Fairview General Hosp. v. Fletcher, Court of Appeals of Ohio Tenth Appellate District, Franklin County, (12/20/1990).

III L. Obstetric

Mississippi State Dep't of Health v. Mississippi Baptist Medical Center, Supreme Court of Mississippi, (10/19/1995).

Providence Hospital of Everett v. State of Washington, Department of Social & Health Services, and A.N. Shinpoch, Secretary of the Department of Social & Health Services, Thurston County Superior Court, (4/13/1989).

Johnston-Willis Ltd. v. Kenley, Court of Appeals of Virginia, (5/3/1988).

III M. Open Heart

Georgia Department of Community Health v. Satilla Health Services, Inc., Court of Appeals of Georgia, (3/17/2004).

Medstar Health v. Maryland Health Care Commission, Court of Appeals of Maryland, (6/18/2003).

St. Joseph Hospital v. Kevin Concannon, Superior Court of Maine, (11/2/2001).

Central Maine Medical Center v. Kevin Concannon and Maine Medical Center, Superior Court of Maine, (9/26/2000).

Frye Regional Med. Ctr. Inc. v. Hunt, Supreme Court of North Carolina, (2/5/1999).

Adventist Healthcare Midatlantic v. Suburban Hosp., Court of Appeals of Maryland, (6/10/1998).

Pennsylvania Dep't of Health v. North Hills Passavant Hosp., Commonwealth Court of Pennsylvania, (4/10/1996).

Maryland Gen. Hosp. v. Maryland Health Resources Planning Commission, Court of Special Appeals of Maryland, (2/14/1995).

Hospital Auth. v. State Health Planning Agency, Court of Appeals of Georgia, (11/19/1993).

Robert Packer Hosp. v. Department of Health, Commonwealth Court of Pennsylvania, (9/7/1993).

In re Timken Mercy Medical Center, Supreme Court of Ohio, (7/3/1991).

Lee Memorial Hosp. v. Department of Health & Rehabilitative Serv., Court of Appeal of Florida First District, (5/9/1990).

Magnolia Hosp. v. Mississippi State Dep't of Health, Supreme Court of Mississippi, (4/4/1990).

Commission on Hospitals & Health Care v. Stamford Hospital, Supreme Court of Connecticut, (8/16/1988).

Sinai Hospital of Baltimore Inc. v. Maryland Health Resources Planning Commission, Court of Appeals of Maryland, (6/10/1986).

State Health Planning Review Bd. v. Piedmont Hospital Inc., Court of Appeals of Georgia, (2/6/1985).

Wausau Hospitals Inc. v. Department of Health & Social Services, Court of Appeals of Wisconsin, (3/18/1980).

State ex rel. Metzler v. Sisters of Charity of Leavenworth Health Services Corp., Supreme Court of Kansas, (1/19/1980).

Iowa State Dep't of Health v. Hertko, Supreme Court of Iowa, (8/29/1979).

St. Joseph's Hospital & Medical Center v. Finley, Superior Court of New Jersey Appellate Division, (10/14/1977).

III N. Pharmacy

Walgreen Co. v. John V. Rullan, United States District Court for the District of Puerto Rico, (9/8/2003).

III O. Provider Specialty

Portland Surgery Center, LLC. v. Department of Human Services, Superior Court of Maine, Kennebec County, (2/23/2004).

Morristown Surgery Center, LLC v. Tennessee Health Facilities Commission, Court of Appeals of Tennessee, at Nashville, (12/15/2003).

Alan D. Gordon v. Lewistown Hospital, United States District Court for the Middle District of Pennsylvania, (7/11/2003).

Jackson HMA, Inc. v. Mississippi State Department of Health, Supreme Court of Mississippi, (4/25/2002).

Albany Surgical, P.C. v. Department of Community Health, Georgia Appeals Court, (1/1/2002).

Adams & Boyle P.C. v. Tennessee Dep't of Health, United States Court of Appeals for the Sixth Circuit, (2/9/2001).

Adams & Boyle P.C. v. Tennessee Dep't of Health, United States Court of Appeals for the Sixth Circuit, (2/9/2001).

Johnston Ambulatory Surgical Associates, LTD. v. Patricia Nolan, In Her Capacity as Director of the Rhode Island Department of Health et al., Supreme Court of Rhode Island, (7/12/2000).

Armstrong Surgical Ctr. Inc. v. Armstrong County Memorial Hosp., United States Court of Appeals For the Third Circuit, (6/26/2000).

Dimensions Med. Ctr. v. Elmhurst Outpatient Surgery Ctr., Appellate Court of Illinois, Fourth District, (9/29/1999).

Carle Found. v. Illinois Health Facilities Planning Board, Appellate Court of Illinois, First District Fifth Division, (8/13/1999).

Biloxi HMA Inc. v. Singing River Hosp., Supreme Court of Mississippi, (7/29/1999).

Mississippi State Dep't of Health v. Natchez Community Hosp., Supreme Court of Mississippi, (7/29/1999).

Access Ctr. for Health v. Health Facilities Planning Bd., Appellate Court of Illinois, Second District, (9/17/1996).

In re Midwest Eye Ctr., Court of Appeals of Ohio Tenth Appellate District, Franklin County, (5/30/1995).

Cabinet for Human Resources v. Women's Health Serv., Court of Appeals of Kentucky, (6/24/1994).

HCA Health Serv. v. Roach, Supreme Court of Georgia, (2/7/1994).

Catawba Memorial Hosp. v. North Carolina Dep't of Human Resources, Court of Appeals of North Carolina, (11/16/1993).

Iredell Memorial Hosp. v. North Carolina Dep't of Human Resources etc., Court of Appeals of North Carolina, (8/6/1991).

Jeannette Dist. Memorial Hosp. v. Department of Health, Commonwealth Court of Pennsylvania, (7/12/1991).

Appeal of Psychiatric Institutes of America v. Supreme Court of New Hampshire, (8/23/1989).

Alabama Nursing Home Ass'n v. Alabama State Health Planning Agency, Court of Civil Appeals of Alabama, (1/13/1989).

Cincinnati Ambulatory Surgery Center v. Certificate of Need Review Board, Court of Appeals of Ohio Tenth Appellate District, Franklin County, (12/13/1988).

Grandview Surgical Center Inc. v. Holy Spirit Hospital of Sisters of Christian Charity, Commonwealth Court of Pennsylvania, (11/19/1987).

Florida Hospital v. Department of Health & Rehabilitative Services, Court of Appeal of Florida First District, (5/14/1987).

Humana of Fla. Inc. v. Department of Health & Rehabilitative Serv., Court of Appeals of Florida First District, (9/11/1986).

Arnot-Ogden Memorial Hospital v. Guthrie Clinic Inc., Supreme Court of New York, Appellate Division, Third Department, (7/17/1986).

Medivision of East Broward County, Inc. v. Department of Health & Rehabilitative Services, Court of Appeals of Florida First District, (5/15/1986).

Shoolman v. Health Facilities Appeals Bd. (1980), Appeals Court of Massachusetts, Suffolk, (12/11/1980).

III P. Radiation Therapy

Northside Hospital, Inc. v. McCord et al., Court of Appeals of Georgia, (7/19/2000).

McLeod Regional Medical Center v. South Carolina Department of Health and Environmental Control, State of South Carolina Administrative Law Judge Division, (6/7/1996).

SSM Health Care v. Missouri Health Facilities Review Comm., Supreme Court of Missouri, (3/21/1995).

Associates in Radiation Oncology P.A. v. Siegel M.P.H., Superior Court of New Jersey Appellate Division, (3/8/1994).

St. Francis Hosp. v. Appeals Bd. of Dep't of Health & Social Serv., Superior Court of Delaware New Castle, (8/12/1993).

Powers v. Commonwealth Dep't of Health, Commonwealth Court of Pennsylvania, (1/22/1990).

Department of Health v. Lutheran Hospitals & Homes Soc., Supreme Court of Nebraska, (12/11/1987).

Bio-Medical Applications of Arlington Inc. v. Kenley, Court of Appeals of Virginia, (7/7/1987).

Roanoke Memorial Hospitals v. Kenley, Court of Appeals of Virginia, (1/6/1987).

Bio-Medical Applications of Arlington Inc. v. Kenley, Circuit Court of Arlington County Virginia, (6/4/1984).

In re Review of Decision of Kansas Corp. Com. etc., Supreme Court of Kansas, (2/19/1983).

III Q. Transplant

State Health Commissioner v. Sentara Norfolk General Hospital, Supreme Court of Virginia, (9/15/2000).

CON STATUTES AND REGULATIONS

ALABAMA

CON Statute Title: Control and Regulation of Development of Certain Health Care Facilities
CON Statute Citation: Code of Ala. 22-21-260
Year CON Statute Enacted: 1975
CON Regulations Title: State Health Planning and Development Agency Administrative Code
CON Regulations Citation: Ala. Admin. Code sec. 410-1-6-(.01-.18)

ALASKA

CON Statute Title: Certificate of Need Program
CON Statute Citation: Alaska Stat. 18.07
CON Regulations Title: Alaska Certificate of Need Regulations
CON Regulations Citation: Sec. 7 AAC 07-(.010-.030)

ARKANSAS

CON Statute Title: Health Services Permit Agency
CON Statute Citation: Ark.Code Ann. Sec. 20-8-(103-110)
Year CON Statute Enacted: 2003
CON Regulations Title: Health Services Permit Commission
CON Regulations Citation: HSC Regulations 001

CONNECTICUT

CON Statute Title: Office of Health Care Access Act
CON Statute Citation: Conn. Gen. Stat. 19a610-662
CON Regulations Title: OHCA Administrative Regulations
CON Regulations Citation: Sec. 19a-643-1

DELAWARE

CON Statute Title: Health Planning and Resource Management
CON Statute Citation: 16 Del. C. sec. 9301-9311
Year CON Statute Enacted: 2004
CON Regulations Title: Bylaws of Delaware Health Resources Board
CON Regulations Citation: 61 Del. Laws, c 393, sec1
Year CON Regulations Enacted: 1999

FLORIDA

CON Statute Title: Health Facility and Services Development Act
CON Statute Citation: Fla. Stat. 408.031-408.045
Year CON Statute Enacted: 2003

CON Regulations Title: Procedures for the Administration of Sections 408.031-408.045, Florida Statutes, Health Facility and Services Development Act

CON Regulations Citation: 59C-(1.001-1.050)

GEORGIA

CON Statute Title: State Health Planning and Development

CON Statute Citation: O.C.G.A. 31-6-(1-2,20-22,40-50,70)

CON Regulations Title: State Health Planning Agency

CON Regulations Citation: Ga. Comp. R. & Regs. R. 272-2-(.01-.12)

HAWAII

CON Statute Title: Health Planning and Resources Development and Health Care Cost Control

CON Statute Citation: HRS 323D-2, HRS 323 D-41-55

CON Regulations Title: Department of Health State of Hawaii State Health Planning and Development Agency Certificate of Need Program

CON Regulations Citation: Title 11, Chapter 186

ILLINOIS

CON Statute Title: Illinois Health Facilites Planning Act

CON Statute Citation: 20 ILCS 3960/1 et seq.

Year CON Statute Enacted: 1974

CON Regulations Title: Public Health Health Facilities Planning Board

CON Regulations Citation: Title 77, Chapter 2, Section 1120-1130

IOWA

CON Statute Title: Health Facilites Council

CON Statute Citation: Iowa Code sec. 135.(61-85)

CON Regulations Title: Certificate of Need Program

CON Regulations Citation: Chapter 202

KENTUCKY

CON Statute Title: Licensure and Regulation of Health Facilities and Services

CON Statute Citation: KRS 216B.015 et seq

CON Regulations Title: Certificate of need administrative regulation

CON Regulations Citation: 900 KAR 6:020,040,050

LOUISIANA

CON Statute Title: Facility Need Review

CON Statute Citation: La. R.S. 40:2116

Year CON Statute Enacted: 2003

CON Regulations Title: Facility Need Review

CON Regulations Citation: Chapter 125 sec. 12501

Year CON Regulations Enacted: 1995

MAINE

CON Statute Title: Maine Certificate of Need Act
CON Statute Citation: 22 M.R.S. 326
CON Regulations Title: Main Certificate of Need Procedures Manual for Health Care Facilities
CON Regulations Citation: 10-144 Chapter 503

MARYLAND

CON Statute Title: Certificate of Need - Health Care Facilities
CON Statute Citation: 19-120
Year CON Statute Enacted: 2003
CON Regulations Title: Determination of Certificate of Need for Health Care Facilities
CON Regulations Citation: 10.24.01.00
Year CON Regulations Enacted: 2003

MASSACHUSETTS

CON Statute Title: Substantial Capital Expenditure or Substantial Change in Services
CON Statute Citation: Massachusetts General Laws, Chapter 111, s. 25C
CON Regulations Title: Massachusetts Determination of Need Regulations
CON Regulations Citation: 105 CMR 100.000-102.000

MICHIGAN

CON Statute Title: Certificate of Need
CON Statute Citation: Part 222 333.22201-333.22260
CON Regulations Title: Michigan Administrative Code
CON Regulations Citation: MICH. ADMIN. CODE R 325.9101 - 325.9525

MISSISSIPPI

CON Statute Title: Health Care Certificate of Need Law of 1979
CON Statute Citation: Miss. Code Ann. 41-7
CON Regulations Title: Mississippi State Dept. of Health: Division of Health Planning and Resource Development
CON Regulations Citation: Dept of Health: Certificate of Need Review Manual
Year CON Regulations Enacted: 2002

MISSOURI

CON Statute Title: Missouri Certificate of Need Law
CON Statute Citation: 197.300 to 197.366 R.S.Mo.
CON Regulations Title: Rules of Dept of Health and Senior Services: Missouri Health Facilities Review Committee: Certificate of Need Program
CON Regulations Citation: Title 19, Division 60, Chapter 50

MONTANA

CON Statute Title: Health and Safety: Hospitals and Related Facilities General Provisions
CON Statute Citation: Mont. Code Anno., 50-5-101 et seq
CON Regulations Title: Certificate of Need
CON Regulations Citation: 37.106

NEBRASKA

CON Statute Title: Nebraska Health Care Certificate of Need Act
CON Statute Citation: Sections 71-5801 to 71-5870
CON Regulations Title: HHS Finance and Support Manual
CON Regulations Citation: Ch. 12-011

NEVADA

CON Statute Title: Planning for the Provision of Health Care
CON Statute Citation: NRS Chapter 439A
CON Regulations Title: Planning for the Provision of Health Care
CON Regulations Citation: Chapter 439A

NEW HAMPSHIRE

CON Statute Title: Certificate of Need Review of Proposed New Institutional Health Services
CON Statute Citation: RSA Chapter 151-C
CON Regulations Title: Health Services Planning and Review Board
CON Regulations Citation: Chapter He-Hea 100

NEW JERSEY

CON Statute Title: Health Care Facilities Planning Act
CON Statute Citation: N.J. Stat. Ann. 26:2H-1 to 26:2H-26
CON Regulations Title: Certificate of Need: Application and Review Process
CON Regulations Citation: N.J.A.C. Title 8, Chapter 33

NEW YORK

CON Statute Title: Public Health Law
CON Statute Citation: NY CLS Pub Health prec 2800
Year CON Statute Enacted: 1965
CON Regulations Title: Hospital Establishmet
CON Regulations Citation: Subchapter B

NORTH CAROLINA

CON Statute Title: Certificate of Need Law
CON Statute Citation: N.C. Gen. Stat. 131E
Year CON Statute Enacted: 2001
CON Regulations Title: Certificate of Need Regulation
CON Regulations Citation: Subchapter 14C

OHIO

CON Statute Title: Certificates of Need
CON Statute Citation: Title 37, Chapter 3702
CON Regulations Title: Ohio Adminstrative Code: Certificate of Need
CON Regulations Citation: 3701-12

OKLAHOMA

CON Statute Title: LTC Certificate of Need Act; Psychiatric and Chemical Dependency Facility Certificate of Need Act

CON Statute Citation: 63 Okl. St. 1-85; 63 Okl. St. 1-88

CON Regulations Title: Oklahoma State Department of Health Certificate of Need Standards for Health Care Facility Acquisitions

CON Regulations Citation: Title 310, Chapter 620

OREGON

CON Statute Title: Certificates of Need for Health Services

CON Statute Citation: Title 36, Chapter 442

CON Regulations Title: Procedural Rules

CON Regulations Citation: 333-001-0000 et seq

RHODE ISLAND

CON Statute Title: Health Care Certificate of Need Act of Rhode Island

CON Statute Citation: R.I. Gen. Laws 23-15

CON Regulations Title: Rules and Regulations for Determination of Need for New Health Care Equipment and New Institutional Health Services

CON Regulations Citation: R23-15-CON

Year CON Regulations Enacted: 2000

SOUTH CAROLINA

CON Statute Title: State Certification of Need and Health Facility Licensure Act

CON Statute Citation: S.C. Code Ann. 44-7

CON Regulations Title: Certification of Need for Health Facilities and Services

CON Regulations Citation: Regulation No. 61-15

TENNESSEE

CON Statute Title: Tennessee Health Services and Planning Act of 2002

CON Statute Citation: Tenn. Code Ann. 68-11

Year CON Statute Enacted: 2002

CON Regulations Title: Rules of the Tennessee Health Facilities Commission: Certificate of Need Program - Scope and Procedures

CON Regulations Citation: Chapter 0720-3

Year CON Regulations Enacted: 1999

VERMONT

CON Statute Title: Health Facility Planning

CON Statute Citation: 18 V.S.A. sec. 9434-9442

CON Regulations Title: Certificate of Need Regulations

CON Regulations Citation: Regulation H-99-3

Year CON Regulations Enacted: 1999

VIRGINIA

CON Statute Title: Medical Care Facilities Certificate of Public Need
CON Statute Citation: Va. Code Ann. 32-1
CON Regulations Title: Virginia Medical Care Facilities Certificate of Public Need Rules and Regulations
CON Regulations Citation: 12 VAC 50220
Year CON Regulations Enacted: 2003

WASHINGTON

CON Statute Title: State Health Planning and Resources Development Act
CON Statute Citation: Rev. Code Wash. (ARCW) 70.38
CON Regulations Title: Washington Adminstrative Code
CON Regulations Citation: WAC 246-310

WASHINGTON D.C.

CON Statute Title: Health Services Planning
CON Statute Citation: D.C. Code sec. 44-(406-420)
CON Regulations Title: Public Health and Medicine
CON Regulations Citation: Title 22
Year CON Regulations Enacted: 1986

WEST VIRGINIA

CON Statute Title: Certificate of Need
CON Statute Citation: W. Va. Code 16-2D
CON Regulations Title: Certificate of Need Rule
CON Regulations Citation: 65-7-1
Year CON Regulations Enacted: 2000

WISCONSIN

CON Statute Title: Regulation of Health Services: Resource Allocation Program - Long Term Care
CON Statute Citation: Wis. Stat. sec 150
CON Regulations Title: Wisconsin Administrative Code: Long-Term Care Facility Bed Additions and Capital Expenditures Review
CON Regulations Citation: Chapter HFS 122

APPLICATION OF CON LAWS TO ASSETS AND SERVICES BY STATE

ALABAMA

STATE CON AGENCY CONTACTS

State Department Overseeing CON

Name of state CON department:	State Health Planning and Development Agency
URL address for state CON organization:	http://www.shpda.state.al.us/main.htm

CON Administrative Office Information

Name of state CON office:	Statewide Health Coordinating Council Hierarchy for state CON administrative office: Governor: Certificate of Need Review Board: State Health Planning and Development Agency
CON organization contact person:	James E. Sanders
Title of CON contact person:	Deputy Director
Email address of CON contact:	jsanders@shpda.state.al.us
Mailing address for state CON office:	100 North Union Street
Mailing address for state CON office:	Suite 870
City where state CON office is located:	Montgomery
State for mailing address:	Alabama
Zip code for CON office:	36104-
Phone number for CON contact:	(334) 242-4103
Fax number for CON contact:	(334) 242-4113

State CON Decision Making Body (DMB)

Name of DMB:	State Health Planning and Development Agency
Title of person DMB reports to:	Governor
Title of person appointing DMB members:	Governor

Composition of CON DMB:

Number of people in the DMB:	9
Number of association reps in DMB:	3
Number of consumers in DMB:	3
Number of healthcare providers in DMB:	3

EQUIPMENT REGULATION AND DATA

Subject to CON (Y/N):

Is any equipment subject to CON?:	False
Are air ambulances subject to CON?:	False
Are cardiac cath labs subject to CON?:	True
Are CT scanners subject to CON?:	False
Are gamma knives subject to CON?:	True
Are linear accelerators subject to CON?:	True
Is lithotropsy subject to CON?:	False
Is mobile high tech subject to CON?:	False
Are MRI scanners subject to CON?:	False
Are PET scanners subject to CON?:	False
Is radiation therapy subject to CON?:	True
Is renal dialysis subject to CON?:	True
Are swing beds subject to CON?:	True
Is ultra-sound subject to CON?:	True

Dollar Threshold for CON Application:

Dollar threshold for any equipment application:	$2,000,000

Additional Criteria Used to Determine Need:

Additional criteria used to determine need for any equipment: no CON needed to replace equipment

Additional criteria used to determine need for cardiac cath lab: criteria to expand existing service are different than criteria to establish new service; existing facilities must have performed an average of 1,000 procedures; applicant must project at least 600 or 750 procedures depending on whether equipment is diagnostic or diagnostic/therapeutic.

FACILITIES REGULATION AND DATA

Subject to CON (Y/N):

Is any facility subject to CON?	False
Are hospitals subject to CON?	True
Are nursing homes subject to CON?	True
Are residential care facilities subject to CON?	False
Are psychiatric facilities subject to CON?	True
Are ambulatory surgery centers subject to CON?	True
Are ICF/MRs subject to CON?	True
Is long term care subject to CON?	True
Are medical office buildings subject to CON?	False
Are rehabilitation facilities subject to CON?	True
Are renal dialysis facilities subject to CON?	True
Are RCF/Assisted Living facilities subject to CON?	True
Are subacute care facilities subject to CON?	False
Are substance abuse facilities subject to CON?	True
Are swing beds subject to CON?	True

Subject to CON (Y/N) (Continued)

Are other facilities subject to CON? public health centers; skilled or intermediate care units operated in veterans' nursing homes and veterans' homes

Project Dollar Threshold Requiring CON Application:

Dollar threshold for any facility application: $expenditure exceeding $4,000,000; change in existing bed capacity or conversion of beds

Capacity Requirements – Beds / Population:

Capacity requirement-beds/population for nursing homes: 40 beds per 1,000 population 65 and older

Capacity requirement-beds/population for psychiatric facilities: 37.1 beds per 100,000 population

Capacity requirement-beds/population for rehabilitation facility: 12 beds per 100,000 population

Capacity requirement-beds/population for RCF/Assisted Living facility: 15 beds per 1,000 population 65 and older

Capacity Requirements – Facilities / Population:

Capacity requirement-facilities/population for a RCF/Assisted Living facility: 15 beds per 1,000 population 65 and older

Additional Criteria Used to Determine Need:

Additional criteria used to determine need for a hospital: bed need cannot exceed 5% of combined average daily census of all acute care hospitals in county and contiguous counties

Additional criteria used to determine need for a nursing home: county's annual occupancy must be at least 97% before additional beds are approved

Additional criteria used to determine need for a psychiatric facility: bed need may be adjusted if applicant can prove population's needs are not being met within the region by showing average occupancy is at least 75%

Additional criteria used to determine need for a long term care facility: bed need for proposed LTC hospital shall be for no more than 5% of the combined average daily census of all participating hospitals

Additional criteria used to determine need for a renal dialysis facility: optimal utilization = 80% of present capacity or 9.6 dialysis treatments per station per week

Additional criteria used to determine need for a RCF/Assisted Living facility: facility must have at least 8 beds

Additional criteria used to determine need for a substance abuse facility: complex calculation of bed need considering population

Additional criteria used to determine need for other facilities: for existing facilities, the quality of care provided by the facility will be considered

Notes Including Bed Limits and Moratoria:

Notes including bed limits/moratoria for any facility: use population estimates or projections published by the Center for Business and Economic Research, University of Alabama; the community reaction to the facility should be considered; the contribution of the facility in meeting health related needs of a traditionally medically underserved group should be considered

Notes including bed limits/moratoria for a hospital: temporary utilization of beds for different service not considered a conversion if does not exceed 20% of unit

Notes including bed limits/moratoria for an ambulatory surgery center: committee to develop criteria

Notes including bed limits/moratoria for a renal dialysis facility: present capacity defined as two shifts per day, six days a week; no CON needed for facilities located in certain areas with less than 10 hemodialysis units

SERVICES REGULATION AND DATA

Subject to CON (Y/N):

Are all services subject to CON?:	False
Are nursing home services subject to CON?:	True
Are acute care services subject to CON?:	True
Are air ambulance subject to CON?:	False
Is burn care subject to CON?:	False
Is cardiac catheterization subject to CON?:	True
Is CT scanning subject to CON?:	False
Is gamma knife service subject to CON?:	True
Is home health subject to CON?:	True
Is linear accelerator service subject to CON?:	True
Is lithotripsy service subject to CON?:	False
Is long term care subject to CON?:	True
Is mobile high tech service subject to CON?:	False
Is MRI scanning subject to CON?:	False
Is neo-natal intensive care subject to CON?:	True
Are obstetrical services subject to CON?:	True
Is open heart surgery subject to CON?:	True
Is organ transplantation subject to CON?:	True
Is PET scanning subject to CON?:	False
Are psychiatric services subject to CON?:	True
Is radiation therapy subject to CON?:	False
Are rehabilitation services subject to CON?:	True
Is renal dialysis subject to CON?:	True
Is RCF/Assisted Living subject to CON?:	False
Is subacute care subject to CON?:	False
Is substance abuse subject to CON?:	True
Are swing beds subject to CON?:	True
Is utlra-sound subject to CON?:	True

Dollar Threshold for CON Application:

Dollar threshold for any service application:	$800,000

Utilization Requirements (Facilities or Services/Population):

Utilization requirement-services/population for home health: 160 per 1000 persons served age 65 and older

Additional Criteria Used to Determine Need:

Additional criteria used to determine need for any service: Use population estimates or projections published by the Center for Business and Economic Research, University of Alabama; expansion of services may be reviewed more favorably than the establishment of new services; consider how service will serve needs of traditionally medically underserved groups; for existing services, the quality of care provided by the service will be considered

Additional criteria used to determine need for home health: Must provide minimun range of home health services

Additional criteria used to determine need for open heart surgery: Criteria for adult is different from pediatric;

adult - project 200 (150 CAGB) annually; pediatrics - 100 annually; existing units must operate at minimum utilization (350 adult, 130 peds)

Additional criteria used to determine need for organ transplantation: All existing services must operate at 80% capacity

Additional criteria used to determine need for radiation therapy: Planning policy - average 300 cancer cases annually; no approvals unless each existing unit performing at least 6000 treatments per year

Additional criteria used to determine need for rehabilitation: Regional occupancy must be at least 75% before additional beds can be approved

Additional criteria used to determine need for swing beds: hospitals limited to 10 swing beds; average length of stay cannot exceed 30 days

CON STATUTES AND REGULATIONS

CON Statutes:

CON Statute Title: Control and Regulation of Development of Certain Health Care Facilities
CON Statute Citation: Code of Ala. 22-21-260
Year CON Statute Enacted: 1975

CON Regulations:

CON Regulations Title: State Health Planning and Development Agency Administrative Code
CON Regulations Citation: Ala. Admin. Code sec. 410-1-6-(.01-.18)

STATE NOTE

Alabama requires a certificate of need ("CON") for most new health services except for certain diagnostic services and the replacement of medical equipment. The statute requires the consideration of several state plans such as the State Health Plan. The statute provides that kidney dialysis treatment centers are exempted from the CON requirement if located in certain types of communities and have less than a specified number of freestanding hemodialysis units. The planning policies, found in the regulations, contain optimal utilization of the service or equipment that must be met before the service can be initiated or expanded. The regulations contain methodologies to calculate need which consider the incidence rate of certain diseases and the population of the county.

ALASKA

STATE CON AGENCY CONTACTS

State Department Overseeing CON	
Name of state CON department:	Department of Health and Human Services
URL address for state CON organization:	http://www.hss.state.ak.us/dph/chems cert_of_need/
CON Administrative Office Information	
Name of state CON office:	Facilities & Planning Section
Hierarchy for state CON administrative office:	
Governor: Dept. of Health and Social Services:	Facilities & Planning Section
CON organization contact person:	David Pierce
Title of CON contact person:	Coordinator
Email address of CON contact:	david_pierce@health.state.ak.us
Mailing address for state CON office:	PO Box 110616
City where state CON office is located:	Juneau
State for mailing address:	Alaska
Zip code for CON office:	99811-
Phone number for CON contact:	(907) 465-3001
Fax number for CON contact:	(907) 465-4101
State CON Decision Making Body (DMB)	
Name of DMB:	Commissioner of Health & Social Services
Title of person DMB reports to:	Governor
Title of person appointing DMB members:	N/A
Composition of CON DMB:	
Number of people in the DMB:	1
Number of consumers in DMB:	N/A
Number of healthcare providers in DMB:	N/A

EQUIPMENT REGULATION AND DATA

Subject to CON (Y/N):	
Is any equipment subject to CON?:	True
Are air ambulances subject to CON?:	True
Are cardiac cath labs subject to CON?:	True
Are CT scanners subject to CON?:	True
Are gamma knives subject to CON?:	True
Are linear accelerators subject to CON?:	True
Is lithotropsy subject to CON?:	True

Subject to CON (Y/N) (Continued)

Is mobile high tech subject to CON?:	True
Are MRI scanners subject to CON?:	True
Are PET scanners subject to CON?:	True
Is radiation therapy subject to CON?:	True
Is renal dialysis subject to CON?:	True
Are swing beds subject to CON?:	True
Is ultra-sound subject to CON?:	True

FACILITIES REGULATION AND DATA

Subject to CON (Y/N):

Is any facility subject to CON?	False
Are hospitals subject to CON?	True
Are nursing homes subject to CON?	True
Are residential care facilities subject to CON?	True
Are psychiatric facilities subject to CON?	True
Are ambulatory surgery centers subject to CON?	True
Are ICF/MRs subject to CON?	True
Is long term care subject to CON?	True
Are medical office buildings subject to CON?	False
Are rehabilitation facilities subject to CON?	True
Are renal dialysis facilities subject to CON?	True
Are RCF/Assisted Living facilities subject to CON?	False
Are subacute care facilities subject to CON?	True
Are substance abuse facilities subject to CON?	True
Are swing beds subject to CON?	True
Are other facilities subject to CON?	tuberculosis hospital; skilled nursing facility

Project Dollar Threshold Requiring CON Application:

Dollar threshold for any facility application:	$1,000,000

Notes Including Bed Limits and Moratoria:

Notes including bed limits/moratoria for an ambulatory surgery center: can relocate ASC to a new site in same community without obtaining CON as long as the number of services provided does not increase

SERVICES REGULATION AND DATA

Subject to CON (Y/N):

Are all services subject to CON?:	False
Are nursing home services subject to CON?:	True
Are acute care services subject to CON?:	True
Are air ambulance subject to CON?:	True
Is burn care subject to CON?:	True
Is cardiac catheterization subject to CON?:	True
Is CT scanning subject to CON?:	True
Is gamma knife service subject to CON?:	True
Is home health subject to CON?:	True

Subject to CON (Y/N) (Continued)

Is linear accelerator service subject to CON?:	True
Is lithotripsy service subject to CON?:	True
Is long term care subject to CON?:	True
Is mobile high tech service subject to CON?:	False
Is MRI scanning subject to CON?:	True
Is neo-natal intensive care subject to CON?:	True
Are obstetrical services subject to CON?:	True
Is open heart surgery subject to CON?:	True
Is organ transplantation subject to CON?:	True
Is PET scanning subject to CON?:	True
Are psychiatric services subject to CON?:	True
Is radiation therapy subject to CON?:	True
Are rehabilitation services subject to CON?:	True
Is renal dialysis subject to CON?:	True
Is RCF/Assisted Living subject to CON?:	False
Is subacute care subject to CON?:	True
Is substance abuse subject to CON?:	True
Are swing beds subject to CON?:	True
Is utlra-sound subject to CON?:	True

CON STATUTES AND REGULATIONS

CON Statutes:

CON Statute Title: Certificate of Need Program
CON Statute Citation: Alaska Stat. 18.07

CON Regulations:

CON Regulations Title: Alaska Certificate of Need Regulations
CON Regulations Citation: Sec. 7 AAC 07-(.010-.030)

STATE NOTE

Alaska requires a certificate of need ("CON") for most healthcare services. The statute says that a CON can only be granted for non-nursing home services if the availability of existing healthcare resources are less than the projected requirement but the regulations do not define how the projected requirement is calculated. The statute directs the department to develop review standards for CONs for nursing homes but the regulations do not contain review standards.

ARKANSAS

STATE CON AGENCY CONTACTS

State Department Overseeing CON

Name of state CON department:	Health Services Permit Agency
URL address for state CON organization:	http://www.arhspa.org/

CON Administrative Office Information

Name of state CON office:	Health Services Permit Agency Hierarchy for state CON administrative office: Governor: Health Services Permit Agency
CON organization contact person:	Debra Frazier
Title of CON contact person:	Director
Email address of CON contact:	dfrazier@healthyarkansas.com
Mailing address for state CON office:	Freeway Medical Tower
Mailing address for state CON office:	5800 West 10th Street, Suite 805
City where state CON office is located:	Little Rock
State for mailing address:	Arkansas
Zip code for CON office:	72205-
Phone number for CON contact:	(501) 661-2509
Fax number for CON contact:	(501) 661-2399

State CON Decision Making Body (DMB)

Name of DMB:	Health Services Permit Commission
Title of person DMB reports to:	Governor
Title of person appointing DMB members:	Governor

Composition of CON DMB:

Number of people in the DMB:	9
Number of CON agency reps in DMB:	1
Number of association reps in DMB:	6
Number of consumers in DMB:	1
Number of healthcare providers in DMB:	1

EQUIPMENT REGULATION AND DATA

Subject to CON (Y/N):

Is any equipment subject to CON?:	False
Are air ambulances subject to CON?:	False
Are cardiac cath labs subject to CON?:	False
Are CT scanners subject to CON?:	False
Are gamma knives subject to CON?:	False

Subject to CON (Y/N) (Continued)

Are linear accelerators subject to CON?:	False
Is lithotropsy subject to CON?:	False
Is mobile high tech subject to CON?:	False
Are MRI scanners subject to CON?:	False
Are PET scanners subject to CON?:	False
Is radiation therapy subject to CON?:	False
Is renal dialysis subject to CON?:	False
Are swing beds subject to CON?:	False
Is ultra-sound subject to CON?:	False

Utilization Requirements (Facilities or Services/Population):

Utilization requirement-services/population for home health: 3 agencies for area with 30,000-50,000 population

FACILITIES REGULATION AND DATA

Subject to CON (Y/N):

Is any facility subject to CON?	False
Are hospitals subject to CON?	False
Are nursing homes subject to CON?	True
Are residential care facilities subject to CON?	True
Are psychiatric facilities subject to CON?	True
Are ambulatory surgery centers subject to CON?	False
Are ICF/MRs subject to CON?	True
Is long term care subject to CON?	True
Are medical office buildings subject to CON?	False
Are rehabilitation facilities subject to CON?	False
Are renal dialysis facilities subject to CON?	False
Are RCF/Assisted Living facilities subject to CON?	True
Are subacute care facilities subject to CON?	False
Are substance abuse facilities subject to CON?	False
Are swing beds subject to CON?	False
Are other facilities subject to CON?	imaging centers; freestanding radiation therapy centers

Project Dollar Threshold Requiring CON Application:

Dollar threshold for any facility application:	$500,000 or additional bed capacity
Dollar threshold for a nursing home application:	$500,000
Dollar threshold for a long term care facility application:	$movement of LTC from one site to another requires approval

Capacity Requirements – Beds / Population:

Capacity requirement-beds/population for nursing homes: 10.8 beds per 1000 population 65-74

Capacity requirement-beds/population for psychiatric facilities: 0.385 beds per 1000 age 6-17; 0.300 beds 18-21

Capacity requirement-beds/population for RCF/Assisted Living facility: 5 beds per 1000 persons aged 65 or older

Capacity Requirements – Facilities / Population:

Capacity requirement-facilities/population for a RCF/Assisted Living facility: 5 beds per 1000 persons aged 65 or older

Additional Criteria Used to Determine Need:

Additional criteria used to determine need for any facility: whether project can be adequately staffed when completed; economically feasible; fosters cost containment; is needed

Additional criteria used to determine need for a nursing home: county must have occupancy of at least 70% to show need; applicants with 96% occupancy are eligible to increase their capacity by 10%; applicants proposing to replace facilities are eligible for 20% increase in capacity; applicants proposing to expand to 70 beds are eligible to expand to 70 beds; applicants with between 60 and 70 beds are eligible for 10 bed increase; nursing home may acquire up to 10% of its capacity if home has 90% occupancy and acquires beds from a facility with 70% or less occupancy; nursing homes that commenced operations between 1996 and 2000 may add up to 10% of their capacity if they averaged 96% occupancy

Additional criteria used to determine need for a psychiatric facility: existing facility may be approved for up to 10 additional beds if had average occupancy of 90%

Additional criteria used to determine need for a RCF/Assisted Living facility: ALF may acquire 10% of their licensed beds or 10 beds (whichever greater) if applicant has at least 90% occupancy; exception to population based need formula exists when 75% of beds in county are occupied by persons under 65; if need is not projected beds may be approved if facility had high occupancy (85%+)

Notes Including Bed Limits and Moratoria:

Notes including bed limits/moratoria for a hospital: hospitals not subject to review except if hospital seeks to add LTC beds or convert acute beds to LTC beds or to add/expand home health services

Notes including bed limits/moratoria for a nursing home: may convert from 10 to 80 beds to assisted living

Notes including bed limits/moratoria for an ICF/MR: moratorium on ICF

SERVICES REGULATION AND DATA

Subject to CON (Y/N):

Are all services subject to CON?:	False
Are nursing home services subject to CON?:	True
Are acute care services subject to CON?:	False
Are air ambulance subject to CON?:	False
Is burn care subject to CON?:	False
Is cardiac catheterization subject to CON?:	False
Is CT scanning subject to CON?:	False
Is gamma knife service subject to CON?:	False
Is home health subject to CON?:	True
Is linear accelerator service subject to CON?:	False
Is lithotripsy service subject to CON?:	False
Is long term care subject to CON?:	True
Is mobile high tech service subject to CON?:	False
Is MRI scanning subject to CON?:	False
Is neo-natal intensive care subject to CON?:	False
Are obstetrical services subject to CON?:	False

Subject to CON (Y/N) (Continued)

Is open heart surgery subject to CON?:	False
Is organ transplantation subject to CON?:	False
Is PET scanning subject to CON?:	False
Are psychiatric services subject to CON?:	True
Is radiation therapy subject to CON?:	False
Are rehabilitation services subject to CON?:	False
Is renal dialysis subject to CON?:	False
Is RCF/Assisted Living subject to CON?:	True
Is subacute care subject to CON?:	False
Is substance abuse subject to CON?:	False
Are swing beds subject to CON?:	False
Is utlra-sound subject to CON?:	False

CON STATUTES AND REGULATIONS

CON Statutes:

CON Statute Title: Health Services Permit Agency
CON Statute Citation: Ark.Code Ann. Sec. 20-8-(103-110)
Year CON Statute Enacted: 2003

CON Regulations:

CON Regulations Title: Health Services Permit Commission
CON Regulations Citation: HSC Regulations 001

STATE NOTE

Arkansas requires a certificate of need ("CON") for only certain services, including long-term care and home health. The regulations specify "need" for the service and contain a minimum occupancy or utilization rate for existing services. The regulations pertaining to home health contain different criteria based on the size of the area. If a facility has a "high" occupancy rate (defined in the regulation), "need" does not need to be demonstrated. The regulations also specify criteria for converting beds.

CONNECTICUT

STATE CON AGENCY CONTACTS

State Department Overseeing CON

Name of state CON department:	Office of Health Care Access
URL address for state CON organization:	http://www.ct.gov/ohca/site/default.asp

CON Administrative Office Information

Name of state CON office:	Office of Health Care Access Hierarchy for state CON administrative office: Governor: Dept. of Public Health: Office of Health Care Access
CON organization contact person:	Susan Cole-England
Title of CON contact person:	Program Service Team Leader
Email address of CON contact:	Susan.Coleengland@po.state.ct.us
Mailing address for state CON office:	410 Capitol Avenue
Mailing address for state CON office:	MS#13HCA, PO Box 340308
City where state CON office is located:	Hartford
State for mailing address:	Connecticut
Zip code for CON office:	06134-
Phone number for CON contact:	(860) 418-7038
Fax number for CON contact:	(860) 418-7053

State CON Decision Making Body (DMB)

Name of DMB:	Office of Health Care Access
Title of person DMB reports to:	Governor
Title of person appointing DMB members:	Governor

Composition of CON DMB:

Number of people in the DMB:	N/A
Number of consumers in DMB:	N/A
Number of healthcare providers in DMB:	N/A

EQUIPMENT REGULATION AND DATA

Subject to CON (Y/N):

Is any equipment subject to CON?:	False
Are air ambulances subject to CON?:	True
Are cardiac cath labs subject to CON?:	True
Are CT scanners subject to CON?:	True
Are gamma knives subject to CON?:	True
Are linear accelerators subject to CON?:	True
Is lithotropsy subject to CON?:	True

Subject to CON (Y/N) (Continued)

Is mobile high tech subject to CON?:	True
Are MRI scanners subject to CON?:	True
Are PET scanners subject to CON?:	True
Is radiation therapy subject to CON?:	True
Is renal dialysis subject to CON?:	False
Are swing beds subject to CON?:	True
Is ultra-sound subject to CON?:	True

Dollar Threshold for CON Application:

Dollar threshold for any equipment application: $400,000

Additional Criteria Used to Determine Need:

Additional criteria used to determine need for any equipment: no CON needed for replacement equipment if cost of replacement equipment does not exceed 110% of original cost

FACILITIES REGULATION AND DATA

Subject to CON (Y/N):

Is any facility subject to CON?	True
Are hospitals subject to CON?	True
Are nursing homes subject to CON?	True
Are residential care facilities subject to CON?	True
Are psychiatric facilities subject to CON?	True
Are ambulatory surgery centers subject to CON?	True
Are ICF/MRs subject to CON?	True
Is long term care subject to CON?	True
Are medical office buildings subject to CON?	True
Are rehabilitation facilities subject to CON?	True
Are renal dialysis facilities subject to CON?	False
Are RCF/Assisted Living facilities subject to CON?	False
Are subacute care facilities subject to CON?	False
Are substance abuse facilities subject to CON?	True
Are swing beds subject to CON?	True

Are other facilities subject to CON? outpatient clinics; clinical lab; central service; nonprofit health centers; rest homes; diagnostic treatment centers

Project Dollar Threshold Requiring CON Application:

Dollar threshold for any facility application: $1,000,000

Additional Criteria Used to Determine Need:

Additional criteria used to determine need for any facility: evidence state health plan was considered; long term plan was considered; alternative sources of financing; identificatoin of increases in net patient revenue; evidence regional accessibility will be enhanced

Notes Including Bed Limits and Moratoria:

Notes including bed limits/moratoria for any facility: state operated facilities, including hospitals, are subject to CON requirements; community health centers are exempt; school-based health care centers are exempt

Notes including bed limits/moratoria for a nursing home: moratorium on beds
Notes including bed limits/moratoria for a psychiatric facility: moratorium on beds
Notes including bed limits/moratoria for a long term care facility: moratorium on LTC until 6/30/07
Notes including bed limits/moratoria for swing beds: moratorium

CON STATUTES AND REGULATIONS

CON Statutes:

CON Statute Title:	Office of Health Care Access Act
CON Statute Citation:	Conn. Gen. Stat. 19a610-662

CON Regulations:

CON Regulations Title:	OHCA Administrative Regulations
CON Regulations Citation:	Sec. 19a-643-1

SERVICES REGULATION AND DATA

Subject to CON (Y/N):

Are all services subject to CON?:	False
Are nursing home services subject to CON?:	True
Are acute care services subject to CON?:	True
Are air ambulance subject to CON?:	True
Is burn care subject to CON?:	True
Is cardiac catheterization subject to CON?:	True
Is CT scanning subject to CON?:	True
Is gamma knife service subject to CON?:	True
Is home health subject to CON?:	True
Is linear accelerator service subject to CON?:	True
Is lithotripsy service subject to CON?:	True
Is long term care subject to CON?:	True
Is mobile high tech service subject to CON?:	True
Is MRI scanning subject to CON?:	True
Is neo-natal intensive care subject to CON?:	True
Are obstetrical services subject to CON?:	True
Is open heart surgery subject to CON?:	True
Is organ transplantation subject to CON?:	True
Is PET scanning subject to CON?:	True
Are psychiatric services subject to CON?:	True
Is radiation therapy subject to CON?:	True
Are rehabilitation services subject to CON?:	True
Is renal dialysis subject to CON?:	False
Is RCF/Assisted Living subject to CON?:	False
Is subacute care subject to CON?:	False
Is substance abuse subject to CON?:	True
Are swing beds subject to CON?:	True
Is utlra-sound subject to CON?:	True

Dollar Threshold for CON Application:

Dollar threshold for any service application:	$1,000,000

STATE NOTE

The healthcare facilities and institutions covered by the Conn. CON program are very broad and include: outpatient clinics; imaging centers; clinical laboratory or central service facilities serving one or more healthcare facilities; rest homes; NP health centers; diagnostic and treatment facilities; and lastly, state health care facilities or institutions (meaning a hospital or other such facility or institution operated by the state providing services which are eligible for reimbursement under Title XVIII or XIX).

Under Conn. Statutes, Section 19a-630, "health care facility or institution" includes any parent company, subsidiary, affiliate or joint venture or any combination thereof, of any such facility or institution, but does not include any health care facility operated by a non-profit educational institution solely for the students, faculty and staff of such institution and their dependents...

Section 19a-630a defines "affiliate" under the program such that if a facility or institution transfers control or ownership to an affiliate, that transaction is subject to CON review.

3. Conn. Statutes, Section 19a-638 is the key CON provision, as it tells when a health care facility/ institution/person may be subject to a CON review by the state. There are several features under this section worth noting:
4. There are a number of facilities/institutions which are either exempt from having to submit CON applications or who may have the CON application waived under certain conditions. These exceptions are as follows:

Under Conn. Statutes, Section 19a-639a(a), 12 types of facilities may be exempt from having to meet CON, some of which again don't fall into an easy category:

1) Outpatient clinic or program operated exclusively by or contracted to be operated exclusively for a municipality or municipal agency, a health district or board of education; 2) a residential facility for the mentally retarded; 3) outpatient rehabilitation service agency that was in operation on 1/1/98, that is operated exclusively on an outpatient basis; 4) a program of ambulatory services established and conducted by a HMO; 5) a clinic operated by the Americares Foundation; and 6) a rest home.

Under Conn. Statutes, Section 19a-639b, the Office of Health Care Access may grant an exemption from CON for any nonprofit facility/institution/provider if that nonprofit entity is proposing a "capital expenditure" of not more than one million dollars and the expenditure does not in fact exceed one million dollars".

Lastly, under Conn. Statutes, Section 19a-639c, a waiver may be granted to a facility, institution, or provider proposing to "replace major medical equipment, imaging equipment".

DELAWARE

STATE CON AGENCY CONTACTS

State Department Overseeing CON	
Name of state CON department:	Bureau of Health Planning and Resource Management
URL address for state CON organization:	http://www.state.de.us/dhss/dph/index.html
CON Administrative Office Information	
Name of state CON office:	Bureau of Health Planning & Resource Management Hierarchy for state CON administrative office: Governor: Dept. of Health and Social Services: Health Systems Management Section: Bureau of Helath Planning & Resource Management
CON organization contact person:	Kae Johnson
Title of CON contact person:	Director
Email address of CON contact:	kae.johnson@state.de.us
Mailing address for state CON office:	655 S. Bay Road
Mailing address for state CON office:	Blue Hen Corporate Center
City where state CON office is located:	Dover
State for mailing address:	Delaware
Zip code for CON office:	19910-
Phone number for CON contact:	(302) 741-2960
Fax number for CON contact:	(302) 741-2970
State CON Decision Making Body (DMB)	
Name of DMB:	Delaware Health Resources Board
Title of person DMB reports to:	Governor
Title of person appointing DMB members:	Governor
Composition of CON DMB:	
Number of people in the DMB:	20
Number of association reps in DMB:	3
Number of consumers in DMB:	9
Number of healthcare providers in DMB:	3

EQUIPMENT REGULATION AND DATA

Subject to CON (Y/N):	
Is any equipment subject to CON?:	False
Are air ambulances subject to CON?:	True
Are cardiac cath labs subject to CON?:	True
Are CT scanners subject to CON?:	True

Subject to CON (Y/N) (Continued)

Are gamma knives subject to CON?:	True
Are linear accelerators subject to CON?:	True
Is lithotropsy subject to CON?:	True
Is mobile high tech subject to CON?:	True
Are MRI scanners subject to CON?:	True
Are PET scanners subject to CON?:	True
Is radiation therapy subject to CON?:	True
Is renal dialysis subject to CON?:	True
Are swing beds subject to CON?:	True
Is ultra-sound subject to CON?:	False

Dollar Threshold for CON Application:

Dollar threshold for any equipment application: $5,000,000

Additional Criteria Used to Determine Need:

Additional criteria used to determine need for any equipment: no treshold for new medical technology or designated technology; do not need CON for replacement equipment

Additional criteria used to determine need for cardiac cath lab: no threshold

FACILITIES REGULATION AND DATA

Subject to CON (Y/N):

Is any facility subject to CON?	False
Are hospitals subject to CON?	True
Are nursing homes subject to CON?	True
Are residential care facilities subject to CON?	False
Are psychiatric facilities subject to CON?	False
Are ambulatory surgery centers subject to CON?	True
Are ICF/MRs subject to CON?	False
Is long term care subject to CON?	True
Are medical office buildings subject to CON?	False
Are rehabilitation facilities subject to CON?	False
Are renal dialysis facilities subject to CON?	False
Are RCF/Assisted Living facilities subject to CON?	False
Are subacute care facilities subject to CON?	False
Are substance abuse facilities subject to CON?	False
Are swing beds subject to CON?	False

Project Dollar Threshold Requiring CON Application:

Dollar threshold for any facility application: $5,000,000; change in bed capacity; construction of healthcare facility

Notes Including Bed Limits and Moratoria:

Notes including bed limits/moratoria for a hospital: no hospitals offering obstetrical beds shall be established in DE for the next five years

SERVICES REGULATION AND DATA

Subject to CON (Y/N):

Are all services subject to CON?:	False
Are nursing home services subject to CON?:	True
Are acute care services subject to CON?:	True
Are air ambulance subject to CON?:	True
Is burn care subject to CON?:	True
Is cardiac catheterization subject to CON?:	True
Is CT scanning subject to CON?:	True
Is gamma knife service subject to CON?:	True
Is home health subject to CON?:	False
Is linear accelerator service subject to CON?:	True
Is lithotripsy service subject to CON?:	True
Is long term care subject to CON?:	True
Is mobile high tech service subject to CON?:	False
Is MRI scanning subject to CON?:	True
Is neo-natal intensive care subject to CON?:	True
Are obstetrical services subject to CON?:	True
Is open heart surgery subject to CON?:	True
Is organ transplantation subject to CON?:	True
Is PET scanning subject to CON?:	True
Are psychiatric services subject to CON?:	True
Is radiation therapy subject to CON?:	True
Are rehabilitation services subject to CON?:	True
Is renal dialysis subject to CON?:	False
Is RCF/Assisted Living subject to CON?:	True
Is subacute care subject to CON?:	True
Is substance abuse subject to CON?:	True
Are swing beds subject to CON?:	True
Is utlra-sound subject to CON?:	True

Additional Criteria Used to Determine Need:

Additional criteria used to determine need for nursing home: Desired occupancy rate of 90%; preference for projects with bed complements of at least 100 beds, especially increases in bed complements of smaller facilities resulting in at least 100 beds

Additional criteria used to determine need for acute care: Hospital should have 90% occupancy rate; desired occupancy rate of 87.5%

Additional criteria used to determine need for long term care: Supply of state beds is allocated to each county based on patient origin

CON STATUTES AND REGULATIONS

CON Statutes:

CON Statute Title: Health Planning and Resource Management
CON Statute Citation: 16 Del. C. sec. 9301-9311
Year CON Statute Enacted: 2004

CON Regulations:

CON Regulations Title: Bylaws of Delaware Health Resources Board
CON Regulations Citation: 61 Del. Laws, c 393, sec1
Year CON Regulations Enacted: 1999

STATE NOTE

Delaware requires a certificate of need ("CON") to establish most healthcare services. The criteria for CON applications are contained the Bylaws of the Health Resources Board. The bylaws contain calculations to determine need for a service. The calculations consider a desired occupancy rate and the planning area's population. However, there are not standards for each service requiring a CON. Delaware's Health Resources Board and all laws regulating health planning and resources management will sunset on June 30, 2005.

FLORIDA

STATE CON AGENCY CONTACTS

State Department Overseeing CON

Name of state CON department:	Agency for Health Care Administration
URL address for state CON organization:	http://www.fdhc.state.fl.us/MCHQ CON_FA/

CON Administrative Office Information

Name of state CON office:	Health Facility Regulation Hierarchy for state CON administrative office: Governor: Agency for Health Care Administration: Health Facility Regulation
CON organization contact person:	Jeff Gregg
Title of CON contact person:	Bureau Chief
Email address of CON contact:	greggj@fdhc.state.fl.us
Mailing address for state CON office:	Health Facility Regulation
Mailing address for state CON office:	2727 Mahan Dr., Bldg. 3
City where state CON office is located:	Tallahassee
State for mailing address:	Florida
Zip code for CON office:	32308
Phone number for CON contact:	(850) 048-8862
Fax number for CON contact:	(850) 922-6964

State CON Decision Making Body (DMB)

Name of DMB:	Health Facilities Regulation
Title of person DMB reports to:	Agency for Health Care Administration
Title of person appointing DMB members:	N/A

Composition of CON DMB:

Number of people in the DMB:	1
Number of CON agency reps in DMB:	1
Number of consumers in DMB:	N/A
Number of healthcare providers in DMB:	N/A

EQUIPMENT REGULATION AND DATA

Subject to CON (Y/N):

Is any equipment subject to CON?:	False
Are air ambulances subject to CON?:	False
Are cardiac cath labs subject to CON?:	False
Are CT scanners subject to CON?:	False

Subject to CON (Y/N) (Continued)

Are gamma knives subject to CON?:	False
Are linear accelerators subject to CON?:	False
Is lithotropsy subject to CON?:	False
Is mobile high tech subject to CON?:	False
Are MRI scanners subject to CON?:	False
Are PET scanners subject to CON?:	False
Is radiation therapy subject to CON?:	False
Is renal dialysis subject to CON?:	False
Are swing beds subject to CON?:	False
Is ultra-sound subject to CON?:	False

FACILITIES REGULATION AND DATA

Subject to CON (Y/N):

Is any facility subject to CON?	False
Are hospitals subject to CON?	True
Are nursing homes subject to CON?	False
Are residential care facilities subject to CON?	False
Are psychiatric facilities subject to CON?	True
Are ambulatory surgery centers subject to CON?	False
Are ICF/MRs subject to CON?	True
Is long term care subject to CON?	True
Are medical office buildings subject to CON?	False
Are rehabilitation facilities subject to CON?	False
Are renal dialysis facilities subject to CON?	False
Are RCF/Assisted Living facilities subject to CON?	False
Are subacute care facilities subject to CON?	True
Are substance abuse facilities subject to CON?	True
Are swing beds subject to CON?	False
Are other facilities subject to CON?	skilled nursing units; hospice

Project Dollar Threshold Requiring CON Application:

Dollar threshold for any facility application: $addition of new beds; establishment of new facility; conversion of facility

Additional Criteria Used to Determine Need:

Additional criteria used to determine need for any facility: consider need in relation to applicable district health plan; consider availablity, quality of care, accessibility, and the extent of utilization of existing facilities in district; ability of applicant to provide quality of care; need in service district of applicant for services that are not reasonably and economically accessible in adjoining areas; needs of research and educational facilities; availability of resources; immediate and long-term financial feasibility of the proposal

Additional criteria used to determine need for a hospital: applications for additional acute care beds will not be approved unless average occupancy rate for existing beds in subdistrict exceeds 75%

Additional criteria used to determine need for a nursing home: complex need formula considering population and estimated bed rate and number of nursing facility beds

Additional criteria used to determine need for a psychiatric facility: minimum size of facility is 40 beds; optimal occupancy is 75%

Additional criteria used to determine need for an ICF/MR: proposal cannot be for more than 60 beds divided into living units of not more than 15 beds each; proposal for conversion to ICF/MR provides for division of facility into living units of not more than 25 beds

Additional criteria used to determine need for a rehabilitation facility: desired occupancy is 85%; complex need formula; preference given to disproportionate share hospital or designated trauma center

Additional criteria used to determine need for a substance abuse facility: desired occupancy is 75%

Additional criteria used to determine need for other facilities: .75 is desired occupancy rate for skilled nursing units

Additional Criteria Used to Determine Need:

Additional criteria used to determine need for burn care: Desired occupancy rate is 80%; preference given to applicants proposing to convert existing medical and surgical beds to burn unit beds

Additional criteria used to determine need for cardiac catheterization: Minimum volume for establishment of new adult cardiac catheterization program is 300 admissions; pediatric cardiac catherization programs shall be established on a regional basis; new pediatric cardiac catheterization program will not be approved unless the number of live births exceeds 30,000; pediatric programs must project 150 catherizations per year; programs serving both pediatric and adult patients shall project 350 procedures

Additional criteria used to determine need for open heart surgery: Additional program will not normally be approved if there is an adult open heart surgery program in the district; preference given to programs in counties meeting certain criteria; optimal utilization is 300 operations; different requirements for services in certain counties

Additional criteria used to determine need for organ transplantation: Liver, adult allogenic bone marrow, pediatric allogenic and autologous bone marrow, lung, heart and lung, pancreas and islet cells, and intestines transplant programs restricted to teaching or research hospitals; separate CON is required for pediatric organ transplant programs by type

SERVICES REGULATION AND DATA

Subject to CON (Y/N):

Are all services subject to CON?:	False
Are nursing home services subject to CON?:	True
Are acute care services subject to CON?:	True
Are air ambulance subject to CON?:	False
Is burn care subject to CON?:	True
Is cardiac catheterization subject to CON?:	False
Is CT scanning subject to CON?:	False
Is gamma knife service subject to CON?:	False
Is home health subject to CON?:	False
Is linear accelerator service subject to CON?:	False
Is lithotripsy service subject to CON?:	False
Is long term care subject to CON?:	True
Is mobile high tech service subject to CON?:	False
Is MRI scanning subject to CON?:	False
Is neo-natal intensive care subject to CON?:	True
Are obstetrical services subject to CON?:	False
Is open heart surgery subject to CON?:	True

Subject to CON (Y/N) (Continued)

Is organ transplantation subject to CON?:	True
Is PET scanning subject to CON?:	False
Are psychiatric services subject to CON?:	True
Is radiation therapy subject to CON?:	False
Are rehabilitation services subject to CON?:	True
Is renal dialysis subject to CON?:	False
Is RCF/Assisted Living subject to CON?:	False
Is subacute care subject to CON?:	True
Is substance abuse subject to CON?:	True
Are swing beds subject to CON?:	True
Is utlra-sound subject to CON?:	False
Are other services subject to CON?:	pediatric oncology and hematology; neonatal and pedatric cardiac and vascular surgery

CON STATUTES AND REGULATIONS

CON Statutes:

CON Statute Title: Health Facility and Services Development Act
CON Statute Citation: Fla. Stat. 408.031-408.045
Year CON Statute Enacted: 2003

CON Regulations:

CON Regulations Title: Procedures for the Administration of Sections 408.031-408.045, Florida Statutes, Health Facility and Services Development Act
CON Regulations Citation: 59C-(1.001-1.050)

STATE NOTE

Florida requires a certificate of need ("CON") for most healthcare services. The statutes specify that before additional nursing facility beds can be approved, it must be demonstrated that the need cannot be met through home or community-based services. The regulations proscribe complex calculations for "need" which consider the number of facilities in the region and the area's population.

GEORGIA

STATE CON AGENCY CONTACTS

State Department Overseeing CON	
Name of state CON department:	Department of Community Health
URL address for state CON organization:	http://www.communityhealth.state.ga.us
CON Administrative Office Information	
Name of state CON office:	Division of Health Planning Hierarchy for state CON administrative office: Governor: Dept. of Community Health: Division of Health Planning
CON organization contact person:	Rathelia Stroud
Title of CON contact person:	Director Certificate of Need Program
Email address of CON contact:	rstroud@dch.state.ga.us
Mailing address for state CON office:	2 Peachtree Street NW
Mailing address for state CON office:	40th Floor
City where state CON office is located:	Atlanta
State for mailing address:	Georgia
Zip code for CON office:	30303
Phone number for CON contact:	(404) 656-0436
Fax number for CON contact:	(404) 656-0442
State CON Decision Making Body (DMB)	
Name of DMB:	Health Planning Review Board
Title of person DMB reports to:	Commisioner of Community Health
Title of person appointing DMB members:	Governor, subject to Senate confirm.
Composition of CON DMB:	
Number of people in the DMB:	11
Number of consumers in DMB:	10
Number of healthcare providers in DMB:	10

EQUIPMENT REGULATION AND DATA

Subject to CON (Y/N):	
Is any equipment subject to CON?:	False
Are air ambulances subject to CON?:	False
Are cardiac cath labs subject to CON?:	True
Are CT scanners subject to CON?:	True
Are gamma knives subject to CON?:	True
Are linear accelerators subject to CON?:	False

Subject to CON (Y/N) (Continued)

Is lithotropsy subject to CON?:	True
Is mobile high tech subject to CON?:	True
Are MRI scanners subject to CON?:	True
Are PET scanners subject to CON?:	True
Is radiation therapy subject to CON?:	True
Is renal dialysis subject to CON?:	False
Are swing beds subject to CON?:	False
Is ultra-sound subject to CON?:	False

Dollar Threshold for CON Application:

Dollar threshold for any equipment application:	$500000

FACILITIES REGULATION AND DATA

Subject to CON (Y/N):

Is any facility subject to CON?	False
Are hospitals subject to CON?	True
Are nursing homes subject to CON?	True
Are residential care facilities subject to CON?	True
Are psychiatric facilities subject to CON?	True
Are ambulatory surgery centers subject to CON?	True
Are ICF/MRs subject to CON?	True
Is long term care subject to CON?	True
Are medical office buildings subject to CON?	False
Are rehabilitation facilities subject to CON?	True
Are renal dialysis facilities subject to CON?	False
Are RCF/Assisted Living facilities subject to CON?	True
Are subacute care facilities subject to CON?	True
Are substance abuse facilities subject to CON?	True
Are swing beds subject to CON?	False
Are other facilities subject to CON?	podiatric facilities, skilled nursing facilities, personal care homes (RCF with 25 beds); facilties which are devoted to the provision of treatment and rehabilitative care for periods continuing for 24 hours or longer for persons who have traumatic brain injury

Project Dollar Threshold Requiring CON Application:

Dollar threshold for any facility application: $CON required for new institutional health service (the construction, development, or other establishment of a new health care facility; any expenditure in excess of $900,000; any increase in the bed capacity; clinical health services not offered regularly

Dollar threshold for an ambulatory surgery center application: $1,000,000

Capacity Requirements – Beds / Population:

Capacity requirement-beds/population for psychiatric facilities: bed need varies based on program

Capacity requirement-beds/population for ICF/MRs:

Capacity requirement-beds/population for RCF/Assisted Living facility: 18/1000 to 60/1000 based on pop. char.

Capacity Requirements – Facilities / Population:

Capacity requirement-facilities/population for a hospital: Rur. Hosp.=65%; Non-rur. Hosp.=75%; teach hos.=70%

Capacity requirement-facilities/population for a residential care facility: adult programs=80%+; child prog.=75%+

Capacity requirement-facilities/population for a psychiatric facility: >=85%

Capacity requirement-facilities/population for an ambulatory surgery center: 80 percent aggregate utilization rate

Capacity requirement-facilities/population for a RCF/Assisted Living facility: 18/1000 to 60/1000 based on pop. char.

Additional Criteria Used to Determine Need:

Additional criteria used to determine need for a hospital: New hospital must be at least 50 beds if in rural county and at least 100 if located in non-rural. Need for new, replacement, or expanded hospital determined through demand-based forecasting. A new hospital shall be approved only if the total target service area population is at least 50,000 persons.

Additional criteria used to determine need for a nursing home: Need determined through numerical, supply-oriented need method

Additional criteria used to determine need for a psychiatric facility: Minimum bed size: new psych program=8; new psych acute care hospitals=50; aggregate of any and all acute psych program in general hospital=15. Must get approval to add new beds as opposed to using existing hospital beds

Additional criteria used to determine need for an ambulatory surgery center: A proposed multi-specialty ambulatory surgery service shall have a minimum of three operating rooms and a limited purpose ambulatory surgery service shall have a minimum of two operating rooms.

Notes Including Bed Limits and Moratoria:

Notes including bed limits/moratoria for a hospital: No CON for transfer of facility.

Notes including bed limits/moratoria for a psychiatric facility: CON not required in public sector as long as beds proposed within state system does not exceed number needed statewide

Notes including bed limits/moratoria for an ambulatory surgery center: Freestanding ambulatory surgery centers require CON. If ambulatory surgery service is part of hospital, no CON is required.

Notes including bed limits/moratoria for other facilities: Residential facility must have at least 25 beds to qualify as a personal care home

Utilization Requirements (Procedures/Population):

Utilization requirement-procedures/population for home health: A range of 4 to 185 based on population

Utilization Requirements (Facilities or Services/Population):

Utilization requirement-services/population for obsterical services: Occupancy rate shall equal or exceed 75%

Additional Criteria Used to Determine Need:

Additional criteria used to determine need for cardiac catheterization: The need for new or expanded adult card cath services shall be determined thorugh application of a numerical need mehod and an analysis of service demand. The numerical need for new or expanded adult card cath services shall be determined by a population based formula. In the case of an approved service, service volume should be projected in accordance with the volume projections in the approved application. An applicant for a new or expanded adult cardiac cath service must project and, if approved, shall document that the proposed service will be performing a minimum of 1040 adult cardiac cath procedure equivalents within three years of initiation of the service and annually thereafter within the authorized guidelines for such services.

Additional criteria used to determine need for obstetrical: The need for a new or expanded Obstetric Service, Neonatal Intermediate Care Service and Neonatal Intensive Care Service shall be determined through application of a Numerical Need method and an assessment of the aggregate occupancy rate of exising services. The numerical need shall be determined through the application of a demand-based forecasting model. An applicant shall document the impact on existing and approved services in the planning area with the goal of minimizing adverse impact on the delivery system.

Additional criteria used to determine need for open heart surgery: Standards: 1)3 yrs card cath in acute care hospital; 2)minimum of 250 procedures in previous 2 years; 3) Projected to perform 300 procedures in next 3 years; 4)exidting and approved services not predicted to have an adverse impact as a result of new service. New service must be capable of implementing intraaortic balloon assist and cardio procedures including minimum of: repair and replacement of heart valves; card. Revascularization; card. Trauma; congenital defects; acute aortic dissection. Must submit written plan to Department.

Additional criteria used to determine need for radiation therapy: The need for a new or expanded radiation therapy service shall be determined through the application of a Numerical Need method and an assesment of the aggregate utilization rate of exisiting services. The numerical need shall be determined through the application of a demand-based forecasting model. For services which are performing below 80% of optimal utilization, the application shall document that it will not cause such exising service to fall more than 10% below its current utilization.

Additional criteria used to determine need for rehabilitation: Min Bed Size: Comprehensive Inpatient Phys. Rehab. Program for Spinal Cord Disorders=20, 10 for children; New unit in freestanding rehab hospital=40 for adult and children programs

Additional criteria used to determine need for others: The need for an ambulatory surgery service is determined using a complicated numerical need method and an assessment of the aggregate utilization rate of existing services. The numerical need shall be determined by a demographic formula which includes the number of ambulatory surgery services cases in a planning area.

SERVICES REGULATION AND DATA

Subject to CON (Y/N):

Are all services subject to CON?:	False
Are nursing home services subject to CON?:	True
Are acute care services subject to CON?:	True
Are air ambulance subject to CON?:	False
Is burn care subject to CON?:	True
Is cardiac catheterization subject to CON?:	False
Is CT scanning subject to CON?:	False
Is gamma knife service subject to CON?:	False
Is home health subject to CON?:	False
Is linear accelerator service subject to CON?:	False
Is lithotripsy service subject to CON?:	False
Is long term care subject to CON?:	True
Is mobile high tech service subject to CON?:	False
Is MRI scanning subject to CON?:	False
Is neo-natal intensive care subject to CON?:	True

Subject to CON (Y/N) (Continued)

Are obstetrical services subject to CON?:	False
Is open heart surgery subject to CON?:	True
Is organ transplantation subject to CON?:	True
Is PET scanning subject to CON?:	False
Are psychiatric services subject to CON?:	True
Is radiation therapy subject to CON?:	False
Are rehabilitation services subject to CON?:	True
Is renal dialysis subject to CON?:	False
Is RCF/Assisted Living subject to CON?:	False
Is subacute care subject to CON?:	True
Is substance abuse subject to CON?:	True
Are swing beds subject to CON?:	True
Is utlra-sound subject to CON?:	False
Are other services subject to CON?:	pediatric oncology and hematology; neonatal and pedatric cardiac and vascular surgery

CON STATUTES AND REGULATIONS

CON Statutes:

CON Statute Title: State Health Planning and Development
CON Statute Citation: O.C.G.A. 31-6-(1-2,20-22,40-50,70)

CON Regulations:

CON Regulations Title: State Health Planning Agency
CON Regulations Citation: Ga. Comp. R. & Regs. R. 272-2-(.01-.12)

STATE NOTE

Georgia requires a certificate of need ("CON") for most healthcare services. The regulations contain complex calculations of "need." The calculations consider a desired utilization rate, the area's population, and actual utilization of the service by existing providers. The criteria to expand or replace an existing service are different than the standards to establish a new service.

HAWAII

STATE CON AGENCY CONTACTS

State Department Overseeing CON

Name of state CON department:	State Health Planning & Development Agency
URL address for state CON organization:	http://www.state.hi.us/health/shpda/

CON Administrative Office Information

Name of state CON office:	State Health Planning & Development Agency Hierarchy for state CON administrative office: Governor: Dept. of Health: State Health Planning & Development Agency
CON organization contact person:	David Sakamoto, MD
Title of CON contact person:	Administrator
Email address of CON contact:	david@shpda.org
Mailing address for state CON office:	1177 Alakea Street, Rm 402
Mailing address for state CON office:	
City where state CON office is located:	Honolulu
State for mailing address:	Hawaii
Zip code for CON office:	96813-
Phone number for CON contact:	(808) 587-0788
Fax number for CON contact:	(808) 587-0783

State CON Decision Making Body (DMB)

Name of DMB:	Statewide Health Coordinating Council: Review Panel
Title of person DMB reports to:	Governor
Title of person appointing DMB members:	Statewide Health Coordinating Council

Composition of CON DMB:

Number of consumers in DMB:	Majority of review panel members, which includes 1 member per county

EQUIPMENT REGULATION AND DATA

Subject to CON (Y/N):

Is any equipment subject to CON?:	True
Are air ambulances subject to CON?:	True
Are cardiac cath labs subject to CON?:	True
Are CT scanners subject to CON?:	True

Subject to CON (Y/N) (Continued)

Are gamma knives subject to CON?:	True
Are linear accelerators subject to CON?:	True
Is lithotropsy subject to CON?:	True
Is mobile high tech subject to CON?:	True
Are MRI scanners subject to CON?:	True
Are PET scanners subject to CON?:	True
Is radiation therapy subject to CON?:	True
Is renal dialysis subject to CON?:	True
Are swing beds subject to CON?:	True
Is ultra-sound subject to CON?:	True

FACILITIES REGULATION AND DATA

Subject to CON (Y/N):

Is any facility subject to CON?	False
Are hospitals subject to CON?	True
Are nursing homes subject to CON?	True
Are residential care facilities subject to CON?	False
Are psychiatric facilities subject to CON?	True
Are ambulatory surgery centers subject to CON?	True
Are ICF/MRs subject to CON?	True
Is long term care subject to CON?	True
Are medical office buildings subject to CON?	False
Are rehabilitation facilities subject to CON?	True
Are renal dialysis facilities subject to CON?	True
Are RCF/Assisted Living facilities subject to CON?	False
Are subacute care facilities subject to CON?	True
Are substance abuse facilities subject to CON?	True
Are swing beds subject to CON?	True
Are other facilities subject to CON?	HMOs and others providing similarly organized services regardless of nomenclature

Project Dollar Threshold Requiring CON Application:

Dollar threshold for any facility application: $4,000,000 for cap.exp; $1,000,000 for new or replacement med. equip; $400,000 for used med. Equip

Notes Including Bed Limits and Moratoria:

Notes including bed limits/moratoria for any facility: CON exemptions: bed changes that involve 10% or ten beds of existing licensed bed types, whichever is less, of a facility's total existing licensed beds within a two-year period; and replacement of existing equipment with its modern-day equivalent

Notes including bed limits/moratoria for a RCF/Assisted Living facility: Extended care adult residential care homes and assisted living facilites are exempt from CON

SERVICES REGULATION AND DATA

Subject to CON (Y/N):

Are all services subject to CON?:	True
Are nursing home services subject to CON?:	False

Subject to CON (Y/N) (Continued)

Are acute care services subject to CON?:	True
Are air ambulance subject to CON?:	False
Is burn care subject to CON?:	False
Is cardiac catheterization subject to CON?:	True
Is CT scanning subject to CON?:	True
Is gamma knife service subject to CON?:	True
Is home health subject to CON?:	True
Is linear accelerator service subject to CON?:	False
Is lithotripsy service subject to CON?:	True
Is long term care subject to CON?:	True
Is mobile high tech service subject to CON?:	True
Is MRI scanning subject to CON?:	True
Is neo-natal intensive care subject to CON?:	True
Are obstetrical services subject to CON?:	True
Is open heart surgery subject to CON?:	True
Is organ transplantation subject to CON?:	False
Is PET scanning subject to CON?:	True
Are psychiatric services subject to CON?:	True
Is radiation therapy subject to CON?:	True
Are rehabilitation services subject to CON?:	True
Is renal dialysis subject to CON?:	False
Is RCF/Assisted Living subject to CON?:	True
Is subacute care subject to CON?:	True
Is substance abuse subject to CON?:	True
Are swing beds subject to CON?:	False
Is utlra-sound subject to CON?:	False
Are other services subject to CON?:	surgery; general medical care; inpatient nursing care; coronary care

Additional Criteria Used to Determine Need:

Additional criteria used to determine need for any service: Expenditure minimum means $4,000,000 for capital expenditures; $1,000,000 for new or replacement medical equipment and $400,000 for used medical equipment. Under CON, cannot: construct, expand, alter, convert, develop, initiate, or modify health care facility or health care services in the State that requires total capital expenditure in excess of expenditure minimum; substantially modify or increase scope of health services; or change class of usage of the bed complement of health care facility, or relocate beds from one facility to another unless CON issued. Change of health care service requiring CON: adding or deleting any standard category of health care service; and changing of location, unless the change doesn't affect the delivery of service to the target group. The addition or deletion of any bed service category requires a CON

CON STATUTES AND REGULATIONS

CON Statutes:

CON Statute Title: Health Planning and Resources Development and Health Care Cost Control
CON Statute Citation: HRS 323D-2, HRS 323 D-41-55

CON Regulations:

CON Regulations Title: Department of Health State of Hawaii State Health Planning and Development Agency Certificate of Need Program

CON Regulations Citation: Title 11, Chapter 186

STATE NOTE

Hawaii requires a certificate of need ("CON") for most healthcare services. The rules state that the agency must consider the "need" for the service but does not detail how "need" is determined.

ILLINOIS

STATE CON AGENCY CONTACTS

State Department Overseeing CON	
Name of state CON department:	Health Facilities Planning Board
URL address for state CON organization:	http://www.idph.state.il.us/about/hfpb.htm
CON Administrative Office Information	
Name of state CON office:	Health Facilites Planning Board Hierarchy for state CON administrative office: Governor: Departement of Public Health: Division of Facilities Development
CON organization contact person:	Jeffrey Mark
Title of CON contact person:	Executive Secretary
Email address of CON contact:	jmark@idph.state.il.us
Mailing address for state CON office:	525 W. Jefferson St.
City where state CON office is located:	Springfield
State for mailing address:	Illinois
Zip code for CON office:	62761-
Phone number for CON contact:	(217) 782-3516
Fax number for CON contact:	(217) 785-4308
State CON Decision Making Body (DMB)	
Name of DMB:	Health Facilities Planning Board
Title of person DMB reports to:	Department of Health
Title of person appointing DMB members:	Governor
Composition of CON DMB:	
Number of people in the DMB:	9-member State Board

EQUIPMENT REGULATION AND DATA

Subject to CON (Y/N):	
Is any equipment subject to CON?:	True
Are air ambulances subject to CON?:	False
Are cardiac cath labs subject to CON?:	True
Are CT scanners subject to CON?:	False
Are gamma knives subject to CON?:	False
Are linear accelerators subject to CON?:	True
Is lithotropsy subject to CON?:	True
Is mobile high tech subject to CON?:	False
Are MRI scanners subject to CON?:	False

Subject to CON (Y/N) (Continued)

Are PET scanners subject to CON?:	False
Is radiation therapy subject to CON?:	True
Is renal dialysis subject to CON?:	True
Are swing beds subject to CON?:	True
Is ultra-sound subject to CON?:	False
Is other equipment subject to CON?:	Post-Surg. Recov. Care Ctrs: Child

Dollar Threshold for CON Application:

Dollar threshold for any equipment application: $6,000,000 capital expenditure minimum for major medical equipment and all other capital expenditures

Additional Criteria Used to Determine Need:

Additional criteria used to determine need for any equipment: CON exemption: acquisition or replacement of equipment by health care facilty that does not substantially change bed count or scope of facility and that does not exceed the lesser of $4 million or 10% of facility operating revenues.

FACILITIES REGULATION AND DATA

Subject to CON (Y/N):

Is any facility subject to CON?	False
Are hospitals subject to CON?	True
Are nursing homes subject to CON?	True
Are residential care facilities subject to CON?	False
Are psychiatric facilities subject to CON?	True
Are ambulatory surgery centers subject to CON?	True
Are ICF/MRs subject to CON?	True
Is long term care subject to CON?	True
Are medical office buildings subject to CON?	False
Are rehabilitation facilities subject to CON?	True
Are renal dialysis facilities subject to CON?	True
Are RCF/Assisted Living facilities subject to CON?	False
Are subacute care facilities subject to CON?	True
Are substance abuse facilities subject to CON?	False
Are swing beds subject to CON?	True

Project Dollar Threshold Requiring CON Application:

Dollar threshold for any facility application: $6,000,000 capital expenditure minimum for major medical equipment and all other capital expenditures

Notes Including Bed Limits and Moratoria:

Notes including bed limits/moratoria for any facility: The state of Illinois CON Regulations include detailed cost data, financial feasibility data, and economic feasibility data.

SERVICES REGULATION AND DATA

Subject to CON (Y/N):

Are all services subject to CON?:	False
Are nursing home services subject to CON?:	False
Are acute care services subject to CON?:	True
Are air ambulance subject to CON?:	False
Is burn care subject to CON?:	False
Is cardiac catheterization subject to CON?:	True
Is CT scanning subject to CON?:	False
Is gamma knife service subject to CON?:	False
Is home health subject to CON?:	False
Is linear accelerator service subject to CON?:	False
Is lithotripsy service subject to CON?:	False
Is long term care subject to CON?:	True
Is mobile high tech service subject to CON?:	False
Is MRI scanning subject to CON?:	False
Is neo-natal intensive care subject to CON?:	True
Are obstetrical services subject to CON?:	True
Is open heart surgery subject to CON?:	True
Is organ transplantation subject to CON?:	True
Is PET scanning subject to CON?:	True
Are psychiatric services subject to CON?:	True
Is radiation therapy subject to CON?:	True
Are rehabilitation services subject to CON?:	True
Is renal dialysis subject to CON?:	True
Is RCF/Assisted Living subject to CON?:	False
Is subacute care subject to CON?:	True
Is substance abuse subject to CON?:	False
Are swing beds subject to CON?:	True
Is utlra-sound subject to CON?:	False

Additional Criteria Used to Determine Need:

Additional criteria used to determine need for any service: No person shall construct, modify or establish a health care facility or acquire major medical equipment without first obtaining a permit or exemption from the State Board (requires total capital expenditure in excess of capital expenditure minimum

Additional criteria used to determine need for neonatal intensive care: CON exemption: proposed project limited to the establishment or expansion of a neonatal intensive care service or beds

CON STATUTES AND REGULATIONS

CON Statutes:

CON Statute Title: Illinois Health Facilites Planning Act
CON Statute Citation: 20 ILCS 3960/1 et seq.
Year CON Statute Enacted: 1974

CON Regulations:

CON Regulations Title: Public Health Health Facilities Planning Board
CON Regulations Citation: Title 77, Chapter 2, Section 1120-1130

STATE NOTE

Illinois requires a certificate of need ("CON") to establish most healthcare services. The Illinois regulations contain extensive information concerning project and related cost data which applicants must include in the CON application. Similarly, Illinois requires applicants to submit detailed information on both financial and economic feasibility of proposed projects. In addition to requiring extensive data from applicants, Illinois regulations require CON holders to submit annual progress reports to the Agency every twelve (12) months from the permit issuance date until the project is completed, at which time the Agency requires notification of completion.

IOWA

STATE CON AGENCY CONTACTS

State Department Overseeing CON

Name of state CON department:	Department of Public Health
URL address for state CON organization:	http://www.idph.state.ia.us/docert_of_need.asp

CON Administrative Office Information

Name of state CON office:	Certificate of Need Program Hierarchy for state CON administrative office: Governor: Department of Public Health: Director's Office: CON Program
CON organization contact person:	Barb Nervig
Title of CON contact person:	Program Manager
Email address of CON contact:	bnervig@idph.state.ia.us
Mailing address for state CON office:	321 E 12th St.
Mailing address for state CON office:	Lucas State Office Bldg
City where state CON office is located:	Des Moines
State for mailing address:	Iowa
Zip code for CON office:	50319-0075
Phone number for CON contact:	(515) 281-4344
Fax number for CON contact:	(515) 281-6475

State CON Decision Making Body (DMB)

Name of DMB:	Health Facilities Council
Title of person DMB reports to:	Department of Public Health
Title of person appointing DMB members:	Governor

Composition of CON DMB:

Number of people in the DMB:	5
Number of association reps in DMB:	1
Number of consumers in DMB:	3
Number of healthcare providers in DMB:	1

EQUIPMENT REGULATION AND DATA

Subject to CON (Y/N):

Is any equipment subject to CON?:	False
Are air ambulances subject to CON?:	True
Are cardiac cath labs subject to CON?:	True
Are CT scanners subject to CON?:	True

Subject to CON (Y/N) (Continued)

Are gamma knives subject to CON?:	True
Are linear accelerators subject to CON?:	True
Is lithotropsy subject to CON?:	True
Is mobile high tech subject to CON?:	True
Are MRI scanners subject to CON?:	True
Are PET scanners subject to CON?:	True
Is radiation therapy subject to CON?:	True
Is renal dialysis subject to CON?:	True
Are swing beds subject to CON?:	True
Is ultra-sound subject to CON?:	False

Dollar Threshold for CON Application:

Dollar threshold for any equipment application:	$1,500,000

FACILITIES REGULATION AND DATA

Subject to CON (Y/N):

Is any facility subject to CON?	False
Are hospitals subject to CON?	True
Are nursing homes subject to CON?	True
Are residential care facilities subject to CON?	False
Are psychiatric facilities subject to CON?	True
Are ambulatory surgery centers subject to CON?	True
Are ICF/MRs subject to CON?	True
Is long term care subject to CON?	True
Are medical office buildings subject to CON?	False
Are rehabilitation facilities subject to CON?	False
Are renal dialysis facilities subject to CON?	False
Are RCF/Assisted Living facilities subject to CON?	False
Are subacute care facilities subject to CON?	False
Are substance abuse facilities subject to CON?	False
Are swing beds subject to CON?	False
Are other facilities subject to CON?	Birth Center, Organized Outpatient Health Facility

Project Dollar Threshold Requiring CON Application:

Dollar threshold for any facility application:	$1,500,000

Additional Criteria Used to Determine Need:

Additional criteria used to determine need for an ICF/MR: 3% of mentally retarded in total population, and 8% mentally retarded population need services outside their homes

Additional criteria used to determine need for a renal dialysis facility: No additional or expanded renal dialysis centers or facilities unless stations within 90 minute travel time perform at rate of at least 7 dialyses per station per week. No increase in dialysis stations if less than 35 percent of ESRD patients in catchment area of that center are on home or self-care dialysis. Applicant must identify large unserved population within 90 minutes travel time of proposed site.

Notes Including Bed Limits and Moratoria:

Notes including bed limits/moratoria for any facility: a permanent change in bed capacity. CON exclusions: reduction in bed capacity of an institutional health facility; and deletion of one or more health services

Notes including bed limits/moratoria for a hospital: Subject to CON: construction, development, or relocation of health facility

Notes including bed limits/moratoria for a nursing home: Subject to CON: construction, development, or relocation of health facility. CON exclusions: remedial care for patients in any institution conducted for those who rely only on prayer or spiritual treatment

Notes including bed limits/moratoria for a psychiatric facility: Subject to CON: construction, development, or relocation of health facility

Notes including bed limits/moratoria for an ICF/MR: Subject to CON: construction, development, or relocation of health facility

Notes including bed limits/moratoria for a long term care facility: Subject to CON: construction, development, or relocation of health facility

Notes including bed limits/moratoria for a renal dialysis facility: CON exclusions: hemodialysis services provided by a hospital or freestanding facility

Notes including bed limits/moratoria for a RCF/Assisted Living facility: Subject to CON: construction, development, or relocation of health facility

Notes including bed limits/moratoria for other facilities: Subject to CON: construction, development, or relocation of health facility

SERVICES REGULATION AND DATA

Subject to CON (Y/N):

Are all services subject to CON?:	False
Are nursing home services subject to CON?:	True
Are acute care services subject to CON?:	True
Are air ambulance subject to CON?:	False
Is burn care subject to CON?:	False
Is cardiac catheterization subject to CON?:	True
Is CT scanning subject to CON?:	False
Is gamma knife service subject to CON?:	False
Is home health subject to CON?:	False
Is linear accelerator service subject to CON?:	True
Is lithotripsy service subject to CON?:	False
Is long term care subject to CON?:	True
Is mobile high tech service subject to CON?:	False
Is MRI scanning subject to CON?:	False
Is neo-natal intensive care subject to CON?:	False
Are obstetrical services subject to CON?:	False
Is open heart surgery subject to CON?:	True
Is organ transplantation subject to CON?:	True
Is PET scanning subject to CON?:	True
Are psychiatric services subject to CON?:	True
Is radiation therapy subject to CON?:	True
Are rehabilitation services subject to CON?:	False
Is renal dialysis subject to CON?:	True
Is RCF/Assisted Living subject to CON?:	False

Subject to CON (Y/N) (Continued)

Is subacute care subject to CON?:	False
Is substance abuse subject to CON?:	False
Are swing beds subject to CON?:	False
Is utlra-sound subject to CON?:	False
Are other services subject to CON?:	Mobile Health Service

Dollar Threshold for CON Application:

Dollar threshold for any service application:	$500,000
Dollar threshold for other service application:	$1,500,000

Additional Criteria Used to Determine Need:

Additional criteria used to determine need for acute care: Number of acute care beds needed by each hospital in the future is a function of the number of patient days of acute care that will be needed by Iowa citizens, with allowance for the needs of specific population groups and for the travel distance to and location of the hospital

Additional criteria used to determine need for cardiac catheterization: Minimum Utilization: adult cardiac cath labs projected to operate at min of 300 caths per yr; and ped cath labs should project a minimum of 150 caths per yr. Expansions Adult: no units opened unless number of studies per yr is greater than 500 within 2 hr service area; no additional units that would reduce volume of existing units below 500 adult caths, 200 of which are intracardiac or coronary artery caths; no new cardiac cath unit opened in any facility not performing open heart surgery. Expansions Pediatric Card Cath: no additional unit unless number of studies is more than 250 within 2 hr surface travel time; no additional unit that would reduce volume of existing units below 150; and no unit opened in facility not performing open heart surgery

Additional criteria used to determine need for CT scanning: Determination of Need: (1) area with no other scanners- must perform at least 30,000 general imaging procedures in last year or demonstrate performance of 1500 HECTs; (2) area with one or more scanners- average level of utilization at least 3,000 HECTs in past year; (3) replace scanner with another scanner- use of current scanner at least at operating capacity level during last year or below operating capacity level but above 1500 HECT level

Additional criteria used to determine need for MRI scanning: (1) Area with no other MRI units- must document CT procedure volume of at least 4500 CT procedures during past year, (2)Area with 1+ MRI units - other MRI unit in area must be operating at a minimum of 3,000 MRI procedures annually, if below that level, future projections should be above or proof of why it was so low is required. (3)Replacing MRI Unit-existing MRI unit must be operating at a level of at least 3,000 procedures annually, if below future utilization must be predicted above that level, or proof of why level was so low is required. (4)Adding Additional MRI Unit-existing MRI unit must be operating at level of at least 3,500 procedures annually, and applicant must demonstrate a demand for a significant amount over 3,500 procedures annually.

Additional criteria used to determine need for neonatal intensive care: Minimum Utilization: each perinatal center service area should have no more than four neonatal intensive care beds per 1,000 live births. Expansions: expanding or new units must be endorsed by Iowa Dept of Public Health Perinatal Standards Committee

Additional criteria used to determine need for obstetrical: Travel time to level I obstetrical unit should not exceed 30 minutes for 80 percent of population served

Additional criteria used to determine need for open heart surgery: Min Utilization: adult cardiovascular surgical programs should project annual minimum rate of over 200; and pediatric cardiovascular surgical units should project minimum of 100 ped heart operations after first year, at least 75 of which must be open heart procedures. Expansions Adult: no additional surgery units unless each existing unit within 3 hrs is operating at 130 surgeries per yr; no additional surgery units if reduces volume of existing services below 350 procedures annually; surgery units granted only to institutions which demonstrate underserved population of 500,000 people. Expansions Pediatric: no additional surgery units unless each existing unit within 3 hrs operates at 130 surgeries per year; no units approved that reduce existing services below 130 annually, 75 of which are open heart; demonstrate unserved population base of 2.5 million with 30,000 live births per year

Additional criteria used to determine need for organ transplantation: Renal transplantation centers should perform 25+ transplants annually with service area population of at least 2,000,000 people. Each transplant center should perform at least 50 annual transplants before additional facilities open.

Additional criteria used to determine need for PET scanning: (1) Area with no PET Units: must show reasonable potential utilization of PET unit based on diversified patient case mix and have other diagnostic capabilities, on site or through referral arrangements (2) Area with 1+ PET Unit- existing PET units in area must be operating at minimum of 1,000 PET procedures during past year

Additional criteria used to determine need for radiation therapy: Minimum Utilization: low energy unit should serve at least 200,000 people, and treat at least 300 new patients annually; medium energy unit placed in facilities treating minimum of 500 new patients annually; and high energy units in facilities with minimum of 750 new patients annually. Expansions: no approved units unless existing units performing at least 6,000 treatments per year; new units must identify unserved population base of 200,000 within 90 minute radius; no new units if they will reduce existing unit treatments to less than 6,000 treatments per year and which would result in less than 300 projected new patients per year for that existing unit; and new conjoint centers justified if more than 3,000 new patients are currently treated in existing center

Additional criteria used to determine need for RCF or Assisted Living: Formula for Beds Needed in Five Years:

Additional criteria used to determine need for substance abuse: Existing programs should operate at least 85% occupancy in units of less than 20 beds, and 90% occupancy in units with 20+ beds befor new beds are approved. Hospital seeking expansion of substance abuse unit must show occupancy 90%+ for the past two years.

Additional criteria used to determine need for others: Minimum Utilization: all pediatric units should operate at least at 60-75% minimal occupancy based on the number of beds in the facility

CON STATUTES AND REGULATIONS

CON Statutes:

CON Statute Title: Health Facilites Council
CON Statute Citation: Iowa Code sec. 135.(61-85)

CON Regulations:

CON Regulations Title: Certificate of Need Program
CON Regulations Citation: Chapter 202

STATE NOTE

Iowa requires a certificate of need ("CON") for most inpatient and outpatient services. The CON regulations contain complex calculations to determine "need" for the service within the area. The formula considers utilization and population. Some of the calculations are different if the county is "rural." Applicants must project a minimum utilization of the service within a specific time period. There are different formulas for adult versus pediatric services.

KENTUCKY

STATE CON AGENCY CONTACTS

State Department Overseeing CON

Name of state CON department:	Cabinet for Health Services
URL address for state CON organization:	http://chs.state.ky.us/cofn/

CON Administrative Office Information

Name of state CON office:	Certificate of Need Office
	Hierarchy for state CON administrative office:
	Governor: Cabinet for Health Services:
	Certificate of Need Office
CON organization contact person:	John Gray
Title of CON contact person:	Executive Director
Email address of CON contact:	John.Gray@mail.state.ky.us
Mailing address for state CON office:	275 E. Main St.
Mailing address for state CON office:	HS1E-D
City where state CON office is located:	Frankfort
State for mailing address:	Kentucky
Zip code for CON office:	40621-
Phone number for CON contact:	(502) 564-9589
Fax number for CON contact:	(502) 564-0302

State CON Decision Making Body (DMB)

Name of DMB:	CHS Administrative Hearings Branch
Title of person DMB reports to:	Governor
Title of person appointing DMB members:	Cabinet for Health Services

Composition of CON DMB:

Number of people in the DMB:	6
Number of consumers in DMB:	N/A
Number of healthcare providers in DMB:	N/A

EQUIPMENT REGULATION AND DATA

Subject to CON (Y/N):

Is any equipment subject to CON?:	False
Are air ambulances subject to CON?:	False
Are cardiac cath labs subject to CON?:	True
Are CT scanners subject to CON?:	True
Are gamma knives subject to CON?:	True
Are linear accelerators subject to CON?:	True

Subject to CON (Y/N) (Continued)

Is lithotropsy subject to CON?:	True
Is mobile high tech subject to CON?:	True
Are MRI scanners subject to CON?:	True
Are PET scanners subject to CON?:	False
Is radiation therapy subject to CON?:	True
Is renal dialysis subject to CON?:	False
Are swing beds subject to CON?:	False
Is ultra-sound subject to CON?:	False
Is other equipment subject to CON?:	Mobile Services

Dollar Threshold for CON Application:

Dollar threshold for any equipment application:	$1,870,973 for Major Medical Equipment

FACILITIES REGULATION AND DATA

Subject to CON (Y/N):

Is any facility subject to CON?	False
Are hospitals subject to CON?	True
Are nursing homes subject to CON?	True
Are residential care facilities subject to CON?	True
Are psychiatric facilities subject to CON?	True
Are ambulatory surgery centers subject to CON?	True
Are ICF/MRs subject to CON?	True
Is long term care subject to CON?	True
Are medical office buildings subject to CON?	False
Are rehabilitation facilities subject to CON?	True
Are renal dialysis facilities subject to CON?	False
Are RCF/Assisted Living facilities subject to CON?	True
Are subacute care facilities subject to CON?	True
Are substance abuse facilities subject to CON?	True
Are swing beds subject to CON?	False
Are other facilities subject to CON?	Mobile Services

Project Dollar Threshold Requiring CON Application:

Dollar threshold for any facility application:	$1,870,973 (adjusted annually)
Dollar threshold for a medical office building application:	$600,000

Capacity Requirements – Beds / Population:

Capacity requirement-beds/population for psychiatric facilities: (16-48 beds)/(275,000-550,000 population)

Notes Including Bed Limits and Moratoria:

Notes including bed limits/moratoria for any facility: A CON shall be required for the acquisition of a health facility or major medical equipment only if: (1) the notice required is not filed and the arrangement will require the obligation of a capital expenditure which exceeds the capital expenditure minimum; or (2) the cabinet finds within 30 days after the date it received notice that the health services or bed capacity of the health facility will be substantially changed in being acquired. A CON will be required for the acquisition of major medical equipment solely for research, or the making or obligating of a capital expenditure solely for research by a health facility, only if: (1) the notice required by this section is not filed; or the cabinet finds that the project or transaction for which notice is given will affect the charges of the facility other than services which are included in the research, will change the bed capacity of the facility, or will change the medical or other patient care services of the facility which were offered before the acquisition, offering, making or obligation

Notes including bed limits/moratoria for a hospital: Acute care hospital or critical access hospital designated as a swing bed hospital shall not be required to obtain a CON to utilize its licensed acute or critical access hospital beds as swing beds. For swing bed hospital to add new acute or critical access hospital beds which may be utilized as swing beds, the hospital's proposal requires a CON.

Notes including bed limits/moratoria for a nursing home: No continuing care retirement community nursing home beds shall be established after July 31, 2004 without affirmative actions of the General Assembly.

Notes including bed limits/moratoria for a psychiatric facility: CON exemptions: psychiatric care where chemical dependency services are provided. CON Requirement: a CON is required for all psychiatric residential treatment facilities.

Notes including bed limits/moratoria for an ICF/MR: Certificate of need not required for respite-service beds in intermediate care facility for the mentally retarded

Notes including bed limits/moratoria for a medical office building: CON exemptions: the relocation of hospital administrative or outpatient services into medical office buildings which are on or contiguous to the premises of the hospital or the following health services provided on site in an existing health facility when the cost is less than $600,000.

Notes including bed limits/moratoria for a RCF/Assisted Living facility: A continuing care retirement community's nursing home beds shall not be certified as Medicaid eligible unless a CON has been issued authorizing applications for Medicaid certification. Also, a continuing care retirement community shall not change the level of care licensure status of its beds without a CON

Notes including bed limits/moratoria for swing beds: Acute care hospital or critical access hospital designated as a swing bed hospital shall not be required to obtain a CON to utilize its licensed acute or critical access hospital beds as swing beds. For swing bed hospital to add new acute or critical access hospital beds which may be utilized as swing beds, the hospital's proposal requires a CON.

Notes including bed limits/moratoria for other facilities: CON exemptions: level one and level two of neonatal care; cardiac cath and open heart surgery where cardiac cath services are in place as of July 15, 1990

SERVICES REGULATION AND DATA

Subject to CON (Y/N):

Are all services subject to CON?:	False
Are nursing home services subject to CON?:	True
Are acute care services subject to CON?:	True
Are air ambulance subject to CON?:	False
Is burn care subject to CON?:	True
Is cardiac catheterization subject to CON?:	True
Is CT scanning subject to CON?:	True
Is gamma knife service subject to CON?:	True
Is home health subject to CON?:	True
Is linear accelerator service subject to CON?:	True
Is lithotripsy service subject to CON?:	True
Is long term care subject to CON?:	True
Is mobile high tech service subject to CON?:	True
Is MRI scanning subject to CON?:	True
Is neo-natal intensive care subject to CON?:	True

Subject to CON (Y/N) (Continued)

Are obstetrical services subject to CON?:	False
Is open heart surgery subject to CON?:	True
Is organ transplantation subject to CON?:	True
Is PET scanning subject to CON?:	True
Are psychiatric services subject to CON?:	True
Is radiation therapy subject to CON?:	True
Are rehabilitation services subject to CON?:	False
Is renal dialysis subject to CON?:	True
Is RCF/Assisted Living subject to CON?:	False
Is subacute care subject to CON?:	True
Is substance abuse subject to CON?:	True
Are swing beds subject to CON?:	False
Is utlra-sound subject to CON?:	False
Are other services subject to CON?:	Mobile Services

Dollar Threshold for CON Application:

Dollar threshold for any service application: $1,870,973

Additional Criteria Used to Determine Need:

Additional criteria used to determine need for any service: Unless otherwise stated, no person shall do any of the following without first obtaining a CON: (1)establish a health facility; (2)obligate capital expenditure which exceeds capital expenditure minimum; (3) make substantial change in bed capacity; (4)make a substantial change in a health service; (5) make a substantial change in a project; or (6) acquire major medical equipment

CON STATUTES AND REGULATIONS

CON Statutes:

CON Statute Title: Licensure and Regulation of Health Facilities and Services
CON Statute Citation: KRS 216B.015 et seq

CON Regulations:

CON Regulations Title: Certificate of need administrative regulation
CON Regulations Citation: 900 KAR 6:020,040,050

STATE NOTE

Kentucky requires a certificate of need ("CON") for most healthcare services. The regulations specify that the proposed project must be consistent with the State Health Plan. The regulations contain complex calculations of "need" for the service which consider the occupancy of existing providers and the population of the area. The project must also be financially feasible.

LOUISIANA

STATE CON AGENCY CONTACTS

State Department Overseeing CON

Name of state CON department:	Department of Health and Hospitals
URL address for state CON organization:	http://www.dhh.state.la.us/offices.asp

CON Administrative Office Information

Name of state CON office:	Bureau of Health Services Financing Hierarchy for state CON administrative office: Governor: Department of Health & Hospitals: Bureau of Health Services Financing
CON organization contact person:	James Taylor
Title of CON contact person:	Program Manager
Email address of CON contact:	jhtaylor@dhh.la.gov
Mailing address for state CON office:	Bureau of Health Services Financing
Mailing address for state CON office:	P.O. Box 3767
City where state CON office is located:	Baton Rouge
State for mailing address:	Louisiana
Zip code for CON office:	70821-
Phone number for CON contact:	(225) 342-3881
Fax number for CON contact:	(225) 342-3893

State CON Decision Making Body (DMB)

Name of DMB:	Department of Health Administrative Hearings
Title of person DMB reports to:	Governor
Title of person appointing DMB members:	Governor

Composition of CON DMB:

Number of people in the DMB:	N/A
Number of consumers in DMB:	N/A
Number of healthcare providers in DMB:	N/A

EQUIPMENT REGULATION AND DATA

Subject to CON (Y/N):

Is any equipment subject to CON?:	False
Are air ambulances subject to CON?:	False
Are cardiac cath labs subject to CON?:	False
Are CT scanners subject to CON?:	False

Subject to CON (Y/N) (Continued)

Are gamma knives subject to CON?:	False
Are linear accelerators subject to CON?:	False
Is lithotropsy subject to CON?:	False
Is mobile high tech subject to CON?:	False
Are MRI scanners subject to CON?:	False
Are PET scanners subject to CON?:	False
Is radiation therapy subject to CON?:	False
Is renal dialysis subject to CON?:	False
Are swing beds subject to CON?:	False
Is ultra-sound subject to CON?:	False

FACILITIES REGULATION AND DATA

Subject to CON (Y/N):

Is any facility subject to CON?	False
Are hospitals subject to CON?	False
Are nursing homes subject to CON?	False
Are residential care facilities subject to CON?	False
Are psychiatric facilities subject to CON?	False
Are ambulatory surgery centers subject to CON?	False
Are ICF/MRs subject to CON?	True
Is long term care subject to CON?	True
Are medical office buildings subject to CON?	False
Are rehabilitation facilities subject to CON?	False
Are renal dialysis facilities subject to CON?	False
Are RCF/Assisted Living facilities subject to CON?	False
Are subacute care facilities subject to CON?	False
Are substance abuse facilities subject to CON?	False
Are swing beds subject to CON?	False

Additional Criteria Used to Determine Need:

Additional criteria used to determine need for a long term care facility: facility with 98% occupancy may apply for additional beds

Notes Including Bed Limits and Moratoria:

Notes including bed limits/moratoria for an ICF/MR: recommended bed to population ratio has been achieved

SERVICES REGULATION AND DATA

Subject to CON (Y/N):

Are all services subject to CON?:	False
Are nursing home services subject to CON?:	False
Are acute care services subject to CON?:	False
Are air ambulance subject to CON?:	False
Is burn care subject to CON?:	False
Is cardiac catheterization subject to CON?:	False

Subject to CON (Y/N) (Continued)

Is CT scanning subject to CON?:	False
Is gamma knife service subject to CON?:	False
Is home health subject to CON?:	False
Is linear accelerator service subject to CON?:	True
Is lithotripsy service subject to CON?:	False
Is long term care subject to CON?:	True
Is mobile high tech service subject to CON?:	False
Is MRI scanning subject to CON?:	False
Is neo-natal intensive care subject to CON?:	False
Are obstetrical services subject to CON?:	False
Is open heart surgery subject to CON?:	False
Is organ transplantation subject to CON?:	False
Is PET scanning subject to CON?:	False
Are psychiatric services subject to CON?:	False
Is radiation therapy subject to CON?:	False
Are rehabilitation services subject to CON?:	False
Is renal dialysis subject to CON?:	False
Is RCF/Assisted Living subject to CON?:	False
Is subacute care subject to CON?:	False
Is substance abuse subject to CON?:	False
Are swing beds subject to CON?:	False
Is utlra-sound subject to CON?:	False

CON STATUTES AND REGULATIONS

CON Statutes:

CON Statute Title: Facility Need Review
CON Statute Citation: La. R.S. 40:2116
Year CON Statute Enacted: 2003

CON Regulations:

CON Regulations Title: Facility Need Review
CON Regulations Citation: Chapter 125 sec. 12501
Year CON Regulations Enacted: 1995

STATE NOTE

The Louisiana Department of Health and Hospitals ("LDHH") conducts a facility need review process for long term care facilities, including skilled nursing facilities (SNF) and intermediate care facilities for the mentally retarded (ICF/MR), to determine if there is a need for additional beds in the state's Title XIX Program. Need for an additional service is determined on the basis of a bed-to-population ratio. Alternatively, if a need for additional beds is determined through a study conducted by the LDHH, a Request for Proposals (RFP) will be issued and then proposals will be evaluated before final approval or denial (La. Admin. Code §12503(B)(9)(b)(iii)).

MAINE

STATE CON AGENCY CONTACTS

State Department Overseeing CON

Name of state CON department:	Bureau of Medical Services
URL address for state CON organization:	http://www.state.me.us/bms/

CON Administrative Office Information

Name of state CON office:	Division of Finance & Reimbursement Services Hierarchy for state CON administrative office: Governor: Department of Human Services: Bureau of Medical Services: Division of Finance & Reimbursement Services
CON organization contact person:	Bill Perfetto
Title of CON contact person:	Assistant Director and Certificate of Need
Email address of CON contact:	bill.perfetto@maine.gov
Mailing address for state CON office:	Bureau of Medical Services
Mailing address for state CON office:	422 Civic Center Drive
City where state CON office is located:	Augusta
State for mailing address:	Maine
Zip code for CON office:	04333-
Phone number for CON contact:	(207) 287-2769
Fax number for CON contact:	(207) 287-1788

State CON Decision Making Body (DMB)

Name of DMB:	Certificate of Need Advisory Committee
Title of person DMB reports to:	Department of Human Services
Title of person appointing DMB members:	Governor (9 of the 10 members)

Composition of CON DMB:

Number of people in the DMB:	10
Number of CON agency reps in DMB:	1
Number of consumers in DMB:	5
Number of healthcare providers in DMB:	4

EQUIPMENT REGULATION AND DATA

Subject to CON (Y/N):

Is any equipment subject to CON?:	False
Are air ambulances subject to CON?:	True

Subject to CON (Y/N) (Continued)

Are cardiac cath labs subject to CON?:	True
Are CT scanners subject to CON?:	True
Are gamma knives subject to CON?:	True
Are linear accelerators subject to CON?:	True
Is lithotropsy subject to CON?:	True
Is mobile high tech subject to CON?:	True
Are MRI scanners subject to CON?:	True
Are PET scanners subject to CON?:	True
Is radiation therapy subject to CON?:	True
Is renal dialysis subject to CON?:	True
Are swing beds subject to CON?:	True
Is ultra-sound subject to CON?:	True

Dollar Threshold for CON Application:

Dollar threshold for any equipment application:	$1,200,000

FACILITIES REGULATION AND DATA

Subject to CON (Y/N):

Is any facility subject to CON?	False
Are hospitals subject to CON?	True
Are nursing homes subject to CON?	True
Are residential care facilities subject to CON?	False
Are psychiatric facilities subject to CON?	True
Are ambulatory surgery centers subject to CON?	True
Are ICF/MRs subject to CON?	True
Is long term care subject to CON?	True
Are medical office buildings subject to CON?	False
Are rehabilitation facilities subject to CON?	True
Are renal dialysis facilities subject to CON?	True
Are RCF/Assisted Living facilities subject to CON?	False
Are subacute care facilities subject to CON?	False
Are substance abuse facilities subject to CON?	True
Are swing beds subject to CON?	True

Project Dollar Threshold Requiring CON Application:

Dollar threshold for any facility application:	$2,400,000
Dollar threshold for a nursing home application:	$510,000

SERVICES REGULATION AND DATA

Subject to CON (Y/N):

Are all services subject to CON?:	False
Are nursing home services subject to CON?:	True
Are acute care services subject to CON?:	True
Are air ambulance subject to CON?:	True
Is burn care subject to CON?:	True

Subject to CON (Y/N) (Continued)

Is cardiac catheterization subject to CON?:	True
Is CT scanning subject to CON?:	True
Is gamma knife service subject to CON?:	True
Is home health subject to CON?:	False
Is linear accelerator service subject to CON?:	True
Is lithotripsy service subject to CON?:	True
Is long term care subject to CON?:	True
Is mobile high tech service subject to CON?:	True
Is MRI scanning subject to CON?:	True
Is neo-natal intensive care subject to CON?:	True
Are obstetrical services subject to CON?:	True
Is open heart surgery subject to CON?:	True
Is organ transplantation subject to CON?:	True
Is PET scanning subject to CON?:	True
Are psychiatric services subject to CON?:	True
Is radiation therapy subject to CON?:	True
Are rehabilitation services subject to CON?:	True
Is renal dialysis subject to CON?:	True
Is RCF/Assisted Living subject to CON?:	False
Is subacute care subject to CON?:	False
Is substance abuse subject to CON?:	True
Are swing beds subject to CON?:	True
Is utlra-sound subject to CON?:	True

Dollar Threshold for CON Application:

Dollar threshold for any service application:	$110,000

CON STATUTES AND REGULATIONS

CON Statutes:

CON Statute Title: Maine Certificate of Need Act
CON Statute Citation: 22 M.R.S. 326

CON Regulations:

CON Regulations Title: Main Certificate of Need Procedures Manual for Health Care Facilities
CON Regulations Citation: 10-144 Chapter 503

STATE NOTE

The Maine Department of Human Services administers a certificate of need (CON) process for capital expenditures exceeding two million four hundred thousand dollars ($2,400,000); purchases of major medical equipment exceeding one million two hundred thousand dollars ($1,200,000); and, the establishment of new services with a capital expenditure exceeding one hundred ten thousand dollars ($110,000) [Note: this is adjusted to four hundred thousand dollars ($400,000 in the third year of facility operation]. CON approval is determined not on the basis of specific standards, but rather guideline criteria including: the applicant's ability to provide the service; the economic feasibility of the project; the public need for the project; and, the impact that the project has on existing providers (Maine Certificate of Need Procedures Manual, Chapter 10).

MARYLAND

STATE CON AGENCY CONTACTS

State Department Overseeing CON	
Name of state CON department:	Maryland Health Care Commission
URL address for state CON organization:	http://www.mhcc.state.md.us certificateofneed/_certificateofneed.htm
CON Administrative Office Information	
Name of state CON office:	Certificate of Need Program Hierarchy for state CON administrative office: Governor: Department of Human Resources: MD Health Care Commission: CON Program
CON organization contact person:	Susan Panek
Title of CON contact person:	Chief
Email address of CON contact:	spanek@mhcc.state.md.us
Mailing address for state CON office:	Certificate of Need Program
Mailing address for state CON office:	4160 Patterson Avenue
City where state CON office is located:	Baltimore
State for mailing address:	Maryland
Zip code for CON office:	21215
Phone number for CON contact:	(410) 764-3282
Fax number for CON contact:	(410) 358-1311
State CON Decision Making Body (DMB)	
Name of DMB:	Maryland Health Care Commission
Title of person DMB reports to:	Governor
Title of person appointing DMB members:	Governor
Composition of CON DMB:	
Number of people in the DMB:	13
Number of consumers in DMB:	7
Number of healthcare providers in DMB:	4

EQUIPMENT REGULATION AND DATA

Subject to CON (Y/N):	
Is any equipment subject to CON?:	False
Are air ambulances subject to CON?:	False

Subject to CON (Y/N) (Continued)

Are cardiac cath labs subject to CON?:	False
Are CT scanners subject to CON?:	False
Are gamma knives subject to CON?:	False
Are linear accelerators subject to CON?:	False
Is lithotropsy subject to CON?:	False
Is mobile high tech subject to CON?:	False
Are MRI scanners subject to CON?:	False
Are PET scanners subject to CON?:	False
Is radiation therapy subject to CON?:	False
Is renal dialysis subject to CON?:	False
Are swing beds subject to CON?:	False
Is ultra-sound subject to CON?:	False

Dollar Threshold for CON Application:

Dollar threshold for any equipment application:	$1,250,000

FACILITIES REGULATION AND DATA

Subject to CON (Y/N):

Is any facility subject to CON?	False
Are hospitals subject to CON?	True
Are nursing homes subject to CON?	False
Are residential care facilities subject to CON?	False
Are psychiatric facilities subject to CON?	True
Are ambulatory surgery centers subject to CON?	True
Are ICF/MRs subject to CON?	True
Is long term care subject to CON?	True
Are medical office buildings subject to CON?	False
Are rehabilitation facilities subject to CON?	True
Are renal dialysis facilities subject to CON?	False
Are RCF/Assisted Living facilities subject to CON?	False
Are subacute care facilities subject to CON?	True
Are substance abuse facilities subject to CON?	True
Are swing beds subject to CON?	False

SERVICES REGULATION AND DATA

Subject to CON (Y/N):

Are all services subject to CON?:	False
Are nursing home services subject to CON?:	False
Are acute care services subject to CON?:	True
Are air ambulance subject to CON?:	False
Is burn care subject to CON?:	True
Is cardiac catheterization subject to CON?:	True
Is CT scanning subject to CON?:	False
Is gamma knife service subject to CON?:	False
Is home health subject to CON?:	True

Subject to CON (Y/N) (Continued)

Is linear accelerator service subject to CON?:	False
Is lithotripsy service subject to CON?:	False
Is long term care subject to CON?:	True
Is mobile high tech service subject to CON?:	False
Is MRI scanning subject to CON?:	False
Is neo-natal intensive care subject to CON?:	True
Are obstetrical services subject to CON?:	True
Is open heart surgery subject to CON?:	True
Is organ transplantation subject to CON?:	True
Is PET scanning subject to CON?:	False
Are psychiatric services subject to CON?:	True
Is radiation therapy subject to CON?:	False
Are rehabilitation services subject to CON?:	True
Is renal dialysis subject to CON?:	False
Is RCF/Assisted Living subject to CON?:	False
Is subacute care subject to CON?:	True
Is substance abuse subject to CON?:	True
Are swing beds subject to CON?:	False
Is utlra-sound subject to CON?:	False
Are other services subject to CON?:	hospice; pediatrics beds; chronic care; comprehensive care

CON STATUTES AND REGULATIONS

CON Statutes:

CON Statute Title: Certificate of Need - Health Care Facilities
CON Statute Citation: 19-120
Year CON Statute Enacted: 2003

CON Regulations:

CON Regulations Title: Determination of Certificate of Need for Health Care Facilities
CON Regulations Citation: 10.24.01.00
Year CON Regulations Enacted: 2003

STATE NOTE

The Maryland Health Care Commission ("MHCC") is responsible for the determination of certificate of need (CON) for healthcare facilities. Capital expenditures exceeding one million five hundred and fifty thousand dollars *($1,550,000)* and any new services, regardless of amount expended, are subject to CON approval. The MHCC, in determining if a CON should be issued, evaluate applicants on the basis of: the state's health plan; need for the service; alternatives which are most cost effective; the financial and non-financial viability of the proposal; the applicant's compliance with other certificate of need laws; and, the impact on existing providers (Md. Regs. Code 10.24.01.08(G)(3)).

MASSACHUSETTS

STATE CON AGENCY CONTACTS

State Department Overseeing CON

Name of state CON department:	Determination of Need Program
URL address for state CON organization:	http://www.state.ma.us/dph/dhcq/don.htm

CON Administrative Office Information

Name of state CON office:	Determination of Need Program Hierarchy for state CON administrative office: Governor: Department of Public Health: Determination of Need Program
CON organization contact person:	Joyce E. James
Title of CON contact person:	Director
Email address of CON contact:	Joyce.James@state.ma.us
Mailing address for state CON office:	2 Boylston Street
Mailing address for state CON office:	3rd
City where state CON office is located:	Boston
State for mailing address:	Massachusetts
Zip code for CON office:	02116-
Phone number for CON contact:	(617) 753-5002
Fax number for CON contact:	(617) 338-5183

State CON Decision Making Body (DMB)

Name of DMB:	Public Health Council
Title of person DMB reports to:	Department of Public Health
Title of person appointing DMB members:	Department of Public Health

Composition of CON DMB:

Number of people in the DMB:	9
Number of CON agency reps in DMB:	1
Number of consumers in DMB:	5
Number of healthcare providers in DMB:	3

EQUIPMENT REGULATION AND DATA

Subject to CON (Y/N):

Is any equipment subject to CON?:	False
Are air ambulances subject to CON?:	True
Are cardiac cath labs subject to CON?:	False
Are CT scanners subject to CON?:	False

Subject to CON (Y/N) (Continued)

Are gamma knives subject to CON?:	True
Are linear accelerators subject to CON?:	True
Is lithotropsy subject to CON?:	True
Is mobile high tech subject to CON?:	False
Are MRI scanners subject to CON?:	True
Are PET scanners subject to CON?:	True
Is radiation therapy subject to CON?:	True
Is renal dialysis subject to CON?:	False
Are swing beds subject to CON?:	False
Is ultra-sound subject to CON?:	False

Dollar Threshold for CON Application:

Dollar threshold for any equipment application:	$150,000

FACILITIES REGULATION AND DATA

Subject to CON (Y/N):

Is any facility subject to CON?	False
Are hospitals subject to CON?	False
Are nursing homes subject to CON?	True
Are residential care facilities subject to CON?	False
Are psychiatric facilities subject to CON?	True
Are ambulatory surgery centers subject to CON?	True
Are ICF/MRs subject to CON?	True
Is long term care subject to CON?	True
Are medical office buildings subject to CON?	False
Are rehabilitation facilities subject to CON?	True
Are renal dialysis facilities subject to CON?	True
Are RCF/Assisted Living facilities subject to CON?	False
Are subacute care facilities subject to CON?	False
Are substance abuse facilities subject to CON?	True
Are swing beds subject to CON?	False
Are other facilities subject to CON?	comprehensive cancer center; institution for unwed mothers; clinic; rest home; clinical laboratory; public medical institution

Project Dollar Threshold Requiring CON Application:

Dollar threshold for any facility application:	$800,000/acquisitions; 350,000/new service
Dollar threshold for a hospital application:	$7,500,000
Dollar threshold for other facility applications:	$7,500,000

Notes Including Bed Limits and Moratoria:

Notes including bed limits/moratoria for a long term care facility: moratorium on LTC beds

SERVICES REGULATION AND DATA

Subject to CON (Y/N):

Are all services subject to CON?:	False
Are nursing home services subject to CON?:	True
Are acute care services subject to CON?:	False
Are air ambulance subject to CON?:	True
Is burn care subject to CON?:	False
Is cardiac catheterization subject to CON?:	False
Is CT scanning subject to CON?:	False
Is gamma knife service subject to CON?:	True
Is home health subject to CON?:	False
Is linear accelerator service subject to CON?:	False
Is lithotripsy service subject to CON?:	True
Is long term care subject to CON?:	True
Is mobile high tech service subject to CON?:	False
Is MRI scanning subject to CON?:	True
Is neo-natal intensive care subject to CON?:	True
Are obstetrical services subject to CON?:	False
Is open heart surgery subject to CON?:	True
Is organ transplantation subject to CON?:	True
Is PET scanning subject to CON?:	True
Are psychiatric services subject to CON?:	True
Is radiation therapy subject to CON?:	True
Are rehabilitation services subject to CON?:	True
Is renal dialysis subject to CON?:	True
Is RCF/Assisted Living subject to CON?:	False
Is subacute care subject to CON?:	False
Is substance abuse subject to CON?:	True
Are swing beds subject to CON?:	False
Is utlra-sound subject to CON?:	False

Dollar Threshold for CON Application:

Dollar threshold for any service application:	$350,000

Additional Criteria Used to Determine Need:

Additional criteria used to determine need for any service: Need CON for innovative service or new technology not provided in a health care facility

CON STATUTES AND REGULATIONS

CON Statutes:

CON Statute Title: Substantial Capital Expenditure or Substantial Change in Services
CON Statute Citation: Massachusetts General Laws, Chapter 111, s. 25C

CON Regulations:

CON Regulations Title: Massachusetts Determination of Need Regulations
CON Regulations Citation: 105 CMR 100.000-102.000

STATE NOTE

Massachusetts "Determination of Need" program includes several unconventional facilities: institutions for the care of unwed mothers or clinics; rest homes or charitable homes for the aged; clinical laboratories; and public medical institutions.

The following are specific applicable definitions:

"Acute-care hospital" are defined as containing a majority of medical-surgical, pediatric, obstetric and maternity beds.

"Innovative service" is a service or procedure such as dialysis, transplant services, cardiac catheterization, angioplasty and neonatal intensive care, which for reasons of quality, access, or cost is determined to be innovative.

"Major movable equipment" is equipment that is not permanently attached to the building and that has a depreciable life of 3 or more years.

"New technology" is equipment, including, but not limited to, magnetic resonance images; lithotripters, and linear accelerators OR a service.

A "substantial capital expenditure" by a facility triggers DON review and as such, a "substantial capital expenditure" is (1) the expenditure, or obligation of a sum of money for construction of a "health care facility", which under generally accepted accounting principles is not properly chargeable as an expense of operation and maintenance, or is made by lease or comparable arrangement, and which exceeds or may reasonably be regarded as leading to an expenditure for construction in excess of the "expenditure minimum" or (2) the obtaining by lease or comparable arrangement, by donation, or by transfer for less than fair market value in excess of the "expenditure minimum".

"Expenditure minimum" with respect to "substantial capital expenditures", shall mean, with respect to expenditure and acquisitions made by or for (1) "acute-care hospitals" and "comprehensive cancer centers" … "Acute-care hospitals" has been labeled as "hospital", while the "comprehensive cancer centers" are labeled as "other facility" under this definition.

Under, Mass. Regulation, Section 100.536, in making determinations of need, Massachusetts will accept as supporting documentation any statistical or other factual material, which is reliable. Under this Section, Massachusetts may take official notice of utilization data.

MICHIGAN

STATE CON AGENCY CONTACTS

State Department Overseeing CON

Name of state CON department:	Department of Community Health
URL address for state CON organization:	http://www.michigan.gov/mdch/0,1607,7-1322945_5106—,00.html

CON Administrative Office Information

Name of state CON office:	Department of Community Health Hierarchy for state CON administrative office: Governor: Department of Community Health: Certificate of Need Section
CON organization contact person:	Larry Horvath
Title of CON contact person:	Manager
Email address of CON contact:	horvath1@michigan.gov
Mailing address for state CON office:	320 S Walnut Street
Mailing address for state CON office:	320 S. Walnut St., Lewis Cass Bldg.
City where state CON office is located:	Lansing
State for mailing address:	Michigan
Zip code for CON office:	48913-
Phone number for CON contact:	(517) 241-3343
Fax number for CON contact:	(517) 241-2962

State CON Decision Making Body (DMB)

Name of DMB:	Certificate of Need Commission
Title of person DMB reports to:	Governor
Title of person appointing DMB members:	Governor

Composition of CON DMB:

Number of people in the DMB:	11
Number of consumers in DMB:	5
Number of healthcare providers in DMB:	6

Equipment Regulation and Data

Subject to CON (Y/N):

Is any equipment subject to CON?:	False
Are air ambulances subject to CON?:	True
Are cardiac cath labs subject to CON?:	True
Are CT scanners subject to CON?:	True
Are gamma knives subject to CON?:	True

Subject to CON (Y/N) (Continued)

Are linear accelerators subject to CON?:	True
Is lithotropsy subject to CON?:	True
Is mobile high tech subject to CON?:	True
Are MRI scanners subject to CON?:	True
Are PET scanners subject to CON?:	True
Is radiation therapy subject to CON?:	True
Is renal dialysis subject to CON?:	False
Are swing beds subject to CON?:	True
Is ultra-sound subject to CON?:	False

FACILITIES REGULATION AND DATA

Subject to CON (Y/N):

Is any facility subject to CON?	False
Are hospitals subject to CON?	True
Are nursing homes subject to CON?	True
Are residential care facilities subject to CON?	True
Are psychiatric facilities subject to CON?	True
Are ambulatory surgery centers subject to CON?	True
Are ICF/MRs subject to CON?	False
Is long term care subject to CON?	True
Are medical office buildings subject to CON?	False
Are rehabilitation facilities subject to CON?	False
Are renal dialysis facilities subject to CON?	False
Are RCF/Assisted Living facilities subject to CON?	False
Are subacute care facilities subject to CON?	False
Are substance abuse facilities subject to CON?	False
Are swing beds subject to CON?	False

Notes Including Bed Limits and Moratoria:

Notes including bed limits/moratoria for a nursing home:	moratorium on nursing home beds

SERVICES REGULATION AND DATA

Subject to CON (Y/N):

Are all services subject to CON?:	False
Are nursing home services subject to CON?:	True
Are acute care services subject to CON?:	True
Are air ambulance subject to CON?:	True
Is burn care subject to CON?:	False
Is cardiac catheterization subject to CON?:	True
Is CT scanning subject to CON?:	True
Is gamma knife service subject to CON?:	True
Is home health subject to CON?:	False
Is linear accelerator service subject to CON?:	False
Is lithotripsy service subject to CON?:	True
Is long term care subject to CON?:	True

Subject to CON (Y/N) (Continued)

Is mobile high tech service subject to CON?:	True
Is MRI scanning subject to CON?:	True
Is neo-natal intensive care subject to CON?:	True
Are obstetrical services subject to CON?:	False
Is open heart surgery subject to CON?:	True
Is organ transplantation subject to CON?:	True
Is PET scanning subject to CON?:	True
Are psychiatric services subject to CON?:	True
Is radiation therapy subject to CON?:	True
Are rehabilitation services subject to CON?:	False
Is renal dialysis subject to CON?:	False
Is RCF/Assisted Living subject to CON?:	False
Is subacute care subject to CON?:	False
Is substance abuse subject to CON?:	False
Are swing beds subject to CON?:	True
Is utlra-sound subject to CON?:	False
Are other services subject to CON?:	surgical services; bone marrow transplantation service

Additional Criteria Used to Determine Need:

Additional criteria used to determine need for nursing home: Regulations contain calculated bed need for planning area; statewide pool of additional nursing home beds of 2% of beds needed are allocated to the planning areas

Additional criteria used to determine need for acute care: Replacement beds applicant must demonstrate that project will result in 200 beds if in metropolitan areas or 50 beds in rural area; regulations contain bed need by health service area

Additional criteria used to determine need for air ambulance: Different criteria for initiating/expanding/replacing service

Additional criteria used to determine need for cardiac catheterization: Adult desired utilization = 300 procedures; different criteria for rural locations; different criteria for initiating/expanding/replacing service

Additional criteria used to determine need for CT scanning: Desired utilization = 7,500 procedures/year (fixed) 3,500 procedures/year (mobile); different criteria for hospital; no volume requirements for PET/CT hybrid

Additional criteria used to determine need for gamma knives: Desired utilization = 1,000 visits per year

Additional criteria used to determine need for lithotripsy: Desired utilization = 1,000 procedures/year; to expand must have performed 1,800 procedures per year

Additional criteria used to determine need for long term care: Regulations contain calculated bed need for planning area

Additional criteria used to determine need for MRI scanning: Desired utilization = 6,000 procedures/year(fixed) 5,500 procedures/year(mobile); applicant must project from 400 to 600 procedures depending on location of service

Additional criteria used to determine need for neonatal intensive care: To initiate service unmet need = 15 NICU beds & 600 or 2000 live births based on whether hospital is located in a rural or metropolitan area; to expand must show that project will not result in a surplus of NICU beds

Additional criteria used to determine need for open heart surgery: Different utilization for pediatric and adult services; desired utilization = 300 adult 100 pediatric;

Additional criteria used to determine need for organ transplantation: Different criteria for type of transplantation; maximum number of heart/lung or lung transplantation services in planning area is 3; minimum utilization for heart/lung or lung transplantation service is 12; maximum number of liver transplantation services in planning area is 3; minimum utilization for liver transplantation services = 12; pancreas transplantation service - project 12 procedures/year

Additional criteria used to determine need for PET scanning: Different criteria for fixed and mobile services; different criteria to initiate/expand/replace services

Additional criteria used to determine need for psychiatric services: Bed need calculated in regulations; need calculated for adult and child/adolescent beds

Additional criteria used to determine need for radiation therapy: Desired utilization = 8,000 visits per year; exception for rural locations and hospitals with more than 90 beds; to expand need 10,000 visits per year; to replace 5,500 visits per year

Additional criteria used to determine need for others: Desired occupancy = 1,200 cases/year; to expand/ replace need desired occupancy or minimum hours of use (from 1,600 to 1,800 depending on facility type); exception for hospital in rural county; bone marrow transplantation only 3 adult services and 2 pediatrics services in planning area

CON STATUTES AND REGULATIONS

CON Statutes:

CON Statute Title: Certificate of Need

CON Statute Citation: Part 222 333.22201-333.22260

CON Regulations:

CON Regulations Title: Michigan Administrative Code

CON Regulations Citation: MICH. ADMIN. CODE R 325.9101 - 325.9525

STATE NOTE

Michigan has a very complicated certificate of need ("CON") regulatory scheme. A CON is required for most healthcare services. The Michigan Certificate of Need Commission ("Commission") has promulgated review standards for each service requiring a CON. There are different standards for initiating and replacing each service. There are often different review standards for pediatric versus adult services or fixed versus mobile services. The requirements to initiate a service set out a minimum number of projected services. To replace a service, the unit must have performed a minimum number of services and the applicant must project a minimum number of services will be performed. For the bed-based services, the review standards contain a methodology to determine the bed need for the health planning region. The review standards contain an appendix listing the calculating the bed need using the methodology.

MISSISSIPPI

STATE CON AGENCY CONTACTS

State Department Overseeing CON

Name of state CON department:	Department of Community Health-Certificate of Need
URL address for state CON organization:	http://www.msdh.state.ms.us/msdhsite/index.cfm/30,0,84,html

CON Administrative Office Information

Name of state CON office:	State Department of Health Hierarchy for state CON administrative office: Governor: Mississippi State Department of Health
CON organization contact person:	Rachel Pittman
Title of CON contact person:	Chief
Email address of CON contact:	rachel.pittman@msdh.state.ms.us
Mailing address for state CON office:	570 E. Woodrow Wilson
Mailing address for state CON office:	PO Box 1700
City where state CON office is located:	Jackson
State for mailing address:	Mississippi
Zip code for CON office:	39215-
Phone number for CON contact:	(601) 576-7874
Fax number for CON contact:	(601) 576-7530

State CON Decision Making Body (DMB)

Name of DMB:	State Health Officer
Title of person DMB reports to:	Dept. of Heatlh
Title of person appointing DMB members:	Governor

Composition of CON DMB:

Number of people in the DMB:	1

EQUIPMENT REGULATION AND DATA

Subject to CON (Y/N):

Is any equipment subject to CON?:	True
Are air ambulances subject to CON?:	True
Are cardiac cath labs subject to CON?:	True
Are CT scanners subject to CON?:	True
Are gamma knives subject to CON?:	True
Are linear accelerators subject to CON?:	True

Subject to CON (Y/N) (Continued)

Is lithotropsy subject to CON?:	True
Is mobile high tech subject to CON?:	True
Are MRI scanners subject to CON?:	True
Are PET scanners subject to CON?:	True
Is radiation therapy subject to CON?:	True
Is renal dialysis subject to CON?:	True
Are swing beds subject to CON?:	True
Is ultra-sound subject to CON?:	True

Dollar Threshold for CON Application:

Dollar threshold for any equipment application: $1,500,000

Additional Criteria Used to Determine Need:

Additional criteria used to determine need for any equipment: must be consistent with State Health Plan

FACILITIES REGULATION AND DATA

Subject to CON (Y/N):

Is any facility subject to CON?	False
Are hospitals subject to CON?	True
Are nursing homes subject to CON?	False
Are residential care facilities subject to CON?	False
Are psychiatric facilities subject to CON?	True
Are ambulatory surgery centers subject to CON?	True
Are ICF/MRs subject to CON?	True
Is long term care subject to CON?	True
Are medical office buildings subject to CON?	True
Are rehabilitation facilities subject to CON?	True
Are renal dialysis facilities subject to CON?	True
Are RCF/Assisted Living facilities subject to CON?	False
Are subacute care facilities subject to CON?	False
Are substance abuse facilities subject to CON?	True
Are swing beds subject to CON?	True
Are other facilities subject to CON?	geriatric psychiatric beds

Project Dollar Threshold Requiring CON Application:

Dollar threshold for any facility application: $2,000,000

Additional Criteria Used to Determine Need:

Additional criteria used to determine need for any facility: must be consistent with State Health Plan

Additional criteria used to determine need for a nursing home: bed need = .5 beds per 1,000 population aged 64 and under; 14 beds per 1,000 population aged 65-74; 59 beds per 1,000 population aged 75-84; 179 beds per 1,000 population aged 85+

Additional criteria used to determine need for an ambulatory surgery center: ASC must serve area with 60,000 population within 30 minutes driving time or 25 miles; only approve multi-specialty centers; minimum surgeries must be 1,000 surgeries; optimum capacity is 800 surgeries/room/year

Notes Including Bed Limits and Moratoria:

Notes including bed limits/moratoria for any facility: relocation requires CON; change in ownership requires CON

Notes including bed limits/moratoria for a nursing home: moratorium on nursing home beds

Notes including bed limits/moratoria for an ICF/MR: moratorium on ICF/MR beds; temporary suspension of moratorium for 60 nursing facility beds for individuals with Alzheimer's

SERVICES REGULATION AND DATA

Subject to CON (Y/N):

Are all services subject to CON?:	False
Are nursing home services subject to CON?:	True
Are acute care services subject to CON?:	True
Are air ambulance subject to CON?:	False
Is burn care subject to CON?:	False
Is cardiac catheterization subject to CON?:	True
Is CT scanning subject to CON?:	False
Is gamma knife service subject to CON?:	True
Is home health subject to CON?:	True
Is linear accelerator service subject to CON?:	False
Is lithotripsy service subject to CON?:	True
Is long term care subject to CON?:	True
Is mobile high tech service subject to CON?:	False
Is MRI scanning subject to CON?:	True
Is neo-natal intensive care subject to CON?:	True
Are obstetrical services subject to CON?:	True
Is open heart surgery subject to CON?:	True
Is organ transplantation subject to CON?:	False
Is PET scanning subject to CON?:	True
Are psychiatric services subject to CON?:	True
Is radiation therapy subject to CON?:	True
Are rehabilitation services subject to CON?:	True
Is renal dialysis subject to CON?:	True
Is RCF/Assisted Living subject to CON?:	False
Is subacute care subject to CON?:	False
Is substance abuse subject to CON?:	True
Are swing beds subject to CON?:	True
Is utlra-sound subject to CON?:	False
Are other services subject to CON?:	new institutional health service; invasive diagnostic imaging services

Dollar Threshold for CON Application:

Dollar Threshold for neo-natal intensive care application: $2,000,000

Additional Criteria Used to Determine Need:

Additional criteria used to determine need for any service: Must be consistent with State Health Plan; if criteria have not been adopted, application shall be deferred until department adopts criteria

Additional criteria used to determine need for home health: Need exists if county had fewer home health visits per 1,000 elderly population than average number of visits per 1,000 elderly population in ten-state region

Additional criteria used to determine need for neonatal intensive care: 1 intensive care bed per 1,000 live births; 3 intermediate care beds per 1,000 live births; single unit should have at least 15 beds; optimal occupancy = 75%

Additional criteria used to determine need for obstetrical: Expect to deliver minimum of 150 babies in 1st year & 250 babies by 2nd year; optimal occupancy = 60%

Additional criteria used to determine need for rehabilitation: MS is over bedded with Level 1 beds; 41 additional Level II CMR beds are needed; no methodology for children's comprehensive medical rehabilitation services

Additional criteria used to determine need for renal dialysis: Applications only accepted from July 1 through September 1; service area is area within 30 miles of existing facility; facilities within area must have minimum utilization of 80%; need threshold is 749 dialysis visits per station per year; must project 50% utilization within 1 year and 75% by 3rd year; no application shall be approved for project with less than 4 stations; renal transplantation service must serve 3.5 million people

Additional criteria used to determine need for others: Need CON to add more than 10 beds or 10% of capacity

CON STATUTES AND REGULATIONS

CON Statutes:

CON Statute Title: Health Care Certificate of Need Law of 1979

CON Statute Citation: Miss. Code Ann. 41-7

CON Regulations:

CON Regulations Title: Mississippi State Dept. of Health: Division of Health Planning and Resource Development

CON Regulations Citation: Dept of Health: Certificate of Need Review Manual

Year CON Regulations Enacted: 2002

STATE NOTE

A certificate of need ("CON") is required for any "capital expenditure," the establishment of a "new health care facility," or the offering of a "new institutional health service." Most healthcare services fall within the rule's definition of a "health service." Regulations defining the calculation of "need" have been promulgated for every service. Most calculations consider actual utilization and the population of the service area.

MISSOURI

STATE CON AGENCY CONTACTS

State Department Overseeing CON

Name of state CON department:	Department of Health and Senior Services
URL address for state CON organization:	http://www.dhss.state.mo.us/con

CON Administrative Office Information

Name of state CON office:	Missouri Certificate of Need Program Hierarchy for state CON administrative office: Governor: DHSS: MHFRC: CON Program
CON organization contact person:	Thomas R. Piper
Title of CON contact person:	Director
Email address of CON contact:	tpiper@mail.state.mo.us
Mailing address for state CON office:	915G Leslie Blvd.
City where state CON office is located:	Jefferson City
State for mailing address:	Missouri
Zip code for CON office:	65101-
Phone number for CON contact:	(573) 751-6403
Fax number for CON contact:	(573) 751-7894

State CON Decision Making Body (DMB)

Name of DMB:	Missouri Health Facilities Review Committee
Title of person DMB reports to:	Department of Health and Senior Services
Title of person appointing DMB members:	

Composition of CON DMB:

Number of people in the DMB:	9
Number of legislators in DMB:	4
Number of consumers in DMB:	1
Number of healthcare providers in DMB:	2

EQUIPMENT REGULATION AND DATA

Subject to CON (Y/N):

Is any equipment subject to CON?:	False
Are air ambulances subject to CON?:	False
Are cardiac cath labs subject to CON?:	True
Are CT scanners subject to CON?:	True
Are gamma knives subject to CON?:	True
Are linear accelerators subject to CON?:	False
Is lithotropsy subject to CON?:	True

Subject to CON (Y/N) (Continued)

Is mobile high tech subject to CON?:	True
Are MRI scanners subject to CON?:	True
Are PET scanners subject to CON?:	True
Is radiation therapy subject to CON?:	True
Is renal dialysis subject to CON?:	True
Are swing beds subject to CON?:	False
Is ultra-sound subject to CON?:	False

Dollar Threshold for CON Application:

Dollar threshold for cardiac cath lab application:	$1,000,000
Dollar threshold for CT scanner application:	$1,000,000
Dollar threshold for gamma knife application:	$1,000,000
Dollar threshold for linear accelerator application:	$1,000,000
Dollar threshold for lithotropsy application:	$1,000,000
Dollar threshold for MRI scanner application:	$1,000,000
Dollar threshold for PET scanner application:	$1,000,000
Dollar threshold for renal dialysis application:	$1,000,000

Utilization Requirements (Procedures/Population):

Utilization Requirement-Procedures/Population for cardiac cath lab:	Adult: 1/500 Ped: 1/250
Utilization Requirement-Procedures/Population for gamma knives:	1/200
Utilization Requirement-Procedures/Population for linear accelerators:	1/3,500
Utilization Requirement-Procedures/Population for lithotropsy:	1/1,000
Utilization Requirement-Procedures/Population for MRI scanners:	1/2,000
Utilization Requirement-Procedures/Population for PET scanners:	1/1,000
Utilization Requirement-Procedures/Population for renal dialysis:	1/200
Utilization Requirement-Procedures/Population for other equipment:	Adult open heart surg: 1/200 Ped open heart surgery: 1/100; General surgery: 1/750; Excimer laser: 1/1,800

Utilization Requirements (Equipment/Population):

Utilization Requirement-Equipment/Population for cardiac cath labs:	1/50,000
Utilization Requirement-Equipment/Population for gamma knives:	1/7,500,000
Utilization Requirement-Equipment/Population for linear accelerators:	1/100,000
Utilization Requirement-Equipment/Population for lithotropsy:	1/1,000,000
Utilization Requirement-Equipment/Population for MRI scanners:	1/100,000
Utilization Requirement-Equipment/Population for PET scanners:	1/500,000
Utilization Requirement-Equipment/Population for other equipment:	Adult and Ped.open heart surgery rooms:1/100,000; Excimer laser: 1/500,000

FACILITIES REGULATION AND DATA

Subject to CON (Y/N):

Is any facility subject to CON?	False
Are hospitals subject to CON?	True
Are nursing homes subject to CON?	True
Are residential care facilities subject to CON?	True
Are psychiatric facilities subject to CON?	False
Are ambulatory surgery centers subject to CON?	False
Are ICF/MRs subject to CON?	True
Is long term care subject to CON?	True
Are medical office buildings subject to CON?	False
Are rehabilitation facilities subject to CON?	False
Are renal dialysis facilities subject to CON?	True
Are RCF/Assisted Living facilities subject to CON?	True
Are subacute care facilities subject to CON?	False
Are substance abuse facilities subject to CON?	False
Are swing beds subject to CON?	False
Are other facilities subject to CON?	skilled nursing facility

Project Dollar Threshold Requiring CON Application:

Dollar threshold for a residential care facility application:	$600,000
Dollar threshold for a long term care facility application:	$600,000
Dollar threshold for a RCF/Assisted Living facility application:	$600,000

Additional Criteria Used to Determine Need:

Additional criteria used to determine need for a hospital: Proposal for new hospital must include documentation that the proposed costs per square ft are reasonable when compared to the latest RS Means Construction Cost Data, document sufficient financing available to assure project completion, and document financial feasibility

Additional criteria used to determine need for a nursing home: Proposal for new nursing home must include documentation that the proposed costs per square ft are reasonable when compared to the latest RS Means Construction Cost Data, document sufficient financing available to assure project completion, and document financial feasibility

Additional criteria used to determine need for a residential care facility: Proposal for new RCF must include documentation that the proposed costs per square ft are reasonable when compared to the latest RS Means Construction Cost Data, document sufficient financing available to assure project completion, and document financial feasibility

Additional criteria used to determine need for a RCF/Assisted Living facility: Proposal for new RCF must include documentation that the proposed costs per square ft are reasonable when compared to the latest RS Means Construction Cost Data, document sufficient financing available to assure project completion, and document financial feasibility

Notes Including Bed Limits and Moratoria:

Notes including bed limits/moratoria for a hospital: Health Care Facility Defined: construction of new hospital considerd a health care facility. Bed Requirements: (1)Med Surg Bed (1/570); Ped Bed (1/8,330); Psych Bed (1/2,080); Sub Abuse (1/20,000); Inpatient Rehab (1/9,090); and OB bed (1/5,880)

Notes including bed limits/moratoria for a residential care facility: Approval of additional RCF beds based on service area need determined to be 16 beds per 1,000 population age 65+ minus the current supply of RCF beds shown in the Inventory of Residential Care Facility Beds

Notes including bed limits/moratoria for a long term care facility: Health Care Facility Defined: LTC beds in a hospital only if residential care facility, intermediate care facility or skilled nursing facility is physically attached to hospital. Bed Requirements: average occupancy for all licensed and available LTC beds located within 15 miles of proposed site exceed ninety percent during at least each of the most recent four consecutive calender quarters at time of filing

SERVICES REGULATION AND DATA

Subject to CON (Y/N):

Are all services subject to CON?:	False
Are nursing home services subject to CON?:	False
Are acute care services subject to CON?:	True
Are air ambulance subject to CON?:	False
Is burn care subject to CON?:	True
Is cardiac catheterization subject to CON?:	True
Is CT scanning subject to CON?:	True
Is gamma knife service subject to CON?:	True
Is home health subject to CON?:	False
Is linear accelerator service subject to CON?:	False
Is lithotripsy service subject to CON?:	True
Is long term care subject to CON?:	True
Is mobile high tech service subject to CON?:	True
Is MRI scanning subject to CON?:	True
Is neo-natal intensive care subject to CON?:	True
Are obstetrical services subject to CON?:	True
Is open heart surgery subject to CON?:	True
Is organ transplantation subject to CON?:	True
Is PET scanning subject to CON?:	True
Are psychiatric services subject to CON?:	False
Is radiation therapy subject to CON?:	True
Are rehabilitation services subject to CON?:	False
Is renal dialysis subject to CON?:	True
Is RCF/Assisted Living subject to CON?:	True
Is subacute care subject to CON?:	False
Is substance abuse subject to CON?:	False
Are swing beds subject to CON?:	False
Is utlra-sound subject to CON?:	False

Additional Criteria Used to Determine Need:

Additional criteria used to determine need for any service: Must show how proposed service will be affordable to population in the proposed service area by documenting how proposal will impact current patient charges and by demonstrating that proposed service will be responsive to the medically indigent through fee waivers, reduced charges, or structured payments

CON STATUTES AND REGULATIONS

CON Statutes:

CON Statute Title: Missouri Certificate of Need Law
CON Statute Citation: 197.300 to 197.366 R.S.Mo.

CON Regulations:

CON Regulations Title: Rules of Dept of Health and Senior Services: Missouri Health Facilities Review Committee: Certificate of Need Program
CON Regulations Citation: Title 19, Division 60, Chapter 50

STATE NOTE

Missouri requires a certificate of need ("CON") for most healthcare services. The regulations contain criteria for each service with "unmet need" a function of the community rate of one unit per the population specified for the service. The regulations also contain a minimum utilization for the type of service in the service area before new service can be initiated or existing service expanded. The regulations also contain a requirement of "financial feasibility" which specify that the proposed costs are reasonable when compared to data produced by the CON program.

MONTANA

STATE CON AGENCY CONTACTS

State Department Overseeing CON	
Name of state CON department:	Department of Public Health and Human Services
URL address for state CON organization:	http://www.dphhs.state.mt.us/about_us/divisions/quality_assurance certificate_of_need/certificate_of_need.htm
CON Administrative Office Information	
Name of state CON office:	Certificate of Need Program Hierarchy for state CON administrative office: Governor: Department of Public Health and Human Services
CON organization contact person:	Pamela Sourbeer
Title of CON contact person:	Admin. Officer
Email address of CON contact:	psourbeer@state.mt.us
Mailing address for state CON office:	Dept of Public Health and Human Services
Mailing address for state CON office:	P.O. Box 202953
City where state CON office is located:	Helena
State for mailing address:	Montana
Zip code for CON office:	59620-
Phone number for CON contact:	(406) 444-9519
Fax number for CON contact:	(406) 444-1742
State CON Decision Making Body (DMB)	
Name of DMB:	Director, Dept of Public Health and Human Services
Title of person DMB reports to:	Governor
Title of person appointing DMB members:	Governor
Composition of CON DMB:	
Number of people in the DMB:	1
Number of CON agency reps in DMB:	1

EQUIPMENT REGULATION AND DATA

Subject to CON (Y/N):	
Is any equipment subject to CON?:	False
Are air ambulances subject to CON?:	False
Are cardiac cath labs subject to CON?:	False

Subject to CON (Y/N) (Continued)

Are CT scanners subject to CON?:	False
Are gamma knives subject to CON?:	False
Are linear accelerators subject to CON?:	False
Is lithotropsy subject to CON?:	False
Is mobile high tech subject to CON?:	False
Are MRI scanners subject to CON?:	False
Are PET scanners subject to CON?:	False
Is radiation therapy subject to CON?:	False
Is renal dialysis subject to CON?:	False
Are swing beds subject to CON?:	True
Is ultra-sound subject to CON?:	False

FACILITIES REGULATION AND DATA

Subject to CON (Y/N):

Is any facility subject to CON?	False
Are hospitals subject to CON?	False
Are nursing homes subject to CON?	False
Are residential care facilities subject to CON?	False
Are psychiatric facilities subject to CON?	False
Are ambulatory surgery centers subject to CON?	True
Are ICF/MRs subject to CON?	True
Is long term care subject to CON?	True
Are medical office buildings subject to CON?	False
Are rehabilitation facilities subject to CON?	True
Are renal dialysis facilities subject to CON?	False
Are RCF/Assisted Living facilities subject to CON?	False
Are subacute care facilities subject to CON?	False
Are substance abuse facilities subject to CON?	True
Are swing beds subject to CON?	True

Project Dollar Threshold Requiring CON Application:

Dollar threshold for any facility application:	$1,500,000

Additional Criteria Used to Determine Need:

Additional criteria used to determine need for swing beds: CON Requirement: avg occupancy level of at least 95% during the 3 yrs prior to the date of the application for CON; and no more than 50% of the excess bed capacity of the hospital or medical assistance facility will be approved as swing beds.

Notes Including Bed Limits and Moratoria:

Notes including bed limits/moratoria for any facility: CON requirement: any capital expenditure of a health care facility that exceeds $1.5 million, other than to acquire an existing health care facility; and a capital expenditure by any person to acquire 50% or more of an existing health care facility. CON Exemptions: construction of state-owned facility and repair or replacement of a facility damaged or destroyed as a result of fire, storm, civil disturbance, or an act of God if the use of the facility after repair or replacement is within the scope of the facility's original license.

SERVICES REGULATION AND DATA

Subject to CON (Y/N):

Are all services subject to CON?:	False
Are nursing home services subject to CON?:	True
Are acute care services subject to CON?:	True
Are air ambulance subject to CON?:	False
Is burn care subject to CON?:	False
Is cardiac catheterization subject to CON?:	False
Is CT scanning subject to CON?:	False
Is gamma knife service subject to CON?:	False
Is home health subject to CON?:	True
Is linear accelerator service subject to CON?:	False
Is lithotripsy service subject to CON?:	False
Is long term care subject to CON?:	True
Is mobile high tech service subject to CON?:	False
Is MRI scanning subject to CON?:	False
Is neo-natal intensive care subject to CON?:	False
Are obstetrical services subject to CON?:	False
Is open heart surgery subject to CON?:	False
Is organ transplantation subject to CON?:	False
Is PET scanning subject to CON?:	False
Are psychiatric services subject to CON?:	False
Is radiation therapy subject to CON?:	False
Are rehabilitation services subject to CON?:	True
Is renal dialysis subject to CON?:	False
Is RCF/Assisted Living subject to CON?:	False
Is subacute care subject to CON?:	False
Is substance abuse subject to CON?:	True
Are swing beds subject to CON?:	True
Is utlra-sound subject to CON?:	False

Dollar Threshold for CON Application:

Dollar threshold for any service application:	$150,000

Additional Criteria Used to Determine Need:

Additional criteria used to determine need for nursing home: CON Requirement: a change in bed capacity of health care facility through an increase in the number of beds or a relocation of beds from one health care facility or site to another, unless; the number of beds involved is 10 or less or 10% or less of the licensed beds

Additional criteria used to determine need for acute care: CON Requirement: a change in bed capacity of health care facility through an increase in the number of beds or a relocation of beds from one health care facility or site to another, unless; the number of beds involved is 10 or less or 10% or less of the licensed beds

Additional criteria used to determine need for swing beds: CON Requirement: a change in bed capacity of health care facility through an increase in the number of beds or a relocation of beds from one health care facility or site to another, unless the number of beds involved is 10 or less or 10% or less of the licensed beds

CON STATUTES AND REGULATIONS

CON Statutes:

CON Statute Title: Health and Safety: Hospitals and Related Facilities General Provisions
CON Statute Citation: Mont. Code Anno., 50-5-101 et seq

CON Regulations:

CON Regulations Title: Certificate of Need
CON Regulations Citation: 37.106

STATE NOTE

Montana requires a certificate of need ("CON") to add new health services with capital expenditures above a minimum amount. Some criteria for healthcare are detailed in the regulations but others are contained in the Montana Health Care Facilities Plan which is updated annually. The regulations and facilities plan contain complex formals to calculate need. The formulas consider average utilization of the health service for a specific time period and the county's population. Some of the formulas are different based on the county's size.

NEBRASKA

STATE CON AGENCY CONTACTS

State Department Overseeing CON	
Name of state CON department:	Dept of Health & Human Services Reg. & Licensure
URL address for state CON organization:	http://www.hhs.state.ne.us/crl/crlindex.htm
CON Administrative Office Information	
Name of state CON office:	NE Health and Human Services Regulation and Licen.
	Hierarchy for state CON administrative office: Governor: HHS: Reg. and Licens.
CON organization contact person:	Claire Titus
Title of CON contact person:	Section Program Manager
Email address of CON contact:	claire.titus@hhs.state.ne.us
Mailing address for state CON office:	301 Centennial Mall South, 3rd Floor
Mailing address for state CON office:	PO Box 94986
City where state CON office is located:	Lincoln
State for mailing address:	Nebraska
Zip code for CON office:	68509-
Phone number for CON contact:	(402) 471-4963
Fax number for CON contact:	(402) 471-3577
State CON Decision Making Body (DMB)	
Name of DMB:	Dept of Health & Human Services Reg. & Licensure
Title of person DMB reports to:	Health and Human Services
Title of person appointing DMB members:	

EQUIPMENT REGULATION AND DATA

Subject to CON (Y/N):	
Is any equipment subject to CON?:	False
Are air ambulances subject to CON?:	False
Are cardiac cath labs subject to CON?:	False
Are CT scanners subject to CON?:	False
Are gamma knives subject to CON?:	False
Are linear accelerators subject to CON?:	False
Is lithotropsy subject to CON?:	False
Is mobile high tech subject to CON?:	False
Are MRI scanners subject to CON?:	False

Subject to CON (Y/N) (Continued)

Are PET scanners subject to CON?:	False
Is radiation therapy subject to CON?:	False
Is renal dialysis subject to CON?:	False
Are swing beds subject to CON?:	False
Is ultra-sound subject to CON?:	False

FACILITIES REGULATION AND DATA

Subject to CON (Y/N):

Is any facility subject to CON?	False
Are hospitals subject to CON?	False
Are nursing homes subject to CON?	True
Are residential care facilities subject to CON?	False
Are psychiatric facilities subject to CON?	False
Are ambulatory surgery centers subject to CON?	False
Are ICF/MRs subject to CON?	False
Is long term care subject to CON?	True
Are medical office buildings subject to CON?	False
Are rehabilitation facilities subject to CON?	True
Are renal dialysis facilities subject to CON?	False
Are RCF/Assisted Living facilities subject to CON?	False
Are subacute care facilities subject to CON?	False
Are substance abuse facilities subject to CON?	False
Are swing beds subject to CON?	False

Notes Including Bed Limits and Moratoria:

Notes including bed limits/moratoria for a long term care facility: All LTC beds which require a CON under section 71-5829.03 are subject to a moratorium

Notes including bed limits/moratoria for a rehabilitation facility: All rehab beds which require CON are subject to moratorium

SERVICES REGULATION AND DATA

Subject to CON (Y/N):

Are all services subject to CON?:	False
Are nursing home services subject to CON?:	True
Are acute care services subject to CON?:	False
Are air ambulance subject to CON?:	False
Is burn care subject to CON?:	False
Is cardiac catheterization subject to CON?:	False
Is CT scanning subject to CON?:	False
Is gamma knife service subject to CON?:	False
Is home health subject to CON?:	False
Is linear accelerator service subject to CON?:	False
Is lithotripsy service subject to CON?:	False
Is long term care subject to CON?:	True
Is mobile high tech service subject to CON?:	False

Subject to CON (Y/N) (Continued)

Is MRI scanning subject to CON?:	False
Is neo-natal intensive care subject to CON?:	False
Are obstetrical services subject to CON?:	False
Is open heart surgery subject to CON?:	False
Is organ transplantation subject to CON?:	False
Is PET scanning subject to CON?:	False
Are psychiatric services subject to CON?:	False
Is radiation therapy subject to CON?:	False
Are rehabilitation services subject to CON?:	True
Is renal dialysis subject to CON?:	False
Is RCF/Assisted Living subject to CON?:	True
Is subacute care subject to CON?:	False
Is substance abuse subject to CON?:	False
Are swing beds subject to CON?:	False
Is utlra-sound subject to CON?:	False
Are other services subject to CON?:	Any change by a domiciliary facility to convert domiciliary beds to long-term care beds

Additional Criteria Used to Determine Need:

Additional criteria used to determine need for long term care: LTC bed need is equal to the population, multiplied by the utilization rate goal, and the result divided by the minimum occupancy rate goal.

Additional criteria used to determine need for rehabilitation: If the avg occupancy for all rehab beds located in Nebraska has exceeded 90% occupancy during the most recent 3 consecutive calendar quarters as reported at the time of the filing of the application, the dept may grant an exception to the moratorium and issue a CON

CON STATUTES AND REGULATIONS

CON Statutes:

CON Statute Title: Nebraska Health Care Certificate of Need Act
CON Statute Citation: Sections 71-5801 to 71-5870

CON Regulations:

CON Regulations Title: HHS Finance and Support Manual
CON Regulations Citation: Ch. 12-011

STATE NOTE

Nebraska requires a certificate of need ("CON") only for long-term care beds and rehabilitation beds. Per the statute, there is currently a moratorium on new long-term care beds and rehabilitation beds. The statutes allows a certificate of need to be granted for these services if there is an unmet need. The calculation to determine unmet need requires that current facilities within the service area have a minimum occupancy rate.

NEVADA

STATE CON AGENCY CONTACTS

State Department Overseeing CON

Name of state CON department:	Nevada State Health Division
URL address for state CON organization:	http://health2k.state.nv.us/vs/letter.htm

CON Administrative Office Information

Name of state CON office:	Bureau of Health Planning & Statistics Hierarchy for state CON administrative office: Governor: Dept. of Human Resources: Bureau of Health Planning & Statistics
CON organization contact person:	Mary Griffith, RN
Title of CON contact person:	Health Resource Analyst
Email address of CON contact:	mgriffith@nvhd.state.nv.us
Mailing address for state CON office:	505 E. King St.
Mailing address for state CON office:	Room 102
City where state CON office is located:	Carson City
State for mailing address:	Nevada
Zip code for CON office:	89701-
Phone number for CON contact:	(775) 684-4180
Fax number for CON contact:	(775) 684-4156

State CON Decision Making Body (DMB)

Name of DMB:	Director of Department of Human Resources
Title of person DMB reports to:	Governor
Title of person appointing DMB members:	Governor

Composition of CON DMB:

Number of people in the DMB:	1

EQUIPMENT REGULATION AND DATA

Subject to CON (Y/N):

Is any equipment subject to CON?:	False
Are air ambulances subject to CON?:	False
Are cardiac cath labs subject to CON?:	False
Are CT scanners subject to CON?:	False
Are gamma knives subject to CON?:	False
Are linear accelerators subject to CON?:	False
Is lithotropsy subject to CON?:	False
Is mobile high tech subject to CON?:	False
Are MRI scanners subject to CON?:	False

Subject to CON (Y/N) (Continued)

Are PET scanners subject to CON?:	False
Is radiation therapy subject to CON?:	False
Is renal dialysis subject to CON?:	False
Are swing beds subject to CON?:	False
Is ultra-sound subject to CON?:	False

FACILITIES REGULATION AND DATA

Subject to CON (Y/N):

Is any facility subject to CON?	False
Are hospitals subject to CON?	True
Are nursing homes subject to CON?	False
Are residential care facilities subject to CON?	False
Are psychiatric facilities subject to CON?	False
Are ambulatory surgery centers subject to CON?	True
Are ICF/MRs subject to CON?	True
Is long term care subject to CON?	True
Are medical office buildings subject to CON?	False
Are rehabilitation facilities subject to CON?	True
Are renal dialysis facilities subject to CON?	False
Are RCF/Assisted Living facilities subject to CON?	False
Are subacute care facilities subject to CON?	True
Are substance abuse facilities subject to CON?	True
Are swing beds subject to CON?	False

Project Dollar Threshold Requiring CON Application:

Dollar threshold for any facility application:	$2,000,000

Additional Criteria Used to Determine Need:

Additional criteria used to determine need for any facility: Applicant must prove that population to be served has a need for the project based upon: (1)id of the population to be served; (2)projected numbers of persons who will have a need for the proposed service; and (3)a showing that the existing providers of the proposed service in the area cannot or will not meet the projected need of the population to be served.

Notes Including Bed Limits and Moratoria:

Notes including bed limits/moratoria for any facility: Health facility means a facility in or through which health services are provided, except for the office of a practitioner used solely to provide routine services for health to his patients. In a county whose population is less than 100,000, no person may undertake any proposed expenditure for new construction by or on behalf of a health facility in excess of $2,000,000 without written approval of the Director. CON Exemption: any project for the development of hospital in unincorporated town if: (1)population of town is more than 24,000; (2)no other hospitals exist; (3)no other hospital has been approved for construction or qualified for an exemption from approval for construction in the town; and (4)town is at least 45 minute drive from nearest center for treatment of trauma434

SERVICES REGULATION AND DATA

Subject to CON (Y/N):

Are all services subject to CON?:	False
Are nursing home services subject to CON?:	True
Are acute care services subject to CON?:	True
Are air ambulance subject to CON?:	True
Is burn care subject to CON?:	False
Is cardiac catheterization subject to CON?:	False
Is CT scanning subject to CON?:	False
Is gamma knife service subject to CON?:	False
Is home health subject to CON?:	False
Is linear accelerator service subject to CON?:	False
Is lithotripsy service subject to CON?:	False
Is long term care subject to CON?:	True
Is mobile high tech service subject to CON?:	False
Is MRI scanning subject to CON?:	False
Is neo-natal intensive care subject to CON?:	False
Are obstetrical services subject to CON?:	False
Is open heart surgery subject to CON?:	False
Is organ transplantation subject to CON?:	False
Is PET scanning subject to CON?:	False
Are psychiatric services subject to CON?:	False
Is radiation therapy subject to CON?:	False
Are rehabilitation services subject to CON?:	True
Is renal dialysis subject to CON?:	True
Is RCF/Assisted Living subject to CON?:	False
Is subacute care subject to CON?:	False
Is substance abuse subject to CON?:	False
Are swing beds subject to CON?:	False
Is utlra-sound subject to CON?:	False

Additional Criteria Used to Determine Need:

Additional criteria used to determine need for air ambulance: No person may operate or undertake any proposed expenditure for the operation of a new medical helicopter that will provide medical helicopter services in an area located within 150 miles from the base of an existing medical helicopter without first applying for and obtaining the written approval of the State Health Officer.

CON STATUTES AND REGULATIONS

CON Statutes:

CON Statute Title: Planning for the Provision of Health Care
CON Statute Citation: NRS Chapter 439A

CON Regulations:

CON Regulations Title: Planning for the Provision of Health Care
CON Regulations Citation: Chapter 439A

STATE NOTE

Nevada requires a certificate of need ("CON") only for the construction of a "health facility" in a county whose population is less than 100,000 (§ 439A.100.1). The applicant is required to demonstrate need for the proposed service (NAC 439A.605). The state has not promulgated specific methodologies for defining need for a service.

NEW HAMPSHIRE

STATE CON AGENCY CONTACTS

State Department Overseeing CON

Name of state CON department:	Department of Health and Human Services
URL address for state CON organization:	http://www.dhhs.state.nh.us?DHHS?HSPR/default.htm

CON Administrative Office Information

Name of state CON office:	Health Services Planning & Review Hierarchy for state CON administrative office: Governor: Department of Health and Human Services
CON organization contact person:	Margaret Heatley
Title of CON contact person:	Administrator
Email address of CON contact:	m.heatley@dhhs.state.nh.us
Mailing address for state CON office:	29 Hazen Drive
City where state CON office is located:	Concord
State for mailing address:	New Hampshire
Zip code for CON office:	03301
Phone number for CON contact:	(603) 271-4606
Fax number for CON contact:	(603) 271-4141

State CON Decision Making Body (DMB)

Name of DMB:	Health Services Planning and Review Board
Title of person DMB reports to:	Office of Community & Public Health
Title of person appointing DMB members:	Governor and Council

Composition of CON DMB:

Number of people in the DMB:	9
Number of CON agency reps in DMB:	1
Number of consumers in DMB:	4
Number of healthcare providers in DMB:	4

EQUIPMENT REGULATION AND DATA

Subject to CON (Y/N):

Is any equipment subject to CON?:	False
Are air ambulances subject to CON?:	False
Are cardiac cath labs subject to CON?:	True
Are CT scanners subject to CON?:	True
Are gamma knives subject to CON?:	False

Subject to CON (Y/N) (Continued)

Are linear accelerators subject to CON?:	False
Is lithotropsy subject to CON?:	True
Is mobile high tech subject to CON?:	True
Are MRI scanners subject to CON?:	True
Are PET scanners subject to CON?:	True
Is radiation therapy subject to CON?:	True
Is renal dialysis subject to CON?:	False
Are swing beds subject to CON?:	False
Is ultra-sound subject to CON?:	False

Dollar Threshold for CON Application:

Dollar threshold for any equipment application:	$400,000

FACILITIES REGULATION AND DATA

Subject to CON (Y/N):

Is any facility subject to CON?	False
Are hospitals subject to CON?	True
Are nursing homes subject to CON?	True
Are residential care facilities subject to CON?	False
Are psychiatric facilities subject to CON?	True
Are ambulatory surgery centers subject to CON?	True
Are ICF/MRs subject to CON?	False
Is long term care subject to CON?	True
Are medical office buildings subject to CON?	False
Are rehabilitation facilities subject to CON?	True
Are renal dialysis facilities subject to CON?	False
Are RCF/Assisted Living facilities subject to CON?	False
Are subacute care facilities subject to CON?	False
Are substance abuse facilities subject to CON?	True
Are swing beds subject to CON?	False
Are other facilities subject to CON?	specialty hospital

Project Dollar Threshold Requiring CON Application:

Dollar threshold for a hospital application: $1,759,512
Dollar threshold for a nursing home application: $1,173,000
Dollar threshold for a psychiatric facility application: $1,173,000
Dollar threshold for an ambulatory surgery center application: $1,173,000
Dollar threshold for a rehabilitational facility application: $1,173,000
Dollar threshold for other facility applications: $1,173,000

Capacity Requirements – Beds / Population:

Capacity requirement-beds/population for hospitals: 3.1/1,000
Capacity requirement-beds/population for nursing homes: 40/1,000 persons over age 65 living in region
Capacity requirement-beds/population for ICF/MRs:
Capacity requirement-beds/population for rehabilitation facility: 12/100,000

Capacity requirement-beds/population for other facilities: SNF: 40/1,000 persons over age 65 living in region

Notes Including Bed Limits and Moratoria:

Notes including bed limits/moratoria for any facility: Institutions or homes which provide remedial care or treatment only to residents or patients who rely solely upon treatment by prayer or spiritual means in accordance with the creed or attendance of any recognized church or religious denomination

Notes including bed limits/moratoria for a nursing home: No CON granted by board for any nursing home, skilled nursing facility, intermediate care facility or rehab facility from the effective date of Ch. 310, laws of 1995, dept of health and human services reorganization act, through the period ending December 31, 2006, except that a CON shall be issued for replacement or renovation of existing beds

Notes including bed limits/moratoria for an ambulatory surgery center: The threshold amount for construction of ambulatory surgical centers within the service area of a hospital with fewer than 70 general hospital beds licensed by the department of health and human services shall be $500,000

Notes including bed limits/moratoria for an ICF/MR: No CON granted by board for any nursing home, skilled nursing facility, intermediate care facility or rehab facility from the effective date of Ch. 310, laws of 1995, dept of health and human services reorganization act, through the period ending December 31, 2006, except that a CON shall be issued for replacement or renovation of existing beds

Notes including bed limits/moratoria for a long term care facility: Service area for new LTC facility to include those towns and cities located within a 15 mile radius or 45 minute drive of proposed facility. Bed Need = Region Population Aged 65+ x 40

Notes including bed limits/moratoria for a rehabilitation facility: No CON granted by board for any nursing home, skilled nursing facility, intermediate care facility or rehab facility from the effective date of Ch. 310, laws of 1995, dept of health and human services reorganization act, through the period ending December 31, 2006, except that a CON shall be issued for replacement or renovation of existing beds

Notes including bed limits/moratoria for other facilities: No CON granted by board for any nursing home, skilled nursing facility, intermediate care facility or rehab facility from the effective date of Ch. 310, laws of 1995, dept of health and human services reorganization act, through the period ending December 31, 2006, except that a CON shall be issued for replacement or renovation of existing beds

SERVICES REGULATION AND DATA

Subject to CON (Y/N):

Are all services subject to CON?:	False
Are nursing home services subject to CON?:	True
Are acute care services subject to CON?:	True
Are air ambulance subject to CON?:	False
Is burn care subject to CON?:	False
Is cardiac catheterization subject to CON?:	True
Is CT scanning subject to CON?:	True
Is gamma knife service subject to CON?:	False
Is home health subject to CON?:	False
Is linear accelerator service subject to CON?:	True
Is lithotripsy service subject to CON?:	True
Is long term care subject to CON?:	True
Is mobile high tech service subject to CON?:	True
Is MRI scanning subject to CON?:	True
Is neo-natal intensive care subject to CON?:	False

Subject to CON (Y/N) (Continued)

Are obstetrical services subject to CON?:	False
Is open heart surgery subject to CON?:	True
Is organ transplantation subject to CON?:	False
Is PET scanning subject to CON?:	True
Are psychiatric services subject to CON?:	True
Is radiation therapy subject to CON?:	True
Are rehabilitation services subject to CON?:	True
Is renal dialysis subject to CON?:	False
Is RCF/Assisted Living subject to CON?:	False
Is subacute care subject to CON?:	False
Is substance abuse subject to CON?:	True
Are swing beds subject to CON?:	False
Is utlra-sound subject to CON?:	False

Additional Criteria Used to Determine Need:

Additional criteria used to determine need for acute care: New Health Service: increase of more than 10 beds or 10 percent of the total bed complement, whichever is less, during a 2-yr period. Medical and Surgical Bed Minimum Occupancy (75%) and Optimal Occupancy(90%)

Additional criteria used to determine need for cardiac catheterization: Adult diagnostic cardiac cath services shall only be provided on the campus of an acute care facility. No new adult open hearth surgery program approved unless it can be demonstrated that the proposed program can retain number of patients needed to assure a minimum volume of 250 cases annually per facility. No new service shall be approved if the intro of that service causes the volume in any facility dedicated for adult open heart surgery in the State to drop below 350 adult open heart surgery cases per year.

Additional criteria used to determine need for obstetrical: OB Bed Minimum Occupancy (60%) and Optimal Occupancy(85%)

Additional criteria used to determine need for PET scanning: No licensed facility or consortium shall apply for CON for a fixed unit until: (1) it is making 1200 referrals per yr to a mobile PET vendor based on previous 12 months of operation; or (2) a report can be made to the board proving projected volume of, at least 1000 scans per yr. No applicant shall add an additional fixed unit under the provisions of RSA 151-C:5, II(d) until it is performing a total of 1200 scans per yr on the first unit based on the previous 12 months of operation

Additional criteria used to determine need for psychiatric services: Psychiatric Bed Minimum Occupancy (70%) and Optimal Occupancy(90%)

Additional criteria used to determine need for radiation therapy: The proposed equipment shall treat minimum of 325 patients annually by the end of third yr of operations, an avg of 6,500 annual procedures shall be performed by each machine in the facility by the end of the third year of operation, and all existing services which have a current radiation therapy mkt share of greater than 30% of the proposed service area are performing an avg of 7,000 procedures per machine at that site during the most recent full yr of operation

Additional criteria used to determine need for others: Pediatrics Bed Minimum Occupancy Less than 40 Beds (60%) and Optimal Occupancy Less than 40 Beds(85%); Minimum Occupancy More than 40 Beds (65%) and Optimal Occupancy More than 40 Beds(90%); ICU/CCU Bed Minimum Occupancy (60%) and Optimal Occupancy(85%)

CON STATUTES AND REGULATIONS

CON Statutes:

CON Statute Title: Certificate of Need Review of Proposed New Institutional Health Services
CON Statute Citation: RSA Chapter 151-C

CON Regulations:

CON Regulations Title: Health Services Planning and Review Board
CON Regulations Citation: Chapter He-Hea 100

STATE NOTE

New Hampshire requires a certificate of need ("CON") to establish any new "institutional health service." The statute defines "institutional health service" to include most inpatient services and the acquisition of medical equipment by an outpatient provider which more than a threshold amount. There is a different threshold amount for each type of service.

NEW JERSEY

STATE CON AGENCY CONTACTS

State Department Overseeing CON	
Name of state CON department:	Certificate of Need & Acute Care Licensure
URL address for state CON organization:	http://www.state.nj.us/health/hcsa/hcsadmin.htm#CN
CON Administrative Office Information	
Name of state CON office:	State Health Planning Board Hierarchy for state CON administrative office: Governor:NJ Dept. of Health:CON&Acute Lic. Program
CON organization contact person:	John Calabria
Title of CON contact person:	Director
Email address of CON contact:	john.calabria@doh.state.nj.us
Mailing address for state CON office:	P.O. Box 360, John Fitch Plaza
City where state CON office is located:	Trenton
State for mailing address:	New Jersey
Zip code for CON office:	08625
Phone number for CON contact:	(609) 292-8773
Fax number for CON contact:	(609) 292-3780
State CON Decision Making Body (DMB)	
Name of DMB:	Commissioner of Health
Title of person DMB reports to:	Governor
Title of person appointing DMB members:	Governor
Composition of CON DMB:	
Number of people in the DMB:	1
Number of CON agency reps in DMB:	1

EQUIPMENT REGULATION AND DATA

Subject to CON (Y/N):	
Is any equipment subject to CON?:	False
Are air ambulances subject to CON?:	False
Are cardiac cath labs subject to CON?:	False
Are CT scanners subject to CON?:	False
Are gamma knives subject to CON?:	False
Are linear accelerators subject to CON?:	False
Is lithotropsy subject to CON?:	False

Subject to CON (Y/N) (Continued)

Is mobile high tech subject to CON?:	False
Are MRI scanners subject to CON?:	False
Are PET scanners subject to CON?:	False
Is radiation therapy subject to CON?:	False
Is renal dialysis subject to CON?:	False
Are swing beds subject to CON?:	False
Is ultra-sound subject to CON?:	False

Dollar Threshold for CON Application:

Dollar threshold for any equipment application: $2,000,000

Additional Criteria Used to Determine Need:

Additional criteria used to determine need for any equipment: CON Exemptions: replacement of existing major moveable equipment

Additional criteria used to determine need for cardiac cath lab: CON Exemptions: addition of cardiac cath equipment by a general hospital licensed to provide full service invasive cardiac diagnostic services; replacement of equipment

FACILITIES REGULATION AND DATA

Subject to CON (Y/N):

Is any facility subject to CON?	False
Are hospitals subject to CON?	True
Are nursing homes subject to CON?	False
Are residential care facilities subject to CON?	False
Are psychiatric facilities subject to CON?	True
Are ambulatory surgery centers subject to CON?	False
Are ICF/MRs subject to CON?	True
Is long term care subject to CON?	True
Are medical office buildings subject to CON?	False
Are rehabilitation facilities subject to CON?	True
Are renal dialysis facilities subject to CON?	False
Are RCF/Assisted Living facilities subject to CON?	False
Are subacute care facilities subject to CON?	False
Are substance abuse facilities subject to CON?	False
Are swing beds subject to CON?	False

Project Dollar Threshold Requiring CON Application:

Dollar threshold for any facility application: $2,000,000

Additional Criteria Used to Determine Need:

Additional criteria used to determine need for a rehabilitation facility: CON Requirements: minimum size of new, freestanding rehab hospital shall be 60 beds; and minimum size of non-freestanding rehab hospital located within another type of licensed health care facility shall be 30 beds.

Notes Including Bed Limits and Moratoria:

Notes including bed limits/moratoria for any facility: Health Care Facility Defined: excludes institutions that provide healing solely by prayer and excluding such bioanalytical labs that are independently owned and operated. CON Exemptions: capital improvements and renovations to health care facilities; ambulatory care facilities; transfer of ownership interest except in the case of an acute care hospital. CON applicants must show how proposed project will promote access to low income persons, racial and ethnic minorities, women, disabled persons, the elderly, and persons with HIV infections and other persons who are unable to obtain care

Notes including bed limits/moratoria for a nursing home: CON Exemptions: nursing home which proposes to increase the total number of licensed beds contained therein by not more than 10 beds or 10% of its licensed bed capacity, whichever is less, within a period of five years; nursing home affiliated with a well established religious body or denomination and reserves at least 65% of its licensed bed capacity for patients who are members of that religious body or denomination

Notes including bed limits/moratoria for a residential care facility: CON Exemptions: residential health care facility

Notes including bed limits/moratoria for an ambulatory surgery center: CON Exemptions: ambulatory surgery facilities; ambulatory care

Notes including bed limits/moratoria for a renal dialysis facility: CON Exemptions: Chronic or acute renal dialysis facilities

SERVICES REGULATION AND DATA

Subject to CON (Y/N):

Are all services subject to CON?:	False
Are nursing home services subject to CON?:	False
Are acute care services subject to CON?:	True
Are air ambulance subject to CON?:	True
Is burn care subject to CON?:	True
Is cardiac catheterization subject to CON?:	True
Is CT scanning subject to CON?:	False
Is gamma knife service subject to CON?:	False
Is home health subject to CON?:	True
Is linear accelerator service subject to CON?:	False
Is lithotripsy service subject to CON?:	False
Is long term care subject to CON?:	True
Is mobile high tech service subject to CON?:	False
Is MRI scanning subject to CON?:	False
Is neo-natal intensive care subject to CON?:	True
Are obstetrical services subject to CON?:	False
Is open heart surgery subject to CON?:	True
Is organ transplantation subject to CON?:	True
Is PET scanning subject to CON?:	False
Are psychiatric services subject to CON?:	True
Is radiation therapy subject to CON?:	False
Are rehabilitation services subject to CON?:	True
Is renal dialysis subject to CON?:	True
Is RCF/Assisted Living subject to CON?:	False
Is subacute care subject to CON?:	False

Subject to CON (Y/N) (Continued)

Is substance abuse subject to CON?:	False
Are swing beds subject to CON?:	False
Is utlra-sound subject to CON?:	False
Are other services subject to CON?:	central service agency, mobile intensive care or advanced life support service, organ bank, trauma service, any other new health care technologies that the Dept identifies as having a Statewide or regional impact

Additional Criteria Used to Determine Need:

Additional criteria used to determine need for acute care: CON Exemptions: additions of medical/surgical; adult itensive care and adult critical care beds in hospitals; hosptial based subacute care unit

Additional criteria used to determine need for cardiac catheterization: All cardiac cath procedures, regardless of the category, shall be performed in a hospital-based facility where inpatient services are available on site. At a minimum, the non-invasive lab shall include the capability to perform the following: Electrocardiography; Exercise Stress Testing; Echocardiography; Ambulatory Electrocardiographic Monitoring; and Nuclear Cardiology. CON Requirement for Adult Cardiovascular Surgical Units: ability to achieve annual volume of 350 open heart surgical cases by end of third year of operation and annually thereafter. CON Requirements Pediatric Cardiac Diagnostic and Surgical Services: proposed center must perform at least 150 pediatric open and closed heart surgery procedures per year, at least 75 of which must be open heart procedures, for each operating room utilized for pediatric open heart surgery by end of third year of operation and each year thereafter. CON Requirements Card Surg Center PTCA Services: must perform minimum of 200 PTCA procedures per year by third year of operation

Additional criteria used to determine need for long term care: CON Requirement Bed Addition: avg occupancy rate for existing licensed long term acute care beds for the six most recent quarters prior to submission of the CON application exceeds 85 percent. CON Requirement for Newly Licenced LTAC Beds: existing LTAC hospitals within one hour travel time of applicant have been operating at 80% occupancy of licensed beds for the latest four quarters of utilization data

Additional criteria used to determine need for neonatal intensive care: CON Requirements: hospital in full compliance with rules set forth ; CON applicant has become general member or is a member in good standing of MCHC; documentation that CON applicant has notified appropriate MCHC of change in services planned in accordance with the application; and CON applicant's intent and ability to assure access to patient care services

Additional criteria used to determine need for obstetrical: CON Exemptions: basic obstetric and pediatric services and birth centers, including additions of basic obstetric and pediatric beds in hospitals

Additional criteria used to determine need for organ transplantation: CON Requirements: Kidney Transplant-25 minimum procedures; Heart Transplant-12 minimum procedures; Liver Transplant-15 minimum procedures; and Pancreas Transplant-15 minimum procedures

Additional criteria used to determine need for rehabilitation: CON Exemptions: comprehensive outpatient rehab services

Additional criteria used to determine need for substance abuse: CON Exemptions: residential drug and alcohol services; medical detox program (hospital based)

CON STATUTES AND REGULATIONS

CON Statutes:

CON Statute Title: Health Care Facilities Planning Act
CON Statute Citation: N.J. Stat. Ann. 26:2H-1 to 26:2H-26

CON Regulations:

CON Regulations Title: Certificate of Need: Application and Review Process
CON Regulations Citation: N.J.A.C. Title 8, Chapter 33

STATE NOTE

A certificate of need ("CON") is required to construct or expand a "health care facility" or to institute a "new health care service" (§ 26:2H-7). The statutory definitions of "health care facility" and "health care service" are very broad but in 1998, the New Jersey legislature eliminated certificate of need ("CON") requirements for many services (§ 26:2H-6.1(h)(i)) therefore many services falling within the statutory definitions of "health care facility" and "health care service" do not require a CON(§ 26:2H-7a). A CON is not required for equipment involving "new technology" (§ 26:2H-7d). The State Health Planning Board ("Board") has not promulgated specific utilization requirements for most services requiring a CON. The Board is not required to demonstrate lack of need for a proposed service when denying a CON application (8.33-4.9).

NEW YORK

STATE CON AGENCY CONTACTS

State Department Overseeing CON	
Name of state CON department:	Division of Health Facilities Planning (CON)
URL address for state CON organization:	http://health2k.state.nv.us/vs/letter.htm
CON Administrative Office Information	
Name of state CON office:	Division of Health Facilities Planning Hierarchy for state CON administrative office: Governor: NY State Dept. of Health: Division of Health Facilities Planning
CON organization contact person:	Neal Benjamin
Title of CON contact person:	Director
Email address of CON contact:	cpd02@health.state.ny.us
Mailing address for state CON office:	Headley Park Place
Mailing address for state CON office:	433 River Street
City where state CON office is located:	Troy
State for mailing address:	New York
Zip code for CON office:	12180
Phone number for CON contact:	(518) 402-0966
Fax number for CON contact:	(518) 402-0971
State CON Decision Making Body (DMB)	
Name of DMB:	Commissioner of Health (existing providers)
Title of person DMB reports to:	
Title of person appointing DMB members:	
Composition of CON DMB:	
Number of people in the DMB:	1

EQUIPMENT REGULATION AND DATA

Subject to CON (Y/N):	
Is any equipment subject to CON?:	False
Are air ambulances subject to CON?:	False
Are cardiac cath labs subject to CON?:	True
Are CT scanners subject to CON?:	True
Are gamma knives subject to CON?:	False
Are linear accelerators subject to CON?:	True
Is lithotropsy subject to CON?:	True
Is mobile high tech subject to CON?:	True

Subject to CON (Y/N) (Continued)

Are MRI scanners subject to CON?:	True
Are PET scanners subject to CON?:	True
Is radiation therapy subject to CON?:	True
Is renal dialysis subject to CON?:	True
Are swing beds subject to CON?:	True
Is ultra-sound subject to CON?:	False

Utilization Requirements (Equipment/Population):

Utilization Requirement-Equipment/Population for lithotropsy: 1 unit/2.5 million residents

FACILITIES REGULATION AND DATA

Subject to CON (Y/N):

Is any facility subject to CON?	False
Are hospitals subject to CON?	True
Are nursing homes subject to CON?	True
Are residential care facilities subject to CON?	True
Are psychiatric facilities subject to CON?	True
Are ambulatory surgery centers subject to CON?	True
Are ICF/MRs subject to CON?	True
Is long term care subject to CON?	True
Are medical office buildings subject to CON?	False
Are rehabilitation facilities subject to CON?	True
Are renal dialysis facilities subject to CON?	True
Are RCF/Assisted Living facilities subject to CON?	False
Are subacute care facilities subject to CON?	False
Are substance abuse facilities subject to CON?	True
Are swing beds subject to CON?	True
Are other facilities subject to CON?	public health center; diagnostic center; treatment center; dental clinic; dental dispensary; tuberculosis; chronic disease hospital; maternity hospital; lying-in asylum; outpatient department; outpatient lodge; dispensary; laboratory

Additional Criteria Used to Determine Need:

Additional criteria used to determine need for a hospital: methodology to calculate bed need; considers population, discharges, and desired occupancy levels. Medical/surgical .85 urban/.80 rural; pediatric .70 urban/.65 rural; obstetric .75 urban/.70 rural

Additional criteria used to determine need for an ambulatory surgery center: public need if documentation that project is financially feasible, will enance access, the facility's hours will enhance access, and documentation that facility will safely serve patients.

Additional criteria used to determine need for an ICF/MR: regulations contain projected estimates of public need by county; total estimated bed need = 120,838

Notes Including Bed Limits and Moratoria:

Notes including bed limits/moratoria for any facility: no CON needed for institution serving members of recognized religious organization; need CON for transfer of 10% or more ownership in facility

Notes including bed limits/moratoria for a hospital: planning area is the county

Notes including bed limits/moratoria for an ambulatory surgery center: need CON for construction/establish of new ASC/services or extention of existing services

SERVICES REGULATION AND DATA

Subject to CON (Y/N):

Are all services subject to CON?:	False
Are nursing home services subject to CON?:	False
Are acute care services subject to CON?:	True
Are air ambulance subject to CON?:	False
Is burn care subject to CON?:	True
Is cardiac catheterization subject to CON?:	True
Is CT scanning subject to CON?:	True
Is gamma knife service subject to CON?:	True
Is home health subject to CON?:	True
Is linear accelerator service subject to CON?:	False
Is lithotripsy service subject to CON?:	True
Is long term care subject to CON?:	True
Is mobile high tech service subject to CON?:	True
Is MRI scanning subject to CON?:	True
Is neo-natal intensive care subject to CON?:	True
Are obstetrical services subject to CON?:	True
Is open heart surgery subject to CON?:	True
Is organ transplantation subject to CON?:	True
Is PET scanning subject to CON?:	True
Are psychiatric services subject to CON?:	True
Is radiation therapy subject to CON?:	True
Are rehabilitation services subject to CON?:	True
Is renal dialysis subject to CON?:	True
Is RCF/Assisted Living subject to CON?:	True
Is subacute care subject to CON?:	False
Is substance abuse subject to CON?:	True
Are swing beds subject to CON?:	True
Is utlra-sound subject to CON?:	True
Are other services subject to CON?:	liver transplantation services; bone marrow transplantation; adult day care programs

Additional Criteria Used to Determine Need:

Additional criteria used to determine need for cardiac catheterization: Use area is area within 100 mile radius of facility; planning should ensure 80% of population of planning area resides within 100 miles of cardiac cath service; project annual volume of 500 cases within 3 years

Additional criteria used to determine need for organ transplantation: Heart transplantation - minimum of 14 transplants/year, no additional services will be approved until each existing serviced performs at least 30 transplants/year

Additional criteria used to determine need for rehabilitation: Beds for brain-injured patients should have 90% occupancy;

Additional criteria used to determine need for renal dialysis: Public need if demonstrate that project is financially feasible, proposed service will enhance access to services, evidence that facility's hours will promote availability of services, facility's ability to serve dialysis patients, if proposal is to add 12 or more stations, evidence that approval will not jeopardize the quality or financial viability of existing dialysis facilities within the planning area.

Additional criteria used to determine need for others: Minimum of 20 liver transplants/year; no additional liver transplantation service approved until each existing service performs 50 transplantations per year; priority given to applicants proposing to provide service within the facility's current capacity; number of people expected to be bone marrow transplant candidates are 13.2 per million/year; capacity of each bone marrow transplant bed is 6 patients/year; bone marrow transplantation service shall have minimum of 4 beds; adult day care - capacity = .04 registrants/1000 population aged 20-64, 2.5 registrants/1000 population aged 65-74, 3.65 registrants/1000 population aged 75+

CON STATUTES AND REGULATIONS

CON Statutes:

CON Statute Title: Public Health Law
CON Statute Citation: NY CLS Pub Health prec 2800
Year CON Statute Enacted: 1965

CON Regulations:

CON Regulations Title: Hospital Establishmet
CON Regulations Citation: Subchapter B

STATE NOTE

New York requires written approval from the Public Health Council before the establishment of a "hospital." The statute's definition of "hospital" includes almost every kind of health service, including outpatient care. New York's regulations provide for a complex calculation of "need" for each type of service. Need is based on the area's population and expected utilization of the service as well as actual utilization in the past.

NORTH CAROLINA

STATE CON AGENCY CONTACTS

State Department Overseeing CON	
Name of state CON department:	State Health Planning and Development Agency
URL address for state CON organization:	http://facility-services.state.nc.us conpage.htm
CON Administrative Office Information	
Name of state CON office:	Certificate of Need Section Hierarchy for state CON administrative office: Governor: Dept. of Health and Human Services: Division of Facility Services: Certificate of Need Section
CON organization contact person:	Lee Hoffman
Title of CON contact person:	Chief
Email address of CON contact:	Lee.Hoffman@ncmail.net
Mailing address for state CON office:	Certificate of Need Section
Mailing address for state CON office:	2704 Mail Service Center
City where state CON office is located:	Raleigh
State for mailing address:	North Carolina
Zip code for CON office:	27699
Phone number for CON contact:	(919) 855-3763
Fax number for CON contact:	(919) 733-8139
State CON Decision Making Body (DMB)	
Name of DMB:	Department of Health and Human Services
Title of person DMB reports to:	Governor
Composition of CON DMB:	
Number of people in the DMB:	1
Number of CON agency reps in DMB:	1

EQUIPMENT REGULATION AND DATA

Subject to CON (Y/N):	
Is any equipment subject to CON?:	False
Are air ambulances subject to CON?:	True
Are cardiac cath labs subject to CON?:	True

Subject to CON (Y/N) (Continued)

Are CT scanners subject to CON?:	True
Are gamma knives subject to CON?:	True
Are linear accelerators subject to CON?:	True
Is lithotropsy subject to CON?:	True
Is mobile high tech subject to CON?:	True
Are MRI scanners subject to CON?:	True
Are PET scanners subject to CON?:	True
Is radiation therapy subject to CON?:	True
Is renal dialysis subject to CON?:	True
Are swing beds subject to CON?:	False
Is ultra-sound subject to CON?:	False
Is other equipment subject to CON?:	cardiac angioplasty equipment; heart bypass machine

Additional Criteria Used to Determine Need:

Additional criteria used to determine need for cardiac cath lab: desired occupancy is 80%; project perform at least 225 procedures/year by 3rd year

FACILITIES REGULATION AND DATA

Subject to CON (Y/N):

Is any facility subject to CON?	False
Are hospitals subject to CON?	True
Are nursing homes subject to CON?	True
Are residential care facilities subject to CON?	True
Are psychiatric facilities subject to CON?	True
Are ambulatory surgery centers subject to CON?	True
Are ICF/MRs subject to CON?	True
Is long term care subject to CON?	True
Are medical office buildings subject to CON?	False
Are rehabilitation facilities subject to CON?	True
Are renal dialysis facilities subject to CON?	True
Are RCF/Assisted Living facilities subject to CON?	True
Are subacute care facilities subject to CON?	False
Are substance abuse facilities subject to CON?	True
Are swing beds subject to CON?	False
Are other facilities subject to CON?	diagnostic center

Additional Criteria Used to Determine Need:

Additional criteria used to determine need for a psychiatric facility: desired occupancy is 75%

Additional criteria used to determine need for an ambulatory surgery center: project perform 2.7 surgical cases/day for inpatient room/4.3 cases per day for ambulatory operating room; need CON to convert specialty ASC to multi-specialty ASC; different volume for endoscopy procedures

Additional criteria used to determine need for a rehabilitation facility: desired occupancy is 80%

Additional criteria used to determine need for a substance abuse facility: desired occupancy is 75% for facilities with 1-15 beds & 85% for facilities with 16 or more beds

Additional criteria used to determine need for other facilities: existing services operating at 80% utilization

Notes Including Bed Limits and Moratoria:

Notes including bed limits/moratoria for a nursing home: average occupancy within planning area should be 90%

Notes including bed limits/moratoria for an ICF/MR: desired occupancy is 90%

Notes including bed limits/moratoria for a RCF/Assisted Living facility: desired occupancy is 85%

SERVICES REGULATION AND DATA

Subject to CON (Y/N):

Are all services subject to CON?:	False
Are nursing home services subject to CON?:	False
Are acute care services subject to CON?:	False
Are air ambulance subject to CON?:	True
Is burn care subject to CON?:	True
Is cardiac catheterization subject to CON?:	True
Is CT scanning subject to CON?:	False
Is gamma knife service subject to CON?:	True
Is home health subject to CON?:	True
Is linear accelerator service subject to CON?:	False
Is lithotripsy service subject to CON?:	True
Is long term care subject to CON?:	False
Is mobile high tech service subject to CON?:	False
Is MRI scanning subject to CON?:	False
Is neo-natal intensive care subject to CON?:	True
Are obstetrical services subject to CON?:	False
Is open heart surgery subject to CON?:	True
Is organ transplantation subject to CON?:	True
Is PET scanning subject to CON?:	False
Are psychiatric services subject to CON?:	False
Is radiation therapy subject to CON?:	False
Are rehabilitation services subject to CON?:	True
Is renal dialysis subject to CON?:	True
Is RCF/Assisted Living subject to CON?:	True
Is subacute care subject to CON?:	False
Is substance abuse subject to CON?:	True
Are swing beds subject to CON?:	False
Is utlra-sound subject to CON?:	False
Are other services subject to CON?:	intensive care services; pediatric intensive care services; hospice; end-stage renal disease services;bone marrow transplantation service

Additional Criteria Used to Determine Need:

Additional criteria used to determine need for cardiac catheterization: Project 60% utilization; open heart surgery must be provided at same facility

Additional criteria used to determine need for home health: Minimum need is in State Medical Facilities Plan

Additional criteria used to determine need for neonatal intensive care: Project 50% utilization during 1st year & 65% during 3rd year; staffing requirements in regulations

Additional criteria used to determine need for open heart surgery: Should perform at least 4 caths per quarter

Additional criteria used to determine need for renal dialysis: Utilization is 3.2 patients per station per week

Additional criteria used to determine need for others: Intensive care beds - desired occupancy is 70% for facilities with 20 or more beds, 65% for facilities with 10-19 beds, 60% for facilities with 1-9 beds

CON STATUTES AND REGULATIONS

CON Statutes:

CON Statute Title: Certificate of Need Law
CON Statute Citation: N.C. Gen. Stat. 131E
Year CON Statute Enacted: 2001

CON Regulations:

CON Regulations Title: Certificate of Need Regulation
CON Regulations Citation: Subchapter 14C

STATE NOTE

North Carolina requires a Certificate of Need ("CON") for any "new institutional health service." However, a hospital established to serve a minority population that would otherwise not have been served does not need to obtain a CON to transfer up to sixty-five (65) beds to nursing care facility beds if the hospital continues to serve the minority population (§ 131E-178(a)). Generally, in order to obtain a CON to add new beds, the applicant must demonstrate that the average occupancy for the facility exceeded a minimum amount and the projected occupancy exceeds a minimum amount. In order to obtain a CON to acquire a proposed item of medical equipment, the applicant must demonstrate that the utilization rate for the equipment shall exceed a minimum amount. For certain types of medical equipment, e.g. fixed cardiac catheterization lab, the applicant must demonstrate that the item of equipment will perform more than a specified number of procedures in a year. In addition to the utilization requirements, the applicant must demonstrate that it meets certain staffing and support service requirement. For example, an applicant for a CON to initiate open-heart surgery services must demonstrate that the facility provides certain services such as electrocardiography laboratory and testing services (10A NCAC 14C.1704).

OHIO

STATE CON AGENCY CONTACTS

State Department Overseeing CON

Name of state CON department:	Office of Public Affairs Dept of Health
URL address for state CON organization:	http://www.odh.ohio.gov/ODHPrograms/CERTN/certneed1.htm

CON Administrative Office Information

Name of state CON office:	Certificate of Need Program Hierarchy for state CON administrative office: Governor: Dept. of Health: Certificate of Need Program
CON organization contact person:	Christine Kenney

Title of CON contact person:

Email address of CON contact:	ckenney@gw.odh.state.oh.us
Mailing address for state CON office:	246 North High Street
Mailing address for state CON office:	P.O. Box 118
City where state CON office is located:	Columbus
State for mailing address:	Ohio
Zip code for CON office:	43216
Phone number for CON contact:	(614) 466-3325
Fax number for CON contact:	(614) 752-4157

State CON Decision Making Body (DMB)

Name of DMB:	Board of Trustees of the Health Service Agency
Title of person DMB reports to:	Governor
Title of person appointing DMB members:	Agency's membership

Composition of CON DMB:

Number of consumers in DMB:	Majority of trustees, not more than 75%.
Number of healthcare providers in DMB:	All other non-consumer trustees.

EQUIPMENT REGULATION AND DATA

Subject to CON (Y/N):

Is any equipment subject to CON?:	False
Are air ambulances subject to CON?:	False
Are cardiac cath labs subject to CON?:	False
Are CT scanners subject to CON?:	False
Are gamma knives subject to CON?:	False
Are linear accelerators subject to CON?:	False

Subject to CON (Y/N) (Continued)

Is lithotropsy subject to CON?:	False
Is mobile high tech subject to CON?:	False
Are MRI scanners subject to CON?:	False
Are PET scanners subject to CON?:	False
Is radiation therapy subject to CON?:	False
Is renal dialysis subject to CON?:	False
Are swing beds subject to CON?:	False
Is ultra-sound subject to CON?:	False

FACILITIES REGULATION AND DATA

Subject to CON (Y/N):

Is any facility subject to CON?	False
Are hospitals subject to CON?	True
Are nursing homes subject to CON?	False
Are residential care facilities subject to CON?	False
Are psychiatric facilities subject to CON?	False
Are ambulatory surgery centers subject to CON?	False
Are ICF/MRs subject to CON?	False
Is long term care subject to CON?	True
Are medical office buildings subject to CON?	False
Are rehabilitation facilities subject to CON?	False
Are renal dialysis facilities subject to CON?	False
Are RCF/Assisted Living facilities subject to CON?	False
Are subacute care facilities subject to CON?	False
Are substance abuse facilities subject to CON?	False
Are swing beds subject to CON?	False

Project Dollar Threshold Requiring CON Application:

Dollar threshold for any facility application:	$2,000,000 renovations

Additional Criteria Used to Determine Need:

Additional criteria used to determine need for a long term care facility: Director must consider the relationship of the project to the most current edition of the "State Health Plan"

Notes Including Bed Limits and Moratoria:

Notes including bed limits/moratoria for a long term care facility: CON Exemptions: facility been in operation for not less than one hundred twenty years; located in an inner city area; operating as a nonprofit entity; and for addition of up to 30 LTC beds

SERVICES REGULATION AND DATA

Subject to CON (Y/N):

Are all services subject to CON?:	False
Are nursing home services subject to CON?:	False
Are acute care services subject to CON?:	False
Are air ambulance subject to CON?:	False
Is burn care subject to CON?:	False

Subject to CON (Y/N) (Continued)

Is cardiac catheterization subject to CON?:	False
Is CT scanning subject to CON?:	False
Is gamma knife service subject to CON?:	False
Is home health subject to CON?:	False
Is linear accelerator service subject to CON?:	False
Is lithotripsy service subject to CON?:	False
Is long term care subject to CON?:	True
Is mobile high tech service subject to CON?:	False
Is MRI scanning subject to CON?:	False
Is neo-natal intensive care subject to CON?:	False
Are obstetrical services subject to CON?:	False
Is open heart surgery subject to CON?:	False
Is organ transplantation subject to CON?:	False
Is PET scanning subject to CON?:	False
Are psychiatric services subject to CON?:	False
Is radiation therapy subject to CON?:	False
Are rehabilitation services subject to CON?:	False
Is renal dialysis subject to CON?:	False
Is RCF/Assisted Living subject to CON?:	False
Is subacute care subject to CON?:	False
Is substance abuse subject to CON?:	False
Are swing beds subject to CON?:	False
Is utlra-sound subject to CON?:	False

Additional Criteria Used to Determine Need:

Additional criteria used to determine need for neonatal intensive care: CON Exemptions: changes in perinatal bed capacity or pediatric intensive care bed capacity

CON STATUTES AND REGULATIONS

CON Statutes:

CON Statute Title: Certificates of Need
CON Statute Citation: Title 37, Chapter 3702

CON Regulations:

CON Regulations Title: Ohio Adminstrative Code: Certificate of Need
CON Regulations Citation: 3701-12

STATE NOTE

Ohio required a certificate of need ("CON") for most health services until 1995 when the statute was amended to gradually phase out the CON requirement for all services except long term care. The CON requirements were phased out by 1997. The only facilities currently requiring a CON are "long-term care facilities" which includes nursing homes and skilled nursing facilities. The regulations set out a calculation to determine the "need" for long-term care beds for each county. The county's population of people aged seventy-five (75) and over are multiplied by the ratio of existing and approved beds to the statewide population aged seventy-five (75) and over. This is multiplied by the county's risk adjustment (measure of the risk of a county resident entering a long-term care facility) ratio.

OKLAHOMA

STATE CON AGENCY CONTACTS

State Department Overseeing CON	
Name of state CON department:	Health Resources Development Service
URL address for state CON organization:	http://www.health.state.ok.us/program/condiv/
CON Administrative Office Information	
Name of state CON office:	Health Facility Systems Hierarchy for state CON administrative office: Governor: Dept. of Health: Health Resources Development Service: Health Facility Systems
CON organization contact person:	Henry F. Hartsell, Jr PhD
Title of CON contact person:	Chief
Email address of CON contact:	hank@health.state.ok.us
Mailing address for state CON office:	Oklahoma State Department of Health
Mailing address for state CON office:	1000 NE 10th St
City where state CON office is located:	Oklahoma City
State for mailing address:	Oklahoma
Zip code for CON office:	73117
Phone number for CON contact:	(405) 271-6868
Fax number for CON contact:	(405) 271-7360
State CON Decision Making Body (DMB)	
Name of DMB:	Department of Health
Title of person DMB reports to:	Commissioner of Health
Title of person appointing DMB members:	Governor

EQUIPMENT REGULATION AND DATA

Subject to CON (Y/N):	
Is any equipment subject to CON?:	False
Are air ambulances subject to CON?:	False
Are cardiac cath labs subject to CON?:	False
Are CT scanners subject to CON?:	False
Are gamma knives subject to CON?:	False
Are linear accelerators subject to CON?:	False
Is lithotropsy subject to CON?:	False
Is mobile high tech subject to CON?:	False
Are MRI scanners subject to CON?:	False
Are PET scanners subject to CON?:	False
Is radiation therapy subject to CON?:	False

Subject to CON (Y/N) (Continued)

Is renal dialysis subject to CON?:	False
Are swing beds subject to CON?:	False
Is ultra-sound subject to CON?:	False

Facilities Regulation and Data

Subject to CON (Y/N):

Is any facility subject to CON?	False
Are hospitals subject to CON?	False
Are nursing homes subject to CON?	True
Are residential care facilities subject to CON?	False
Are psychiatric facilities subject to CON?	True
Are ambulatory surgery centers subject to CON?	False
Are ICF/MRs subject to CON?	True
Is long term care subject to CON?	True
Are medical office buildings subject to CON?	False
Are rehabilitation facilities subject to CON?	False
Are renal dialysis facilities subject to CON?	False
Are RCF/Assisted Living facilities subject to CON?	False
Are subacute care facilities subject to CON?	True
Are substance abuse facilities subject to CON?	True
Are swing beds subject to CON?	False

Project Dollar Threshold Requiring CON Application:

Dollar threshold for a psychiatric facility application: $500,000
Dollar threshold for a substance abuse facility application: $500,000

Capacity Requirements – Beds / Population:

Capacity requirement-beds/population for nursing homes: 152/1000
Capacity requirement-beds/population for psychiatric facilities: 117/100,000

Capacity requirement-beds/population for ICF/MRs:

Capacity requirement-beds/population for a substance abuse facility: 117/100,000

Additional Criteria Used to Determine Need:

Additional criteria used to determine need for a nursing home: No application shall cause an excessive increase in the bed to population ratio of a service area. The determination of whether or not an increase is excessive shall be based on the percentage of increase a project will cause in an area's bed to population ratio, and on a comparison of the area's bed to population ratio against the statewide ratio

Additional criteria used to determine need for an ICF/MR: No additional ICF/MR beds, whether proposed through construction or conversion of existing space, shall be approved for any existing ICF/MR unless it has maintained an occupancy rate of at least 95%

Notes Including Bed Limits and Moratoria:

Notes including bed limits/moratoria for a nursing home: service area for an LNF shall be presumed to be a map mileage of fifteen miles from the location of the facility, except that the service area shall be a radius of seven and one-half miles for any facility located in the corporate limits of Tulsa or Ok City, and any municipality contiguous with boundaries of Tulsa or OK City

Notes including bed limits/moratoria for a psychiatric facility: The provisions of the Psychiatric and Chemical Dependency Facility CON Act shall not apply to any hospital; CON required for Acquisition of a facility; the service area for a psych and/or chemical dependency application shall be the mental health service area in which the service is to be located

Notes including bed limits/moratoria for an ICF/MR: For review purposes under these standards, the service area for an ICF/MR shall be the Mentally Retarded School Service Region

Notes including bed limits/moratoria for a long term care facility: need CON to establish, expand, or acquire long term care facility

Notes including bed limits/moratoria for a substance abuse facility: the service area for a psych and/or chemical dependency application shall be the mental health service area in which the service is to be located

SERVICES REGULATION AND DATA

Subject to CON (Y/N):

Are all services subject to CON?:	False
Are nursing home services subject to CON?:	False
Are acute care services subject to CON?:	False
Are air ambulance subject to CON?:	False
Is burn care subject to CON?:	False
Is cardiac catheterization subject to CON?:	False
Is CT scanning subject to CON?:	False
Is gamma knife service subject to CON?:	False
Is home health subject to CON?:	False
Is linear accelerator service subject to CON?:	False
Is lithotripsy service subject to CON?:	False
Is long term care subject to CON?:	True
Is mobile high tech service subject to CON?:	False
Is MRI scanning subject to CON?:	False
Is neo-natal intensive care subject to CON?:	False
Are obstetrical services subject to CON?:	False
Is open heart surgery subject to CON?:	False
Is organ transplantation subject to CON?:	False
Is PET scanning subject to CON?:	False
Are psychiatric services subject to CON?:	True
Is radiation therapy subject to CON?:	False
Are rehabilitation services subject to CON?:	False
Is renal dialysis subject to CON?:	False
Is RCF/Assisted Living subject to CON?:	False
Is subacute care subject to CON?:	True
Is substance abuse subject to CON?:	True
Are swing beds subject to CON?:	False
Is utlra-sound subject to CON?:	False
Are other services subject to CON?:	Skilled Nursing Care

Dollar Threshold for CON Application:

Dollar threshold for psychiatric services application:	$500,000
Dollar threshold for substance abuse application:	$500,000

CON STATUTES AND REGULATIONS

CON Statutes:

CON Statute Title: LTC Certificate of Need Act; Psychiatric and Chemical Dependency Facility Certificate of Need Act

CON Statute Citation: 63 Okl. St. 1-85; 63 Okl. St. 1-88

CON Regulations:

CON Regulations Title: Oklahoma State Department of Health Certificate of Need Standards for Health Care Facility Acquisitions

CON Regulations Citation: Title 310, Chapter 620

STATE NOTE

Oklahoma has two (2) certificate of need ("CON") laws, the "Long-Term Care Certificate of Need Act" and the "Psychiatric and Chemical Dependency Facility Certificate of Need Act." A CON is required to construct, acquire, or expand long-term care services, nursing home services, health and habitation services for mentally retarded or developmentally disabled persons, psychiatric care services, and chemical abuse services. The primary difference the two (2) acts is the party with authority to issue a CON. The State Commissioner of Health has authority to issue a CON for long-term care services, nursing home services, and health and habitation services for mentally or developmentally disabled persons. The State Department of Health has authority to issue a CON for psychiatric care services and chemical abuse services.

OREGON

STATE CON AGENCY CONTACTS

State Department Overseeing CON

Name of state CON department:	Certificate of Need Program
URL address for state CON organization:	http://www.dhs.state.or.us/index.html

CON Administrative Office Information

Name of state CON office:	Certificate of Need Program Hierarchy for state CON administrative office: Governor: Dept. of Human Services/Health Services: Certificate of Need Program
CON organization contact person:	Jana Fussell
Title of CON contact person:	CON Coordinator
Email address of CON contact:	jana.fussell@state.or.us
Mailing address for state CON office:	800 NE Oregon Street, Suite 925
Mailing address for state CON office:	Suite 925
City where state CON office is located:	Portland
State for mailing address:	Oregon
Zip code for CON office:	97232
Phone number for CON contact:	(503) 731-4320
Fax number for CON contact:	(503) 731-4078

State CON Decision Making Body (DMB)

Name of DMB:	Public Health Officer
Title of person DMB reports to:	Dept. of Human Services/HealthServices

Composition of CON DMB:

Number of people in the DMB:	1

EQUIPMENT REGULATION AND DATA

Subject to CON (Y/N):

Is any equipment subject to CON?:	False
Are air ambulances subject to CON?:	False
Are cardiac cath labs subject to CON?:	False
Are CT scanners subject to CON?:	False
Are gamma knives subject to CON?:	False
Are linear accelerators subject to CON?:	False
Is lithotropsy subject to CON?:	False
Is mobile high tech subject to CON?:	False
Are MRI scanners subject to CON?:	False

Subject to CON (Y/N) (Continued)

Are PET scanners subject to CON?:	False
Is radiation therapy subject to CON?:	False
Is renal dialysis subject to CON?:	False
Are swing beds subject to CON?:	True
Is ultra-sound subject to CON?:	False

FACILITIES REGULATION AND DATA

Subject to CON (Y/N):

Is any facility subject to CON?	False
Are hospitals subject to CON?	True
Are nursing homes subject to CON?	False
Are residential care facilities subject to CON?	False
Are psychiatric facilities subject to CON?	False
Are ambulatory surgery centers subject to CON?	False
Are ICF/MRs subject to CON?	True
Is long term care subject to CON?	True
Are medical office buildings subject to CON?	False
Are rehabilitation facilities subject to CON?	False
Are renal dialysis facilities subject to CON?	False
Are RCF/Assisted Living facilities subject to CON?	False
Are subacute care facilities subject to CON?	False
Are substance abuse facilities subject to CON?	False
Are swing beds subject to CON?	True
Are other facilities subject to CON?	skilled nursing

Capacity Requirements – Beds / Population:

Capacity requirement-beds/population for nursing homes: 40/1,000
Capacity requirement-beds/population for rehabilitation facility: 7/100,000

Additional Criteria Used to Determine Need:

Additional criteria used to determine need for a hospital: Bed Need Methodology for Proposed New Hospitals: (1) determine service area of applicant facility as those zip codes from which either ten percent or more of the hospital's discharges are reasonably expected to originate, or in which the hospital would have at least a 20 percent market share; (2) determine the estimated population for the hospital service area identified; and (3)determine current year hospital service area and historical health service area population-based discharge and patient day use-rates from statewide patient origin studies

Additional criteria used to determine need for a rehabilitation facility: CON Requirements: (1) rehab units must have an annual occupancy rate of at least 85 percent prior to expansion of any bed capacities, and expansion should be such that the unit can maintain a minimal occupancy rate of 75 percent on unit capacity, within 1-1/2 years of CON approval; (2) new rehab unit must show it will be able to achieve and maintain a minimal annual occupancy rate of 75 percent of unit capacity within three years of CON approval.

Notes Including Bed Limits and Moratoria:

Notes including bed limits/moratoria for a hospital: Rural hospitals are exempted from CON.

Notes including bed limits/moratoria for a nursing home: Need for Nursing Home Beds: clinical and epidemiological research indicates that, on average, 30 nursing home beds per 1,000 persons age 65 and over would meet the need for care for those functional deficits for which nursing home care is medically necessary and cost effective

Notes including bed limits/moratoria for an ambulatory surgery center: CON Exemptions: ASC performing only ophthalmic

Notes including bed limits/moratoria for other facilities: Number of Freestanding Hospice Facilities that can be approved is limited to six

SERVICES REGULATION AND DATA

Subject to CON (Y/N):

Are all services subject to CON?:	False
Are nursing home services subject to CON?:	False
Are acute care services subject to CON?:	False
Are air ambulance subject to CON?:	False
Is burn care subject to CON?:	True
Is cardiac catheterization subject to CON?:	True
Is CT scanning subject to CON?:	False
Is gamma knife service subject to CON?:	False
Is home health subject to CON?:	False
Is linear accelerator service subject to CON?:	False
Is lithotripsy service subject to CON?:	True
Is long term care subject to CON?:	True
Is mobile high tech service subject to CON?:	False
Is MRI scanning subject to CON?:	True
Is neo-natal intensive care subject to CON?:	True
Are obstetrical services subject to CON?:	False
Is open heart surgery subject to CON?:	True
Is organ transplantation subject to CON?:	True
Is PET scanning subject to CON?:	True
Are psychiatric services subject to CON?:	True
Is radiation therapy subject to CON?:	True
Are rehabilitation services subject to CON?:	False
Is renal dialysis subject to CON?:	False
Is RCF/Assisted Living subject to CON?:	False
Is subacute care subject to CON?:	False
Is substance abuse subject to CON?:	False
Are swing beds subject to CON?:	True
Is utlra-sound subject to CON?:	False
Are other services subject to CON?:	trauma care

Dollar Threshold for CON Application:

Dollar threshold for any service application:	$500,000

Additional Criteria Used to Determine Need:

Additional criteria used to determine need for any service: A new hospital health service is any health services except basic health services as defined in ORS 442.315(9) that were not offered in or through the hospital on a regular basis within the 12-month period prior to the time such services are proposed to be offered, provided that the annual operating expenses exceed $500,000 in the first full year of operation at normal levels of utilization

Additional criteria used to determine need for psychiatric services: CON Requirements: if proposed project would result in .40 beds, other than those run by the state Mental Health and Developmental Disability Services Division, per 1,000 population in the third year following date of the letter of intent, a complete description of all alternatives available in the service area shall be required

CON STATUTES AND REGULATIONS

CON Statutes:

CON Statute Title: Certificates of Need for Health Services
CON Statute Citation: Title 36, Chapter 442

CON Regulations:

CON Regulations Title: Procedural Rules
CON Regulations Citation: 333-001-0000 et seq

STATE NOTE

Oregon requires a certificate of need ("CON") for most "hospital services," meaning that the service requires a CON if offered by a hospital, skilled nursing facility, or intermediate care facility. The regulations contain a methodology to calculate need for the service which considers population and statewide discharge and patient day use-rates.

RHODE ISLAND

STATE CON AGENCY CONTACTS

State Department Overseeing CON

Name of state CON department:	Office of Health Systems Development
URL address for state CON organization:	http://www.health.ri.gov/hsr/healthsystems/Home.htm

CON Administrative Office Information

Name of state CON office:	Office of Health Systems Development Hierarchy for state CON administrative office: Governor: Department of Health: Office of Health Systems Development
CON organization contact person:	John X. Donahue
Title of CON contact person:	Chief
Email address of CON contact:	JohnD@doh.state.ri.us
Mailing address for state CON office:	Three Capitol Hill, Room 407
City where state CON office is located:	Providence
State for mailing address:	Rhode Island
Zip code for CON office:	02908
Phone number for CON contact:	(401) 222-2788
Fax number for CON contact:	(401) 273-4350

State CON Decision Making Body (DMB)

Name of DMB:	Department of Health
Title of person DMB reports to:	Governor

EQUIPMENT REGULATION AND DATA

Subject to CON (Y/N):

Is any equipment subject to CON?:	False
Are air ambulances subject to CON?:	False
Are cardiac cath labs subject to CON?:	True
Are CT scanners subject to CON?:	True
Are gamma knives subject to CON?:	True
Are linear accelerators subject to CON?:	False
Is lithotropsy subject to CON?:	False
Is mobile high tech subject to CON?:	True
Are MRI scanners subject to CON?:	True
Are PET scanners subject to CON?:	True
Is radiation therapy subject to CON?:	True
Is renal dialysis subject to CON?:	False

Subject to CON (Y/N) (Continued)

Are swing beds subject to CON?:	True
Is ultra-sound subject to CON?:	False

Dollar Threshold for CON Application:

Dollar threshold for any equipment application:	$1,000,000

FACILITIES REGULATION AND DATA

Subject to CON (Y/N):

Is any facility subject to CON?	False
Are hospitals subject to CON?	True
Are nursing homes subject to CON?	True
Are residential care facilities subject to CON?	False
Are psychiatric facilities subject to CON?	True
Are ambulatory surgery centers subject to CON?	True
Are ICF/MRs subject to CON?	False
Is long term care subject to CON?	True
Are medical office buildings subject to CON?	False
Are rehabilitation facilities subject to CON?	True
Are renal dialysis facilities subject to CON?	False
Are RCF/Assisted Living facilities subject to CON?	False
Are subacute care facilities subject to CON?	True
Are substance abuse facilities subject to CON?	True
Are swing beds subject to CON?	True
Are other facilities subject to CON?	inpatient hospice care

Additional Criteria Used to Determine Need:

Additional criteria used to determine need for any equipment: CON Exemptions: any application which proposes one for one equipment replacement

SERVICES REGULATION AND DATA

Subject to CON (Y/N):

Are all services subject to CON?:	False
Are nursing home services subject to CON?:	False
Are acute care services subject to CON?:	True
Are air ambulance subject to CON?:	False
Is burn care subject to CON?:	False
Is cardiac catheterization subject to CON?:	True
Is CT scanning subject to CON?:	True
Is gamma knife service subject to CON?:	True
Is home health subject to CON?:	False
Is linear accelerator service subject to CON?:	False
Is lithotripsy service subject to CON?:	False
Is long term care subject to CON?:	True
Is mobile high tech service subject to CON?:	True
Is MRI scanning subject to CON?:	True

Subject to CON (Y/N) (Continued)

Is neo-natal intensive care subject to CON?:	True
Are obstetrical services subject to CON?:	True
Is open heart surgery subject to CON?:	True
Is organ transplantation subject to CON?:	True
Is PET scanning subject to CON?:	True
Are psychiatric services subject to CON?:	True
Is radiation therapy subject to CON?:	True
Are rehabilitation services subject to CON?:	True
Is renal dialysis subject to CON?:	False
Is RCF/Assisted Living subject to CON?:	False
Is subacute care subject to CON?:	True
Is substance abuse subject to CON?:	True
Are swing beds subject to CON?:	True
Is utlra-sound subject to CON?:	False

Dollar Threshold for CON Application:

Dollar threshold for any service application:	$2,000,000

CON STATUTES AND REGULATIONS

CON Statutes:

CON Statute Title: Health Care Certificate of Need Act of Rhode Island
CON Statute Citation: R.I. Gen. Laws 23-15

CON Regulations:

CON Regulations Title: Rules and Regulations for Determination of Need for New Health Care Equipment and New Institutional Health Services
CON Regulations Citation: R23-15-CON
Year CON Regulations Enacted: 2000

STATE NOTE

Rhode Island requires a certificate of need ("CON") for most healthcare facilities. However, no CON is required to replace medical equipment. The regulations state that a CON should not be granted unless it is demonstrated that there is a "need" for the service, but the regulations do not define what constitutes "need." The regulations contain no standards or criteria to determine need.

SOUTH CAROLINA

STATE CON AGENCY CONTACTS

State Department Overseeing CON	
Name of state CON department:	Bureau of Health Facilities and Services Developme
URL address for state CON organization:	http://www.scdhec.net/hr/cofn
CON Administrative Office Information	
Name of state CON office:	Division of Planning & CON Hierarchy for state CON administrative office: Governor: Dept. of Helath & Evironmental Control: Divison of Planning & CON
CON organization contact person:	Albert Whiteside
Title of CON contact person:	Director
Email address of CON contact:	whitesan@columb54.dhec.state.sc.us
Mailing address for state CON office:	DHEC, Division of Planning & CON
Mailing address for state CON office:	2600 Bull Street
City where state CON office is located:	Columbia
State for mailing address:	South Carolina
Zip code for CON office:	29201
Phone number for CON contact:	(803) 545-4200
Fax number for CON contact:	(803) 545-4579
State CON Decision Making Body (DMB)	
Name of DMB:	State Board of Health and Environmental Control
Title of person DMB reports to:	Governor
Title of person appointing DMB members:	Governor
Composition of CON DMB:	
Number of people in the DMB:	7
Number of CON agency reps in DMB:	7

EQUIPMENT REGULATION AND DATA

Subject to CON (Y/N):	
Is any equipment subject to CON?:	False
Are air ambulances subject to CON?:	False
Are cardiac cath labs subject to CON?:	True
Are CT scanners subject to CON?:	True
Are gamma knives subject to CON?:	True

Subject to CON (Y/N) (Continued)

Are linear accelerators subject to CON?:	True
Is lithotropsy subject to CON?:	True
Is mobile high tech subject to CON?:	True
Are MRI scanners subject to CON?:	True
Are PET scanners subject to CON?:	True
Is radiation therapy subject to CON?:	True
Is renal dialysis subject to CON?:	False
Are swing beds subject to CON?:	False
Is ultra-sound subject to CON?:	False

Dollar Threshold for CON Application:

Dollar threshold for any equipment application:	$600,000

FACILITIES REGULATION AND DATA

Subject to CON (Y/N):

Is any facility subject to CON?	False
Are hospitals subject to CON?	True
Are nursing homes subject to CON?	True
Are residential care facilities subject to CON?	False
Are psychiatric facilities subject to CON?	True
Are ambulatory surgery centers subject to CON?	True
Are ICF/MRs subject to CON?	True
Is long term care subject to CON?	True
Are medical office buildings subject to CON?	False
Are rehabilitation facilities subject to CON?	True
Are renal dialysis facilities subject to CON?	False
Are RCF/Assisted Living facilities subject to CON?	False
Are subacute care facilities subject to CON?	True
Are substance abuse facilities subject to CON?	True
Are swing beds subject to CON?	False
Are other facilities subject to CON?	tuberculosis hospital; hospice

Project Dollar Threshold Requiring CON Application:

Dollar threshold for any facility application:	$2,000,000

Notes Including Bed Limits and Moratoria:

Notes including bed limits/moratoria for an ambulatory surgery center: must have 2 operating rooms except if restricted to endoscopic procedures

SERVICES REGULATION AND DATA

Subject to CON (Y/N):

Are all services subject to CON?:	False
Are nursing home services subject to CON?:	False
Are acute care services subject to CON?:	True
Are air ambulance subject to CON?:	False
Is burn care subject to CON?:	False

Subject to CON (Y/N) (Continued)

Is cardiac catheterization subject to CON?:	True
Is CT scanning subject to CON?:	True
Is gamma knife service subject to CON?:	True
Is home health subject to CON?:	True
Is linear accelerator service subject to CON?:	False
Is lithotripsy service subject to CON?:	True
Is long term care subject to CON?:	True
Is mobile high tech service subject to CON?:	True
Is MRI scanning subject to CON?:	True
Is neo-natal intensive care subject to CON?:	True
Are obstetrical services subject to CON?:	True
Is open heart surgery subject to CON?:	True
Is organ transplantation subject to CON?:	False
Is PET scanning subject to CON?:	True
Are psychiatric services subject to CON?:	True
Is radiation therapy subject to CON?:	True
Are rehabilitation services subject to CON?:	True
Is renal dialysis subject to CON?:	False
Is RCF/Assisted Living subject to CON?:	False
Is subacute care subject to CON?:	True
Is substance abuse subject to CON?:	True
Are swing beds subject to CON?:	False
Is utlra-sound subject to CON?:	False

Dollar Threshold for CON Application:

Dollar threshold for any service application:	$1,000,000

Additional Criteria Used to Determine Need:

Additional criteria used to determine need for acute care: Desired occupancy - 0-174 bed hospitals = 65%, 175-349 bed hospital = 70%, 350+ bed hospitals = 75%; also consider compliance with need outlined in state health plan, community need documentation, distribution, acceptability, financial feasibility, cost containment and adverse effects on other facilities

Additional criteria used to determine need for cardiac catheterization: Desired capacity is 1,200 procedures/ year; service area is all facilities within 45 minutes one way automobile travel time; new services only approved if existing labs in area had 80% utilization

Additional criteria used to determine need for neonatal intensive care: Desired occupancy is 65%; SC has 1.5 neonatal intensive care bassinets and 5.1 neonatal intermediate care bassinets per 1,000 births

Additional criteria used to determine need for obstetrical: Desired occupancy is 65% for Level I and 75% for Levels II, IIE, III and RPCs

Additional criteria used to determine need for open heart surgery: Minimum of 350 open heart surgery procedures per open heart surgery unit for adult services

Additional criteria used to determine need for radiation therapy: Desired utilization is 5,600 treatments/year

CON STATUTES AND REGULATIONS

CON Statutes:

CON Statute Title: State Certification of Need and Health Facility Licensure Act
CON Statute Citation: S.C. Code Ann. 44-7

CON Regulations:

CON Regulations Title: Certification of Need for Health Facilities and Services
CON Regulations Citation: Regulation No. 61-15

STATE NOTE

South Carolina requires a certificate of need ("CON") for most healthcare services. The standards for review of a CON application are found in the South Carolina Health Plan. The plan contains complex calculations of "need" which consider population and a desired occupancy rate. The state health plan details the need for the service in each South Carolina county.

TENNESSEE

STATE CON AGENCY CONTACTS

State Department Overseeing CON	
Name of state CON department:	Health Services Development Agency
URL address for state CON organization:	http://www.tn.gov/hsda/cert_need_sum.html
CON Administrative Office Information	
Name of state CON office:	Certificate of Need Program Hierarchy for state CON administrative office: Governor: Health Services and Development Agency: CON Program
CON organization contact person:	Melanie Hill
Title of CON contact person:	Acting Executive Director
Email address of CON contact:	Melanie.Hill@state.tn.us
Mailing address for state CON office:	500 Deaderick Street
Mailing address for state CON office:	Suite 850
City where state CON office is located:	Nashville
State for mailing address:	Tennessee
Zip code for CON office:	37243
Phone number for CON contact:	(615) 741-2364
Fax number for CON contact:	(615) 532-9884
State CON Decision Making Body (DMB)	
Name of DMB:	Health Services and Development Agency
Title of person DMB reports to:	Governor
Title of person appointing DMB members:	Governor
Composition of CON DMB:	
Number of people in the DMB:	10
Number of legislators in DMB:	2
Number of healthcare providers in DMB:	4

EQUIPMENT REGULATION AND DATA

Subject to CON (Y/N):	
Is any equipment subject to CON?:	False
Are air ambulances subject to CON?:	True
Are cardiac cath labs subject to CON?:	True
Are CT scanners subject to CON?:	False
Are gamma knives subject to CON?:	False
Are linear accelerators subject to CON?:	True

Subject to CON (Y/N) (Continued)

Is lithotropsy subject to CON?:	True
Is mobile high tech subject to CON?:	False
Are MRI scanners subject to CON?:	True
Are PET scanners subject to CON?:	True
Is radiation therapy subject to CON?:	True
Is renal dialysis subject to CON?:	False
Are swing beds subject to CON?:	True
Is ultra-sound subject to CON?:	False

Dollar Threshold for CON Application:

Dollar threshold for any equipment application:	$1,500,000

Utilization Requirements (Equipment/Population):

Utilization Requirement-Equipment/Population for lithotropsy: 1 ESWL unit/250,000
Utilization Requirement-Equipment/Population for radiation therapy: 1 unit/120,000

FACILITIES REGULATION AND DATA

Subject to CON (Y/N):

Is any facility subject to CON?	False
Are hospitals subject to CON?	True
Are nursing homes subject to CON?	True
Are residential care facilities subject to CON?	False
Are psychiatric facilities subject to CON?	True
Are ambulatory surgery centers subject to CON?	True
Are ICF/MRs subject to CON?	True
Is long term care subject to CON?	True
Are medical office buildings subject to CON?	False
Are rehabilitation facilities subject to CON?	True
Are renal dialysis facilities subject to CON?	False
Are RCF/Assisted Living facilities subject to CON?	False
Are subacute care facilities subject to CON?	True
Are substance abuse facilities subject to CON?	True
Are swing beds subject to CON?	True
Are other facilities subject to CON?	recuperation center; birthing center; outpatient diagnostic center; residential hospice

Project Dollar Threshold Requiring CON Application:

Dollar threshold for any facility application:	$2,000,000
Dollar threshold for a hospital application:	$5,000,000

Capacity Requirements – Beds / Population:

Capacity requirement-beds/population for psychiatric facilities: 30 beds/100,000
Capacity requirement-beds/population for ICF/MRs:
Capacity requirement-beds/population for long term care facilities:
Capacity requirement-beds/population for rehabilitation facility: 10 beds/100,000 population

Additional Criteria Used to Determine Need:

Additional criteria used to determine need for a nursing home: county bed need = .0004 x pop. 65 and under+ .01 x pop. 65-74 + .04 x pop. 75-84 + .15 x pop. 85 and over

Additional criteria used to determine need for an ambulatory surgery center: perform at least 800 operations per room per year; current utilization must be 80%

Additional criteria used to determine need for an ICF/MR: projected need is .032% of the general population

Additional criteria used to determine need for a long term care facility: minimum size of 20 beds

Additional criteria used to determine need for a rehabilitation facility: desired occupancy: 20-30 bed unit = 75%, 31-50 bed unit = 80%, 51+ bed = 85%

Notes Including Bed Limits and Moratoria:

Notes including bed limits/moratoria for any facility: no CON needed if premises exclusively used as the professional office of a physician

Notes including bed limits/moratoria for a hospital: hospital with less than 100 beds may increase its capacity by 10 beds within obtaining a CON

SERVICES REGULATION AND DATA

Subject to CON (Y/N):

Are all services subject to CON?:	False
Are nursing home services subject to CON?:	False
Are acute care services subject to CON?:	True
Are air ambulance subject to CON?:	True
Is burn care subject to CON?:	True
Is cardiac catheterization subject to CON?:	True
Is CT scanning subject to CON?:	False
Is gamma knife service subject to CON?:	False
Is home health subject to CON?:	True
Is linear accelerator service subject to CON?:	False
Is lithotripsy service subject to CON?:	True
Is long term care subject to CON?:	True
Is mobile high tech service subject to CON?:	True
Is MRI scanning subject to CON?:	True
Is neo-natal intensive care subject to CON?:	True
Are obstetrical services subject to CON?:	True
Is open heart surgery subject to CON?:	True
Is organ transplantation subject to CON?:	False
Is PET scanning subject to CON?:	True
Are psychiatric services subject to CON?:	True
Is radiation therapy subject to CON?:	True
Are rehabilitation services subject to CON?:	True
Is renal dialysis subject to CON?:	False
Is RCF/Assisted Living subject to CON?:	False
Is subacute care subject to CON?:	True
Is substance abuse subject to CON?:	True
Are swing beds subject to CON?:	True
Is utlra-sound subject to CON?:	False
Are other services subject to CON?:	hospice

Utilization Requirements (Facilities or Services/Population):

Utilization requirement-services/population for burn care: 1 unit/225,000 persons

Additional Criteria Used to Determine Need:

Additional criteria used to determine need for nursing home: Commission may consider approving new nursing home beds in excess of need standard if all facilities in service area have 90% occupancy; facility should have 90% occupancy after 2 years; no additional beds for service area unless each facility with 50 or more beds had occupancy of 95%; free-standing nursing home must have capacity of 30 beds; nursing home seeking to expand must have occupancy rate of 95%

Additional criteria used to determine need for acute care: Formula to calculate projected need in regulations with average daily census; new hospital beds can be approved in excess of need if all existing hospitals in service area had 80% occupancy

Additional criteria used to determine need for burn care: Have minimum of 12 beds with 6-9 beds for adults & 3-6 beds for pediatric patients; existing services must have occupancy rate of 70%; proposed burn unit must project treating 50 patients

Additional criteria used to determine need for cardiac catheterization: Minimum number of procedures: adult = 500, pediatric = 200; majority of population of service area should live within 45 miles of facility; existing programs must have 80% utilization

Additional criteria used to determine need for home health: 1.5% of total population is need estimate

Additional criteria used to determine need for long term care: Minimum occupancy of 85%

Additional criteria used to determine need for neonatal intensive care: 8 beds per 1,000 live births; single neonatal special care unit shall have a minimum of 15 beds

Additional criteria used to determine need for open heart surgery: Adult programs should perform at least 200 operations per year by 3rd year; pediatric programs should perform at least 100 procedures/year by 3rd year; no new programs can be approved unless operations performed exceeds 350 for adult & 130 for pediatrics; no approval if program will cause caseload of other programs within service area to drop below 350 adult or 130 pediatric; maximum travel time to hospitals providing open heart surgery should be maximum one-way driving time of 2 hours for 90% of population

Additional criteria used to determine need for swing beds: County bed need = .0005 x pop. 65 and under + .0120 x pop. 65-74 + .06 x pop. 75-84 + .15 x pop. 85 and over; commission may consider approving new beds in excess of need standard is all facilities had 90% occupancy; nursing home should have 90% occupancy or 95% occupancy for facility with more than 50 beds;

Additional criteria used to determine need for others: Hospice inpatient bed need is 20% of average daily hospice census divided by expected occupancy rate of .85

CON STATUTES AND REGULATIONS

CON Statutes:

CON Statute Title: Tennessee Health Services and Planning Act of 2002
CON Statute Citation: Tenn. Code Ann. 68-11
Year CON Statute Enacted: 2002

CON Regulations:

CON Regulations Title: Rules of the Tennessee Health Facilities Commission: Certificate of Need Program - Scope and Procedures
CON Regulations Citation: Chapter 0720-3
Year CON Regulations Enacted: 1999

STATE NOTE

Tennessee requires a certificate of need ("CON") for most services. The criteria for new services are found in the Health Guidelines for Growth which was last updated in 2000. The guidelines contains minimum utilization for each service and calculations of need based on population.

VERMONT

STATE CON AGENCY CONTACTS

State Department Overseeing CON

Name of state CON department:	Division of Health Care Administration
URL address for state CON organization:	http://www.bishca.state.vt.us/HcaDiv/CON_/CON_Main_Index.htm

CON Administrative Office Information

Name of state CON office:	Certificate of Need Program Hierarchy for state CON administrative office: Governor: Dept. of Banking, Insurance, Securities & Health: Division of Health Care Administration: CON Program
CON organization contact person:	Paulette Thabault
Title of CON contact person:	Deputy Commissioner, Health Care Administration
Mailing address for state CON office:	89 Main Street
Mailing address for state CON office:	Drawer 20
City where state CON office is located:	Montpelier
State for mailing address:	Vermont
Zip code for CON office:	05620
Phone number for CON contact:	(802) 828-2900
Fax number for CON contact:	(802) 828-2949

State CON Decision Making Body (DMB)

Name of DMB:	Public Oversight Commission
Title of person DMB reports to:	Commissioner of Div. of Health Care Administration
Title of person appointing DMB members:	Governor

Composition of CON DMB:

Number of people in the DMB:	13
Number of association reps in DMB:	1
Number of consumers in DMB:	11

EQUIPMENT REGULATION AND DATA

Subject to CON (Y/N):

Is any equipment subject to CON?:	False
Are air ambulances subject to CON?:	True

Subject to CON (Y/N) (Continued)

Are cardiac cath labs subject to CON?:	True
Are CT scanners subject to CON?:	True
Are gamma knives subject to CON?:	True
Are linear accelerators subject to CON?:	True
Is lithotropsy subject to CON?:	True
Is mobile high tech subject to CON?:	True
Are MRI scanners subject to CON?:	True
Are PET scanners subject to CON?:	True
Is radiation therapy subject to CON?:	True
Is renal dialysis subject to CON?:	True
Are swing beds subject to CON?:	True
Is ultra-sound subject to CON?:	False

Dollar Threshold for CON Application:

Dollar threshold for any equipment application:	$1,000,000

FACILITIES REGULATION AND DATA

Subject to CON (Y/N):

Is any facility subject to CON?	False
Are hospitals subject to CON?	True
Are nursing homes subject to CON?	True
Are residential care facilities subject to CON?	False
Are psychiatric facilities subject to CON?	True
Are ambulatory surgery centers subject to CON?	True
Are ICF/MRs subject to CON?	True
Is long term care subject to CON?	True
Are medical office buildings subject to CON?	False
Are rehabilitation facilities subject to CON?	True
Are renal dialysis facilities subject to CON?	True
Are RCF/Assisted Living facilities subject to CON?	False
Are subacute care facilities subject to CON?	True
Are substance abuse facilities subject to CON?	True
Are swing beds subject to CON?	True

Project Dollar Threshold Requiring CON Application:

Dollar threshold for any facility application:	$1,500,000
Dollar threshold for a hospital application:	$3,000,000

SERVICES REGULATION AND DATA

Subject to CON (Y/N):

Are all services subject to CON?:	False
Are nursing home services subject to CON?:	True
Are acute care services subject to CON?:	True
Are air ambulance subject to CON?:	True
Is burn care subject to CON?:	True

Subject to CON (Y/N) (Continued)

Is cardiac catheterization subject to CON?:	True
Is CT scanning subject to CON?:	True
Is gamma knife service subject to CON?:	True
Is home health subject to CON?:	True
Is linear accelerator service subject to CON?:	True
Is lithotripsy service subject to CON?:	True
Is long term care subject to CON?:	True
Is mobile high tech service subject to CON?:	True
Is MRI scanning subject to CON?:	True
Is neo-natal intensive care subject to CON?:	True
Are obstetrical services subject to CON?:	True
Is open heart surgery subject to CON?:	True
Is organ transplantation subject to CON?:	True
Is PET scanning subject to CON?:	True
Are psychiatric services subject to CON?:	True
Is radiation therapy subject to CON?:	True
Are rehabilitation services subject to CON?:	True
Is renal dialysis subject to CON?:	True
Is RCF/Assisted Living subject to CON?:	False
Is subacute care subject to CON?:	False
Is substance abuse subject to CON?:	True
Are swing beds subject to CON?:	True
Is utlra-sound subject to CON?:	False

Dollar Threshold for CON Application:

Dollar threshold for any service application:	$500,000

Additional Criteria Used to Determine Need:

Additional criteria used to determine need for home health: No threshold for home health.

CON STATUTES AND REGULATIONS

CON Statutes:

CON Statute Title: Health Facility Planning
CON Statute Citation: 18 V.S.A. sec. 9434-9442

CON Regulations:

CON Regulations Title: Certificate of Need Regulations
CON Regulations Citation: Regulation H-99-3
Year CON Regulations Enacted: 1999

STATE NOTE

Vermont requires a certificate of need ("CON") to offer most healthcare services. The minimum threshold requiring a CON is different if the facility is a hospital. The department publishes "Certificate of Need Guidelines" outlining the need for healthcare services. The guidelines specify that there is no need to certain healthcare services, i.e. air ambulance, in Vermont. The guidelines state that new technology should only be introduced at Vermont's tertiary care hospital and that other services, i.e. kidney dialysis, should only be provided by certain named providers.

VIRGINIA

STATE CON AGENCY CONTACTS

State Department Overseeing CON	
Name of state CON department:	Ctr. For Quality Health Care & Consumer Protection
URL address for state CON organization:	http://www.vdh.state.va.us/quality/copn
CON Administrative Office Information	
Name of state CON office:	Certificate of Public Need Program Hierarchy for state CON administrative office: Governor: VA Dept. of Health: Ctr. For Quality Health Care & Consumer Protection: Certificate of Public Need Program
CON organization contact person:	Erik Bodin
Title of CON contact person:	Director
Email address of CON contact:	erik.bodin@vdh.virginia.gov
Mailing address for state CON office:	3600 W. Broad St.
Mailing address for state CON office:	Suite 216
City where state CON office is located:	Richmond
State for mailing address:	Virginia
Zip code for CON office:	23230
Phone number for CON contact:	(804) 367-2126
Fax number for CON contact:	(804) 367-2206
State CON Decision Making Body (DMB)	
Name of DMB:	Health Commissioner of Dept. of Health
Title of person DMB reports to:	Governor
Title of person appointing DMB members:	Governor
Composition of CON DMB:	
Number of people in the DMB:	1
Number of CON agency reps in DMB:	1

EQUIPMENT REGULATION AND DATA

Subject to CON (Y/N):

Is any equipment subject to CON?:	False
Are air ambulances subject to CON?:	False
Are cardiac cath labs subject to CON?:	True
Are CT scanners subject to CON?:	True
Are gamma knives subject to CON?:	True
Are linear accelerators subject to CON?:	False
Is lithotropsy subject to CON?:	True
Is mobile high tech subject to CON?:	True
Are MRI scanners subject to CON?:	True
Are PET scanners subject to CON?:	True
Is radiation therapy subject to CON?:	True
Is renal dialysis subject to CON?:	False
Are swing beds subject to CON?:	False
Is ultra-sound subject to CON?:	False

FACILITIES REGULATION AND DATA

Subject to CON (Y/N):

Is any facility subject to CON?	True
Are hospitals subject to CON?	True
Are nursing homes subject to CON?	True
Are residential care facilities subject to CON?	False
Are psychiatric facilities subject to CON?	True
Are ambulatory surgery centers subject to CON?	True
Are ICF/MRs subject to CON?	True
Is long term care subject to CON?	True
Are medical office buildings subject to CON?	False
Are rehabilitation facilities subject to CON?	True
Are renal dialysis facilities subject to CON?	False
Are RCF/Assisted Living facilities subject to CON?	False
Are subacute care facilities subject to CON?	False
Are substance abuse facilities subject to CON?	True
Are swing beds subject to CON?	False
Are other facilities subject to CON?	sanitariums

Project Dollar Threshold Requiring CON Application:

Dollar threshold for any facility application:	$5,000,000

Notes Including Bed Limits and Moratoria:

Notes including bed limits/moratoria for a long term care facility:	moratorium on LTC beds

SERVICES REGULATION AND DATA

Subject to CON (Y/N):

Are all services subject to CON?:	False
Are nursing home services subject to CON?:	True
Are acute care services subject to CON?:	True
Are air ambulance subject to CON?:	False
Is burn care subject to CON?:	False
Is cardiac catheterization subject to CON?:	True
Is CT scanning subject to CON?:	True
Is gamma knife service subject to CON?:	True
Is home health subject to CON?:	False
Is linear accelerator service subject to CON?:	False
Is lithotripsy service subject to CON?:	True
Is long term care subject to CON?:	True
Is mobile high tech service subject to CON?:	False
Is MRI scanning subject to CON?:	True
Is neo-natal intensive care subject to CON?:	True
Are obstetrical services subject to CON?:	True
Is open heart surgery subject to CON?:	True
Is organ transplantation subject to CON?:	True
Is PET scanning subject to CON?:	True
Are psychiatric services subject to CON?:	True
Is radiation therapy subject to CON?:	True
Are rehabilitation services subject to CON?:	True
Is renal dialysis subject to CON?:	False
Is RCF/Assisted Living subject to CON?:	False
Is subacute care subject to CON?:	False
Is substance abuse subject to CON?:	True
Are swing beds subject to CON?:	False
Is utlra-sound subject to CON?:	False
Are other services subject to CON?:	magnetic source imaging; nuclear medicine imaging; extended care facility; skilled nursing facility

CON STATUTES AND REGULATIONS

CON Statutes:

CON Statute Title:	Medical Care Facilities Certificate of Public Need
CON Statute Citation:	Va. Code Ann. 32-1

CON Regulations:

CON Regulations Title:	Virginia Medical Care Facilities Certificate of Public Need Rules and Regulations
CON Regulations Citation:	12 VAC 50220
Year CON Regulations Enacted:	2003

STATE NOTE

Virginia requires a certificate of need ("CON") for most healthcare services. The regulations specify that the service be provided within a minimum "driving time" from most of the population in the "planning district." The regulations pertaining to some services specify a different minimum "driving time" for rural areas. Calculation of "need" is set out in the regulations and is a complex formula. Need considers population and the number of beds in the planning area. The regulations also specify a minimum utilization percentage for existing services.

WASHINGTON

STATE CON AGENCY CONTACTS

State Department Overseeing CON

Name of state CON department:	Facilities and Services Licensing
URL address for state CON organization:	http://www.doh.wa.gov/hsqa/fsl/CRS/certificate_need.htm

CON Administrative Office Information

Name of state CON office:	Construction Review Services Hierarchy for state CON administrative office: Governor: Dept. of Health: Health Systems Quality Assurance: Facilities and Services Licensing: Construction Review Services
CON organization contact person:	Jans Sigman
Title of CON contact person:	Manager
Email address of CON contact:	fslcon@doh.wa.gov
Mailing address for state CON office:	P.O. Box 47852
City where state CON office is located:	Olympia
State for mailing address:	Washington
Zip code for CON office:	98504-7852
Phone number for CON contact:	(360) 236-2905
Fax number for CON contact:	(360) 236-2901

State CON Decision Making Body (DMB)

Name of DMB:	Secretary of Dept. of Health
Title of person DMB reports to:	Governor
Title of person appointing DMB members:	Governor

Composition of CON DMB:

Number of people in the DMB:	1

EQUIPMENT REGULATION AND DATA

Subject to CON (Y/N):

Is any equipment subject to CON?:	False
Are air ambulances subject to CON?:	False
Are cardiac cath labs subject to CON?:	True
Are CT scanners subject to CON?:	False
Are gamma knives subject to CON?:	False
Are linear accelerators subject to CON?:	False
Is lithotropsy subject to CON?:	False

Subject to CON (Y/N) (Continued)

Is mobile high tech subject to CON?:	False
Are MRI scanners subject to CON?:	False
Are PET scanners subject to CON?:	False
Is radiation therapy subject to CON?:	False
Is renal dialysis subject to CON?:	True
Are swing beds subject to CON?:	True
Is ultra-sound subject to CON?:	False

FACILITIES REGULATION AND DATA

Subject to CON (Y/N):

Is any facility subject to CON?	False
Are hospitals subject to CON?	True
Are nursing homes subject to CON?	True
Are residential care facilities subject to CON?	False
Are psychiatric facilities subject to CON?	True
Are ambulatory surgery centers subject to CON?	True
Are ICF/MRs subject to CON?	False
Is long term care subject to CON?	True
Are medical office buildings subject to CON?	False
Are rehabilitation facilities subject to CON?	True
Are renal dialysis facilities subject to CON?	True
Are RCF/Assisted Living facilities subject to CON?	False
Are subacute care facilities subject to CON?	False
Are substance abuse facilities subject to CON?	True
Are swing beds subject to CON?	False
Are other facilities subject to CON?	hospice; kidney disease treatment centers

Capacity Requirements – Beds / Population:

Capacity requirement-beds/population for nursing homes: 40 beds per 1,000 persons aged 65 and older

Notes Including Bed Limits and Moratoria:

Notes including bed limits/moratoria for an ambulatory surgery center: ASC should have a minimum of 2 operating rooms

SERVICES REGULATION AND DATA

Subject to CON (Y/N):

Are all services subject to CON?:	True
Are nursing home services subject to CON?:	True
Are acute care services subject to CON?:	True
Are air ambulance subject to CON?:	False
Is burn care subject to CON?:	True
Is cardiac catheterization subject to CON?:	True
Is CT scanning subject to CON?:	False
Is gamma knife service subject to CON?:	False
Is home health subject to CON?:	True

Subject to CON (Y/N) (Continued)

Is linear accelerator service subject to CON?:	False
Is lithotripsy service subject to CON?:	False
Is long term care subject to CON?:	True
Is mobile high tech service subject to CON?:	False
Is MRI scanning subject to CON?:	False
Is neo-natal intensive care subject to CON?:	True
Are obstetrical services subject to CON?:	True
Is open heart surgery subject to CON?:	True
Is organ transplantation subject to CON?:	True
Is PET scanning subject to CON?:	False
Are psychiatric services subject to CON?:	True
Is radiation therapy subject to CON?:	False
Are rehabilitation services subject to CON?:	True
Is renal dialysis subject to CON?:	True
Is RCF/Assisted Living subject to CON?:	False
Is subacute care subject to CON?:	True
Is substance abuse subject to CON?:	False
Are swing beds subject to CON?:	True
Is utlra-sound subject to CON?:	False
Are other services subject to CON?:	inpatient pediatric services; kidney transplantation service; new tertiary health service

Dollar Threshold for CON Application:

Dollar threshold for nursing home application: $1,000,000

Additional Criteria Used to Determine Need:

Additional criteria used to determine need for open heart surgery: Minimum of 250 procedures per year; hospitals applying must demonstrate that they can meet 110% of minimum volume standard

Additional criteria used to determine need for renal dialysis: Operate at 748.8 dialyses per nontraining station per year; new services if existing stations operate at 936 dialyses per year

Additional criteria used to determine need for others: Kidney transplant services must perform at least 15 transplants a year

CON STATUTES AND REGULATIONS

CON Statutes:

CON Statute Title: State Health Planning and Resources Development Act
CON Statute Citation: Rev. Code Wash. (ARCW) 70.38

CON Regulations:

CON Regulations Title: Washington Adminstrative Code
CON Regulations Citation: WAC 246-310

STATE NOTE

Washington requires a certificate of need ("CON") for most healthcare services above the expenditure minimum as prescribed in the statute. The regulations contain criteria for new services. There are minimum utilization numbers for existing equipment and a minimum projected utilization for new equipment.

WASHINGTON D.C.

STATE CON AGENCY CONTACTS

State Department Overseeing CON	
Name of state CON department:	State Health Planning and Development Agency
URL address for state CON organization:	http://dchealth.dc.gov/services/administration_offices/shpda/services.shtm
CON Administrative Office Information	
Name of state CON office:	State Health Planning and Development Agency Hierarchy for state CON administrative office: Mayor: State Health Planning & Development Agency
CON organization contact person:	Amha Selassie
Title of CON contact person:	Chief of Project Review
Email address of CON contact:	aselassie@dchealth.com
Mailing address for state CON office:	825 North Capitol Street NE
City where state CON office is located:	Washington
State for mailing address:	Washington D.C.
Zip code for CON office:	20002
Phone number for CON contact:	(202) 442-5875
Fax number for CON contact:	(202) 442-9035
State CON Decision Making Body (DMB)	
Name of DMB:	SHPDA Director advised by Project Review Cmte.
Title of person DMB reports to:	Mayor
Title of person appointing DMB members:	Mayor
Composition of CON DMB:	
Number of people in the DMB:	1

EQUIPMENT REGULATION AND DATA

Subject to CON (Y/N):	
Is any equipment subject to CON?:	False
Are air ambulances subject to CON?:	False
Are cardiac cath labs subject to CON?:	True
Are CT scanners subject to CON?:	True
Are gamma knives subject to CON?:	True
Are linear accelerators subject to CON?:	False
Is lithotropsy subject to CON?:	True

Subject to CON (Y/N) (Continued)

Is mobile high tech subject to CON?:	True
Are MRI scanners subject to CON?:	True
Are PET scanners subject to CON?:	True
Is radiation therapy subject to CON?:	True
Is renal dialysis subject to CON?:	True
Are swing beds subject to CON?:	True
Is ultra-sound subject to CON?:	False

Dollar Threshold for CON Application:

Dollar threshold for any equipment application:	$400,000

FACILITIES REGULATION AND DATA

Subject to CON (Y/N):

Is any facility subject to CON?	False
Are hospitals subject to CON?	True
Are nursing homes subject to CON?	True
Are residential care facilities subject to CON?	False
Are psychiatric facilities subject to CON?	True
Are ambulatory surgery centers subject to CON?	True
Are ICF/MRs subject to CON?	False
Is long term care subject to CON?	True
Are medical office buildings subject to CON?	False
Are rehabilitation facilities subject to CON?	True
Are renal dialysis facilities subject to CON?	True
Are RCF/Assisted Living facilities subject to CON?	False
Are subacute care facilities subject to CON?	True
Are substance abuse facilities subject to CON?	True
Are swing beds subject to CON?	True

Project Dollar Threshold Requiring CON Application:

Dollar threshold for any facility application:	$2,500,000

SERVICES REGULATION AND DATA

Subject to CON (Y/N):

Are all services subject to CON?:	False
Are nursing home services subject to CON?:	True
Are acute care services subject to CON?:	True
Are air ambulance subject to CON?:	False
Is burn care subject to CON?:	True
Is cardiac catheterization subject to CON?:	True
Is CT scanning subject to CON?:	True
Is gamma knife service subject to CON?:	True
Is home health subject to CON?:	True
Is linear accelerator service subject to CON?:	True
Is lithotripsy service subject to CON?:	True

Subject to CON (Y/N) (Continued)

Is long term care subject to CON?:	True
Is mobile high tech service subject to CON?:	True
Is MRI scanning subject to CON?:	True
Is neo-natal intensive care subject to CON?:	True
Are obstetrical services subject to CON?:	True
Is open heart surgery subject to CON?:	True
Is organ transplantation subject to CON?:	True
Is PET scanning subject to CON?:	True
Are psychiatric services subject to CON?:	True
Is radiation therapy subject to CON?:	True
Are rehabilitation services subject to CON?:	True
Is renal dialysis subject to CON?:	True
Is RCF/Assisted Living subject to CON?:	False
Is subacute care subject to CON?:	True
Is substance abuse subject to CON?:	True
Are swing beds subject to CON?:	True
Is utlra-sound subject to CON?:	False

Are other services subject to CON?: cardiac surgery; coronary care services; newborn services; pediatric services; pediatric cardiac surgery services; clinical laboratory services; emergency medical services; occupational therapy services; hospice; diagnostic radiology & ultrasound services; primary care services; skilled nursing services; renal transplantaion services

Dollar Threshold for CON Application:

Dollar threshold for any service application: $600,000

Additional Criteria Used to Determine Need:

Additional criteria used to determine need for any service: Utilization should be 80% by 3rd year; no CON needed for services provided by physicians, dentists, HMOs and other individual healthcare providers

CON STATUTES AND REGULATIONS

CON Statutes:

CON Statute Title: Health Services Planning
CON Statute Citation: D.C. Code sec. 44-(406-420)

CON Regulations:

CON Regulations Title: Public Health and Medicine
CON Regulations Citation: Title 22
Year CON Regulations Enacted: 1986

STATE NOTE

The District of Columbia requires a certificate of need ("CON") for most new healthcare services. The regulations set out general criteria for all projects which require that the project be consistent with the facility's long range development plan. The regulations do not contain specific minimum criteria to establish a new service but require that the project not negatively impact available services. The regulations require that the applicant demonstrate a projection of a minimum utilization of the new service. There are also financial criteria.

WEST VIRGINIA

STATE CON AGENCY CONTACTS

State Department Overseeing CON

Name of state CON department:	Health Care Authority
URL address for state CON organization:	http://www.hcawv.org/con1.htm

CON Administrative Office Information

Name of state CON office:	Certificate of Need Program
	Hierarchy for state CON administrative office: Governor: Health Care Authority: Certificate of Need Program
CON organization contact person:	Dayle Stepp
Title of CON contact person:	CON Director
Email address of CON contact:	dstepp@hcawv.org
Mailing address for state CON office:	100 Dee Drive
City where state CON office is located:	Charleston
State for mailing address:	West Virginia
Zip code for CON office:	25311-1600
Phone number for CON contact:	(304) 558-7000
Fax number for CON contact:	(304) 558-7001

State CON Decision Making Body (DMB)

Name of DMB:	Health Care Authority
Title of person DMB reports to:	Governor
Title of person appointing DMB members:	Governor

EQUIPMENT REGULATION AND DATA

Subject to CON (Y/N):

Is any equipment subject to CON?:	False
Are air ambulances subject to CON?:	False
Are cardiac cath labs subject to CON?:	True
Are CT scanners subject to CON?:	False
Are gamma knives subject to CON?:	False
Are linear accelerators subject to CON?:	True
Is lithotropsy subject to CON?:	True
Is mobile high tech subject to CON?:	True
Are MRI scanners subject to CON?:	True
Are PET scanners subject to CON?:	True
Is radiation therapy subject to CON?:	True
Is renal dialysis subject to CON?:	True

Subject to CON (Y/N) (Continued)

Are swing beds subject to CON?:	True
Is ultra-sound subject to CON?:	True

Dollar Threshold for CON Application:

Dollar threshold for any equipment application:	$2,000,000

Additional Criteria Used to Determine Need:

Additional criteria used to determine need for any equipment: no CON needed for equipment acquired by a clinical laboratory

FACILITIES REGULATION AND DATA

Subject to CON (Y/N):

Is any facility subject to CON?	True
Are hospitals subject to CON?	True
Are nursing homes subject to CON?	True
Are residential care facilities subject to CON?	False
Are psychiatric facilities subject to CON?	True
Are ambulatory surgery centers subject to CON?	True
Are ICF/MRs subject to CON?	True
Is long term care subject to CON?	True
Are medical office buildings subject to CON?	False
Are rehabilitation facilities subject to CON?	True
Are renal dialysis facilities subject to CON?	True
Are RCF/Assisted Living facilities subject to CON?	False
Are subacute care facilities subject to CON?	True
Are substance abuse facilities subject to CON?	True
Are swing beds subject to CON?	True

Project Dollar Threshold Requiring CON Application:

Dollar threshold for any facility application:	$2,000,000

Capacity Requirements – Beds / Population:

Capacity requirement-beds/population for rehabilitation facility: 13 beds per 100,000

Notes Including Bed Limits and Moratoria:

Notes including bed limits/moratoria for any facility: no facility can add skilled nursing or intermediate care beds

Notes including bed limits/moratoria for an ICF/MR: moratorium on new ICF/MR beds

SERVICES REGULATION AND DATA

Subject to CON (Y/N):

Are all services subject to CON?:	True
Are nursing home services subject to CON?:	True
Are acute care services subject to CON?:	True
Are air ambulance subject to CON?:	False
Is burn care subject to CON?:	True

Subject to CON (Y/N) (Continued)

Is cardiac catheterization subject to CON?:	True
Is CT scanning subject to CON?:	False
Is gamma knife service subject to CON?:	True
Is home health subject to CON?:	True
Is linear accelerator service subject to CON?:	True
Is lithotripsy service subject to CON?:	True
Is long term care subject to CON?:	True
Is mobile high tech service subject to CON?:	True
Is MRI scanning subject to CON?:	True
Is neo-natal intensive care subject to CON?:	True
Are obstetrical services subject to CON?:	True
Is open heart surgery subject to CON?:	True
Is organ transplantation subject to CON?:	True
Is PET scanning subject to CON?:	True
Are psychiatric services subject to CON?:	True
Is radiation therapy subject to CON?:	True
Are rehabilitation services subject to CON?:	True
Is renal dialysis subject to CON?:	True
Is RCF/Assisted Living subject to CON?:	False
Is subacute care subject to CON?:	True
Is substance abuse subject to CON?:	True
Are swing beds subject to CON?:	True
Is utlra-sound subject to CON?:	False
Are other services subject to CON?:	ultrasound; mammography; fluoroscopy; nuclear imaging; densitometry; discrete inpatient psychiatric units; pediatric intensive care; surgical services; hospice; in-home personalcare services; ventilator services for nursing facility bed

Additional Criteria Used to Determine Need:

Additional criteria used to determine need for acute care: Proposal will be approved if resulting bed supply in area 5 years in the future is less than or equal to the bed need based on the application of the Normative Age Adjusted Use Rates; additional acute care beds in excess of the bed need will be considered if resulting bed supply for the area will not exceed the bed need by the greater of 30 beds or 5% of the bed need; use rate calculation found in regulations

Additional criteria used to determine need for cardiac catheterization: Perform at least 1,000 procedures per year; for new unit project at least 250 procedures per by by 36 months; for new service existing services within 2 hours driving time must have performed at least 500 surgeries during preceding year

Additional criteria used to determine need for neonatal intensive care: Number of NICU beds shall not exced 4 beds per 1000 live births; level II NICU services shall be considered only at hospitals performing at least 1,100 deliveries a year

Additional criteria used to determine need for obstetrical: Level II and level III units shall perform at least 1,100 deliveries per year; level I units shall perform at least 750 deliveries per year; new level I units will only be considered based on less than 750 deliveries per year if the absence of the service would result in a population of at least 5,000 being more than 30 minutes normal driving time from another obstetric unit

Additional criteria used to determine need for psychiatric services: Average occupancy should be 85%

CON STATUTES AND REGULATIONS

CON Statutes:

CON Statute Title: Certificate of Need
CON Statute Citation: W. Va. Code 16-2D

CON Regulations:

CON Regulations Title: Certificate of Need Rule
CON Regulations Citation: 65-7-1
Year CON Regulations Enacted: 2000

STATE NOTE

West Virginia requires a certificate of need ("CON") to establish most healthcare services requiring a capital expenditure above the minimum stated in the statute. The standards for offering new healthcare services are found outside of the regulations and are approved by the governor. Need for most services is a complex calculation considering population and a minimum occupancy/utilization for the service. The calculation also includes an estimate of in and out migration. The standards include an estimated percent of the population that will need the service. For some services, e.g. birthing centers, the calculation is different for facilities located in 'underserved' areas. The need calculations also consider driving times of the state's population.

WISCONSIN

STATE CON AGENCY CONTACTS

State Department Overseeing CON

Name of state CON department:	Division of Health Care Financing
URL address for state CON organization:	http://dhfs.wisconsin.gov/aboutDHFS DHCF/ dhcf.htm

CON Administrative Office Information

Name of state CON office:	Bureau of Health Care Benefits Hierarchy for state CON administrative office: Governor: Dept. of Health & Family Services: Div. Of Health Care Financing: Bureau of Health Care Benefits
CON organization contact person:	C. David Lund
Title of CON contact person:	Chief, Nursing Home Section
Email address of CON contact:	lundcd@dhfs.state.wi.us
Mailing address for state CON office:	1 West Wilson St.
City where state CON office is located:	Madison
State for mailing address:	Wisconsin
Zip code for CON office:	53702
Phone number for CON contact:	(608) 266-2021
Fax number for CON contact:	(608) 267-2832

State CON Decision Making Body (DMB)

Name of DMB:	Secretary of the Dept. of Health & Family Services
Title of person DMB reports to:	Governor
Title of person appointing DMB members:	Governor

Composition of CON DMB:

Number of people in the DMB:	1
Number of CON agency reps in DMB:	1

EQUIPMENT REGULATION AND DATA

Subject to CON (Y/N):

Is any equipment subject to CON?:	False
Are air ambulances subject to CON?:	False
Are cardiac cath labs subject to CON?:	False
Are CT scanners subject to CON?:	False
Are gamma knives subject to CON?:	False

Subject to CON (Y/N) (Continued)

Are linear accelerators subject to CON?:	False
Is lithotropsy subject to CON?:	False
Is mobile high tech subject to CON?:	False
Are MRI scanners subject to CON?:	False
Are PET scanners subject to CON?:	False
Is radiation therapy subject to CON?:	False
Is renal dialysis subject to CON?:	False
Are swing beds subject to CON?:	False
Is ultra-sound subject to CON?:	False

Dollar Threshold for CON Application:

Dollar threshold for any equipment application:	$196,000

Additional Criteria Used to Determine Need:

Additional criteria used to determine need for any equipment: only need CON if equipment purchased by nursing home

FACILITIES REGULATION AND DATA

Subject to CON (Y/N):

Is any facility subject to CON?	False
Are hospitals subject to CON?	False
Are nursing homes subject to CON?	True
Are residential care facilities subject to CON?	False
Are psychiatric facilities subject to CON?	False
Are ambulatory surgery centers subject to CON?	False
Are ICF/MRs subject to CON?	True
Is long term care subject to CON?	True
Are medical office buildings subject to CON?	False
Are rehabilitation facilities subject to CON?	False
Are renal dialysis facilities subject to CON?	False
Are RCF/Assisted Living facilities subject to CON?	False
Are subacute care facilities subject to CON?	True
Are substance abuse facilities subject to CON?	False
Are swing beds subject to CON?	False

Additional Criteria Used to Determine Need:

Additional criteria used to determine need for a nursing home: maximum number of beds statewide = 51,795

Additional criteria used to determine need for an ICF/MR: maximum number of beds statewide = 3,704

SERVICES REGULATION AND DATA

Subject to CON (Y/N):

Are all services subject to CON?:	False
Are nursing home services subject to CON?:	True
Are acute care services subject to CON?:	False
Are air ambulance subject to CON?:	False
Is burn care subject to CON?:	False

Subject to CON (Y/N) (Continued)

Is cardiac catheterization subject to CON?:	False
Is CT scanning subject to CON?:	False
Is gamma knife service subject to CON?:	False
Is home health subject to CON?:	False
Is linear accelerator service subject to CON?:	False
Is lithotripsy service subject to CON?:	False
Is long term care subject to CON?:	True
Is mobile high tech service subject to CON?:	False
Is MRI scanning subject to CON?:	False
Is neo-natal intensive care subject to CON?:	False
Are obstetrical services subject to CON?:	False
Is open heart surgery subject to CON?:	False
Is organ transplantation subject to CON?:	False
Is PET scanning subject to CON?:	False
Are psychiatric services subject to CON?:	False
Is radiation therapy subject to CON?:	False
Are rehabilitation services subject to CON?:	False
Is renal dialysis subject to CON?:	False
Is RCF/Assisted Living subject to CON?:	False
Is subacute care subject to CON?:	True
Is substance abuse subject to CON?:	False
Are swing beds subject to CON?:	False
Is utlra-sound subject to CON?:	False
Are other services subject to CON?:	partial or total conversion of nursing home to facility serving developmentally disabled

Dollar Threshold for CON Application:

Dollar threshold for nursing home application:	$1,000,000

CON STATUTES AND REGULATIONS

CON Statutes:

CON Statute Title: Regulation of Health Services: Resource Allocation Program - Long Term Care
CON Statute Citation: Wis. Stat. sec 150

CON Regulations:

CON Regulations Title: Wisconsin Administrative Code: Long-Term Care Facility Bed Additions and Capital Expenditures Review
CON Regulations Citation: Chapter HFS 122

STATE NOTE

Wisconsin requires a certificate of need ("CON") for nursing homes, long-term care facilities, and facilities for the developmentally disabled. The statute contains a statewide bed limit for beds in these facilities. The regulations contain "bed allocation methodology" to allocate beds to the planning area. The formula considers the planning area's population and nursing home utilization.

GLOSSARY

This glossary is intended to provide a general industry understanding of the terms included. Please be advised that state CON statutes and regulations might contain definitions of these terms that may differ from the general definitions provided below. It is therefore important to review the definitions section of a state's CON statutes and regulations for specific information on the terminology used in that state. This glossary is not intended to provide legal advice.

1. **Ambulatory Services:** Healthcare services provided on an outpatient basis, without admission for an overnight stay in a hospital.
2. **Antitrust (see also Clayton Act; and Sherman Act):** Refers to opposition to trusts or legislation passed to protect commerce and trade from unlawful restraint, unfair business practices, such as price fixing or price discrimination, and monopolies.
3. **Acquisition:** Obtaining legal title.
4. **Average Age of Plant:** Equal to the accumulated depreciation divided by the depreciation expense.
5. **Average Length of Stay:** Mean stay counted by days of all or part of inpatients discharged over a given period; calculated by dividing the number of inpatient days by the number of discharges.
6. **Barriers to Entry:** Market conditions that raise the entry costs for firms wanting to enter the market above the costs of firms already in the market.
7. **Bed Capacity:** Number of beds that a hospital has set up and staffed for use (See also bed supply).
8. **Bed Supply (see also supply; oversupply; and capacity):** Supply of hospital beds located in a region, usually expressed as beds per region, or beds per 1000 people.
9. **Business Coalition:** Organization of companies formed to address a range of healthcare issues affecting the employees of the individual companies.
10. **Capacity (see also excess capacity):** May alternately refer to the maximum amount of healthcare services that can be provided by existing providers or the number of providers or equipment. Capacity is sometimes expressed as a ratio of providers or equipment to population.
11. **Capital Costs (see also capital expenditures):** The costs associated with investing in a new facility, new service, or new equipment, excluding operational costs.
12. **Capital Expenditures:** Funds spent on additions or improvements, excluding operational and maintenance costs.
13. **Certificate of Need (CON):** Approval, usually issued by a state health planning agency, for healthcare organizations that propose to construct or modify a healthcare facility, purchase major medical equipment, or offer a new or different health service.
14. **Certificate of Public Necessity:** See Certificate of Need.
15. **Certificate of Public Need:** See Certificate of Need.
16. **Certificate of Public Review:** See Certificate of Need.
17. **Charity Care:** Free or subsidized health services provided to indigent persons with limited or no healthcare coverage.
18. **Clayton Act of 1914:** Antitrust act meant to strengthen the Sherman Act by allowing prosecutors to bring charges with respect to potential anti-competitive business practices, such as exclusive dealings and price discrimination which may lead to the creation of a monopoly in a given area of commerce.

19. **CON Laws:** Laws enacted to reduce the amount of increasing healthcare costs by eliminating unnecessary duplication and maldistribution of health facilities.
20. **CON Program:** A state regulatory program designed to help contain healthcare costs, and improve access to care.
21. **CON Review:** A process which examines financial feasibility, consistency with the state health plan, and need.
22. **Cost Overrun:** Any increase in cost of a project approved by a CON program. CON statutes and/or regulations usually require that applicants file notice of any cost overrun with the CON agency.
23. **Debt per bed:** Total bonds issued plus loans divided by number of beds in the hospital.
24. **Determinate of Need Necessity:** See Certificate of Need.
25. **Determination of Duplication of Services:** See Certificate of Need.
26. **Ethics in Patient Referrals Act of 1989 ("Stark Laws"):** Legislation which prohibits a physician from referring patients to designated health services such as laboratories, radiology services, diagnostic services, physical therapy, home health services, pharmacies, occupational therapy, and distributors of medical equipment in which the physician has a financial interest.
27. **Excess Capacity:** The proposition that under monopolistic conditions, free entry of firms will result in normal profit, but with too many firms, each producing at too low a rate of output to exploit economies of scale; The difference between actual output and output necessary to achieve full economies of scale.
28. **Expedited Review:** Nonsubstantive and less burdensome review of certain applications.
29. **Facility Need Review:** See Certificate of Need.
30. **For Profit Hospital:** Hospital without not for profit status.
31. **Freestanding:** Facility that is not affiliated with a hospital.
32. **Healthcare Facility:** Facility where healthcare services are provided. Usually defined in the CON statute or CON regulations.
33. **Health Systems Agency (HSA):** Organization or unit of local government intended to provide a network of health planning and resource development services, including development of a health service plan, conducting certificate of need reviews and reviewing proposed use of federal health funds in each of several health service areas established under the National Health Planning and Resources Development Act of 1974.
34. **Health Maintenance Organization (HMO):** Organization designed to maintain health and provide comprehensive healthcare services on a pre-paid basis to voluntarily enrolled patients within a designated population.
35. **Health Planning:** Planning concerned with improving health, improving access to healthcare, or promoting maximum efficiency of health resources for an area, population, health facility or health program.
36. **Health Planning Agency:** A unit of state government organized under the Health Planning and Resources Development Act of 1974 to perform health planning and development functions such as, administering certificate of need programs and preparing a state health plan.
37. **Hill-Burton Act of 1946 (Hospital Survey and Construction Act):** Created a federal program of financial assistance for the construction and modernization of healthcare facilities.
38. **HMO Act of 1973:** Assisted in the establishment and expansion of HMOs and legally defined the term "health maintenance organization".
39. **Horizontal Consolidation:** Two hospitals (i.e. competitors) fuse into one entity.
40. **Integrated Delivery System:** Operationally and clinically integrated organization which provides a full range of health services, including physician services, hospital services and ancillary services.
41. **Letter of Approval:** A state issued document which confirms the granting of a Certificate of Need.
42. **Letter of Intent (LOI):** A written request for CON applications and forms submitted by an individual who intends to submit a CON application. The CON statute or regulations usually contain detailed descriptions of the information needed in the letter of intent.

43. **Major Medical Equipment:** Medical clinical equipment intended for use in the diagnosis or treatment of medical conditions. Usually defined in the CON statute or regulations.
44. **Market Competition:** An economic situation in which there are a large number of buyers and sellers of the same product that have access to perfect information and there is freedom of entry for new sellers into the market.
45. **Monopoly:** An economic situation in which one seller controls the entire output of a particular good or service. There is no competition and the seller sets the price of the good or service in order to maximize profit.
46. **Moratorium:** A period during which no new services can be initiated.
47. **National Health Planning and Resources Development Act ("NHPRDA") of 1974:** Authorized major federal reorganization of health planning programs, including Hill-Burton and set up health systems areas and governing agencies.
48. **Net Patient Revenue:** Revenue for patient care only, not including revenue from other operations such as cafeteria, parking, research or educational activities.
49. **Non-hospital Facilities:** An outpatient facility, such as a clinic, or imaging center.
50. **Nonprofit Hospital:** Hospital with not-for-profit status.
51. **Occupancy Rate:** Percent of beds that are occupied during a specified period.
52. **Oligopoly:** A type of market in which there are a small number of firms accounting for a large proportion of output and employment so that their actions directly impact their competitors and the price of the good or service they are all selling.
53. **Omnibus Budget Reconciliation Act of 1993 ("OBRA 1993/Stark II"):** Adjustments made to the Stark Law of 1989. Stark II regulations provide more flexibility in contracting and they expand the exceptions created in the Stark Law. Stark II clarified the definition of a designated health service and excluded services personally performed by the referring physician from the definition of referral.
54. **Oversupply:** An economic situation in which the quantity of a good or service that sellers wish to sell is greater than the quantity that buyer wish to buy, causing sellers to lower their prices.
55. **Patient Choice:** The idea that patients should be able to choose their own physicians without pressure from a managed care organization.
56. **Price Fixing:** Cooperation in the setting of price ranges by competing firms.
57. **Professional Standards Review Organizations ("PSROs"):** A physician sponsored organization formed in 1972 under the Social Security Act amendments to review medical services available under Medicare, Medicaid, and maternal child health programs.
58. **Prospective Payment System (PPS):** A system which has set reimbursement rates for a given period of time prior to and regardless of actual costs incurred. This system is used for Medicare Part A reimbursement, which bases payment on the patient's diagnosis upon admission to the hospital.
59. **Prospective Pricing:** Method of third party payment by which rates for services are established in advance of the coming fiscal year, and providers are paid these rates regardless of the actual costs incurred.
60. **Public Necessity:** A reasonably necessary, although not necessarily essential or absolutely indispensable, good or service for a community or population.
61. **Relative Value Unit (RVU):** Unit of measurement designed to permit comparison between the amount of resources used to perform various services within a department or in similar departments in different hospitals by assigning weights to factors involved in performance of the service, such as personnel time and level of skill.
62. **Religious Facility:** Facility created exclusively for members of a recognized religious denomination or for those who rely exclusively upon treatment by prayer alone for healing in accordance with the tenets or practices of any recognized religious denomination. The facilities are often exempted from CON requirements.

63. **Resource Based Relative Value Systems (RBRVS):** System used to develop the relative procedural resource weighting Relative Value Unites (RVUs) used in the Medicare physician fee schedule.
64. **Roemer Effect:** Close correlation between bed supply per 1000 population and hospital days per 1000 population. The theory that "A bed built is a bed to be filled."
65. **Rural Healthcare Provider/Hospital:** A provider or hospital which is designated by the United States Government Health Care Financing Administration as rural.
66. **Self-referral:** Referral of patients by physician to a testing or treatment facility with which they have a financial interest.
67. **Service Area (Geographic market service area):** A geographic area covered by a network of providers. The service area may be defined in the CON statute or regulations.
68. **Sherman Antitrust Act of 1890:** Legislation designed to control the market power of large firms by making it illegal to set up monopolies or participate in any activities restraining trade.
69. **Social Security Act Amendments of 1972, Section 1122:** Denies payment under Medicare and Medicaid for capital expenditures not approved by state planning agencies.
70. **Stark Bill:** See Ethics in Patient Referral Act of 1989.
71. **Stark II:** See Omnibus Budget Reconciliation Act of 1993.
72. **Statements of Antitrust:** In 1993, 1994, and 1996, the Justice Department and the Federal Trade Commission issued Statements of Antitrust Enforcement Policy in Healthcare describing the legal standards for prosecution for anti-competitive actions related to hospital mergers and joint ventures, physician networks, multi-provider networks, and other groups. The statements include descriptions of safety zones or Safe Harbors, and criteria for determining compliance. The 1996 Statements expanded the Rule of Reason for physician networks, providing an overall approach to determining anti-competitiveness.
73. **State Health Plan:** Comprehensive plan produced by the state outlining the state's health goals.
74. **Supply:** The flow of a good or service into a market to meet a demand.
75. **"Supply creating demand":** Additional demand created by asymmetric information between the provider and the patient.
76. **Total Profit Margin:** Calculated by subtracting total expenses from total sales and reported as a single amount.
77. **Utilization Rate:** Percent of the facility's capacity that is used during a specified time period.
78. **Vertical Integration:** ownership or control of production and distribution of a good from raw material until sale to customer.

www.ingramcontent.com/pod-product-compliance
Lightning Source LLC
LaVergne TN
LVHW080115011026
849160LV00013B/1111